EVID

LONGMAN LAW SERIES

GENERAL EDITORS

PROFESSOR I. H. DENNIS, *University College London*
PROFESSOR R. W. RIDEOUT, *University College London*
PROFESSOR J. A. USHER, *University of Exeter*

PUBLISHED TITLES

PETER STONE,
The Conflict of Laws
CHRISTOPHER HARDING AND ANN SHERLOCK,
European Community Law: Text and Materials
ANDREW LE SUEUR AND MAURICE SUNKIN,
Public Law
ROGER J. SMITH,
Property Law
ANDREW CHOO,
Evidence: Text and Materials

ANDREW CHOO

EVIDENCE
Text and Materials

LONGMAN

LONDON AND NEW YORK

Addison Wesley Longman Limited
Edinburgh Gate
Harlow
Essex CM20 2JE
United Kingdom
and Associated Companies throughout the world

*Published in the United States of America
by Addison Wesley Longman, New York*

First published 1998

ISBN 0 582-08756-2 PPR

British Library Cataloguing-in-Publication Data

A catalogue record for this book is available from the British Library

Library of Congress Cataloging-in-Publication Data

Choo, Andrew L.-T.
    Evidence : text and materials / Andrew Choo.
    p.   cm. — (Longman law series)
    Includes bibliographical references and index.
    ISBN 0-582-08756-2 (ppr)
    1. Evidence (Law)—Great Britain—Cases. I. Title. II. Series.
KD7498.C48   1998
347.41'06—dc21
                                                                97-31550
                                                                CIP

Set by 35 in 10/12pt Plantin
Produced through Longman Malaysia, CLP

CONTENTS

Preface   x
Acknowledgements   xi
Table of Cases   xiv
Table of Legislation   xxviii
Table of Orders, Rules and Regulations   xxxii

CHAPTER 1: INTRODUCTION   I

1. Relevance, admissibility and weight   3
2. Terminology   8
   (a) Testimony   8
   (b) Real evidence   9
   (c) Hearsay evidence   12
   (d) Circumstantial evidence   12
3. The allocation of responsibility   16
4. Exclusionary rules and exclusionary discretions   23
5. Civil evidence and criminal evidence   27
6. Issues in criminal evidence   28
7. The implications of trial by jury   33
8. Law reform   37
9. Organisation of book   38

CHAPTER 2: BURDEN AND STANDARD OF PROOF   40

1. Burden of proof   40
   (a) The legal burden and the evidential burden   40
   (b) Incidence of legal burden   41
2. Standard of proof   57
   (a) Criminal trials   57
   (b) Civil trials   61
   (c) The United States: A third standard   68

CHAPTER 3: WITNESSES   73

1. Competence and compellability   73
   (a) The accused   75
   (b) The accused's spouse   81
   (c) Mental disability   84
   (d) Children   86
   (e) Bankers   88
   (f) Judges   88
2. Corroboration and supporting evidence   89
3. Vulnerable witnesses   104
   (a) Complainants in sexual cases   105
   (b) Children   119

CHAPTER 4: THE COURSE OF EVIDENCE   131

1. The adversarial tradition   131
2. The course of the trial   134
3. Adducing evidence   139
   (a) Civil proceedings   139
   (b) Criminal proceedings   140
   (c) Adducing evidence after closing the case   154
4. Examination-in-chief   155
   (a) No leading questions   155
   (b) Hostile witnesses   158
   (c) Evidence of prior consistent statements in criminal trials   161
   (d) Evidence of prior consistent statements in civil trials   174
   (e) Refreshing memory   175
5. Cross-examination   184
   (a) The purposes of cross-examination   184
   (b) Limitations on cross-examination   187
   (c) The rule in *Browne v Dunn*   189
   (d) The collateral-finality rule   189
6. Re-examination   206

CHAPTER 5: SIMILAR-FACT EVIDENCE   207

1. The modern law   208
2. The problem of possible contamination   223
3. The similar-facts rule and identification evidence   230
4. Joinder and severance   235
5. Possession of incriminating articles   237
6. Statutory exceptions to the general prohibition   241
7. Civil trials   242

CHAPTER 6: CROSS-EXAMINATION OF THE ACCUSED   245

1. Introduction   245
   (a) The relationship between provisos (e) and (f)   246
   (b) Proviso (f): some general issues   252
2. Requirement of leave   254
3. Section 1(f)(i)   254
4. Section 1(f)(ii): First limb   255
   (a) What is the relevance of evidence of good character?   257
   (b) What is meant by 'good character'?   263
   (c) Cross-examination under the first limb of s 1(f)(ii)   264
5. Section 1(f)(ii): Second limb   265
   (a) The law   265
   (b) Practical implications   279
   (c) Reform   283
6. Section 1(f)(iii)   284
7. A general evaluation   288

CHAPTER 7: HEARSAY EVIDENCE   292

1. Introduction   292
2. The rule against hearsay in civil proceedings   295
3. The rule against hearsay in criminal proceedings   300
   (a) Applications of the rule   300
   (b) Evasions of the rule   304
   (c) Implied assertions   316
   (d) Common law exceptions to the rule   321
   (e) Statutory exceptions to the rule   332
   (f) The implications of the European Convention on
       Human Rights   358
   (g) Reform   360

CHAPTER 8: CONFESSION EVIDENCE AND RELATED MATTERS   369

1. Introduction   369
2. No requirement for supporting evidence   371
3. Mandatory exclusion   373
   (a) Oppression   374
   (b) Words or conduct conducive to unreliability   378
4. Discretionary exclusion   385
   (a) Police lies   387
   (b) Denial of access to legal advice   389
   (c) Recording requirements   396
   (d) The limitations of discretionary exclusion   402
5. The respective functions of judge and jury   403

6. Police and Criminal Evidence Act 1984, s 77   405
7. Withdrawal of case from jury   407
8. Partly adverse statements   407
9. 'Fruit of the poisonous tree'   408
10. Erosion of the right to silence in the face of police questioning   410

CHAPTER 9: IMPROPERLY OBTAINED NON-CONFESSION EVIDENCE   433

1. The road traffic cases   434
2. Violations of the Police and Criminal Evidence Act 1984
   (or the Codes of Practice)   438
3. Entrapment situations, undercover police activity generally
   and electronic listening devices   442
4. Evidence obtained improperly outside the jurisdiction   458
5. Is there a clear rationale for the exclusion of improperly
   obtained evidence?   458

CHAPTER 10: IDENTIFICATION EVIDENCE   467

1. The problem   467
2. The solution   471
   (a) Warnings to the jury   472
   (b) Discretionary exclusion of identification evidence   479

CHAPTER 11: EXPERT OPINION EVIDENCE   490

1. Admissibility   493
   (a) Express statutory provisions   494
   (b) Mens rea, defences and credibility   494
   (c) Confessions   501
   (d) Obscenity   501
   (e) DNA evidence   502
   (f) Bayes Theorem   506
   (g) Further illustrations   517
   (h) Other jurisdictions   519
2. The implications of the rule against hearsay   524
3. 'Ultimate issues'   528
4. Duties and responsibilities of expert witnesses   530
5. Reform   531

CHAPTER 12: PUBLIC INTEREST IMMUNITY   537

1. A shift in judicial attitudes   538
2. National security and analogous concerns   546
3. Proper functioning of the public service   547

4. Criminal cases   548
   (a) Disclosure of the identity of police informers   548
   (b) Disclosure of the location of police observation points   559
   (c) General comments   560
5. Confidentiality   563

CHAPTER 13: LEGAL PROFESSIONAL PRIVILEGE   574

1. The concept of privilege   574
2. What is legal professional privilege?   575
   (a) Collateral facts and pre-existing documents   577
   (b) 'Legal adviser'   578
   (c) Communications between client and legal adviser   578
   (d) Communications with third parties   581
3. Waiver   586
4. Facilitation of crime or fraud   588
5. An 'absolute' doctrine?   593
6. Secondary evidence   599

Bibliography   606
Index   620

PREFACE

This book contains a treatment of a number of key topics in the law of evidence. Its main purpose is to enable readers to engage with extracts from primary materials as well as from periodical and other literature. The text accompanying the extracts is intended to provide critical commentary, as well as to serve as a guide to using and working with the extracts. The book aims to stimulate readers to think about the issues themselves and to work out their own position on the issues, rather than forcefully to advance a particular thesis or a blueprint for reform.

Extracts from recent cases have generally been presented to the exclusion of extracts from earlier ones, particularly where a recent decision contains a comprehensive discussion of the older authorities.

Material from other jurisdictions is presented in some cases where it throws special light on the issue under discussion. This may be the case, for example, where the material reflects an approach which is different from that adopted in England but which is particularly innovative, or where the approach adopted is the same as that adopted in England and the material encapsulates this approach in a clear and succinct manner.

I would like to express my sincere gratitude to Professor Ian Dennis of University College London for reading an earlier draft of the book on behalf of Longman and making a number of suggestions for improvement.

I have generally been able to take account of material available to me on 1 May 1997, although it has been possible in some instances to incorporate material which became available subsequently. I have treated all recent statutory provisions as if they were completely in force.

Professor Andrew Choo
Brunel University
August 1997

ACKNOWLEDGEMENTS

We are grateful to the following for permission to reproduce copyright material:

Australian Government Publishing Service for reproduction of the Evidence Act 1995, ss 53, 102–104, 114, 130, 138
© Commonwealth of Australia (1998)
All legislative material is produced by permission but does not purport to be the official or authorised version. It is subject to Commonwealth of Australia copyright. The Copyright Act 1968 permits certain reproduction and publication of Commonwealth legislation. In particular, s 182A of the Act enables a complete copy to be made by or on behalf of a particular person. For reproduction or publication beyond that permitted by the Act, permission should be sought in writing from the Australia Government Publishing Service. Requests in the first instance should be addressed to the Manager, Commonwealth Information Services, Australian Government Publishing Service, GPO Box 84, Canberra ACT 2601.

Blackstone Press Ltd for an extract from EJ Imwinkelried, 'The Next Step in Conceptualizing the Presentation of Expert Evidence as Education: The Case for Didactic Trial Procedures' (1997) 1(2) *International Journal of Evidence and Proof* 128, 132.

Blackwell Publishers for extracts from A Stein, 'After *Hunt*. The Burden of Proof, Risk of Non-Persuasion and Judicial Pragmatism' (1991) 54 *Modern Law Review* 570, 571–572 and ALE Newbold, 'The Crime/Fraud Exception to Legal Professional Privilege' (1990) 53 *Modern Law Review* 472, 481–483.

Butterworths, London for extracts from R Bagshaw, *Cross and Wilkins: Outline of the Law of Evidence* (1996) pp 3–4; M Zander, *Cases and Materials on the English Legal System* (7th ed, 1996) p 236; and C Tapper, *Cross and Tapper on Evidence* (8th ed, 1995) pp 296, 483.

Butterworths Pty Ltd, Australia for extracts from J Hunter and K Cronin, *Evidence, Advocacy and Ethical Practice: A Criminal Trial Commentary* (1995) pp 363–364, 394–395.

Cambridge Law Journal for an extract from R Munday, 'The Paradox of Cross-examination to Credit – Simply Too Close for Comfort' [1994] *Cambridge Law Journal* 303, 324.

Cambridge University Press for an extract from BL Cutler and SD Penrod, *Mistaken Identification: The Eyewitness, Psychology, and the Law* (1995) pp 101–106.

Canada Lawbook Inc for excerpts reproduced from Dominion Law Reports with the permission of Canada Law Book Inc, through the Canadian Copyright Licensing Agency.

Criminal Law Forum for an extract from K Mack, 'Continuing Barriers to Women's Credibility: A Feminist Perspective on the Proof Process' (1993) 4 *Criminal Law Forum* 327, 350–352.

Her Majesty's Stationery Office. The material herein which is Crown Copyright is reproduced by kind permission of the Controller of Her Majesty's Stationery Office.

Northwestern University Press for an extract from W Twining, *Rethinking Evidence: Exploratory Essays* (1994) pp 185–186.

Oxford University Press for extracts from AAS Zuckerman, *The Principles of Criminal Evidence* (1989) pp 4–6, 95–96, 290–292, 343, 345–350, 352; CAG Jones, *Expert Witness: Science, Medicine, and the Practice of the Law* (1994) pp 126–127; M McConville, J Hodgson, L Bridges and A Pavlovic, *Standing Accused: The Organisation and Practices of Criminal Defence Lawyers in Britain* (1994) pp 216–220; and A McColgan, 'Common Law and the Relevance of Sexual History Evidence' (1996) 16 *Oxford Journal of Legal Studies* 275, 285.

SLS Legal Publications (NI) for extracts from JC Smith, 'The Presumption of Innocence' (1987) 38 *Northern Ireland Legal Quarterly* 223, 231–233, 235–236 and M Newark, 'Opening Up the Collateral Issue Rule' (1992) 43 *Northern Ireland Legal Quarterly* 166, 176.

Stanford University Press for an extract from Herbert L Packer, *The Limits of the Criminal Sanction* (1969) 154, 158–160, 162–166 © 1968 Herbert L Packer.

Sweet & Maxwell for extracts from AAS Zuckerman, 'Miscarriage of Justice and Judicial Responsibility' [1991] *Criminal Law Review* 492, 499–500; LSE Jury Project, 'Juries and the Rules of Evidence' [1973] *Criminal Law Review* 208, 209–210; S Dorah, 'Similar Facts and the Shadow of Collusion: A Matter of Judicial Responsibility', *Archbold News*, 12 December 1995, 5, 708;

D Wolchover and A Heaton-Armstrong, *Wolchover and Heaton-Armstrong on Confession Evidence* (1996) p 698; J Stone, 'Burden of Proof and the Judicial Process: A Commentary on *Joseph Steamship Ltd v Imperial Smelting Corporation Ltd*' (1944) 60 *Law Quarterly Review* 262, 278; RD Mackay and AM Colman, 'Excluding Expert Evidence: A Tale of Ordinary Folk and Common Experience' [1991] *Criminal Law Review* 800, 809; and extracts from the European Human Rights Reports.

Victim Support for an extract from Victim Support, *Women, Rape and the Criminal Justice System* (1996) pp 15–17. Inquiries can be made to Victim Support National Office, Cranmer House, 39 Brixton Road, London SW9 6DZ (Tel: 0171 735 9166 ; Fax 0171 582 5712).

West Publishing Corporation for extracts from US case reports which are reprinted from West's National Reporter System with permission of the West Publishing Corporation and for an extract from JW Strong (ed), *McCormick on Evidence* (4th ed, 1992) pp 39–41.

TABLE OF CASES

A (LL) v B (A) [1995] 4 SCR 536; sub nom R v Beharriell 555
Abrath v North Eastern Railway Co (1883) 11 QBD 440, CA........................55
Addington v Texas, 441 US 418 (1979) (US Supreme Court) 68–72
Aegis Blaze, The [1986] 1 Lloyd's Rep 203, CA 576
Air Canada v Secretary of State for Trade [1983] 2 AC 394, HL........541–544, 547, 567
Ajodha v The State [1982] AC 220, PC 404
Alexander v Rayson [1936] 1 KB 169 138–139
Anderson v Bank of British Columbia, 2 Ch D 644 584
Anderson v Whalley (1852) 3 Car & K 54 (Nisi Prius).........................175–176
Anderton v Waring [1986] RTR 74..53
Ankin v London and North Eastern Railway Co [1930] 1 KB 527 582
Apothecaries' Co v Bentley (1824) 1 C & P 538 47
Arizona v Evans, 115 S Ct 1185 (1995) (US Supreme Court) 461–462
Artner v Austria, 39/1991/291/362 (unreported) 359
Asch v Austria (1991) 15 EHRR 597...358, 359
Asiatic Petroleum Co Ltd v Anglo-Persian Oil Co [1916] 1 KB 822 546
Associated Provincial Picture Houses v Wednesbury Corp [1948] 1 KB 223. 25, 94, 441, 442
Att.-Gen. v Briant (1846) 15 M & W 169 557
Att.-Gen. v Hitchcock (1847) 1 Ex 91 (Exchequer Division) 190, 194, 201
Att.-Gen.'s Ref (No 3 of 1979) (1979) 69 Cr App R 411, CA.......................176
Balabel v Air India [1988] Ch 317, CA 580
Balfour v Foreign Office [1994] 1 WLR 681 ....545, 546
Balkanbank v Taher, *The Times*, 19 February 1994 586
Bank of England v Vagliano Bros [1891] AC 107 ....442, 443
Barclays Bank v Eustice [1995] 4 All ER 511, CA................................589
Bater v Bater [1951] P 35, CA...61–2, 63
Beckford v R (1993) 97 Cr App R 409 475
Beresford v Justices of St Albans (1905) 22 TLR 1..............................13
Bisaillon v Keable [1983] 2 SCR 60 ....551, 552, 553, 554
Blake v DPP (1992) 97 Cr App R 169 560
Blunt v Park Lane Hotel Ltd [1942] 2 KB 253 574
Bramblevale, Re [1970] Ch 128 62–3
Bratty v Att.-Gen. for Northern Ireland [1963] AC 386 41
Brind v Secretary of State for the Home Department [1991] 1 All ER 720 453
Briscoe v Briscoe [1968] P 501, P, D & A.......................................140
British Coal Corpn v Dennis Rye [1988] 1 WLR 1113 588
British Railways Board v Herrington [1972] AC 877..............................14
Brown v Eastern & Midlands Railway Co (1889) 22 QBD 391 243
Brown v Foster (1857) 1 H & N 736 577
Browne v Dunn (1893) 6 R 67 189
Buccleuch, Duke of, v Metropolitan Board of Works (1872) LR 5 HL 418 88
Buckley v Law Society (No 2) [1984] 3 All ER 313 548
Burmah Oil Co v Bank of England [1980] AC 1090, HL 541, 543, 547
Butler v Board of Trade [1971] Ch 680 ....588, 601, 602, 603

Buttes Gas and Oil Co v Hammer (No 3) [1982] AC 888 . . . . 546, 586
Calcraft v Guest [1898] 1 QB 759 . . . . 599, 601, 603, 604
Callis v Gunn [1964] 1 QB 495 373
Castle v Cross [1984] 1 WLR 1372 351
Causton v Mann Egerton (Johnsons) Ltd [1974] 1 WLR 162 596
Chambers v Bernasconi (1834) 1 C M & R 347 322
Champneys v Peck (1816) 1 Stark 404 323
Chandrasekera v R [1937] AC 220 316
Chaunt v United States, 364 US 350, 5 L Ed 2d 120, 81 S Ct 147 (1960) 69
Chundawadra v Immigration Appeal Tribunal [1988] Imm AR 161 454
Clifford v Clifford [1961] 1 WLR 1274, CA 195, 196
Collins v R (1987) 38 DLR (4th) 508, SCC 460–461
Conway v Rimmer [1968] AC 910 . . . . 538, 539, 540, 543, 546, 547, 563
Cotgrave v Cooney [1987] Crim LR 272 53
Crofter Hand Woven Harris Tweed Co v Veitch [1942] AC 435 585
Crompton (A) v Customs & Excise [1974] AC 405 548
Crosdale v R [1995] 1 WLR 864, PC 136–138
Crossland v DPP [1988] 3 All ER 712, DC 90
D (Infants), Re [1970] 1 WLR 599 548
D v National Society for the Prevention of Cruelty to Children [1978] AC 171. . . . 547, 557, 558, 583, 584
Daley v R [1994] 1 AC 117 474
Daniels v DPP (1991) 156 JP 543 438
Daubert v Merrell Dow Pharmaceuticals Inc, 113 S Ct 2786 (1993) (US Supreme Court) 519–523
Davie v Edinburgh Magistrates [1953] SC 34 493
Dawson v The Queen (1961) 106 CLR 1 59
De L'Isle (Viscount) v Times Newspapers [1987] 3 All ER 499 25
Dellow's Will Trusts, Re [1964] 1 WLR 451 63
Delta v France (1990) 16 EHRR 574 . . . . 358, 359
Demeter v R (1977) 75 DLR (3d) 251 322
Derby & Co and Others v Weldon and Others, *The Times*, 9 November 1990 531
Derby & Co Ltd v Weldon (No 8) [1990] 3 All ER 762 . . . . 603, 604
Dickinson v Yates; Lettice v Chief Constable of the Lancashire Constabulary [1986] CA Transcript 554 197
Domican v R (1992) 173 CLR 555 479
Doorson v Netherlands (1996) 22 EHRR 330 . . . . 358, 359
Dover District Council v Sherred, *The Times*, 11 February 1997; LEXIS transcript 493
DPP v A & BC Chewing Gum Ltd [1968] 1 QB 159 . . . . 502, 528
DPP v Godwin [1991] RTR 303, DC 25, 437–438
DPP v Jordan [1977] AC 699 502
DPP v Kilbourne [1973] AC 729, HL 3–4
DPP v M [1997] 2 All ER 749 88
DPP v McGladrigan [1991] RTR 297, DC 436–437
DPP v McKeown [1997] 1 WLR 295, HL 349–355
DPP v P [1991] 2 AC 447, HL 208–217, 219, 225, 227, 236, 240, 255
DPP v Ping Lin [1976] AC 574 373
Dubai Bank Ltd v Galadari (No 7) [1992] 1 WLR 106 577
Duncan v Cammell, Laird & Co [1942] AC 624. . . . . 537, 538, 539, 546
Dwyer v Collins (1852) 21 LJ Ex 225 577
E (SA) (A Minor) (Wardship: Court's Duty), Re [1984] 1 WLR 156 597
Elias v Pasmore [1934] 2 KB 164 463
English & American Insurance Co v Herbert Smith [1988] FSR 232 . . . . 599, 600
English Exporters v Eldonwall Ltd [1973] Ch 415 (Ch D) 524, 527
Enoch and Zaretzky, Bock & Co, Re [1910] 1 KB 327, CA 140
Ewer v Ambrose (1825) 3 B & C 746, KBD 158
Fayed v Al-Tajir [1987] 2 All ER 396 547
Ferguson v R [1979] 1 WLR 94 59
Freemantle v R [1994] 1 WLR 1437 479
Frye v US, 54 App DC 46 (1923) 519, 520, 524

G (A Minor) (Child Abuse: Standard of Proof), Re [1987] 1 WLR 1461..............67
G v DPP [1997] 2 All ER 755...88
Gaskin v Liverpool Council [1980] 1 WLR 1549..............................548
Gatland v Metropolitan Police Commissioner [1968] 2 QB 279 ....52, 53
General Accident Corpn v Tanter [1984] 1 WLR 100 586
Gilbey v Great Western Railway Co (1910) 102 LT 202, CA 330
Glasgow Corporation v Central Land Board, 1956 SC (HL) 1.....................542
Glendarroch, The [1894] P 226...57
Goddard v Nationwide [1986] 3 WLR 734................599, 600, 601, 602–603, 604
Goodwin v UK (1996) 22 EHRR 123 (ECHR) 569–572
Great Atlantic Insurance v Home Insurance [1981] 1 WLR 529 586
Greenough v Eccles (1859) 5 CB (NS) 786 159
Gregory v Tavernor (1833) 6 C & P 280 ....178, 179
Guinness Peat Ltd v Fitzroy Robinson [1987] 1 WLR 1027, CA 585–586, 599
H (Minors), Re [1996] 2 WLR 8, HL 66–7
H v H (Minors) (Child Abuse: Evidence) [1990] Fam 86 67
H v Schering Chemicals [1983] 1 WLR 143, DC 526–527
Hales v Kerr [1908] 2 KB 601...243
Halford v Brookes, The Times, 3 October 1991 ....63, 66
Halford v Sharples [1992] 3 All ER 624.................................559
Hall v The Queen [1971] 1 WLR 298....................................414
Harmony Shipping Co SA v Saudi Europe Line [1979] 1 WLR 1380................596
Hehir v Commissioner of Police of the Metropolis [1982] 2 All ER 335............559
Hennessy v Wright (1888) 21 QBD 509 546
Henry Coxon, The (1878) 3 PD 156....................................323
Heyne v Fischel & Co (1913) 30 TLR 190 331
Higham v Ridgway (1808) 10 East 109.................................321–322
Hindes v Edwards, The Times, 9 October 1987 25
Hirst and Agu v The Chief Constable of the West Yorkshire Police [1987] Crim LR 330 .52
HM Advocate v AE, 1937 JC 96.......................................211
Hobbs v Tinling [1929] 2 KB 1, CA 188
Hoch v R (1988) 165 CLR 292, HCA 229–230
Hollingham v Head (1858) 4 CB (NS) 388 6–7
Homes v Newman [1931] 2 Ch 112 328
Howe v Malkin (1878) 40 LT 196.....................................328
Hubbard v Pitt [1975] 1 All ER 7.....................................52
Hudson v DPP [1992] RTR 27..433
IBM Corp v Phoenix International [1995] 1 All ER 413, Ch D..................600–601
Ibrahim v R [1914] AC 599...373
Ikarian Reefer, The [1993] FSR 563 (Commercial Court)....................530–531
Illinois v Krull, 107 S Ct 1160 (1987).....................................462
Inquiry under the Company Securities (Insider Dealing) Act 1985, Re [1988] AC 660...566
Ioannou v Demetriou [1952] AC 84 331
Ireland v UK (1978) 2 EHRR 25 377
Isgrò v Italy, 1/1990/192/252 (unreported) 358, 359
ITC Ltd v Video Exchange [1982] Ch 431, Ch D 601, 603
J, Re [1990] FCR 193...531
Jayesena v The Queen [1970] AC 618 47
Jones v DPP [1962] AC 635, HL 246–249, 250, 251, 252
Jones v Godrich (1845) 5 Moo PC 16 577
Jones v R (1997) 71 ALJR 538 169
Joseph Constantine Steamship Line v Imperial Smelting Corpn [1942] AC 154, HL ...55–6
K (Infants), Re [1965] AC 201...597
Kershaw v Whelan [1996] 1 WLR 358 588
Kostovski v Netherlands (1989) 12 EHRR 434 ....358, 359
Kuruma v R [1955] AC 197...439
L (A Minor), Re [1996] 2 WLR 395, HL.............................595–599
Lam Chi-ming v R [1991] 2 AC 212 ....409, 441
Lau Pak Ngam v The Queen [1966] Crim LR 443...........................182
Laurie v Raglan Building Co [1942] 1 KB 152..............................139

Lawrence v Chester Chronicle, *The Times*, 8 February 1986 62
Li Shu-Ling v R [1989] 1 AC 270, PC. 369–370
Lilley v Pettit [1946] KB 401 331
Lillicrap v Nalder & Son [1993] 1 WLR 94 587
Lobban v R [1995] 1 WLR 877, PC. 23–4, 313
Lonrho plc v Fayed (No 4) [1994] 2 WLR 209 564
Lord Ashburton v Pape [1913] 2 Ch 469 . . . . 599, 602, 603, 604
Lord Stafford's Case (1680) 7 How St Tr 1400. 201
Lowery v R [1974] AC 85, PC 311, 495–496
Lüdi v Switzerland (1992) 15 EHRR 173 . . . . .358, 359
Lui Mei Lin v The Queen [1989] AC 288 . . . . .312, 314
Lyell v Kennedy (1884) 27 Ch D 1. 577
M (A Minor) (Appeal) (No 2), Re [1994] 1 FLR 59 67
M (A Minor) (Disclosure of Material), Re [1990] 2 FLR 36 548
M and R (Minors), Re [1996] 4 All ER 239. . . . . 68, 497, 502, 528
M'Naghten's Case (1843) 10 Cl & F 200. . . . . 42, 43, 46
Makanjuola v Commissioner of the Metropolis [1992] 3 All ER 617 559
Makin v Att.-Gen. for New South Wales [1894] AC 57 . . . . 4, 208, 209, 210, 239, 240, 251
Mallows v Harris [1979] RTR 404 53
Malone v Commissioner of Police of the Metropolis (No 2) [1979] 2 All ER 620 449
Malone v UK (1984) 7 EHRR 14 449
Mancini v DPP [1942] AC 1. . . . . 41, 46, 47
Marks v Beyfus (1890) 25 QBD 494, CA. 554, 555, 557
Marks v Lahee (1837) 3 Bing (NC) 408 323
Martin v Nicholls [1994] Crim LR 218. 486
Massachusetts v Sheppard, 104 S Ct 3424 (1984) 462
Matto v Wolverhampton Crown Court [1987] RTR 337 435
Maugham v Hubbard (1828) 8 B & C 14. 181
Maves v Grand Trunk Pacific R Co (1913) 14 DLR 70 (Alberta SC). 155–158
Maxwell v DPP [1935] AC 309, HL. 249, 253, 265, 273, 276
McCarthy v Melita, The (Owners) (1923) 16 BWCC 222 332
McGreevy v DPP [1973] 1 WLR 276 60
McKinney v R (1991) 171 CLR 468 372
McLoughlin v O'Brien [1983] 1 AC 410. 493
Mechanical and General Inventions Co and Lehwess v Austin and the Austin Motor Co [1935]
    AC 346 187–188
Melik & Co v Norwich Union [1980] 1 Lloyd's Rep 523 585
Mercer v Denne [1905] 2 Ch 538 . . . . 322, 331
Mezzo v R (1986) 30 DLR (4th) 161 478
Miller v Minister of Pensions [1947] 2 All ER 372, KBD 57–58, 61
Mills v Mills (1920) 36 TLR 772. 322
Mills v R [1995] 1 WLR 511 . . . . 323, 325–327
Minter v Priest [1930] AC 558. 579
Mohd Ali bin Burut v Public Prosecutor [1995] 2 AC 579, PC 376–377
Mood Music Publishing Co v De Wolfe Ltd [1976] Ch 119, CA 242–243
Moor v Moor [1954] 1 WLR 927 158
Moore v Ransome's Dock Committee (1898) 14 TLR 539 243
Moorov v HM Advocate, 1930 JC 68 211
Munro, Brice & Co v War Risks Association [1918] 2 KB 78 56
Murdoch v Taylor [1965] AC 574 . . . . 24, 285–287, 311, 312
Murphy v R (1989) 167 CLR 94, HCA 499
Murray v UK (1996) 22 EHRR 29 (ECHR) 81, 428–429
Myers v DPP [1965] AC 1001, HL. 292, 304, 305, 308, 317, 527
N (A Minor), Re [1996] 4 All ER 225 497
Nagy v Weston [1965] 1 All ER 78 52
Nederlandse Reassurantie Groep Holding NV v Bacon & Woodrow [1995] 1 All ER 976 (Com-
    mercial Court) 580–581, 587–588
Neill v North Antrim Magistrates' Court (1992) 97 Cr App R 121 336
Neilson v Laugharne [1981] 1 All ER 829 559
Nembhard v R [1981] 1 WLR 1515. . . . . 323, 324

New Victoria Hospital v Ryan [1993] ICR 201 578
Nimmo v Alexander Cowan & Sons [1968] AC 107 ....48, 49
Noor Mohamed v The King [1949] AC 182 275
Norwich Pharmacal v Customs & Excise [1974] AC 133 548
O'Rourke v Darbishire [1920] AC 581 579
Ogden v London Electric Railway Co, 49 TLR 543 ....582, 583
Ogg v HM Advocate, 1938 JC 152 211
Osenton (Charles) & Co v Johnston [1942] AC 130 24
Oxfordshire County Council v M [1994] Fam 151..............595, 596, 597, 598
Pan-American World Airways Inc v Department of Trade [1976] 1 Lloyd's Rep 257 454
Parkes v R [1976] 1 WLR 1251, PC 413–415
Parkin v Moon (1836) 7 Car & P 408 184
Patel v Mehtab (1980) 5 HLR 78 493
Patterson v New York, 432 US 197 (1977) 28
People v Callen, 194 Cal App 3d 558 (1987) 551
People v Collins, 438 P 2d 33 (1968) 515
Perrie v HM Advocate, 1991 JC 27...312
Pfennig v R (1995) 127 ALR 99 ....219, 220, 222, 227
Polivitte v Commercial Union Assurance Co plc [1987] 1 Lloyd's Rep 379 531
Post Office v Estuary Radio Ltd [1967] 1 WLR 1396 63
Practice Direction (Crime: Spent Convictions) [1975] 1 WLR 1065 196
Practice Direction: Crown Court (Defendant's Evidence) [1995] 2 Cr App R 192, CC ...80
Practice Direction (Submission of No Case) [1962] 1 WLR 227, DC..............138
Prince v Samo (1838) 7 Ad & E 627.......................................206
Printers & Finishers v Holloway [1965] 1 WLR 1 602
Public Prosecutor v Yuvaraj [1970] 2 WLR 226 61
R v Abadom [1983] 1 WLR 126, CA 524–526
R v Abraham (1848) 3 Cox CC 430 (Assizes) 172
R v Ackinclose [1996] Crim LR 747...80
R v Acton JJ, ex p McMullen (1990) 92 Cr App R 98, CA 336
R v Adams (Denis) [1996] 2 Cr App R 467, CA 506
R v Ahluwalia [1992] 4 All ER 889 497
R v Alladice (1988) 87 Cr App R 380, CA 393, 441
R v Anderson [1988] QB 678, CA 250–252, 255
R v Andrews (Donald) [1987] AC 281, HL..............................325–327
R v Argent (1996) 161 JP 190, CA 418–424
R v Ashford Magistrates' Court, ex p Hilden (1992) 156 JP 869...............336, 337
R v Ataou [1988] QB 798 ....593, 594
R v Atkinson [1984] 2 NZLR 381 21
R v Aziz [1995] 3 WLR 53, HL...262, 408
R v B [1997] 2 Cr App R 88, CA...237–241
R v B (KG) [1993] 1 SCR 740 366
R v Bailey [1995] 2 Cr App R 262 406
R v Baker (1912) 7 Cr App R 252 256
R v Ball [1911] AC 47, HL 14
R v Barnes [1994] Crim LR 691; LEXIS transcript 116
R v Barnes [1995] 2 Cr App R 491, CA 231–235
R v Barrington [1981] 1 All ER 1132 219
R v Barsoum, 12 October 1993 (unreported).............................277, 278
R v Barton [1973] 1 WLR 115..594
R v Barton (1986) 85 Cr App R 5...116
R v Beattie (1989) 89 Cr App R 302 195
R v Beck [1982] 1 WLR 461 101
R v Beckford and Daley [1991] Crim LR 833 ....307, 309, 310, 313
R v Bedford, 93 Cr App R 113 227
R v Bellamy (1985) 82 Cr App R 222, CA...............................84–5, 86
R v Bellis [1966] 1 WLR 234...258
R v Benjamin (1913) 8 Cr App R 146 170
R v Bentley [1991] Crim LR 620...474
R v Berrada (Note) (1989) 91 Cr App R 131................................258, 259

R v Bird (1996) 161 JP 96, CA 337–338
R v Black, 23 February 1995 (unreported) 233
R v Blastland [1986] AC 41 .... 7, 306, 308, 312, 313, 328–329, 330
R v Bliss (1837) 7 Ad & E 550 328
R v Boal [1965] 1 QB 402 77
R v Boardman [1975] AC 421 .... 208, 209, 215, 242
R v Bond [1906] 2 KB 389 239
R v Bracewell (1978) 68 Cr App R 44 310
R v Braithwaite; R v John, 24 November 1983 (unreported) 274, 275, 276
R v Bray (1988) 88 Cr App R 354 335
R v Britton [1987] 1 WLR 539, CA 178–179
R v Britzman [1983] 1 WLR 350, CA 270–271
R v Brooks (1990) 92 Cr App R 36 216
R v Brown (1988) 89 Cr App R 97, CA 115–116
R v Brown [1997] 1 Cr App R 112, CA 150–152
R v Brown [1997] Crim LR 502 235
R v Brown (Winston) [1997] 3 WLR 447, HL 141, 148
R v Bryant [1979] QB 108 258
R v Bryce [1992] 4 All ER 567 443
R v Brydon (1995) 129 DLR (4th) 1 60
R v Buckley (1873) 13 Cox CC 293 329
R v Burge [1996] 1 Cr App R 163, CA 103–104
R v Burke (1985) 82 Cr App R 156 .... 274, 276, 278
R v Busby (1981) 75 Cr App R 79, CA 190–191, 193, 202, 203, 204
R v Butler (1986) 84 Cr App R 12 219
R v Butterwasser [1948] 1 KB 4 267
R v Buzalek and Schiffer [1991] Crim LR 116 263
R v Cain [1994] 1 WLR 1449, CA 261
R v Campbell [1983] Crim LR 174 85
R v Campbell [1995] 1 Cr App R 522 405
R v Campbell and Williams [1993] Crim LR 448 .... 307, 308, 309, 310, 315
R v Camplin [1978] AC 705 497
R v Canale [1990] 2 All ER 187 .... 400, 441
R v Cape [1996] 1 Cr App R 191 474
R v Cargill (1913) 8 Cr App R 224 26
R v Carr-Briant [1943] KB 607 .... 60, 61
R v Carrington (1993) 99 Cr App R 376, CA 339–341
R v Carroll (1993) 99 Cr App R 381, CA 91–2
R v Carter (1996) 161 JP 207, CA 254
R v Castillo [1996] 1 Cr App R 438, CA 335
R v CCC, ex p Francis & Francis [1989] AC 346 .... 575, 589–592
R v Chard (1971) 56 Cr App R 268, CA 494–495
R v Chaulk (1990) 62 CCC (3d) 193 43
R v Chiarantano [1990] OJ No 2603 (QL) (Ont CA) 554
R v Chief Constable of West Midlands, ex p Wiley [1995] 1 AC 274, HL 538–541,
                                                                          547, 559
R v Ching (1976) 63 Cr App R 7, CA 59
R v Chinn (1996) 160 JP 765 267
R v Chitson [1909] 2 KB 945 247
R v Christie [1914] AC 545, HL 4, 5, 23, 173, 414
R v Christou [1992] 1 QB 979 .... 386, 443
R v Christou [1996] 2 WLR 620 235–237
R v City of Birmingham DC, ex p O [1982] 2 All ER 356 548
R v Clark [1955] 2 QB 469 269
R v Clarke [1995] 2 Cr App R 425, CA 518–519
R v Clarke (Leslie) (1977) 67 Cr App R 398 216
R v Cokar [1960] 2 QB 207, CCA 255
R v Cole (1914) 28 Cr App R 43 239
R v Cole [1990] 1 WLR 866, CA 344–345
R v Coles [1995] 1 Cr App R 157 495

R v Condron (1996) 161 JP 1, CA 415–418, 588
R v Constantinou (1989) 91 Cr App R 74 306
R v Conti (1973) 58 Cr App R 387.. 77
R v Conway (1990) 91 Cr App R 143.. 482
R v Cook [1959] 2 QB 340 .... 269, 275
R v Cook [1987] QB 417, CA 305–306
R v Cooke [1995] 1 Cr App R 318, CA 438–439, 442, 458
R v Coulman (1912) 20 Cr App R 106 256
R v Cowan [1995] 3 WLR 818, CA 78–9, 416
R v Cox (1884) 14 QBD 153, CCR 588, 603
R v Cox (1986) 84 Cr App R 132 115
R v Cox [1991] Crim LR 276 406
R v Crampton (1990) 92 Cr App R 369, CA 378–381
R v Crawford (Charisse), The Times, 10 June 1997 285
R v Cummings [1948] 1 All ER 551 .... 166, 167
R v D, The Times, 15 November 1995; LEXIS transcript, CA 87
R v Da Silva [1990] 1 WLR 31, CA........................... 176–177, 178
R v Dalloz (1908) 1 Cr App R 258 13
R v Davis (1975) 62 Cr App R 194 .... 10, 11
R v Davis [1993] 1 WLR 613, CA 561–562, 563
R v Deakin [1994] 4 All ER 769.. 74
R v Deen, 21 December 1993 (unreported) 503
R v Derby Magistrates' Court, ex p B [1995] 3 WLR 681, HL...... 576, 593–595, 596, 599
R v Doheny [1997] 1 Cr App R 369, CA...................................... 502–506
R v Donaldson (1976) 64 Cr App R 59 170
R v Downes and Rawlinson, The Times, 10 December 1993..................... 408
R v Downey [1995] 1 Cr App R 547 .... 232, 233
R v Dragic [1996] 2 Cr App R 232 346
R v Dunbar [1958] 1 QB 1 61
R v Duncalf [1979] 1 WLR 918 273
R v Duncan (1981) 73 Cr App R 359 .... 259, 264, 408
R v Dunford (1990) 91 Cr App R 150 394
R v Dunkley [1927] 1 KB 323 254
R v Dunn (1990) 91 Cr App R 237, CA 400–401
R v Durbin [1995] 2 Cr App R 84, CA... 263
R v Edwards [1975] QB 27 .... 46, 49
R v Edwards (1983) 77 Cr App R 5 61
R v Edwards [1991] 1 WLR 207 .... 191, 202–203, 205
R v Eleftheriou, The Times, 2 March 1993 176
R v Ellis [1910] 2 KB 746, CCA 256–257
R v Emmerson (1990) 92 Cr App R 284 377
R v Everett [1988] Crim LR 826.. 501
R v Exall (1866) 4 F & F 922 12
R v Farnham JJ, ex p Gibson (1991) 155 JP 792 77
R v Fenelley [1989] Crim LR 142 441
R v Fenlon (1980) 71 Cr App R 307 189
R v Fergus (1993) 98 Cr App R 313, CA 476–477, 478
R v Ferguson (1909) 2 Cr App R 250 256
R v Fowkes, The Times, 8 March 1856 173
R v Foxley [1995] 2 Cr App R 523, CA.. 342
R v France and France [1979] Crim LR 48.............................. 272, 273
R v French (1993) 97 Cr App R 421 346
R v Friend [1997] 2 All ER 1011 80
R v Frost (1839) 9 C & P 129 154
R v Fulling [1987] QB 426, CA 374, 442
R v Funderburk [1990] 1 WLR 587 .... 116, 191, 192–195, 202, 205
R v Galbraith [1981] 1 WLR 1040, CA............... 134–135, 136, 372, 407
R v Gale (1987) (unreported).. 239
R v Gallagher [1974] 1 WLR 1204, CA 14–15
R v Garofoli [1990] 2 SCR 1421 553

R v Gentles, 30 April 1993 (No 92/3162/W2) (unreported) 19, 20
R v Genus [1996] Crim LR 502 104
R v Gill [1963] 1 WLR 841 41
R v Glennon (1992) 66 ALJR 344 25
R v Gloster (1888) 16 Cox CC 471 331
R v Goldenberg (1988) 88 Cr App R 285, CA 378
R v Golder [1960] 3 All ER 457 . . . . 160, 161
R v Gonzales de Arango (1991) 96 Cr App R 399 335
R v Governor of Brixton Prison, ex p Levin [1997] 3 WLR 117 347
R v Governor of Pentonville Prison, ex p Chinoy [1992] 1 All ER 317 . . . . 443, 458
R v Grafton [1993] QB 101, CA 152–153
R v Grant [1944] 2 All ER 311 75
R v Grant [1996] 1 Cr App R 73, CA 8
R v Grant [1996] 2 Cr App R 272 235
R v Gray (1973) 58 Cr App R 177 60
R v Grayson [1993] Crim LR 864 408
R v Greenacre (1837) 8 C & P 35 42
R v Grout (1909) 3 Cr App R 64 269
R v Gunning (1980) 98 Cr App R 303, CA 153–154
R v H [1994] Crim LR 205 262
R v H [1995] 2 AC 596 . . . . 224–228, 229
R v Hacker [1994] 1 WLR 1659 . . . . 241, 242
R v Hall [1973] QB 496 332
R v Halpin [1975] QB 907 331
R v Hamid and Hamid (1979) 69 Cr App R 324 91
R v Hampshire [1995] 3 WLR 260, CA 87
R v Hants County Council, ex p Ellerton [1985] 1 WLR 749, CA 64–5
R v Hardy (1994) 45 BCAC 146 553
R v Haringey JJ, ex p DPP [1996] 2 WLR 114 153
R v Harron [1996] 2 Cr App R 457 104
R v Hart (1932) 23 Cr App R 202 189
R v Harz [1967] AC 760 5
R v Hawkins (1996) 141 DLR (4th) 193, SCC 366–367
R v Hayes (1976) 64 Cr App R 194 85
R v Heaton [1993] Crim LR 593 501
R v Hennessy (1978) 68 Cr App R 419 557
R v Hepworth [1955] 2 QB 600, CCA 58
R v Herrox, 5 October 1993, CA 263
R v Hester [1973] AC 296 . . . . 102, 103
R v Hewitt (1991) 95 Cr App R 81 560
R v Hill [1996] Crim LR 419 104
R v Hilton [1972] 1 QB 421 77
R v Hind (1860) 8 Cox CC 300 324
R v Hogan [1997] Crim LR 349 342
R v Home Secretary, ex p Khawaja [1984] AC 74, HL 63–4
R v Hope and Others [1994] Crim LR 118 . . . . 475, 476
R v Horseferry Road Magistrates' Court, ex p Bennett [1994] 1 AC 42 445
R v Horseferry Road Magistrates' Court, ex p Bennett (No 2) [1994] 1 All ER 189 563
R v Horwood (1969) 53 Cr App R 619 239
R v Howes [1996] 2 Cr App R 490, CA 117
R v Hudson [1912] 2 KB 464 269
R v Hunt [1987] AC 352 . . . . 46–50, 51, 52, 53
R v Hunter (1987) 57 CR (3d) 1 (Ont CA) 550
R v Hurst [1995] 1 Cr App R 82, CA 334–335, 497
R v Hutchinson (1822) 2 B & C 608n 324
R v Hutchinson (1985) 82 Cr App R 51, CA 154–155
R v Ilyas [1996] Crim LR 810 342
R v Inch (1989) 91 Cr App R 51 517
R v Inder (1977) 67 Cr App R 143 216
R v Jackson [1996] 2 Cr App R 420 527

R v Jelen; R v Katz (1989) 90 Cr App R 456 443
R v Jenkins (1869) 29 LT 372 323
R v Jenkins (1945) 31 Cr App R 1 .... 269, 271, 275
R v Jiminez-Paez (1993) 98 Cr App R 239 335
R v Johnson (Kenneth) [1988] 1 WLR 1377, CA 558, 559–560
R v Johnson [1995] 2 Cr App R 41 219
R v Jones (1923) 17 Cr App R 117 269
R v Jurtyn (1958) 28 CR 295 324
R v K (1992) 97 Cr App R 342 545
R v Kabariti (1990) 92 Cr App R 362 .... 259, 263
R v Keane [1994] 1 WLR 746 .... 147, 549, 550, 562
R v Kearley [1992] 2 AC 228 ....5, 37, 316–318, 319, 327
R v Keenan [1990] 2 QB 54, CA 397–400, 440
R v Kemble [1990] 1 WLR 1111 74
R v Kennaway [1917] 1 KB 25 .... 247, 248
R v Kenny, The Times, 27 July 1993 405
R v Khan [1990] 2 SCR 531 .... 366, 367
R v Khan, 9 August 1990 (unreported) 276, 277, 278
R v Khan (Sultan) [1996] 3 All ER 289, HL 386, 447–457, 458
R v Kilbourne [1973] AC 729 .... 102, 211, 213
R v King [1983] 1 WLR 411 577
R v Kritz [1950] 1 KB 82 52
R v Lamont [1989] Crim LR 813 406
R v Lasseur [1991] Crim LR 53 269
R v Latif [1996] 1 WLR 104, HL 444–446, 465
R v Lawless (1993) 98 Cr App R 342, CA 186–187
R v Lawrence [1977] Crim LR 492 .... 112, 114, 115
R v Lee (1912) 7 Cr App R 31 165
R v Lee [1996] 2 Cr App R 266 123
R v Lee [1996] Crim LR 825 219
R v Lee (Paul) [1976] 1 WLR 71, CA 257
R v Leipert (1997) 143 DLR (4th) 38, SCC 550
R v Lewes Justices, ex p Secretary of State for the Home Department [1973] AC 388 .. 540,
                                                                                    548
R v Lewis (1982) 76 Cr App R 33 239
R v Lillyman [1896] 2 QB 167 .... 163, 164
R v Lloyd (1830) 4 Car & P 233 324
R v Lobell [1957] 1 QB 547 41
R v Lockley [1995] 2 Cr App R 554, CA 341–342, 346
R v Lovelock, The Times, 5 June 1997 8
R v Lucas [1981] QB 720 .... 103, 104
R v Lydon (1986) 85 Cr App R 221, CA 301–302
R v M [1996] 2 Cr App R 56, CA 126–128
R v MacKenney (1981) 76 Cr App R 271 497
R v Maggs (1990) 91 Cr App R 243, CA 10
R v Makanjuola [1995] 1 WLR 1348, CA 93–4, 97, 99, 100
R v Martin [1996] Crim LR 589 336
R v Masih [1986] Crim LR 395 495
R v Mason [1988] 1 WLR 139, CA 387–388
R v Maw [1994] Crim LR 841; LEXIS transcript, CA 160–161
R v McCarthy [1996] Crim LR 818; LEXIS transcript, CA 439–442, 458
R v McGillivray (1992) 97 Cr App R 237, CA 333–334
R v McGovern (1990) 92 Cr App R 228, CA 381–385
R v McGranaghan (Note) [1995] 1 Cr App R 559 .... 231, 232, 233, 235
R v McGuin [1982] 1 NZLR 13 22
R v McGuire (1985) 81 Cr App R 323 322
R v McKenzie [1993] 1 WLR 453, CA 135, 407
R v McLean (1967) 52 Cr App R 80, CA 302–303, 305
R v McLeod [1994] 1 WLR 1500, CA 271–279
R v Mead (1824) 2 B & C 605 324

R v Meads [1996] Crim LR 519 .... 203, 519
R v Mendy (1976) 64 Cr App R 4, CA 201
R v Miah [1997] 2 Cr App R 12 261
R v Milk Marketing Board, ex p Austin, *The Times*, 21 March 1983.............. 65, 66
R v Miller [1952] 2 All ER 667................................... 24, 310, 312
R v Miller (1996) 161 JP 158, CA..265
R v Minister of Agriculture and Fisheries, ex p Graham [1955] 2 QB 140.............332
R v Mitchell (1892) 17 Cox CC 503 415
R v Moghal (1977) 65 Cr App R 56 .... 329, 330
R v Moon [1969] 1 WLR 1705...54
R v Morris (1969) 54 Cr App R 69 219
R v Morris [1995] 2 Cr App R 69 8
R v Moss (1990) 91 Cr App R 371..406
R v Mussell, 27 February 1995 (unreported) 477
R v Mustafa (1976) 65 Cr App R 26 239
R v Myers [1997] 3 WLR 552, HL.......................................307-315
R v Nagah (1990) 155 JP 229 482
R v Napper (1995) 161 JP 16 80
R v Neale (Paul) (1977) 65 Cr App R 304....................................24
R v Newton and Carpenter (1859) 1 F & F 641 324
R v Nicholas (1846) 2 Car & K 246 (Assizes)................................331
R v Norton [1910] 2 KB 496, CCA 412-413
R v O'Boyle (1990) 92 Cr App R 202 314
R v O'Brien (1977) 76 DLR (3d) 513 322
R v O'Connor [1995] 4 SCR 411 555
R v Oakley (1979) 70 Cr App R 7 518
R v Oliver [1944] KB 68 .... 48, 49
R v Osborne [1905] 1 KB 551 ....163, 164, 165
R v Osbourne [1973] QB 678, CA 305
R v Owen (1985) 83 Cr App R 100 .... 276, 278
R v Oyesiku (1971) 56 Cr App R 240, CA 169-170
R v P [1991] 2 AC 447..197, 200
R v Palmer (1993) 99 Cr App R 83 75
R v Paris (1992) 97 Cr App R 99, CA..................................... 375-376
R v Parmar (1987) 34 CCC (3d) 260 (Ont HCJ) 553
R v Parris (1988) 89 Cr App R 68 .... 395, 443
R v Pattinson [1996] 1 Cr App R 51, CA 477-478
R v Paul [1920] 2 KB 183 77
R v Pearce (1979) 69 Cr App R 365, CA 170-171
R v Peterborough Justices, ex p Hicks [1977] 1 WLR 1371 577
R v Phillips (1936) 26 Cr App R 17 193
R v Pieterson [1995] 1 WLR 293, CA 13-14
R v Podola [1960] 1 QB 325 61
R v Police Complaints Board, ex p Madden [1983] 1 WLR 447 65
R v Polin [1991] Crim LR 293 408
R v Pook (1871) 13 Cox CC 172n 330
R v Powell [1985] 1 WLR 1364 .... 274, 276, 278
R v Prager [1972] 1 WLR 260..373
R v Preston [1993] 4 All ER 638 450
R v Price [1996] Crim LR 738 80
R v Price (Herbert) [1969] 1 QB 541 102
R v Putland and Sorrell [1946] 1 All ER 85 49
R v Quinn [1995] 1 Cr App R 480, CA.................................. 487-488
R v R [1994] 1 WLR 758, CA 577
R v R [1996] Crim LR 815 100
R v R (D) (1996) 107 CCC (3d) 289..528
R v Rance (1975) 62 Cr App R 118 221
R v Rankine [1986] 2 All ER 566 558
R v Raphaie [1996] Crim LR 812; LEXIS transcript, CA 403
R v Rawlings and Broadbent (Practice Note) [1995] 1 WLR 178 ....126, 127

R v Reading (1965) 50 Cr App R 98. 239
R v Redd [1923] 1 KB 104 257
R v Reid [1989] Crim LR 719 311
R v Rennie (1981) 74 Cr App R 207 381
R v Reynolds [1989] Crim LR 220 495
R v Rice [1963] 1 QB 857 . . . . 304, 312
R v Richardson (1967) 51 Cr App R 381 77
R v Richardson [1969] 1 QB 299, CA 203–204
R v Richardson [1971] 2 QB 484, CA 182
R v Richens, The Times, 25 November 1992 . . . . 259, 260
R v Rider (1986) 83 Cr App R 207, CA 92
R v Robb (1991) 93 Cr App R 161 517
R v Roberts [1942] 1 All ER 187, CCA 161
R v Roberts (John Marcus) (1984) 80 Cr App R 89. 152
R v Robertson [1968] 1 WLR 1767 43
R v Robinson [1994] 3 All ER 346, CA 498
R v Robinson [1996] Crim LR 417 104
R v Robinson, 37 Cr App R 95 211
R v Rogers (1994) 158 JP 909, CA 321–322
R v Rouse [1904] 1 KB 184. 269
R v Rowson [1986] QB 174 . . . . 311, 314
R v Rowton (1865) 10 Cox CC 25 264
R v Roy [1992] Crim LR 185 221
R v Rudd (1948) 32 Cr App R 138 77
R v Russell (1968) 52 Cr App R 147. 102
R v Russell-Jones [1995] 1 Cr App R 538 . . . . 150, 152
R v Ryder [1994] 2 All ER 859 227
R v Sabouri, 20 January 1997 (unreported) 238
R v Samuel (1956) 40 Cr App R 8, CCA. 256, 265
R v Samuel [1988] QB 615 . . . . 393–394, 395, 436, 437, 443
R v Sang [1980] AC 402 . . . . 23, 386, 433, 439, 441, 443, 451, 452, 458
R v Sat-Bhambra (1988) 88 Cr App R 55 387
R v Scaife (1836) 2 Lewin 150 324
R v Scarrott [1978] QB 1016 25
R v Scott (1921) 86 JP 69 47
R v Scott (1984) 79 Cr App R 49, CA 155
R v Scott [1990] 3 SCR 979 . . . . 551, 554
R v Seaboyer (1991) 83 DLR (4th) 193, SCC 105–108, 111, 555
R v Sealby [1965] 1 All ER 701. 331
R v Sekhon (1986) 85 Cr App R 19, CA 180, 181
R v Selvey See Selvey v DPP
R v Setz-Dempsey (1993) 98 Cr App R 23, CA 334, 346
R v Sharp [1988] 1 All ER 65 408
R v Sharrock [1948] 1 All ER 145. 75
R v Shaw, The Times, 31 December 1992 260
R v Sheean (1908) 21 Cox CC 561 269
R v Shephard [1993] AC 380, HL 347, 349
R v Silcott, The Times, 9 December 1991 501
R v Simmonds [1969] 1 QB 685 . . . . 176, 181
R v Simmonds [1996] Crim LR 816 88
R v Simpson (1993) 99 Cr App R 48 219
R v Sims [1946] KB 531. 211
R v Slater [1995] 1 Cr App R 584, CA 475–476
R v Smith (1915) 11 Cr App R 229, CCA .5, 215, 218–219
R v Smith [1992] 2 SCR 915 . . . . 366, 367
R v Smith [1994] Crim LR 458. 121
R v Smith (Brian) 16 February 1995 (unreported), CA. 19, 20
R v Smurthwaite [1994] 1 All ER 898, CA 442–443, 446
R v South Ribble Magistrates, ex p Cochrane [1996] 2 Cr App R 544, DC 177–178
R v Spencer [1987] AC 128, HL. 101

R v Springer [1996] Crim LR 903, CA 125
R v Stafford [1968] 3 All ER 752 60
R v Stamford [1972] 2 QB 391 ....501, 502
R v Stannard (1837) 7 C & P 673 ....258, 259
R v Stewart and Sappleton (1989) 89 Cr App R 273 10–12
R v Stinchcombe [1991] 3 SCR 326 ....554, 555
R v Stockwell (1993) 97 Cr App R 260, CA 493, 518, 519, 528
R v Storey and Anwar (1968) 52 Cr App R 334 170
R v Straffen [1952] 2 QB 911, CCA 215, 217–218
R v Stretton and McCallion (1986) 86 Cr App R 7 186
R v Strudwick (1993) 99 Cr App R 326 499
R v Sweet-Escott (1971) 55 Cr App R 316 ....188, 193
R v Symonds (1924) 18 Cr App R 100, CCA 77
R v Tanner (1977) 66 Cr App R 56 270
R v Taylor (1928) 21 Cr App R 20 12
R v Theodosi [1993] RTR 179 517
R v Thompson (1976) 64 Cr App R 96, CA 159
R v Thompson (1981) 74 Cr App R 315 266
R v Thompson [1982] QB 647 332
R v Thompson [1995] 2 Cr App R 589 24
R v Thomson [1912] 3 KB 19 330
R v Thornton [1995] 1 Cr App R 578 ....475, 476
R v Tiplady (1995) 159 JP 548, CA 483–487
R v Tolson (1864) 4 F & F 103 305
R v Tompkins, 67 Cr App R 181 603
R v Toner (1991) 93 Cr App R 382, CA 495
R v Tooke (1989) 90 Cr App R 417, CA 171–172
R v Treacy [1944] 2 All ER 229 312
R v Tregear [1967] 2 QB 574 153
R v Tudor, 18 July 1988 (unreported) 216
R v Turnbull [1977] QB 224 .... 29, 234, 372, 472–473, 474, 475, 476, 477, 478
R v Turner (1816) 5 M & S 206 47
R v Turner [1944] KB 463 269
R v Turner (Bryan James) (1975) 61 Cr App R 67 .... 75, 306, 308, 310, 313
R v Turner (Terence) [1975] QB 834, CA 496–497, 499
R v Turner [1995] 1 WLR 264, CA 548–550
R v Twiss (1918) 13 Cr App R 177 239
R v U (FJ) [1995] 3 SCR 764 (SCC) 366, 367
R v Uljee [1982] 1 NZLR 561 603
R v Valentine [1996] 2 Cr App R 213, CA 162–168
R v Varley [1982] 2 All ER 519, CA 284–285
R v Vickers [1972] Crim LR 101 ....272, 277, 278
R v Viola [1982] 1 WLR 1138, CA 24, 112–115, 117
R v Virgo (1978) 67 Cr App R 323 179
R v Vye [1993] 1 WLR 471, CA 258–261, 262
R v Wainwright (1875) 13 Cox CC 171 330
R v Walker [1996] Crim LR 742; LEXIS transcript, CA 94–100
R v Walsh (1989) 91 Cr App R 161, CA 394–395
R v Ward (Judith Theresa) [1993] 1 WLR 619, CA 141, 490–491, 501, 549
R v Warickshall (1783) 1 Leach 263 409
R v Waters (1997) 161 JP 249, CA 336
R v Watson (1913) 8 Cr App R 249 275
R v Watts [1983] 3 All ER 101 ....273, 274, 275, 276, 278
R v Webb (1994) 74 A Crim R 436 20
R v Weightman [1993] 2 All ER 577, CA 501
R v Welstead [1996] 1 Cr App R 59 125
R v West [1996] 2 Cr App R 390 ....219, 220, 221
R v Westwell [1976] 2 All ER 812, CA 183
R v Wilbourne (1917) 12 Cr App R 280 165
R v Wilmot (1988) 89 Cr App R 341 418

R v Winfield [1939] 4 All ER 164, CCA..264
R v Wood [1994] Crim LR 222 407
R v Woodcock (1789) 1 Leach 500 323
R v Wright (1821) Russ & R 456 528
R v Wright (1989) 90 Cr App R 325 ....205, 238, 240, 241
R v X (1989) 91 Cr App R 36, CA 121
R v Young [1995] 2 WLR 430 35-6
R v Zarrabi, *The Times*, 23 February 1985 54
R v Zoppola-Barraza [1994] Crim LR 833 ....262, 263
Ratten v R [1972] AC 378 327
Rawson v Haigh (1824) 2 Bing 99 328
Read v Bishop of Lincoln [1892] AC 644...332
Reid v R (1989) 90 Cr App R 121 476
Rex Co v Muirhead (1926) 136 LT 568 602
Rex v.... See R v...
Reynolds v Phoenix Assurance Co [1978] 2 Lloyd's Rep 22 197
Rogers v Secretary of State for the Home Department; Gaming Board for GB v Rogers [1972]
    2 All ER 1057 558
Rowlands v De Vecchi (1882) Cab & El 10.......................................323
Rush & Tomkins v GLC [1989] AC 1280, HL.............................574-575
Saïdi v France (1993) 17 EHRR 251...358, 359
Saunders v UK (1996) 23 EHRR 313 (ECHR) 430-432
Savage v Chief Constable of Hampshire [1997] 2 All ER 631, CA 556-559
Saxton (Dec'd), Re [1962] 1 WLR 968...596
Schenk v Switzerland (1988) 13 EHRR 242......................................455, 457
Schneiderman v United States, 320 US 118, 87 L Ed 1796, 63 S Ct 1333 (1943)........69
Science Research Council v Nassé [1980] AC 1028, HL 563-564
Scott v R; Barnes v R [1989] AC 1242, PC.................................453, 474
Secretary of State for Defence v Guardian Newspapers Ltd [1984] Ch 156 ....565, 566, 567
Selvey v DPP [1970] AC 304, HL 269, 270, 271, 273, 274, 275, 276, 278
Senat v Senat [1965] P 172 179
Shand v R [1996] 1 WLR 67...474, 479
Simon v Simon [1936] P 17...322
Smith v Blakey (1867) LR 2 QB 326 322
Sodeman v R [1936] 2 All ER 1138..61
Solicitor, A, Re [1993] QB 69 ....65, 66
Solicitor General of Canada v Royal Commission of Inquiry into Confidentiality of Health
    Records in Ontario [1981] 2 SCR 494 552
Southwark and Vauxhall Water Co v Quick (1878) 3 QBD 315....................583
Sparks v R [1964] AC 964, PC...303
State v Schwab, 409 NW 2d 876 (1987)..288
Statue of Liberty, The [1968] 1 WLR 739 351
Stirland v DPP [1944] AC 315, HL 252-253, 263-264
Sturla v Freccia (1880) 5 App Cas 623..331
Subramaniam v Public Prosecutor [1956] 1 WLR 965, PC 300-301
Sussex Peerage case (1844) 11 Cl & Finley 85..............................321, 322
Svenska v Sun Alliance [1995] 2 Lloyd's Rep 84.................................581
Talbot, Lord v Cusack (1864) 17 ICLR 213 181
Taylor v Anderton [1995] 1 WLR 447 541
Teper v R [1952] AC 480, HL 13, 293
Thomas v Commissioner of Police [1997] 1 All ER 747, CA..................196-200
Thomas v DPP [1991] RTR 292, DC 435-436, 438
Thompson v DPP (1918) 13 Cr App R 61..239
Thorpe v Chief Constable of Manchester [1989] 1 WLR 665, CA 243
Tickle v Tickle [1968] 1 WLR 937, P, D & A.....................................331
Tippett v Maryland, 436 F 2d 1153 (1971); sub nom Murel v Baltimore City Criminal Court,
    407 US 355 (1972) 69
Toohey v Metropolitan Police Commissioners [1965] AC 595, HL..........203, 204, 497
United States v Davis, 835 F 2d 274 (11th Cir 1988) 529
United States v Manley, 893 F 2d 1221 (11th Cir) 529

TABLE OF CASES

Unterpertinger v Austria (1986) 13 EHRR 175 359
US v Giraldo, 822 F 2d 205 (2nd Cir 1987) 320
US v Leon, 104 S Ct 3405 (1984) 462
US v Long, 905 F 2d 1572 (DC Cir 1990) 319, 320
US v Thigpen, 4 F 3d 1573 (11th Cir 1993) 529
US v Zenni, 492 F Supp 464 (ED Ky 1980) 320
Ventouris v Mountain [1991] 1 WLR 607 577
Ventouris v Mountain (No 2) [1992] 1 WLR 887 2
W, Re, *The Times*, 22&23 November 1990 25
W (Minors) (Sexual Abuse: Standard of Proof), Re [1994] 1 FLR 419 67
Wallace v R [1997] 1 Cr App R 396, PC 19–23
Wallace Smith Trust Co v Deloitte [1996] 4 All ER 403 . . . . .545, 564
Walters v R [1969] 2 AC 26, PC 58, 59
Walton v R (1989) 166 CLR 283 330
Ward v James [1966] 1 QB 273 24–5
Warren v Warren [1996] 4 All ER 664, CA 88
Waugh v British Railways Board [1980] AC 521, HL 581–585, 596
Waugh v R [1950] AC 203 324
Webster v Chapman (James) & Co [1989] 3 All ER 939 603
Wharf Properties v Eric Cumine Associates (1991) 29 Con LR 84, PC 189
Wheeler v Le Marchant (1881) 17 Ch D 675 581
White v Taylor [1969] 1 Ch 150 331
Whitehouse v Jordan [1981] 1 WLR 246 530
Windisch v Austria (1990) 13 EHRR 281 . . . . .358, 359
Winship, Re, 397 US 358, 25 L Ed 2d 368, 90 S Ct 1068, 51 Ohio Ops 2d 323 (1970)
. . . . .68, 70
Witham v Holloway (1995) 69 ALJR 847 63
Wong Kam-Ming v R [1980] AC 247 404
Woodby v INS, 385 US 276, 17 L Ed 2d 362, 87 S Ct 483 (1966) 69
Woodhouse v Hall (1980) 72 Cr App R 39, DC 301
Woolley v North London Railway Co (1869) LR 4 CP 602 581
Woolmington v DPP [1935] AC 462, HL 41–2, 44, 46, 47
Worrall v Reich [1955] 1 QB 296 596
Wright v Doe d Tatham (1837) 7 Ad & E 313 318–319
Wright v Wright (1948) 77 CLR 191 64
X Ltd v Morgan-Grampian Ltd [1991] 1 AC 1 . . . . 564, 565–569
Young v Rank [1950] 2 KB 510 139

TABLE OF LEGISLATION

Aboriginal Affairs Planning Authority Act 1972 (WA) 20, 21
Administration of Justice Act 1985
s.33 578
Administration of Justice (Miscellaneous Provisions) Act 1933 149
Bankers' Books Evidence Act 1879
s.6 88
Charter of Rights and Freedoms (Can)..111, 550, 554, 555
s.1 43
s.11(d).............................43
s.24(2)............. 460, 461, 462, 465
Children Act 1989
Pt IV.................. 595, 597, 598
s.1(1)............................595
s.10(1)(b).......................598
s.31(2)............................68
s.31(5)...........................598
s.34(5)...........................598
s.96 86
s.105(1) 86
Children and Young Persons Act 1933
s.1 122
s.38(1).........................85, 86
Civil Evidence Act 1968
Pt.1 352
s.10(1)(c).........................352
Civil Evidence Act 1972
s.3 530
Civil Evidence Act 1995 ...... 38, 159, 181, 195, 300
s.1 295
s.1(2)(a) 12, 292
ss.2–5 298
s.2 295–296
s.3 296
s.4 296
s.5 296–297
s.6(1).............................175
s.6(2).............................175
s.7 ....297, 298
s.10 298
s.14 298
Civil Rights Act (US) 464

Companies Act 1985
s.434 430
s.434(5).........................432
s.436 .... 430, 432
Contempt of Court Act 1981
s.8 ....33, 34
s.8(1).............................33
s.10 .... 564, 565, 566, 568
s.19 567
Copyright, Design and Patents Act 1988
s.280 578
Crimes Act 1900 (NSW)
s.409B 118
Criminal Appeal Act 1968
s.2(1)..............................61
Sched.2, para.1A 333, 338
Criminal Appeal Act 1995
s.9 122
s.11 122
Criminal Attempts Act 1981
s.2(2)(g) 92
Criminal Code (Can) 43
s.27 111
Criminal Damage Act 1971
s.1 456
Criminal Evidence Act 1898..........289
s.1 .... 75, 250, 251
s.1(e)............ 245, 246 et seq, 574
s.1(f)..196, 198, 245, 246 et seq, 311, 574
s.1(f)(i) 245, 246, 249, 254–255, 268, 273
s.1(f)(ii). 245–246, 255–284, 285, 286, 288
s.1(f)(iii) 23, 246, 268, 284–288, 311
s.1(g)..............................77
Criminal Justice Act 1925
s.13(3).......................265, 266
Criminal Justice Act 1967.............266
s.9 .... 265, 357–358
Criminal Justice Act 1987
s.4.............. 15, 149, 411, 426, 427
s.6 .... 15, 342, 411, 426, 427
s.8 17
Criminal Justice Act 1988
Pt.II 266, 332
Pt.VI 390, 392

s.23 . . . . 265, 332, 333, 337,
                        338, 343, 344, 347
s.23(2). 332, 342
s.23(2)(b) 335
s.23(3). 332, 342
s.23(3)(b) 336, 337, 338
s.24 . . . . 323, 332, 338–339,
                        341, 342, 343, 344, 347
s.24(1)(i)–(iii) 340, 341
s.24(2)(a) 340
s.24(4). 341
s.25 . . . . 342–343, 344
s.25(2). 344
s.26 343–344
s.30 . . . . 358, 527–528
s.32 . . . . 121–122, 125
s.32(2). 128
s.32(2)(a)–(c) 129
s.32A. 123–125, 358
s.32A(2) 129
s.33A. 86–87
s.33A(1)–(3) 86
s.34A. 128
Sched.2. 266
Sched.2, para.1. 347
Sched.2, para.3. 347
Sched.13, para.6. 362
Criminal Justice Act 1991
s.52 86
s.53 . . . . . 15, 128–129, 149, 411, 426, 427
Sched.6, para.5. . . . 15, 343, 411, 426, 427
Criminal Justice and Public Order Act 1994
. . . . 38, 86, 92, 396
s.32 . . . . 93, 100
s.32(1). 93, 97
s.32(3). 93
s.34 . . . . 411–412, 415, 416,
                        421, 424, 425, 432, 588
s.34(1)(a) 421
s.34(2)(c) 416
s.34(2)(d) 421
s.34(3). 416
s.34(4). 421
s.34(5). 412
s.35 . . . . 75–76, 77, 81, 268, 416, 428
s.35(1). 78, 80
s.35(2). 80
s.36 .425–426, 432
s.37 . . . . 425, 426–427, 428, 432
s.38(3). 75, 79, 427–428
s.38(6). 428
Criminal Justice (International Co-operation)
Act 1990
s.3 . . . . .339, 343, 362
Criminal Law Act 1977
s.54 82
Criminal Procedure Act 1865 – ('Lord
Denman's Act')
s.3 159
s.4 . . . . .191–192, 193, 195, 205, 314

s.5 . . . . .192, 195, 312
s.6 195
Criminal Procedure and Investigations Act
1996 491
s.1 141–142
s.3 142
s.3(1). 147
s.3(6). 537
s.5 . . . . 142–143, 148
s.6 143
s.7 143–144
s.7(5). 537
s.8 144
s.8(5). 537
s.9 144–145
s.9(8). 537
s.10. 145
s.11. 146
s.20 149
s.30 17
s.39 17
s.40 17
s.41 18
Sched.2, para.1. 355–356
Sched.2, para.2. . . . . . . 265, 266, 355, 356
Criminal Procedure (Insanity) Act 1964
s.4 43
s.4(6). 494
s.4A(2) 365
s.6 43
Criminal Procedure (Insanity and Unfitness to
Plead) Act 1991
s.1(1). 494
Customs and Excise Management Act 1979
. 447
s.50(3). 445
s.170(2). 445
Documentary Evidence Act 1868
s.2 298
Documentary Evidence Act 1882
s.2 298
European Convention on Human Rights 1950
Art.3 377
Art.6 . . . . 430, 431, 455, 457
Art.6(1) 81, 428, 429, 430,
                        454, 455, 457
Art.6(2) 81, 428, 429, 430
Art.6(3)(d) 358, 359, 360
Art.8 . . .449, 452, 453, 454, 455, 456, 457
Art.8(2) 450
Art.10 . . . . 569, 570, 572
Art.10(1) 569
Art.10(2) 569, 570, 571, 572
Art.13 . . . . .453, 454
Evidence Act 1995 (Commonwealth of Aus-
tralia) .38, 283, 585
s.18 83
s.18(2). 83
s.18(6). 83, 84
s.18(7). 83, 84

s.39 206
s.53 9
s.54 9
s.59(1) 319
s.102 188
s.103 189
s.104 289–290
s.114 488–489
s.130 545
s.138 459
s.140 62
Evidence Act 1995 (New South Wales). . . 38
Evidence (Colonial Statutes) Act 1907
 s.1 298
Evidence (Foreign, Dominion and Colonial
Documents) Act 1933
 s.1 298
Factories Act 1961
 s.29(1) 48
Highways Act 1959
 s.121(1) 52
 s.140 52
Highways Act 1980
 s.137(1) 52
 s.161 52
Homicide Act 1957
 s.2(2) 45
Indecency with Children Act 1960. . .82, 122
Indian Evidence Act 1872
 s.148 188
Indictments Act 1915
 s.4 236
 s.5(3) 236, 237
Intelligence Services Act 1994
 s.2(2)(a) 451
 s.5(4) 451
Interception of Communications Act 1985
449
 s.9 . . . . .450, 452
Legal Aid Act 1988
 s.20(4) 129
Magistrates' Courts Act 1952
 s.81 45
Magistrates' Courts Act 1980
 s.101 . . . . 45, 49, 51, 52, 53
Mental Health Act 1959 101
Mental Health Act 1983 101
Misuse of Drugs Act 1971 . . . . 50, 447
 s.5 46
Motor Car Act 1903 90
Oaths Act 1978
 s.1 73–74
 s.4 74
 s.5 . . . . .74, 84
Oaths and Evidence (Overseas Authorities and
Countries) Act 1963
 s.5 298
Obscene Publications Act 1959
 s.4 494

Official Secrets Act 1911
 s.1 402
 s.1(2) 241
Perjury Act 1911
 s.1 74
 s.1(1) 92
 s.13 . . . . .29, 91, 92
Police Act 1996
 s.101(2) 405
Police Act 1997
 Pt.III 458
 s.93(2) 458
Police and Criminal Evidence Act 1984. . 32,
 384, 397
 Pt.II. 589, 590
 Pt.III 398
 Pt.IV 398
 Pt.V 398
 Pt.VI 433
 s.2(2) 440
 s.2(3) 440
 ss.8–22 589
 s.8 590
 s.10 . . . . 575–576, 577, 590
 s.10(1) 590, 591
 s.10(1)(a)–(c) .577
 s.10(2) 589, 590, 591, 592
 s.24(5) 463
 s.41 392
 s.58 . . . . 382, 393, 394, 395, 400
 s.58(1)–(11) 389–390
 s.58(1) 382
 s.62(10) 15
 s.63 439
 s.65 439
 s.66 389
 s.67 487
 s.69 . . . . .333, 338, 351, 352, 353, 355
 s.69(1) 347, 349, 353, 354, 355
 s.68(1)(a) 353
 s.69(1)(b) 349, 352, 353
 s.76 . . . . .307, 308, 313, 333, 338,
 372, 373, 374 et seq,
 408–409, 439, 446
 s.76(1) 313
 s.76(2) 307, 310, 313, 314,
 315, 376, 381,
 382, 404
 s.76(2)(a) 374, 377, 382
 s.76(2)(b) . . . 374, 378, 379, 381, 382, 385
 s.76(3) 379
 s.76(8) 374, 377
 s.77 . . . . 104, 405, 406, 407
 s.77(1) 29
 s.78 . . . . 9, 20, 152, 225, 229, 307,
 310, 365, 372, 381, 382, 386,
 387 et seq, 435, 436, 437, 439,
 442, 443, 448, 452, 453, 454,
 456, 484, 485

s.78(1)...... 24, 228, 387, 389, 395, 396,
400, 402, 433, 434, 437,
438, 446, 447, 453, 457,
458, 459, 471, 472
s.79 154
s.80 82
s.80(1)–(8) 81–82
s.81 149
s.82(1) 369, 431
s.82(3) 225, 228, 386
Sched.3, Pt.II, para.8...... 348, 349, 354
Sched.3, Pt.II, para.9 348
Sched.3, Pt.II, para.11 348
Sched.3, Pt.II, para.12 348
Code C............. 390–392, 396–397
Code C, Annex B 392–393
Code D..................... 479–482
Code E 401–402
Prevention of Corruption Act 1906 44
Prevention of Corruption Act 1916
s.2 44
Prevention of Crime Act 1953 53
s.1(1) 44
Prevention of Terrorism (Temporary Provi-
sions) Act 1989 396
s.14(1)(a)...................... 401
s.20(1)......................... 402
Sched.5, para.6................... 401
Protection of Children Act 1978..... 82, 122
Public Bodies Corrupt Practices Act 1889 44
Rehabilitation of Offenders Act 1974.... 196
s.4(1)....................... 195, 197
s.7(3) 195, 197, 199, 200

Road Traffic Act 1988 349
s.5 .... 350, 437
s.5(1)........................ 350, 351
s.6 .... 437, 438
s.7(1) 350, 355
s.7(6) 350, 355
Road Traffic Offenders Act 1988
s.16 .... 350, 351
Road Traffic Regulations Act 1984
s.89 .... 29, 89
s.89(1) 90
s.89(2) 90
Security Service Act 1989 448
Sexual Offences Act 1956 .... 82, 122
s.30(2) 45
s.47 53
Sexual Offences Act 1967 .... 82, 122
Sexual Offences (Amendment) Act 1976. 193
s.2 .... 111, 112, 113, 116, 117, 118
s.2(1).......................... 118
s.2(2).......................... 118
Theft Act 1968
s.27(3).......................241, 242
s.27(3)(b) 242
Trade Descriptions Act 1968
s.1(1)(b)........................483
Treason Act 1795
s.1 89
Trial of Lunatics Act 1833 494
United States Code (US)
Title 18, s.109A 223
Title 18, s.513................... 223
Wireless Telegraphy Act 1949 63

TABLE OF ORDERS, RULES AND REGULATIONS

Consumer Rationing (Consolidation) Order 1944 (SR & O 1944 No 800)
   Art.4 49
   Art.4(1) 50
   Sched.1 50
County Court Rules 1981 (SI 1981 No 1687)
   Ord.20
     rr.15–17 300
Criminal Evidence (Northern Ireland) Order 1988 (SI 1988 No 1987)
   Art.4 428
   Art.4(5) 428
   Art.6 . . . . 428, 429
Crown Court (Advance Notice of Expert Evidence) Rules 1987 (SI 1987 No 716). . . .491
   r.3(1) 149
   r.3(2) 149
   r.5 149
Crown Court (Criminal Procedure and Investigations Act 1996) (Disclosure) Rules 1997
. 563
Emergency Regulations 1951 (Malaya). . .300
Family Proceedings Rules 1991 (SI 1991 No 1247) 598
Federal Rules of Civil Procedure (US)
   Rule 50(a) 522
Federal Rules of Evidence (US)
   Rule 104(a) 521
   Rule 403 522
   Rule 413 222–223
   Rule 414 . . . . .222, 223
   Rule 415 . . . . .222, 223
   Rule 701 521
   Rule 702 . . . . .520, 522, 523
   Rule 703 . . . . .521, 522

Rule 704 529
Rule 704(b) 529, 530
Rule 706 522
Rule 801(a) 319, 320
Rule 803 360
Rule 804 360
Rule 807 360–361
Fire Services (Discipline) Regulations 1948
. 64
   Sched., para.(7)(a) 65
   Sched., para.(11)(c) 65
Indictment Rules 1971 (SI 1971 No 1253)
   r.9 236
Magistrates' Courts (Advance Notice of Expert Evidence) Rules 1997 150
Magistrates' Courts (Criminal Procedure and Investigations Act 1996) (Disclosure) Rules 1997 563
Misuse of Drugs Regulations 1973 46
Police (Discipline) Regulations 1977
   Sched.2 65
Rules of the Supreme Court 1965 (SI 1965 No 1776)
   Ord.24
     r.13 543
     r.13(1) 543
     r.13(2) 543
   Ord.38
     r.21 298–299
     r.22 . . . . .298, 299
     r.23 . . . . .298, 299
     r.37 583
Sugar (Control) Order 1940 (SR & O 1940 No 1068)
   Art.2 48

I

INTRODUCTION

Evidence is the information with which the matters requiring proof in a trial are proved. The study of evidence, therefore, is the study of the process by which such matters are proved in court. In very broad terms, the law of evidence may be said to be concerned with the following questions:

(1) What is the extent to which particular types of evidence may be considered in a case? In a criminal trial, for example, the issue may arise as to whether evidence that the person accused has previously been involved in other misconduct can be introduced. If it can be introduced, precisely what use may the jury make of the evidence? If it cannot be introduced, what is the justification for this restriction on the free admissibility of evidence?
(2) Are there principles governing the manner in which evidence which has been admitted is to be evaluated?
(3) By which party in a case must evidence be presented?
(4) What are the principles governing the course of evidence in a trial?

Questions such as these will form the basis of the discussions later in this chapter and in subsequent chapters. For the present, it is sufficient to explore briefly the theoretical context of the English law of evidence. In particular, it should be noted that this law is generally considered to embody a 'rationalist' approach:

Extract 1.0

W Twining, *Rethinking Evidence: Exploratory Essays* (1994) 185–6

. . . the common law of evidence, and the perception of Evidence as a distinct field of study, were relatively late developments. Many of the technical refinements, which led to the perception of the Anglo-American law of evidence as being peculiar, developed in the period 1770 to 1830. Nearly all specialized secondary writings about the common law of evidence since Gilbert have proceeded on very similar assumptions that belong to a remarkably homogeneous intellectual tradition that may be called 'The Rationalist Tradition of Evidence Scholarship'. These assumptions relate, firstly, to the aims and nature

I

of 'rational' adjudication and, secondly, to what is involved in 'proving' disputed matters of fact by 'rational' means.

The key ideas can be restated as follows: Firstly, the central *purpose* of adjudication is 'rectitude of decision', that is the correct application of substantive law to facts proved to be true on the basis of relevant evidence presented to the tribunal. However, the pursuit of truth in adjudication has to be constrained by other, 'extrinsic' values. These subordinate ends, or side-constraints, were summarized by the utilitarian jurist Jeremy Bentham (1748–1832) in the classic phrase 'vexation, expense and delay'; non-utilitarians have expressed some of the central values in terms of ideas of 'procedural fairness' or 'due process'.

Secondly, the pursuit of truth as a means to justice under the law is to be pursued by *rational* means. Evidence scholars have almost without exception adopted a conception of 'rational' fact-finding that comes from a single philosophical tradition, English empiricism, as exemplified by Locke, Bentham, John Stuart Mill and, in modern times, A J Ayer....

... certain features of that tradition deserve attention. Firstly, the idea that adjective law (evidence and procedure) is concerned with the correct implementation of substantive law (Truth and Justice under the Law) fits well with the ideology of Liberal Legalism, exemplified by the classic notion of the Rule of Law. But it fits equally well (if not better) with Damaška's ideal type of the managerial state in which adjudicators are bureaucratic officials charged with implementing state policy through the efficient application of precise rules. This need not surprise us; but it is significant in that it suggests that the idea that adjudication is concerned with the correct application of existing laws to true facts is shared by standard versions of liberal and socialist theories of law.

Secondly, Civilian lawyers have pointed out that the set of assumptions embodied in the Rationalist Tradition fits civilian conceptions of procedure and evidence. Indeed, they ask, do they not fit the 'inquisitorial' systems of procedure better than 'adversarial'? If so, how is it that the Rationalist Model is a rational reconstruction of the underlying assumptions of *common law* discourse about evidence? A short answer is first that common law procedural arrangements deviate in many important respects from the pure adversarial model ... ; and secondly, a great deal of our law of evidence is concerned with side-constraints on the pursuit of truth (what Wigmore called 'rules of *extrinsic* policy') rather than upholding rectitude of decision. Thirdly, the history of the Anglo-American law of evidence is marked by a series of long-running debates. At one extreme, Jeremy Bentham argued that all binding rules of evidence should be abolished. At the other extreme, it has been argued that the law of evidence embodies both the accumulated wisdom of centuries of practical experience and some fundamental notions of procedural fairness, especially in respect of safeguards of persons accused of crime. The latter include the presumption of innocence; the right to silence and the privilege against self-incrimination; exclusion of evidence of character (or disposition – including evidence of past convictions); the hearsay rule and, in the United States, the exclusion of evidence that has been obtained by illegal or unfair means. Such debates are often portrayed as differences between 'Right Wing' proponents of Law-and-Order and 'Left Wing' or Civil Libertarian defenders of the rights of persons suspected of crime. The issues are much more complex than that. However, the debates do fit a recognizable pattern: they are, by and large, debates *within* a single intellectual and ideological tradition; they are repeated across time and across geographical boundaries: for example, they have been repeated, with local variations, in England, Scotland, the United States, Australia, Canada, India – and, indeed, in nearly all common law jurisdictions; similarly recent arguments about criminal evidence in England in the period 1972–85 can be found in almost identical terms in debates in the first half of the nineteenth century. Not surprisingly, the outcome has almost invariably ended in compromise, a 'balancing' of the interests of the community in enforcing the criminal law and in avoiding the wrongful conviction of innocent persons. From time to time the balance shifts in one direction or another, with a general trend towards the reduction in scope and importance of the technical rules of evidence. However, no common law country has yet implemented Bentham's proposals for total abolition of the technical rules. One possibly surprising feature of those debates is that it is the proponents of 'Law-and-Order', generally regarded as conservatives or reactionaries, who claim to have reason on their side and who attribute the survival of the technical rules to the sinister economic interests of a privileged group, the legal profession.

Scholars such as Twining[1] have criticised the English law of evidence for being too heavily focused on questions of whether particular evidence is to be admitted or excluded, and for its consequent marginalisation of questions of how particular evidence which has been admitted is to be evaluated. As will be seen in the course of this book, this criticism is to a large extent justified. Putting aside the law's expectation that those responsible for evaluating evidence are apprised in appropriate circumstances of its possible unreliability, the actual process of evaluating evidence is considered to be a question of fact with which the law of evidence has little concern.

It is necessary now to turn to an examination of a number of basic concepts which are built upon in the rest of the book.

1. RELEVANCE, ADMISSIBILITY AND WEIGHT

The fundamental concepts of the *relevance, admissibility* and *weight* of evidence are discussed in the following extract:

Extract 1.1.1

DPP v Kilbourne [1973] AC 729, 756–7 (HL)

LORD SIMON OF GLAISDALE: Evidence is relevant if it is logically probative or disprobative of some matter which requires proof. I do not pause to analyse what is involved in 'logical probativeness,' except to note that the term

---

[1] See generally W Twining, *Rethinking Evidence: Exploratory Essays* (1994).

3

does not of itself express the element of experience which is so significant of its operation in law, and possibly elsewhere. It is sufficient to say, even at the risk of etymological tautology, that relevant (ie, logically probative or disprobative) evidence is evidence which makes the matter which requires proof more or less probable. . . . Evidence is admissible if it may be lawfully adduced at a trial. 'Weight' of evidence is the degree of probability (both intrinsically and inferentially) which is attached to it by the tribunal of fact once it is established to be relevant and admissible in law (though its relevance may exceptionally, as will appear, be dependent on its evaluation by the tribunal of fact).

Exceptionally evidence which is irrelevant to a fact which is in issue is admitted to lay the foundation for other, relevant, evidence (eg, evidence of an unsuccessful search for a missing relevant document, in order to lay the foundation for secondary evidence of the document). Apart from such exceptional cases no evidence which is irrelevant to a fact in issue is admissible. But some relevant evidence is nevertheless inadmissible. To cite a famous passage from the opinion of Lord Herschell LC in *Makin v Attorney-General for New South Wales* [1894] AC 57, 65:

'It is undoubtedly not competent for the prosecution to adduce evidence tending to show that the accused has been guilty of criminal acts other than those covered in the indictment, for the purpose of leading to the conclusion that the accused is a person likely from his criminal conduct or character to have committed the offence for which he is being tried. On the other hand, the mere fact that the evidence adduced tends to show the commission of other crimes does not render it inadmissible if it is relevant to an issue before the jury and it may be so relevant if it bears upon the question whether the acts alleged to constitute the crime charged in the indictment were designed or accidental, or to rebut a defence which would otherwise be open to the accused.'

That what was declared to be inadmissible in the first sentence of this passage is nevertheless relevant (ie, logically probative) can be seen from numerous studies of offences in which recidivists are matched against first offenders, and by considering that it has never been doubted that evidence of motive (which can be viewed as propensity to commit the particular offence charged, in contradistinction to propensity to commit offences generally of the type charged) is relevant. All relevant evidence is prima facie admissible. The reason why the type of evidence referred to by Lord Herschell LC in the first sentence of the passage is inadmissible is, not because it is irrelevant, but because its logically probative significance is considered to be grossly outweighed by its prejudice to the accused, so that a fair trial is endangered if it is admitted; the law therefore exceptionally excludes this relevant evidence: whereas in the circumstances referred to in the second sentence the logically probative significance of the evidence is markedly greater. (See also Lord Moulton in *Rex v Christie* [1914] AC 545, 559, 560.)

Not all admissible evidence is universally relevant. Admissible evidence may be relevant to one count of an indictment and not to another. It may be admissible against one accused (or party) but not another. It may be admissible to rebut a defence but inadmissible to reinforce the case for the prosecution.

The summing up of Scrutton J in *Rex v Smith* ('The Brides in the Bath' case: see the report in the *'Notable British Trials'* series, at pp 276–278) was a striking example; the jury was directed to consider the drowning of other newly-wedded and well-insured wives of the accused for the purpose only of rebutting a defence of accidental death by drowning, but not otherwise for the purpose of positive proof of the murder charged. (See also Lord Atkinson, Lord Parker concurring, in *Rex v Christie* [1914] AC 545, 553.)

As the above extract indicates, an item of evidence is considered relevant if it renders a matter requiring proof *more probable than it would be without that evidence*. Thus, an item of evidence is relevant so long as it has some probative value or probative force, however little.[2] As has been put by Thesiger J in *R v Harz*, 'the word "relevant" is to all intents and purposes synonymous with the phrase "of probative value"'.[3] And in *R v Kearley* Lord Oliver of Aylmerton observed:

> 'Relevant' cannot, I think, be better defined than in article 1 of *Stephen's Digest of the Law of Evidence*, 12th ed (1936), p 3 that is to say, that the word means that
>
>> 'any two facts to which it is applied are so related to each other that according to the common course of events one either taken by itself or in connection with other facts proves or renders probable the past, present, or future existence or non-existence of the other.'
>
> To put it, perhaps, more succinctly, a fact to be relevant must be probative . . .[4]

Unless it is excluded by some exclusionary rule, such as the hearsay rule or the similar-facts rule, all relevant evidence is presumptively admissible. Such evidence is said to be 'legally admissible', 'admissible as a matter of law' or 'prima facie admissible'. It may, however, be excluded by the trial judge in the exercise of an exclusionary discretion.

An alternative approach to relevance is that advocated by Wigmore.[5] On this approach, a distinction is made between logical relevance and legal relevance. Evidence is not prima facie admissible unless it is legally relevant. An item of evidence which is relevant in the normal sense of rendering a fact in issue more probable than it would be without the evidence is logically relevant, but it is not necessarily legally relevant. To be legally relevant, it may be necessary for that item of evidence to possess some 'plus value' in the shape of additional probative value:

Logical relevance + 'Plus value' = Sufficient relevance/Legal relevance

It would seem that this concept of 'plus value' is simply a vehicle for facilitating consideration of any disadvantages of admitting the evidence. Put

---

[2] 'It is enough if the item could reasonably show that a fact is slightly more probable than it would appear without that evidence': E W Cleary, *McCormick on Evidence* (3rd ed 1984) 542.
[3] [1967] AC 760, 785.
[4] [1992] 2 AC 228, 263.
[5] J H Wigmore, *Evidence in Trials at Common Law (Vol 1A)* (rev by P Tillers, 1983) 969. Such an approach is also taken by L H Hoffmann, 'Similar Facts after *Boardman*' (1975) 91 *Law Quarterly Review* 193, 204–6.

another way, plus value is the additional probative value required for the total probative value of the evidence to outweigh such possible considerations as prejudice to the defendant, the introduction of collateral issues, delay, confusion of the jury, and so on.[6] On the orthodox approach to relevance, however, such considerations would be taken into account in the exercise of *discretion*, rather than in determining whether the evidence is 'relevant' in the first place. The Wigmore approach has often been criticised for obscuring the precise basis on which a decision on admissibility has been reached: the mere fact that an item of evidence is legally irrelevant does not tell us whether it is legally irrelevant because it lacks probative value completely, or because of considerations which do not relate to probative value.[7] On the other hand, a court taking the orthodox approach which treats evidence with some probative value, however little, as relevant, but subject to be excluded on a variety of other grounds, would be more likely to articulate the precise basis on which a particular item of evidence is to be excluded.[8]

Whenever a discussion of 'relevance' is encountered in the cases, the following question should therefore be asked: in precisely what sense is the court using the term 'relevance'? Consider, for example, the following case:

Extract 1.1.2

Hollingham v Head (1858) 4 CB (NS) 388, 390–2; 140 ER 1135, 1136–7 (Common Pleas)

WILLES J: The question is, whether, in an action for goods sold and delivered, it is competent to the defendant to set up by way of defence that the plaintiff has entered into contracts with third persons in a particular form, with the view of thereby inducing the jury to come to the conclusion that the contract sued upon was not as represented by the plaintiff. I am clearly of opinion that it was not competent to the defendant to do so. The case put forward on the part of the plaintiff, was, that the defendant bought of him a quantity of a certain article called 'Rival Guano,' at a given price per ton. The

---

[6] R O Lempert and S A Saltzburg, *A Modern Approach to Evidence: Text, Problems, Transcripts and Cases* (2nd ed 1982) 153: 'Now this concept of plus value is confusing; it is not clear what it would be. In fact it is probably a less precise way of acknowledging, as modern courts do, that even relevant evidence may be excluded if it seems likely to be prejudicial, misleading or unduly time-consuming. . . . The judge's task is to balance the probative value of and need for the evidence against the harm likely to result from admission.' See also E W Cleary, *McCormick on Evidence* (3rd ed 1984) 548 ('This notion of "plus value" is at best an imprecise way to say that the probative value and the need for the evidence must outweigh the harm likely to result from admission . . .'); W Twining, *Theories of Evidence: Bentham and Wigmore* (1985) 154.
[7] E W Cleary, *McCormick on Evidence* (3rd ed 1984) 548 n 45: 'The phrase "legal relevance" is misleading inasmuch as it blurs the distinction between evidence that is excluded because it lacks all probative force as to an issue that is of consequence to the outcome of the case and evidence that has probative worth but is excluded on other grounds.'
[8] See, however, the defence of the Wigmore approach in J H Wigmore, *Evidence in Trials at Common Law (Vol 1A)* (rev by P Tillers, 1983) 973–4.

defendant, on the other hand, insists that it was one of the terms of the contract that he was not to pay for the article unless it turned out to be equal to Peruvian guano. The plaintiff, having given evidence in support of his case, was asked on cross-examination by the defendant's counsel whether he had not entered into contracts for the sale of his guano to other persons upon the terms suggested, viz to be paid for only on condition that it proved equal to Peruvian guano. That question was disallowed as not being competent evidence for the purpose of establishing that the contract was made subject to that condition. . . . I am of opinion that the evidence was properly disallowed, as not being relevant to the issue. It is not easy in all cases to draw the line, and to define with accuracy where probability ceases and speculation begins: but we are bound to lay down the rule to the best of our ability. No doubt, the rule as to confining the evidence to that which is relevant and pertinent to the issue, is one of great importance, not only as regards the particular case, but also with reference to saving the time of the court, and preventing the minds of the jury from being drawn away from the real point they have to decide. This rule is nowhere more clearly laid down than in the very able treatise by Mr Best upon the Principles of Evidence, 2nd edit 319. 'Of all rules of evidence,' he says, 'the most universal and most obvious is this, – that the evidence adduced should be alike directed and confined to the matters which are in dispute, or form the subject of investigation. Its theoretical propriety can never be matter of doubt, whatever difficulties may arise in its application. The tribunal is created to determine matters in dispute between contending parties, or which otherwise require proof; and anything which is neither directly nor indirectly relevant to those matters ought at once to be put aside, as beyond the jurisdiction of the tribunal, as tending to distract its attention and to waste its time.' . . . Now, it appears to me that the evidence proposed to be given in this case, if admitted, would not have shewn that it was more probable that the contract was subject to the condition insisted upon by the defendant . . . To admit such speculative evidence would I think be fraught with great danger.

The evidence in question, it will be noted, was held to be inadmissible because it was 'irrelevant'. But surely the evidence would in fact have rendered the fact that the contract was subject to the condition more probable than it would have been in the absence of the evidence. By 'relevance', therefore, Willes J must have meant legal relevance: what he must effectively have been saying was that the evidence, even if logically relevant, should not be treated as admissible because of considerations such as saving court time and preventing the trier of fact from being distracted. See also the decision of the House of Lords in *R v Blastland*,[9] discussed in Chapter 7.

Where an item of evidence has been admitted in a criminal trial on indictment, it is up to the jury to decide how much *weight* to place on the evidence. That is, the final decision on how compelling the evidence is, and how far it goes in proving the matter requiring proof, is within the province of the jury. There may be circumstances, however, where relevant evidence ought not to be left to the jury without an accompanying judicial warning:

[9] [1986] AC 41.

Extract 1.1.3

R v Grant [1996] 1 Cr App R 73, 78 (CA)

LORD TAYLOR CJ: In our judgment the finding of money, whether in the home of the appellant or perhaps, more cogently, in the possession of the appellant when away from his home, and in conjunction with a substantial quantity of drugs, is capable of being relevant to the issue of whether there was proved an intent to supply. It is a matter for the jury to decide whether the presence of money, in all the circumstances, is indicative of an ongoing trading in the drugs, so that the presence of the drugs at the time of the arrest is capable of being construed as possession with intent to supply. We therefore consider that the learned judge in the present case was justified in allowing the evidence of the £912.50 to be admitted before the jury.

However, in [*R v Morris* [1995] 2 Cr App R 69], . . . the Court said that where such evidence was admitted it was incumbent upon the judge to give a direction to the jury as to the way in which they should approach the question of whether the finding of the money is probative of the necessary intent . . . In our judgment it is necessary, in the circumstances, for the judge to indicate that any explanation for the money which has been put forward by way of an innocent explanation by the accused would have to be rejected by the jury before they could regard the finding of the money as relevant to the offence. Again the jury should be directed that if there was any possibility of the money being in the accused's possession for reasons other than drug dealing, then the evidence would not be probative. If, on the other hand, the jury were to come to the conclusion that the presence of the money indicated not merely past dealing, but an ongoing dealing in drugs, then finding the money, together with the drugs in question, would be a matter which the jury could take into account in considering whether the necessary intent had been proved.

See also *R v Lovelock*.[10]

For a general discussion of relevance see Law Commission (Consultation Paper No 141), *Criminal Law – Evidence in Criminal Proceedings: Previous Misconduct of a Defendant – A Consultation Paper* (1996) 97.

2. TERMINOLOGY

For the sake of convenience, a number of items of terminology will be introduced at this point.

(a) Testimony

Testimonial evidence is oral evidence. Thus, the testimony of a witness consists of the oral statements made in court by that witness.

---

[10] (1997) *The Times*, 5 June.

(b) Real evidence

Real evidence is evidence which may be inspected by the trier of fact. Examples of real evidence include:

(1) material objects such as the alleged murder weapon;
(2) documents;
(3) the demeanour of witnesses.

Out-of-court inspections of, for example, the scene of the crime may be permitted in appropriate circumstances. Such inspections are known as 'views'. The following provisions in the Australian Evidence Act 1995[11] on views, as well as demonstrations and experiments, may be said to reflect the position in England:

Extract 1.2.1

Evidence Act 1995 (Australia), s 53

53. Views

(1) A judge may, on application, order that a demonstration, experiment or inspection be held.

(2) A judge is not to make an order unless he or she is satisfied that:
    (a) the parties will be given a reasonable opportunity to be present; and
    (b) the judge and, if there is a jury, the jury will be present.

(3) Without limiting the matters that the judge may take into account in deciding whether to make an order, the judge is to take into account the following:
    (a) whether the parties will be present;
    (b) whether the demonstration, experiment or inspection will, in the court's opinion, assist the court in resolving issues of fact or understanding the evidence;
    (c) the danger that the demonstration, experiment or inspection might be unfairly prejudicial, might be misleading or confusing or might cause or result in undue waste of time;
    (d) in the case of a demonstration – the extent to which the demonstration will properly reproduce the conduct or event to be demonstrated;
    (e) in the case of an inspection – the extent to which the place or thing to be inspected has materially altered.

(4) The court (including, if there is a jury, the jury) is not to conduct an experiment in the course of its deliberations.

(5) This section does not apply in relation to the inspection of an exhibit by the court or, if there is a jury, by the jury.

54. Views to be evidence

The court (including, if there is a jury, the jury) may draw any reasonable inference from what it sees, hears or otherwise notices during a demonstration, experiment or inspection.

---

[11] This Act is discussed below.

The supply of a tape measure to the jury was considered by the Court of Appeal in the following case:

Extract 1.2.2

R v Maggs (1990) 91 Cr App R 243, 245-7 (CA)

THE LORD CHIEF JUSTICE: After the jury had retired to consider their verdict and after a direction, as to which no complaint of any sort is made, they sent a message asking if they could borrow a tape measure. The judge asked counsel whether there was any objection. There was no objection. Counsel then appearing on that particular day for the appellant was not counsel appearing for him today, Mr Jafferjee, but someone who was standing in for Mr Jafferjee for the day, Mr Jafferjee having to be elsewhere. However, neither counsel raised any objection. What happened then, we are told, was that inquiries were made for a tape measure. The first object which was available was a police surveyor's tape and that, rather than the simple tape measure which the jury had asked for, was handed to them.

It is submitted by counsel today that that was a material irregularity. The complying with the jury's request in that respect was something, it is suggested, which should never have happened and invalidates the conviction.

It is well established that no fresh evidence can be given to the jury after they have retired. The *locus classicus* for that principle is to be found in the case of *Davis* (1975) 62 Cr App R 194. Turning to the judgment of the Court delivered by Lord Widgery CJ, one finds at p 201 this passage:

> 'The principle which arises out of this incident is one which is now well established, and it is that the jury may not when they have once retired to consider their verdict be given any additional evidence, any additional matter or material to assist them. They can come back and ask the judge to repeat for their benefit evidence which has been given, but they cannot come back and ask for anything new and the judge must not allow them to have anything new.'

That principle is well established and is known to all courts. It does not however meet the situation which exists in the instant case, where there is a request for equipment rather than a request for evidence. That is a matter which was the subject of a decision of another division of this Court last year, the case being *Stewart and Sappleton* (1989) 89 Cr App R 273. The facts of the case are perhaps important, and they are set out in the headnote, which I will accordingly read:

> 'Both appellants were stopped by customs officers at Heathrow airport and concealed in the holdalls they were carrying were found in respect of Angela Stewart 1.87 kilogrammes of cannabis and in respect of Sappleton 1.8 kilogrammes of the same drug. They were charged with importing cannabis. At their trial much emphasis was placed by the prosecution upon the obvious change in the weight of the flimsy holdalls by the addition of

1.87 and 1.8 kilogrammes of cannabis. The appellants denied that they were aware of any change in the weight of the holdalls. The jury retired . . . Thereafter the jury sent a note to the Court that they be provided with weighing scales in the jury room to conduct experiments with the exhibits. Counsel for the appellants objected to that course; but the trial judge agreed, after warning the jury of the dangers of experiments. The jury returned 41 minutes later with unanimous verdicts of guilty against the appellants.'

McKinnon J delivering the judgment of the Court, at p 276 of the report had this to say:

'The general principle is now well established. It is that the jury may not when they have once retired to consider their verdict be given any additional evidence, any additional matter or material to assist them (see *Davis* (1975) 62 Cr App R 194, 201) where Lord Widgery CJ said: . . .'

and the learned judge quotes part of the passage which we have cited. McKinnon J continued:

'To provide the jury with a ruler or magnifying glass for the purpose of reading a scale on a map or document already in evidence would be giving them something new. The better and safer course, as it seems to us, would be for the judge to ask the jury for what purpose they wanted the ruler or magnifying glass. Once that purpose was known, then the information sought by the jury, if it was already in evidence, could be given to them without difficulty. That approach seems to us to avoid difficulties that could well arise from the jury advancing new theories and then seeking to resolve them in the absence of the accused and without any assistance from the judge or counsel . . . To provide the jury with scales without asking for what purpose they were required was, in our view, a material irregularity.'

Accordingly the appeals were allowed and the convictions were quashed. One observes that the purpose for which the scales were required was apparently clear. They wanted to conduct experiments with the exhibits.

The observations in that judgment with regard to a ruler or a magnifying glass are plainly *obiter*. In so far as that passage seeks to lay down a general principle, we think, with respect, that the words are rather too wide. Equipment which is required or designed to enable a jury to carry out unsupervised scientific experiments in their room, and scales in the drug case came clearly within that category, are not permissible. On the other hand, in our judgment, a magnifying glass or a ruler, or come to that a tape measure, do not normally raise even the possibility of any such experiments. Indeed they are the sort of objects which any member of the jury might easily have in his pocket when summoned to serve upon the jury, and there could be no possible objection to his using it in the jury room.

The fact that a surveyor's tape measure was supplied in the instant case did cause us to hesitate. But it is clear the request which was made by the jury in this case was simply for a tape measure, and the reason why the surveyor's tape was supplied was because that was the first thing that came to hand which apparently supplied the jury's needs.

We have no doubt that what the jury required the tape for was to see what the measurements on the plan, measurements being expressed, one observes, in metres, looked like in real life. The suggestion that they were intending to carry out some experiment as to what happened between the car in the present case and the bicycle, we regard as fanciful. Counsel were correct, in our judgment, to raise no objection to the supplying to the jury of a tape measure and the judge was not in error in allowing it to be supplied. Consequently there was no material irregularity.

(c) Hearsay evidence

Hearsay evidence is evidence of 'a statement made otherwise than by a person while giving oral evidence in the proceedings which is tendered as evidence of the matters stated'.[12] As will be seen in Chapter 7, hearsay evidence is now admissible in civil trials by virtue of the Civil Evidence Act 1995. In criminal trials, however, hearsay evidence is inadmissible unless it falls within one of the defined exceptions to the rule.

(d) Circumstantial evidence

The testimony of a witness about a fact in issue perceived by that witness constitutes *direct* evidence. This is to be distinguished from *circumstantial* evidence, which is evidence from which a fact in issue may be inferred.

Extract 1.2.3

R v Exall (1866) 4 F & F 922, 929; 176 ER 850, 853 (Assizes)

POLLOCK CB: It has been said that circumstantial evidence is to be considered as a chain, and each piece of evidence as a link in the chain, but that is not so, for then, if any one link broke, the chain would fall. It is more like the case of a rope composed of several cords. One strand of the cord might be insufficient to sustain the weight, but three stranded together may be quite of sufficient strength.

Thus it may be in circumstantial evidence – there may be a combination of circumstances, no one of which would raise a reasonable conviction, or more than a mere suspicion; but the whole, taken together, may create a strong conclusion of guilt, that is, with as much certainty as human affairs can require or admit of.

Whilst, however, 'it is no derogation of evidence to say that it is circumstantial',[13] such evidence must be approached with caution:

---

[12] Civil Evidence Act 1995, s 1(2)(a).
[13] *R v Taylor* (1928) 21 Cr App R 20, 21.

Extract 1.2.4

Teper v R [1952] AC 480, 489 (HL)

LORD NORMAND: Circumstantial evidence may sometimes be conclusive, but it must always be narrowly examined, if only because evidence of this kind may be fabricated to cast suspicion on another. Joseph commanded the steward of his house, 'put my cup, the silver cup in the sack's mouth of the youngest,' and when the cup was found there Benjamin's brethren too hastily assumed that he must have stolen it. It is also necessary before drawing the inference of the accused's guilt from circumstantial evidence to be sure that there are no other co-existing circumstances which would weaken or destroy the inference.

The following are some examples of circumstantial evidence:

(i) Opportunity

Circumstantial evidence of opportunity to commit a crime may be provided, for example, by evidence of the presence of the accused at the time of, and at the scene of, the crime.

(ii) Fingerprints and bodily samples

The fact that an object found at the scene of the crime bore the accused's fingerprints constitutes circumstantial evidence of the identity of the perpetrator, as does the fact that samples taken from the accused's body match those taken from the victim.

(iii) Continuance

The fact that an event was taking place at a certain point in time may give rise to the inference that it was also taking place at a (sufficiently proximate) prior[14] or subsequent[15] point in time.

(iv) Reactions of tracker dogs

Extract 1.2.5

R v Pieterson [1995] 1 WLR 293, 297–8 (CA)

LORD TAYLOR OF GOSFORTH CJ: In our judgment, if a dog handler can establish that a dog has been properly trained and that over a period of time

---

[14] See R v Dalloz (1908) 1 Cr App R 258.
[15] See Beresford v Justices of St Albans (1905) 22 TLR 1.

the dog's reactions indicate that it is a reliable pointer to the existence of a scent from a particular individual, then that evidence should properly be admitted.

However, it is important to emphasise two safeguards. First, the proper foundation must be laid by detailed evidence establishing the reliability of the dog in question. Secondly, the judge must, in giving his directions to the jury, alert them to the care that they need to take and to look with circumspection at the evidence of tracker dogs, having regard to the fact that the dog may not always be reliable and cannot be cross-examined.

(v) Motive

Extract 1.2.6

R v Ball [1911] AC 47, 68 (HL)

LORD ATKINSON: Surely in an ordinary prosecution for murder you can prove previous acts or words of the accused to shew he entertained feelings of enmity towards the deceased, and this is evidence not merely of the malicious mind with which he killed the deceased, but of the fact that he killed him. You can give in evidence the enmity of the accused towards the deceased to prove that the accused took the deceased's life. Evidence of motive necessarily goes to prove the fact of the homicide by the accused, as well as his 'malice aforethought,' inasmuch as it is more probable that men are killed by those who have some motive for killing them than by those who have not.

(vi) Adverse inferences

In civil trials, the failure of one party to give evidence or call witnesses may give rise to the inference that the *other* party's version of the facts withheld by the first party is correct.[16] The implications of the failure, in a criminal trial, to call a potential witness (other than the accused) is discussed in the following case:

Extract 1.2.7

R v Gallagher [1974] 1 WLR 1204, 1211 (CA)

MEGAW LJ: It is permissible for a judge in an appropriate case to tell the jury that they are entitled to take into account the fact that a potential witness who has not been called has not indeed been called. It is of course clear that

---

[16] *British Railways Board v Herrington* [1972] AC 877, 930 per Lord Diplock.

14

in making any such comment, the judge must exercise care . . . But, it would be wrong and inappropriate to seek to tie the hands of the trial judge by laying down or attempting to lay down any particular formulae, because it must depend essentially upon the infinitely varying facts of different cases. . . .

. . . In this sort of matter great care must be taken to avoid the possibility that injustice may be done by leaving the jury under the impression that the failure to call a particular witness is something of importance where in fact there may have been some perfectly good and valid reason why a witness should not be called, which would not bear upon the jury's decision. But, it is impossible to take the view that the failure to call a witness cannot in a proper case be a matter to be taken into account by the jury as a part of the whole of the material upon which they have to decide.

Adverse inferences may be drawn in appropriate circumstances from an accused's refusal to consent to the taking of an intimate sample:

Extract 1.2.8

Police and Criminal Evidence Act 1984, s 62(10)

62. Intimate samples

(10) Where the appropriate consent to the taking of an intimate sample from a person was refused without good cause, in any proceedings against that person for an offence –

    (a) the court, in determining –

        (i) whether to commit that person for trial; or

        (ii) whether there is a case to answer; and

    (aa) a judge, in deciding whether to grant an application made by the accused under –

        (i) section 6 of the Criminal Justice Act 1987 (application for dismissal of charge of serious fraud in respect of which notice of transfer has been given under section 4 of that Act); or

        (ii) paragraph 5 of Schedule 6 to the Criminal Justice Act 1991 (application for dismissal of charge of violent or sexual offence involving child in respect of which notice of transfer has been given under section 53 of that Act); and

    (b) the court or jury, in determining whether that person is guilty of the offence charged,

may draw such inferences from the refusal as appear proper.

As we shall see later in the book, adverse inferences may also be drawn, in appropriate circumstances, from:

(1) the accused's failure to mention facts when questioned or charged;[17]

(2) the accused's failure or refusal to account for objects, substances or marks;[18]

---

[17] See Ch 8.
[18] See Ch 8.

(3) the accused's failure or refusal to account for presence at a particular place;[19]
(4) the accused's failure to make adequate advance disclosure of his or her defence;[20]
(5) the accused's silence at trial.[21]

3. THE ALLOCATION OF RESPONSIBILITY

Questions arising in a trial may be classified either as questions of law or as questions of fact, and are determined by the trier of law and trier of fact respectively. In jury trials, the trial judge is the trier of law while the jury is the trier of fact. In trials without a jury, the trial judge or magistrate acts as both trier of law and trier of fact. Questions of law include questions relating to the following matters:

(1) The substantive law.
(2) The competence of witnesses.
(3) Whether particular evidence should be admitted or excluded.
(4) Whether an issue should be withdrawn from the jury.
(5) The directions which should be given to the jury.

Questions of fact include questions relating to the following matters:

(a) The credibility of witnesses.
(b) The weight to be accorded to evidence.
(c) Whether the facts in issue have been proved.

In criminal trials on indictment, the jury is usually sent out of the courtroom before discussions take place about whether a particular item of evidence should be admitted or excluded. This is because, in the course of such discussions, reference to the evidence in question is often inevitable. A decision on whether to admit or exclude the evidence may be dependent on the existence of particular facts. For example, as we shall see in Chapter 8, a confession by an accused person is not admissible as prosecution evidence unless the following facts are established: that the confession was not obtained by oppression, and that the confession was not obtained in consequence of words or conduct conducive to unreliability. A further example may be provided by an issue which will be examined in detail in Chapter 7. Evidence which would otherwise be inadmissible hearsay is admissible in criminal proceedings under an exception to the hearsay rule if the fact that the hearsay statement was made sufficiently soon after the event which

---

[19] See Ch 8.
[20] See Ch 4.
[21] See Ch 3.

16

precipitated it, so that the mind of the maker of the statement would still have been dominated by the event, can be established. Where the facts on which the trial judge's decision would depend are in dispute, he or she must hear evidence from witnesses to determine the facts. Such evidence is given on a special form of oath known as a voir dire.[22] A hearing on the voir dire is known also as a 'trial within a trial'.

The traditional procedure involves determinations of whether evidence should be excluded being made at the point of the trial at which it is sought to adduce the evidence; it is only if the evidence is so crucial that the prosecution cannot even open its case without referring to it that a determination of whether it should be excluded may take place immediately after the jury has been sworn. However, this traditional procedure now stands alongside the provision made by the Criminal Procedure and Investigations Act 1996 for pre-trial determinations of whether evidence should be excluded:

Extract 1.3.1

Criminal Procedure and Investigations Act 1996, ss 39, 40

39. Meaning of pre-trial hearing
    (1) For the purposes of this Part a hearing is a pre-trial hearing if it relates to a trial on indictment and it takes place –
        (a) after the accused has been committed for trial for the offence concerned or after the proceedings for the trial have been transferred to the Crown Court, and
        (b) before the start of the trial.
    (2) ...
    (3) For the purposes of this section the start of a trial on indictment occurs when a jury is sworn to consider the issue of guilt or fitness to plead or, if the court accepts a plea of guilty before a jury is sworn, when that plea is accepted; but this is subject to section 8 of the Criminal Justice Act 1987 and section 30 of this Act (preparatory hearings).

40. Power to make rulings
    (1) A judge may make at a pre-trial hearing a ruling as to –
        (a) any question as to the admissibility of evidence;
        (b) any other question of law relating to the case concerned.
    (2) A ruling may be made under this section –
        (a) on an application by a party to the case, or
        (b) of the judge's own motion.

---

[22] 'The title of the procedure comes from the French "vrai dire" and the Latin "veritatem dicere" literally to "tell the truth". "Voir" (sometimes spelt "voire") is the Norman-French for "vrai" and reflects the long lineage of this judicial procedure': Mr Justice J H Phillips, 'The Voir Dire' (1989) 63 *Australian Law Journal* 46, 46.

(3) Subject to subsection (4), a ruling made under this section has binding effect from the time it is made until the case against the accused or, if there is more than one, against each of them is disposed of; and the case against an accused is disposed of if –
    (a) he is acquitted or convicted, or
    (b) the prosecutor decides not to proceed with the case against him.

(4) A judge may discharge or vary (or further vary) a ruling made under this section if it appears to him that it is in the interests of justice to do so; and a judge may act under this subsection –
    (a) on an application by a party to the case, or
    (b) of the judge's own motion.

(5) No application may be made under subsection (4)(a) unless there has been a material change of circumstances since the ruling was made or, if a previous application has been made, since the application (or last application) was made.

(6) The judge referred to in subsection (4) need not be the judge who made the ruling or, if it has been varied, the judge (or any of the judges) who varied it.

(7) . . .

The reporting of matters pertaining to a pre-trial hearing before the conclusion of the relevant trial is prohibited by s 41.

The obvious advantage of a pre-trial hearing is that it avoids the need for the jury to be excluded from the courtroom for an indefinite period while a trial within a trial takes place. Further, and perhaps more importantly, a pre-trial hearing would obviate the need for full-scale preparations for a trial which could very well be abandoned later if the accused changes his or her plea to guilty after defence attempts to obtain exclusion fail, or if the prosecution decides not to proceed after defence attempts to obtain exclusion succeed. However, 'it is possible that the parties' knowledge that a jury has not been empanelled means that there is less pressure on them to co-operate at the pre-trial stage than during the trial proper', and thus there is a danger that pre-trial hearings may themselves become slow-moving affairs which do little to alleviate the problem of delay in the criminal justice process generally. Problems in relation to pre-trial hearings may also be caused by the possible 'lack of continuity of judge and counsel, and the [lack of] incentives for lawyers to do more work at an early stage'.[23]

See generally A Edwards, 'The Criminal Procedure and Investigations Act 1996: (2) The Procedural Aspects' [1997] *Criminal Law Review* 321.

Whilst it is obviously helpful for the precise reasons for admitting or excluding a particular item of evidence to be articulated as clearly as possible, there is no requirement that this be invariably done:

---

[23] M Redmayne, 'Process Gains and Process Values: The Criminal Procedure and Investigations Act 1996' (1997) 60 *Modern Law Review* 79, 88.

Extract 1.3.2

Wallace v R [1997] 1 Cr App R 396, 403–8 (PC)

LORD MUSTILL: The first ground advanced on behalf of the appellants was not raised in the Court of Appeal of Jamaica, or foreshadowed by their printed case. Nevertheless, their Lordships allowed it to be pursued . . . It relies on the fact that the trial judge, when announcing his decision that the statements were admissible in evidence, gave no reasons beyond saying that he found that the statements were given voluntarily by both the accused. The appellants contend for a rule of general application that a judge should always express his reasons for any procedural ruling given during a trial. Their Lordships are wholly unpersuaded that a rule so broadly framed is now the law, or that it should be laid down for the future. It is convenient to begin with the four authorities cited in argument. The first was the unreported decision of the English Court of Appeal (Criminal Division) in *Gentles*, April 30, 1993 (No 92/3162/W2). The relevant passage from the judgment of the court, delivered by Wright J reads as follows:

> 'First of all, we have to observe that when the court is dealing with any submission of this kind, where the judicial ruling which is being sought requires a finding, whether of fact or of law, it is incumbent on the trial judge to make clear, albeit in brief terms, what his finding is upon the matters in dispute, so as to enable everyone, including, in appropriate cases, this court, to understand the factual and judicial basis upon which the ruling is made. A simple: "I am against you" in this context is not acceptable in such terms. A judgment, albeit in short and simple terms, was clearly called for in the present case. If it is necessary to do so, a brief adjournment for the trial judge to collect his or her thoughts and set out the basis for his or her ruling is to be taken.'

It will be noted that this statement is qualified by references to 'any submission of this kind' and 'in the present case'. So qualified, and set in the context of the facts, it can readily be sustained. Evidence had been tendered on a *voir dire* of a conversation taking place at the defendant's home between himself and a police officer. For the defendant it was objected that the conversation was an 'interview' within paragraph C11.A of the Criminal Code of Practice, and therefore should have been held at a police station. It seems that a submission under section 78 of the Police and Criminal Evidence Act 1984 was also involved. The trial judge overruled the objection. Although pressed by counsel on both sides to explain whether this was because she did not regard the conversation as an interview, or whether the circumstances were such that it need not have been held at a police station, or whether she was exercising whatever discretion might exist, she declined to go further. The Court of Appeal was therefore left to explore the matter completely afresh. The present case is quite different.

The same must be said of the appellants' next authority, *Smith (Brian)*, February 16, 1995, another decision of the English Court of Appeal. An important part of the evidence against the applicant in a drug related offence was to be given by an undercover police officer. Before the jury were sworn the applicant's counsel applied *ex parte* for an order that the prosecution should disclose the relationship between the officer and two other men who featured in the story, and in particular should state whether they too were policemen. This information was said to be needed as a basis for a possible defence of entrapment. This application was refused by the trial judge. When the trial began there was a new application on the *voir dire* to exclude the evidence of the officer, pursuant to the discretion conferred by section 78. This application was also refused, without reasons being given. Exception was taken to this feature on appeal, and the court was referred to the passage from *Gentles* quoted above. The Court observed:

> 'We, of course, loyally accept the nature of that guidance, but it is clear that the Court of Appeal, in the case of *Gentles*, did not have a case such as the present in mind, where the judge had to consider the impact upon his decision of material he had been provided with in an *ex parte* hearing, and had to be very careful not to disclose matters, in order to elucidate his ruling, which might cause the very damage which the *ex parte* hearing had been intended to avoid.
>
> We do not think that the case of *Gentles*, while being of general application, can really be said to apply with full rigour in this case.'

This decision supports the present appellants only to the limited extent that the statement in *Gentles* was treated by the Court in *Smith (Brian)* as being of general application, whilst for the reasons given their Lordships believe that it was limited to the facts of that particular case. (Their Lordships note that in *Smith (Brian)*, which was an application for leave to appeal, the Court did not have the assistance of counsel for the prosecution.) Apart from this, however, the decision illustrates very well that there are circumstances where it would be misguided for the court to give reasons, and that there cannot be a rule of general application such as the appellants propound.

The two remaining authorities were decided in the Criminal Courts of Appeal of Western Australia and New Zealand, respectively. The first was *Webb* (1994) 74 A Crim R 436. This concerned the admissibility of a confession by a person of Aboriginal descent, to which special conditions were applied by the Aboriginal Affairs Planning Authority Act 1972 (WA). The appellant's conviction was quashed on the ground that the judge had given no reasons for admitting his confession in evidence. It would be possible to explain this decision by reference to the special provisions of the Act, but it is plain that the Court had wider principles in mind. It is sufficient to quote the following passages from the judgments of Malcolm CJ and Ipp J (at pp 439 and 445):

> 'I accept that in certain circumstances it may be undesirable for a judge to give detailed reasons for decision on a *voir dire*. This may be the case where the judge has decided that confessional evidence is admissible because the allegations which have been made by the accused to the effect that it was involuntary are incredible, or the judge has otherwise reached an unfavourable conclusion about the credibility of the accused as a witness. There is a natural reluctance to say too much in case the views expressed are communicated to the jury, even if only after the trial has

been concluded. Given that a degree of circumspection may be required, I am nonetheless of the opinion that there is an obligation on a judge to give reasons for ruling on the admissibility of evidence following a *voir dire*. The obligation applies whether the issue raised is voluntariness or fairness at common law or is referable to the statutory criteria specified in the Aboriginal Affairs Planning Authority Act. Not to give such reasons would unfairly deprive the accused of his or her right of appeal or at least unjustly circumscribe it.

The relevant Australian authorities have been collected by Ipp J. I agree with his Honour that, in the circumstances of this case, the failure of the learned Commissioner to give any reasons for his decision to admit the confessional material was an error of law. . . .'

'Cases can arise where the admissibility of confessional material involves issues of voluntariness alone. It can occur that those issues depend for their resolution merely upon credibility disputes. In cases of that kind the basis of the presiding judge's decision to admit the confessional material may be apparent solely from the issues raised during the *voir dire*. Where, however, there are a multiplicity of issues that arise in regard to the admissibility of confessional material, the mere fact that the judge holds that the material is admissible does not necessarily indicate that he or she has applied the proper tests in so holding, or that all relevant factors have been taken into account. In such circumstances, without the court giving reasons, it is not possible to ascertain whether the decision was made according to law. . . .'

The remaining authority was *Atkinson* [1984] 2 NZLR 381. Delivering the judgment of the Court, Hardie Boys J said (at p 383):

'In *Awatere* [1982] 1 NZLR 644, this Court considered whether there is a general obligation for a judge to give reasons for his decision. It was held that there is not but it was pointed out that it must always be good judicial practice to give reasons and failure to follow that practice might, depending on the circumstances, jeopardise the decision on appeal. For example, the potential appellant might have been seen to be unduly prejudiced by the omission, or the appellate Court may have to infer that there are in fact no adequate reasons to support the decision. Thus whether or not reasons should be given and if so how fully expressed they should be will depend on the nature of the individual case.

Mr Larsen submitted that it is apparent from the judge's decision, coming as it did at the conclusion of a lengthy hearing and after reference had been made to relevant authorities, that he must have rejected the appellant's version of events where it was in conflict with that of the police officer; for he conceded that if the judge had been in any doubt about any of the appellant's allegations then he must have excluded the statement. The judge's remarks may well be read in that way, and there may indeed be cases in this area of admissibility of statements, as in others, that are sufficiently plain and straightforward for the mere rejection of one account and the acceptance of another to be a sufficient discharge of the judicial duty. In other cases there may be no necessity to give more than quite brief reasons. In every case however it is essential for the judge to make it clear that he has properly applied his mind to the issues before him and has proceeded to his conclusion on the correct legal basis. Even if the issue be no more than a determination of where the truth lies, it must be made apparent that he has correctly directed himself on the all important point of the standard of proof: as to which see *McGuin* [1982] 1 NZLR 13.'

Their Lordships doubt whether these and other passages support the proposed general rule to its full extent, but if so they must respectfully disagree. Undoubtedly there will be occasions when good practice requires a reasoned ruling. For example, where the judge decides a question of law sufficient, but no more, must be displayed of his reasoning to enable a review on appeal. Again, on a mixed question of law and fact the judge should state his findings of fact so that the law can be put in context. Similarly, the exercise of a discretion will often call for an account (however brief) of the judge's reasoning, especially where the issue concerns the existence of the discretion as well as the way in which it should be exercised. These are no more than examples. In every case it will depend on the circumstances whether reasons should be given, and if so with what particularity. Frequently, there will be everything to gain and little to lose by the giving of reasons, even if only briefly. But other situations are different, as the present case well shows.

Here, the trial judge was faced with an irreconcilable conflict of evidence between the police officers and the defendant, turning on credibility alone. No principles of law were in issue, and there was no discretion to be exercised. The only question was whether the judge believed one set of witnesses or the other. His ruling leaves the answer in no doubt. Simply to announce that he accepted the account given by the officers and the justice, and found the appellants' story unworthy of credit would not have advanced an appeal. Furthermore, although in cases where reasons are given it is prudent for the judge to say no more than strictly necessary, it is hard to see how a mere summary would have been appropriate in the present case; for there was always the risk that if anything was omitted in the interests of brevity the defendants would argue on appeal that the judge had overlooked it. In practice, he could scarcely stop short of a fully reasoned analysis. Their Lordships can see nothing to recommend such a course, and good reason not to follow it. In a case hinging on confessions the tasks of the judge and of the jury, although technically distinct, are in reality very much the same. The decision of the jury is announced in a non-speaking verdict at the end of the trial. For the judge to expound in detail almost at the beginning of the trial his reasons for preferring one story to the other would wholly unbalance the proceedings. His reasons, which would be given in the presence of the public, the advocates and the defendants would inevitably leave their mark not only on the future conduct of the trial but also on its atmosphere. Furthermore, although a jury may well have a general inkling of what happens on a *voir dire* the risk that a lapse in security would allow the jury to learn why the judge considered the defendants' evidence unworthy even to raise a serious doubt as to the voluntary nature of the evidence was too serious to justify whatever gain, if any, there might be at the appellate level. In truth, nobody in the present case who had heard the evidence, the cross-examination and the submissions of counsel could have doubted why the judge decided as he did. It is not surprising that none of the counsel asked the judge to explain his ruling.

In rejecting the first ground of appeal their Lordships are neither stating a general rule as to the giving of reasons for interlocutory decisions, nor recognising categories of situation in which reasons should always or should never be given. In every instance, it is for the judge to decide whether the interests of justice call for the giving of reasons, and if so with what degree of particularity.

4. EXCLUSIONARY RULES AND EXCLUSIONARY DISCRETIONS

As seen above, relevant evidence is liable to exclusion not only pursuant to the application of an exclusionary rule, but also in the exercise of an exclusionary discretion. The most important exclusionary discretion is the discretion, in criminal cases, to exclude prosecution evidence on the ground that its probative value is outweighed by its prejudicial effect.

Extract 1.4.1

Lobban v R [1995] 1 WLR 877, 886–7 (PC)

LORD STEYN: Two principles are clearly established. First, a trial judge in a criminal trial always has a discretion to refuse to admit evidence, which is tendered by the prosecution, if in his opinion its prejudicial effect outweighs its probative value. This power has probably existed since *Rex v Christie* [1914] AC 545 but, in any event, it was expressly affirmed by the House of Lords in *Reg v Sang* [1980] AC 402. The power is based on a judge's duty in a criminal trial to ensure that a defendant receives a fair trial. The width of the discretion is circumscribed by the purpose for which it exists. . . .

The second principle is lucidly summarised by *Keane, The Modern Law of Evidence*, 3rd ed (1994). The author states, at p 36:

'the discretion may only be exercised in relation to evidence tendered by the *prosecution*. There is no discretion to exclude, at the request of one co-accused, evidence tendered by another. Thus although, as we have seen, there is a discretion to exclude similar fact evidence tendered by the prosecution, such evidence, when tendered by an accused to show the misconduct on another occasion of a co-accused is, if relevant to the defence of the accused, admissible whether or not it prejudices the co-accused. Similarly, there is no discretion to prevent an accused from cross-examining a co-accused about his previous convictions and bad character when, as a matter of law, he becomes entitled to do so pursuant to section 1(*f*)(iii), Criminal Evidence Act 1898, ie where the co-accused has "given evidence against" the accused, because, it is said, the accused, in seeking to defend himself, should not be fettered in any way.'

These propositions are amply borne out by the decisions cited by the author, namely *Reg v Miller* [1952] 2 All ER 667, 669; *Reg v Neale (Paul)* (1977) 65 Cr App R 304; *Murdoch v Taylor* [1965] AC 574; *Cross on Evidence*, 7th ed (1990), pp 187–188.

The principle that it is only *prosecution* evidence which is subject to exclusion pursuant to the probative value versus prejudicial effect discretion has not escaped criticism.[24] Such criticism may be justified. It is arguable that the existence of a judicial discretion to exclude defence evidence should be explicitly acknowledged, so that such evidence should not automatically be admitted if it is considered 'relevant' and is not subject to an exclusionary rule. The concept of 'relevance' is, as seen above, an imprecise one. This being the case, it may be desirable to acknowledge openly the existence of an exclusionary discretion in the context of defence evidence, so that the precise reasons for excluding such evidence in a particular case are at least more likely to be articulated, rather than cloaked in a finding of 'irrelevance'. Interestingly, the Court of Appeal stated recently that 'we should not like it to be thought that we have concluded that such a discretion can never exist, although the authorities make it difficult to hold that it does'.[25]

Another important exclusionary discretion is that provided for by s 78(1) of the Police and Criminal Evidence Act 1984. This enables prosecution evidence to be excluded in the interests of ensuring the fairness of a trial.

The essential difference between exclusionary rules and exclusionary discretions relates to the attitude of appellate courts. An appeal on the basis of an allegedly erroneous exercise of discretion is not treated by an appellate court in the same way as an appeal on the basis of an alleged misapplication of a rule of law. If, on applying an exclusionary rule, a trial judge in a Crown Court concludes that the evidence should not be excluded, the Court of Appeal will not hesitate to substitute its own conclusion if it disagrees with that reached by the trial judge. It is immaterial that the trial judge may have, in reaching his or her conclusion, taken all relevant factors into account and left irrelevant factors out of consideration.[26] However, where a decision is reached pursuant to judicial discretion and this decision is the subject of an appeal, the appellate court will interfere with the decision only in limited circumstances. In considering the issue of the circumstances in which the Court of Appeal should interfere with a decision reached pursuant to judicial discretion, Lord Denning MR said in *Ward v James*:

> The true proposition was stated by Lord Wright in *Charles Osenton & Co v Johnston*.[27] This court can and will, interfere if it is satisfied that the judge was wrong. Thus it will interfere if it can see that the judge has given no weight (or

---

[24] R Pattenden, *Judicial Discretion and Criminal Litigation* (1990) 259.
[25] *R v Thompson* [1995] 2 Cr App R 589, 597.
[26] See *R v Viola* (1982) 75 Cr App R 125, 130–1.
[27] [1942] AC 130.

no sufficient weight) to those considerations which ought to have weighed with him. . . . Conversely it will interfere if it can see that he has been influenced by other considerations which ought not to have weighed with him, or not weighed so much with him . . .[28]

And in *R v Scarrott*, Scarman LJ observed that so long as a trial judge 'does not err in law, takes into account all relevant matters and excludes consideration of irrelevant matters, his discretion will stand'.[29]

As their name suggests, exclusionary discretions are 'discretionary' in nature, in the sense that the tests to be applied by trial judges in deciding whether to exercise such discretions are typically flexible and open-textured. In other words, a degree of latitude is accorded to the trial judge in deciding whether to exclude the evidence. By contrast, exclusionary rules are traditionally more rigid, often prescribing that where certain conditions are satisfied, a particular consequence will automatically follow. A classic example of this, as we shall see in Chapter 7, is the rule against hearsay in criminal proceedings. Where, in a criminal trial, an item of evidence falls within the definition of hearsay, it must automatically be excluded, unless it comes within one of the defined exceptions to the rule. In recent times, however, there has been a trend towards making exclusionary rules more 'discretionary' in nature. As will be seen in Chapter 5, the test for determining whether the prosecution can lead evidence of an accused's past misconduct is a case in point: the test is a flexible one which permits trial judges considerable latitude in coming to a conclusion in the context of a particular case. However, because the determination of the admissibility of such evidence is required pursuant to a rule of law, appellate courts should substitute their own conclusion if they disagree with that reached by the trial judge.

There has been much debate as to the desirability of allowing trial judges more discretion (whether in the context of exclusionary rules or exclusionary discretions) in determining whether evidence should be admitted or excluded. Wigmore once denounced the idea of increased discretion in the law of evidence in colourful terms: 'Is it not probable that in these proposed large

---

[28] [1966] 1 QB 273, 293.

[29] [1978] QB 1016, 1028. 'In my opinion a judge reaches a decision in the exercise of his "discretion" . . . where, on the facts found by or agreed before him and on the law correctly stated by him, he is required in the exercise of his judicial function to decide between two or more courses of action without any further rules governing the decision which he should make, other than that he must act judicially. It is just because this is the nature of such a task facing a judge that this court is restricted by the authorities to the extent to which it can interfere. Unless his decision is perverse in the *Wednesbury* sense (see *Associated Provincial Picture Houses Ltd v Wednesbury Corp* [1947] 2 All ER 680, [1948] 1 KB 223), it must be one to which a judge, acting judicially, could come': *Viscount De L'Isle v Times Newspapers* [1987] 3 All ER 499, 504 per May LJ. See also *Hindes v Edwards* (1987) *The Times*, 9 October; *Re W* (1990) *The Times*, 22 and 23 November; *R v Glennon* (1992) 66 ALJR 344, 348 per Mason CJ and Toohey J (an exercise of discretion should not be overturned unless the trial judge 'took into account some extraneous consideration, failed to take into account a relevant consideration or mistook the facts . . .'); *DPP v Godwin* [1991] RTR 303, 308 (extracted in Ch 9).

areas of "discretion" the Law of Evidence will suffer . . . a relapse into that primal condition of chaos, described in Genesis 1:2, when the Earth "was without form and void"?'[30] Courts in earlier times, too, viewed the notion of judicial discretion with some suspicion.[31] The issue of the relative merits and demerits of discretionary, as opposed to rule-based, approaches to the law of criminal evidence and procedure continues to be the subject of a good deal of discussion.[32] The main objection voiced to vesting considerable discretion in trial judges is that the resulting uncertainty and unpredictability would make preparation for trial, and planning and decision-making generally, more difficult.[33] This is an argument on which it is easy to place too much weight. It is unlikely that uncertainty and unpredictability would pose a problem after the emergence of a substantial body of case law which lays down clear guidelines in the form of factors to be taken into account by a trial judge in deciding whether to admit or exclude the evidence. An appropriate balance should be able to be struck between maintaining flexibility, and considerations such as the promotion of certainty and predictability.[34] Further, the objection assumes that there is certainty and predictability where the determination of whether to admit or exclude is governed by rigid tests. This is far from being the case:[35] as will be seen in Chapter 7, criminal courts regularly misapply the hearsay rule, or evade it altogether, in order to achieve the admissibility of highly cogent evidence. Paradoxically, therefore, the introduction of a more discretionary approach might well increase, rather than decrease, certainty and predictability.

Where exclusionary discretions are encountered in the law of evidence, it is important to determine whether clear guidelines have been laid down by the courts to govern the exercise of the particular discretion, and if so, to assess whether these guidelines clearly reflect the rationale for the existence of the discretion.

---

[30] J H Wigmore, 'The American Law Institute Code of Evidence Rules: A Dissent' (1942) 28 *American Bar Association Journal* 23, 24.

[31] See, eg, *R v Cargill* (1913) 8 Cr App R 224, 229.

[32] See A L-T Choo, *Abuse of Process and Judicial Stays of Criminal Proceedings* (1993) 119–30, and the references cited therein. See also A M Gleeson, 'Individualised Justice – The Holy Grail' (1995) 69 *Australian Law Journal* 421; C E Schneider, 'Discretion and Rules: A Lawyer's View' in K Hawkins (ed), *The Uses of Discretion* (1992); C R Sunstein, 'Problems with Rules' (1995) 83 *California Law Review* 953; Law Commission (Consultation Paper No 141), *Criminal Law – Evidence in Criminal Proceedings: Previous Misconduct of a Defendant – A Consultation Paper* (1996) 149–50; S Walker, *Taming the System: The Control of Discretion in Criminal Justice 1950–1990* (1993).

[33] See generally C E Schneider, 'Discretion and Rules: A Lawyer's View' in K Hawkins (ed), *The Uses of Discretion* (1992) 76–7.

[34] See generally A M Gleeson, 'Individualised Justice – The Holy Grail' (1995) 69 *Australian Law Journal* 421.

[35] See C T McCormick, 'The Borderland of Hearsay' (1930) 39 *Yale Law Journal* 489, 503 ('[It is assumed that a fixed categorical approach to admissibility] enable[s] the lawyer preparing his case to know in advance with fair certainty what he can get in, and what he cannot. If a question as to admissibility does arise, the judge who has no time for subtle discrimination in the heat of trial can make a decision in his stride, as it were. This is splendid, and the only difficulty is that it does not work').

5. CIVIL EVIDENCE AND CRIMINAL EVIDENCE

What are the fundamental differences between civil procedure and criminal procedure? Do these differences suggest that there should, in reality, be not one, but two, 'laws' of evidence?

Extract 1.5.1

A A S Zuckerman, *The Principles of Criminal Evidence* (1989) 4–6

A number of important factors set apart our criminal and civil procedures. Unlike the civil trial, the criminal trial is not concerned with resolving a dispute between symmetrically competing claims, but is devoted to an examination of the conduct of the accused. Its object is to determine whether the accused has transgressed a criminal prohibition and whether he should be punished. The proceedings take the form of a charge brought by the state against an individual. . . . On the one hand are ranged the investigative and prosecuting authorities of the state and, on the other, there is the individual accused. This imbalance calls for special measures to ensure that the individual suspect or accused is protected from abuse by the organs of the state. . . .

The object of the criminal trial is to punish offenders. Punishment . . . can mark the convict with a moral condemnation that may hurt more than imprisonment and could inflict permanent injury upon the convict's self-respect and standing in the community. A legal system which respects the rights of the individual has to devise a criminal procedure that affords due protection from punishment to the innocent citizen and the law of criminal evidence includes several measures for achieving this end.

It is an important function of the criminal process to promote observance of the law. To this end its verdicts have to command public approval. Hence not only must the criminal process protect the innocent but it must also be seen to be doing so. . . .

Public confidence in the administration of criminal justice depends also on its ability to provide the community with satisfactory protection from crime. . . .

In civil procedure, where the aim is essentially to settle disputes between citizens, hardly any of these concerns figure to any important extent. Since the civil process is not principally concerned with affording the individual protection from the state's organs, it does not have to adopt special measures to protect the innocent from punishment or reflect the community's need for protection from crime.

As will be seen in this book, because of the inherent differences between civil and criminal litigation, the exclusionary rules and exclusionary discretions applicable in criminal proceedings have largely no application in civil proceedings. As has been observed in the Court of Appeal:

> The modern tendency in civil proceedings is to admit all relevant evidence, and the judge should be trusted to give only proper weight to evidence which is not the best evidence . . .[36]

---

[36] *Ventouris v Mountain (No 2)* [1992] 1 WLR 887, 899 per Balcombe LJ.

Numerous illustrations of the manner in which the principles of civil and criminal evidence differ will be encountered in the course of this book. For the present, a number of examples will suffice:

(1) There is a presumption in criminal cases that every issue be proved by the prosecution as the party bringing the action. In civil cases, however, there is no presumption that the plaintiff prove every issue.
(2) The similar-facts rule, which renders evidence of a defendant's misconduct on other occasions prima facie inadmissible in criminal cases, has no general application in civil cases.
(3) The rule against hearsay has been effectively abolished in civil cases, but remains applicable (subject to exceptions) in criminal cases.

6. ISSUES IN CRIMINAL EVIDENCE

It is important, given the special position of criminal evidence, to identify the considerations upon which the law of criminal evidence is premised. Essentially, it may be said that underlying the principles of criminal evidence are considerations of both intrinsic policy and extrinsic policy. The concern of intrinsic policy is with the promotion of accurate fact-finding, or, in other words, with what Jeremy Bentham called 'rectitude of decision'.[37] The need to ensure that evidence is as reliable as possible is especially important in the case of prosecution evidence, because the admission of unreliable prosecution evidence could lead to the wrongful conviction of an innocent person. 'People have', in the words of Ronald Dworkin, 'a profound right not to be convicted of crimes of which they are innocent.'[38] The crucial question for the evidence lawyer, however, is how far the law of criminal evidence should go in protecting the innocent from wrongful conviction. If the right of the innocent not to be convicted were to be regarded as an absolute right (in other words, if what we are seeking is maximum protection of the innocent), then it is arguable that prosecution evidence like confession evidence and identification evidence should never be permitted in criminal trials. A blanket ban on such evidence would, however, probably have the effect of leading to the widespread acquittal of the guilty, and would therefore be regarded as unpalatable. It is clearly not required 'that every conceivable step be taken, at whatever cost, to eliminate the possibility of convicting an innocent person'.[39] In examining intrinsic policy considerations, therefore, it is important not to lose sight of the underlying tension between, on the one hand, the pressure to admit all relevant prosecution evidence, and, on the other hand, the need to protect the innocent from conviction.

---

[37] J Bentham, *Rationale of Judicial Evidence, Specially Applied to English Practice (Vol 1)* (1827) (reprinted 1978) 1.
[38] R Dworkin, *A Matter of Principle* (1986) 72.
[39] *Patterson v New York* 432 US 197, 208 (1977).

As we shall see throughout this book, a number of evidential principles are justified in English law on the ground that they ensure the reliability of evidence. Two examples are the rule against hearsay and the general prohibition against the adduction in chief by the prosecution of evidence of an accused's past misconduct. Concerns about reliability also underlie the principles relating to corroboration and supporting evidence. Certain types of evidence require to be corroborated by other evidence in order to be admissible,[40] and it is mandatory, or normal practice, for warnings to be issued to the jury about the danger of convicting on the basis of certain types of evidence if unsupported by other evidence.[41]

It should be noted that evidence may be excluded in English law not only because of its potential unreliability, but also because of considerations of *extrinsic* policy which do not relate to reliability. Such considerations as the importance of upholding values and protecting the moral integrity of the criminal justice system may dictate that evidence should sometimes be excluded even if reliable. Thus Galligan has written that

> there are two distinct issues: (i) one concerns rules about the probative value of evidence; (ii) the other concerns rules about the exclusion of evidence for reasons other than reasons of evidentiary value. The question in (i) is how to deal with evidence the probative value of which is in doubt, or which, although of probative value, contains a degree of risk that it will be used improperly. . . . The guiding objective in these cases is rectitude of outcome; the question is, given some such uncertainty or defect, how best is rectitude achieved; what is the most rational procedure for obtaining an accurate outcome. These are issues *internal* to proof. In (ii) the issue is whether certain kinds of evidence, which are likely to be of probative value and therefore relevant in achieving rectitude, should be excluded, in order to advance other values or policies . . . These are issues *external* to proof; they are based on values which compete with rectitude. The exclusion of evidence in order to uphold those values may mean the loss of probative evidence and thus a lower level of accuracy. The distinction between (i) and (ii) is fundamental, since (i) is concerned with the rationality of proof, while (ii) is concerned with the conflict of values.[42]

The issue of extrinsic policy considerations is best illustrated by reference to the problem of improperly obtained evidence, discussed in Chapter 9. Suppose that a piece of prosecution evidence has been obtained illegally by the police, but that there is no suggestion that this evidence may be unreliable. If the sole concern of the courts were with intrinsic policy considerations, it would have to be said that there is no reason to exclude the evidence. This

---

[40] See Perjury Act 1911, s 13; Road Traffic Regulation Act 1984, s 89.
[41] Eg, warnings are required in relation to identification evidence (*R v Turnbull* [1977] QB 224) and evidence of a confession made by a mentally handicapped person not in the presence of an independent person (Police and Criminal Evidence Act 1984, s 77(1)).
[42] D J Galligan, 'More Scepticism about Scepticism' (1988) 8 *Oxford Journal of Legal Studies* 249, 255 (emphasis in original). See also T J Reed, 'Evidentiary Failures: A Structural Theory of Evidence Applied to Hearsay Issues' (1994) 18 *American Journal of Trial Advocacy* 353, 362.

would be the case despite the seriousness of the police illegality. Yet the courts have acknowledged that improperly obtained, yet reliable, evidence is liable to exclusion in certain circumstances. The exact rationale for such exclusion will be explored in Chapter 9, but for present purposes one should note the extension of the courts' exclusionary jurisdiction beyond the confines of considerations of intrinsic policy. When progressing through this book, it is important to assess how well considerations of intrinsic and/or extrinsic policy are accommodated within the individual doctrines of the law of criminal evidence that are encountered.

An examination of the extent to which considerations of intrinsic and extrinsic policy are accommodated within a criminal justice system can be usefully undertaken against the background of Herbert Packer's diametrically opposed models of the criminal process.

Extract 1.6.1

H L Packer, *The Limits of the Criminal Sanction* (1969) 154, 158–60, 162–6

The models are polarities, and so are the schemes of value that underlie them. A person who subscribed to all of the values underlying one model to the exclusion of all of the values underlying the other would be rightly viewed as a fanatic. The values are presented here as an aid to analysis, not as a program for action.

. . .

Crime Control Values. The value system that underlies the Crime Control Model is based on the proposition that the repression of criminal conduct is by far the most important function to be performed by the criminal process. . . . If the laws go unenforced – which is to say, if it is perceived that there is a high percentage of failure to apprehend and convict in the criminal process – a general disregard for legal controls tends to develop. . . . The claim ultimately is that the criminal process is a positive guarantor of social freedom. In order to achieve this high purpose, the Crime Control Model requires that primary attention be paid to the efficiency with which the criminal process operates to screen suspects, determine guilt, and secure appropriate dispositions of persons convicted of crime.

. . . By 'efficiency' we mean the system's capacity to apprehend, try, convict, and dispose of a high proportion of criminal offenders whose offenses become known. . . .

The model, in order to operate successfully, must produce a high rate of apprehension and conviction, and must do so in a context where the magnitudes being dealt with are very large and the resources for dealing with them are very limited. There must then be a premium on speed and finality. Speed, in turn, depends on informality and on uniformity; finality depends on minimizing the occasions for challenge. The process must not be cluttered up with ceremonious rituals that do not advance the progress of a case. Facts can be established more quickly through interrogation in a police station than through the formal process of examination and cross-examination in a court. It follows that extra-judicial processes should be preferred to judicial processes, informal operations to formal ones. But informality is not enough; there must also be uniformity. Routine, stereotyped procedures are essential if large numbers are being handled. The model that will operate successfully on these presuppositions must be an administrative, almost a managerial, model. The image that comes to mind is an assembly-line conveyor belt down which moves an endless stream of cases, never stopping, carrying the cases to workers who stand at fixed stations and who perform on each case as it comes by the same small but essential operation that brings it one step closer to being a finished product, or, to exchange the metaphor for the reality, a closed file. The criminal process, in this model, is seen as a screening process in which each successive stage − pre-arrest investigation, arrest, post-arrest investigation, preparation for trial, trial or entry of plea, conviction, disposition − involves a series of routinized operations whose success is gauged primarily by their tendency to pass the case along to a successful conclusion.

What is a successful conclusion? One that throws off at an early stage those cases in which it appears unlikely that the person apprehended is an offender and then secures, as expeditiously as possible, the conviction of the rest, with a minimum of occasions for challenge, let alone post-audit. By the application of administrative expertness, primarily that of the police and prosecutors, an early determination of probable innocence or guilt emerges. Those who are probably innocent are screened out. Those who are probably guilty are passed quickly through the remaining stages of the process. . . .

. . . It might be said of the Crime Control Model that, when reduced to its barest essentials and operating at its most successful pitch, it offers two possibilities: an administrative fact-finding process leading (1) to exoneration of the suspect or (2) to the entry of a plea of guilty.

Due Process Values. . . .

The Due Process Model encounters its rival on the Crime Control Model's own ground in respect to the reliability of fact-finding processes. The Crime Control Model, as we have suggested, places heavy reliance on the ability of investigative and prosecutorial officers, acting in an informal setting in which their distinctive skills are given full sway, to elicit and reconstruct a tolerably accurate account of what actually took place in an alleged criminal event. The Due Process Model rejects this premise and substitutes for it a view of informal, nonadjudicative fact-finding that stresses the possibility of error. People are notoriously poor observers of disturbing events − the more emotion-arousing the context, the greater the possibility that recollection will be incorrect; confessions and admissions by persons in police custody may be induced by physical or psychological coercion so that the police end up hearing what the suspect thinks they want to hear rather than the truth; witnesses may be animated by a bias or interest that no one would trouble to discover except one specially charged with protecting the interests of the accused (as the police are not). Considerations of this kind all lead to a rejection of informal fact-finding processes as definitive of factual guilt and to an insistence on formal, adjudicative, adversary fact-finding processes in which the factual case against the accused is publicly heard by an impartial tribunal and is evaluated only after the accused has had a full opportunity to discredit the case against him. Even then, the distrust of fact-finding processes that animates the Due Process Model is not dissipated. The possibilities of human error being what they are, further scrutiny is necessary, or at least must be available, in case facts have been overlooked or suppressed in the heat of battle. . . .

. . .

The combination of stigma and loss of liberty that is embodied in the end result of the criminal process is viewed as being the heaviest deprivation that government can inflict on the individual. Furthermore, the processes that culminate in these highly afflictive sanctions are seen as in themselves coercive, restricting, and demeaning. Power is always subject to abuse – sometimes subtle, other times, as in the criminal process, open and ugly. Precisely because of its potency in subjecting the individual to the coercive power of the state, the criminal process must, in this model, be subjected to controls that prevent it from operating with maximal efficiency. According to this ideology, maximal efficiency means maximal tyranny. And, although no one would assert that minimal efficiency means minimal tyranny, the proponents of the Due Process Model would accept with considerable equanimity a substantial diminution in the efficiency with which the criminal process operates in the interest of preventing official oppression of the individual.

Finally, consideration must be given to the relationship between the principles of criminal evidence and the possible production of miscarriages of justice. The past decade has witnessed the exposure of a number of spectacular miscarriages of justice, notably the cases of the Guildford Four, Birmingham Six and, most recently, Bridgewater Three. This gives rise to the question of what part, if any, the principles of criminal evidence might have been able to play in preventing such miscarriages.

Extract 1.6.2

A A S Zuckerman, 'Miscarriage of Justice and Judicial Responsibility'
[1991] *Criminal Law Review* 492, 499–500

. . . the police, although justly criticised in some respects, are not alone to blame for the deterioration in the administration of criminal justice. The contribution of the courts to the present state of affairs must not be overlooked. The refusal of the courts, before [the Police and Criminal Evidence Act 1984] came into effect, to insist on the observance of the Judges' Rules gave an unambiguous message to the police that they were not required to allow the suspect access to a solicitor, nor to maintain a contemporaneous and accurate record of the interrogation. The police reacted accordingly, with the result that suspects were left to face police interrogation unaided by legal advice while police officers were relatively free to record the suspects' statements as they saw fit. This, as the outcomes of the Guildford Four and Birmingham Six cases have shown, has proved a recipe for much injustice. . . .

. . .

The fundamental principles of criminal evidence, which are by and large the creatures of the common law, are sound and stand witness to great achievements of English law. It is in the implementation of these principles that the courts have not been wholly successful. Two main failings may be identified in this respect. The judiciary has traditionally preferred to forego close supervision of the proceedings in the police station and has left the police with too much discretion and too little guidance as to what is proper or improper in the search for a confession. Second, the courts have been slow to adapt the rules of criminal evidence to changing circumstances, with the result that some of these rules have become empty technical artifacts. So much so that one gets the impression that as these venerable rules have grown less apt for their purpose, so the courts have devoted more attention to their cosmetic application.

Consideration should be given when proceeding through this book, and in particular Chapters 8 (confessions) and 9 (improperly obtained evidence), to the extent to which Zuckerman's comments are justified.

7. THE IMPLICATIONS OF TRIAL BY JURY

It is fair to say that the existence of some of the major exclusionary rules of criminal evidence is attributable, at least in part, to the phenomenon of trial by jury. This is despite the fact that, statistically, trials on indictment account for only a small percentage of all criminal trials. Thus, the rule against hearsay in criminal trials is often justified on the ground that juries cannot be expected to assess properly the reliability of hearsay evidence on a case-by-case basis, and thus it is preferable that a general ban on such evidence be maintained. The general ban on evidence of an accused's past misconduct is justified on the ground that such evidence may be misused by the jury.

Are such assumptions about the jury really justified? The short answer to this is that we simply have no way of knowing for certain. To conduct serious empirical research in England into how juries handle evidence is a difficult enterprise owing to s 8 of the Contempt of Court Act 1981, which effectively makes it illegal to ask juries questions about their deliberations in actual trials:

Extract 1.7.1

Contempt of Court Act 1981, s 8(1)

8. Confidentiality of jury's deliberations

(1) Subject to subsection (2) below, it is a contempt of court to obtain, disclose or solicit any particulars of statements made, opinions expressed, arguments advanced or votes cast by members of a jury in the course of their deliberations in any legal proceedings.

Any empirical research on juries and the principles of criminal evidence must therefore be based on simulated 'trials' involving mock jurors. The need to rely on simulations means that subjects are not exposed to the atmosphere, drama and tension of a real trial, and may not therefore (consciously or otherwise) react in the same way as they would in the context of a real trial. The repeal of s 8 of the Contempt of Court Act 1981, as recommended by the Runciman Royal Commission on Criminal Justice[43] and as advocated by many, would enable 'real' juries to be questioned about how evidence was evaluated in their deliberations. But the lack of definitive empirical evidence has not deterred the law from making (often unstated) assumptions about what juries can and cannot cope with. While, for example, juries are assumed to be incapable of evaluating hearsay evidence fairly, they are expected to be able to obey instructions from the trial judge to treat certain evidence as relevant only to 'credit' (that is, the credibility of a particular witness), rather than as relevant to the facts in issue in the case. The extent to which juries can comprehend and comply with such an instruction is, at best, speculative.

It might be tempting to argue that, given the uncertainty about whether juries are capable of what is expected of them, it would be fairer to move to a system of trial by judge alone. The obvious problem with this suggestion is that – any considerations pertaining to the intrinsic value of jury trial aside – it is premised on a further assumption: that professional judges would necessarily perform better than lay jurors. As Zuckerman has observed: 'Given that common-sense reasoning and moral sentiment influence fact-finding whether by judge or jury it is difficult to see what can be achieved by a change from lay judges to professional ones. Furthermore, if professional judges become triers of fact, the amount of prejudicial evidence will increase due to the assumption in judicial circles that professional judges are immune from prejudice and need not necessarily be kept ignorant of such evidence.'[44] Surely, if the system of jury trial is regarded as being of intrinsic value and as a fundamental facet of the criminal justice system, it is the principles of criminal evidence which should be adapted to fit properly into the system. It is not the system that should be tinkered with to enable the principles of criminal evidence to be accommodated within it.

At present, debate continues on whether complex fraud trials (which are notorious for the complex evidence which they can generate) should be heard by a panel of one judge and two expert assessors or a panel of three judges, instead of by a judge and jury.[45]

---

[43] Royal Commission on Criminal Justice, *Report* (Cm 2263) (1993) 2.

[44] A A S Zuckerman, *The Principles of Criminal Evidence* (1989) 262 n 36. Note also the colourful comment, in relation to evidence of an accused's propensity for wrongdoing, by M R Damaška, 'Propensity Evidence in Continental Legal Systems' (1994) 70 *Chicago-Kent Law Review* 55, 65: 'Unfortunately, there is no solid ground in psychology for the belief that only novice factfinders succumb to the temptation of drawing negative conclusions from a person's unsavory life history, while professional adjudicators are immune, even in close cases, to the syren's call of these inferences.'

[45] I King, 'SFO Chief Seeks Review of Jury Role in Fraud Cases', *The Guardian*, 25 June 1996, 18; G Langdon-Down, 'Hung on the Issue of Juries', *The Independent*, Section Two, 24 January 1996, 14; M Levi, 'When the Quality of Mercy is Strained', *The Times Higher Education Supplement*, 4 October 1996, 20. See also the report of the Roskill Committee: Lord Roskill, *Fraud Trials Committee Report* (1986).

Whilst it is to be hoped that it represents a highly untypical illustration of jury decision-making, an interesting insight into jury deliberations is provided by the following case:

Extract 1.7.2

R v Young [1995] 2 WLR 430, 434, 436–8 (CA)

LORD TAYLOR OF GOSFORTH CJ: In brief, the allegation was that whilst in the hotel, using an ouija board, some members of the jury purported to make contact with the deceased Harry Fuller and to have received certain information from him bearing upon the case. . . .
. . .
   Whilst there were differences of detail, the affidavits gave a reasonably clear and consistent account of what occurred in the hotel. After dinner, there was conversation amongst some of the jurors about ouija boards. One of the bailiffs spoke out strongly against them as did a lady juror, and the other bailiff agreed, saying 'not to be so stupid.' At about 11 pm the bailiffs conducted the jurors to their rooms. Thereafter it is clear that four jurors, the foreman and three women, got together in the room of one of the women. An ouija board was set up.
   The word 'ouija' is simply a combination of the French word 'oui' and the German word 'ja' and means therefore 'yes, yes.' An ouija board is used at a séance to seek messages from the spirits of absent or deceased persons. In this case there was no formal board. Letters of the alphabet were printed on scraps of paper and a glass was used as a pointer. Those present each put a finger on the glass which then moved towards a succession of letters, thereby purporting to reveal a message. At least some of those present began this procedure as a joke or 'harmless prank.' After purporting to receive messages from persons known or related to two of the jurors (one of them being deceased), the matter proceeded as follows, according to one of those present:

'Ray then asked, "Is anyone there?" The glass went to "yes." Ray said, "Who is it?" The glass spelt out "Harry Fuller." When I say the glass spelt it out, I mean it went to each letter. I realised Fuller was the subject of the evidence we were hearing. Ray said, "Who killed you?" The glass spelt out "Stephen Young done it." Ray said, "How?" The glass spelt "shot." Ray said something else and the glass spelt "shotgun and pistol." Ray said, "Where is the gun?" The glass spelt "Police." Ray also asked who killed Nicola, and the glass spelt out "Stephen Young." Ray then cut up paper and put numbers 0 to 10 on them and put them in an inner circle. The alphabet was on an outer circle. Previously Ray had asked the motive and the glass spelt out "money." Ray asked where it was and the glass spelt "case." He then asked how much had been taken and the glass spelt out "63,000." Ray asked where the money was now and the glass spelt out "bag." Ray asked where and the glass spelt out

35

"Harry Brinklow, room above office." We then discussed among ourselves what we should do and the glass spelt out "Tell police." I said "We can't." It then spelt out "later, us and you." It continued, "Vote guilty tomorrow." During this time Ray made notes. It is only right to say I was crying by this time and the other ladies were upset as well. We realised it had gone too far and we ended the exercise. Ray threw the paper away. We retired to our rooms and agreed not to relate what we'd done to anyone.'

Despite that agreement, it is clear that the matter was discussed at breakfast with other jurors who had not been present at the ouija board and one of them was told (in addition to the account given above) that 'Walther PPK' was mentioned as having emerged from the session. A gun of that type had been referred to in the evidence as had the name Harry Brinklow.
. . .

In our view, what occurred in the present case was not merely objectionable but amounted to a material irregularity. Although many, perhaps most, people would regard attempts to communicate with the dead as futile, there can be no doubt that the four jurors were going through the motions of asking questions to that end and apparently receiving answers. It seems to us that what matters is not whether the answers were truly from the deceased, but whether the jurors believed them to be so or whether they may have been influenced by the answers received during this exercise or experiment.

Was it merely a drunken game which the court should disregard, as Mr Lawson suggests? We do not think it can be laughed off in that way. The three women jurors were upset about what emerged. One was crying and took the view that it had gone too far. Why, if it was just a game? And why, when the verdict had been unanimous, should one juror (not one of the four) have been sufficiently concerned to consult a solicitor and make a statement about what had happened?

Is Mr Lawson right in saying that what occurred was no different from jurors influencing each other? There is, in our view, a clear distinction between the views of one juror however strongly expressed, intended to influence others, and on the other hand revelations purporting to come from outside the jury and to be invested with some external authority however specious. We stress that the answers which upset the jurors went to the heart of the case. They purported to deal with points which had been expressly raised by the evidence and they were strongly adverse to the appellant.

Having considered all the circumstances, we concluded there was a real danger that what occurred during this misguided ouija session may have influenced some jurors and may thereby have prejudiced the appellant. For those reasons we allowed the appeal but ordered a retrial.

Reference will be made at appropriate points in this book to the results of some of the relevant empirical research on jury decision-making undertaken in England and abroad. One example of such research on juries and the principles of criminal evidence is the LSE Jury Project in England:

Extract 1.7.3

LSE Jury Project, 'Juries and the Rules of Evidence' [1973]
Criminal Law Review 208, 209–10

The research takes an experimental form. Groups of jurors have been invited to listen to a tape-recording re-enacted from the transcript of a real trial, and then to reach a verdict upon what they have heard. The experiments have been conducted under laboratory conditions so that the jurors could be observed and their deliberations recorded for later analysis. . . . we set about observing how different applications of particular rules of evidence might affect the verdicts given by jurors.

There are drawbacks in using laboratory experimentation as a means of discovering how actual juries operate 'on the job.' If the experimental trial consists of a tape recording of spoken voices (as was the case in . . . our own experiments), the 'jurors' are deprived of the myriad impressions made up of things seen in the court room. Even if the experiment is set up on a grand and expensive scale, using a filmed trial, or even a trial performed by actors, the jury will know that they are not deciding the fate of an actual defendant. . . . [However,] [o]ur observation of the course of [the mock jurors'] discussions showed them to be deeply immersed, entirely serious, often vehemently argumentative, to all appearances oblivious that the situation was only an experiment.

Additionally, in 1995, the Home Office commissioned the Centre for Socio-Legal Studies at the University of Oxford to conduct research, again with mock trials, into the effect on mock juries of knowing that the defendant had a prior conviction.[46]

Of some interest also is the *Crown Court Study* undertaken for the Runciman Royal Commission on Criminal Justice. This study was based on every case completed in the last two weeks of February 1992 in all Crown Courts in England but three, and involved administering questionnaires to those regarded as the main actors in each case – the judge, the prosecution and defence barristers, the defence solicitor, the CPS, the police, the court clerk, the defendant and the members of the jury.[47]

8. LAW REFORM

English courts are generally reluctant to engage in reform of the law of evidence, preferring to leave such matters to the legislature. This is well illustrated by the 1992 decision on hearsay of the House of Lords in *R v Kearley*[48]

---

[46] Law Commission (Consultation Paper No 141), *Criminal Law – Evidence in Criminal Proceedings: Previous Misconduct of a Defendant – A Consultation Paper* (1996) Appendix D.

[47] M Zander and P Henderson, *The Royal Commission on Criminal Justice: Crown Court Study* (1993).

[48] [1992] 2 AC 228.

(discussed in Chapter 7), in which the majority, while deprecating the result they reached, felt nonetheless constrained into reaching it by the law, which in their view could be changed only by Parliament. In contrast, the courts in Canada and Australia have been generally far more innovative and reformist in their approach to evidence doctrine. Some references will be made in this book to developments in these countries.

In England, legislation is occasionally passed which makes fundamental changes to the law of evidence. Examples in recent years include the Criminal Justice and Public Order Act 1994 (which changed the law in relation to the right to silence at both the pre-trial and trial stages, and the law relating to corroboration) and the Civil Evidence Act 1995 (which effectively abolished the hearsay rule in civil proceedings). The Runciman Royal Commission on Criminal Justice recommended in 1993 that the law of criminal evidence be subjected to a review by the Law Commission.[49] The Law Commission has recently issued its Consultation Paper on evidence of a defendant's previous misconduct in criminal proceedings,[50] and its final report on criminal hearsay.[51]

In contrast with the piecemeal legislative reform being witnessed in England, there has been legislative activity of a more fundamental nature in Australia.[52] On 18 April 1995, the Evidence Act 1995 (Commonwealth of Australia) came into force in the Australian Federal jurisdiction. This legislation covers nearly all aspects of the law of evidence. A number of references will be made to this legislation throughout this book. For convenience, the Act will be referred to simply as the 'Australian Evidence Act', even though it is applicable only in the Australian Federal jurisdiction and in the courts of the Australian Capital Territory. It is expected, however, that the Act will provide a model for similar legislation in some of the Australian States in the next few years. Indeed, on 1 September 1995, a virtually identical statute, the Evidence Act 1995 (New South Wales), came into force in the State of New South Wales.

9. ORGANISATION OF BOOK

The order of the rest of the book is as follows. Chapter 2 examines how it is to be determined which party bears the burden of proving a particular issue in a trial, and to what standard the burden of proving a particular issue requires to be discharged. Chapter 3 looks at a number of issues pertaining

---

[49] Royal Commission on Criminal Justice, *Report* (Cm 2263) (1993) 125, 126.
[50] Law Commission (Consultation Paper No 141), *Criminal Law – Evidence in Criminal Proceedings: Previous Misconduct of a Defendant – A Consultation Paper* (1996), discussed briefly in 'Previous Misconduct of a Defendant', *Archbold News*, 15 August 1996, 6.
[51] Law Commission (Law Com No 245), *Evidence in Criminal Proceedings: Hearsay and Related Topics* (1997).
[52] See generally I Dennis, 'Codification and Reform of Evidence Law in Australia' [1996] *Criminal Law Review* 477.

to witnesses, and Chapter 4 considers the principles governing the course of evidence in a trial. The following two chapters are concerned with the broad issue of evidence of the character of the accused in a criminal trial. Chapter 5 examines the extent to which evidence of the accused's misconduct on other occasions may be adduced in chief by the prosecution, while Chapter 6 looks at the extent to which the prosecution may cross-examine the accused with a view to eliciting evidence of his or her bad character, or of his or her prior offences. In Chapter 7, the extent to which hearsay evidence may be admitted in civil and criminal trials is considered. Chapters 8 and 9 are concerned with the relationship between pre-trial police powers and the principles of evidence. Chapters 10 and 11 deal with two types of evidence which have given rise to substantial miscarriages of justice: identification evidence and expert opinion evidence respectively. Chapters 12 and 13 examine two doctrines which allow a party to refrain from disclosing or giving evidence of material, not on the basis of its actual or potential unreliability, but because of considerations of extrinsic policy. These are, respectively, the doctrines of public interest immunity and legal professional privilege.

2

BURDEN AND STANDARD OF PROOF

This chapter is divided into two parts. The first part is concerned with the manner in which a dispute as to which party bears the burden of proving a particular issue in a trial should be resolved. The question may arise in a criminal trial as to whether it is the prosecution or defence which bears the burden of proving a certain issue, and in a civil trial as to whether it is the plaintiff or defendant who bears the burden of proving a certain issue. Another question which may arise concerns the standard to which the burden of proving a particular issue requires to be discharged. This is the subject of the second part of the chapter.

1. BURDEN OF PROOF

(a) The legal burden and the evidential burden

The *legal burden of proof* is the probative burden, and relates to the duty of a party to prove a fact in issue to the trier of fact by the end of the trial. Failure to discharge this burden means that the issue will be decided in favour of the other party. The legal burden of proof, which is most commonly known simply as the 'burden of proof',[1] is therefore the final, or ultimate, burden of proving a particular fact. The *evidential burden of proof*, by contrast, is merely a provisional burden.[2] It relates to the duty of a party to make a matter a 'live issue' at the trial – in other words, to adduce sufficient evidence of a particular issue to satisfy the judge that the issue should be left to the trier of fact for its consideration. The question whether a legal burden has been discharged is, therefore, a question of fact, while the question whether an evidential burden has been discharged is a question of law.

Generally, the party which bears the legal burden of proving a particular issue also bears the evidential burden in relation to that issue. In criminal trials, however, this is not always the case. It is true that both the legal and

---

[1] It is also known as the 'risk of non-persuasion', the 'fixed burden of proof' and the 'persuasive burden'.
[2] It is also known as the 'burden of adducing evidence' and the 'burden of passing the judge'.

the evidential burden in relation to actus reus and mens rea fall on the prosecution. Where, however, the defence wishes to raise the defence of self-defence,[3] duress,[4] provocation[5] or non-insane automatism,[6] then, unless sufficient evidence to support the defence has already emerged during the trial, the defence has an evidential burden to discharge. It must introduce sufficient evidence to satisfy the trial judge that the defence in question should be left to the jury for its consideration. The legal burden of proving to the jury that the defendant was not acting in self-defence, under duress, as a result of provocation, or in a state of non-insane automatism (as the case may be) then falls on the prosecution.

(b) Incidence of legal burden

(i) Criminal trials

THE *WOOLMINGTON* RULE

Extract 2.1.1

Woolmington v DPP [1935] AC 462, 473, 481–2 (HL)

VISCOUNT SANKEY LC: It is true . . . that there is apparent authority for the law as laid down by the learned judge. But your Lordships' House has had the advantage of a prolonged and exhaustive inquiry dealing with the matter in debate from the earliest times, an advantage which was not shared by either of the Courts below. . . .

. . .

. . . Throughout the web of the English Criminal Law one golden thread is always to be seen, that it is the duty of the prosecution to prove the prisoner's guilt subject to what I have already said as to the defence of insanity and subject also to any statutory exception. If, at the end of and on the whole of the case, there is a reasonable doubt, created by the evidence given by either the prosecution or the prisoner, as to whether the prisoner killed the deceased with a malicious intention, the prosecution has not made out the case and the prisoner is entitled to an acquittal. No matter what the charge or where the trial, the principle that the prosecution must prove the guilt of the prisoner is part of the common law of England and no attempt to whittle it down can be entertained. . . . It is not the law of England to say, as was said in the summing-up in the present case: 'if the Crown satisfy you that this woman died at the prisoner's hands then he has to show that there are circumstances to be found in the evidence which has been given from the witness-box in this

---

[3] *R v Lobell* [1957] 1 QB 547.
[4] *R v Gill* [1963] 1 WLR 841.
[5] *Mancini v DPP* [1942] AC 1.
[6] *Bratty v A-G for NI* [1963] AC 386.

case which alleviate the crime so that it is only manslaughter or which excuse the homicide altogether by showing it was a pure accident.' If the proposition laid down by Sir Michael Foster or in the summing-up in *Rex v Greenacre* [(1837) 8 C & P 35] means this, those authorities are wrong.

The position, then, may be stated simply. In a criminal trial, the prosecution generally bears the legal burden of proving every issue. In general, therefore, actus reus, mens rea and the lack of a defence must all be proved by the prosecution. This reflects the principle of the presumption of innocence. In a criminal trial, the might of a 'strong' state is ranged against a 'weak' individual. If a conviction results, serious consequences may flow from this, including the possible deprivation of liberty. It is appropriate, therefore, for the prosecution to have to prove the defendant's guilt, rather than for the defendant to have to prove his or her own innocence. In a recent article, three reasons for the presumption of innocence have been identified.[7] First, 'whenever the burden of proof on any particular issue rests with the defendant it follows that the jury or magistrates must convict in cases in which they remain undecided about facts material to that issue'. Secondly, 'for as long as criminal proceedings are initiated and structured by the prosecutor's presentation of a prima facie case to answer on specified charges – as opposed, say, to requiring each of us to undergo monthly confessionals before an inquisitor – placing the burden of proof on a defendant will often deprive him of a fair opportunity to answer the allegations against him'. Finally, 'the prosecution has access to investigative resources which are vastly superior to those available to most defendants in criminal cases'.

The '*Woolmington* rule' is, however, subject to two broad exceptions. First, there is the defence of insanity. An accused who raises insanity or insane automatism as a defence (or who argues unfitness to plead) bears the legal burden of proving it:

Extract 2.1.2

M'Naghten's Case (1843) 10 Cl & F 200, 210; 8 ER 718, 722 (HL)

LORD TINDAL CJ: . . . we have to submit our opinion to be, that the jurors ought to be told in all cases that every man is to be presumed to be sane, and to possess a sufficient degree of reason to be responsible for his crimes, until the contrary be proved to their satisfaction; and that to establish a defence on the ground of insanity, it must be clearly proved that, at the time of the committing of the act, the party accused was labouring under such a defect of reason, from disease of the mind, as not to know the nature and quality of the act he was doing; or, if he did know it, that he did not know he was doing what was wrong.

---

[7] P Roberts, 'Taking the Burden of Proof Seriously' [1995] *Criminal Law Review* 783, 785–7.

Is it justifiable for the defence of insanity to be treated differently from the other common-law defences in English law where burden of proof is concerned? A number of arguments in support of this strategy have been advanced. It has been argued, for example, that, there being a presumption of sanity (as made clear in *M'Naghten* itself), it must be for the accused to prove his or her insanity. This, however, is a non sequitur. All the word 'presumption' means in this context is that insanity will not be an issue in a trial until the evidential burden in relation to the issue is discharged – that is, until sufficient evidence is adduced to make it a 'live issue'. In this sense, there is surely equally a 'presumption' that the accused was not acting in self-defence, under duress, as a result of provocation, or in a state of non-insane automatism, yet the legal burden of proof in relation to these defences lies on the prosecution. Secondly, it has been argued that to place the legal burden on the prosecution would be to impose a burden which would be very difficult to discharge, thus making it easy for the defence to make false claims of insanity. Again, however, there are other common-law defences in relation to which the prosecution bears legal burdens which may be similarly difficult to discharge. Thirdly, it is said that to place the legal burden on the defence would not cause unfairness, since insanity is a matter which would be peculiarly within the knowledge of the accused. But so is mens rea, which must be proved by the prosecution. For a much fuller discussion of these, and related, issues, see the perceptive article by T H Jones, 'Insanity, Automatism, and the Burden of Proof on the Accused' (1995) 111 *Law Quarterly Review* 475. See also T H Jones, 'Insanity and the Burden of Proof on the Accused: A Human Rights Approach' in J F Nijboer and J M Reijntjes (eds), *Proceedings of the First World Conference on New Trends in Criminal Investigation and Evidence* (1997).

The Supreme Court of Canada has been confronted with the issue of whether the presumption of sanity embodied in the Canadian Criminal Code violated the presumption of innocence guaranteed by s 11(d) of the Canadian Charter of Rights and Freedoms. The majority of the Supreme Court held that it did, but that the placing of the legal burden on the accused constituted a reasonable limit within the meaning of s 1[8] of the Charter.[9]

It is to be noted that, where an accused charged with murder raises the defence *either* of insanity or of diminished responsibility, s 6 of the Criminal Procedure (Insanity) Act 1964 permits the prosecution to adduce evidence to prove the *other* defence. In this situation, the legal burden of proof falls on the prosecution. In a similar vein, s 4 of the same Act allows the issue of unfitness to plead and stand trial to be raised either by the defence or by the prosecution, and where raised by the prosecution, the legal burden of proving the issue falls on the prosecution.[10]

---

[8] 'The *Canadian Charter of Rights and Freedoms* guarantees the rights and freedoms set out in it subject only to such reasonable limits prescribed by law as can be demonstrably justified in a free and democratic society.'
[9] *R v Chaulk* (1990) 62 CCC (3d) 193.
[10] *R v Robertson* [1968] 1 WLR 1767.

The second broad exception to the *Woolmington* rule arises where a statutory provision places the legal burden of proving a particular issue on the defendant. As Ashworth and Blake found in their empirical study, there is no shortage of examples of legislation which places the legal burden of proving particular issues on the defendant. They remark:

> It is a fair conclusion from the evidence presented here that many of those who prepare, draft and enact criminal legislation for England and Wales either fail to recognise these violations of the presumption of innocence, or disagree with the presumption of innocence or its application in this sphere, or fail to appreciate what can be achieved by placing only an evidential burden (rather than the legal burden) on defendants in respect of defences.[11]

EXPRESS STATUTORY EXCEPTIONS

On occasion, the legal burden of proving a particular issue is placed *expressly* on the defendant by statute:

Extract 2.1.3

Prevention of Corruption Act 1916, s 2

2. Presumption of corruption in certain cases
Where in any proceedings against a person for an offence under the Prevention of Corruption Act 1906, or the Public Bodies Corrupt Practices Act 1889, it is proved that any money, gift, or other consideration has been paid or given to or received by a person in the employment of His Majesty or any Government Department or a public body by or from a person, or agent of a person, holding or seeking to obtain a contract from His Majesty or any Government Department or public body, the money, gift, or consideration shall be deemed to have been paid or given and received corruptly as such inducement or reward as is mentioned in such Act unless the contrary is proved.

Extract 2.1.4

Prevention of Crime Act 1953, s 1(1)

1. Prohibition of the carrying of offensive weapons without lawful authority or reasonable excuse
(1) Any person who without lawful authority or reasonable excuse, the proof whereof shall lie on him, has with him in any public place any offensive weapon shall be guilty of an offence . . .

---

[11] A Ashworth and M Blake, 'The Presumption of Innocence in English Criminal Law' [1996] *Criminal Law Review* 306, 315.

44

Extract 2.1.5

Sexual Offences Act 1956, s 30(2)

30. Man living on earnings of prostitution

(2) For the purposes of this section a man who lives with or is habitually in the company of a prostitute, or who exercises control, direction or influence over a prostitute's movements in a way which shows he is aiding, abetting or compelling her prostitution with others, shall be presumed to be knowingly living on the earnings of prostitution, unless he proves the contrary.

Extract 2.1.6

Homicide Act 1957, s 2(2)

2. Persons suffering from diminished responsibility

(2) On a charge of murder, it shall be for the defence to prove that the person charged is by virtue of this section not liable to be convicted of murder.

IMPLIED STATUTORY EXCEPTIONS: SUMMARY TRIALS

In summary trials, the following statutory provision governs the issue of how it is to be determined whether the legislature has impliedly placed the legal burden of proof in relation to a particular issue on the defendant:

Extract 2.1.7

Magistrates' Courts Act 1980, s 101 (formerly Magistrates' Courts Act 1952, s 81)

101. Onus of proving exceptions, etc

Where the defendant to an information or complaint relies for his defence on any exception, exemption, proviso, excuse or qualification, whether or not it accompanies the description of the offence or matter of complaint in the enactment creating the offence or on which the complaint is founded, the burden of proving the exception, exemption, proviso, excuse or qualification shall be on him; and this notwithstanding that the information or complaint contains an allegation negativing the exception, exemption, proviso, excuse or qualification.

The crucial issue, therefore, is to determine whether the defendant is relying for his or her defence on an *exception, exemption, proviso, excuse* or *qualification*. If so, then the legal burden of proof in relation to the particular issue falls on the defendant. As will now be seen, s 101 has been held to encapsulate the common law, and, accordingly, the same approach is to be taken in trials on indictment.

IMPLIED STATUTORY EXCEPTIONS: TRIALS ON INDICTMENT

The entire issue of implied statutory exceptions and trials on indictment was the subject of extensive consideration by the Court of Appeal in *R v Edwards*[12] and by the House of Lords in *R v Hunt*.[13] Below is an extract from the decision in *Hunt*, in which *Edwards* was discussed in detail.

Extract 2.1.8

R v Hunt [1987] AC 352, 368–70, 374–8 (HL)

The accused was charged, under s 5 of the Misuse of Drugs Act 1971, with the unlawful possession of morphine. In his defence, he wanted to rely on the Misuse of Drugs Regulations 1973, which provided that s 5 did not apply to any preparation of morphine containing 0.2% of morphine or less. The question for the House of Lords was which party bore the legal burden of proof in relation to the issue of the percentage of morphine.

LORD GRIFFITHS: The appellant submits that in using the phrase 'any statutory exception' Lord Sankey LC [in *Woolmington*] was referring to statutory exceptions in which Parliament had by the use of express words placed the burden of proof on the accused, in the same way as the judges in *M'Naghten's Case* (1843) 10 Cl & Fin 200 had expressly placed the burden of proving insanity upon the accused. There are, of course, many examples of such statutory drafting . . .

The appellant also relies upon a passage in the speech of Viscount Simon LC in *Mancini v Director of Public Prosecutions* [1942] AC 1 in which he said, at p 11:

'*Woolmington's* case is concerned with explaining and reinforcing the rule that the prosecution must prove the charge it makes beyond reasonable doubt, and, consequently, that if, on the material before the jury, there is a reasonable doubt, the prisoner should have the benefit of it. The rule is of general application in all charges under the criminal law. The only exceptions arise, as explained in *Woolmington's* case, in the defence of insanity and in offences where onus of proof is specially dealt with by statute.'

It is submitted that the use of the word 'specially' indicates that Lord Simon LC considered that the reference in *Woolmington* [1935] AC 462 was limited to express statutory burdens of proof.

From this premise, it is argued that as it is well settled that if a defendant raises any of the common law defences such as accident, self-defence, provocation or duress and there is evidence to support such a defence the judge must leave it to the jury with a direction that the burden is on the prosecution to negative that defence, so it must follow that if a defendant raises any

---

[12] [1975] QB 27.
[13] [1987] AC 352.

statutory defence the same rule must apply, and provided there is evidence to support such a defence the burden lies on the prosecution to negative it, the only exceptions to this rule being those cases in which the statute has by express words placed the burden of proving the defence upon the defendant.

However, in *Woolmington* the House was not concerned to consider the nature of a statutory defence or upon whom the burden of proving it might lie. The House was considering a defence of accident to a charge of murder and were concerned to correct a special rule which appeared to have emerged in charges of murder whereby once it was proved that the defendant had killed the deceased a burden was held to lie upon the defendant to excuse himself by proving that it was the result of an accident or that he had been provoked to do so or had acted in self-defence. This in effect relieved the prosecution of the burden of proving an essential element in the crime of murder, namely the malicious intent and placed the burden upon the accused to disprove it. It was this aberration that was so trenchantly corrected by Lord Sankey LC in the passage already cited [1935] AC 462, 481–482. In *Mancini* the House dealt with the duty of the judge to lay before the jury any line of defence which the facts might reasonably support and they also dealt with the particular nature of the defence of provocation. In neither appeal was the House concerned with a statutory defence and no argument was addressed on the nature or scope of statutory exceptions.

Before the decision in *Woolmington* [1935] AC 462 there had been a number of cases in which in trials on indictment the courts had held that the burden of establishing a statutory defence fell upon the defendant although the statute did not expressly so provide: see for example *Rex v Turner* (1816) 5 M & S 206, a decision under the Gaming Acts, and *Apothecaries' Co v Bentley* (1824) 1 C & P 538 and *Rex v Scott* (1921) 86 JP 69, decisions in which it was held that the defendant had the burden of proving that he was licensed to perform an otherwise prohibited act.

I cannot accept that either Viscount Sankey LC or Lord Simon LC intended to cast doubt on these long-standing decisions without having had the benefit of any argument addressed to the House on the question of statutory exceptions. I am, therefore, unwilling to read the reference to 'any statutory exception' in *Woolmington*, at p 481, in the restricted sense in which the appellant invites us to read it. It is also to be observed that Lord Devlin in *Jayesena v The Queen* [1970] AC 618, a decision of the Privy Council, commenting upon *Woolmington* said, at p 623:

'The House laid it down that, save in the case of insanity or of a statutory defence, there was no burden laid on the prisoner to prove his innocence and that it was sufficient for him to raise a doubt as to his guilt.'

Lord Devlin does not appear to restrict a statutory defence to one in which the burden of proof is expressly placed upon the defendant.

. . .

I would summarise the position thus far by saying that *Woolmington* [1935] AC 462 did not lay down a rule that the burden of proving a statutory defence only lay upon the defendant if the statute specifically so provided: that a statute can, on its true construction, place a burden of proof on the defendant although it does not do so expressly: that if a burden of proof is placed on the defendant it is the same burden whether the case be tried summarily or on indictment, namely, a burden that has to be discharged on the balance of probabilities.

The real difficulty in these cases lies in determining upon whom Parliament intended to place the burden of proof when the statute has not expressly so provided. It presents particularly difficult problems of construction when what might be regarded as a matter of defence appears in a clause creating the offence rather than in some subsequent proviso from which it may more readily be inferred that it was intended to provide for a separate defence which a defendant must set up and prove if he wishes to avail himself of it. This difficulty was acutely demonstrated in *Nimmo v Alexander Cowan & Sons Ltd* [1968] AC 107. S 29(1) of the Factories Act 1961 provides:

'There shall, so far as is reasonably practicable, be provided and main-tained safe means of access to every place at which any person has at any time to work, and every such place shall, so far as is reasonably practica-ble, be made and kept safe for any person working there.'

The question before the House was whether the burden of proving that it was not reasonably practicable to make the working place safe lay upon the defendant or the plaintiff in a civil action. However, as the section also created a summary offence the same question would have arisen in a prosecution. In the event, the House divided three to two on the construction of the section, Lord Reid and Lord Wilberforce holding that the section required the plaintiff or prosecution to prove that it was reasonably practicable to make the working place safe, the majority, Lord Guest, Lord Upjohn and Lord Pearson, holding that if the plaintiff or prosecution proved that the working place was not safe it was for the defendant to excuse himself by proving that it was not reason-ably practicable to make it safe. However, their Lordships were in agreement that if the linguistic construction of the statute did not clearly indicate upon whom the burden should lie the court should look to other considerations to determine the intention of Parliament such as the mischief at which the Act was aimed and practical considerations affecting the burden of proof and, in particular, the ease or difficulty that the respective parties would encounter in discharging the burden. I regard this last consideration as one of great import-ance for surely Parliament can never lightly be taken to have intended to impose an onerous duty on a defendant to prove his innocence in a criminal case, and a court should be very slow to draw any such inference from the language of a statute.

When all the cases are analysed, those in which the courts have held that the burden lies on the defendant are cases in which the burden can be easily discharged. This point can be demonstrated by what, at first blush, appear to be two almost indistinguishable cases that arose under wartime regulations. In *Rex v Oliver* [1944] KB 68 the defendant was prosecuted for selling sugar without a licence. The material part of the Sugar (Control) Order 1940 (SR & O 1940 No 1068) by article 2 provided:

'Subject to any directions given or except under and in accordance with the terms of a licence permit or other authority granted by or on behalf of the Minister no ... wholesaler shall by way of trade ... supply ... any sugar.'

The Court of Criminal Appeal held that this placed the burden upon the defendant to prove that he had the necessary licence to sell sugar. In *Rex v Putland and Sorrell* [1946] 1 All ER 85, the defendant was charged with acquiring silk stockings without surrendering clothing coupons. The material part of the Consumer Rationing (Consolidation) Order 1944 (SR & O 1944 No 800), article 4 provided: 'A person shall not acquire rationed goods ... without surrendering ... coupons.' The Court of Criminal Appeal there held that the burden was upon the prosecution to prove that the clothing had been bought without the surrender of coupons. The real distinction between these two cases lies in the comparative difficulty which would face a defendant in discharging the burden of proof.

In *Oliver's* case [1944] KB 68 it would have been a simple matter for the defendant to prove that he had a licence if such was the case but in the case of purchase of casual articles of clothing it might, as the court pointed out in *Putland's* case, be a matter of the utmost difficulty for a defendant to establish that he had given the appropriate number of coupons for them. It appears to me that it was this consideration that led the court to construe that particular regulation as imposing the burden of proving that coupons had not been surrendered upon the prosecution.

In *Reg v Edwards* [1975] QB 27, 39–40 the Court of Appeal expressed their conclusion in the form of an exception to what they said was the fundamental rule of our criminal law that the prosecution must prove every element of the offence charged. They said that the exception

'is limited to offences arising under enactments which prohibit the doing of an act save in specified circumstances or by persons of specified classes or with specified qualifications or with the licence or permission of specified authorities.'

I have little doubt that the occasions upon which a statute will be construed as imposing a burden of proof upon a defendant which do not fall within this formulation are likely to be exceedingly rare. But I find it difficult to fit *Nimmo v Alexander Cowan & Sons Ltd* [1968] AC 107 into this formula, and I would prefer to adopt the formula as an excellent guide to construction rather than as an exception to a rule. In the final analysis each case must turn upon the construction of the particular legislation to determine whether the defence is an exception within the meaning of s 101 of the Act of 1980 which the Court of Appeal rightly decided reflects the rule for trials on indictment. With this one qualification I regard *Reg v Edwards* as rightly decided.

My Lords, I am, of course, well aware of the body of distinguished academic opinion that urges that wherever a burden of proof is placed upon a defendant by statute the burden should be an evidential burden and not a persuasive burden, and that it has the support of the distinguished signatories to the 11th Report of the Criminal Law Revision Committee, Evidence (General) (1972) (Cmnd 4991). My Lords, such a fundamental change is, in my view, a matter for Parliament and not a decision of your Lordships' House.

...

... The prosecution must prove as an essential element of the offence the possession of a prohibited substance and the burden therefore lies upon the prosecution to prove not only that the powder contained morphine but also that it was not morphine in the form permitted by regulation 4(1) and Schedule 1 thereunder.

I do not share the anxieties of the Court of Appeal that this may place an undue burden on the prosecution. It must be extremely rare for a prosecution to be brought under the Act of 1971 without the substance in question having been analysed. If it has been analysed there will be no difficulty in producing evidence to show that it does not fall within Schedule 1 to the Regulations. I pause here to observe that the analyst was in court during this trial and could, no doubt, have given this evidence if called upon to do so. In future the evidence can, of course, be included in the analyst's report. On the other hand if the burden of proof is placed upon the defendant he may be faced with very real practical difficulties in discharging it. The suspected substance is usually seized by the police for the purposes of analysis and there is no statutory provision entitling the defendant to a proportion of it. Often there is very little of the substance and if it has already been analysed by the prosecution it may have been destroyed in the process. In those cases, which I would surmise are very rare, in which it is intended to prosecute without an analyst's report there will have to be evidence from which the inference can be drawn that the substance was a prohibited drug and such evidence may well permit of the inference that it was not one of the relatively harmless types of compounds containing little more than traces of the drugs which are contained in Schedule 1 to the Regulations.

Finally, my Lords, as this question of construction is obviously one of real difficulty I have regard to the fact that offences involving the misuse of hard drugs are among the most serious in the criminal calendar and, subject to certain special defences the burden whereof is specifically placed upon the defendant, they are absolute. In these circumstances, it seems to me right to resolve any ambiguity in favour of the defendant and to place the burden of proving the nature of the substance involved in so serious an offence upon the prosecution.

The House of Lords in *Hunt* confirms, therefore, that legal burdens may be placed on the defence impliedly as well as expressly. In determining whether Parliament has impliedly placed a legal burden on the defence, the court is to consider factors such as the language of the statute; the mischief at which the statute was aimed; and practical considerations such as the ease or difficulty which the respective parties would encounter in discharging the burden. Despite the fact that this approach led in *Hunt* to the conclusion that the burden of proof was borne by the prosecution, such an approach is open to criticism. Trials on indictment, it must be remembered, differ from summary trials in a number of important respects: they are inherently more 'serious' and formal affairs, and have the potential to lead to far more drastic consequences for those found guilty. Would it, therefore, be more consistent with the presumption of innocence for the law to embrace a principle whereby, in trials on indictment, legal burdens can be placed on defendants by the legislature *expressly* only, and not by implication? The adoption of such a principle would mean, of course, that, in the case of offences triable either way, the location of the burden of proof may differ according to whether the offence is being tried summarily or on indictment. Lord Griffiths commented that 'the law would have developed on absurd lines if in respect of the same offence the burden of proof today differed according to whether the case was being heard by the magistrates or on indictment'.[14] It may be doubted, however, whether this should be a matter of real concern. After all, for the reasons stated earlier in the chapter, a Crown Court prosecution would by its nature be of a completely different dimension from a prosecution in the magistrates' court for precisely the same offence.

It has also been argued that it may be inappropriate to treat as a relevant consideration the ease or difficulty which the respective parties would encounter in discharging the legal burden if placed on either of them:

Extract 2.1.9

A Stein, 'After *Hunt*: The Burden of Proof, Risk of Non-Persuasion and Judicial Pragmatism' (1991) 54 *Modern Law Review* 570, 571–2

... classification of defences as falling within the ambit of section 101 should not merely be independent of their syntax or sectional location in criminal law statutes, but must also be independent of forensic contingencies, such as the ease or difficulty encountered by the parties in proving various facts. Section 101 deals with the allocation of the risk of non-persuasion, not merely with the burden of adducing evidence, and the mere fact that the accused holds the relevant information or has a better or even exclusive access to evidence does not alone support the view that he should therefore carry that risk. This fact can only justify an imposition of a duty on the accused to put forward such evidence that he possesses. Once the accused produces his evidence for examination at the trial, his advantage evaporates and should therefore not be used against him any further.

Hence, classification of defences for the purposes of section 101 can cogently be made only on the grounds of their substance. Those defences which are no different from ordinary protestations of innocence should not be subject to a less favourable treatment in allocating the risk of non-persuasion. Section 101 should therefore apply solely to 'excuses,' that is, defences which, on individual grounds, as a matter of leniency and concession to human frailty, exonerate or mitigate the responsibility of those who committed a criminally blameworthy act. It cannot properly be interpreted as including 'justifications,' those defences which render the act in question unblameworthy, making the actor's claim of innocence no different from any other form of saying 'I did nothing wrong.' If the rules allocating the risk of non-persuasion in criminal cases are to be carried through consistently, and an interpreter's standpoint is that like cases should always be treated alike, this interpretive possibility would be the only one available.

It [may] therefore [be] submitted that the guidelines laid down in *Hunt* are inadequate. Without discriminating between various defences on the grounds

---

[14] *R v Hunt* [1987] AC 352, 373.

of their substance, the courts could hardly be certain about when to be 'very slow' in imposing the risk of non-persuasion on the accused by classifying his defence as falling within section 101. What the courts will almost always be certain about would be that the accused holds better knowledge of the facts that can prove or refute his defence. When the charges brought against the accused are not too serious, he would probably end up bearing the risk of non-persuasion in respect of both 'excuses' and 'justifications.'

Are you persuaded by these arguments?

The following extract demonstrates that the law in this area is littered with inconsistencies and anomalies which the decision in *Hunt* does little to ameliorate:

Extract 2.1.10

J C Smith, 'The Presumption of Innocence' (1987) 38 *Northern Ireland Legal Quarterly* 223, 231–3, 235–6

The haphazard application of section 101

Prior to *Hunt*, the leading case which established that section 101 imposes a legal burden of proof, and not merely an evidential burden on the defendant, was *Gatland v Metropolitan Police Commissioner* [1968] 2 QB 279; [1968] 2 All ER 100. That was a case under section 140 of the Highways Act 1959 (section 161 of the Highways Act 1980) under which it is an offence: 'If a person, without lawful authority or excuse, deposits any thing whatever on a highway . . .'. Lord Parker CJ, giving the judgment of the Divisional Court, stated that the effect of section 101 was that it was for the accused to raise and prove lawful authority or excuse. In *Hunt* Lord Ackner stated that it was accepted that this decision was correct. . . .

But there is another section of the Highways Act (section 121(1) of the 1959 Act and section 137(1) of the 1980 Act) which provides that it is an offence: 'If a person, without lawful authority or excuse, in any way wilfully obstructs . . .'. In the leading case of *Nagy v Weston* [1965] 1 All ER 78 Lord Parker CJ, not referring to section 101, accepted the submission of counsel that the prosecution had to prove that there was no lawful authority or reasonable excuse. In *Hubbard v Pitt* [1975] 1 All ER 7 Lord Denning MR, not mentioning either *Gatland* or section 101, regarded Lord Parker's judgment on this point as 'authoritative'; and in the very recent case of *Hirst and Agu v The Chief Constable of the West Yorkshire Police* [1987] Crim LR 330 the Divisional Court cited it as binding authority, again without referring to *Gatland* or section 101. But, I have to ask, what is the difference between –

If a person, without lawful authority or excuse, deposits any thing on a highway. . . .

and

If a person, without lawful authority or excuse, in any way wilfully obstructs . . . ?

I can see no relevant difference. If section 101 applies to the one, it surely applies to the other. Of course, the obstruction section is the more important one in practice and its interpretation has serious implications for civil liberties because those taking part in demonstrations or picketing are likely to find themselves charged with an offence under this section. To impose on such persons the burden of proving that every obstruction of the highway which they might have caused was done with lawful authority or excuse would be a grave step. To deduce from this that Parliament intended to exclude the effect of section 101 from the obstruction offence, though not from another offence under the same statute, in respect of which Parliament has used exactly the same language, would seem to be to indulge in fiction of an arbitrary and undesirable kind. Of course, the courts have not done that. They and counsel have behaved as if section 101 did not exist. But section 101 is there, its authority and effect is confirmed by the House of Lords in *Hunt*.
. . .

Perhaps most striking of all is the treatment of the legislation relating to drinking and driving which makes it an offence to fail, 'without reasonable excuse', to provide a specimen of breath or a laboratory specimen as the case may be. These provisions have been very strictly construed against the defendant. The courts have taken a very narrow view of what is capable of being a reasonable excuse, no doubt because they consider that it is in the interest of public safety on the roads to do so. Yet they seem consistently to have held, without reference to section 101, that the only burden on the defendant is an evidential burden and that the burden of proof of absence of reasonable excuse is on the prosecution (*Mallows v Harris* [1979] RTR 404, 410; *Anderton v Waring* [1986] RTR 74, 80; *Cotgrave v Cooney* [1987] Crim LR 272).
. . .

Parliament itself seems to have no confidence in the effectiveness of section 101 and any equivalent rule of common law – else, why provide in section 47 of the Sexual Offences Act 1956 –

> Where in any of the foregoing sections the description of an offence is expressed to be subject to exceptions mentioned in the section, proof of the exception is to lie on the person relying on it?

Section 101 is supposed to do this job already for summary trials and the common law rule for trial on indictment. Why provide in the Prevention of Crime Act 1953 that it is an offence for a person to have with him an offensive weapon in a public place without lawful authority or excuse 'the proof whereof shall lie on him'? Again, section 101 as interpreted in *Gatland* and the common law do this. Many other examples could be cited.

Further reading

A Ashworth and M Blake, 'The Presumption of Innocence in English Criminal Law' [1996] *Criminal Law Review* 306

F Bennion, 'Statutory Exceptions: A Third Knot in the Golden Thread?' [1988] *Criminal Law Review* 31

D J Birch, 'Hunting the Snark: The Elusive Statutory Exception' [1988] *Criminal Law Review* 221

P Healy, 'Proof and Policy: No Golden Threads' [1987] *Criminal Law Review* 355

P Mirfield, 'The Legacy of *Hunt*' [1988] *Criminal Law Review* 19

— 'An Ungrateful Reply' [1988] *Criminal Law Review* 233

P Roberts, 'Taking the Burden of Proof Seriously' [1995] *Criminal Law Review* 783

J C Smith, 'The Presumption of Innocence' (1987) 38 *Northern Ireland Legal Quarterly* 223

A Stein, 'After *Hunt*: The Burden of Proof, Risk of Non-Persuasion and Judicial Pragmatism' (1991) 54 *Modern Law Review* 570

A A S Zuckerman, 'No Third Exception to the Woolmington Rule' (1987) 103 *Law Quarterly Review* 170

— 'The Third Exception to the Woolmington Rule' (1976) 92 *Law Quarterly Review* 402

EFFECT OF MISDIRECTION

A misdirection (or failure to give a direction) to the jury in a criminal trial on burden of proof can lead to the quashing of a conviction on appeal. In *R v Zarrabi*,[15] the trial judge informed the jury that he was going to deal with the burden of proof, but in fact directed them on the standard of proof. The Court of Appeal held that this constituted a misdirection and quashed the conviction. The conviction in *R v Moon*[16] was quashed because the jury had been directed that the legal burden of proof in relation to self-defence fell on the accused.

(ii) Civil trials

The principle in civil trials is that the party asserting an issue essential to his or her case bears the legal burden of proof in relation to that issue. In a tort action for negligence, the plaintiff bears the legal burden of proving the existence of a duty of care, breach of that duty, and the consequential loss. If the defendant wishes to raise a defence such as volenti non fit injuria or contributory negligence, then he or she bears the legal burden of proving it. In a similar vein, the plaintiff in a contract action bears the legal burden of proving the existence of a contract, breach of that contract, and the consequential loss. The legal burden of proving a defence such as discharge by agreement or frustration falls on the defendant. Unlike criminal trials, there is no presumption in civil trials, where in theory the parties are 'equals', that the party bringing the action bears the legal burden of proof in relation to every issue.

[15] (1985) *The Times*, 23 February.
[16] [1969] 1 WLR 1705.

A party upon whom the legal burden in relation to a particular issue falls bears that burden even if this means having to 'prove a negative':

Extract 2.1.11

***Abrath v North Eastern Railway Co* (1883) 11 QBD 440, 457, 462 (CA)**

BOWEN LJ: Now in an action for malicious prosecution the plaintiff has the burden throughout of establishing that the circumstances of the prosecution were such that a judge can see no reasonable or probable cause for instituting it. In one sense that is the assertion of a negative, and we have been pressed with the proposition that when a negative is to be made out the onus of proof shifts. That is not so. If the assertion of a negative is an essential part of the plaintiff's case, the proof of the assertion still rests upon the plaintiff. The terms 'negative' and 'affirmative' are after all relative and not absolute. In dealing with a question of negligence, that term may be considered either as negative or affirmative according to the definition adopted in measuring the duty which is neglected. Wherever a person asserts affirmatively as part of his case that a certain state of facts is present or is absent, or that a particular thing is insufficient for a particular purpose, that is an averment which he is bound to prove positively. . . .

. . .

. . . Who had to make good their point as to the proposition whether the defendants had taken reasonable and proper care to inform themselves of the true state of the case? The defendants were not bound to make good anything. It was the plaintiff's duty to shew the absence of reasonable care . . .

The principle that the party asserting an issue essential to his or her case bears the legal burden of proving it may, however, be more easily stated than applied. How is it to be determined whether a particular issue is essential to a party's case?

Extract 2.1.12

***Joseph Constantine Steamship Line Ltd v Imperial Smelting Corpn Ltd* [1942] AC 154, 177 (HL)**

1. A ship on charter was destroyed by an explosion.
2. The charterers brought an action claiming damages from the owners for failure to load.
3. The owners raised the defence of frustration.
4. The issue arose whether the owners bore the legal burden of proving that the explosion (the frustrating event) was *not* their fault, or whether the charterers bore the legal burden of proving that the explosion *was* the fault of the owners.

55

LORD RUSSELL OF KILLOWEN: The rival contentions may be stated thus: (1.) The appellants say: 'Frustration will excuse unless it is proved to be self-induced.' (2.) The respondents say: 'Frustration will not excuse unless it is proved not to be self-induced.'.

My Lords, in my opinion the appellants' contention is correct. In coming to this conclusion I am influenced by three considerations. First, the proving of a negative, a task always difficult and often impossible, would be a most exceptional burden to impose on a litigant. Secondly, I know of no case of frustration in the books, in which an attempt has been made, or called for, to prove the suggested negative. Thirdly, the statement of the doctrine in the authorities does not in any way compel us to adopt the contention of the respondents.

Extract 2.1.13

J Stone, 'Burden of Proof and the Judicial Process: A Commentary on *Joseph Constantine Steamship, Ltd v Imperial Smelting Corporation, Ltd*' (1944) 60 *Law Quarterly Review* 262, 278

Let it be assumed then that in the great majority of frustration cases no fault of the parties was operative; and let it be assumed that in these cases the impossibility of proof mentioned by the Lords is present. A rule requiring the defendant pleading frustration to negative fault will then *ex hypothesi* do injustice to the great majority of defendants. While on the other hand, a rule requiring the plaintiff to prove fault will *ex hypothesi* do injustice to only a small minority of plaintiffs.

This consideration seems to support decisively the rule laid down in the House of Lords in all cases where, though human fault may be present, the circumstances make proof of it either way impossible. Moreover, in those cases where the circumstances do not make proof impossible the rule laid down by the House of Lords is preferable on the ground taken by some of the Lords that an affirmative is easier to prove than a negative. For there will be proportionately less cases of injustice through failure of proof among plaintiffs required to prove the affirmative, than there would be among defendants who had to prove the negative.

These arguments on policy, which are either explicit or implicit in the speeches of all the members of the House of Lords, seem not only unanswerable in themselves: they also seem to be quite conclusive of the point at issue, always assuming that there was no decisive precedent on the matter. It has been seen that the absence of any such precedent was freely recognised by all the members of the House.

Do you agree with Stone that, in the absence of binding precedent, the matter is to be resolved by examining considerations of policy?

In *Munro, Brice & Co v War Risks Association*,[17] it was held that in an action on a policy insuring against loss by perils of the sea, with a clause excepting loss by capture, seizure and consequences of hostilities, a plaintiff

---

[17] [1918] 2 KB 78.

56

whose ship had been lost at sea did not bear the legal burden of proving that
it had not been lost by the excepted causes. The legal burden of proving that
it *had* been so lost fell on the defendant. The court took the view 'that . . . when
in an action upon a policy of marine insurance the assured has proved that
his ship was sunk at sea, he has made out a prima facie case against his
underwriters on that policy, and that it is for them to set up the free of capture and seizure exception and to bring themselves within it if they can'.[18]
This decision may be compared with that reached in *The Glendarroch*.[19] The
plaintiffs brought an action for the non-delivery of goods shipped under a bill
of lading. The goods had been damaged by sea water through the stranding
of the vessel. The bill of lading exempted the defendants from liability for
loss or damage occasioned by perils of the sea, provided that the defendants
were not negligent. The Court of Appeal held as follows:[20]

(1) The plaintiffs bore the legal burden of proving the contract and the non-
delivery of the goods.
(2) If the defendants relied on the exemption clause, then the legal burden
fell on them to prove that the damage was caused by a peril of the sea.
(3) If, however, the plaintiffs then relied on the proviso, they bore the
legal burden of proving that the damage was caused by the defendants'
negligence.

2. STANDARD OF PROOF

If a party bears the legal burden of proving a particular issue, to what standard does that party need to discharge the burden?

(a) Criminal trials

(i) Where the prosecution bears the legal burden

Where the prosecution bears the legal burden of proving a particular issue,
it must be proved 'beyond reasonable doubt'. What exactly is meant by this
phrase? Should it, or any other phrase, be used in directing the jury?

Extract 2.2.1

Miller v Minister of Pensions [1947] 2 All ER 372, 373 (KBD)

DENNING J: . . . the . . . degree of cogency . . . required in a criminal case
before an accused person is found guilty . . . is well settled. It need not reach

---

[18] At 88.
[19] [1894] P 226.
[20] At 231.

certainty, but it must carry a high degree of probability. Proof beyond reasonable doubt does not mean proof beyond the shadow of a doubt. The law would fail to protect the community if it admitted fanciful possibilities to deflect the course of justice. If the evidence is so strong against a man as to leave only a remote possibility in his favour which can be dismissed with the sentence 'of course it is possible, but not in the least probable,' the case is proved beyond reasonable doubt, but nothing short of that will suffice.

Extract 2.2.2

R v Hepworth [1955] 2 QB 600, 603–4 (CCA)

LORD GODDARD CJ: . . . one would be on safe ground if one said in a criminal case to a jury: 'You must be satisfied beyond reasonable doubt' and one could also say: 'You, the jury, must be completely satisfied,' or better still: 'You must feel sure of the prisoner's guilt.' But I desire to repeat what I said in *Rex v Kritz* [1950] 1 KB 82, 89: 'It is not the particular formula that matters: it is the effect of the summing-up. If the jury are made to understand that they have to be satisfied and must not return a verdict against a defendant unless they feel sure, and that the onus is all the time on the prosecution and not on the defence,' that is enough. I should be very sorry if it were thought that these cases should depend on the use of a particular formula or particular word or words. The point is that the jury should be directed first, that the onus is always on the prosecution; secondly, that before they convict they must feel sure of the accused's guilt. If that is done, that will be enough.
. . .
    For the reasons I have endeavoured to give – I hope it will not be thought that we are laying down any particular form of words, but we are saying it is desirable that something more should be said than merely 'satisfied' – we think that the conviction should be quashed.

Extract 2.2.3

Walters v R [1969] 2 AC 26, 29–31 (PC)

LORD DIPLOCK: At the trial of the petitioner the judge thought it desirable to explain to the jury what was meant by the time-honoured phrase 'a reasonable doubt'. In the course of doing so he said:

> 'a reasonable doubt is that quality and kind of doubt which, when you are dealing with matters of importance in your own affairs, you allow to influence you one way or the other.'

. . .
    By the time he sums up the judge at the trial has had an opportunity of observing the jurors. In their Lordships' view it is best left to his discretion to choose the most appropriate set of words in which to make *that* jury understand that they must not return a verdict against a defendant unless they

are sure of his guilt; and if the judge feels that any of them, through unfamiliarity with court procedure, are in danger of thinking that they are engaged in some task more esoteric than applying to the evidence adduced at the trial the common sense with which they approach matters of importance to them in their ordinary lives, then the use of such analogies as that used by Small J in the present case, whether in the words in which he expressed it or in those used in any of the other cases to which reference has been made, may be helpful and is in their Lordships' view unexceptionable. Their Lordships would deprecate any attempt to lay down some precise formula or to draw fine distinctions between one set of words and another. It is the effect of the summing-up as a whole that matters.

Extract 2.2.4

Ferguson v R [1979] 1 WLR 94, 98–9 (PC)

LORD SCARMAN: In *Walters v The Queen* [1969] 2 AC 26 their Lordships had to consider a direction almost identical in part with that in this case. Delivering the judgment in that case (which was not an appeal, but an application for special leave to appeal) Lord Diplock pointed out that a distinction between 'objective' and 'subjective' tests is not apt in this context. The Board expressed the view in that case that the formula used in summing up does not matter so long as it is made clear to the jury, whatever words are used, that they must not return a verdict against a defendant unless they are sure of his guilt. Their Lordships' Board agree with these comments, with one reservation. Though the law requires no particular formula, judges are wise, as a general rule, to adopt one.

The time-honoured formula is that the jury must be satisfied beyond reasonable doubt. As Dixon CJ said in *Dawson v The Queen* (1961) 106 CLR 1, 18, attempts to substitute other expressions have never prospered. It is generally sufficient and safe to direct a jury that they must be satisfied beyond reasonable doubt so that they feel sure of the defendant's guilt. Nevertheless, other words will suffice, so long as the message is clear.

Extract 2.2.5

R v Ching (1976) 63 Cr App R 7, 10–11 (CA)

The jury were directed as follows: '... A reasonable doubt, it has been said, is a doubt to which you can give a reason as opposed to a mere fanciful sort of speculation such as "Well, nothing in this world is certain nothing in this world can be proved." ... It is sometimes said the sort of matter which might influence you if you were to consider some business matter. A matter, for example, of a mortgage concerning your house, or something of that nature. ...'

LAWTON LJ: Mr Latham said that the judge did not stress that the relevant doubts were those which have to be overcome in *important* business affairs.

What he did was to pick an example, which for sensible people would be an important matter. We can see nothing wrong in his so doing.

. . .

There is no reason for saying in this case that the verdict was unsafe. As I said earlier, and I repeat, this is one of a large number of cases which have come before this Court in recent years, raising fine points about the terms in which judges have directed the jury as to the standard of proof. We point out and emphasise that if judges stopped trying to define that which is almost impossible to define there would be fewer appeals. We hope there will not be any more for some considerable time.

The preceding case may be contrasted with *R v Gray*.[21] The trial judge defined a 'reasonable doubt' as 'a doubt based upon good reason and not a fanciful doubt', and as 'the sort of doubt which might affect you in the conduct of your *everyday affairs*'. The Court of Appeal held that if the trial judge had referred to *important affairs* then the direction would have been unobjectionable, but 'everyday affairs' might have suggested to the jury a standard of proof which was too low.

In *R v Stafford*[22] the trial judge told the jury to 'remember that a reasonable doubt is one for which you could give reasons if you were asked'. On appeal, the Court of Appeal disapproved of this definition.

In *McGreevy v DPP*,[23] the House of Lords expressed the view that 'it would be undesirable to lay it down as a rule which would bind judges that a direction to a jury in cases where circumstantial evidence is the basis of the prosecution case must be given in some special form, provided always that in suitable terms it is made plain to a jury that they must not convict unless they are satisfied of guilt beyond all reasonable doubt'.[24]

Note also the following recent comment by Lamer CJC, delivering the judgment of the Supreme Court of Canada in *R v Brydon*:

. . . in my opinion instructing a jury that proof beyond a reasonable doubt *is not met* if the jurors can only conclude that the accused is 'probably' or 'likely' guilty is quite a useful manner in which to convey the meaning of such an elusive concept.[25]

See generally J C Smith, 'Satisfying the Jury' [1988] *Criminal Law Review* 335.

(ii) Where the defence bears the legal burden

Where the defence bears the legal burden of proving a particular issue, it need only be proved 'on the balance of probabilities': see, for example, *R v*

[21] (1973) 58 Cr App R 177.
[22] [1968] 3 All ER 752.
[23] [1973] 1 WLR 276.
[24] At 285.
[25] (1995) 129 DLR (4th) 1, 11 (emphasis in original).

Carr-Briant,[26] *R v Dunbar*[27] and *Public Prosecutor v Yuvaraj*[28] (cases where the burden was placed on the defence expressly by statute); *Sodeman v R*[29] (insanity); *R v Podola*[30] (unfitness to plead). Proof 'on the balance of probabilities' is the civil standard of proof, which will be considered in detail later.

(iii) Effect of misdirection

A misdirection (or failure to give a direction) to the jury in a criminal trial on standard of proof can lead to the quashing of a conviction on appeal. However, in *R v Edwards*,[31] although the trial judge had failed to direct the jury on standard of proof, the evidence against the accused was considered to be so overwhelming that a reasonable jury, properly directed on standard of proof, would inevitably have convicted him. Accordingly, the 'proviso' which was then contained in s 2(1) of the Criminal Appeal Act 1968 was applied and the conviction upheld.

(b) Civil trials

(i) The general rule

Where a legal burden requires to be discharged in civil proceedings, the relevant standard of proof is proof 'on the balance of probabilities'. What does this mean?

Extract 2.2.6

Miller v Minister of Pensions [1947] 2 All ER 372, 374 (KBD)

DENNING J: It must carry a reasonable degree of probability, but not so high as is required in a criminal case. If the evidence is such that the tribunal can say: 'We think it more probable than not,' the burden is discharged, but, if the probabilities are equal, it is not.

Extract 2.2.7

Bater v Bater [1951] P 35, 37 (CA)

DENNING LJ: . . . in civil cases, the case must be proved by a preponderance of probability, but there may be degrees of probability within that standard. The degree depends on the subject-matter. A civil court, when considering

---

[26] [1943] KB 607.
[27] [1958] 1 QB 1.
[28] [1970] 2 WLR 226.
[29] [1936] 2 All ER 1138.
[30] [1960] 1 QB 325.
[31] (1983) 77 Cr App R 5.

a charge of fraud, will naturally require for itself a higher degree of probability than that which it would require when asking if negligence is established. It does not adopt so high a degree as a criminal court, even when it is considering a charge of a criminal nature; but still it does require a degree of probability which is commensurate with the occasion. Likewise, a divorce court should require a degree of probability which is proportionate to the subject-matter.

Section 140 of the Australian Evidence Act 1995 makes specific provision regarding the standard of proof in civil proceedings.

Extract 2.2.8

Evidence Act 1995 (Australia), s 140

140. Civil proceedings: standard of proof
(1) In a civil proceeding, the court must find the case of a party proved if it is satisfied that the case has been proved on the balance of probabilities.
(2) Without limiting the matters that the court may take into account in deciding whether it is so satisfied, it is to take into account:
   (a) the nature of the cause of action or defence; and
   (b) the nature of the subject-matter of the proceeding; and
   (c) the gravity of the matters alleged.

Does this reflect the position in England?

Defamation actions are civil actions but tried with a jury. The Court of Appeal held in *Lawrence v Chester Chronicle*[32] that, in trials of defamation actions, it was not generally necessary for the jury to be directed that the civil standard of proof was a flexible one which varied according to the seriousness of the alleged defamatory statement; in most cases this was a matter for the jury's common sense.

Further reading

D Hamer, 'The Civil Standard of Proof Uncertainty: Probability, Belief and Justice' (1994) 16 *Sydney Law Review* 506

(ii) Contempt of court

It is well established that contempt of court must be proved beyond reasonable doubt, even if the alleged contempt was of a civil court. In *Re Bramblevale Ltd*, Lord Denning MR remarked:

---

[32] (1986) *The Times*, 8 February.

4414

3445344343434443

2. STANDARD OF PROOF

A contempt of court is an offence of a criminal character. A man may be sent to prison for it. It must be satisfactorily proved. To use the time-honoured phrase, it must be proved beyond reasonable doubt.[33]

(iii) Allegations of criminal conduct

It has generally been held, consistently with what was said in *Bater v Bater*, that allegations of criminal conduct in civil proceedings need be proved on the balance of probabilities only, and not beyond reasonable doubt. Examples include *Re Dellow's Will Trusts*[34] (civil proceedings – issue of whether a wife had killed her husband) and *Post Office v Estuary Radio Ltd*[35] (application for an injunction under the Wireless Telegraphy Act 1949 – allegation of a criminal offence under the same Act). In *Halford v Brookes*,[36] by contrast, a different approach was taken. The plaintiff brought a tort action for damages in respect of the murder of her daughter, whom she alleged had been murdered by the defendants. It was held that the allegation of murder had to be proved beyond reasonable doubt: the court considered that nobody, whether in a civil or criminal court, should be declared guilty of murder unless the tribunal was sure that there was no other sensible conclusion. Do you favour this approach? Is it not justifiable for such serious allegations as murder to have to be proved beyond reasonable doubt, even if they are made in civil proceedings? If so, then how 'serious' do you consider the allegation needs to be before proof beyond reasonable doubt is required?

(iv) Quasi-criminal proceedings

The issue of the standard to which the executive had to prove that an individual had obtained leave to enter the United Kingdom by deception was considered by the House of Lords in the following case.

Extract 2.2.9

R v Home Secretary, ex p Khawaja [1984] AC 74, 112–14 (HL)

The applicant was detained as an illegal entrant. He applied for judicial review of the order detaining him.

---

[33] [1970] Ch 128, 137. See also the recent decision of the High Court of Australia in *Witham v Holloway* (1995) 69 ALJR 847 and C J Miller, 'Proof of Civil Contempt' (1996) 112 *Law Quarterly Review* 539.
[34] [1964] 1 WLR 451.
[35] [1967] 1 WLR 1396.
[36] (1991) *The Times*, 3 October.

63

LORD SCARMAN: The law is less certain as to the standard of proof. The choice is commonly thought to be between proof beyond reasonable doubt, as in criminal cases, and the civil standard of the balance of probabilities . . .
. . .

My Lords, I would adopt as appropriate to cases of restraint put by the executive upon the liberty of the individual the civil standard flexibly applied in the way set forth in the cases . . . It is not necessary to import into the civil proceedings of judicial review the formula devised by judges for the guidance of juries in criminal cases. Liberty is at stake: that is . . . a grave matter. The reviewing court will therefore require to be satisfied that the facts which are required for the justification of the restraint put upon liberty do exist. The flexibility of the civil standard of proof suffices to ensure that the court will require the high degree of probability which is appropriate to what is at stake. '. . . the nature and gravity of an issue necessarily determines the manner of attaining reasonable satisfaction of the truth of the issue': Dixon J in *Wright v Wright* (1948) 77 CLR 191, 210. I would, therefore, adopt the civil standard flexibly applied in the way described in the case law . . . And I completely agree with the observation made by my noble and learned friend, Lord Bridge of Harwich, that the difficulties of proof in many immigration cases afford no valid ground for lowering the standard of proof required.

Accordingly, it is enough to say that, where the burden lies on the executive to justify the exercise of a power of detention, the facts relied on as justification must be proved to the satisfaction of the court. A preponderance of probability suffices: but the degree of probability must be such that the court is satisfied. The strictness of the criminal formula is unnecessary to enable justice to be done: and its lack of flexibility in a jurisdiction where the technicalities of the law of evidence must not be allowed to become the master of the court could be a positive disadvantage inhibiting the efficacy of the developing safeguard of judicial review in the field of public law.

For these reasons I conclude that in these two appeals, once the applicant had shown, as each did, that he had entered the United Kingdom with the leave of the immigration officer, the burden of proving that he had obtained leave by deception was upon the executive and the standard of proof was the balance of probabilities.

To what standard do disciplinary offences need to be proved in disciplinary proceedings?

Extract 2.2.10

R v Hants CC, ex p Ellerton [1985] 1 WLR 749, 753–4 (CA)

O'CONNOR LJ: I have no doubt that proceedings under the provisions of the Fire Services (Discipline) Regulations 1948 are not criminal proceedings. The disciplinary tribunal and the fire authority are domestic tribunals, and in the absence of any express provision in the Act or Regulations prima facie the civil standard of proof is appropriate. Mr Scrivener recognised this, but advanced two reasons for saying that we should declare that offences under these Regulations must be proved beyond reasonable doubt.

First, he submitted that this statutory code is couched in the language of the criminal law for the Regulations talk about 'offences,' 'the accused,' 'charges,' 'punishments,' and that this language used in relation to a disciplined force is enough to take proof of 'offences' out of the civil standard into the criminal. I cannot accept this submission. It is only necessary to look at the Schedule to the Regulations which sets out the 'Code of offences against discipline.' As the offences may lead to dismissal, reduction in rank, stoppage of pay, reprimand or caution, one would expect them to be of varying degrees of seriousness. There is a long list of offences, none of which are necessarily criminal, save perhaps wilful damage to clothing. Some crimes might also involve breaches of the code, for example a fireman who stole property while fighting a fire would offend against paragraphs (7)(a) 'improperly [using] his position as a member of the fire brigade for his private advantage,' and probably (11)(c) as well (acting 'in a manner likely to bring discredit on the reputation of the fire brigade'). The fact that the language of the criminal law is used to lay down the procedure for adjudicating upon a whole series of activities which form no part of the criminal law, but do form part of the relationship between master and servant, does not persuade me that we should depart from the prima facie rule.

Secondly, Mr Scrivener submitted that it was recognised that the criminal standard was used in disciplinary proceedings under the Police (Discipline) Regulations 1977 and that by analogy the same standard should be used for firemen. Broadly speaking, the code of offences found in Schedule 2 to those Regulations are not all that different to the fire services regulations, but I do not wish to say more on the topic of the police regulations, since we have not heard argument from the Police Federation, beyond saying that I doubt that the proposition asserted by McNeill J in *Reg v Police Complaints Board, Ex parte Madden* [1983] 1 WLR 447 is correct. . . .

. . .

Lastly, Mr Scrivener submitted that even if the civil standard of proof is the appropriate standard there was no evidence that the tribunal appreciated that the standard is flexible. Like the judge I see no reason to think that the members of the tribunal would not have realised that the more serious the alleged offence against discipline so the greater the degree of probability required to tip the balance.

In *R v Milk Marketing Board, ex p Austin*,[37] however, it was held that when a person's livelihood was at stake the standard of proof should be no lower than that applicable in criminal proceedings. A similar approach was taken in *Re a Solicitor*,[38] where the issue was the standard of proof which had to be applied by a disciplinary tribunal in determining an allegation of misconduct. The Divisional Court stated: 'It seems to us, if we may respectfully say so, that it is not altogether helpful if the burden of proof is left somewhere undefined between the criminal and the civil standards. We conclude that at

[37] (1983) *The Times*, 21 March.
[38] [1993] QB 69.

least in cases such as the present, where what is alleged is tantamount to a criminal offence, the tribunal should apply the criminal standard of proof, that is to say proof to the point where they feel sure that the charges are proved or, put in another way, proof beyond reasonable doubt.'[39] Like *Halford v Brookes*, therefore, *Austin* and *Re a Solicitor* seem to be out of step with the general approach of speaking in terms of a 'flexible' balance-of-probabilities standard of proof in civil proceedings. It may be argued that, where the livelihood or liberty of a person is at stake, proof beyond reasonable doubt should be required. After all, as has been seen above, the justification for the adoption of the criminal standard in proceedings for contempt of court is that such proceedings are 'of a criminal character'. Should not the same reasoning apply in the case of other quasi-criminal proceedings?

See generally A A S Zuckerman, 'Evidence' [1985] *All ER Review* 155, 156–7.

(v) Allegations of sexual abuse in care proceedings

Until recently, there was considerable uncertainty about the relevant standard of proof where allegations of sexual abuse were made in care proceedings, with suggestions made in some cases that such allegations had to be proved to a standard higher than proof on a balance of probabilities. This issue is addressed in the following extract from the speech of Lord Nicholls of Birkenhead in *Re H (Minors)*.[40] In this extract, Lord Nicholls also makes some general observations about the standard of proof required in non-criminal proceedings. Do you consider that his observations constitute a good clarification and rationalisation of this area of the law?

Extract 2.2.11

Re H (Minors) [1996] 2 WLR 8, 23–5 (HL)

LORD NICHOLLS OF BIRKENHEAD: Where the matters in issue are facts the standard of proof required in non-criminal proceedings is the preponderance of probability, usually referred to as the balance of probability. This is the established general principle. There are exceptions such as contempt of court applications, but I can see no reason for thinking that family proceedings are, or should be, an exception. . . . Despite their special features, family proceedings remain essentially a form of civil proceedings. Family proceedings often raise very serious issues, but so do other forms of civil proceedings.

The balance of probability standard means that a court is satisfied an event occurred if the court considers that, on the evidence, the occurrence of the event was more likely than not. When assessing the probabilities the court will

[39] At 81.
[40] [1996] 2 WLR 8.

have in mind as a factor, to whatever extent is appropriate in the particular case, that the more serious the allegation the less likely it is that the event occurred and, hence, the stronger should be the evidence before the court concludes that the allegation is established on the balance of probability. Fraud is usually less likely than negligence. Deliberate physical injury is usually less likely than accidental physical injury. A stepfather is usually less likely to have repeatedly raped and had non-consensual oral sex with his under age stepdaughter than on some occasion to have lost his temper and slapped her. Built into the preponderance of probability standard is a generous degree of flexibility in respect of the seriousness of the allegation.

Although the result is much the same, this does not mean that where a serious allegation is in issue the standard of proof required is higher. It means only that the inherent probability or improbability of an event is itself a matter to be taken into account when weighing the probabilities and deciding whether, on balance, the event occurred. The more improbable the event, the stronger must be the evidence that it did occur before, on the balance of probability, its occurrence will be established. . . .

. . . This approach also provides a means by which the balance of probability standard can accommodate one's instinctive feeling that even in civil proceedings a court should be more sure before finding serious allegations proved than when deciding less serious or trivial matters.

. . . The law looks for probability, not certainty. Certainty is seldom attainable. But probability is an unsatisfactorily vague criterion because there are degrees of probability. In establishing principles regarding the standard of proof, therefore, the law seeks to define the degree of probability appropriate for different types of proceedings. Proof beyond reasonable doubt, in whatever form of words expressed, is one standard. Proof on a preponderance of probability is another, a lower standard having the in-built flexibility already mentioned. If the balance of probability standard were departed from, and a third standard were substituted in some civil cases, it would be necessary to identify what the standard is and when it would apply. Herein lies a difficulty. If the standard were to be higher than the balance of probability but lower than the criminal standard of proof beyond reasonable doubt, what would it be? The only alternative which suggests itself is that the standard should be commensurate with the gravity of the allegation and the seriousness of the consequences. A formula to this effect has its attraction. But I doubt whether in practice it would add much to the present test in civil cases, and it would risk causing confusion and uncertainty. As at present advised I think it is better to stick to the existing, established law on this subject. I can see no compelling need for a change.

I therefore agree with the recent decisions of the Court of Appeal in several cases involving the care of children, to the effect that the standard of proof is the ordinary civil standard of balance of probability: see *H v H (Minors) (Child Abuse: Evidence)* [1990] Fam 86, 94, 100, *In re M (A Minor) (Appeal) (No 2)* [1994] 1 FLR 59, 67 and *In re W (Minors) (Sexual Abuse: Standard of Proof)* [1994] 1 FLR 419, 424, *per* Balcombe LJ. The Court of Appeal were of the same view in the present case. It follows that the contrary observations . . . in *In re G (A Minor) (Child Abuse: Standard of Proof)* [1987] 1 WLR 1461, 1466 and *In re W (Minors) (Sexual Abuse: Standard of Proof)* [1994] 1 FLR 419, 429, are not an accurate statement of the law.

See also *Re M and R (Minors)*.[41]

It is notable that, in spite of his acknowledgement that this might effectively be the result of his holding, Lord Nicholls was unprepared to state directly that the more serious the allegation, the higher the standard of proof required. Rather, it is the inherent probability or improbability of the event that is the crucial consideration: the more serious the allegation the less likely that the event occurred and, consequently, the stronger the evidence required for the balance of probabilities standard to be satisfied.

See generally A Bainham, 'Sexual Abuse in the Lords' [1996] *Cambridge Law Journal* 209; D Burrows, 'Care Proceedings after *Re H*' (1996) 140 *Solicitors Journal* 94; R Stevens, 'Getting over the Threshold – An Exegesis of Section 31(2) of the Children Act 1989' (1996) 160 *Justice of the Peace* 111.

(c) The United States: A third standard

In the United States, a third standard of proof – that requiring 'clear and convincing evidence' – is recognised. This lies in between the 'proof on the balance of probabilities' and 'proof beyond reasonable doubt' standards. In the following case, this intermediate standard was discussed by the US Supreme Court:

Extract 2.2.12

***Addington v Texas* 441 US 418, 419, 423–33 (1979)**
(US Supreme Court)

BURGER CJ: The question in this case is what standard of proof is required by the Fourteenth Amendment to the Constitution in a civil proceeding brought under state law to commit an individual involuntarily for an indefinite period to a state mental hospital.

. . .

The function of a standard of proof, as that concept is embodied in the Due Process Clause and in the realm of factfinding, is to 'instruct the factfinder concerning the degree of confidence our society thinks he should have in the correctness of factual conclusions for a particular type of adjudication.' In re Winship, 397 US 358, 370, 25 L Ed 2d 368, 90 S Ct 1068, 51 Ohio Ops 2d 323 (1970) (Harlan, J, concurring). The standard serves to allocate the risk of error between the litigants and to indicate the relative importance attached to the ultimate decision.

Generally speaking, the evolution of this area of the law has produced across a continuum three standards or levels of proof for different types of cases. At one end of the spectrum is the typical civil case involving a monetary dispute between private parties. Since society has a minimal concern

---

[41] [1996] 4 All ER 239.

with the outcome of such private suits, plaintiff's burden of proof is a mere preponderance of the evidence. The litigants thus share the risk of error in roughly equal fashion.

In a criminal case, on the other hand, the interests of the defendant are of such magnitude that historically and without any explicit constitutional requirement they have been protected by standards of proof designed to exclude as nearly as possible the likelihood of an erroneous judgment. In the administration of criminal justice, our society imposes almost the entire risk of error upon itself. This is accomplished by requiring under the Due Process Clause that the state prove the guilt of an accused beyond a reasonable doubt. . . .

The intermediate standard, which usually employs some combination of the words 'clear,' 'cogent,' 'unequivocal,' and 'convincing,' is less commonly used, but nonetheless 'is no stranger to the civil law.' Woodby v INS, 385 US 276, 285, 17 L Ed 2d 362, 87 S Ct 483 (1966). . . . One typical use of the standard is in civil cases involving allegations of fraud or some other quasi-criminal wrongdoing by the defendant. The interests at stake in those cases are deemed to be more substantial than mere loss of money and some jurisdictions accordingly reduce the risk to the defendant of having his reputation tarnished erroneously by increasing the plaintiff's burden of proof. Similarly, this Court has used the 'clear, unequivocal and convincing' standard of proof to protect particularly important individual interests in various civil cases. See, eg, Woodby v INS, supra, at 285, 17 L Ed 2d 362, 87 S Ct 483 (deportation); Chaunt v United States, 364 US 350, 353, 5 L Ed 2d 120, 81 S Ct 147 (1960) (denaturalization); Schneiderman v United States, 320 US 118, 125, 159, 87 L Ed 1796, 63 S Ct 1333 (1943) (denaturalization).

Candor suggests that, to a degree, efforts to analyze what lay jurors understand concerning the differences among these three tests or the nuances of a judge's instructions on the law may well be largely an academic exercise; there are no directly relevant empirical studies. Indeed, the ultimate truth as to how the standards of proof affect decisionmaking may well be unknowable, given that factfinding is a process shared by countless thousands of individuals throughout the country. We probably can assume no more than that the difference between a preponderance of the evidence and proof beyond a reasonable doubt probably is better understood than either of them in relation to the intermediate standard of clear and convincing evidence. Nonetheless, even if the particular standard-of-proof catch words do not always make a great difference in a particular case, adopting a 'standard of proof is more than an empty semantic exercise.' Tippett v Maryland, 436 F 2d 1153, 1166 (CA4 1971) (Sobeloff, J, concurring in part and dissenting in part), cert dismissed sub nom Murel v Baltimore City Criminal Court, 407 US 355, 32 L Ed 2d 791, 92 S Ct 2091 (1972). In cases involving individual rights, whether criminal or civil, '[t]he standard of proof [at a minimum] reflects the value society places on individual liberty.' 436 F 2d, at 1166.

In considering what standard should govern in a civil commitment proceeding, we must assess both the extent of the individual's interest in not being involuntarily confined indefinitely and the state's interest in committing the emotionally disturbed under a particular standard of proof. Moreover, we must be mindful that the function of legal process is to minimize the risk of erroneous decisions. . . .

This Court repeatedly has recognized that civil commitment for any purpose constitutes a significant deprivation of liberty that requires due process protection.... Moreover, it is indisputable that involuntary confinement to a mental hospital after a finding of probable dangerousness to self or others can engender adverse social consequences to the individual. Whether we label this phenomena 'stigma' or choose to call it something else is less important than that we recognize that it can occur and that it can have a very significant impact on the individual.

. . .

At one time or another every person exhibits some abnormal behavior which might be perceived by some as symptomatic of a mental or emotional disorder, but which is in fact within a range of conduct that is generally acceptable. Obviously, such behavior is no basis for compelled treatment and surely none for confinement. However, there is the possible risk that a factfinder might decide to commit an individual based solely on a few isolated instances of unusual conduct. Loss of liberty calls for a showing that the individual suffers from something more serious than is demonstrated by idiosyncratic behavior. Increasing the burden of proof is one way to impress the factfinder with the importance of the decision and thereby perhaps to reduce the chances that inappropriate commitments will be ordered.

The individual should not be asked to share equally with society the risk of error when the possible injury to the individual is significantly greater than any possible harm to the state. We conclude that the individual's interest in the outcome of a civil commitment proceeding is of such weight and gravity that due process requires the state to justify confinement by proof more substantial than a mere preponderance of the evidence.

. . .

There are significant reasons why different standards of proof are called for in civil commitment proceedings as opposed to criminal prosecutions. In a civil commitment state power is not exercised in a punitive sense. Unlike the delinquency proceeding in Winship, a civil commitment proceeding can in no sense be equated to a criminal prosecution....

In addition, the 'beyond a reasonable doubt' standard historically has been reserved for criminal cases. This unique standard of proof, not prescribed or defined in the Constitution, is regarded as a critical part of the 'moral force of the criminal law,' In re Winship, 397 US, at 364, 25 L Ed 2d 368, 90 S Ct 1068, 51 Ohio Ops 2d 323, and we should hesitate to apply it too broadly or casually in noncriminal cases....

The heavy standard applied in criminal cases manifests our concern that the risk of error to the individual must be minimized even at the risk that some who are guilty might go free.... The full force of that idea does not apply to a civil commitment. It may be true that an erroneous commitment is sometimes as undesirable as an erroneous conviction ... However, even though an erroneous confinement should be avoided in the first instance, the layers of professional review and observation of the patient's condition, and the concern of family and friends generally will provide continuous opportunities for an erroneous commitment to be corrected. Moreover, it is not true that the release of a genuinely mentally ill person is no worse for the individual than the failure to convict the guilty. One who is suffering from a debilitating mental illness and in need of treatment is neither wholly at liberty nor free of stigma. . . . It cannot be said, therefore, that it is much better for a mentally ill person to 'go free' than for a mentally normal person to be committed. Finally, the initial inquiry in a civil commitment proceeding is very different from the central issue in either a delinquency proceeding or a criminal prosecution. In the latter cases the basic issue is a straightforward factual question – did the accused commit the act alleged? There may be factual issues to resolve in a commitment proceeding, but the factual aspects represent only the beginning of the inquiry. Whether the individual is mentally ill and dangerous to either himself or others and is in need of confined therapy turns on the meaning of the facts which must be interpreted by expert psychiatrists and psychologists. Given the lack of certainty and the fallibility of psychiatric diagnosis, there is a serious question as to whether a state could ever prove beyond a reasonable doubt that an individual is both mentally ill and likely to be dangerous. . . .

The subtleties and nuances of psychiatric diagnosis render certainties virtually beyond reach in most situations. The reasonable-doubt standard of criminal law functions in its realm because there the standard is addressed to specific, knowable facts. Psychiatric diagnosis, in contrast, is to a large extent based on medical 'impressions' drawn from subjective analysis and filtered through the experience of the diagnostician. This process often makes it very difficult for the expert physician to offer definite conclusions about any particular patient. Within the medical discipline, the traditional standard for 'factfinding' is a 'reasonable medical certainty.' If a trained psychiatrist has difficulty with the categorical 'beyond a reasonable doubt' standard, the untrained lay juror – or indeed even a trained judge – who is required to rely upon expert opinion could be forced by the criminal law standard of proof to reject commitment for many patients desperately in need of institutionalized psychiatric care. . . . Such 'freedom' for a mentally ill person would be purchased at a high price.

That practical considerations may limit a constitutionally based burden of proof is demonstrated by the reasonable doubt standard, which is a compromise between what is possible to prove and what protects the rights of the individual. If the state was required to guarantee error-free convictions, it would be required to prove guilt beyond all doubt. . . .

. . .

Having concluded that the preponderance standard falls short of meeting the demands of due process and that the reasonable doubt standard is not required, we turn to a middle level of burden of proof that strikes a fair balance between the rights of the individual and the legitimate concerns of the state. We note that 20 states, most by statute, employ the standard of 'clear and convincing' evidence; three states use 'clear, cogent, and convincing' evidence; and two states require 'clear, unequivocal and convincing' evidence.

. . .

We have concluded that the reasonable doubt standard is inappropriate in civil commitment proceedings because, given the uncertainties of psychiatric diagnosis, it may impose a burden the state cannot meet and thereby erect an unreasonable barrier to needed medical treatment. Similarly, we conclude that use of the term 'unequivocal' is not constitutionally required, although the states are free to use that standard. To meet due process demands, the standard has to inform the factfinder that the proof must be greater than the preponderance of the evidence standard applicable to other categories of civil cases.

Is there anything to be said for the formal adoption of such an intermediate standard of proof in England? After all, as we have seen, it has been effectively (even if not directly) acknowledged in English law that certain matters in civil cases may need to be proved beyond a 'mere' balance of probabilities, although not beyond reasonable doubt. That being so, it is certainly arguable that greater certainty and fairness would result from the express application of an intermediate standard in appropriate situations.

3

WITNESSES

In this chapter three broad issues pertaining to witnesses will be examined. First, we shall consider whether certain categories of people may be incompetent to testify, or, even if competent to testify, may not be compellable to do so. Secondly, we shall consider whether the law requires certain categories of evidence to be supported by other evidence in order to be admissible, or, at least, whether there is a requirement that juries be warned about convicting on the basis of certain categories of evidence if unsupported by other evidence. Thirdly, some issues pertaining to two categories of witnesses who may be regarded as particularly unfairly treated in the trial process – complainants in sexual cases and child witnesses – will be examined.

1. COMPETENCE AND COMPELLABILITY

There is a general rule in modern law that any person is competent to testify (that is, is permitted to testify if he or she wishes to do so). A further general rule states that all competent witnesses are compellable to testify. A compellable witness's refusal to testify may constitute contempt of court. The concern of this section is to identify the main qualifications and exceptions to the two general rules.

Generally, a witness who testifies must give sworn evidence. There is an exception to this in the case of children, as will be discussed below. Sworn evidence is given by a witness who has either taken an oath or made a solemn affirmation.

Extract 3.1.1

Oaths Act 1978, ss 1, 4, 5

1. Manner of administration of oaths

(1) Any oath may be administered and taken in England, Wales or Northern Ireland in the following form and manner: –

The person taking the oath shall hold the New Testament, or, in the case of a Jew, the Old Testament, in his uplifted hand, and shall say or repeat after the officer administering the oath the words 'I swear by Almighty God that . . .', followed by the words of the oath prescribed by law.

(2) The officer shall (unless the person about to take the oath voluntarily objects thereto, or is physically incapable of so taking the oath) administer the oath in the form and manner aforesaid without question.

(3) In the case of a person who is neither a Christian nor a Jew, the oath shall be administered in any lawful manner.

(4) . . .

4. Validity of oaths

(1) . . .

(2) Where an oath has been duly administered and taken, the fact that the person to whom it was administered had, at the time of taking it, no religious belief, shall not for any purpose affect the validity of the oath.

5. Making of solemn affirmations

(1) Any person who objects to being sworn shall be permitted to make his solemn affirmation instead of taking an oath.

(2) Subsection (1) above shall apply in relation to a person to whom it is not reasonably practicable without inconvenience or delay to administer an oath in the manner appropriate to his religious belief as it applies in relation to a person objecting to be sworn.

(3) A person who may be permitted under subsection (2) above to make his solemn affirmation may also be required to do so.

(4) A solemn affirmation shall be of the same force and effect as an oath.

An oath is not invalid simply because, for example, it was taken by a Muslim on the New Testament. As the Court of Appeal stated in *R v Kemble*:

> We take the view that the question of whether the administration of an oath is lawful does not depend upon what may be the considerable intricacies of the particular religion which is adhered to by the witness. It concerns two matters and two matters only in our judgment. First of all, is the oath an oath which appears to the court to be binding on the conscience of the witness? And, if so, secondly, and most importantly, is it an oath which the witness himself considers to be binding upon his conscience?[1]

The offence of perjury is committed where a witness who has taken an oath or made a solemn affirmation wilfully makes a statement which he or she knows to be false or does not believe to be true: Perjury Act 1911, s 1.

The Court of Appeal has made it clear that any expert evidence on the issue of a witness's competence should be heard in the jury's absence: 'The jury would not be assisted in deciding the issue before them by hearing the expert evidence, which was concerned with the capacity of the complainant to tell the truth. As Mr Barnes put it in argument, "What good would it do?"'[2]

[1] [1990] 1 WLR 1111, 1114.
[2] *R v Deakin* [1994] 4 All ER 769, 775.

(a) The accused

It is a well-established principle in English law that accused persons are not competent (and therefore not compellable) witnesses for the *prosecution*.[3] Thus, where two or more people are charged in the same indictment, the prosecution may call one of them to testify against the other(s) only if the person being called ceases to be an accused in the same trial. This may happen in one of four ways: (1) he or she may plead guilty;[4] (2) he or she may be acquitted as a result of a successful submission of no case to answer, or a decision by the prosecution not to offer any evidence; (3) the indictment may be severed and separate trials ordered; (4) the Attorney-General may enter a nolle prosequi. Whether an accomplice against whom proceedings are pending should be called as a prosecution witness only if the prosecution has undertaken to discontinue proceedings against him or her would appear to be a matter within the court's discretion.[5]

For the *defence*, accused persons are competent, but not compellable, witnesses.

Extract 3.1.2

Criminal Evidence Act 1898, s 1

1. Competency of witnesses in criminal cases
Every person charged with an offence shall be a competent witness for the defence at every stage of the proceedings, whether the person so charged is charged solely or jointly with any other person. Provided as follows:

(a) A person so charged shall not be called as a witness in pursuance of this Act except upon his own application;

. . .

(g) Every person called as a witness in pursuance of this Act shall, unless otherwise ordered by the court, give his evidence from the witness box or other place from which the other witnesses give their evidence.

Extract 3.1.3

Criminal Justice and Public Order Act 1994, s 35

35. Effect of accused's silence at trial
(1) At the trial of any person who has attained the age of fourteen years for an offence, subsections (2) and (3) below apply unless −

---

[3] *R v Grant* [1944] 2 All ER 311; *R v Sharrock* [1948] 1 All ER 145.
[4] There does not appear to be a strict rule as to whether the person pleading guilty should be sentenced before testifying; the matter is probably best regarded as being within the court's discretion: *R v Palmer* (1993) 99 Cr App R 83.
[5] *R v Turner* (1975) 61 Cr App R 67.

(a) the accused's guilt is not in issue; or
(b) it appears to the court that the physical or mental condition of the accused makes it undesirable for him to give evidence;

but subsection (2) below does not apply if, at the conclusion of the evidence for the prosecution, his legal representative informs the court that the accused will give evidence or, where he is unrepresented, the court ascertains from him that he will give evidence.

(2) Where this subsection applies, the court shall, at the conclusion of the evidence for the prosecution, satisfy itself (in the case of proceedings on indictment, in the presence of the jury) that the accused is aware that the stage has been reached at which evidence can be given for the defence and that he can, if he wishes, give evidence and that, if he chooses not to give evidence, or having been sworn, without good cause refuses to answer any question, it will be permissible for the court or jury to draw such inferences as appear proper from his failure to give evidence or his refusal, without good cause, to answer any question.

(3) Where this subsection applies, the court or jury, in determining whether the accused is guilty of the offence charged, may draw such inferences as appear proper from the failure of the accused to give evidence or his refusal, without good cause, to answer any question.

(4) This section does not render the accused compellable to give evidence on his own behalf, and he shall accordingly not be guilty of contempt of court by reason of a failure to do so.

(5) For the purposes of this section a person who, having been sworn, refuses to answer any question shall be taken to do so without good cause unless –
(a) he is entitled to refuse to answer the question by virtue of any enactment, whenever passed or made, or on the ground of privilege; or
(b) the court in the exercise of its general discretion excuses him from answering it.

(6) Where the age of any person is material for the purposes of subsection (1) above, his age shall for those purposes be taken to be that which appears to the court to be his age.

(7) This section applies –
(a) in relation to proceedings on indictment for an offence, only if the person charged with the offence is arraigned on or after the commencement of this section;
(b) in relation to proceedings in a magistrates' court, only if the time when the court begins to receive evidence in the proceedings falls after the commencement of this section.

Extract 3.1.4

Criminal Justice and Public Order Act 1994, s 38(3)

38. Interpretation and savings for sections 34, 35, 36 and 37
(3) A person shall not have the proceedings against him transferred to the Crown Court for trial, have a case to answer or be convicted of an offence solely on an inference drawn from such a failure or refusal as is mentioned in section 34(2), 35(3), 36(2) or 37(2).

An accused who does testify renders himself liable to cross-examination by the prosecution as well as by any co-accused, even if he has not actually given evidence against that co-accused.[6] Further, where an accused does testify, the prosecution may use evidence elicited from him (both in evidence-in-chief[7] and in cross-examination[8]) against any co-accused.

It is clear that the same principles apply to testifying on behalf of a co-accused as apply to testifying on one's own behalf. That is, an accused is competent, but not compellable, to testify on behalf of a co-accused. To be compellable, he must have ceased to be an accused in the same trial. He may, for example, have pleaded guilty,[9] been acquitted as a result of a direction to acquit by the trial judge,[10] or become liable to be tried separately as a result of the indictment being severed.[11]

Section 1(g) of the 1898 Act was considered in the following case:

Extract 3.1.5

R v Symonds (1924) 18 Cr App R 100, 101 (CCA)

SWIFT J: The obvious intention of the Criminal Evidence Act, 1898, is that an accused person shall have an opportunity of giving evidence on his own behalf in the same way and from the same place as the witnesses for the prosecution. It is not right to deprive him of the benefit of the statute. There may be cases in which a prisoner is so infirm that he cannot walk from the dock to the witness box without inconvenience or pain. There may be cases where the prisoner exhibits violence which may be more easily quelled in the dock than in the witness box. But apart from cases of such a nature the right of the prisoner to give his evidence from the witness box should not be interfered with . . .

See also *R v Farnham JJ, ex p Gibson*.[12]

As an accused person is not compellable to testify in his own defence, he may be regarded as enjoying the 'right to silence' at his trial. Section 35 of the Criminal Justice and Public Order Act 1994, however, permits adverse inferences to be drawn from such silence in certain circumstances. This represents one of the more controversial areas of the English law of criminal evidence today. That s 35 would inevitably place pressure on defendants to testify is undeniable. The fact that adverse inferences may be drawn in certain circumstances leads, in turn, to the question of the extent to which prosecution counsel,[13] counsel for a co-accused and the trial judge may

---

[6] *R v Hilton* [1972] 1 QB 421.
[7] *R v Rudd* (1948) 32 Cr App R 138.
[8] *R v Paul* [1920] 2 KB 183.
[9] *R v Boal* [1965] 1 QB 402.
[10] *R v Conti* (1973) 58 Cr App R 387.
[11] *R v Richardson* (1967) 51 Cr App R 381.
[12] (1991) 155 JPR 792.
[13] Such comment was forbidden prior to the Criminal Justice and Public Order Act 1994.

comment adversely to the jury on the accused's exercise of the right to silence at trial. The decision of the Court of Appeal in *R v Cowan* provides some guidance on this issue.

Extract 3.1.6

R v Cowan [1995] 3 WLR 818, 823–6 (CA)

LORD TAYLOR OF GOSFORTH CJ: We accept that apart from the mandatory exceptions in section 35(1), it will be open to a court to decline to draw an adverse inference from silence at trial and for a judge to direct or advise a jury against drawing such inference if the circumstances of the case justify such a course. But in our view there would need either to be some evidential basis for doing so or some exceptional factors in the case making that a fair course to take. It must be stressed that the inferences permitted by the section are only such 'as appear proper.' The use of that phrase was no doubt intended to leave a broad discretion to a trial judge to decide in all the circumstances whether any proper inference is capable of being drawn by the jury. If not he should tell them so; otherwise it is for the jury to decide whether in fact an inference should properly be drawn.

By way of guidance, a specimen direction has been suggested by the Judicial Studies Board in the following terms:

'The defendant has not given evidence. That is his right. But, as he has been told, the law is that you may draw such inferences as appear proper from his failure to do so. Failure to give evidence on its own cannot prove guilt but depending on the circumstances, you may hold his failure against him when deciding whether he is guilty. [There is evidence before you on the basis of which the defendant's advocate invites you not to hold it against the defendant that he has not given evidence before you namely . . . If you think that because of this evidence you should not hold it against the defendant that he has not given evidence, do not do so.] But if the evidence he relies on presents no adequate explanation for his absence from the witness box then you may hold his failure to give evidence against him. You do not have to do so. What proper inferences can you draw from the defendant's decision not to give evidence before you? If you conclude that there is a case for him to answer, you may think that the defendant would have gone into the witness box to give you an explanation for or an answer to the case against him. If the only sensible explanation for his decision not to give evidence is that he has no answer to the case against him, or none that could have stood up to cross-examination, then it would be open to you to hold against him his failure to give evidence. It is for you to decide whether it is fair to do so.' (The words in square brackets are to be used only where there is *evidence*.)

We consider that the specimen direction is in general terms a sound guide. It may be necessary to adapt or add to it in the particular circumstances of an individual case. But there are certain essentials which we would highlight.

(1) The judge will have told the jury that the burden of proof remains upon the prosecution throughout and what the required standard is. (2) It is necessary for the judge to make clear to the jury that the defendant is entitled to remain silent. That is his right and his choice. The right of silence remains. (3) An inference from failure to give evidence cannot on its own prove guilt. That is expressly stated in section 38(3) of the Act. (4) Therefore, the jury must be satisfied that the prosecution have established a case to answer before drawing any inferences from silence. Of course, the judge must have thought so or the question whether the defendant was to give evidence would not have arisen. But the jury may not believe the witnesses whose evidence the judge considered sufficient to raise a prima facie case. It must therefore be made clear to them that they must find there to be a case to answer on the prosecution evidence before drawing an adverse inference from the defendant's silence. (5) If, despite any evidence relied upon to explain his silence or in the absence of any such evidence, the jury conclude the silence can only sensibly be attributed to the defendant's having no answer or none that would stand up to cross-examination, they may draw an adverse inference.

It is not possible to anticipate all the circumstances in which a judge might think it right to direct or advise a jury against drawing an adverse inference. Nor would it be wise even to give examples as each case must turn on its own facts. . . .

. . .

We wish to stress, moreover, that this court will not lightly interfere with a judge's exercise of discretion to direct or advise the jury as to the drawing of inferences from silence and as to the nature, extent and degree of such inferences. He is in the best position to have the feel of the case and so long as he gives the jury adequate directions of law as indicated above and leaves the decision to them, this court will be slow to substitute its view for his.

. . .

Finally, we wish to make it clear that the rule against advocates giving evidence dressed up as a submission applies in this context. It cannot be proper for a defence advocate to give to the jury reasons for his client's silence at trial in the absence of evidence to support such reasons.

See generally K Browne, 'An Inference of Guilt?' (1997) 141 *Solicitors Journal* 202; R Munday, '*Cum Tacent Clamant*: Drawing Proper Inferences from a Defendant's Failure to Testify' [1996] *Cambridge Law Journal* 32.

It is arguable that *Cowan* invests too much discretion in trial judges, and that more detailed guidelines should have been provided by the Court of Appeal on the issue of when it would be appropriate for a jury to be advised against drawing adverse inferences. Further, a direction to the jury that 'they must find there to be a case to answer on the prosecution evidence before drawing an adverse inference from the defendant's silence' is likely to prove confusing. Finally, it seems unfair to impose a requirement that evidence be adduced to support any reasons given to the jury for the defendant's silence. The reasons why defendants may choose not to testify are many and varied, and it is often possible merely to speculate as to what these reasons might be in a particular case.

See also *R v Napper*;[14] *R v Price*;[15] *R v Ackinclose*;[16] *R v Friend*.[17]
The following *Practice Direction* has been issued:

Extract 3.1.7

Practice Direction: Crown Court (Defendant's Evidence)
[1995] 2 Cr App R 192, 192–3 (CC)

LORD TAYLOR OF GOSFORTH CJ:

If the accused is legally represented
2. Section 35(1) provides that section 35(2) does *not* apply if at the conclusion of the evidence for the prosecution the accused's legal representative informs the court that the accused will give evidence. This should be done in the presence of the jury. If the representative indicates that the accused will give evidence, the case should proceed in the usual way.
3. If the court is not so informed, or if the court is informed that the accused does *not* intend to give evidence, the judge should in the presence of the jury enquire of the representative in these terms:

> 'Have you advised your client that the stage has now been reached at which he may give evidence and, if he chooses not to do so or, having been sworn, without good cause refuses to answer any question, the jury may draw such inferences as appear proper from his failure to do so?'

4. If the representative replies to the judge that the accused has been so advised, then the case shall proceed. If counsel replies that the accused has not been so advised then the judge shall direct the representative to advise his client of the consequences set out in para 3 hereof and should adjourn briefly for this purpose before proceeding further.

If the accused is not legally represented
5. If the accused is not represented the judge shall at the conclusion of the evidence for the prosecution and in the presence of the jury say to the accused:

> 'You have heard the evidence against you. Now is the time for you to make your defence. You may give evidence on oath, and be cross-examined like any other witness. If you do not give evidence or, having been sworn, without good cause refuse to answer any question the jury may draw such inferences as appear proper. That means they may hold it against you.
>
> You may also call any witness or witnesses whom you have arranged to attend court.
>
> Afterwards you may also, if you wish, address the jury by arguing your case from the dock. But you cannot at that stage give evidence.
>
> Do you now intend to give evidence?'

[14] (1995) 161 JPR 16.
[15] [1996] Crim LR 738.
[16] [1996] Crim LR 747.
[17] [1997] 2 All ER 1011.

In *Murray v UK*[18] (extracted in Chapter 8), the European Court of Human Rights held that the drawing of adverse inferences under the Northern Ireland equivalent of s 35 did not infringe the right to a fair trial guaranteed by art 6(1) of the European Convention on Human Rights, or the principle of the presumption of innocence enshrined in art 6(2) of that Convention.

Further reading

G J Durston, 'A Brief Recap on the Implications of the Abolition of the Right to Silence in the Criminal Justice and Public Order Act 1994' (1996) 160 *Justice of the Peace* 62

J D Jackson, 'Interpreting the Silence Provisions: The Northern Ireland Cases' [1995] *Criminal Law Review* 587

A F Jennings, 'Resounding Silence' (1996) 146 *New Law Journal* 725

— 'Resounding Silence – 2' (1996) 146 *New Law Journal* 764

— 'Resounding Silence – 3' (1996) 146 *New Law Journal* 821

J Michael and B Emmerson, 'Current Topic: The Right to Silence' [1995] *European Human Rights Law Review* 4

P Mirfield, 'Two Side-Effects of Sections 34 to 37 of the Criminal Justice and Public Order Act 1994' [1995] *Criminal Law Review* 612

S Nash, 'Silence as Evidence: Inquisitorial Developments in England and Wales' [1996] *Scots Law Times* 69

R Pattenden, 'Inferences from Silence' [1995] *Criminal Law Review* 602

(b) The accused's spouse

Extract 3.1.8

Police and Criminal Evidence Act 1984, s 80(1)–(8)

80. Competence and compellability of accused's spouse

(1) In any proceedings the wife or husband of the accused shall be competent to give evidence –

    (a) subject to subsection (4) below, for the prosecution; and

    (b) on behalf of the accused or any person jointly charged with the accused.

(2) In any proceedings the wife or husband of the accused shall, subject to subsection (4) below, be compellable to give evidence on behalf of the accused.

(3) In any proceedings the wife or husband of the accused shall, subject to subsection (4) below, be compellable to give evidence for the prosecution or on behalf of any person jointly charged with the accused if and only if –

---

[18] (1996) 22 EHRR 29.

(a) the offence charged involves an assault on, or injury or a threat of injury to, the wife or husband of the accused or a person who was at the material time under the age of sixteen; or

(b) the offence charged is a sexual offence alleged to have been committed in respect of a person who was at the material time under that age; or

(c) the offence charged consists of attempting or conspiring to commit, or of aiding, abetting, counselling, procuring or inciting the commission of, an offence falling within paragraph (a) or (b) above.

(4) Where a husband and wife are jointly charged with an offence neither spouse shall at the trial be competent or compellable by virtue of subsection (1)(a), (2) or (3) above to give evidence in respect of that offence unless that spouse is not, or is no longer, liable to be convicted of that offence at the trial as a result of pleading guilty or for any other reason.

(5) In any proceedings a person who has been but is no longer married to the accused shall be competent and compellable to give evidence as if that person and the accused had never been married.

(6) Where in any proceedings the age of any person at any time is material for the purposes of subsection (3) above, his age at the material time shall for the purposes of that provision be deemed to be or to have been that which appears to the court to be or to have been his age at that time.

(7) In subsection (3)(b) above 'sexual offence' means an offence under the Sexual Offences Act 1956, the Indecency with Children Act 1960, the Sexual Offences Act 1967, section 54 of the Criminal Law Act 1977 or the Protection of Children Act 1978.

(8) The failure of the wife or husband of the accused to give evidence shall not be made the subject of any comment by the prosecution.

What is the rationale underlying the strategy in s 80 of exempting an accused's spouse from the obligation of testifying either for the prosecution or for a co-accused, except in specific circumstances? Do you agree with this rationale? Note the cogent arguments advanced in the following extract:

Extract 3.1.9

A A S Zuckerman, *The Principles of Criminal Evidence* (1989) 290–2

The rationale underlying the spouse's privilege in section 80 ... is ... that compulsion to testify might lead to marital discord. . . . The idea is that if relations between the spouses are poor, a spouse will not be deterred from testifying against the accused but, where harmony subsists, a spouse will decline to do so and thereby preserve the matrimonial accord. . . .

Marital harmony is doubtless very important but in view of contemporary public attitudes the force of this consideration is somewhat limited. When marriage was indissoluble, the souring of relations between the spouses would have condemned them to living together in enmity for the rest of their lives or, alternatively, to separation without the prospect of establishing another family.

However, matrimonial morality and matrimonial policy have undergone radical transformation. If marital relations have deteriorated, the marriage can be brought to an end. Indeed, a very considerable proportion of marriages do in fact end in divorce. It is difficult to imagine that granting spouses immunity from having to testify against each other in criminal proceedings makes an appreciable contribution to the general stability of marriage in our community.

There are further considerations that weaken the justification based on matrimonial harmony. If the wife is accorded a freedom to choose whether or not to testify, her accused husband will in many cases bring pressure to bear on her to refuse to testify when invited to do so by the prosecution. Those who regard it as repugnant to call a wife to testify against her husband (or a husband against his wife) should reflect that the present law holds out a temptation to the accused to exercise unedifying pressure on his or her spouse to refrain from testifying. If the wife succumbs to pressure from her accused husband and declines to impart incriminating information, she is in effect made an unwilling accomplice after the event in that she is helping her husband to escape punishment. A spouse who becomes an instrument in the accused's attempt to avoid conviction suffers moral degradation which is likely to undermine the couple's harmony.

. . .

. . . even if the privilege protects the marital harmony of accused persons, it is doubtful whether this end provides sufficient justification for foregoing evidence of crime and, to that extent, reducing the protection of the community from crime.

The approach of the Australian Evidence Act 1995 may have more to commend it. The Act provides that an accused's spouse, de facto spouse, parent or child is compellable for the prosecution in the case of particular offences against children, and domestic violence offences.[19] In the case of all *other* offences, s 18 provides for a discretionary approach to determining whether an accused's spouse, de facto spouse, parent or child is compellable for the prosecution:

Extract 3.1.10

Evidence Act 1995 (Australia), s 18(2), (6), (7)

18. Compellability of spouses and others in criminal proceedings generally

(2) A person who, when required to give evidence, is the spouse, de facto spouse, parent or child of a defendant may object to being required:
   (a) to give evidence; or
   (b) to give evidence of a communication between the person and the defendant;
as a witness for the prosecution.

---

[19] Section 19.

(6) A person who makes an objection under this section to giving evidence or giving evidence of a communication must not be required to give the evidence if the court finds that:

(a) there is a likelihood that harm would or might be caused (whether directly or indirectly) to the person, or to the relationship between the person and the defendant, if the person gives the evidence; and

(b) the nature and extent of that harm outweighs the desirability of having the evidence given.

(7) Without limiting the matters that may be taken into account by the court for the purposes of subsection (6), it must take into account the following:

(a) the nature and gravity of the offence for which the defendant is being prosecuted;

(b) the substance and importance of any evidence that the person might give and the weight that is likely to be attached to it;

(c) whether any other evidence concerning the matters to which the evidence of the person would relate is reasonably available to the prosecutor;

(d) the nature of the relationship between the defendant and the person;

(e) whether, in giving the evidence, the person would have to disclose matter that was received by the person in confidence from the defendant.

Further reading

P Creighton, 'Spouse Competence and Compellability' [1990] *Criminal Law Review* 34

S Edwards, 'Compelling a Reluctant Spouse' (1989) 139 *New Law Journal* 691

(c) Mental disability

Extract 3.1.11

R v Bellamy (1985) 82 Cr App R 222, 225–6 (CA)

The court was faced with the issue of a mentally handicapped rape complainant.

SIMON BROWN J: As it seems to this Court, the learned judge, although clearly right to investigate whether or not the complainant was a competent witness in so far as having a sufficient understanding of the nature of the proceedings was concerned, ought not to have embarked upon a detailed examination of her theological appreciation.

Applying section 5 of the Oaths Act 1978, given that the judge concluded as he did that the complainant was a competent witness and given that she did not object to being sworn, it is our opinion that he should simply have allowed her to be sworn. Even however, if one took a different view as to that and concluded that the learned judge was entitled also to examine the complainant upon the extent of her belief in God, recent authorities regarding the proper application of section 38(1) of the Children and Young Persons Act 1933 [now repealed] indicate clearly that it is no longer necessary that a witness should have awareness of the divine sanction of the oath in order that that witness may properly be sworn.

This is made abundantly clear by consideration of two decisions of this Court: *Hayes* (1976) 64 Cr App R 194; [1977] 2 All ER 288 and *Campbell* [1983] Crim LR 174. I cite just a short paragraph from each case.

The position in *Hayes* was that two children, respectively aged 12 and 11, had been sworn in a case of gross indecency. They had been examined and had in fact denied having heard of God. The judgment of the Court was given by Bridge LJ (as he then was) in these terms at p 196 and p 290 of the respective reports. 'If the series of questions and answers started with the question "Do you think there is a God?" and the answer "Yes" there would really be no substance in Mr Charlesworth's complaints, but the fact that the earlier questions and answers, on their face, reveal the boy declaring that he is wholly ignorant of the existence of God does lend some force to the submission that if the essence of the sanction of the oath is a divine sanction, and if it is an awareness of that divine sanction which the Court is looking for in a child of tender years, then here was a case where, on the face of it, that awareness was absent. The Court is not convinced that that is really the essence of the Court's duty in the difficult situation where the Court has to determine whether a young person can or cannot properly be permitted to take an oath before giving evidence. It is unrealistic not to recognise that, in the present state of society, amongst the adult population the divine sanction of an oath is probably not generally recognised. The important consideration, we think, when a judge has to decide whether a child should properly be sworn, is whether the child has a sufficient appreciation of the solemnity of the occasion, and the added responsibility to tell the truth, which is involved in taking an oath, over and above the duty to tell the truth which is an ordinary duty of normal social conduct.'

Applying that passage in *Campbell*, May LJ, giving the judgment of the Court, said this: 'The two principles to be followed when considering whether a child should properly be sworn set out in *Hayes* (*supra*) were: that the child had a sufficient appreciation of the seriousness of the occasion and a realisation that taking the oath involved something more than the duty to tell the truth in ordinary day to day life.'

That this complainant had such a realisation is evident and was clearly found by the learned judge, he having noted her evidence that she realised that if she told a lie in the particular circumstances in which she was to give her evidence, then she could 'be put away'.

Those cases of course were concerned with the statute governing the position of children of tender years. A fortiori they would apply where, in regard to adult persons such as this complainant, there is no ruling statutory provision.

The test for determining whether a person is competent to testify notwithstanding mental disability would appear, therefore, to be the same as that which was previously applied to determine the competence of children to give sworn evidence in criminal cases. Does the person in question have a sufficient appreciation of the seriousness of the occasion and a realisation that giving sworn evidence involves something more than the duty to tell the truth in ordinary everyday life?

(d) Children

(i) Civil trials

Extract 3.1.12

Children Act 1989, s 96

96. Evidence given by, or with respect to, children

(1) Subsection (2) applies where a child who is called as a witness in any civil proceedings does not, in the opinion of the court, understand the nature of an oath.

(2) The child's evidence may be heard by the court if, in its opinion –

    (a) he understands that it is his duty to speak the truth; and

    (b) he has sufficient understanding to justify his evidence being heard.

A 'child' is someone under 18: s 105(1). The effect of s 96, therefore, is that a child who understands the nature of an oath should give sworn evidence, while one who does not may give unsworn evidence if the two conditions specified in subs (2) are satisfied.

(ii) Criminal trials

Section 38(1) of the Children and Young Persons Act 1933, mentioned in *Bellamy*, was repealed by s 52 of the Criminal Justice Act 1991, which also inserted ss 33A(1), 33A(2) and 33A(3) into the Criminal Justice Act 1988. Section 33A(2A) was added by the Criminal Justice and Public Order Act 1994.

Extract 3.1.13

Criminal Justice Act 1988, s 33A

33A. Evidence given by children

(1) A child's evidence in criminal proceedings shall be given unsworn.

(2) A deposition of a child's unsworn evidence may be taken for the purposes of criminal proceedings as if that evidence had been given on oath.

(2A) A child's evidence shall be received unless it appears to the court that the child is incapable of giving intelligible testimony.

(3) In this section 'child' means a person under fourteen years of age.

Extract 3.1.14

R v D (1995) *The Times*, 15 November; LEXIS transcript (CA)

SWINTON THOMAS LJ: In our judgment, the test of the competence of a child witness . . . is whether the child is able to understand the questions put to him or her, to communicate, and to give a coherent and comprehensible account of the matters in relation to which he or she is giving evidence. Built into that concept must be an ability to distinguish between truth and fiction or between fact and fantasy. If a child, by reason of extreme youth or for any other reason, is unable to distinguish between truth and fiction or between fact and fantasy, then that child would be unable to give a coherent and comprehensible account of the matters in issue. In our view, the phraseology which we have adopted is more apt to a child witness under the legislation than an ability to distinguish between truth and lies, because (a) the abolition of the requirement of the child to take the oath and (b), perhaps, more importantly, lies by definition are an intentional or deliberate falsehood connoting an ability to tell the difference between lies and the truth. Once a child can give a comprehensible account and distinguish between fact and fiction, whether the child is telling the truth or not is a matter for the jury.

Save, in the case of exceedingly young children, the competence of children to give evidence is likely to arise very rarely and in exceptional circumstances only.

Extract 3.1.15

R v Hampshire [1995] 3 WLR 260, 269 (CA)

AULD J: . . . a judge who considers it necessary to investigate a child's competence to give evidence in addition to or without the benefit of an earlier view of a videotaped interview under section 32A of the Act of 1988 should do so in open court in the presence of the defendant because it is part of the trial, but need not do so in the presence of the jury. The jury's function is to assess the child's evidence, including its weight, from the evidence he or she gives on the facts of the case after the child has been found competent to give it. The exercise of determining competence is not a necessary aid to that function. . . . However, even though a judge is no longer bound to investigate a child's competence to give evidence (unless he has reason to doubt it), he may find it appropriate to remind the child, in the presence of the defendant and the jury, of the importance of telling the truth.

It has been held that 'a child will be capable of giving intelligible testimony if he or she is able to understand questions and to answer them in a manner which is coherent and comprehensible'.[20] Further, 'the test of whether a child is capable of giving intelligible evidence does not require any input from an expert. It is a simple test well within the capacity of a judge or magistrate.'[21]

See also *R v Simmonds*.[22]

(e) Bankers

Extract 3.1.16

Bankers' Books Evidence Act 1879, s 6

6. Case in which banker, etc, not compellable to produce book, etc
A banker or officer of a bank shall not, in any legal proceeding to which the bank is not a party, be compellable to produce any banker's book the contents of which can be proved under this Act, or to appear as a witness to prove the matters, transactions, and accounts therein recorded, unless by order of a judge made for special cause.

(f) Judges

Extract 3.1.17

Warren v Warren [1996] 4 All ER 664, 671 (CA)

LORD WOOLF MR: [A judge is not compellable] to give evidence of those matters of which he became aware relating to and as a result of his perform-ance of his judicial functions. If therefore . . . a murder is committed in the face of the court the judge could be compelled to give evidence as to the murder, since although he would have observed the murder when acting as a judge, the murder did not relate to his functions as a judge. The position is no different from that which would apply if the murder had taken place in the presence of the judge outside the court. It would be a collateral incident (see *Duke of Buccleuch v Metropolitan Board of Works* (1872) LR 5 HL 418 at 433, [1861–73] All ER Rep 654 at 657 and *Phipson* para 19–12).

It is also important to remember that the judge will remain competent to give evidence, and if a situation arises where his evidence is vital, the judge should be able to be relied on not to allow the fact that he cannot be compelled to give evidence to stand in the way of his doing so.

---

[20] *DPP v M* [1997] 2 All ER 749, 753.
[21] *G v DPP* [1997] 2 All ER 755, 759.
[22] [1996] Crim LR 816.

2. CORROBORATION AND SUPPORTING EVIDENCE

The general preference in modern English law for 'qualitative' rather than 'quantitative' controls on evidence may be sharply contrasted with the elaborate system of 'full proofs' and 'fractional proofs' which prevailed on the Continent prior to the end of the 19th century:

> The basic rules might be simplified as follows:
> (a) Full proof always requires judgment.
> (b) Less than full proof never admits judgment.
> (c) The best full proof was two credible witnesses. The concurrence of their testimony was conclusive for guilt or innocence.
> (d) One witness, however credible, constituted only a half-proof and could never of itself suffice for judgment.
> (e) Such half-proof might, however, be sufficient if another half-proof could be supplied. The following counted as a half-proof each:
>   (i) confessions extracted by torture – hence the rule that torture could be applied if there was a half-proof;
>   (ii) entries by tradesmen in their books;
>   (iii) an oath of sincerity and truth specially administered to the party;
>   (iv) rumour or reputation confirmatory of the half-proof.
> (f) Any two half-proofs make a full proof.
> (g) Other factors might be invested with the value of a quarter proof, or an eight[h] proof, two and four of which respectively were equivalent to a half-proof.[23]

Nevertheless, there remain examples in English law of offences of which a person cannot be convicted on the evidence of one witness alone. Treason is an example.[24] Two further examples may be provided by speeding offences and the offence of perjury.

Speeding offences

Extract 3.2.1

Road Traffic Regulation Act 1984, s 89

89. Speeding offences generally

(1) A person who drives a motor vehicle on a road at a speed exceeding a limit imposed by or under any enactment to which this section applies shall be guilty of an offence.

(2) A person prosecuted for such an offence shall not be liable to be convicted solely on the evidence of one witness to the effect that, in the opinion of the witness, the person prosecuted was driving the vehicle at a speed exceeding a specified limit.

---

[23] J Stone (rev W A N Wells), *Evidence: Its History and Policies* (1991) 13–14.
[24] Treason Act 1795, s 1.

Extract 3.2.2

Crossland v DPP [1988] 3 All ER 712, 713, 714–5 (DC)

BINGHAM LJ: The question raised is whether on the true construction of s 89(2) of the Road Traffic Regulation Act 1984, the acting stipendiary magistrate was right in law to find that there was a case to answer when the sole prosecution evidence on the question of speed was that given by a single expert in post-accident reconstruction.

. . .

The question which falls for consideration is the following: is a person prosecuted for an offence of speeding under s 89(1) of the Road Traffic Regulation Act 1984 liable to be convicted on the evidence of one witness to the effect that, having inspected damage to the vehicle driven by the person prosecuted following a collision and having inspected and measured marks on the road at the place of collision and inspected marks on such vehicle, and having carried out certain tests, and having made calculations based on the physical signs observed and the tests carried out (such damage, marks, tests and calculations being described in evidence), he was of opinion that the person prosecuted was driving the vehicle at a speed exceeding a specified limit before the collision?

. . .

. . . It is plain, and indeed common ground between the parties, that [s 89(2)] is intended to prevent the conviction of a defendant on evidence given by a single witness of his unsupported visual impression of a defendant's speed. That is so whether the witness is an untutored bystander or a police officer who may have considerable expertise in visually assessing the speed of moving vehicles. . . .

. . . There is, and can be, no doubt but that the evidence of two witnesses as to their unsupported visual impression of speed will, if the evidence is accepted, suffice to support a conviction. . . .

. . .

. . . did the evidence which he gave at the hearing amount *solely* to the evidence of one witness to the effect that in his opinion the appellant was driving at an excessive speed? In my view it did not because his evidence also described in some detail the objectively determined phenomena on which his expert opinion was based. Those objectively determined phenomena did not of themselves show that the vehicle was being driven at an excessive speed, although in an extreme case they might do so, but having been described in evidence they did, in my judgment, prevent the conviction resting, in the language of the [Motor Car Act 1903], 'merely on the opinion of one witness as to the rate of speed'. The phenomena were, at the time of collision, verifiable by the appellant. She, or her advisers, were in principle as well able as the prosecutor to draw relevant scientific inferences from them and to challenge the prosecutor's calculations. She was not in jeopardy on the strength only of the unsupported visual impression of a single witness and this is the risk against which the subsection is in my judgment intended to give protection.

I would accordingly give an affirmative answer to the question posed by the acting stipendiary magistrate and uphold the conviction.

Perjury

Extract 3.2.3

Perjury Act 1911, s 13

13. Corroboration

A person shall not be liable to be convicted of any offence against this Act, or of any offence declared by any other Act to be perjury or subornation of perjury, or to be punishable as perjury or subornation of perjury, solely upon the evidence of one witness as to the falsity of any statement alleged to be false.

Extract 3.2.4

R v Carroll (1993) 99 Cr App R 381, 384 (CA)

LORD TAYLOR CJ: Although the word 'corroboration' is not mentioned in that section, and although no mention is made in that section of any obligation upon a judge to give any particular direction to a jury, the effect of case law upon this section has been to require that judges should indicate to the jury the need for there to be evidence of more than one witness before a conviction of perjury can be recorded.

Mr Stelling has referred us to *Hamid and Hamid* (1979) 69 Cr App R 324. The judgment of this Court was given by Lawton LJ. . . .

At p 328 the learned Lord Justice said this, having given the history of the provisions in section 13:

'It seems to us therefore that in perjury cases nowadays the judge should approach the statutory requirement as one of corroboration, and that the ordinary practice rule about reminding juries of the need for corroboration should be followed. It is easy to see why this should be so. Occasionally in perjury cases those who prove the falsity of the material statement have no connection whatsoever with the defendant, but in many cases they have. The circumstances may be such that those who are relied upon by the Crown to prove the falsity may have motives of their own for making statements against the defendant which are not true.'

We have looked again at the terms of section 13. It is true that one could construe that section as requiring simply that there should be before the jury evidence of more than one witness as to the falsity of the statement said to have been made.

However, it is possible that, even if the judge looking at the material before the jury comes to his own conclusion that there is more than one witness, or that there is a combination of one witness and some other evidence such as a confession, nevertheless the jury may not accept such evidence.

Accordingly we accept as being correct the passage which we have cited from the judgment of Lawton LJ, and in our opinion it is not merely desirable but it clearly is a requisite to the summing up of the judge under the Perjury Act 1911 that there should be reference to section 13, and the need for the jury to have before it the evidence which they accept of more than one witness; that is to say, either of other witnesses or of one other witness, or at least of some other supporting evidence by way of confession or otherwise, which supplements that of a single witness.

Extract 3.2.5

R v Rider (1986) 83 Cr App R 207, 210 (CA)

MUSTILL LJ: We pause at this stage to notice a curiosity of the law of perjury. There is old authority for the view that falsity of the evidence is not an essential element in the offence of perjury; that a defendant who makes a statement which he believes to be false may properly be convicted even if the statement proves in the event to have been true: see Smith and Hogan, *Criminal Law*, 5th Edn (1983), p 695, and Law Commission Report No 96, para 2.54.

The wording of section 1(1), with its reference to a statement which the defendant 'does not believe to be true', appears to leave open the possibility that this is still the law. . . .

We find it unnecessary to express an opinion whether it is still the law that a true statement may found a conviction for perjury, especially as the question was not explored in argument. What does, however, appear to us is that there is no true inconsistency between section 1(1) and section 13. The latter simply requires more than one witness 'as to the falsity of any statement *alleged to be false.*' Thus in those very rare cases where the prosecution elects to proceed on the basis that the truth or falsehood of the statement forms no part of their case s 13 does not apply and there is no need for any direction on the point.

Attempts

By virtue of s 2(2)(g) of the Criminal Attempts Act 1981, all 'provisions whereby a person may not be convicted or committed for trial on the uncorroborated evidence of one witness (including any provision requiring the evidence of not less than two credible witnesses)' apply also to *attempts* to commit the offences in question.

Prior to the Criminal Justice and Public Order Act 1994, trial judges were obliged to issue a warning to the jury about convicting the accused on the uncorroborated evidence of (1) an alleged accomplice of the accused; or (2) a complainant in a sexual case.

Extract 3.2.6

Criminal Justice and Public Order Act 1994, s 32(1)

32. Abolition of corroboration rules

(1) Any requirement whereby at a trial on indictment it is obligatory for the court to give the jury a warning about convicting the accused on the uncorroborated evidence of a person merely because that person is –

(a) an alleged accomplice of the accused, or

(b) where the offence charged is a sexual offence, the person in respect of whom it is alleged to have been committed,

is hereby abrogated.

Analogous provision is made for summary trials in s 32(3).

The opportunity to consider s 32(1) was presented to the Court of Appeal in the following cases:

Extract 3.2.7

R v Makanjuola [1995] 1 WLR 1348, 1351–2 (CA)

LORD TAYLOR OF GOSFORTH CJ: . . . it is clear that to carry on giving 'discretionary' warnings generally and in the same terms as were previously obligatory would be contrary to the policy and purpose of the Act. Whether, as a matter of discretion, a judge should give any warning and if so its strength and terms must depend upon the content and manner of the witness's evidence, the circumstances of the case and the issues raised. The judge will often consider that no special warning is required at all. Where, however the witness has been shown to be unreliable, he or she may consider it necessary to urge caution. In a more extreme case, if the witness is shown to have lied, to have made previous false complaints, or to bear the defendant some grudge, a stronger warning may be thought appropriate and the judge may suggest it would be wise to look for some supporting material before acting on the impugned witness's evidence. We stress that these observations are merely illustrative of some, not all, of the factors which judges may take into account in measuring where a witness stands in the scale of reliability and what response they should make at that level in their directions to the jury. We also stress that judges are not required to conform to any formula and this court would be slow to interfere with the exercise of discretion by a trial judge who has the advantage of assessing the manner of a witness's evidence as well as its content.

To summarise. (1) Section 32(1) abrogated the requirement to give a corroboration direction in respect of an alleged accomplice or a complainant of a sexual offence, simply because a witness falls into one of those categories. (2) It is a matter for the judge's discretion what, if any warning, he considers appropriate in respect of such a witness as indeed in respect of any other witness in whatever type of case. Whether he chooses to give a warning and in what terms will depend on the circumstances of the case, the issues raised and the content and quality of the witness's evidence. (3) In some cases, it may be appropriate for the judge to warn the jury to exercise caution before acting upon the unsupported evidence of a witness. This will not be so simply because the witness is a complainant of a sexual offence nor will it necessarily be so because a witness is alleged to be an accomplice. There will need to be an evidential basis for suggesting that the evidence of the witness may be unreliable. An evidential basis does not include mere suggestion by cross-examining counsel. (4) If any question arises as to whether the judge should give a special warning in respect of a witness, it is desirable that the question be resolved by discussion with counsel in the absence of the jury before final speeches. (5) Where the judge does decide to give some warning in respect of a witness, it will be appropriate to do so as part of the judge's review of the evidence and his comments as to how the jury should evaluate it rather than as a set-piece legal direction. (6) Where some warning is required, it will be for the judge to decide the strength and terms of the warning. It does not have to be invested with the whole florid regime of the old corroboration rules. (7) ... Attempts to re-impose the straitjacket of the old corroboration rules are strongly to be deprecated. (8) Finally, this court will be disinclined to interfere with a trial judge's exercise of his discretion save in a case where that exercise is unreasonable in the *Wednesbury* sense: see *Associated Provincial Picture Houses Ltd v Wednesbury Corporation* [1948] 1 KB 223.

Extract 3.2.8

R v Walker [1996] Crim LR 742; LEXIS transcript (CA)

EBSWORTH J: This is an appeal by Haughton Alfonso Walker from a conviction at the Crown Court at Birmingham before the Recorder of Birmingham on 24 November 1995. On that day the appellant was convicted, on the unanimous verdict of a jury of rape on counts 1 and 2 of the indictment. He was acquitted on count 3, a further count of rape. . . .

The factual background to this matter may be briefly stated. The complainant was born on 17 February 1981. In 1983 the appellant moved in to live with the complainant's mother and they had lived in the same household since that time, so that the appellant was effectively, although not in law, her stepfather. There was a second child, J, who was born in 1985, being the child of the appellant and the complainant's mother. In 1986, we are told and for these purposes accept, that the child's true father, generally known as B, reappeared on the scene.

. . .

The complication that arose in this case occurred after the defendant had been arrested and after he had been bailed. It had been a condition of his bail that he should not reside with the complainant and her mother and, one assumes, that he would keep away from them. However, in March 1995 he returned to the home.

On a day in March (the specific date is not on the document) the girl wrote a letter to the police in the following terms:

'Dear Police,

I would like to drop the charges on H Walker. I said these things about H because he was too strict and he wouldn't let me play out with my friends. I did have a boyfriend and it wasn't Haughton who done those things to me and I hope that H can forgive me for telling lies. I miss H and I want to live like a normal family. Me and J want H to come back home and see us like he used to. I don't want to see H go to prison. I realise now how serious this is and I'm sorry for wasting your time.'

That letter, on its face, must have been written before the defendant returned to the matrimonial home other than on an occasional basis.

On 15 March the girl and her mother made statements to the police in terms consistent with that letter. The girl in her statement said that in the January, when she had been interviewed on the video, she had said that her mother's boyfriend had been having sex with her for two years. She went on:

'I want to say that I was lying. It wasn't Walker. I have had sex once in July last year with a boy called Peter, 14 or 15 years old.'

She then gave the address at which that boy used to live. She said:

'I knew him for a month. He's moved house now and I don't know where he lives now.'

We are told by Mr Maxwell, who appears for the appellant today, and we accept, that documents disclosed by the Crown to the defence showed that, in the course of the investigation of the retraction of the complaint, the girl M had given a very detailed description of the boy. She said that she had met him in the park; he was 14 or 15; he was a half-caste; he had short black hair, with shapes shaved into the back; he was of medium build; and 5'5" to 5'7".

She went on in her statement of 15 March to say that she had told her mother that she had lied and her mother, not unnaturally, had asked her about it and why she had not mentioned these matters earlier. She had told her mother that she had had sex with her boyfriend and she had given the mother details about these matters. Her mother had asked her if she wanted to drop the charges and she had told her mother that she did. Her mother had suggested that she write the letter to the police, which she did on her own, without any help from her mother, and her mother had not read the letter. She said that she had seen the appellant on two occasions, once before she wrote the letter. She had seen the appellant with her mother but had not talked to him. The second occasion, after she had given her mother the letter, there had been some conversation but not about the police investigation. She ended up by saying she did not want to go to court; 'everything had got very serious'. She said:

'I lied because I wanted my real dad to come back. I'm sorry for wasting the police's time. I want to drop the charges. It's my decision and nobody's told me to do it. I want Walker to come back and be with the family.'

Her mother, C, also made a statement to the police on that same day, 15 March. On that day she supported the girl's retraction and supported her assertion that she had not been put under any pressure to retract that statement. She said, in the course of that statement, that M had told her that the appellant had not touched her; that she had said that he had because she wanted to see her real father; and that she had 'always had a dream that me and her real father would get back together'.

On 20 March 1995 the girl M and her mother made another visit to the police station and on that occasion the girl retracted the statement of 15 March and the content of the earlier letter. She said:

> 'Everything I originally told the police when I was video interviewed was the truth about Walker having sex with me. I understood what would happen as a result of this and I was prepared to go to court over the matter.'

She then went on to say that since that time her mother had been in contact with the appellant. On one occasion he had come and stayed the night; she had hidden. She did not think it would happen again, but it had. This had upset her. She had heard her mother constantly saying that Walker was innocent but that her mother was not calling her a liar. She said that Walker then 'more or less moved back in with us'. There was not direct conversation between them about the court case but it was discussed in her presence and discussed in terms that led her to believe that he might die if he went into prison. Then she began to think, after initially thinking he deserved it, that if he did and if he died it would be all her fault. So she had talked about it again with her mother and decided to retract the charges. However, subsequently she said that she had changed her mind and that what she had originally said was true and that the references to the boy called Peter had all been invented and that she had never had sex with anyone else. Her mother again made a statement on 20 March which effectively supported that assertion.

The complaint made by Mr Maxwell on behalf of the appellant, in essence, is that nowhere in the summing-up does any reference appear to that letter of retraction, to the retraction statement of 20 March and indeed to the further contradictory statement of 20 March. He further complains, in detailed grounds of appeal, that there is no specific warning given to the jury about the potential dangers of Michelle as a witness, in circumstances where there is no evidence to support the complaints that she made. He makes further detailed criticisms about the manner in which the judge dealt with the boyfriend, the possible motive for lying in relation to the natural father, the manner in which, surprisingly in the light of the acquittal, the judge dealt with count 3 of the indictment. He also complains of the manner in which the judge dealt with the detailed descriptions of the incidents, the contradictions which appear between the detailed evidence given at the trial and the earlier versions given by Michelle and the intrinsic improbabilities of the stories.

The summing-up, it has to be said from the outset, does not contain a reference, either specific or by implication, to the fact that Michelle retracted her account and the manner in which the jury should deal with that situation. It also does not give any kind of direction or assistance to the jury as to how they should approach Michelle in circumstances where she had contradicted herself, she had retracted her statement and where the evidence was wholly unsupported.

The purpose of a summing-up is, of course, threefold: it is to direct the jury accurately as to the law, to give them guidance as to the application of that law to the facts of the particular case and to remind them fairly and even-handedly of the evidence. It is the usual practice, and a good one, to summarise the case presented by the Crown and the defence, but the judge cannot and must not be forced into a stereotypical summing-up. It is no part of the judge's role to make a speech for either side or to rehearse the whole of the evidence. Where there has been failure, however, to give a direction in law or a direction is incorrect, it is the duty of counsel to invite the judge's attention to that and to seek correction, and there are circumstances where, prior to the speeches of counsel and the summing-up, it is appropriate for the court and counsel to discuss the directions which are required.

In relation to a situation where, prior to the coming into force of s 32(1) of the Criminal Justice and Public Order Act 1994, a corroboration warning would have been required, this Court in the case of *Makanjuola* said that if the question arose whether a special warning should be given it was desirable that the question be resolved by discussion with counsel in the jury's absence before final speeches, but if such a warning was to be given it should be done as part of the judge's review of the evidence and his comments as to how the jury should evaluate it rather than as a set piece legal direction.

It is common ground that Judge Crawford was not asked before speeches and before summing up to consider whether or not this was a case where a special direction was called for. That we regard as unfortunate.

At the conclusion of the summing-up, when it must have been apparent to counsel that the judge had overlooked or excluded a relevant and significant factual matter and had therefore failed to assist the jury as to the possible evidential and legal significance of that matter, it would have been permissible, and indeed appropriate, for counsel to raise that matter with him. Here no attempt was made by counsel to raise any matter with the judge and we therefore have a situation in which it is necessary to consider the consequences for this conviction of that failure.

We have considered with detailed care the matters raised by Mr Maxwell by way of extensive criticism of the summing-up, but we have come to the conclusion that one, and only one, of those matters causes us concern, and that is the absence of reference to the letter of retraction, followed by the second statement of 20 March and the relevance of those matters to the need to warn the jury as to how they should approach the unsupported evidence of the complainant. The letter of retraction and the following statement admitted lying and gave motives for lying. In a case where the defence was a total denial that the events had occurred, that, in our judgment, was an obviously significant matter which required to be brought to the specific attention of the jury. The statement of 20 March reverting to the original allegation and claiming (we make no comment as to whether or not it was truth or otherwise) that pressure had been created by the defendant being back within the household was also relevant because it went, quite obviously, to the credibility of the witness. On each occasion the complainant's statement had been accompanied by a statement from her mother, who was also a witness who fell to be assessed by the jury. The mother was relevant to the issue of whether or not the girl at the relevant times had a boyfriend and whether that boyfriend could be responsible for her lack of virginity prior to the time she ultimately made a complaint.

The learned Recorder, at page 24 of his summing-up, dealt with the matter in a somewhat oblique way. Having reviewed the medical evidence he said at letter E:

'The doctor thinks that the girl probably had some sexual experience. Of course that raises a question, if you think that she did have some sexual experience, who with? It was suggested to her that she had a boyfriend. Of course one must acknowledge reality and know that girls of 14 do have sexual intercourse these days. Some girls of 14 do and the suggestion was aired that perhaps some boy was responsible for this.

I think all I need say about that is that Michelle denied that there was any boy involved and Mrs Johnson (the mother) said that it could not have happened because she kept this girl under very strict supervision and knew where she went. She rejected the suggestion that her daughter could have had a relationship with somebody else to account for her physical condition.'

That clearly was not an adequate way in which to deal with the retractions the girl had made and the specific reasons that she had given in that retraction for making what she was saying then was a false complaint. The learned Recorder had also dealt with the matter at an earlier stage, at page 9F, of the summing-up, in which he had said:

'You will ask yourself of course: was there any motive for her not to tell the truth? When you are considering whether somebody is telling the truth or lying, motive is something people look at. Is there some motive for lying? There was a suggestion of a motive raised in the course of the case, namely, that she might want to get back to her natural father and made up these stories so as to bring that about. The idea was floated, so I remind you of it for your consideration, but I must also remind you that the girl herself denied it and she said no, she was perfectly happy where she was with her mother and half-brother and, anyway, she said (and I am paraphrasing here) there was no prospect of her going to live with her father who was established with another family, another wife and other children, so it was not a practical possibility anyway. So the girl herself rejected that.

You would have to ask yourself whether there was any other reason why she should make up stories against this defendant. No others have been advanced.'

The summing-up, in that context, made no reference to the circumstances in which the girl herself had raised questions of a boyfriend and raised questions of a motive for lying.

In the course of the summing-up the Recorder had given the jury the standard direction at page 2F as to their right to determine the relevance of evidence whether he referred to it or not and the weight that was to be attached to it. He also, at page 7F, gave the jury a direction as to the importance of credibility in general terms. He said:

'You may think the real issue in this case is whether this happened or not, and if you get beyond the preliminary stages that is what you will have to think about. Did this defendant force sexual intercourse on that child on those three occasions? That will involve your giving very careful consideration to the evidence of all of the witnesses in this case, particularly of course the evidence of Michelle herself and the evidence of the defendant. Put as starkly as perhaps it has to be put: are you satisfied so that you are sure beyond reasonable doubt that the girl was telling the truth? That is the issue for you to decide. Was it true or not? Of course it is not quite the same as saying whether it is truth or lies because you will have to consider the possibility that the girl was fantasising.'

That is all that was said about the manner in which the jury should approach the girl and the considerations that they would need to have in mind in assessing her credibility as a witness.

Mr Cooke sought to say to us at one stage, as he did in his helpful skeleton argument, that all these matters, that is the relevance of the retraction statement to the girl's credibility and her previous inconsistent statements, had been canvassed extensively with the witnesses, both the girl and her mother, and by counsel in their final speeches, but he was forced to concede that that could not, in a case such as this, be sufficient. In our view the jury needed to be reminded by the judge of those matters and of the relevance of that retraction and of the previous inconsistency, and the bald fact is that they were not.

In a case where there was no support for the complaint, merely consistent medical evidence, and where the jury were unsure of her testimony on the third count, in the face of what was in effect an alibi, about which they were fully and fairly directed, we have come to the conclusion that the convictions are unsafe and in the event it is not necessary to consider in detail the other matters of complaint, save to say that we would have taken the view that none of those, individually or collectively, would have rendered the conviction unsafe had the matter of the retraction statement and the need to consider, and in our view give, a special warning in respect of the child Michelle been dealt with. The summing-up dealt quite fairly and in a sufficiently detailed way with the facts of the allegations and enabled the jury to assess the probability or improbability of the actual incidents. It dealt also with the discrepancies and the questions of motive for lying, although in our view not as fully as would have been appropriate, but it did fully draw the defendant's case to the attention of the jury. It is the failure to deal with the crucial matter, which was potentially central to the credibility of the girl, and to do so in specific terms, which leads us to conclude that the conviction cannot stand. This is not a case where it can be said the judge exercised a discretion not to give a direction.

We would wish to reiterate, as we did in the course of argument, that the passage in the case of *Makanjuola*, whereby the Court said that if any question arises as to whether the judge should give a special warning in respect of a witness, it is desirable that the question be resolved by discussion with counsel in the absence of the jury before final speeches, cried out for application in this case and it is a matter, we think, that should always be fully in the minds of counsel when confronted with a situation such as this.

In the circumstances, however, the appeal will be allowed.

See also *R v R*.[25]

The exhortation in *Makanjuola* that it is inappropriate 'to carry on giving "discretionary" warnings generally and in the same terms as were previously obligatory' is very much to be welcomed. Despite this, there is a danger that trial judges might continue to do so with impunity. After all, the prosecution has no right of appeal to the Court of Appeal.[26] Would it have been preferable for s 32 to have been couched in stronger terms, *prohibiting* warnings except in exceptional circumstances? Would such legislation, of itself, suffice? Consider the arguments in the following extract:

Extract 3.2.9

K Mack, 'Continuing Barriers to Women's Credibility: A Feminist Perspective on the Proof Process' (1993) 4 *Criminal Law Forum* 327, 350–2

Perhaps the most important reform will be to educate those in the legal system who believe the myths that belittle women and undermine their credibility. The mere abolition of past rules will not in itself reeducate. Nor will the passage of time necessarily bring changes. . . .

It is also clear that juries need information about the reality of rape and the effects of rape on victims, so that women's testimony can be put into the appropriate context. Expert witnesses can be called to dispel misconceptions the jury may have in evaluating complainants' testimony. It may even be necessary to admit statistical or expert evidence showing the falsity of rape myths once actively endorsed by the law and still accepted by many jurors.

Further and better legislation is essential as well. Experience in Australia has shown that mere abolition of the requirement to warn, which leaves discretion with judges, does not necessarily significantly reduce the frequency, or improve the tenor, of the comments judges make about credibility when women testify about sexual assaults. . . .

What would better legislation look like? . . . The Law Reform Commission of Victoria has recommended a [rule] to the effect that a court shall not give a warning suggesting that complainants in sex cases are an unreliable class of witnesses. A submission to the commission suggested an instruction that, due to the nature of sexual assault, corroborating evidence is often unavailable and no adverse inference should be drawn from that fact. Another possibility is the Canadian approach, which appears expressly and without exception to prohibit the judge from warning that it would be unsafe to convict without

[25] [1996] Crim LR 815.
[26] As K Mack, 'Continuing Barriers to Women's Credibility: A Feminist Perspective on the Proof Process' (1993) 4 *Criminal Law Forum* 327, 348 points out: 'A judge's decision to warn harshly is usually unchallengeable within the legal system. While there is no remedy for the witness whose credibility is impermissibly attacked by improper warnings or improper cross-examination, the defendant can complain after conviction of failure to give a corroboration warning.'

corroboration. To similar effect is a Colorado statute providing that the 'jury shall not be instructed to examine with caution the testimony of the victim solely because of the nature of the charge, nor shall the jury be instructed that such a charge [rape] is easy to make but difficult to defend against, nor shall any similar instruction be given.'

Yet another approach is to institute a form of guided discretion, where a model direction or legislation enumerates factors that judges must consider, and make express findings on, before giving any warning about treating with suspicion the testimony of a witness describing rape. Such a rule should also identify improper statements that are not to be used in jury instructions. This would provide for some flexibility, while still circumscribing the impact of prejudice and false beliefs about women.

See also D J Birch, 'Corroboration: Goodbye to all that?' [1995] *Criminal Law Review* 524; I Dennis, 'The Criminal Justice and Public Order Act 1994: The Evidence Provisions' [1995] *Criminal Law Review* 4; P Lewis, 'Corroboration Reborn' (1996–7) 7 *King's College Law Journal* 140; P Mirfield, ' "Corroboration" after the 1994 Act' [1995] *Criminal Law Review* 448.

Apart from the evidence of alleged accomplices and the evidence of complainants of sexual offences, examples of evidence which may be the subject of a warning by the trial judge to the jury in the exercise of discretion include evidence which may be tainted by an improper motive,[27] and, as the following case suggests, evidence of a witness who is 'suspect' by reason of mental condition or criminal connection.

Extract 3.2.10

R v Spencer [1987] AC 128, 135–6, 141–2, 135 (HL)

LORD ACKNER: My Lords, the appellants in these consolidated appeals were members of the nursing staff at Rampton Hospital, which is a secure hospital catering for patients suffering from mental disorders. The majority of such patients have been sent to Rampton as the result of court orders made under the Mental Health Act 1959 or the Mental Health Act 1983, by reason of their having been convicted of serious crimes. A television programme was shown in 1979 which made a substantial number of allegations of ill-treatment to patients by the nursing staff over a period of some years. This led to police inquiries and resulted in 14 separate trials at the Crown Court at Nottingham. In five of those trials, the defendants were convicted and your Lordships are concerned with two of such trials. . . .

In all the trials, the prosecution case against the nurses depended very largely upon the uncorroborated evidence of a single patient. I say, 'very largely', because there were apparently some alleged incidents of violence

---

[27] *R v Beck* [1982] 1 WLR 461.

which were witnessed by patients who were themselves complainants to other incidents. . . .

. . .

. . . It has been said both in the Court of Appeal and in your Lordships' House, that the obligation to warn a jury does not involve some legalistic ritual to be automatically recited by the judge, or that some particular form of words or incantation has to be used and, if not used, the summing up is faulty and the conviction must be quashed: see *Reg v Russell* (1968) 52 Cr App R 147, 150 *per* Diplock LJ. There is no magic formula which has to be used with regard to any warning which is given to juries: *Reg v Price (Herbert)* [1969] 1 QB 541, 546 *per* Sachs LJ. As this is no mere idle process it follows that there are no set words which must be adopted to express the warning. Rather must the good sense of the matter be expounded with clarity and in the setting of a particular case: *Reg v Hester* [1973] AC 296, 309 *per* Lord Morris of Borth-y-Gest. The summing up should be tailored to suit the circumstances of the particular case: *Reg v Kilbourne* [1973] AC 729, 741 *per* Lord Hailsham of St Marylebone LC.

To my mind the question raised by these appeals is both simple to define and simple to answer. Given that it is common ground that a warning was required as to the way in which the jury should treat the evidence of the complainants, the question is: was that warning sufficient? Did it in clear terms bring home to the jury the danger of basing a conviction on the unconfirmed evidence of the complainants?

. . .

In [some] cases the potential unreliability of the sole or principal witness for the prosecution is obvious for all to see. These were such cases. The complainants were men of bad character. They had been sent to Rampton rather than to an ordinary prison, because they were mentally unbalanced. That they were anti-authoritarian, prone to lie or exaggerate, and could well have old scores which they were seeking to pay off, was not disputed. Notwithstanding that the possibility of their evidence being unreliable was patent, that it was clearly dangerous to prefer their evidence to that of the defendants, all men of good character on whose behalf witnesses had spoken in glowing terms, the judge nevertheless told the jury in the clearest possible terms and repeated himself, that they must approach the evidence of the complainants with great caution. It is common ground that having given that warning, he then identified the very dangers which justified the exercise of great caution. He gave three reasons. First, they were all persons of bad character; secondly, they were all persons suffering from some form of mental disorder, and thirdly, they may have all conspired together to make false allegations. Thus the judge warned the jury of the dangers of relying on the complainants' testimony because, for the reasons which he gave, such testimony could well be unreliable. The judge, however, did not leave the matter there. . . . he pointed out, when dealing with each count, the details of the background of the complainant, his past criminal record, the nature of his mental disturbance and his history in the hospital, and perhaps most important of all, the hospital psychiatrist's view of the personality defects from which the patient suffered . . . he gave the emphatic warning which was required to meet the justice of the case. . . .

The certified point of law is in these terms:

'In a case where the evidence for the Crown is solely that of a witness who is not in one of the accepted categories of suspect witnesses,[28] but who, by reason of his particular mental condition and criminal connection, fulfilled the same criteria, must the judge warn the jury that it is dangerous to convict on his uncorroborated evidence.'

I would amend the question by substituting for the words 'the same criteria' 'analogous criteria.' I would then answer the question in the affirmative, adding, for the sake of clarity, that while it may often be convenient to use the words 'danger' or 'dangerous,' the use of such words is not essential to an adequate warning, so long as the jury are made fully aware of the dangers of convicting on such evidence. Again, for the sake of clarity I would further add that . . . in a case . . . where there exists potential corroborative material, the extent to which the trial judge should make reference to that material depends upon the facts of each case. The overriding rule is that he must put the defence fairly and adequately.

LORD HAILSHAM OF ST MARYLEBONE: . . . the modern cases, quite correctly in my view, are reluctant to insist on any magic formula or incantation, and stress instead the need that each summing up should be tailor-made to suit the requirements of the individual case: cf *Reg v Hester* [1973] AC 296, *per* Lord Morris of Borth-y-Gest at p 309, *per* Lord Pearson at p 321, and *per* Lord Diplock at pp 325, 328. In particular, when as here, it is agreed that no corroboration exists, a disquisition on what can or could amount to such if corroboration were needed is emphatically not required and greatly to be discouraged (*per* Lord Diplock, loc cit). . . . The less juries are confused by superfluous learning and the more their minds are directed to the particular issues relevant to the case before them, the more likely they are, in my view, to arrive at a just verdict.

Prosecution evidence of lies told by a defendant, either in or out of court, may also need to be the subject of a judicial direction in certain circumstances. Guidance as to the circumstances in which a judicial direction concerning a defendant's lies (or a *Lucas*[29] direction, as it is known) may be required is provided in the following case:

Extract 3.2.11

R v Burge [1996] 1 Cr App R 163, 173–4 (CA)

KENNEDY LJ: As there seems to be at the moment a tendency in one appeal after another to assert that there has been no direction, or an inadequate direction, as to lies, it may be helpful if we conclude by summarising the circumstances in which, in our judgment, a *Lucas* direction is usually required. There are four such circumstances but they may overlap:

[28] At the time, mandatory corroboration warnings had to be given in relation to witnesses who fell in these categories.
[29] *R v Lucas* [1981] QB 720.

1. Where the defence relies on an alibi.
2. Where the judge considers it desirable or necessary to suggest that the jury should look for support or corroboration of one piece of evidence from other evidence in the case, and amongst that other evidence draws attention to lies told, or allegedly told, by the defendant.
3. Where the prosecution seek to show that something said, either in or out of the court, in relation to a separate and distinct issue was a lie, and to rely on that lie as evidence of guilt in relation to the charge which is sought to be proved.
4. Where although the prosecution have not adopted the approach to which we have just referred, the judge reasonably envisages that there is a real danger that the jury may do so.

If a *Lucas* direction is given where there is no need for such a direction (as in the normal case where there is a straight conflict of evidence), it will add complexity and do more harm than good. Therefore, in our judgment, a judge would be wise always, before speeches and summing-up in circumstance number four, and perhaps also in other circumstances, to consider with counsel whether, in the instant case, such a direction is in fact required, and, if so, how it should be formulated. If the matter is dealt with in that way, this court will be very slow to interfere with the exercise of the judge's discretion. Further, the judge should, of course, be assisted by counsel in identifying cases where a direction is called for. In particular, this court is unlikely to be persuaded, in cases allegedly falling under number four above, that there was a real danger that the jury would treat a particular lie as evidence of guilt if defence counsel at the trial has not alerted the judge to that danger and asked him to consider whether a direction should be given to meet it. The direction should, if given, so far as possible, be tailored to the circumstances of the case, but it will normally be sufficient if it makes the two basic points:

1. that the lie must be admitted or proved beyond reasonable doubt, and;
2. that the mere fact that the defendant lied is not in itself evidence of guilt since defendants may lie for innocent reasons, so only if the jury is sure that the defendant did not lie for an innocent reason can a lie support the prosecution case.

See also *R v Hill*;[30] *R v Robinson*;[31] *R v Genus*;[32] *R v Harron*.[33]

Of considerable importance, too, is s 77 of the Police and Criminal Evidence Act 1984 (discussed in Chapter 8), which requires warnings about confession evidence in specific circumstances.

3. VULNERABLE WITNESSES

Has the law of criminal evidence struck an appropriate balance between protecting vulnerable witnesses and protecting the innocent from wrongful conviction?

[30] [1996] Crim LR 419.
[31] [1996] Crim LR 417.
[32] [1996] Crim LR 502.
[33] [1996] 2 Cr App R 457.

(a) Complainants in sexual cases

The long-overdue abolition of mandatory warnings to juries about convicting on the uncorroborated evidence of a complainant in a sexual case has been discussed above. Of continuing concern in the context of complainants in sexual cases is the issue of the admissibility of evidence of the complainant's sexual conduct on other occasions. The following extract from the judgment of L'Heureux-Dubé J in *R v Seaboyer*[34] (Supreme Court of Canada) provides a compelling analysis of considerations relevant to this issue, and, more generally, of the treatment by the criminal justice system of complainants in sexual cases. Although her comments are specifically directed at the position in Canada, similar considerations prevail in England.

Extract 3.3.1

R v Seaboyer (1991) 83 DLR (4th) 193, 213–17 (SCC)

L'HEUREUX-DUBÉ J: Rape myths still present formidable obstacles for complainants in their dealings with the very system charged with discovering the truth. Their experience in this regard is illustrated by the following remarks of surprisingly recent vintage:

> Women who say no do not always mean no. It is not just a question of saying no, it is a question of how she says it, how she shows and makes it clear. If she doesn't want it she has only to keep her legs shut and she would not get it without force and there would be marks of force being used.

(Judge David Wild, Cambridge Crown Court, 1982, quoted in Elizabeth Sheehy, 'Canadian Judges and the Law of Rape: Should the Charter Insulate Bias?' 21 Ottawa L Rev 741 (1989), at p 741.)

> Unless you have no worldly experience at all, you'll agree that women occasionally resist at first but later give in to either persuasion or their own instincts.

(Judge Frank Allen, Manitoba Provincial Court, 1984, quoted in Sheehy, 'Canadian Judges and the Law of Rape: Should the Charter Insulate Bias?' 21 Ottawa LR 741, at p 741.)

> . . . it is easy for a man intent upon his own desires to mistake the intentions of a woman or girl who may herself be in two minds about what to do. Even if he makes no mistake it is not unknown for a woman afterwards either to take fright or for some other reason to regret what has happened and seek to justify herself retrospectively by accusing the man of rape.

(Howard, *Criminal Law*, 3rd ed (1977), at p 149.)

> Modern psychiatrists have amply studied the behavior of errant young girls and women coming before the courts in all sorts of cases. Their psychic

---

[34] (1991) 83 DLR (4th) 193.

complexes are multifarious, distorted partly by inherent defects, partly by diseased derangements or abnormal instincts, partly by bad social environment, partly by temporary physiological or emotional conditions. One form taken by these complexes is that of contriving false charges of sexual offenses by men.

(Wigmore, *Evidence in Trials at Common Law*, vol 3A (1970), p 736.)

Regrettably, these remarks demonstrate that many in society hold inappropriate stereotypical beliefs and apply them when the opportunity presents itself.

Feild and Bienen, *ibid*, write at p 139 that, '[t]he results reported in this study confirmed what many writers and researchers studying rape have suggested: extra-evidential factors were found to influence the outcome of the rape trials'. When juries are provided with certain types of information about the complainant, such as evidence regarding past sexual conduct, the weight of the evidence is that they then utilize the myths and stereotypes discussed above and focus on them in 'resolving' the particular legal issues raised by the case. Though these researchers found that the effect of sexual history evidence was more complex than originally thought, they do note at pp 118–9 that:

> Along with race of the defendant, *sexual experience of the victim proved to have important effects on juror decision making as it was involved in four of the seven significant interactions. Support for the reformers' sentiments concerning the elimination of evidence regarding third-party sexual relations is indicated by the presence of these interactions.*
>
> * * *
>
> In the present research, the assailant in the nonprecipitory assault was given a more severe sentence than the offender in the precipitory case indicating that the jurors appeared to attribute blame to the victim when contributory behavior was implied. Several writers (Frederick and Luginbuhl 1976; Jones and Aronson 1973; Landy and Aronson 1969) have documented similar effects. Brooks, Doob, and Kirshenbaum (1975) found that *jurors were more likely to convict a defendant accused of raping a woman with a chaste reputation than an identical defendant charged with assaulting a prostitute. Information on the 'good' or 'bad' character of the victim appears to affect the decisions of the jurors, and the definitions of good or bad are likely to be broadly defined.*

(Emphasis added.)

Similarly, Borgida and White, 'Social Perception of Rape Victims: The Impact of Legal Reform', 2 Law and Hum Behav 339 (1978), report at p 349 that:

> ... when specific evidence of the victim's prior sexual history is admitted in a consent defense rape case ... jurors infer victim consent, carefully and unfavorably scrutinize the victim's credibility and moral character, and tend to attribute more responsibility to the victim ... *Although defendant credibility is a consideration, perceptions of the defendant's general moral character are much less of a consideration than the victim's general moral character.*
>
> * * *
>
> *Jurors are reluctant to convict the defendant when any testimony about prior sexual history is introduced in support of the consent defense.*
>
> * * *

The admission of this evidence seems to enhance the likelihood that jurors make person attributions and attribute more personal responsibility to the victim for the rape. Jurors also are more likely to infer victim consent from testimony about prior sexual history.

(Emphasis added.)

G La Free, who has done extensive research on this issue, suggests that the research is consistent with respect to the conclusion that when the victim allegedly engaged in 'misconduct', acquittals were more likely: 'Variables Affecting Guilty Pleas and Convictions in Rape Cases: Toward a Social Theory of Rape Processing', 58 Social Forces 833 (1980). In this particular study, La Free examined all of the forcible rape cases in an American midwestern city. He defined misconduct for the purpose of his study as either sexual, *ie*, the victim had illegitimate children or was sleeping with her boyfriend, or non-sexual, *ie*, the victim was a runaway or drug dealer. As La Free notes, when one realizes that sexual assault cases are extensively screened prior to trial according to their conformity with mythology, it is surprising that there is much of any 'deviant' behaviour left to trigger the application of stereotype and myth at trial.

In a later study conducted by La Free (G La Free, B Reskin and C A Visher, 'Jurors' Responses to Victims' Behavior and Legal Issues in Sexual Assault Trials', 32 Soc Prob 389 (1985)), post-trial interviews were conducted with jurors who had served in forcible sexual assault cases. At p 392 the authors state that, '[o]ur trial observations suggest that a major avenue for challenging the complainant's victimization in consent and no-sex cases is to encourage jurors to scrutinize her "character"'. They also suggest at p 400 that 'a victim's nontraditional behavior may act as a catalyst, causing jurors' attitudes about how women should behave to affect their judgments under certain conditions'. Also relevant for our purposes are their findings at p 397 that, where the issue at trial is whether the act occurred or whether there was consent:

> Of particular interest are the findings regarding evidence. *Although any evidence that a woman was forced to submit to a sexual act against her will (including use of a weapon or victim injury) might be expected to persuade jurors of the defendant's guilt, neither variable significantly affected jurors' judgments . . .*
>
> * * *
>
> *In contrast, jurors were influenced by a victim's 'character.' They were less likely to believe in a defendant's guilt when the victim had reportedly engaged in sex outside marriage, drank or used drugs, or had been acquainted with the defendant – however briefly – prior to the alleged assault.*

(Emphasis added.)

Although Canadian data are harder to come by, those studies that have been done support the American data. Indeed, it would be somewhat surprising to find that this was not the case. In one Canadian study (K Catton, 'Evidence Regarding the Prior Sexual History of an Alleged Rape Victim – Its Effect on the Perceived Guilt of the Accused', 33 U of T Fac L Rev 165 (1975)), subjects were asked to read a description of a hypothetical rape case. Varied among the descriptions were the nature of the controls placed upon evidence of the complainant's sexual history. At p 173 Catton discusses the results in this fashion:

> ... when jurors heard information regarding an alleged rape victim's prior sexual history with named persons, whether this information was confirmed or denied, this information decreased their perceived guilt of the accused in comparison with the situation where no information relating to the victim's supposed past sex life was heard. *This decrease in the perceived guilt of the accused varied directly with the 'amount' of negative information presented about the victim.*
>
> Although the 'No information' control condition was not as successful as planned ... still the accused was seen as most guilty in this condition where no information at all about the victim's prior sexual history was given. *Any information at all implying that the victim had a prior sex history had the effect of reducing the perceived guilt of the accused regardless of whether this information was verified.*

(Emphasis added.)

Importantly, she finds that even if the prior sexual history of the complainant is denied or fails to be confirmed, the perceived guilt of the accused decreases.

In England, a study of female rape complainants was undertaken recently by Victim Support, a national charity. As part of this study, questionnaires were distributed to Victim Support's Crown Court Witness Service, which offers information and support to witnesses and their families attending trials. The following analysis of responses provides an illuminating insight into the problems experienced in court by female complainants in rape cases:

Extract 3.3.2

Victim Support, *Women, Rape and the Criminal Justice System* (1996) 15–17

The Witness Services surveyed were involved in 590 rape cases in 1995.

COMMON PROBLEMS EXPERIENCED GIVING EVIDENCE AT COURT

Witness Services were asked to list particular problems they were aware of, which were experienced by victims of rape when giving evidence at court. The responses fell into three main areas of concern. These were: cross-examination; lack of protection; waiting times at court and changes to trial dates.

The percentages below refer to the Witness Service returns and not to individual cases.

Cross-examination

- 41% of Witness Services reported that women experienced problems with the nature of questioning during the cross-examination, including feeling it was a character assassination and feeling re-victimised by the defence barrister
- 12% of Witness Services reported that women experienced problems with their past sexual/medical history being brought up during the cross-examination
- 12% of Witness Services reported that women experienced the cross-examination as being made to relive the rape
- 12% of Witness Services reported that women felt sick/ill during the cross-examination
- 12% of Witness Services reported that women experienced problems having to give explicit details to a room full of strangers

Lack of protection

- 41% of Witness Services reported that women experienced problems with the layout of the court building, meeting defendant/supporters, with overcrowded or inadequate waiting areas and with the lack of secure entrances
- 30% of Witness Services reported that women experienced problems having to face defendant/supporters whilst giving evidence
- 30% of Witness Services reported that women experienced problems in not being allowed to give their evidence from behind a screen
- 18% of Witness Services reported that women found the press presence in court problematic
- 12% of Witness Services reported that women experienced problems in having their address read out in court

Waiting times at court and changes to trial dates

- 35% of Witness Services reported that women experienced problems with lengthy waiting periods and changes to trial dates

Witness Services also detailed the improvements they had negotiated to address these problems. These included: practical arrangements for witnesses to avoid contact with defendant/supporters prior to the case; negotiating the use of screens; having the defendant removed from court whilst the witness enters and leaves; and, ensuring that the witness's address was not read out in court.

COMMON REACTIONS TO EXPERIENCES IN COURT

Feeling re-victimised

- 41% of Witness Services reported that women felt they were not believed – for example, a woman was reported as saying it felt: 'like I am the one on trial'. Witness Services reported women feeling as if everything was weighted in the defence's favour

- 41% of Witness Services reported that women felt anger/horror/re-victimised by the nature of the cross-examination
- 35% of Witness Services reported that women felt embarrassed at having to relate intimate details to a room full of strangers
- 30% of Witness Services reported that women felt re-victimised by delays and adjournments
- 12% of Witness Services reported that women stated that the trial was worse than the rape
- 12% of Witness Services reported that women felt that they were made to re-live the rape in court

Fear

- 47% of Witness Services reported that women felt fearful of facing/meeting defendant(s) and supporters

Other comments included: that victims experienced empowerment and relief at having gone through with the trial; that victims felt they had to go through with the trial in order to bring the defendant to justice and to protect others; that victims felt a lack of confidence in, or contact with, the prosecuting counsel; that victims were made to feel unimportant – just a part of the machinery; going through with the trial was a hard thing to do and they would not do it again; the court was a male dominated environment; and that some victims experienced guilt at an acquittal: *'who will be the next victim?'*.

VICTIMS' NEEDS AT COURT

Witness Services were asked to list the most common needs expressed by victims in relation to going to court. These responses fell into four main categories: protection, information, and respect/recognition.

The percentages below refer to the Witness Service returns and not to individual cases.

Protection

- 71% of Witness Services said that witnesses specifically asked for somewhere to wait away from the defendant/supporters, and for security in the court building
- 41% of Witness Services said that witnesses specifically asked to use a screen at court, to avoid having to face the defendant/supporters
- 12% of Witness Services said that witnesses specifically asked to give their evidence via a video link

Information

- 41% of Witness Services said witnesses specifically asked for information/ explanation of the legal process (which the Witness Service can provide) and for information on developments in the case
- 18% of Witness Services said witnesses specifically asked for a pre-court familiarisation visit (the Witness Service provides such visits)

Respect/recognition

- 29% of Witness Services said that witnesses wanted fixed dates and fewer delays
- 24% of Witness Services said that witnesses wanted the prosecution counsel to introduce themselves before the trial
- 18% of Witness Services said that witnesses wanted a change in the nature of questioning
- 12% of Witness Services said that witnesses needed a more sensitive criminal justice system

Victim Support (1996). *Women, rape and the criminal justice system.* London: Victim Support

In *Seaboyer*, the Canadian Supreme Court considered the version of s 276 of the Canadian Criminal Code then in operation. This provided that 'no evidence shall be adduced by or on behalf of the accused concerning the sexual activity of the complainant with any person other than the accused', unless one of three specific conditions was satisfied. The majority of the court declared s 276 unconstitutional on the ground that it violated the fundamental principle, enshrined in the Canadian Charter of Rights and Freedoms, that the innocent should not be punished. As a result of the decision in *Seaboyer*, a new s 276 has been enacted. This is less tightly drafted, according trial judges much greater latitude in admitting evidence of sexual activity. See generally J Temkin, 'Sexual History Evidence – The Ravishment of Section 2' [1993] *Criminal Law Review* 3, 17–19.

In England, the relevant law is contained in section 2 of the Sexual Offences (Amendment) Act 1976, which has been considered by the Court of Appeal on a number of occasions.

Extract 3.3.3

Sexual Offences (Amendment) Act 1976, s 2

2. Restrictions on evidence at trials for rape etc
(1) If at a trial any person is for the time being charged with a rape offence to which he pleads not guilty, then, except with the leave of the judge, no evidence and no question in cross-examination shall be adduced or asked at the trial, by or on behalf of any defendant at the trial, about any sexual experience of a complainant with a person other than that defendant.

(2) The judge shall not give leave in pursuance of the preceding subsection for any evidence or question except on an application made to him in the absence of the jury by or on behalf of a defendant; and on such an application the judge shall give leave if and only if he is satisfied that it would be unfair to that defendant to refuse to allow the evidence to be adduced or the question to be asked.
. . .

III

Extract 3.3.4

R v Viola [1982] 1 WLR 1138, 1141–5 (CA)

At his trial for rape, the defendant argued that the complainant had consented to the sexual intercourse. He was refused leave under s 2 to cross-examine the complainant about her sexual experiences with other men, the proposed questions being based on eyewitness statements regarding incidents with different men some hours before and some hours after the alleged rape.

LORD LANE CJ: It is, we think, apparent from [the words of section 2], without more, that the first question which the judge must ask himself is this: are the questions proposed to be put relevant according to the ordinary common law rules of evidence and relevant to the case as it is being put? If they are not so relevant, that is the end of the matter.
. . .

The second matter which the judge must consider is this. If the questions are relevant, then whether they should be allowed or not will of course depend upon the terms of section 2, which limits the admissibility of relevant evidence. That section has been the subject of judicial consideration first of all by May J in *Reg v Lawrence* [1977] Crim LR 492; a passage, which is taken verbatim from the transcript of the ruling, reads, at p 493:

'The important part of the statute which I think needs construction are the words "if and only if [the judge] is satisfied that it would be unfair to that defendant to refuse to allow the evidence to be adduced or the question to be asked." And, in my judgment, before a judge is satisfied or may be said to be satisfied that to refuse to allow a particular question or a series of questions in cross-examination would be unfair to a defendant he must take the view that it is more likely than not that the particular question or line of cross-examination, if allowed, might reasonably lead the jury, properly directed in the summing up, to take a different view of the complainant's evidence from that which they might take if the question or series of questions was or were not allowed.'

. . .
. . . In the end the judge will have to ask himself the question whether he is satisfied in the terms expounded by May J. It will be a problem for him to apply that dictum to the particular facts of the case. In those circumstances it seems to us it would be both improper and, perhaps more important, very unwise for us to try to say in advance what may or may not be unfair in any particular case.
. . . The judge has to make a judgment as to whether he is satisfied or not in the terms of section 2. But once having reached his judgment on the particular facts, he has no discretion. If he comes to the conclusion that he is satisfied it would be unfair to exclude the evidence, then the evidence has to be admitted and the questions have to be allowed.
. . . this Act . . . was aimed primarily at protecting complainants from cross-examination as to credit, from questions which went merely to credit and no

more. The result is that generally speaking – I use these words advisedly, of course there will always be exceptions – if the proposed questions merely seek to establish that the complainant has had sexual experience with other men to whom she was not married, so as to suggest that for that reason she ought not to be believed under oath, the judge will exclude the evidence. In the present climate of opinion a jury is unlikely to be influenced by such considerations, nor should it be influenced. In other words questions of this sort going simply to credit will seldom be allowed. . . .

On the other hand if the questions are relevant to an issue in the trial in the light of the way the case is being run, for instance relevant to the issue of consent, as opposed merely to credit, they are likely to be admitted, because to exclude a relevant question on an issue in the trial as the trial is being run will usually mean that the jury are being prevented from hearing something which, if they did hear it, might cause them to change their minds about the evidence given by the complainant. But, I repeat, we are very far from laying down any hard and fast rule.

Inevitably in this situation, as in so many similar situations in the law, there is a grey area which exists between the two types of relevance, namely, relevance to credit and relevance to an issue in the case. On one hand evidence of sexual promiscuity may be so strong or so closely contemporaneous in time to the event in issue as to come near to, or indeed to reach the border between mere credit and an issue in the case. Conversely, the relevance of the evidence to an issue in the case may be so slight as to lead the judge to the conclusion that he is far from satisfied that the exclusion of the evidence or the question from the consideration of the jury would be unfair to the defendant.

We have had drawn to our attention some of the difficulties which face a judge. It is perfectly true to say that normally he has to make this decision at an early stage of the trial. It will be, generally speaking, when the complainant's evidence in chief is concluded that counsel in the absence of the jury will make the necessary application under section 2. At this stage it may not be easy for the judge to reach a conclusion, but this is a problem which is continually being faced by judges, sometimes in even more trying circumstances, for example, when he is asked to determine whether a count should be tried separately or whether defendants should be tried separately and so on, before the trial has got under way at all. He has to reach the best conclusion that he can.

The second matter is: is this court entitled to differ from the conclusions of the judge? As already pointed out, this is the exercise of judgment by the judge not an exercise of his discretion. This court is in many respects in as good a position as the judge to reach a conclusion. The judge has certainly heard the complainant give evidence, but only in chief. So far as the proposed questions are concerned, the statements upon which the questions were to be asked or the way in which the matter was going to be put to the jury are presented in exactly the same way to this court as they were to the judge at first instance. We have been told what it was that counsel sought in the course of his submission to the judge and indeed we have been given the statements which were to be the basis of the questions which he was going to ask. So what we have to decide is whether the judge was right or wrong in the conclusion which he reached, applying the test of May J in *Reg v Lawrence* [1977] Crim LR 492, 493. Like so many decisions in the grey area, it is not an easy decision to make. Let me turn therefore to the precise matters about which it was proposed to ask questions.

First of all the presence of the two men in her maisonette very shortly before the alleged rape took place. The facts of that were apparently these. The two men, whose names are not material, called at the maisonette occupied by the complainant, in the hope of finding the complainant's boyfriend, whose name was Willy, present. They arrived some time during the afternoon. They were equipped with a considerable amount of drink, amongst other things a gallon of wine. They discovered that Willy was not there. Nevertheless they went in at the invitation of the complainant. It was not suggested that she knew them very well. Indeed she probably did not, although she was acquainted with them. According to their evidence not only was a good deal of alcohol consumed by them and the complainant, but during the course of the several hours that they were there with her, she made sexual advances to them: she suggested that one or other might like to try out her new bed; she made physical contact with one of them by rubbing his back, and so on; in other words indicated that she would not be averse to sexual intercourse with them. The precise timing is not available, perhaps not surprisingly, but it seems likely that the length of time which elapsed between the departure of these two men and the advent of the appellant was something like an hour and a half. Consequently it is suggested to us, and was suggested to the judge, that in the context of this case this evidence was very much material to an issue in the case, namely, the question of consent, owing, inter alia, to the similarity between the entry of these two men to the maisonette and the entry of the appellant and to the close proximity in time of the two incidents.

The next matter was the fact that she had had sexual intercourse with her boyfriend during the afternoon of September 9, that was about 14 hours after the alleged act of rape. The relevance, it was suggested, in respect of this question was that it was said in the complainant's statement to the police that after the so-called rape her vagina was sore, the inference being that it was because the sexual intercourse had been without consent that she suffered that pain. We are told, although it is not in evidence, that there was some difficulty about the real cause for the girl's soreness; it was suggested perhaps it was the size of the appellant's male member that had caused the soreness rather than the lack of consent.

The final matter which it was sought to introduce was that on the morning of September 9, a very few hours after the alleged act of rape, a woman friend of the complainant had come to her maisonette to pick up the complainant's little boy to take him to school. There was no reason apparently to doubt the veracity of this lady and what she said was that in the maisonette there was lying on the sofa this man naked apart from a pair of slippers.

All those matters have to be read against the somewhat unusual features of this case, the unusual features being first of all the dispute about the injuries, some people saying that they observed them on the Friday, and others apparently saying that they did not earlier on; and the remarkable feature that no complaint was made to anyone apparently between the time of the event, at about midnight on Tuesday night, and Friday.

In those circumstances it seems to us that the presence of the two men in the maisonette prior to the incident in question and the presence of the naked man in the maisonette immediately after the event are matters which went to the question of consent and were matters which could not be regarded as so trivial or of so little relevance as for the judge to be able to say that he was satisfied that no injustice would be done to the appellant by their exclusion from the evidence. . . . These questions were not mere questions as to credit.

It need hardly be said that one differs from a judge on a point such as this with the greatest possible reluctance, and it is only after very serious consideration that we have come to the conclusion that in this particular case the judge was wrong in the conclusion which he reached: he was wrong in respect of the two men in the flat and wrong in respect of the naked man in the flat. We would not say the same of the second of the three allegations, about sexual intercourse with the boyfriend. If the appeal had rested upon that alone, we would not have interfered. We think he was right in the conclusion he reached in respect of that, but he was wrong in respect of the other two.

See also *R v Cox.*[35]

Extract 3.3.5

R v Brown (1988) 89 Cr App R 97, 99–101 (CA)

MAY LJ: After the complainant had given evidence-in-chief, counsel for the appellant applied to the learned judge for leave to cross-examine her about her sexual relations with other men. He relied on the decisions in *Lawrence* [1977] Crim LR 492, and *Viola* (1982) 75 Cr App R 125. He indicated that he wished to put to the complainant, first, the evidence of the police surgeon that she had found signs of venereal disease; secondly, that part of the complainant's own deposition where she described her relationship with her then boy-friend as a 'casual sex relationship,' and which he (the boy-friend) had said had been going on for only some 10 days; thirdly, that the complainant had had a child six months earlier by yet another man. Counsel submitted that this was evidence of promiscuity and that it went to the issue of consent.

. . .

What counsel for the appellant wished to do at the trial in this case, as he told us and as appears from the transcript, was to seek to show that the complainant was promiscuous, that is to say, that not only had she had sexual experience with men to whom she was not married but that she had done so casually and with little discrimination. It was, of course, in any event fundamental to such a submission that there was a factual basis for suggesting sexual promiscuity in this case.

Nevertheless, if the purpose of such questions was merely to show that for that reason the complainant ought not to be believed under oath, then the judge properly excluded the evidence. On the other hand, if the proposed

---

[35] (1986) 84 Cr App R 132.

questions were relevant to the issue of consent, as opposed merely to credit, then they would be likely to be admitted. . . .

. . .

The real inquiry is whether on the facts of the particular case the complainant's attitude to sexual relations could be material upon which in these days a jury could reasonably rely to conclude that the complainant may indeed have consented to the sexual intercourse on the material occasion, despite her evidence to the contrary. It is in every case a question of degree.

Further, the question whether it is unfair to exclude such cross-examination in a case on or near the borderline referred to may be affected by the consideration whether there are other features relevant to consent which could tip the balance between fairness and unfairness. In the present case the complainant did not seek help from her boyfriend when the appellant, on her evidence, was forcing her away from the club. She did not shout out to her friends who were there at the time and who saw what was happening. She did not complain to the taxi-driver the following morning when she was picked up at the appellant's home. May these features have been due to her attitude towards casual sexual relations, and in combination with that attitude sufficiently material to the question whether she consented or not so as to make it unfair to exclude the questions sought to be asked?

In our opinion, this was a case near the borderline. Clearly the complainant was prepared to have intercourse with a number of different men, but we do not think that the mere fact that she was suffering from some venereal disease is necessarily evidence of substantial promiscuity. Before it could be so considered there would have to be cross-examination, largely on a 'fishing basis,' to discover the circumstances in which she came to be infected. There are also the other features to which we have referred.

Nevertheless, although we have not found it easy to reach a decision on this appeal, in the end we do not think that the 'evidence of sexual promiscuity' of the complainant was 'so strong or so closely contemporaneous in time to the event in issue as to . . . reach the border between mere credit and an issue in the case.'

For these reasons we dismiss this appeal.

See also *R v Barton*.[36]

The Court of Appeal has made it clear that, since s 2 deals with sexual experience 'with a person . . .', it 'cannot refer to an inanimate object such as a vibrator'.[37]

It is to be noted that in *R v Funderburk*,[38] extracted in Chapter 4, the Court of Appeal highlighted the blurred distinction in sexual cases between the relevance of sexual history evidence to facts in issue, and the relevance of such evidence to credit.

The following decision of the Court of Appeal affirms that an application for leave under s 2 must be supported by reasonable grounds for making the assertion which leave is being sought to make:

[36] (1986) 85 Cr App R 5.
[37] *R v Barnes* [1994] Crim LR 691; LEXIS transcript.
[38] [1990] 1 WLR 587.

Extract 3.3.6

R v Howes [1996] 2 Cr App R 490, 498 (CA)

EVANS LJ: In our judgment ... no application under section 2 for leave to cross-examine can properly be made unless defence counsel has instructions which provide 'reasonable grounds' for making the assertion which he seeks leave to make; and it follows from this ... that the trial judge can properly ask what the proposed questions are and what support for them counsel has.

The Lord Chief Justice said in *Viola* that the questions proposed to be put must be 'relevant according to the ordinary common law rules of evidence'. Those words, read in isolation, might suggest that they, or perhaps the material on which they are based, must be not only relevant, which is a question of fact and degree, but also admissible in law. We do not consider that they are intended to bear that strict meaning ... relevance, rather than admissibility (if questions in cross-examination can be said to be 'admissible' at all), is the correct test. But we would also hold that where relevance is established the question of admissibility is always likely to be influential on the exercise of the judge's discretion. There will be cases where supporting grounds exist but admissible evidence cannot be produced in court for some reason or another. On the other hand, questions which have no foundation in evidence that would be admissible and could be placed before the jury if it was available for the purpose are likely to be excluded, because those questions amount to the kind of roving inquiry or unfounded assertions based on rumour and gossip which section 2 is intended to exclude.

The extent to which sexual history evidence may appropriately be regarded as relevant to the issue of consent is highly questionable, as the following extract succinctly illustrates:

Extract 3.3.7

A McColgan, 'Common Law and the Relevance of Sexual History Evidence' (1996) 16 *Oxford Journal of Legal Studies* 275, 285

... are women who are or have been sexually active more likely to have consented to sexual activity they characterize as rape than women who are or have not been so active? Is it more likely that a man with a reputation for generosity consented to the appropriation of his possessions, in a case where he alleges theft by the appropriator, than a man who has a reputation for meanness? Of course it is not. Neither his generosity nor her other sexual activities render it more likely that they consented to the activity of which they now complain. It is perhaps more likely, in fact, that the mean man and sexually conservative woman would repent their uncharacteristic behaviour and re-define it subsequently to themselves and others than that the generous man and sexually active woman would re-define behaviour which was not unusual for them.

See also A A S Zuckerman, *The Principles of Criminal Evidence* (1989) 248 n 5. After a survey of the decisions on s 2, Temkin rightly concludes that

> in many cases, it will be an inept defence counsel who is unable by some means or other successfully to apply under section 2. The willingness of the Court of Appeal to see a wide range of evidence as of relevance to consent means that trial judges who refuse to allow in sexual history evidence do so at some considerable risk of a quashed conviction on appeal. This is particularly discouraging as the one thing that does appear to have changed since 1976, if the reported cases are anything to go by, is that some trial judges at least are less inclined to permit sexual history evidence and have clearly understood the purpose of section 2.[39]

An unsuccessful move was made for the inclusion, in the Criminal Procedure and Investigations Bill, of a clause designed to replace subss (1) and (2) of s 2 of the Sexual Offences (Amendment) Act 1976 with the following provisions, which are modelled on those to be found in the relevant New South Wales legislation:[40]

> (1) If at a trial any person is for the time being charged with a sexual offence to which he pleads not guilty, then except with the leave of the judge, no evidence and no question in cross-examination shall be adduced or asked at the trial, by or on behalf of any defendant at the trial, about any sexual experience of a complainant with a person other than that defendant.
>
> (2) The judge shall not give leave in pursuance of the preceding subsection for any evidence or question except on an application to him made in the absence of the jury by or on behalf of a defendant; and on such an application the judge shall give leave if and only if he is satisfied that –
>
>   (a) it is evidence –
>
>   (i) of sexual experience or sexual activity taken part in by the complainant at or about the time of the commission of the alleged sexual offence; and
>
>   (ii) of events which are alleged to form part of a connected series of circumstances in which the alleged sexual offence was committed; or
>
>   (b) (i) the accused person is alleged to have had sexual intercourse with the complainant and the accused person does not concede the sexual intercourse alleged; and
>
>   (ii) it is evidence relevant to whether the presence of semen, pregnancy, disease or injury is attributable to the sexual intercourse alleged; or
>
>   (c) it is evidence relevant to whether at the time of the alleged sexual offence there was present in the complainant a disease which at any relevant time was absent in the accused person; or
>
>   (d) it is evidence relevant to whether the allegation that the sexual offence was committed by the accused person was first made following a realisation or discovery of the presence of pregnancy or disease in the complainant (being a realisation or discovery which took place after the commission of the alleged sexual offence); or

---

[39] J Temkin, 'Sexual History Evidence – The Ravishment of Section 2' [1993] *Criminal Law Review* 3, 17.

[40] Crimes Act 1900 (NSW), s 409B.

(e) it is evidence tending to show that the complainant has, at a different time, made another allegation of a sexual offence which the complainant has subsequently withdrawn, admitted was false or which was unsubstantiated; or

(f) where it has been disclosed or implied in the case for the prosecution against the accused person that the complainant has or may have –

(i) had sexual experience, or lack of sexual experience of a general or specified nature; or

(ii) taken part or not taken part in sexual activity of a general or specified nature; and

(iii) the accused person might be unfairly prejudiced if the complainant could not be cross-examined by or on behalf of the accused person in relation to the disclosure or implication.

(2A) The judge shall not give leave under paragraphs (a) to (f) of subsection (2) above unless he is satisfied that it would be unfair to that defendant to refuse to allow the evidence to be adduced or the question or questions to be asked.

(2B) Where a judge has given leave in accordance with this section for evidence to be adduced or for a question or questions to be asked he shall record or cause to be recorded in writing the nature and scope of the evidence which may be adduced and the question or questions which may be asked and he shall further record or cause to be recorded in writing his reasons for giving leave.

(2C) In considering the nature and scope of the evidence which may be adduced and the question or questions which may be asked the judge shall take into account any distress, humiliation or embarrassment which the complainant might suffer as a result.[41]

Would the introduction of such provisions represent the right way forward? In August 1996, a six-day cross-examination of a rape complainant by the defendant himself (who was later convicted by the jury)[42] led to calls for a curtailment of the right of a defendant in a rape trial to cross-examine the complainant in person.

Further reading

Z Adler, *Rape on Trial* (1987)
S Lees, *Ruling Passions: Sexual Violence, Reputation and the Law* (1997)
J Temkin, *Rape and the Legal Process* (1987)
— (ed), *Rape and the Criminal Justice System* (1995)

(b) Children

Child witnesses have traditionally been regarded with great suspicion. In their book on the evidence of children, Spencer and Flin have marshalled an

---

[41] *Parliamentary Debates (Hansard): House of Commons (Vol 279)* (1996) cols 356–7.
[42] See, eg, *The Independent*, 23 August 1996, p 1.

impressive amount of psychological and other evidence to demonstrate that the following assumptions about children do not withstand close scrutiny:[43]

1. *'Children's memories are unreliable.'* This is a misleading generalisation. What is significant, rather, is that the reliability of a child's memory is dependent to a great extent upon the manner in which he or she is questioned.

2. *'Children are egocentric in two senses: (1) they are not concerned about the impact of their actions (for example, lying) on others; and (2) they are unable to remember details which do not directly interest them.'* While there is evidence that very young children may be egocentric in the first sense, it is unclear whether this kind of egocentrism actually has any effect on a child's veracity. Further, there is no evidence that egocentrism in the second sense is more peculiar to children than to adults.

3. *'Children are particularly suggestible.'* Spencer and Flin point out that 'the psychological research shows that children, like adults, can be suggestible but that this risk can be minimised by the use of sensitive questioning techniques in the hands of a skilled interviewer'.[44]

4. *'Children cannot distinguish fact from fantasy.'* There is, in reality, no evidence suggesting that children routinely fantasise about the sort of incidents which might result in court proceedings. Rather, children's fantasies are characterised by their daily experience and personal knowledge.

5. *'Children are prone to making false allegations.'* There is in fact no evidence to support the assumption that children are more inclined to lie than adults.

We have seen earlier in the chapter that the old rules relating to the competence of child witnesses in criminal proceedings have been replaced with a new principle that all such witnesses are competent unless 'incapable of giving intelligible testimony'. In recent years, a number of other mechanisms designed to protect child witnesses in criminal proceedings have been introduced. These mechanisms, which are of varying degrees of usefulness, will now be examined briefly.

(i) Screens and social workers

Judges may in the exercise of their discretion permit a child witness to give evidence from behind a screen, and allow a social worker to sit with a child witness in court.

---

[43] See J R Spencer and R H Flin, *The Evidence of Children: The Law and the Psychology* (2nd ed 1993) Ch 11. See also G Sattar and R Bull, 'Child Witnesses in Court: Psycho-Legal Issues' (1996) 140 *Solicitors Journal* 401.

[44] J R Spencer and R H Flin, *The Evidence of Children: The Law and the Psychology* (2nd ed 1993) 307.

Extract 3.3.8

R v X (1989) 91 Cr App R 36, 40 (CA)

THE LORD CHIEF JUSTICE: The learned judge has the duty on this and on all other occasions of endeavouring to see that justice is done. Those are high sounding words. What it really means is, he has got to see that the system operates fairly; fairly not only to the defendants but also to the prosecution and also to the witnesses. Sometimes he has to make decisions as to where the balance of fairness lies. He came to the conclusion that in these circumstances the necessity of trying to ensure that these children would be able to give evidence outweighed any possible prejudice to the defendants by the erection of the screen.

This Court agrees with him in that view.

In *R v Smith*,[45] the defendant was charged with rape and gross indecency with a child. During the evidence of the complainant, who was aged 12, a social worker sat beside her. When the complainant broke down in tears, the social worker consoled her and spoke quietly to her. On appeal it was argued, inter alia, that the social worker's talking quietly to the complainant when she broke down in tears constituted an irregularity in the trial. Although this ground of appeal was abandoned, the Court of Appeal dealt with the matter in order to provide guidance for the assistance of courts. The following is the report in the *Criminal Law Review* of what was stated by the Court of Appeal:

> ... it is the judge's task to order a procedure which reduces the strain on child witnesses without prejudicing the interests of the defendant. It is important that anyone providing comfort and support to a child witness should not talk to the complainant while she is giving evidence, and this should be made clear publicly. If a social worker talks or whispers more than a consoling word or two, the suspicion may be aroused that something is being said about the evidence. Anyone fulfilling that role should say as little as possible, preferably nothing, to the witness.[46]

(ii) Live television links

Child witnesses (as well as witnesses who are outside the United Kingdom) may testify through a live television link in certain circumstances:

Extract 3.3.9

Criminal Justice Act 1988, s 32(1), (1A), (2), (3C), (3D), (3E), (6)

32. Evidence through television links

(1) A person other than the accused may give evidence through a live television link in proceedings to which subsection (1A) below applies if –

---

[45] [1994] Crim LR 458.
[46] At 459.

(a) the witness is outside the United Kingdom; or

(b) the witness is a child, or is to be cross-examined following the admission under section 32A below of a video recording of testimony from him, and the offence is one to which subsection (2) below applies,

but evidence may not be so given without the leave of the court.

(1A) This subsection applies –

(a) to trials on indictment, appeals to the criminal division of the Court of Appeal and hearings of references under section 9 of the Criminal Appeal Act 1995; and

(b) to proceedings in youth courts, appeals to the Crown Court arising out of such proceedings and hearings of references under section 11 of the Criminal Appeal Act 1995 so arising.

(2) This subsection applies –

(a) to an offence which involves an assault on, or injury or a threat of injury to, a person;

(b) to an offence under section 1 of the Children and Young Persons Act 1933 (cruelty to persons under 16);

(c) to an offence under the Sexual Offences Act 1956, the Indecency with Children Act 1960, the Sexual Offences Act 1967, section 54 of the Criminal Law Act 1977 or the Protection of Children Act 1978; and

(d) to an offence which consists of attempting or conspiring to commit, or of aiding, abetting, counselling, procuring or inciting the commission of, an offence falling within paragraph (a), (b) or (c) above.

(3C) Where –

(a) the court gives leave for a person to give evidence through a live television link, and

(b) the leave is given by virtue of subsection (1)(b) above,

then, subject to subsection (3D) below, the person concerned may not give evidence otherwise than through a live television link.

(3D) In a case falling within subsection (3C) above the court may give permission for the person to give evidence otherwise than through a live television link if it appears to the court to be in the interests of justice to give such permission.

(3E) Permission may be given under subsection (3D) above –

(a) on an application by a party to the case, or

(b) of the court's own motion;

but no application may be made under paragraph (a) above unless there has been a material change of circumstances since the leave was given by virtue of subsection (1)(b) above.

(6) Subsection (7) of section 32A below shall apply for the purposes of this section as it applies for the purposes of that section, but with the omission of the references to a person being, in the cases there mentioned, under the age of fifteen years or under the age of eighteen years.

The Court of Appeal has made the following comments on the interpretation of subs (2)(a):

In our judgment, an offence involves a threat of injury within the meaning of section 32(2) if its circumstances are such that injury to a person is a real possibility.

It is not necessary, in our view, that the threat of injury to another person referred to in the subsection should be made directly by the offender. It is the conse-quences of the offender's activity, which viewed objectively, must present the threat. If they do, then the unlawful activity, the commission of the offence, involves a threat of injury within the meaning of the subsection.[47]

(iii) Video recordings

In certain circumstances a video recording of an interview with a child wit-ness may be admitted in evidence in place of the child's evidence-in-chief.

Extract 3.3.10

Criminal Justice Act 1988, s 32A(1)–(8)

32A. Video recordings of testimony from child witnesses

(1) This section applies in relation to the following proceedings, namely –

(a) trials on indictment for any offence to which section 32(2) above applies;

(b) appeals to the criminal division of the Court of Appeal and hearings of references under section 9 of the Criminal Appeal Act 1995 in respect of any such offence; and

(c) proceedings in youth courts for any such offence, appeals to the Crown Court arising out of such proceedings and hearings of refer-ences under section 11 of the Criminal Appeal Act 1995 so arising.

(2) In any such proceedings a video recording of an interview which –

(a) is conducted between an adult and a child who is not the accused or one of the accused ('the child witness'); and

(b) relates to any matter in issue in the proceedings,

may, with the leave of the court, be given in evidence in so far as it is not excluded by the court under subsection (3) below.

(3) Where a video recording is tendered in evidence under this section, the court shall (subject to the exercise of any power of the court to exclude evidence which is otherwise admissible) give leave under subsection (2) above unless –

(a) it appears that the child witness will not be available for cross-examination;

(b) any rules of court requiring disclosure of the circumstances in which the recording was made have not been complied with to the satisfac-tion of the court; or

(c) the court is of the opinion, having regard to all the circumstances of the case, that in the interests of justice the recording ought not to be admitted;

and where the court gives such leave it may, if it is of the opinion that in the interests of justice any part of the recording ought not to be admitted, direct that that part shall be excluded.

---

[47] *R v Lee* [1996] 2 Cr App R 266, 269.

(4) In considering whether any part of a recording ought to be excluded under subsection (3) above, the court shall consider whether any prejudice to the accused, or one of the accused, which might result from the admission of that part is outweighed by the desirability of showing the whole, or substantially the whole, of the recorded interview.

(5) Where a video recording is admitted under this section –
  (a) the child witness shall be called by the party who tendered it in evidence;
  (b) that witness shall not be examined in chief on any matter which, in the opinion of the court, has been dealt with adequately in his recorded testimony.

(6) Where a video recording is given in evidence under this section, any statement made by the child witness which is disclosed by the recording shall be treated as if given by that witness in direct oral testimony; and accordingly –
  (a) any such statement shall be admissible evidence of any fact of which such testimony from him would be admissible;
  (b) no such statement shall be capable of corroborating any other evidence given by him;

and in estimating the weight, if any, to be attached to such a statement, regard shall be had to all the circumstances from which any inference can reasonably be drawn (as to its accuracy or otherwise).

(6A) Where the court gives leave under subsection (2) above the child witness shall not give relevant evidence (within the meaning given by subsection (6D) below) otherwise than by means of the video recording; but this is subject to subsection (6B) below.

(6B) In a case falling within subsection (6A) above the court may give permission for the child witness to give relevant evidence (within the meaning given by subsection (6D) below) otherwise than by means of the video recording if it appears to the court to be in the interests of justice to give such permission.

(6C) Permission may be given under subsection (6B) above –
  (a) on an application by a party to the case, or
  (b) of the court's own motion;

but no application may be made under paragraph (a) above unless there has been a material change of circumstances since the leave was given under subsection (2) above.

(6D) For the purposes of subsections (6A) and (6B) above evidence is relevant evidence if –
  (a) it is evidence in chief on behalf of the party who tendered the video recording, and
  (b) it relates to matter which, in the opinion of the court, is dealt with in the recording and which the court has not directed to be excluded under subsection (3) above.

(7) In this section 'child' means a person who –
  (a) in the case of an offence falling within section 32(2)(a) or (b) above, is under fourteen years of age or, if he was under that age when the video recording was made, is under fifteen years of age; or
  (b) in the case of an offence falling within section 32(2)(c) above, is under seventeen years of age or, if he was under that age when the video recording was made, is under eighteen years of age.

(8) Any reference in subsection (7) above to an offence falling within paragraph (a), (b) or (c) of section 32(2) above includes a reference to an offence which consists of attempting or conspiring to commit, or of aiding, abetting, counselling, procuring or inciting the commission of, an offence falling within that paragraph.

It is arguable that these provisions do not go sufficiently far in protecting vulnerable child witnesses,[48] since they still require that the child be subjected to cross-examination (which may, however, be able to be conducted through a live television link[49]). And if there has been a long time lapse between the recorded interview and the cross-examination, the experience of cross-examination may be even more traumatic for the child than cross-examination that takes place immediately after 'normal' examination-in-chief. It is arguable that, as recommended by the Pigot Committee,[50] the interests of child witnesses require that pre-recorded cross-examination be permitted in appropriate circumstances.[51]

It would appear that the jury may have copies of transcripts of a video-recorded interview while the recordings are being played, so long as (1) the transcripts are likely to be helpful to the jury in following the evidence in question; (2) the trial judge makes it clear to the jury that it is the oral evidence on which they should concentrate; and (3) the jury are warned, both at that time and in the summing-up, against placing undue weight on the transcripts. However, a transcript should not normally be permitted to be taken with the jury when they retire unless the defence consents, because of the danger that undue weight might be placed on it.[52]

Extract 3.3.11

R v Springer [1996] Crim LR 903, 903–4 (CA)

The appellant was convicted of two counts of indecent assault and one count of rape. All three counts were specimen counts. The victim was a child who was said to have been aged 4 when the appellant's indecent conduct towards her started. She was 9 at the time of the trial. Her evidence-in-chief was given, pursuant to the provisions of section 32A of the Criminal Justice Act 1988, by way of a video-recorded interview, of which the jury were given a transcript. An application by the defence that the video-recorded interview be excluded, on the ground that the substance of her evidence was hearsay because it

---

[48] Additionally, there is empirical evidence suggesting that the legislature's purpose of securing more general admission of children's evidence has not been realised: see generally B Campbell, 'If Children Accuse, Can there be Justice?', *The Independent*, 17 January 1995, 15.
[49] Section 32.
[50] *Report of the Advisory Group on Video Evidence* (1989).
[51] See generally P Reeves, 'Video Recorded Evidence of Children' (1993) 157 *Justice of the Peace* 229.
[52] *R v Welstead* [1996] 1 Cr App R 59.

came from what she had been told by her mother, had been refused by the judge. The appellant appealed against conviction on the ground that the judge had erred in refusing to exclude the video evidence.

Held, allowing the appeal but ordering a retrial, that although the judge could not be criticised for having permitted the jury to see the video evidence, he had failed to give them any warning about the risks of attaching undue weight to the transcript of that evidence. He had also, amongst a number of other omissions, failed to refer in his summing up to the major point in the defence case that there was at least a risk that the account being forwarded by the victim was not her own account. It behoved a judge, especially in cases such as the present, to give a balanced, clear summing up adverting, where necessary, to specific problems that could arise when video evidence was sought to be adduced before the jury.

That had not been done, leading to the conclusion that the conviction was unsafe.

The Court of Appeal held in *R v Rawlings and Broadbent (Practice Note)*[53] that, where the jury wish to be reminded of *how* the witness spoke in the interview, as opposed to *what* was said by the witness, the trial judge has a discretion to grant a request by the jury to view the video recording again after retiring to consider their verdict.[54] (It may be questioned, however, whether the distinction between how a witness spoke and what he or she said is an entirely clear-cut one.) In addition, the following conditions must be satisfied:

(a) The replay should be in court with judge, counsel and defendant present. (b) The judge should warn the jury that because they are hearing the evidence in chief of the complainant repeated a second time well after all the other evidence, they should guard against the risk of giving it disproportionate weight simply for that reason and should bear well in mind the other evidence in the case. (c) To assist in maintaining a fair balance, he should after the replay of the video, remind the jury of the cross-examination and re-examination of the complainant from his notes whether the jury asked him to do so or not.[55]

The issue arose for consideration again in the following case:

Extract 3.3.12

R v M [1996] 2 Cr App R 56, 60–2 (CA)

KAY J: The principal ground of appeal relates to the playing of the video for the second time. Three separate submissions are made. First, it is submitted that it was wrong to replay the video at all otherwise than at the specific

---

[53] [1995] 1 WLR 178.
[54] See generally D J Birch, 'Play it Again! Replaying Children's Video Evidence', *Archbold News*, 4 April 1996, 6.
[55] [1995] 1 WLR 178, 183.

request of the jury. Secondly, even assuming that it was right that it should be replayed, it is contended that the point of the trial at which this was done was the wrong time for it to happen. Thirdly, it is argued that if the video was to be replayed warnings should have been given in relation to the matter along the lines of those which have since been suggested by this court in *Rawlings and Broadbent* [1995] 2 Cr App R 222; [1995] 1 WLR 178.
. . .

There may be circumstances in which it would be appropriate for a video to be replayed otherwise than at the request of the jury. We do not wish to anticipate every set of circumstances that might arise in such a case. However, we are clear that in normal circumstances it will be inappropriate for a video to be played a second time unless there has been a specific request to that effect from the jury. In general terms the replaying of the video should be a matter to be discouraged. That is because, by its very nature, to replay one aspect of the evidence is a departure from the normal course of events in a criminal trial. Generally speaking any such departure should only take place if there is an exceptional reason that requires such a course to be taken.

In this case we have come to the conclusion that there was no such exceptional reason. The situation here was that matters of detail had been raised by the defence in the course of the cross-examination of the witness but there was nothing which, in our view, demanded that the whole of the video should be replayed. There may be circumstances where in order that the jury may follow a particular line of cross-examination the video requires to be played at that stage so that the witness and the jury can understand the nature of the question that is being put. In such circumstances, a short part of the video may need to be viewed during the course of the questioning, but it is most unlikely that it will require a re-run of the whole. We have come to the conclusion that to replay the video a second time in this case was inappropriate and should not have occurred in the absence of any request from the jury.
. . .

We turn to the second criticism. The second criticism is that the playing of the video after the rest of the evidence had been completed gave it such a prominence that there was a danger that the jury might attach undue weight to it. We think there is merit in the complaint that is made in that regard. It is difficult to understand without reading exactly what was said at the time, how it came about that it was played at that stage. We are satisfied that the learned judge was trying to reach the conclusion that he thought would most assist the jury. However, when one comes to consider the effect that it may have had on the trial, the request of the learned judge's decision was that at the conclusion of the defence case, after all the defence evidence had been heard, there was a replaying of the crucial part of the prosecution case. We are satisfied that such timing cannot have been appropriate and that it is possible it may have had the effect suggested of causing the jury to attach greater significance to the girl's evidence than to the evidence of the defendant and his witnesses which they had only heard the once.

The third and final criticism of this aspect of the case is that if the video was to be replayed, the precautions suggested in the passage in the case of *Rawlings*, to which we have referred ought to have been adopted. . . . So far as we can judge no warning in the terms suggested was given to the jury at any stage. As indicated, we have not seen exactly what was said, but it is quite clear that in the course of summing the case up to the jury no warning of that kind was given. In our judgment if the exceptional course of replaying the video had occurred in the case it required the judge, in the course of his summing-up, even if he had done so at the time, to make clear to the jury that there was a risk of giving it undue weight. The learned judge in his summing-up reminded the jury of the cross-examination but that was at some distance in time from the replaying of the video. We have already made clear our conclusion as to timing and it is sufficient to say that this aspect simply adds to our concerns.

(iv) No cross-examination by accused in person

Extract 3.3.13

Criminal Justice Act 1988, s 34A

34A. Cross-examination of alleged child victims

(1) No person who is charged with an offence to which section 32(2) above applies shall cross-examine in person any witness who:
  (a) is alleged:
      (i) to be a person against whom the offence was committed; or
      (ii) to have witnessed the commission of the offence; and
  (b) is a child, or is to be cross-examined following the admission under section 32A above of a video recording of testimony from him.

(2) Subsection (7) of section 32A above shall apply for the purposes of this section as it applies for the purposes of that section, but with the omission of the references to a person being, in the cases there mentioned, under the age of fifteen years or under the age of eighteen years.

(v) Notices of transfer

In the interests of protecting the welfare of child witnesses, it is possible in certain circumstances for committal proceedings to be bypassed, and the case taken over and proceeded with without delay by the Crown Court.

Extract 3.3.14

Criminal Justice Act 1991, s 53

53. Notices of transfer in certain cases involving children

(1) If a person has been charged with an offence to which section 32(2) of the 1988 Act applies (sexual offences and offences involving violence or cruelty) and the Director of Public Prosecutions is of the opinion –

(a) that the evidence of the offence would be sufficient for the person charged to be committed for trial;
(b) that a child who is alleged –
  (i) to be a person against whom the offence was committed; or
  (ii) to have witnessed the commission of the offence,
    will be called as a witness at the trial; and
(c) that, for the purpose of avoiding any prejudice to the welfare of the child, the case should be taken over and proceeded with without delay by the Crown Court,

a notice ('notice of transfer') certifying that opinion may be given by or on behalf of the Director to the magistrates' court in whose jurisdiction the offence has been charged.

(2) A notice of transfer shall be given before the magistrates' court begins to inquire into the case as examining justices.

(3) On the giving of a notice of transfer the functions of the magistrates' court shall cease in relation to the case except as provided by paragraphs 2 and 3 of Schedule 6 to this Act or by section 20(4) of the Legal Aid Act 1988.

(4) The decision to give a notice of transfer shall not be subject to appeal or liable to be questioned in any court.

(5) Schedule 6 to this Act (which makes further provision in relation to notices of transfer) shall have effect.

(6) In this section 'child' means a person who –
(a) in the case of an offence falling within section 32(2)(a) or (b) of the 1988 Act, is under fourteen years of age or, if he was under that age when any such video recording as is mentioned in section 32(A)(2) of that Act was made in respect of him, is under fifteen years of age; or
(b) in the case of an offence falling within section 32(2)(c) of that Act, is under seventeen years of age or, if he was under that age when any such video recording was made in respect of him, is under eighteen years of age.

(7) Any reference in subsection (6) above to an offence falling within paragraph (a), (b) or (c) of section 32(2) of that Act includes a reference to an offence which consists of attempting or conspiring to commit, or of aiding, abetting, counselling, procuring or inciting the commission of, an offence falling within that paragraph.

Further reading

D J Birch, 'The Criminal Justice Act 1991: (4) Children's Evidence' [1992] *Criminal Law Review* 262 (This contains many references to other useful material.)

R Bull, 'Obtaining Evidence Expertly: The Reliability of Interviews with Child Witnesses' (1992) 1 *Expert Evidence* 5

G Davies, C Wilson, R Mitchell and J Milsom, *Videotaping Children's Evidence: An Evaluation* (1995)

H Dent and R Flin (eds), *Children as Witnesses* (1992)

J Plotnikoff and R Woolfson, *Prosecuting Child Abuse: An Evaluation of the Government's Speedy Progress Policy* (1995)

Report of the Advisory Group on Video Evidence (1989)

A J Solnit, 'Truth Telling: The Child as Witness' (1994) 2 *International Journal of Children's Rights* 61

J R Spencer and R H Flin, *The Evidence of Children: The Law and the Psychology* (2nd ed 1993)

4

THE COURSE OF EVIDENCE

1. THE ADVERSARIAL TRADITION

The Anglo-American model of the trial process is *adversarial* in nature. This is to be distinguished from the *inquisitorial* model, which is that which has traditionally operated in Continental European jurisdictions. The essential difference between the two systems is described by Damaška as follows:

> The adversarial mode of proceeding takes its shape from a contest or a dispute: it unfolds as an engagement of two adversaries before a relatively passive decision maker whose principal duty is to reach a verdict. The nonadversarial mode is structured as an official inquiry. Under the first system, the two adversaries take charge of most procedural action; under the second, officials perform most activities.[1]

The Runciman Royal Commission on Criminal Justice described the differences between criminal procedure in adversarial and inquisitorial jurisdictions thus:

Extract 4.1.1

Royal Commission on Criminal Justice, *Report* (1993) 3

11. The criminal justice system of England and Wales, in common with other jurisdictions which have evolved within the 'Anglo-Saxon' or 'common law' tradition, is often categorised as 'adversarial'. This is in contrast to the so-called 'inquisitorial' system based on the 'Continental' or 'civil law' tradition. In this context, the term 'adversarial' is usually taken to mean the system which has the judge as an umpire who leaves the presentation of the case to the parties (prosecution and defence) on each side. These separately prepare their case and call, examine and cross-examine their witnesses. The term 'inquisitorial' describes the systems where judges may supervise the pre-trial preparation of the evidence by the police and, more important, play a major part in the presentation of the evidence at trial. The judge in 'inquisitorial' systems typically calls and examines the defendant and the witnesses while the lawyers for the prosecution and the defence ask supplementary questions.

[1] M R Damaška, *The Faces of Justice and State Authority: A Comparative Approach to the Legal Process* (1986) 3.

12. It is important not to overstate the differences between the two systems: all adversarial systems contain inquisitorial elements, and vice versa.

See also N Jörg, S Field and C Brants, 'Are Inquisitorial and Adversarial Systems Converging?' in P Fennell, C Harding, N Jörg and B Swart (eds), *Criminal Justice in Europe: A Comparative Study* (1995); J H Langbein, 'Historical Foundations of the Law of Evidence: A View from the Ryder Sources' (1996) 96 *Columbia Law Review* 1168, 1168–9; J F Nijboer, 'Common Law Tradition in Evidence Scholarship Observed from a Continental Perspective' (1993) 41 *American Journal of Comparative Law* 299; J McEwan, *Evidence and the Adversarial Process: The Modern Law* (1992) Ch 1; M Zander, *Cases and Materials on the English Legal System* (7th ed 1996) 283–300.

In this chapter, we examine the rules governing the presentation of a case in court. We shall see how 'adversarial' notions of justice have shaped many of these rules. We shall also see, however, that the commitment of English law to such notions is far from absolute.

The trial is the showpiece of legal proceedings in Anglo-American jurisdictions. This is especially so in the criminal sphere:

Extract 4.1.2

J McEwan, *Evidence and the Adversarial Process: The Modern Law* (1992) 13–14

The theatricality of the English criminal trial might be regarded as one of its most attractive features by those who do not find themselves unwilling participants in it. The traditional dress of the advocates is designed to impress witnesses with the solemnity of the occasion, on the assumption that they are more likely to be truthful in such a setting. There is, however, no evidence that different settings affect the reliability of witnesses ... They are required to stand in a special witness-box and asked to speak up so that the jury can hear them. The accused is placed dramatically in a separate cage, the dock, whereas in some jurisdictions, such as Sweden, he or she sits at a desk.

Orality is one principal feature of the adversarial model. Heavy reliance is placed in the Anglo-American trial process, and particularly in criminal trials, on the oral testimony of witnesses. There are said to be substantial benefits associated with having witnesses testify publicly in open court. It is said, in particular, that observation of a witness's demeanour provides a good indication of the reliability of his or her testimony.

All of us know that, in every-day life, the way a man behaves when he tells a story – his intonations, his fidgetings or composure, his yawns, the use of his eyes, his air of candor or of evasiveness – may furnish valuable clues to his reliability. Such clues are by no means impeccable guides, but they are often immensely helpful.[2]

---

[2] J Frank, *Courts on Trial: Myth and Reality in American Justice* (1950) 21.

The assumption, then, is that a person's demeanour while stating a fact provides valuable clues as to whether he or she is being truthful, whether he or she perceived the fact correctly, and whether his or her memory is functioning effectively. The extent, however, to which this assumption actually reflects reality is a matter of considerable speculation. Wellborn, an American commentator, has presented an impressive body of experimental evidence relating to the utility of demeanour in indicating unreliability.[3] By and large, the experimental research has revealed that demeanour is of little benefit to ordinary observers in assessing whether a person is untruthful. First, observation of facial behaviour appears to be of little value, and there is indeed some evidence which suggests that such observation actually *decreases* the accuracy of lie detection. Secondly, little assistance would appear to be gained from listening to the voice of the respondent, as subjects who merely read transcripts performed just as well as, or even better than, those who heard recordings of the respondent's voice. Finally, there is no compelling evidence that lying is accompanied by distinctive body behaviour which can be discerned by observers.[4] The experimental research has also revealed that demeanour may be of even less assistance in the assessment of the accuracy of a person's perceptions and memory.[5] Thus Wellborn concludes that, consistently, the experiments have demonstrated that the capacity of ordinary people to detect unreliability by observing demeanour is simply a myth.[6] What reforms, then, may it be desirable to introduce?

Extract 4.1.3

L Re, 'Oral v Written Evidence: The Myth of the "Impressive Witness"' (1983) 57 *Australian Law Journal* 679, 689

Since the trial procedure plays an important ceremonial part in the public ritual of judging an offender and setting him apart from law-abiding members of society, it does not seem desirable to advocate its radical revision. Nevertheless, there does appear to be scope for significant reform and modernisation of the techniques currently used for gathering evidence and tendering it to the court. In particular, evidence should be obtained as soon as possible after the event in question in order to ensure greater accuracy. A proposal to introduce a pre-trial procedure in which a neutral official is vested with the power to elicit

---

[3] O G Wellborn III, 'Demeanor' (1991) 76 *Cornell Law Review* 1075. See also J Allan, 'The Working and Rationale of the Hearsay Rule and the Implications of Modern Psychological Knowledge' (1991) 44 *Current Legal Problems* 217, 225–6; L Re, 'Oral v Written Evidence: The Myth of the "Impressive Witness"' (1983) 57 *Australian Law Journal* 679; J R Spencer, 'Orality and the Evidence of Absent Witnesses' [1994] *Criminal Law Review* 628, 637.

[4] See the summary in O G Wellborn III, 'Demeanor' (1991) 76 *Cornell Law Review* 1075, 1088. For details see ibid 1078–88. See also M Stone, 'Instant Lie Detection? Demeanour and Credibility in Criminal Trials' [1991] *Criminal Law Review* 821; P Ekman, *Telling Lies: Clues to Deceit in the Marketplace, Politics, and Marriage* (1992) 291–2.

[5] O G Wellborn III, 'Demeanor' (1991) 76 *Cornell Law Review* 1075, 1088–91.

[6] At 1104.

the story of a witness and record it in advance may be of assistance in achieving the goal of accurate fact-finding. Modern technological aids such as audio and video recording may be useful in this task. Similarly, obtaining an expert's testimony prior to the trial may assist counsel in establishing the facts and may expedite the proceedings. On the other hand, such a change would represent a significant step away from the traditional procedure with its adversary features and surprise tactics. It remains to be seen whether common lawyers would be in favour of such innovative moves, notwithstanding the benefits which could be achieved.

2. THE COURSE OF THE TRIAL

In a trial, the case for the prosecution (in a criminal trial) or plaintiff (in a civil trial) is presented first. Thus, the plaintiff or prosecution calls its witnesses and questions them. This process of questioning one's own witnesses is known as *examination-in-chief*. After a particular witness has been examined in chief, he or she may then be questioned by any of the other parties in the case. This process of questioning witnesses called by another party is known as *cross-examination*. After cross-examination, the witness may be subjected to a re-examination by the party calling him or her. After all the witnesses for the plaintiff/prosecution have been called, the case for the plaintiff/prosecution is closed, and the defence then presents its case by calling its own witnesses. In the same way, each witness is examined in chief, and may then be cross-examined and re-examined. After the defence case is closed, closing speeches are made by counsel for all the parties in the case, and, in a criminal trial on indictment, the trial judge then sums up the case to the jury. In the course of this summing-up, the jury may have to be instructed about a number of the evidential issues which have arisen in the case. As will be seen in the course of this book, alleged misdirections to the jury on such issues provide a fertile ground of appeal.

After the closure of the case for the plaintiff/prosecution, and before defence has started to call its witnesses, a submission of no case to answer may be made by the defence. The relevant principles applicable in criminal trials on indictment were clarified in the following case:

Extract 4.2.1

R v Galbraith [1981] 1 WLR 1039, 1040, 1042 (CA)

LORD LANE CJ: We are told that some doubt exists as to the proper approach to be adopted by the judge at the close of the prosecution case upon a submission of 'no case' . . .

There are two schools of thought: (1) that the judge should stop the case if, in his view, it would be unsafe (alternatively unsafe or unsatisfactory) for the jury to convict; (2) that he should do so only if there is no evidence upon which a jury properly directed could properly convict. Although in many cases the question is one of semantics, and though in many cases each test would produce the same result, this is not necessarily so. A balance has to be struck between on the one hand a usurpation by the judge of the jury's functions and on the other the danger of an unjust conviction.

...

How then should the judge approach a submission of 'no case'? (1) If there is no evidence that the crime alleged has been committed by the defendant, there is no difficulty. The judge will of course stop the case. (2) The difficulty arises where there is some evidence but it is of a tenuous character, for example because of inherent weakness or vagueness or because it is inconsistent with other evidence. (a) Where the judge comes to the conclusion that the prosecution evidence, taken at its highest, is such that a jury properly directed could not properly convict upon it, it is his duty, upon a submission being made, to stop the case. (b) Where however the prosecution evidence is such that its strength or weakness depends on the view to be taken of a witness's reliability, or other matters which are generally speaking within the province of the jury and where on one possible view of the facts there *is* evidence upon which a jury could properly come to the conclusion that the defendant is guilty, then the judge should allow the matter to be tried by the jury. It follows that we think the second of the two schools of thought is to be preferred.

There will of course, as always in this branch of the law, be borderline cases. They can safely be left to the discretion of the judge.

See generally R Pattenden, 'The Submission of No Case – Some Recent Developments' [1982] *Criminal Law Review* 558. It is to be noted that the *Crown Court Study* found that submissions of no case to answer were made in just under one-third of cases, and that 27% of these submissions were successful.[7]

The importance of the existence of such a judicial controlling power is well illustrated by the decision of the Court of Appeal in *R v McKenzie*,[8] examined in Chapter 8. Is, however, the test in *Galbraith* sufficiently wide? Why should it be impermissible for a trial judge to withdraw a case from the jury in circumstances where, if the defendant were to be convicted and were to appeal, the Court of Appeal would be bound to quash the conviction?[9] The Runciman Royal Commission 'recommend[ed] that the Court of Appeal's decision in *Galbraith* be reversed so that a judge may stop any case if he or she takes the view that the prosecution evidence is demonstrably unsafe or unsatisfactory or too weak to be allowed to go to the jury'.[10] Would this be a desirable development in the law? It may be that the *Galbraith* test is, in any event, so flexible that it already enables trial judges to reach decisions on

---

[7] M Zander and P Henderson, *The Royal Commission on Criminal Justice: Crown Court Study* (1993) 124–5.
[8] [1993] 1 WLR 453.
[9] See generally A A S Zuckerman, *The Principles of Criminal Evidence* (1989) 56–8.
[10] Royal Commission on Criminal Justice, *Report* (Cm 2263) (1993) 59.

whether to stop cases in accordance with their own sense of what is required in the interests of justice in the particular case:

> To some extent the matter may be one of semantics. If the judge thinks that the case should be stopped, he will stop it, and he will say that there is no evidence, or no evidence capable of belief. If the judge is not prepared to stop the case, he will reject the submission of no case and say that the matter is one of credibility and weight for the jury.[11]

In the following case, some procedural issues relating to submissions of no case to answer in jury trials were considered by the Privy Council.

Extract 4.2.2

Crosdale v R [1995] 1 WLR 864, 871–3 (PC)

LORD STEYN: . . . the Court of Appeal [of Jamaica] . . . certif[ied] four questions for their Lordships' consideration. The first three questions are general and read as follows:

> '(i) Whether there are any circumstances in which a no case submission should be made in the presence of the jury. (ii) Whether where the defence applies to make a no case submission in the absence of the jury it is right for a judge to refuse the application and to hear the submission in the presence of the jury. (iii) Whether where the defence applies to make a no case submission in the absence of the jury it is right for a judge to inform the jury of his finding that there is a case to answer.'

It is to the first two questions that their Lordships must now turn.

A judge and a jury have separate but complementary functions in a jury trial. The judge has a supervisory role. Thus the judge carries out a filtering process to decide what evidence is to be placed before the jury. Pertinent to the present appeal is another aspect of the judge's supervisory role: the judge may be required to consider whether the prosecution has produced sufficient evidence to justify putting the issue to the jury. Lord Devlin in 'Trial by Jury, The Hamlyn Lectures,' 8th Series (1956 republished in 1988), aptly illustrated the separate roles of the judge and jury. He said, at p 64:

> 'there is in truth a fundamental difference between the question whether there is any evidence and the question whether there is *enough* evidence. I can best illustrate the difference by an analogy. Whether a rope will bear a certain weight and take a certain strain is a question that practical men often have to determine by using their judgment based on their experience. But they base their judgment on the assumption that the rope is what it seems to the eye to be and that it has no concealed defects. It is the business of the manufacturer of the rope to test it, strand by strand if necessary, before he sends it out to see that it has no flaw; that is a job for an expert. It is the business of the judge as the expert who has a mind

---

[11] A Samuels, 'No Case to Answer: The Judge Must Stop the Case: *Galbraith*', *Archbold News*, 14 November 1996, 6, 6.

trained to make examinations of the sort to test the chain of evidence for the weak links before he sends it out to the jury; in other words, it is for him to ascertain whether it has any reliable strength at all and then for the jury to determine how strong it is. . . . The trained mind is the better instrument for detecting flaws in reasoning; but if it can be made sure that the jury handles only solid argument and not sham, the pooled experience of 12 men is the better instrument for arriving at a just verdict. Thus logic and common sense are put together to make the verdict.'

The important point is that the jury cannot assist the judge in his decision as to whether there is sufficient evidence for the judge to place the case before the jury. That part of the proceedings is conducted by the judge alone. And the jury has no interest in that part of the proceedings. There is also no sensible reason why the jury should witness that part of the proceedings. On the contrary, there are substantial reasons why in the interests of an effective and fair determination of the issue whether the defendant has a case to answer the jury should be asked to withdraw. If the jury do not withdraw, there is a risk that they will be influenced by what they hear. In recent times the invariable practice in England has been for the judge to ask the jury to withdraw while such an application is considered by him. The foundation of this practice is to protect the interests of the defendant. It cannot be left to a general discretion of the judge to decide in which cases the jury should be asked to withdraw since it is impossible to predict in advance when a risk of prejudice will arise. In any event, there is no legitimate advantage to be gained by allowing the jury to remain. Moreover, if the jury is asked to withdraw, the submissions of counsel and the testing of the submissions by the judge's questions need not be inhibited. For these reasons their Lordships' response is that irrespective of whether the defence ask for the jury to withdraw or not the judge should invite the jury to withdraw during submissions that a defendant does not have a case to answer. All the jury needs to be told is that a legal matter has arisen on which the ruling of the judge is sought. . . . And their Lordships' ruling applies equally to the trial of a single defendant and joint trial.

It is necessary to refer to one possible qualification which was mentioned in argument. Counsel suggested that the defence may sometimes invite the judge to rule that the jury should remain. If that were to happen, the judge ought to ask the jury to withdraw to hear submissions why he should depart from the ordinary procedure. Their Lordships are sceptical about how realistic the suggestion is that the defence might have a legitimate reason for requesting such a ruling. Certainly, if the defence sought to gain a tactical advantage by making an extra speech before the jury that would not be a legitimate reason for departing from the ordinary practice. Their Lordships are, however, content to assume that in exceptional circumstances the defence might have legitimate reasons for such a request and to leave this point on the basis that the judge in the absence of the jury will hear argument and exercise his discretion on the point. For avoidance of doubt, and since the practice that the jury should withdraw exists for the protection of the defendant, their Lordships make clear that a judge should never entertain a request by the prosecution that the jury should not withdraw.

That brings their Lordships to the third question, namely whether the jury should be present during the judgment on the application that the defendant has no case to answer or whether the jury should subsequently be informed of the judge's reasons for his decision. There is no reason why the jury should be privy to the judge's reasons for his decision. In order to avoid any risk of prejudice to the defendant the jury should not be present during the course of the judgment or be told what the judge's reasons were. If the judge rejects a submission of no case, the jury need know nothing about his decision. No explanation is required. If the judge rules in favour of such a submission on some charges but not on others, or rules in favour of it in respect of some defendants but not others, the jury inevitably will know about the decision. All the jury need then to be told by the judge is that he took his decision for legal reasons. Any further explanation will risk potential prejudice to a defendant or defendants.

The principles applicable to submissions of no case in summary trials were clarified in the following *Practice Direction*:

Extract 4.2.3

Practice Direction (Submission of No Case) [1962] 1 WLR 227, 227 (DC)

LORD PARKER CJ: Without attempting to lay down any principle of law, we think that as a matter of practice justices should be guided by the following considerations.

A submission that there is no case to answer may properly be made and upheld: (a) when there has been no evidence to prove an essential element in the alleged offence; (b) when the evidence adduced by the prosecution has been so discredited as a result of cross-examination or is so manifestly unreliable that no reasonable tribunal could safely convict upon it.

Apart from these two situations a tribunal should not in general be called upon to reach a decision as to conviction or acquittal until the whole of the evidence which either side wishes to tender has been placed before it. If however a submission is made that there is no case to answer, the decision should depend not so much on whether the adjudicating tribunal (if compelled to do so) would at that stage convict or acquit but on whether the evidence is such that a reasonable tribunal might convict. If a reasonable tribunal might convict on the evidence so far laid before it, there is a case to answer.

In civil trials without a jury, the position is as follows:

Extract 4.2.4

Alexander v Rayson [1936] 1 KB 169, 178 (CA)

ROMER LJ: Where an action is being heard by a jury it is, of course, quite usual and often very convenient at the end of the case of the plaintiff, or of the party having the onus of proof, . . . for the opposing party to ask for the ruling of the judge whether there is any case to go to the jury, who are the only judges of fact. It also seems to be not unusual in the King's Bench Division to ask for a similar ruling in actions tried by a judge alone. We think, however, that this is highly inconvenient. For the judge in such cases is also the judge of fact, and we cannot think it right that the judge of fact should be asked to express any opinion upon the evidence until the evidence is completed. Certainly no one would ever dream of asking a jury at the end of a plaintiff's case to say what verdict they would be prepared to give if the defendant called no evidence, and we fail to see why a judge should be asked such a question in cases where he and not a jury is the judge that has to determine the facts. In such cases we venture to think that the responsibility for not calling rebutting evidence should be upon the other party's counsel and upon no one else.

See also *Laurie v Raglan Building Co*;[12] *Young v Rank*.[13]

3. ADDUCING EVIDENCE

(a) Civil proceedings

(i) Pre-trial procedure

The current system of pre-trial procedure in civil proceedings is described succinctly in the following extract:

Extract 4.3.1

**R Bagshaw, *Cross and Wilkins: Outline of the Law of Evidence*
(1996) 3–4**

Before the trial, pleadings are exchanged between the parties. These are intended to clarify the issues. The plaintiff serves the defendant with a 'statement of claim', setting out the facts upon which he relies and the relief which he claims. The defendant counters with his 'defence', a document which he serves on the plaintiff. Generally speaking, facts which are not denied in the defence are deemed to be admitted. The defence may consist of a bare denial of the whole or large parts of the statement of claim, but it may also allege other facts upon which the defendant proposes to rely. Further pleadings may be necessary, but, in many cases, the issues are sufficiently clarified by the statement of claim and defence. A perusal of these documents will often show what facts have to be proved.

After the pleadings are closed, lists of documents are exchanged between the parties. These lists enumerate the documents, relevant to the case, which each party has in its possession. The lists may refer to documents, and yet

---

[12] [1942] 1 KB 152.
[13] [1950] 2 KB 510.

claim privilege from producing them . . . Subject to possible claims of privilege [or public interest immunity], the documents mentioned in the lists are produced for inspection by the opposite party, and copies may be taken. The whole process of the exchange of lists of documents and inspection is called 'discovery'. The object of discovery is partly to prevent one party being surprised by the production of a document at the trial, partly to allow a party access to evidence which may further support its claim, and partly to allow the parties to assess the strength of the opposing cases, in order to facilitate an out-of-court settlement.

From time to time, it may be necessary for the parties to resort to the court for an order to produce a document for inspection. This might happen when a claim to privilege is disputed . . . Applications to the courts for orders in connection with pleadings and discovery are called 'interlocutory' applications.

(ii) Calling witnesses

Does the judge in a civil trial have the power to call witnesses? Is there any particular order in which witnesses should be called in a civil trial?

Extract 4.3.2

Re Enoch and Zaretzky, Bock & Co [1910] 1 KB 327, 333 (CA)

FLETCHER MOULTON LJ: . . . in my opinion it is certainly not the law, that a judge, or any person in a judicial position, such as an arbitrator, has any power himself to call witnesses to fact against the will of either of the parties.

Extract 4.3.3

Briscoe v Briscoe [1968] P 501, 505 (P, D & A)

LANE J: It seems to me to be a matter of quite fundamental importance that counsel should retain the right, which I have always understood them to have, to choose what witnesses to call and in what order.

(b) Criminal proceedings

(i) Pre-trial disclosure

In criminal litigation, the importance of pre-trial disclosure by the prosecution of certain relevant material, in order that the defence is not taken by surprise at trial, cannot be overemphasised. It has been acknowledged by the Court of Appeal that 'in our adversarial system, in which the police and prosecution control the investigatory process, an accused's right to fair disclosure is an inseparable part of his right to a fair trial'.[14] The court has also observed that 'non-disclosure [by the prosecution] is a potent source of injustice and even with the benefit of hindsight, it will often be difficult to say whether or not an undisclosed item of evidence might have shifted the balance or opened up a new line of defence'.[15] Thus, despite the traditional notion of a criminal trial as an adversarial contest between prosecution and defence, the common law evolved a general requirement that the prosecution make pre-trial disclosure to the defence of certain broad categories of material. There was no corresponding common law duty of disclosure on the defence. The main disclosure obligations of the prosecution and defence in a criminal trial are now encapsulated in the following provisions of the Criminal Procedure and Investigations Act 1996:

Extract 4.3.4

**Criminal Procedure and Investigations Act 1996,
ss 1, 3, 5, 6, 7, 8, 9, 10, 11**

1. Application of this Part
(1) This Part applies where –
  (a) a person is charged with a summary offence in respect of which a court proceeds to summary trial and in respect of which he pleads not guilty,
  (b) a person who has attained the age of 18 is charged with an offence which is triable either way, in respect of which a court proceeds to summary trial and in respect of which he pleads not guilty, or
  (c) a person under the age of 18 is charged with an indictable offence in respect of which a court proceeds to summary trial and in respect of which he pleads not guilty.
(2) This Part also applies where –
  (a) a person is charged with an indictable offence and he is committed for trial for the offence concerned,
  (b) a person is charged with an indictable offence and proceedings for the trial of the person on the charge concerned are transferred to the Crown Court by virtue of a notice of transfer given under section 4 of the Criminal Justice Act 1987 (serious or complex fraud),
  (c) a person is charged with an indictable offence and proceedings for the trial of the person on the charge concerned are transferred to the Crown Court by virtue of a notice of transfer served on a magistrates' court under section 53 of the Criminal Justice Act 1991 (certain cases involving children),
  (d) a count charging a person with a summary offence is included in an indictment under the authority of section 40 of the Criminal Justice Act 1988 (common assault etc), or

---

[14] *R v Brown (Winston)* [1994] 1 WLR 1599, 1606. Similar sentiments were expressed when the case reached the House of Lords: *R v Brown (Winston)* [1997] 3 WLR 447.
[15] *R v Ward* [1993] 2 All ER 577, 599.

(e) a bill of indictment charging a person with an indictable offence is preferred under the authority of section 2(2)(b) of the Administration of Justice (Miscellaneous Provisions) Act 1933 (bill preferred by direction of Court of Appeal, or by direction or with consent of a judge).

. . .

3. Primary disclosure by prosecutor

(1) The prosecutor must –

(a) disclose to the accused any prosecution material which has not previously been disclosed to the accused and which in the prosecutor's opinion might undermine the case for the prosecution against the accused, or

(b) give to the accused a written statement that there is no material of a description mentioned in paragraph (a).

(2) For the purposes of this section prosecution material is material –

(a) which is in the prosecutor's possession, and came into his possession in connection with the case for the prosecution against the accused, or

(b) which, in pursuance of a code operative under Part II, he has inspected in connection with the case for the prosecution against the accused.

. . .

(6) Material must not be disclosed under this section to the extent that the court, on an application by the prosecutor, concludes it is not in the public interest to disclose it and orders accordingly.

(7) Material must not be disclosed under this section to the extent that –

(a) it has been intercepted in obedience to a warrant issued under section 2 of the Interception of Communications Act 1985, or

(b) it indicates that such a warrant has been issued or that material has been intercepted in obedience to such a warrant.

(8) The prosecutor must act under this section during the period which, by virtue of section 12, is the relevant period for this section.

5. Compulsory disclosure by accused

(1) Subject to subsections (2) to (4), this section applies where –

(a) this Part applies by virtue of section 1(2), and

(b) the prosecutor complies with section 3 or purports to comply with it.

. . .

(5) Where this section applies, the accused must give a defence statement to the court and the prosecutor.

(6) For the purposes of this section a defence statement is a written statement –

(a) setting out in general terms the nature of the accused's defence,

(b) indicating the matters on which he takes issue with the prosecution, and

(c) setting out, in the case of each such matter, the reason why he takes issue with the prosecution.

(7) If the defence statement discloses an alibi the accused must give particulars of the alibi in the statement, including –

(a) the name and address of any witness the accused believes is able to give evidence in support of the alibi, if the name and address are known to the accused when the statement is given;

(b) any information in the accused's possession which might be of material assistance in finding any such witness, if his name or address is not known to the accused when the statement is given.

(8) For the purposes of this section evidence in support of an alibi is evidence tending to show that by reason of the presence of the accused at a particular place or in a particular area at a particular time he was not, or was unlikely to have been, at the place where the offence is alleged to have been committed at the time of its alleged commission.

(9) The accused must give a defence statement under this section during the period which, by virtue of section 12, is the relevant period for this section.

6. Voluntary disclosure by accused

(1) This section applies where –
  (a) this Part applies by virtue of section 1(1), and
  (b) the prosecutor complies with section 3 or purports to comply with it.

(2) The accused –
  (a) may give a defence statement to the prosecutor, and
  (b) if he does so, must also give such a statement to the court.

(3) Subsections (6) to (8) of section 5 apply for the purposes of this section as they apply for the purposes of that.

(4) If the accused gives a defence statement under this section he must give it during the period which, by virtue of section 12, is the relevant period for this section.

7. Secondary disclosure by prosecutor

(1) This section applies where the accused gives a defence statement under section 5 or 6.

(2) The prosecutor must –
  (a) disclose to the accused any prosecution material which has not previously been disclosed to the accused and which might be reasonably expected to assist the accused's defence as disclosed by the defence statement given under section 5 or 6, or
  (b) give to the accused a written statement that there is no material of a description mentioned in paragraph (a).

(3) For the purposes of this section prosecution material is material –
  (a) which is in the prosecutor's possession and came into his possession in connection with the case for the prosecution against the accused, or
  (b) which, in pursuance of a code operative under Part II, he has inspected in connection with the case for the prosecution against the accused.

. . .

(5) Material must not be disclosed under this section to the extent that the court, on an application by the prosecutor, concludes it is not in the public interest to disclose it and orders accordingly.

(6) Material must not be disclosed under this section to the extent that –

(a) it has been intercepted in obedience to a warrant issued under section 2 of the Interception of Communications Act 1985, or

(b) it indicates that such a warrant has been issued or that material has been intercepted in obedience to such a warrant.

(7) The prosecutor must act under this section during the period which, by virtue of section 12, is the relevant period for this section.

8. Application by accused for disclosure

(1) This section applies where the accused gives a defence statement under section 5 or 6 and the prosecutor complies with section 7 or purports to comply with it or fails to comply with it.

(2) If the accused has at any time reasonable cause to believe that –

(a) there is prosecution material which might be reasonably expected to assist the accused's defence as disclosed by the defence statement given under section 5 or 6, and

(b) the material has not been disclosed to the accused,

the accused may apply to the court for an order requiring the prosecutor to disclose such material to the accused.

(3) For the purposes of this section prosecution material is material –

(a) which is in the prosecutor's possession and came into his possession in connection with the case for the prosecution against the accused,

(b) which, in pursuance of a code operative under Part II, he has inspected in connection with the case for the prosecution against the accused, or

(c) which falls within subsection (4).

(4) Material falls within this subsection if in pursuance of a code operative under Part II the prosecutor must, if he asks for the material, be given a copy of it or be allowed to inspect it in connection with the case for the prosecution against the accused.

(5) Material must not be disclosed under this section to the extent that the court, on an application by the prosecutor, concludes it is not in the public interest to disclose it and orders accordingly.

(6) Material must not be disclosed under this section to the extent that –

(a) it has been intercepted in obedience to a warrant issued under section 2 of the Interception of Communications Act 1985, or

(b) it indicates that such a warrant has been issued or that material has been intercepted in obedience to such a warrant.

9. Continuing duty of prosecutor to disclose

(1) Subsection (2) applies at all times –

(a) after the prosecutor complies with section 3 or purports to comply with it, and

(b) before the accused is acquitted or convicted or the prosecutor decides not to proceed with the case concerned.

(2) The prosecutor must keep under review the question whether at any given time there is prosecution material which –

(a) in his opinion might undermine the case for the prosecution against the accused, and

(b) has not been disclosed to the accused;

and if there is such material at any time the prosecutor must disclose it to the accused as soon as is reasonably practicable.

(3) In applying subsection (2) by reference to any given time the state of affairs at that time (including the case for the prosecution as it stands at that time) must be taken into account.

(4) Subsection (5) applies at all times –

(a) after the prosecutor complies with section 7 or purports to comply with it, and

(b) before the accused is acquitted or convicted or the prosecutor decides not to proceed with the case concerned.

(5) The prosecutor must keep under review the question whether at any given time there is prosecution material which –

(a) might be reasonably expected to assist the accused's defence as disclosed by the defence statement given under section 5 or 6, and

(b) has not been disclosed to the accused;

and if there is such material at any time the prosecutor must disclose it to the accused as soon as is reasonably practicable.

(6) For the purposes of this section prosecution material is material –

(a) which is in the prosecutor's possession and came into his possession in connection with the case for the prosecution against the accused, or

(b) which, in pursuance of a code operative under Part II, he has inspected in connection with the case for the prosecution against the accused.

. . .

(8) Material must not be disclosed under this section to the extent that the court, on an application by the prosecutor, concludes it is not in the public interest to disclose it and orders accordingly.

(9) Material must not be disclosed under this section to the extent that –

(a) it has been intercepted in obedience to a warrant issued under section 2 of the Interception of Communications Act 1985, or

(b) it indicates that such a warrant has been issued or that material has been intercepted in obedience to such a warrant.

10. Prosecutor's failure to observe time limits

(1) This section applies if the prosecutor –

(a) purports to act under section 3 after the end of the period which, by virtue of section 12, is the relevant period for section 3, or

(b) purports to act under section 7 after the end of the period which, by virtue of section 12, is the relevant period for section 7.

(2) Subject to subsection (3), the failure to act during the period concerned does not on its own constitute grounds for staying the proceedings for abuse of process.

(3) Subsection (2) does not prevent the failure constituting such grounds if it involves such delay by the prosecutor that the accused is denied a fair trial.

11. Faults in disclosure by accused

(1) This section applies where section 5 applies and the accused –

(a) fails to give a defence statement under that section,

(b) gives a defence statement under that section but does so after the end of the period which, by virtue of section 12, is the relevant period for section 5,

(c) sets out inconsistent defences in a defence statement given under section 5,

(d) at his trial puts forward a defence which is different from any defence set out in a defence statement given under section 5,

(e) at his trial adduces evidence in support of an alibi without having given particulars of the alibi in a defence statement given under section 5, or

(f) at his trial calls a witness to give evidence in support of an alibi without having complied with subsection (7)(a) or (b) of section 5 as regards the witness in giving a defence statement under that section.

(2) This section also applies where section 6 applies, the accused gives a defence statement under that section, and the accused –

(a) gives the statement after the end of the period which, by virtue of section 12, is the relevant period for section 6,

(b) sets out inconsistent defences in the statement,

(c) at his trial puts forward a defence which is different from any defence set out in the statement,

(d) at his trial adduces evidence in support of an alibi without having given particulars of the alibi in the statement, or

(e) at his trial calls a witness to give evidence in support of an alibi without having complied with subsection (7)(a) or (b) of section 5 (as applied by section 6) as regards the witness in giving the statement.

(3) Where this section applies –

(a) the court or, with the leave of the court, any other party may make such comment as appears appropriate;

(b) the court or jury may draw such inferences as appear proper in deciding whether the accused is guilty of the offence concerned.

(4) Where the accused puts forward a defence which is different from any defence set out in a defence statement given under section 5 or 6, in doing anything under subsection (3) or in deciding whether to do anything under it the court shall have regard –

(a) to the extent of the difference in the defences, and

(b) to whether there is any justification for it.

(5) A person shall not be convicted of an offence solely on an inference drawn under subsection (3).

(6) Any reference in this section to evidence in support of an alibi shall be construed in accordance with section 5.

Discussions of the above provisions may be found in K Browne, 'Primed, Stated and Seconded' (1997) 141 *Solicitors Journal* 336; 'Criminal Procedure and Investigations Act 1996', *Archbold News*, 15 August 1996, 5; R Leng and R D Taylor, *Blackstone's Guide to the Criminal Procedure and Investigations Act 1996* (1996); N Purnell, 'A Brief Guide to Part 1 of the Criminal Procedure and Investigations Act 1996', *Archbold News*, 10 February 1997, 4; M Redmayne, 'Process Gains and Process Values: The Criminal Procedure and Investigations Act 1996' (1997) 60 *Modern Law Review* 79; J Sprack, 'The Criminal Procedure and Investigations Act 1996: (1) The Duty of Disclosure' [1997] *Criminal Law Review* 308. As the provisions indicate, there are essentially three steps in the new scheme of disclosure prescribed by the Act for trials on indictment:

(1) Primary disclosure by the prosecution.
(2) Compulsory disclosure by the defence.
(3) Secondary disclosure by the prosecution.

The following pithy summary of the effect of this scheme is provided by Leng and Taylor:

> ... the new scheme ... aims [in particular] for efficiency by clarifying and narrowing issues at the earliest opportunity, and seeks the conviction of the guilty by preventing ambush defences. These aims are pursued by rationing the defendant's access to the fruits of state investigations and by a carrot and stick approach to encouraging early disclosure of the defence. The carrot is dangled by restricting initial access to prosecution material but with the promise of further disclosure of relevant material once a defence has been disclosed. The stick is the threat of adverse inferences to be drawn against a defendant who raises a defence in court which has not been previously disclosed.[16]

Writing on the disclosure obligations of the prosecution laid down in the Act, Zander notes:

Extract 4.3.5

**M Zander, *Cases and Materials on the English Legal System*
(7th ed 1996) 236**

Section 3(1) requires the prosecutor to disclose to the accused any prosecution material 'which *in the prosecutor's opinion* might undermine the case for the prosecution against the accused' (emphasis supplied), or alternatively to give the accused a written statement that there is no material of that description. (Attempts in both the House of Lords and the Commons to get Ministers to accept that this subjective test should be changed to an objective test were unsuccessful.)

This is to be compared with the definition of what the Lord Chief Justice in [*R v Keane* [1994] 2 All ER 478, 484] said had to be disclosed at common law: 'material which on a sensible appraisal was judged (1) to be relevant or possibly relevant to an issue in the case; or (2) to raise or possibly raise a new issue whose existence is not apparent from the evidence the prosecution propose to use; or (3) to hold a real (as opposed to fanciful) prospect of

---

[16] R Leng and R D Taylor, *Blackstone's Guide to the Criminal Procedure and Investigations Act 1996* (1996) 10.

providing a lead on evidence which goes to (1) or (2)'. In *R v Brown (Winston)* [1994] 1 WLR 1599 it was made clear that the phrase 'an issue in the case' must be given a broad rather than a narrow interpretation . . .

See also J Sprack, 'The Criminal Procedure and Investigations Act 1996: (1) The Duty of Disclosure' [1997] *Criminal Law Review* 308, 309. Do you consider, therefore, that the provisions of the Act on prosecutorial disclosure represent a substantial and unwarranted narrowing of the old common law position?

Criticism may also be levelled at the provisions of the Act relating to the disclosure obligations of the defence in trials on indictment. As Murray has written:

> In one fell swoop the defence has moved from having no [general] obligation of disclosure to having to reveal all. . . . It cannot be fair to demand a full defence to be served against the threat of adverse inference . . . , when the prosecution (against whom there is no sanction) has made incomplete disclosure.
>
> There appears to be no machinery available for the defendant to apply to the court for permission not to serve a defence statement on the grounds that it would be contrary to the interests of justice for him to do so. One can envisage instances where for example the defendant has been the victim of police malpractice, where to be required to disclose to the prosecution such wrongdoing would severely damage the effectiveness of such a defence and possibly threaten the existence of evidence.[17]

What is also notable is that s 5 makes disclosure compulsory for the accused even where the prosecution simply *purports* to comply with its obligation to make primary disclosure.

A number of justifications were put forward by proponents of the introduction of a general defence obligation to make pre-trial disclosure:

> If all the parties had in advance an indication of what the defence would be, this would not only encourage earlier and better preparation of cases but might well result in the prosecution being dropped in the light of the defence disclosure, an earlier resolution through a plea of guilty, or the fixing of an earlier trial date. The length of the trial could also be more readily estimated, leading to a better use of the time both of the court and of those involved in the trial; and there would be kept to a minimum those cases where the defendant withholds his or her defence until the last possible moment in the hope of confusing the jury or evading investigation of a fabricated defence.[18]

It is the last point – concern that lack of a general obligation to make pre-trial disclosure could lead to 'ambush defences' being sprung at a late stage – which proved to be crucial to the decision to introduce such an obligation. In view, however, of the fact that ambush defences were by no means widespread,[19] the fundamental change in the law which was effected by the 1996 Act does not seem justified.

[17] C Murray, 'Fair is Foul and Foul is Fair' (1996) 146 *New Law Journal* 1288, 1290.
[18] Royal Commission on Criminal Justice, *Report* (Cm 2263) (1993) 97.
[19] At 98 n 29.

It is to be noted that, unless specifically repealed, any statutory provisions laying down disclosure obligations are preserved by the 1996 Act.[20] An important example is provided by the Crown Court (Advance Notice of Expert Evidence) Rules 1987, made pursuant to s 81 of the Police and Criminal Evidence Act 1984.

Extract 4.3.6

Crown Court (Advance Notice of Expert Evidence) Rules 1987, rr 3(1), (2), 5

3. – (1) Following –
- (a) the committal for trial of any person;
- (b) the transfer to the Crown Court of any proceedings for the trial of a person by virtue of a notice of transfer given under section 4 of the Criminal Justice Act 1987;
- (c) the transfer to the Crown Court of any proceedings for the trial of a person by virtue of a notice of transfer served on a magistrates' court under section 53 of the Criminal Justice Act 1991;
- (d) the preferment of a bill of indictment charging a person with an offence under the authority of section 2(2)(b) of the Administration of Justice (Miscellaneous Provisions) Act 1933; or
- (e) the making of an order for the retrial of any person,

if any party to the proceedings proposes to adduce expert evidence (whether of fact or opinion) in the proceedings (otherwise than in relation to sentence) he shall as soon as practicable, unless in relation to the evidence in question he has already done so –
- (i) furnish the other party or parties with a statement in writing of any finding or opinion which he proposes to adduce by way of such evidence; and
- (ii) where a request in writing is made to him in that behalf by any other party, provide that party also with a copy of (or if it appears to the party proposing to adduce the evidence to be more practicable, a reasonable opportunity to examine) the record of any observation, test, calculation or other procedure on which such finding or opinion is based and any document or other thing or substance in respect of which any such procedure has been carried out.

(2) A party may by notice in writing waive this right to be furnished with any of the matters mentioned in paragraph (1) above and, in particular, may agree that the statement mentioned ... may be furnished to him orally and not in writing.

5. A party who seeks to adduce expert evidence in any proceedings and who fails to comply with rule 3 above shall not adduce that evidence in those proceedings without the leave of the court.

---

[20] Section 20.

Analogous provisions have now been made in relation to summary trials by the Magistrates' Courts (Advance Notice of Expert Evidence) Rules 1997.

(ii) Prosecutorial obligation to call witnesses

Extract 4.3.7

R v Brown [1997] 1 Cr App R 112, 112–15 (CA)

SCHIEMANN LJ: It appears to be becoming increasingly popular for defence advocates to seek to appeal to this Court in cases where the main ground of appeal is that the judge wrongly refused to direct the prosecution to call or tender a witness whose statement had been included in the committal bundle. This ground of appeal is difficult to sustain, as cases such as *Russell-Jones* [1995] 1 Cr App R 538 show, because they involve asking this Court to review the exercise of the trial judge's discretion, in circumstances where the trial judge himself is reviewing the discretion of the prosecutor.

Submissions in support of this ground of appeal frequently involve citing cases decided long ago and they seldom succeed nowadays, where the defence had the opportunity of themselves calling the relevant witness. A lot of the early case law developed in times when the practice and procedures governing criminal trials were markedly different from those currently existing. In the past many, if not most defendants, on arraignment at Assizes or Quarter Sessions were unrepresented. If a defendant pleaded not guilty and was unable to afford a dock brief, the judge would normally nominate a member of the Bar in court to defend him. Only exceptionally would a solicitor be allocated, for example, if alibi witnesses had to be interviewed. In those days all committals were oral. Disclosure of unused material was a rarity.

Nowadays most defendants will have instructed solicitors on their arrest. Their solicitor will be present and giving advice during interview. There is full disclosure of all unused material well before trial, subject to any PII claim. In such cases the trial judge, before trial, sifts through the PII material, to decide what requires disclosure in the interests of justice. Before the date of arraignment the defence notify the court, the Crown and the probation service whether guilty pleas are expected. On arraignment, if 'not guilty' pleas are entered, a plea and directions hearing takes place, at which, before a Crown Court judge, the issues are defined, the defence is expected to disclose the nature of its defence, admissions are settled, directions given for exchange of expert evidence, witnesses to be called to give oral evidence on the part of the Crown are listed and other directions are given.

The reasoning behind, and indeed expressed in, the old practice of usually calling or tendering a witness named on the back of the indictment is that a failure to do so might result in an unfair trial. The requirement of fairness remains entirely as it was. What has changed in a way which may be relevant in some cases is the procedural ambience in which it has to be satisfied.

We consider that nowadays the primary time when a decision should be made as to whether the Crown should call a witness who, to a greater or lesser degree, may give evidence favourable to the defence is at the plea and directions hearing. Of course circumstances may change thereafter, in which case any decision would have to be reconsidered.

In our judgment:

(1) The prosecution have a discretion in deciding which witnesses it will rely on for the purpose of establishing a prima facie case, whether for committal proceedings or transfer, and will serve their statements accordingly. It must normally disclose any potentially material statement not served.

(2) Counsel for the prosecution must have at court all witnesses whose statements have been served, whether as part of the depositions or as additional evidence, upon whom he intends to rely, unless any such witness is conditionally bound or the defence agree that he need not attend because, for example, his evidence can be admitted.

(3) Counsel for the prosecution enjoys a discretion whether to call or to tender a particular witness whom he has required to attend. Further, counsel may refuse even to tender a witness, notwithstanding that the witness's statement has been included in the depositions, if he decides that the witness is unworthy of belief. Our adversarial system requires counsel for the prosecution to present a case against the defendant. He must always act in the interests of justice and to promote a fair trial, and his discretion must be exercised with these objects in mind. He should not refuse to call a witness merely because his evidence does not fit in exactly with the case he is seeking to prove. But he need not call a witness whose evidence is inconsistent with, or contrary to, the case he is prosecuting since such witnesses's evidence will be unworthy of belief if his case be correct.

(4) Counsel for the prosecution ought normally to call, or offer to call, all the witnesses who give direct evidence of the primary facts of the case unless the prosecutor regards the witness's evidence as unworthy of belief.

(5) It is for counsel for the prosecution to decide which witnesses give direct evidence of the primary facts of the case. He may reasonably take the view that what a particular witness has to say is, at best, marginal.

(6) Counsel for the prosecution is also the primary judge of whether or not a witness to the material events is unworthy of belief.

(7) Counsel for the prosecution, properly exercising his discretion, is not obliged to offer a witness upon whom the Crown does *not* rely merely in order to give the defence material with which to attack the credit of other witnesses on whom the Crown *does* rely. The law does not insist that the prosecution are obliged to call a witness for no purpose other than to assist the defence in its endeavours to destroy the Crown's own case. Such a course would merely serve to confuse a jury. The Crown's obligation is to make such witnesses available to the defence so that the defence can call them if they choose to do so. The jury will then be clear that evidence is led by the party who wishes to rely upon it and can be tested by cross-examination by the other party, if that party wishes to challenge the evidence.

When the Crown serves statements of witnesses on the defence it is an indication that the Crown, at that stage, wished to rely on those witnesses. But there can be a number of reasons why, by the time of the plea and directions hearing or the trial, the Crown no longer wishes to rely on one or more of those witnesses. We instance, by way of example only, a number of possible situations:

1. New evidence – for instance, fingerprint or DNA evidence – becomes available which makes it unnecessary to call persons who had an unsatisfactory view of the commission of the crime;

2. Better and clearer witnesses make themselves available after committal, so that there is no point in relying on a marginally helpful witness who previously was the best available;

3. The prosecution get to hear something which persuades them that the witness is unworthy of belief – that something may vary, from matters discreditable to that witness to an intervening blow on the head causing brain damage;

4. Counsel for the prosecution at trial takes a different view, as to the desirability of calling a witness as a witness of truth, from the view taken at the time of the preparation of the papers for committal.

In general, where the Crown have evidential material upon which they do not seek to rely, it should be made available to the defence and we can see no advantage in distinguishing at trial between those witnesses whom the Crown originally intended to call but in respect of whom the Crown has changed its mind and those whom it never intended to call. Occasionally a last minute change of mind by the Crown may deprive the defence of material which it would have gathered had it not thought that the Crown would call the relevant witness. In such cases, as in others, the Crown must always be alert to the possibility that a decision not to call a witness may not promote a fair trial.

Furthermore, the judge may grant an adjournment or exercise his powers under section 78 of the Police and Criminal Evidence Act 1984 and make appropriate orders if he is satisfied that any decision by counsel for the prosecution may result in unfairness to a defendant in a particular case. We repeat what this Court said in *Russell-Jones* at p 545:

'Plainly, what we have said should not be regarded as a lexicon or rule book to cover all cases in which a prosecutor is called upon to exercise this discretion. There may be special situations to which we have not adverted; and in every case, it is important to emphasise, the judgment to be made is primarily that of the prosecutor, and, in general, the Court will only interfere with it if he has gone wrong in principle.'

(iii) The power of the court to call witnesses

Extract 4.3.8

R v Grafton [1993] QB 101, 107 (CA)

TAYLOR LJ: It is well established that the judge in a criminal trial has power to call a witness. It is, however, a power which should be used most sparingly and rarely exercised: see *Reg v Roberts (John Marcus)* (1984) 80 Cr App

R 89, and the cases therein cited, at p 96. Where the power is exercised, it should be for achieving the ends of justice and fairness. Thus in *Reg v Tregear* [1967] 2 QB 574, a judge's decision to call a witness at a late stage of the trial was upheld because he was 'not seeking to supplement the prosecution.'

Similar principles apply in summary trials: *R v Haringey JJ, ex p DPP.*[21]

The judges in the *Crown Court Study* stated that they were aware in 19% of cases of at least one important witness who was not called by either the prosecution or the defence.[22]

(iv) The power of the court to question witnesses

Extract 4.3.9

R v Gunning (1980) 98 Cr App R 303, 306–7 (CA)

CUMMING-BRUCE LJ: The judge is not an advocate. Under the English and Welsh system of criminal trials he is much more like the umpire at a cricket match. He is certainly not the bowler, whose business it is to get the batsman out. If a judge, without any conscious intention to be unfair, descends into the forum and asks great numbers of pointed questions of the accused when he is giving his evidence in-chief, the jury may very well get the impression that the judge does not believe a word that the witness is saying and by putting these pointed questions, to which there is sometimes only a lame answer, blows the evidence out of the water during the stage that counsel ought to be having the opportunity to bring the evidence of the accused to the attention of the jury in its most impressive pattern and shape. The importance of counsel having that opportunity is not diminished – indeed it is enhanced – if the evidence emerging in-chief is a story that takes a bit of swallowing. If the judge, when the witness is skating over thin ice, asks pointed questions so that the ice seems to crack, the jury may well get the impression, however perfectly the judge may later sum up the case, that the judge has seen through the evidence in-chief so that the jury do not take it very seriously either.

. . .

With some hesitation, this Court has decided that though this evidence given by the appellant was evidence that might well not have carried conviction to the jury if the trial had followed the usual course, the interventions of the judge during the attempts of Mr Hopkins to lead his witness through in-chief were on such a scale and of such a character that though the judge had not got the slightest intention of being unfair, he did, if the matter is considered

---

[21] [1996] 2 WLR 114.
[22] M Zander and P Henderson, *The Royal Commission on Criminal Justice: Crown Court Study* (1993) 110–11.

objectively, prevent the appellant from giving his evidence in-chief in the way in which he should have been allowed to give it, because really Mr Hopkins was not given a fair chance. The best example is the one ... where for a quarter of an hour the judge went on examining the appellant himself while Mr Hopkins was standing there waiting to get a word in edgeways.

This Court reluctantly has formed the view that the irregularity was so significant that the trial must be regarded as a mis-trial in that the appellant did not have the chance that the adversarial system is designed to afford him of developing his evidence under the lead and guidance of defending counsel. For those reasons the conviction is quashed.

(v) Point at which accused to testify

Extract 4.3.10

Police and Criminal Evidence Act 1984, s 79

79. Time for taking accused's evidence
If at the trial of any person for an offence –
   (a) the defence intends to call two or more witnesses to the facts of the case; and
   (b) those witnesses include the accused,
the accused shall be called before the other witness or witnesses unless the court in its discretion otherwise directs.

(c) Adducing evidence after closing the case

There is a discretion to permit a party to adduce further evidence after closing its case:

Extract 4.3.11

R v Hutchinson (1985) 82 Cr App R 51, 58–9 (CA)

WATKINS LJ: The *ex improviso* principle cannot adequately be examined without reference to the expression given to it by Tindal CJ in *Frost* (1839) 9 C & P 129, 195. He said:

'There is no doubt that the general rule is that, where the Crown begins its case like a plaintiff in a civil suit, they cannot afterwards support their case by calling fresh witnesses because they are met by certain evidence that contradicts it. They stand or fall by the evidence they have given. They must close their case before the defence begins; but if any matter arises *ex improviso* which no human ingenuity can foresee on the part of a defendant in a civil suit, or a prisoner in a criminal case, there seems to me no reason why that matter which so arose *ex improviso* may not be answered by contrary evidence on the part of the Crown.'

At that time, of course, an accused person was not permitted by law to give evidence in his own defence.

. . .

The *ex improviso* principle has to be applied by the court with a recognition that the prosecution are expected to react reasonably to what may be suggested as pre-trial warnings of evidence likely to be given which calls for denial beforehand, and for that matter to suggestions put in cross-examination of their witnesses. They are not expected to take notice of fanciful and unreal statements no matter from what source they emanate.

Extract 4.3.12

R v Scott (1984) 79 Cr App R 49, 51–2 (CA)

LAWTON LJ: In our judgment the principle is as follows. If the prosecution could reasonably have foreseen that a particular piece of evidence was necessary to prove their case they should have put it before the court as part of their case. They should not wait until the defendant has given evidence to produce that evidence. Much, however, will turn on what is reasonable. . . .

. . .

. . . If reasonable anticipation were not the test the courts would be cluttered with unnecessary evidence, the expenses of prosecution would rise considerably and justice would tend not to be done.

4. EXAMINATION-IN-CHIEF

(a) No leading questions

As a general rule, it is impermissible to ask leading questions when examining one's witness in chief. The following extract from a Canadian case contains an excellent discussion of the following issues: What is a leading question? Why are such questions generally disallowed in examination-in-chief? Are there any exceptions to the general prohibition?

Extract 4.4.1

Maves v Grand Trunk Pacific R Co (1913) 14 DLR 70, 73–7 (Alberta SC)

BECK J: I find the general subject of leading questions dealt with in a most satisfactory way in Best on Evidence, 11th ed, 624 *et seq*. I quote, italicising what I wish to emphasize: –

The chief rule of practice relative to the interrogation of witnesses is that which prohibits '*leading questions*,' *ie*, questions which directly or indirectly suggest to the witness the answer he is to give. The rule is, that *on material points* a party must not lead his own witnesses, but may lead those of his adversary; in other words, that leading questions are allowed in cross-examination, but not in examination-in-chief. This seems based on two reasons: first, and principally, on the supposition that the witness has a bias in favour of the party bringing him forward, and hostile to his opponent; secondly, that the party calling a witness has an advantage over his adversary, in knowing beforehand what the witness will prove, or, at least, is expected to prove; and that, consequently, if he were allowed to lead, he might interrogate in such a manner as to extract only so much of the knowledge of the witness as would be favourable to his side, or even put a false gloss upon the whole.

I think a third reason may be added, namely, that a witness, though intending to be entirely fair and honest may, owing, for example, to lack of education, of exactness of knowledge of the precise meaning of words or of appreciation at the moment of their precise meaning, or of alertness to see that what is implied in the question requires modification, honestly assent to a leading question which fails to express his real meaning, which he would probably have completely expressed if allowed to do so in his own words.

The author proceeds as follows (Best on Evidence, 11th ed, 625): –

On all matters, however, which are *merely introductory, and form no part of the substance of the enquiry*, it is both allowable *and proper* for a party to lead his own witnesses, as otherwise much time would be wasted to no purpose. It is sometimes said that the test of a leading question is, whether an answer to it by 'Yes' or 'No' would be conclusive upon the matter in issue; but although all such questions undoubtedly come within the rule, it is by no means limited to them. Where 'Yes' or 'No' would be conclusive on any part of the issue, the question would be equally objectionable [. . .] In practice, leading questions are often allowed to pass without objection, sometimes by express, and sometimes by tacit, consent. This latter occurs where the questions relate to matters which, though strictly speaking, in issue, the examining counsel is aware are not meant to be contested by the other side; or where the opposing counsel does not think it worth his while to object.

On the other hand, however, very unfounded objections are constantly taken on this ground. A question is objectionable as leading when it suggests the *answer*, not when it merely directs the attention of the witness to the *subject* respecting which he is questioned [. . .] It should never be forgotten that 'leading' is a relative, not an absolute term. There is no such thing as 'leading' in the abstract – for the identical form of question which would be leading of the grossest kind in one case or state of facts, might be not only unobjectionable, but the very fittest mode of interrogation in another.

So that the *general* rule is that in examining one's own witness, not that no leading questions must be asked, but that *on material points* one must *not* lead his own witness but that on points that are *merely introductory and form no part of the substance* of the inquiry one *should* lead. And the author remarks: –

Although not to lead one's own witness when that is allowable is by no means so bad a fault as leading improperly still *it is a fault*; for it wastes the time of the Court, has a tendency to confuse the witness, and betrays a want of expertness in the advocate: p 627.

. . .

To the general rule, as just stated, against leading, there are several well recognized exceptions which the author puts as follows: –

There are some exceptions to the rule against leading. 1. For the purpose of identifying persons or things, the attention of the witness may be directly pointed to them. 2. Where one witness is called to contradict another as to expressions used by the latter, but which he denies having used, he may be asked directly, 'Did the other witness use such and such expressions'? The authorities are not quite agreed as to the reason of this exception; and some strongly contend that *the memory of the second witness ought first to be exhausted* by his being asked what the other said on the occasion in question. 3. The rule which excludes leading questions being chiefly founded on the assumption that a witness must be taken to have a bias in favour of the party by whom he is called, whenever circumstances shew that this is not the case, and that he is either hostile to that party or unwilling to give evidence, the Judge may, in his discretion, allow the rule to be relaxed. And it would seem that, for the same reason, if the witness shews a strong bias in favour of the cross-examining party, the right of leading him ought to be restrained; but the authorities are not quite clear about this. 4. The rule will be relaxed where the inability of a witness to answer questions put in the regular way obviously arises from defective memory; or, 5. From the complicated nature of the matter as to which he is interrogated.

. . .

In Wigmore on Evidence, sec 777, the rule as to the relaxation of the rule against leading questions is put thus: –

Where the witness is unable without extraneous aid to revive his memory on the desired point – *ie*, where he understands what he is desired to speak about, but cannot recollect what he knows – here *his recollection, being exhausted*, may be aided by a question suggesting the answer,

and sec 778: –

Where there is as yet no exhaustion of memory, but the witness merely does not appreciate the tenor of the desired details and thus is unable to say anything about it, a question calling attention specifically to the details may be allowable, when other means have failed. It may not be necessary to name all the details; the mention of one or more of them may suffice, by association, to stimulate the recollection of the remainder. The common situation of this sort, running, perhaps, throughout the person's entire testimony, is that of a child, or an illiterate or alien adult.

A case which not infrequently arises in practice is that of a witness who recounts a conversation and in doing so omits one or more statements which counsel examining him is instructed formed part of it. The common and proper practice is to ask the witness to repeat the conversation from the beginning. It is often found that in his repetition he gives the lacking statement – possibly omitting one given the first time. This method may be tried more than once, and as a matter of expediency – so as to have the advantage of getting the whole story on the witness' own unaided recollection – counsel might pass on to some other subject and later revert to the conversation, asking him to again state it. But when this method fails, the trial Judge undoubtedly ought to permit a question containing a reference to the subject-matter of the statement which it is supposed has been omitted by the witness. If this method fails, then and not till then – that is when his memory appears to be entirely exhausted, the trial Judge should allow a question to be put to him containing the supposedly omitted matter. It will be, of course, for the jury, or the Judge if there be no jury, to draw a conclusion as to the truthfulness of the witness; although the permitting of a question in a certain form is largely – though I think not wholly – in the discretion of the trial Judge. I should think that, with regard to the class of leading question I have been considering, they should, in every case, be permitted after all the steps which appear to shew the witness' memory to have been exhausted have been taken. If not permitted, great injustice may result. If permitted, the jury or Judge acting as a jury, may, of course, as I have said, disbelieve the answer elicited.

It would seem that evidence elicited by means of an improper leading question is not inadmissible per se, but will carry little or no weight.[23]

(b) Hostile witnesses

An *unfavourable witness* is one who fails to 'come up to proof' or who gives evidence which is unfavourable to the case of the party calling him or her. The extent to which such a situation may be dealt with was considered in the following case:

Extract 4.4.2

Ewer v Ambrose (1825) 3 B & C 746, 750; 107 ER 910, 911–12 (KBD)

HOLROYD J: . . . if a party calls a witness to prove a fact, he cannot, when he finds the witness proves the contrary, give general evidence to shew that that witness is not to be believed on his oath, but he may shew by other evidence that he is mistaken as to the fact which he is called to prove.

[23] *Moor v Moor* [1954] 1 WLR 927, 928.

A *hostile witness*, on the other hand, is one who shows no desire to tell the truth. Hostility may be demonstrated, for example, by the witness's demeanour or by evidence that the witness has made a prior inconsistent statement. In relation to hostile witnesses, s 3 of the Criminal Procedure Act 1865, and the observations of the Lord Chief Justice in *R v Thompson*,[24] are applicable.

Extract 4.4.3

Criminal Procedure Act 1865 ('Lord Denman's Act'), s 3

3. How far witnesses may be discredited by the party producing
A party producing a witness shall not be allowed to impeach his credit by general evidence of bad character; but he may, in case the witness shall in the opinion of the judge prove adverse, contradict him by other evidence, or, by leave of the judge, prove that he has made at other times a statement inconsistent with his present testimony; but before such last-mentioned proof can be given the circumstances of the supposed statement, sufficient to designate the particular occasion, must be mentioned to the witness, and he must be asked whether or not he has made such statement.

'Adverse' in s 3 (which applies to both civil and criminal proceedings) means 'hostile' rather than 'unfavourable': *Greenough v Eccles*.[25] In criminal proceedings, a prior inconsistent statement proved under s 3 will, by virtue of the hearsay rule, be admissible only to discredit the witness and cannot be treated as evidence of the truth of its contents. The Law Commission has recommended, however, that such a statement should be capable of being so treated.[26] In civil proceedings, the Civil Evidence Act 1995 permits such a statement to be admitted as evidence of the facts contained in it, so long as the requirements of the Act (see Chapter 7) are satisfied.

Extract 4.4.4

R v Thompson (1976) 64 Cr App R 96, 99 (CA)

THE LORD CHIEF JUSTICE: ... there is no reason to suppose that the subsequent statutory intervention into this subject has in any way destroyed or removed the basic common law right of the judge in his discretion to allow cross-examination when a witness proves to be hostile.

A number of issues relating to the procedure for declaring a witness to be hostile, and the consequences of a finding of hostility, were discussed succinctly by the Court of Appeal in the following case:

---

[24] (1976) 64 Cr App R 96.
[25] (1859) 5 CB (NS) 786; 141 ER 315.
[26] Law Commission (Law Com No 245), *Evidence in Criminal Proceedings: Hearsay and Related Topics* (1997) 167.

Extract 4.4.5

R v Maw [1994] Crim LR 841; LEXIS transcript (CA)

HOBHOUSE LJ: . . . it is useful to review the position which arises . . . where a prosecution witness gives evidence which is contrary to his statement, or fails to give the evidence expected of him. The first thing that should be done by any prosecutor, and by the trial judge, is to consider the step of inviting the witness to refresh his or her memory from material which it is legitimate to use for that purpose. . . .

It is an undesirable course, following a failure to get the expected answer from the witness, to proceed immediately to treating that witness as hostile. There may be circumstances where the witness is displaying such an excessive degree of hostility, or animus, that that is the only appropriate course. . . . If the witness does not allow his memory to be refreshed, and does not give an explanation of why he chooses to give different evidence, the judge can then go on to consider whether that shows that he should be treated as hostile.

Having decided to treat a witness as hostile, then the witness can not only be cross-examined, but he can be cross-examined on previous statements that he has made. The effect of so doing, if it shows an inconsistency between the evidence that the witness is giving and the previous statement, is simply to undermine or destroy the credibility of that witness. It does not make the statement part of the evidence of that witness. This has been clearly held in *R v Golder* [1960] 3 All ER 457, 45 Cr App Rep 5. Therefore, in any situation where a witness is treated as hostile and is shown to have made previous inconsistent statements, the primary effect of that exercise is to discredit the witness. The Crown will then be unable to place that witness before the jury as a witness upon whose evidence they should convict. Obviously, in some cases the situation is not as stark as that, and each case depends on its own particular facts, but the basic result of challenging a witness's evidence by reference to an out-of-court statement is to undermine or destroy the credit of that witness.

If the witness, as in this case, chooses to adopt and confirm some of the contents of his prior statements, then, to that extent, what he says becomes part of his evidence at the trial and, subject to the jury assessing his credibility and his reliability, it is capable of being accepted. The evidence is what the witness says in the witness box at the trial, not what he has said in the out-of-court statement. . . .

If a witness has been treated as hostile, and has thereafter given evidence, it is necessary for any jury to consider whether that witness is a witness [who] should be treated as creditworthy at all. Once a witness has been attacked in the way that is involved in treating him as a hostile witness, questions of the creditworthiness of the witness arise both for the judge and the jury, and the jury should be clearly directed on that point. . . . It is of fundamental importance for any tribunal to consider whether a witness who has given conflicting evidence is of any creditworthiness at all. It is not proper to go straight to the stage of considering which parts of the evidence are regarded as worthy of acceptance and which are to be rejected.

If the judge considers that the witness is of sufficient creditworthiness to allow the jury to take account of his evidence, then he should give the jury a clear warning about the dangers involved in a witness who contradicts himself. The jury need to be warned that they must consider whether they can give any credence to a witness who gives such inconsistent evidence, and only if they consider that they can, go on to consider what parts of that witness's evidence they can accept.

It should be the task of the prosecution (or other party) who is going to invite the jury to rely upon the evidence of a witness who is being treated as hostile, to explore the inconsistencies in the witness's evidence and the reluctance of the witness to testify. This point was referred to in the case of *Golder* and in other cases. If there is no explanation for the inconsistencies, then it is obvious that the evidence of that witness is less satisfactory. If the witness can give an explanation for the inconsistency, or his initial reluctance to testify, then it may be that that sets at rest any anxieties there may be about his evidence and enables him to be treated as fully creditworthy.

See generally M Newark, 'The Hostile Witness and the Adversary System' [1986] *Criminal Law Review* 441; R Pattenden, 'The Hostile Witness' (1992) 56 *Journal of Criminal Law* 414.

(c) Evidence of prior consistent statements in criminal trials

Extract 4.4.6

R v Roberts [1942] 1 All ER 187, 191 (CCA)

HUMPHREYS J: The rule relating to this is sometimes put in this way, that a party is not permitted to make evidence for himself. . . . So, in a criminal case, an accused person is not permitted to call evidence to show that, after he was charged with a criminal offence, he told a number of persons what his defence was going to be, and the reason for the rule appears to us to be that such testimony has no evidential value. It is because it does not assist in the elucidation of the matters in dispute that the evidence is said to be inadmissible on the ground that it is irrelevant.

As the above extract from *Roberts* indicates, the rule against prior consistent statements (also known as the rule against narrative or the rule against self-corroboration) renders out-of-court statements by a witness that are consistent with his or her present testimony in court inadmissible in evidence. A number of exceptions to the rule against prior consistent statements have, however, evolved. As will now be seen, it is possible, in appropriate circumstances, for evidence to be adduced of (1) prompt, voluntary complaints in sexual cases; (2) statements which serve to rebut allegations of recent fabrication; (3) statements made on accusation; (4) statements made on the discovery of incriminating articles; (5) statements of prior identification of the accused; and (6) statements that are admissible as part of the res gestae.

See generally R N Gooderson, 'Previous Consistent Statements' [1968] *Cambridge Law Journal* 64.

(i) Complaints in sexual cases

Evidence of previous complaints of victims in sexual cases is admissible, as an exception to the rule against prior consistent statements, in certain circumstances. What precisely are these circumstances? For what purpose is such evidence admissible? Can evidence be given only of the *fact* of the previous complaint, or is evidence of the *substance* of the complaint also admissible? Is this area of the law justifiable? Such questions should be borne in mind when considering the decision of the Court of Appeal in the following case, in which all the main earlier authorities are discussed:

Extract 4.4.7

R v Valentine **[1996] 2 Cr App R 213, 214–15, 216, 218, 220–5 (CA)**

ROCH LJ: At about 11.30 pm on May 22, 1992, the complainant, W was walking from Andover town centre to her home when she met the appellant, who was a complete stranger to her. He asked her if she knew of somewhere where he could get a drink. She told him that there was an Indian restaurant nearby. He insisted that she join him and she did so. They left the restaurant together at about 12.30 am and began to walk towards her home. The appellant suggested that they cut across a football ground and W agreed. The prosecution's case was that when they reached the middle of the playing field, the appellant threatened W with a table knife and forced her to have sexual intercourse with him against her will.

The appellant's defence was that intercourse had taken place but with W's consent.

. . .

She went home reaching her home at about 2.30 am. Her parents and her elder brother were in the house but they were asleep.

Next morning she went to her brother's bedroom and told him that she had been attacked with a knife. She did not mention any details to him as she had wanted to forget the incident. She did show him the cuts on her hand which he had caused when she grabbed the knife. She told him that she did not want to tell her parents.

She went to work that afternoon and in the evening met two friends, Andrew Smith and Richard Gould. She told the jury that she spoke to Andrew Smith and at first told him what she had told her brother, namely that she had been attacked with a knife. Subsequently when speaking to Andrew Smith on his

own she had told him that she had been raped. She had not gone into the details of the rape but had told him that it happened on the football field.
. . .

Prior to Andrew Smith and Richard Gould giving evidence, counsel for the appellant, Mr Grey, had sought a ruling that that evidence be excluded as being inadmissible. Two grounds were relied upon: first, that the complaints to Andrew Smith had been made by W in answer to questions put to her by Smith; and secondly, that the complaints had not been made on the first reasonable opportunity W had had for making complaints. The judge ruled that evidence admissible.

. . . Mr Gibson-Lee did not place much reliance upon the point that these complaints were made in answer to questions by Mr Smith. The main thrust of Mr Gibson-Lee's submission . . . was that these complaints had not been made at the first reasonable opportunity. The judge should have ruled these complaints inadmissible or alternatively he should have permitted the prosecution to prove the bare fact that W made a complaint of rape to Mr Smith but not the terms in which the complaint was made. Subsidiary to that submission Mr Gibson-Lee pointed out that nowhere in the summing-up did the judge expressly direct the jury that this part of the evidence was not evidence of the truth of the facts alleged in W's complaint but merely went to her consistency and credibility as a witness.
. . .

The leading authority on complaints in cases of sexual offences is *Lillyman* [1896] 2 QB 167, the judgment of the Court of Crown Cases Reserved being delivered by Hawkins J. At p 170 of the report Hawkins J stated [of] such evidence:

'It clearly is not admissible as evidence of the facts complained of: those facts must therefore be established, if at all, upon oath by the prosecutrix or other credible witness, and, strictly speaking, evidence of them ought to be given before evidence of the complaint is admitted. The complaint can only be used as evidence of the consistency . . . of the prosecutrix with the story told by her in the witness box, and as being inconsistent with her consent to that of which she complains.'

The court in its judgment then went on to trace the history of the use of complaints in rape cases, pointing out that historically the making of a complaint immediately after the alleged offence was:

'in order to prevent malicious accusations.' (p 171).

In the later case of *Osborne* [1905] 1 KB 551 at p 559 Ridley J, in giving the judgment of the Court of Crown Cases Reserved, referred to the fact that:

'. . . in early times it was incumbent on the woman who brought an appeal of rape to prove that while the offence was recent she raised "hue and cry" in the neighbouring towns, she shewed her injuries and clothing to men, and that the appellee might raise as a defence the denial that she had raised the hue and cry.'

Returning to the case of *Lillyman*, Hawkins J quoted from *Hawkins' Pleas of the Crown* this passage:

'It is a strong presumption, but not a conclusive presumption against a woman that she made no complaint in a reasonable time after the fact.' (p 170).

In *Lillyman's* case the principal issue was whether the whole of the alleged complaint should be placed before the jury or whether the evidence should be limited to the bare fact that a complaint had been made. The court was not considering what amounted to a reasonable time after the fact. In that case the complainant, a girl under the age of 16, complained to her mistress, in the absence of the defendant very shortly after the commission of the acts charged against the defendant. The prosecution were permitted by the trial judge, Hawkins J, to lead evidence from the girl and from her mistress not merely of the fact of the complaint but the details of the complaints made. Further the decision in *Lillyman* established that evidence of recent complaint was admissible in cases of sexual offences other than rape.

In *Osborne* it was decided that evidence of recent complaint could be given in a case where consent was not an issue by virtue of the complainant being under the age of consent. In *Osborne* Ridley J cited a passage from *Hale's Pleas of the Crown*, namely:

'For instance, if the witness be of good fame, if she presently discovered the offence, made pursuit after the offender, shewed circumstances and signs of the injury ... these and the like are concurring evidences to give greater probability to her testimony, when proved by others as well as herself. But on the other side, if she concealed the injury for any considerable time after she had opportunity to complain, ... and she made no outcry when the fact was supposed to be done, when and where it is probable she might be heard by others; these and the like circumstances carry a strong presumption, that her testimony is false or feigned.'

Ridley J observed:

'We think these words may be adopted as stating the law accurately, and they indicate that these complaints are to be admitted, not only because they bear on the question of consent, but also because they bear on the probability of her testimony in a case in which, without such or other corroboration, reliance might not be placed on her testimony.'

It is to be observed that this passage from the judgment suggests that a late complaint could be given in evidence as being relevant to the complainant's credibility at the instigation of the defence, as being favourable to their case.

At the end of the judgment in that case Ridley J said:

'We are, at the same time, not insensible of the great importance of carefully observing the proper limits within which such evidence should be given. It is only to cases of this kind that the authorities on which our judgment rests apply; and our judgment also is restricted to them. It applies only where there is a complaint not elicited by questions of a leading and inducing or intimidating character, and only when it is made at the first opportunity after the offence which reasonably offers itself. Within such bounds, we think the evidence should be put before the jury, the judge being careful to inform the jury that the statement is not evidence of the facts complained of, and must not be regarded by them, if believed, as other than corroborative of the complainant's credibility, and, when consent is in issue, of the absence of consent.'

The decision in *Osborne* established the basic criteria for determining which complaints were admissible and which were not. Subsequent cases provide illustrations of the development of the law in this field, for it must be recognised that the trend has been to widen the scope of complaints which are to be admitted in evidence. The case of *Lee* (1912) 7 Cr App R 31 was a case where the complainant claimed to have made an immediate complaint to the mother of the defendant, who was not called by the prosecution. The complainant then went home and told her father about a cut upon her thumb which she alleged had been inflicted in the struggle with Lee but said nothing to her father about an indecent assault. Later the complainant spoke to a Mrs Mussett and told her the whole story. That was some hour and a half to two hours after the alleged indecent assault. Giving the judgment of the court, Hamilton J said at p 33:

'It is now contended that the evidence of Mrs Mussett is not within the proposition in the judgment of Ridley J in *Osborne* . . . , that such evidence "is admissible 'only when' a complaint is made at the first opportunity after the offence which reasonably offers itself." We think that no one could cavil at the lapse of time within which the complaint to Mrs Mussett was made – namely, within one and a half hours; clearly this was as early an opportunity as could reasonably be expected to offer itself, leaving out the complaint to Mrs Lee. It is contended that the second complaint was not admissible after the first complaint to Mrs Lee, or that, the fact of the complaint to Mrs Lee having been elicited, the prosecution could not fortify it by Mrs Mussett's evidence. It must depend on the circumstances of each case whether it can be said that the complaint was made on the first reasonable opportunity which offers itself. But here we think that both the first complaint was in fact put in evidence on the cross-examination, and the second complaint was available.'

The headnote states the principle to be derived in these terms:

'. . . an early complaint is not necessarily excluded because there has been a previous complaint.'

A similar decision was reached by Lord Reading CJ in the case of *Wilbourne* (1917) 12 Cr App R 280. There the charge was one of rape against a medical practitioner, the rape taking place in a dispensary at about 5.30 pm. The complainant met her sister shortly after leaving the dispensary and made a complaint to her in answer to a question put by her sister. The trial judge did not admit that evidence. Evidence was given by the complainant's mother that when her daughters returned home at about 7 pm she noticed that the complainant had been crying. The sister had then said to the complainant that she should tell her mother all about it and the mother asked what had been going on. The complainant then said: 'Why that doctor has insulted me.' The mother then asked: 'What has he been doing to you?' And the complainant said: 'It is not what he has said but what he has done,' and then told her mother the story which she told the jury from the witness box. The trial judge rejected an argument that evidence of a complaint could only be given by the first person to whom the complaint was made. The judge's ruling that the complaint to the mother was admissible was upheld on appeal.

A more recent authority is *Cummings* [1948] 1 All ER 551, where the complainant alleged that she had been raped during an evening by Cummings. At the time she was living at a Landworker's camp. She did not complain to the camp warden that evening, although she saw him. She said she did not complain to the camp warden because he was a friend of Cummings. There was also a female welfare officer at the camp, who was known to the complainant, although there was no evidence that the complainant knew the Welfare Officer was available for her to speak to. The complainant made no complaint to other girls of her age living in the same hut at the camp. However, the next day, as early as she could, the complainant went from the camp to a much older woman who lived two miles away who was known to her and to whom she did make a complaint.

The trial judge permitted evidence of that complaint to be given and the appeal was mounted on the basis that as the complainant had not made a complaint immediately the evidence of that complaint ought not to have been admitted. In the course of giving the judgment of the Court of Criminal Appeal Lord Goddard CJ said at p 552:

'Who is to decide whether the complaint is made as speedily as could reasonably be expected? Surely it must be the judge who tries the case. There is no one else who can decide it. The evidence is tendered, and he has to give a decision there and then whether it is admissible or not. It must, therefore, be a matter for him to decide and a matter for his discretion if he applies the right principle. There is no question here that Hallett J did apply the right principle. He had clearly in mind the fact that there must be an early complaint. Whether it was reasonable to expect the prosecutrix to complain the moment she got back to the Camp to a man who she hardly knew, or whether it was more reasonable that she should wait till the morning and complain to Mrs Watson, her friend, were matters that the learned judge had to take into account. He did take them into account, and he came to the conclusion that in the circumstances the complaint next morning was in reasonable time. If a judge has such facts before him, applies the right principle, and directs his mind to the right question, which is whether or not the prosecutrix did what was reasonable, this Court cannot interfere.'

We accept that passage as a correct statement of the law and of the approach of this Court to a trial judge's ruling on the admissibility of complaints in cases of sexual offences.

The authorities establish that a complaint can be recent and admissible, although it may not have been made at the first opportunity which presented itself. What is the first reasonable opportunity will depend on the circumstances including the character of the complainant and the relationship between the complainant and the person to whom she complained and the persons to whom she might have complained but did not do so. It is enough if it is the first reasonable opportunity. Further, a complaint will not be inadmissible merely because there has been an earlier complaint, provided that the complaint can fairly be said to have been made as speedily as could reasonably be expected. This is not to say that it is permissible to allow the Crown to lead evidence that the same complaint has been made by the complainant in substantially the same terms on several occasions soon after the alleged offence, where that would be prejudicial in that it might incline the jury to regard the contents of individual complaints as evidence of the truth of what they assert. The complaint has to be made within a reasonable time of the alleged offence and on the first occasion that reasonably offers itself for the complainant concerned to make the complaint that was made in the terms in which it was made.

We now have greater understanding that those who are the victims of sexual offences, be they male or female, often need time before they can bring themselves to tell what has been done to them; that some victims will find it impossible to complain to anyone other than a parent or member of their family whereas others may feel it quite impossible to tell their parents or members of their family.

Turning to the present case, we consider that the judge applied the principles applicable correctly and adopted the approach laid down by Lord Goddard in *Cummings*. We are content that we should follow Lord Goddard's approach and say that this Court cannot interfere in a case such as the present where the judge has such facts before him, applied the right principle and directed his mind to the right questions.

The judge saw and heard the complainant. He assessed her as a person who was tense and who would bottle up this matter until she found a friend of her own age to confide in. We would echo the further words of Lord Goddard:

'In the circumstances, we think that there was nothing which could oblige this court to say that the complaint was not made as speedily as could reasonably be expected.'

The subsidiary point raised by Mr Gibson-Lee is that in his summing-up the judge did not in terms tell the jury that the complaints made by W were not evidence of the facts complained of and related only to her credibility. It is correct that the judge did not use those words in directing the jury. On the other hand, at p 17A of the summing-up the judge said to the jury:

'You have to ask yourselves whether the course of the complaint which is why you have heard it as far as W is concerned here is so out of the norm as to make you think she cannot be telling you the truth when she says, "This was rape and not an act of intercourse which I subsequently regretted." That is the crucial question you have to ask yourselves.'

When at the end of the summing-up, at p 60G of the transcript, the judge said:

'Note the course of her complaints, members of the jury. She does not complain of rape at first, she complains of sexual intercourse having certainly happened. She does not complain of rape and then later on adds a knife for good measure, thinking out how she is going to concoct a story.

What she complains of was the knife. That is what she said to A. 'There was a knife that was held at me.' Only much later, hours later, to Andrew Smith does she bring herself to say anything about sex, and as I said to you to Dr Weaver she does not even mention oral sex. Does that help as to the way things came out? Is the prosecution right in saying this is a young woman reluctant to mention the sexual element but content to mention the knife? Or is it as the defence suggest a young woman inventing her story and improving it as it goes along?'

From those passages it must have been clear to the jury that the relevance of the evidence of complaints was to enable the jury to decide whether the complainant was inventing her story and adding to it as it went along, as the defence claimed, or whether she was someone who could only bring herself to complain of the sexual element of the attack on her when she had the opportunity to speak to a trusted friend of her own age alone, as the Crown claimed. We are confident that the jury would have understood that this evidence went to the credibility of the complainant, both the prosecution and the defence having used the evidence of complaints for its proper purpose and the judge having reminded the jury that the prosecution and defence were relying on that evidence in that way. We conclude that there was no material misdirection in this case and this appeal is dismissed.

The doctrine of complaints in sexual cases would appear to have had its roots in the old 'hue and cry' requirement:

Extract 4.4.8

C F H Tapper, *Cross and Tapper on Evidence* (8th ed 1995) 296

In the Middle Ages it was essential that the victim should have raised the hue and cry if an appeal of rape were to succeed. By the beginning of the eighteenth century, when the modern law of evidence was beginning to take shape, the absence of complaint was no longer an absolute bar to success, but Hawkins still referred to the strong presumption against a prosecutrix in a case of rape if she made no complaint within a reasonable time of the alleged offence. If the absence of such complaint could tell against a prosecutrix it seemed to follow that the fact of having made a complaint ought to tell in her favour, and if failure to complain could be proved by the defence then the fact of making a complaint should be capable of proof by the prosecution.

The more flexible and enlightened approach[27] advocated in *Valentine* to determining whether a complaint was made at the first reasonable opportunity is to be welcomed. There is no principled reason, however, why complaints in sexual cases should be singled out by the law for special treatment.

[27] See also Law Commission (Consultation Paper No 138), *Criminal Law – Evidence in Criminal Proceedings: Hearsay and Related Topics – A Consultation Paper* (1995) 187; J Temkin, *Rape and the Legal Process* (1987) 145–6.

Prompt complaints about non-sexual offences do not constitute an exception to the rule against prior consistent statements. It is clear that the recognition of such an exception in the context of sexual offences must have stemmed from the old, and discredited, assumption that the natural reaction of a genuine victim of such an offence would be to seize the first opportunity to tell someone about what happened.

The High Court of Australia has recently emphasised the importance of explaining carefully to the jury the distinction between permissible and impermissible uses of evidence of a complaint: 'The distinction may not be an easy one for a jury to grasp but this does not detract from the need for the distinction to be carefully explained.'[28]

(ii) Statements rebutting allegations of recent fabrication

It may be suggested in the course of cross-examination of a witness that that witness's testimony was recently fabricated. In such a situation, the party calling the witness may seek, typically in the course of re-examining that witness, to adduce evidence of a prior consistent statement to support his or her credit.

Extract 4.4.9

R v Oyesiku (1971) 56 Cr App R 240, 245-7 (CA)

KARMINSKI LJ: Our attention has . . . been drawn to a recent decision in the High Court of Australia, *Nominal Defendant v Clements* (1961) 104 CLR 476. I desire to read only one passage from the full judgment of Dixon CJ. He said this (at p 479): 'The rule of evidence under which it was let in is well recognised and of long standing. If the credit of a witness is impugned as to some material fact to which he deposes upon the ground that his account is a late invention or has been lately devised or reconstructed, even though not with conscious dishonesty, that makes admissible a statement to the same effect as the account he gave as a witness, if it was made by the witness contemporaneously with the event or at a time sufficiently early to be inconsistent with the suggestion that his account is a late invention or reconstruction. But, inasmuch as the rule forms a definite exception to the general principle excluding statements made out of court and admits a possibly self-serving statement made by the witness, great care is called for in applying it. The judge at the trial must determine for himself upon the conduct of the trial before him whether a case for applying the rule of evidence has arisen and, from the nature of the matter, if there be an appeal, great weight should be given to his opinion by the appellate court. It is evident however that the judge at the trial must exercise care in assuring himself not only that the account

---

[28] *Jones v R* (1997) 71 ALJR 538, 539.

given by the witness in his testimony is attacked on the ground of recent invention or reconstruction or that a foundation for such an attack has been laid by the party, but also that the contents of the statement are in fact to the like effect as his account given in his evidence and that having regard to the time and circumstances in which it was made it rationally tends to answer the attack. It is obvious that it may not be easy sometimes to be sure that counsel is laying a foundation for impugning the witness's account of a material incident or fact as a recently invented, devised or reconstructed story. Counsel himself may proceed with a subtlety which is the outcome of caution in pursuing what may prove a dangerous course. That is one reason why the trial judge's opinion has a peculiar importance.'

. . . That judgment of the Chief Justice of Australia, although technically not binding upon us, is a decision of the greatest persuasive power, and one which this Court gratefully accepts as a correct statement of the law . . .

See also *R v Benjamin*.[29]

(iii) *Statements made on accusation*

Extract 4.4.10

R v Pearce (1979) 69 Cr App R 365, 369–70 (CA)

THE LORD CHIEF JUSTICE: In our view the present case can be disposed of within the principles stated in *Storey and Anwar* (1968) 52 Cr App R 334 and *Donaldson* (1976) 64 Cr App R 59. Those decisions will be found to contain all the guidance that is necessary in practice. We would ourselves summarise the principles as follows:

(1) A statement which contains an admission is always admissible as a declaration against interest and is evidence of the facts admitted. With this exception a statement made by an accused person is never evidence of the facts in the statement.

(2) (a) A statement that is not an admission is admissible to show the attitude of the accused at the time when he made it. This however is not to be limited to a statement made on the first encounter with the police. The reference in *Storey* to the reaction of the accused 'when first taxed' should not be read as circumscribing the limits of admissibility. The longer the time that has elapsed after the first encounter the less the weight which will be attached to the denial. The judge is able to direct the jury about the value of such statements. (b) A statement that is not in itself an admission is admissible if it is made in the same context as an admission, whether in the course of an interview, or in the form of a voluntary statement. It would be unfair to admit only the statements against interest while excluding part of the same interview

[29] (1913) 8 Cr App R 146.

or series of interviews. It is the duty of the prosecution to present the case fairly to the jury; to exclude answers which are favourable to the accused while admitting those unfavourable would be misleading. (c) The prosecution may wish to draw attention to inconsistent denials. A denial does not become an admission because it is inconsistent with another denial. There must be many cases however where convictions have resulted from such inconsistencies between two denials.

(3) Although in practice most statements are given in evidence even when they are largely self-serving, there may be a rare occasion when an accused produces a carefully prepared written statement to the police, with a view to it being made part of the prosecution evidence. The trial judge would plainly exclude such a statement as inadmissible.

In the light of the principles which we have ventured to state, there can be no reason for casting doubt on . . . the practice of admitting statements by the accused even when their evidential value is small.

It would appear, however, that a statement made on accusation will be inadmissible in evidence if the accused's reaction has already been adequately proved:

Extract 4.4.11

R v Tooke (1989) 90 Cr App R 417, 421–2 (CA)

THE LORD CHIEF JUSTICE: What happened here was this. The incident happened shortly after 9 o'clock in the evening. The bar manager, Mr Campion, gave evidence before the jury that immediately afterwards these two men were each blaming the other, the appellant was blaming the victim, the victim was blaming the appellant. Then Police Constable Dinnage appears, no doubt having been summoned by the licensee, because there was a disturbance. He approaches the appellant, and one can imagine the situation: the policeman asked 'What is going on here?' and the answer comes from the appellant saying that he had been the victim of an assault in the toilet of the Bristol Arms. That evidence was admitted and no doubt properly admitted without anyone suggesting otherwise, although it was plainly evidence which was self-exculpatory so far as this appellant was concerned. It was obviously spontaneous. It was very soon after the event and it was to that extent relevant to show what the immediate reaction of the appellant had been at the time or shortly after the incident.

He is then taken down to the police station, or goes down to the police station voluntarily, because he certainly had not been arrested, and at 9.40 makes a witness statement in the usual form, which is the subject of these proceedings, a statement which the judge refused to admit.

Now it is submitted to us by Mr Harris in his attractive argument that first of all this was a spontaneous statement, and there is no doubt that that is true. There is no suggestion that he had time to consult a solicitor or had very much time to think about the matter at all before the witness statement was made.

The next question is whether that statement was relevant. Perhaps put in another way, whether a witness statement added anything to the evidence which was already before the jury about this man's reaction to the suggestion that he had committed an assault.

In our judgment it was not relevant. All that evidence was before the jury in two shapes: first of all in what Mr Campion had said and secondly, from what Police Constable Dinnage had said. Consequently it was not relevant nor did it add anything to the weight of the other testimony.

Mr Harris submits that it was only right that the jury should know that this man went to the police station voluntarily and there voluntarily made a statement as a witness. That is perfectly true and there could have been no objection at all to that evidence being extracted from Police Constable Dinnage. Mr Harris seems to have thought that he was in some way being inhibited by the learned judge from adducing that evidence. But as we read the transcript of events that is certainly not the case.

The evidence in any event, if it had been admitted, would not have been evidence of the facts contained in the statement. It would only have been relevant to show this man's reaction, and I repeat myself in saying, his reaction was amply proved.

It seems to us, in those circumstances, that the necessary foundation for the admission of this evidence was absent and the learned judge was correct in ruling that the evidence should not be admitted.

(iv) Statements made on discovery of incriminating articles

Exculpatory statements made by an accused when incriminating articles were found in his or her possession would be admissible in evidence, if the accused testifies to the same effect at trial, of his or her consistency.

Extract 4.4.12

R v Abraham (1848) 3 Cox CC 430 (Assizes)

INDICTMENT for burglary.

. . .

The evidence was, that some glass jars, which had been taken from the prosecutor's shop, were found in the prisoner's house, not concealed. The prisoner had said, before any suspicion was excited, that he had found them in a field.

. . .

ALDERSON, B, in summing up, said, that if it was proved that the prisoner had given such an account of his possession of the stolen property to his neighbours, before suspicion existed, or search made, he had not the slightest doubt that, *valeat quantum*, it would be good evidence for the prisoner.

(v) Statements of prior identification of accused

Extract 4.4.13

R v Christie [1914] AC 545, 551 (HL)

VISCOUNT HALDANE LC: Had the boy, after he had identified the accused in the dock, been asked if he had identified the accused in the field as the man who assaulted him, and answered affirmatively, then that fact might also have been proved by the policeman and the mother who saw the identification. Its relevancy is to shew that the boy was able to identify at the time and to exclude the idea that the identification of the prisoner in the dock was an afterthought or a mistake. But beyond the mere fact of such identification the examination ought not to have proceeded.

(vi) Statements admissible as part of the res gestae

Illustrative of this exception is the case of *R v Fowkes*,[30] which is described by Stephen in the following terms:

Extract 4.4.14

Sir J F Stephen, *A Digest of the Law of Evidence* (12th ed by Sir H L Stephen and L F Sturge, 1946) 7–8

The question was, whether A murdered B by shooting him.
   The fact that a witness in the room with B when he was shot, saw a man with a gun in his hand pass a window opening into the room in which B was shot, and thereupon exclaimed, 'There's butcher!' (a name by which A was known), was allowed to be proved by Lord Campbell, LCJ.

Such a statement would presumably be admissible not only as evidence of consistency but also as evidence of the truth of its contents, since, as will be seen in Chapter 7, statements forming part of the res gestae are admissible in evidence as an exception to the hearsay rule.

(vii) Reform

The Law Commission has recommended that a witness's prior consistent statements be admissible in evidence for their truth in any one of three situations:[31]

[30] (1856) *The Times*, 8 March.
[31] Law Commission (Law Com No 245), *Evidence in Criminal Proceedings: Hearsay and Related Topics* (1997) 154–8.

(1) to rebut a suggestion that his or her oral evidence has been fabricated;
(2) if the statement identifies or describes a person, object or place, *and* the witness indicates that to the best of his belief he made the statement and it states the truth;
(3) if the statement constitutes a prompt complaint. A statement would be admissible in evidence on this basis if the following conditions are satisfied;

    (a) the witness claims to be a person against whom an offence to which the proceedings relate has been committed;

    (b) the previous statement consists of a complaint about conduct which would, if proved, constitute the offence or part of the offence;

    (c) the complaint was made as soon as could reasonably be expected after the alleged conduct;

    (d) the complaint was not made as a result of a threat or promise;

    (e) before the statement is adduced in evidence the witness gives oral evidence in connection with its subject matter;

    (f) the witness indicates that, to the best of his or her belief, he or she made the statement and it states the truth.

It is arguable that this approach would be unduly narrow, and that a witness's prior consistent statements should be admissible in evidence for their truth so long as they are regarded as sufficiently reliable to be admitted in evidence. It is true that, in contrast with the position in relation to prior inconsistent statements, there appears to be no necessity for the admissibility in evidence for their truth of statements of witnesses which are, by definition, *consistent* with their present testimony. However, evidence of statements about an event made by a witness at an earlier time (and hence closer to the time of the event) may, if it exists, be just the type of evidence which a jury would expect to hear in addition to statements about the same event made in court. In his article about countering negative inferences associated with the absence of evidence, Saltzburg[32] has put forward the argument that, when certain issues are raised in jury trials, juries often develop expectations about the evidence which will be adduced for their consideration. The failure of a party to satisfy these expectations may result in negative (and often unfair) inferences being drawn against that party by the jury.

(d) Evidence of prior consistent statements in civil trials

The position with respect to evidence of prior consistent statements in civil trials is now governed by the following statutory provision.

---

[32] S A Saltzburg, 'A Special Aspect of Relevance: Countering Negative Inferences Associated with the Absence of Evidence' (1978) 66 *California Law Review* 1011.

Extract 4.4.15

Civil Evidence Act 1995, s 6(1), (2)

6. Previous statements of witnesses

(1) Subject as follows, the provisions of this Act as to hearsay evidence in civil proceedings apply equally (but with any necessary modifications) in relation to a previous statement made by a person called as a witness in the proceedings.

(2) A party who has called or intends to call a person as a witness in civil proceedings may not in those proceedings adduce evidence of a previous statement made by that person, except –

(a) with the leave of the court, or

(b) for the purpose of rebutting a suggestion that his evidence has been fabricated.

This shall not be construed as preventing a witness statement (that is, a written statement of oral evidence which a party to the proceedings intends to lead) from being adopted by a witness in giving evidence or treated as his evidence.

Thus, in civil trials, prior consistent statements are admissible in evidence either with the leave of the court or for the purpose of rebutting an allegation of fabrication. Because the Civil Evidence Act 1995 has effectively abolished the hearsay rule in civil proceedings, such statements will be admissible in evidence for their truth, subject to the relevant provisions of the Act (see Chapter 7) being satisfied.

(e) Refreshing memory

(i) In court

A witness may, while testifying, be permitted to refresh his or her memory from an entry in a document if it was made or verified by the witness contemporaneously with the events in question.

See generally R R Jerrard, 'The Police Officer's Notebook' (1993) 157 *Justice of the Peace* 5; M Newark and A Samuels, 'Refreshing Memory' [1978] *Criminal Law Review* 408.

MADE OR VERIFIED BY THE WITNESS

The entry in the document, if not actually made by the witness, must at least have been verified by him or her.

Extract 4.4.16

Anderson v Whalley (1852) 3 Car & K 54, 54–5; 175 ER 460, 460 (Nisi Prius)

Case for the negligent navigation of a vessel, whereby the vessel was injured. In the course of the cause the captain of the defendant's vessel was put into the witness box. He deposed that the ship's log, which he produced, was written by the mate, and that the mate was and had been for some time serving abroad on the coast of Portugal; that he had himself read the log about a week after it was written; that the matters to which it referred were then fresh in his mind, and he at that time thought the narrative it contained to be correct.

It was then proposed that the witness should refresh his memory by looking at the log-book.

Byles, Serjt, for the plaintiffs, objected. The witness had not himself written the log-book, and therefore could not be allowed to refresh his memory by it. The absence of the mate was not an excuse.

Crowder, *contra*.

The learned Judge overruled the objection.

Compare *R v Eleftheriou*.[33]

'CONTEMPORANEOUSLY'

The requirement of contemporaneity is interpreted flexibly by the courts:

Extract 4.4.17

A-G's Reference (No 3 of 1979) (1979) 69 Cr App R 411, 414 (CA)

THE LORD CHIEF JUSTICE: Looking at paragraph 515 of *Archbold* (40th ed), a book available to all the judges, one finds this: 'The rule may be stated as follows: a witness may refresh his memory by reference to any writing made or verified by himself concerning and contemporaneously with, the facts to which he testifies. "Contemporaneously" is a somewhat misleading word in the context of the memory refreshing rule. It is sufficient, for the purposes of the rule, if the writing was made or verified at a time when the facts were still fresh in the witness' memory.' That, in our view, is the correct rule.

See also *R v Simmonds*.[34]

Even where the contemporaneity requirement is not satisfied, however, a witness may, subject to certain conditions being satisfied, be permitted to stop testifying for a short while in order to refresh his or her memory from a document:

Extract 4.4.18

R v Da Silva [1990] 1 WLR 31, 36 (CA)

STUART-SMITH LJ: In our judgment, . . . it should be open to the judge, in the exercise of his discretion and in the interests of justice, to permit a witness

---

[33] (1993) *The Times*, 2 March.
[34] [1969] 1 QB 685.

who has begun to give evidence to refresh his memory from a statement made near to the time of events in question, even though it does not come within the definition of contemporaneous, provided he is satisfied: (1) that the witness indicates that he cannot now recall the details of events because of the lapse of time since they took place; (2) that he made a statement much nearer the time of the events and that the contents of the statement represented his recollection at the time he made it; (3) that he had not read the statement before coming into the witness box; (4) that he wished to have an opportunity to read the statement before he continued to give evidence.

We do not think that it matters whether the witness withdraws from the witness box and reads his statement, as he would do if he had had the opportunity before entering the witness box, or whether he reads it in the witness box. What is important is that if the former course is adopted, no communication must be had with the witness, other than to see that he can read the statement in peace. Moreover, if either course is adopted, the statement must be removed from him when he comes to give his evidence and he should not be permitted to refer to it again, unlike a contemporaneous statement which may be used to refresh memory while giving evidence.

It would appear that what was said in *Da Silva* has not been treated as being prescriptive, and that the trial judge is vested with considerable discretion in determining the issue:

Extract 4.4.18

R v South Ribble Magistrates, ex p Cochrane
[1996] 2 Cr App R 544, 550, 552–3 (DC)

HENRY LJ: I do not understand the court there to be saying, as a matter of law, that once a witness was in the witness box he could only refer to his previous non-contemporaneous statement if all four criteria were satisfied. It was permissive, not expressed by way of invariable limitation. That, it seems to me, is supported from the tenor of the judgment when read as a whole.

. . .

. . . Take, for example, the long case: serious frauds require considerable preparation from witnesses who routinely have their own copies of their statements which may run to hundreds of pages. Clearly they will refer to them in the days or weeks they may spend in the witness box. They will have studied those statements both before and during their time in the witness box, and the course of justice is helped and not hindered by that because in complicated matters it is necessary that witnesses should be properly prepared, otherwise matters are reduced to a memory test and justice is not assisted. What is said there will apply equally to the confused, flustered and nervous old lady. Whether she has read her statement before she goes into the witness box or not, if she was confused and flustered when she first read it before giving evidence, she may very well need to read it again and the discretion should lie in the trial judge to allow her to do so.

Finally, in relation to the relevance as to whether a witness has taken the opportunity to read their statement before going into the witness box, there can be no logical difference between someone who has read the statement and for some reason not taken it in properly and one who has never read it at all. It seems to me that the judge has a real discretion as to whether to permit a witness to refresh his memory from a non-contemporaneous document. By 'real discretion' I mean a strong discretion, a choice of alternatives free of binding criteria. I do not mean the so-called weak discretion which is not a true judicial discretion at all, but simply a binding rule of law to be followed by the judge.

... *Da Silva*, as I read it, does not take away the judge's genuine, strong discretion. The judge in a *Da Silva* case would look at the *Da Silva* criteria. If they existed he would be confident that, in the words of the judgment, it would be open to him to admit reference in the witness box to a non-contemporary statement if the criteria would be made out. However, he would not be bound in all circumstances (and I numerated just two) to forbid such reference if those criteria were not satisfied.

The objection taken to this view that I have formed is the familiar one of floodgates. I reject that emphatically. Modern appellate practice recognises more and more that the trial judge has the best opportunity of getting these discretionary decisions right. We can safely rely on the trial judge to follow the twin lodestars of the requirements of fairness and the requirements of justice. Where, as here, there is a strong discretion, the appellate courts will give a generous margin of appreciation to the trial judge in his exercise of that discretion.

STATUS OF MEMORY-REFRESHING DOCUMENTS

What are the precise uses to which a memory-refreshing document may be put? This question was considered by the Court of Appeal in the following cases:

Extract 4.4.19

R v Britton [1987] 1 WLR 539, 541–4 (CA)

LORD LANE CJ: ... cross-examining counsel is entitled to inspect the note in order to check its contents. He can do so without making the document evidence. Indeed he may go further and cross-examine upon it. If he does so and succeeds in confining his cross-examination to those parts of it which have already been used by the witness to refresh his memory, he does not make it evidence. If on the other hand he strays beyond that part of the note which has been so used, the party calling him ... may insist on it being treated as evidence in the case, which will thereupon become an exhibit.

The cases upon which that common law rule is based ... are these. *Gregory v Tavernor* (1833) 6 C & P 280, 281 where Gurney B observed:

'The memorandum itself is not evidence; and particular entries only are used by the witness to refresh his memory. The defendant's counsel may cross-examine on those entries, without making them his evidence. The defendant's counsel cannot go into evidence of the contents of other parts of the book without making it his evidence; but he may cross-examine on the entries already referred to, and the jury may also see those entries if they wish to do so.'

More recently Sir Jocelyn Simon P in *Senat v Senat* [1965] P 172, 177 observed:

'... In my view the mere inspection of a document does not render it evidence which counsel inspecting it is bound to put in. I think that the true rules are as follows: Where a document is used to refresh a witness's memory, cross-examining counsel may inspect that document in order to check it, without making it evidence. Moreover he may cross-examine upon it without making it evidence provided that his cross-examination does not go further than the parts which are used for refreshing the memory of the witness: *Gregory v Tavernor* (1833) 6 C & P 280. But if a party calls for and inspects a document held by the other party, he is bound to put it in evidence if he is required to do so: ...'

...

What the effect of exhibiting such a document might be is another matter. The decision of this court in *Reg v Virgo* (1978) 67 Cr App R 323, shows that their effect is solely to show consistency in the witness producing them, and they are not to be used as evidence of the truth of the facts stated in the aide-mémoire. ...

...

It is to be observed that in *Cross on Evidence*, 6th ed (1985) pp 254–255 the following passage appears:

'There is an old general rule, inadequately explored in the modern authorities, that, if a party calls for and inspects a document held by the other party, he is bound to put it in evidence if required to do so. But ...' – and then he cites the passage from *Senat v Senat* [1965] P 172, 177 which we have already quoted, and goes on – 'If, therefore, a witness refreshes his memory concerning a date or an address by referring to a diary, he may be cross-examined about the terms or form of the entries used to refresh his memory without there being any question of the right of the party calling him to insist that the diary should become evidence in the case. On the other hand, if the witness is cross-examined about other parts of the diary, the party calling him may insist on its being treated as evidence in the case.'

We respectfully adopt that passage. It is, in the view of this court, still good law . . .

...

... As indicated by this court in *Reg v Virgo*, 67 Cr App R 323 in any particular case where the judge takes the view that the interests of justice so require, he will have a discretion to refuse to allow the document to go before the jury, if this could give rise to prejudice to the defendant.

Extract 4.4.20

R v Sekhon (1986) 85 Cr App R 19, 22–3 (CA)

WOOLF LJ: ... the documents used by the witness for the purpose of refreshing his memory must be available for inspection by the other parties who can cross-examine on the basis of that document if it is relevant to do so. In the majority of cases the fact that there is such cross-examination will not make the record evidence in the case, nor will it be necessary for a jury to inspect the document, and it will not be appropriate for the record to become an exhibit.

 ... Where however the nature of the cross-examination involves a suggestion that the witness has subsequently made up his evidence, which will usually involve, if not expressly at least by implication, the allegation that the record is concocted, the record may be admissible to rebut this suggestion and, if the nature of the record assists as to this, to show whether or not it is genuine, that is to say whether or not it has the appearance of being a contemporaneous record which has not subsequently been altered.

 ... Where the record is inconsistent with the witness's evidence, it can be admitted as evidence of this inconsistency.

 .∴. It is also appropriate for the record to be put before the jury where it is difficult for the jury to follow the cross-examination of the witness who has refreshed his memory, without having the record or, in practice, copies of the records before them.

 ... However, subject to the exception mentioned below, in the cases referred to where the record is permitted to go before the jury, it will not be placed before them as evidence of the truth of the contents of the record, and it will not amount to corroboration of the evidence given by the witness refreshing his memory from the record. It will on the one hand be before them for the more limited purpose of being a 'tool' ... to assist the jury to evaluate the truth of the evidence given in the witness box by the witness. Whether in these circumstances it is appropriate to treat the document as an exhibit is of no practical importance. In a case involving a lot of documents, it may be appropriate to give it an exhibit number just to identify the document.

 ... There may be cases where it is also convenient to use the record as an aide memoire as to the witness's evidence where the evidence is long and involved. However care should be exercised in adopting this course in cases where the evidence, and therefore the record, is bitterly contested, because of the danger that the use of the document for this purpose could result in the jury misunderstanding its status and lead to their wrongly regarding the document as being evidence in itself.

 ... Although normally the document when admitted is not evidence of the truth of its contents, in those cases where it provides, because of its nature, material by which its authenticity can be judged, then in respect of that material and only for the purpose of assessing its authenticity it can amount to evidence in the case.

In essence, therefore, there are two main points which are worthy of note when considering the status of memory-refreshing documents. The first concerns the situation where, in the course of cross-examining on a memory-refreshing document, the cross-examining party strays into parts of the document which have not been used by the witness to refresh memory. This entitles the party calling the witness to insist that these parts of the document be treated as evidence in the case. In criminal cases such evidence would, by virtue of the rule against hearsay, go only to the credit of the witness (to demonstrate consistency). The Law Commission has recommended, however, that it be admissible to establish the truth of any facts asserted.[35] It would be admissible for this purpose in civil cases, provided that the relevant requirements of the Civil Evidence Act 1995 (see Chapter 7) are satisfied.

The second point, which emerges from *Sekhon*, relates to an allegation made in a criminal case that a record in a document which a witness has used to refresh memory was concocted. In such a situation the party calling the witness is entitled, in order to rebut the allegation by establishing the genuineness of the record, to put the record in evidence to demonstrate that it has the appearance of being a contemporaneous record which has not been altered subsequently.

It is clear that, in many cases, the memory of the witness is not actually 'refreshed' by consulting the memory-refreshing document, and that he or she is merely testifying to the accuracy of the document.[36] In such a situation, the document is effectively being admitted, 'through' the testimony of the witness, as evidence of the facts contained therein – a clear evasion of the rule against hearsay in criminal cases.[37] It is noteworthy that the Law Commission recommends in its report on criminal hearsay that, if

(1) a witness does not, and cannot reasonably be expected to, remember a matter well enough to be able to give oral evidence of it,
(2) the witness previously made a statement of that matter when it was fresh in his or her memory, and
(3) the witness indicates that, to the best of his or her belief, he or she made the statement and it is true,

the statement should be admissible as evidence of that matter.[38]

(ii) Out of court

The issue of refreshing memory out of court is discussed in the following cases:

---

[35] Law Commission (Law Com No 245), *Evidence in Criminal Proceedings: Hearsay and Related Topics* (1997) 164.

[36] *Maugham v Hubbard* (1828) 8 B & C 14; 108 ER 948; *Lord Talbot v Cusack* (1864) 17 ICLR 213, 220 per Hayes J; *R v Simmonds* [1969] 1 QB 685.

[37] See generally A Ashworth and R Pattenden, 'Reliability, Hearsay Evidence and the English Criminal Trial' (1986) 102 *Law Quarterly Review* 292, 298–300; A A S Zuckerman, *The Principles of Criminal Evidence* (1989) 187–92. The rule against hearsay will be considered in detail in Ch 7 of this book.

[38] Law Commission (Law Com No 245), *Evidence in Criminal Proceedings: Hearsay and Related Topics* (1997) 163.

Extract 4.4.21

R v Richardson [1971] 2 QB 484, 489–90 (CA)

SACHS LJ: Is there, then, anything wrong in the witnesses in this case having been offered an opportunity to see that which they were entitled to ask for and to be shown on request? In a case such as the present, is justice more likely to be done if a witness may not see a statement made by him at a time very much closer to that of the incident?

Curiously enough, these questions are very bare of authority. Indeed, the only case which has a direct bearing on this issue is one which was decided not in this country but on appeal in the Supreme Court of Hong Kong in 1966: *Lau Pak Ngam v The Queen* [1966] Crim LR 443. In the view of each member of this court this case contains some sage observations, two of which are apt to be quoted. One of them is:

> 'Testimony in the witness-box becomes more a test of memory than of truthfulness if witnesses are deprived of the opportunity of checking their recollection beforehand by reference to statements or notes made at a time closer to the events in question.'

The other is:

> 'Refusal of access to statements would tend to create difficulties for honest witnesses but be likely to do little to hamper dishonest witnesses.'

With those views this court agrees. It is true that by the practice of the courts of this country a line is drawn at the moment when a witness enters the witness-box; when giving evidence there in chief he cannot refresh his memory except by a document which, to quote the words of *Phipson on Evidence*, 11th ed (1970), p 634, para 1528: 'must have been written either at the time of the transaction or so shortly afterwards that the facts were fresh in his memory.' (Incidentally, this definition does provide a measure of elasticity and should not be taken to confine witnesses to an over-short period.) This is, moreover, a practice which the courts can enforce: when a witness is in the box the court can see that he complies with it.

The courts, however, must take care not to deprive themselves by new, artificial rules of practice of the best chances of learning the truth. The courts are under no compulsion unnecessarily to follow on a matter of practice the lure of the rules of logic in order to produce unreasonable results which would hinder the course of justice. Obviously it would be wrong if several witnesses were handed statements in circumstances which enabled one to compare with another what each had said. But there can be no general rule (which, incidentally, would be unenforceable, unlike the rule as to what can be done in the witness-box) that witnesses may not before trial see the statements which they made at some period reasonably close to the time of the event which is the subject of the trial. Indeed, one can imagine many cases, particularly those of a complex nature, where such a rule would militate very greatly against the interests of justice.

Extract 4.4.22

R v Westwell [1976] 2 All ER 812, 814–15 (CA)

BRIDGE LJ: There is no general rule that prospective witnesses may not, before giving evidence at a trial, see the statements which they made at or near the time of the events of which they are to testify. They may see them whether they make a request to do so or merely accept an offer to allow them to do so. On the other hand, there is no rule that witnesses must be allowed to see their statements before giving evidence. There may be cases where there is reason to suppose that the witness has some sinister or improper purpose in wanting to see his statement and it is in the interests of justice that he should be denied the opportunity. . . . However, in most cases and particularly where, as often happens, there is a long interval between the alleged offence and the trial, the interests of justice are likely to be best served and witnesses will be more fairly treated if, before giving evidence, they are allowed to refresh their recollection by reference to their own statements made near the time of the events in question. . . . We have all, from time to time, seen the plight of an apparently honest witness, subjected to captious questioning about minor differences between his evidence in the witness box and the statement he made long ago and has never seen since, although his tormentor has it in his hand and has studied it in detail. Although such cross-examination frequently generates in the jury obvious sympathy with the witness and obvious irritation with the cross-examiner, it must leave a witness who has come to court to do his honest best with a smarting sense of having been treated unfairly.

. . .

. . . In some cases the fact that a witness has read his statement before going into the witness box may be relevant to the weight which can properly be attached to his evidence and injustice might be caused to the defendant if the jury were left in ignorance of that fact.

Accordingly, if the prosecution is aware that statements have been seen by witnesses it will be appropriate to inform the defence. But if, for any reason, this is not done, the omission cannot of itself be a ground for acquittal. If the prosecution tell the defence that the witness has been allowed to see his statement the defence can make such use of the information as it thinks prudent, but in any event the defence, where such a fact may be material, can ask the witness directly when giving evidence whether the witness has recently seen his statement. Where such information is material it does not ultimately matter whether it is volunteered by the prosecution or elicited by the defence. If the mere fact that the prosecution had not volunteered the information were a bar to conviction, this would be an artificial and arbitrary rule more appropriate to a game or a sporting contest than to a judicial process. The question for the court is whether, in the event, the trial can be continued without prejudice or risk of injustice to the defendant.

Is the liberal attitude of the law to refreshing memory out of court justifiable? See generally M N Howard, 'Refreshment of Memory out of Court' [1972] *Criminal Law Review* 351.

5. CROSS-EXAMINATION

(a) The purposes of cross-examination

Cross-examination, described by Wigmore as 'beyond any doubt the greatest legal engine ever invented for the discovery of truth',[39] is said to constitute a powerful weapon in exposing the possible unreliability of that witness's testimony. The purpose of cross-examination is twofold: first, to elicit evidence supporting the cross-examining party's version of the facts, and, secondly, to discredit the evidence of the witness. The two essential restrictions which apply to examination-in-chief do not apply to cross-examination. In *Parkin v Moon*, Alderson B observed: 'I apprehend you may put a leading question to an unwilling witness on the examination in chief at the discretion of the Judge; but you may *always* put a leading question in cross-examination, whether a witness be unwilling or not.'[40] Further, questions may be asked in cross-examination which go solely to the credit of the witness. The functions which cross-examination is meant to serve may be illuminated further by the instruction in the 'art' of cross-examination provided in the following extract:

Extract 4.5.1

J W Strong (ed), *McCormick on Evidence* (4th ed 1992) 39–41

Preparation is the key. Certainly, some lawyers seem to have a native talent for conducting effective cross-examination. A great Victorian advocate, Montagu Williams, seemed to share this view when he said, 'I am by trade a reader of faces and minds.' Today, however, the stress is upon thorough preparation, not upon sudden sallies of inspiration. Improvisation is often necessary but its results are small compared to those from planned questions based on facts dug out before trial. The steps in preparation are explained in many of the works concerning the art of cross-examination. Not all steps can be taken as to all adverse witnesses. Nor can every case bear the expense of thorough preparation. Nevertheless, preparation before trial is the only soil from which, in the day-to-day run of cases, successful cross-examination can grow. . . .

No cross-examination without a purpose. As we have seen, these purposes may be, first, to elicit new facts, qualifying the direct, or in some states bearing on any issue in the case; second, to test the story of the witness by exploring its details and implications, in the hope of disclosing inconsistencies or impossibilities; and third, to prove out of the mouth of the witness, impeaching facts known to the cross-examiner such as prior contradictory statements, bias and conviction of crime. In considering any of these objectives, but particularly the latter two, the cross-examiner must be conscious that the odds are slanted against him. An unfavorable answer is more damaging when

---

[39] J H Wigmore (rev J H Chadbourn), *Evidence in Trials at Common Law (Vol 5)* (1974) 32.
[40] (1836) 7 Car & P 408, 409; 173 ER 181, 181–2 (emphasis added).

elicited on cross-examination. It is hard for a cross-examiner to win his case on cross-examination; it is easy for him to lose it. Accordingly, if the witness has done no harm on direct examination, a cross-examination for the second or third purpose is usually ill-advised. There remains the witness whose direct testimony has been damaging, or even threatens to be destructive of the cross-examiner's case if the jury believes it. Cross-examination will usually be needed, and whether the object shall be a skirting reconnaissance distant from the crucial issues, or a frontal attack on the story or the credit of the witness, will depend on the availability of impeaching material disclosed by preparation and on a judgment of the risks and advantages of the holding defence or the counterattack.

A question directed to a crucial or critical fact on which the outcome of the case depends should seldom be asked an adverse witness unless the cross-examiner is reasonably confident the answer will be favorable. Similarly, broad questions which open the door for an eager witness to reinforce his direct testimony with corroborating circumstances, eg, 'How do you explain?' or 'How did it happen?' are usually ill-advised. If a discrepant fact has been drawn out on cross-examination, it is often better to wait and stress the inconsistency in argument than to press the witness with it. It is the responsibility of the proponent's counsel to elicit an explanation, if any, on redirect.

In conducting a testing or exploratory examination, for obvious reasons it is inadvisable to follow the order of the witness's direct testimony. 'If the witness is falsifying, jump quickly with rapid-fire questions from one point of the narrative to the other, without time or opportunity for a connected narrative: backward, forward, forward, backward from the middle to the beginning, etc.'

Cross-examine for the jury, not for your client. It is often a temptation to the cross-examiner to display his wit and skill before his client, or to feed the vengeful feelings of the latter toward opposing witnesses by tripping and humiliating them upon cross-examination. Frequently these small victories upon collateral inquiries are easy to secure. The odds between the experienced advocate and the witness, nervous in new surroundings, are not even. The cross-examiner needs constantly to remind himself that the jury is keenly aware of this inequality of position, and that each juror is prone to imagine himself in the shoes of the witness. Better results with the witness, and a better impression upon the jury will usually flow from tact and consideration than from bulldozing and ridicule. The cloak falls more easily in the sunshine than in the hurricane. In the rare case when the cross-examiner is convinced that a crucial witness is dishonest and that he can demonstrate it, the attack must be pressed home to the jugular. But the cross-examiner should always be mindful of his duty to use his skills and weapons justly and fairly, and also of the need so to conduct himself that the jury, with its latent sympathy for witnesses, will be impressed with his fairness.

Make one or two big points; end on a high note. When the cross-examiner has led up to and secured an important admission, he should not dull the edge of the effect by too many explanatory details, nor risk a recantation by calling for a repetition. He should pass on to another important point if he has one, and end the examination when his last big point is made. 'When you have struck oil stop boring.'

While the above generalities are worthwhile general guideposts, the cross-examiner must adapt his techniques to the specific situation he faces. Of course, different experts might well use different techniques in cross-examining the same witness at a particular trial.

Contrary to popular belief, the utility of cross-examination in ensuring the reliability of evidence may be limited. Cross-examination may well be of little use in exposing a witness's insincerity;[41] 'it is, in truth, quite doubtful whether it is not the honest but weak or timid witness, rather than the rogue, who most often goes down under the fire of a cross-examination'.[42] It is also possible that the efficacy of cross-examination in exposing the faulty perception by a witness of the events supposedly 'witnessed' may not be as high as may be assumed.[43] Additionally, suggesting facts to a witness in cross-examination may actually distort, rather than assist, his or her memory.[44]

What is the position where a witness who has been examined in-chief is unable to be cross-examined?

Extract 4.5.2

R v Lawless (1993) 98 Cr App R 342, 351 (CA)

WATKINS LJ: There are two authorities which bear upon the difficult decision which the judge had to make.

The first is *Stretton and McCallion* (1986) 86 Cr App R 7, a case in which this Court upheld a conviction of two men of sexual offences against an epileptic and mentally-handicapped woman who was unable to continue with her evidence after she had been cross-examined for some time by counsel, who appeared for both defendants. As Lawton LJ observed in giving the judgment of the court, counsel had virtually finished cross-examining her on all the matters with which one of them was concerned, and, save in a most general way, had not started to cross-examine her upon the specific matters involving the other defendant. There was other evidence, provided in large part by the defendants themselves, confirming much of the complainant's account of the incident in question save on the issue of consent. There was also evidence of lies by the defendants which, the judge directed the jury,

---

[41] T Finman, 'Implied Assertions as Hearsay: Some Criticisms of the Uniform Rules of Evidence' (1962) 14 *Stanford Law Review* 682, 690; R C Park, 'A Subject Matter Approach to Hearsay Reform' (1987) 86 *Michigan Law Review* 51, 96; E Swift, 'A Foundation Fact Approach to Hearsay' (1987) 75 *California Law Review* 1339, 1357 n 50. See also J Allan, 'The Working and Rationale of the Hearsay Rule and the Implications of Modern Psychological Knowledge' (1991) 44 *Current Legal Problems* 217.

[42] J W Strong (ed), *McCormick on Evidence* (4th ed 1992) 41.

[43] E A Scallen, 'Constitutional Dimensions of Hearsay Reform: Toward a Three-Dimensional Confrontation Clause' (1992) 76 *Minnesota Law Review* 623, 627 n 15.

[44] Australian Law Reform Commission, *Evidence (Vol 1)* (Report No 26: Interim) (1985) 362; Scottish Law Commission, *Evidence: Report on Hearsay Evidence in Criminal Proceedings* (Scot Law Com No 149) (1995) 16.

were capable of corroborating her evidence on that issue. The problem had thus arisen at a later stage of the witness's evidence in that case than in this, and there was other evidence going to the essential issue. The judge decided to allow the trial to continue and to deal with it by a direction which invited the jury to acquit both defendants if they were not sure that the cross-examination of her by the defendants' counsel had sufficiently probed and tested the complainant's evidence so as to enable them to judge fairly her credibility.

The other case is *Wyatt* [1990] Crim LR 343, in which a child complainant of indecent assault gave evidence in chief and was cross-examined on it for about 15 to 20 minutes before becoming too distressed to continue. There was strong corroborative evidence of her complaint. The judge does not appear to have given the jury a warning of the sort given by the judge in *Stretton and McCallion*; but he did direct them fairly on the evidence of the girl and left it to them to determine her credibility. The conviction was upheld.

The circumstances of both those cases are a long way from those here.

In our view, it is at least doubtful whether any direction, however strongly expressed, could have overcome the powerful prejudice of Davison's damning evidence going *wholly* unchallenged and untested by cross-examination. For the reasons given by the appellants' counsel, he was the central figure in the inter-related offences of corruption, deception and fraud with which the appellants were charged. His was the only direct evidence of corruption which, if accepted by the jury, gave meaning to the prosecution case against each of them on their involvement with Davison in deceiving and defrauding their employer. There was a sharp issue between him on the one hand, and Lawless and Basford on the other, whether he had given them respectively goods and services or whether they had paid him for them in cash or in work. There was also the difficulty of the conflicting direction which the judge would have to give in an attempt to do justice to all the defendants, one that would undermine his evidence against Lawless and Basford whilst at the same time putting it forward as support for Smith.

(b) Limitations on cross-examination

The right to cross-examine is, naturally, subject to some limitations:

Extract 4.5.3

Mechanical and General Inventions Co and Lehwess v Austin and the Austin Motor Co [1935] AC 346, 359–60 (HL)

VISCOUNT SANKEY LC: Cross-examination is a powerful and valuable weapon for the purpose of testing the veracity of a witness and the accuracy and completeness of his story. It is entrusted to the hands of counsel in the confidence that it will be used with discretion; and with due regard to the assistance to be rendered by it to the Court, not forgetting at the same time the burden that is imposed upon the witness. . . .

... It is right to make due allowance for the irritation caused by the strain and stress of a long and complicated case, but a protracted and irrelevant cross-examination not only adds to the cost of litigation, but is a waste of public time. Such a cross-examination becomes indefensible when it is conducted ... without restraint and without the courtesy and consideration which a witness is entitled to expect in a Court of law. It is not sufficient for the due administration of justice to have a learned, patient and impartial judge. Equally with him, the solicitors who prepare the case and the counsel who present it to the Court are taking part in the great task of doing justice between man and man.

Extract 4.5.4

Hobbs v Tinling [1929] 2 KB 1, 50–1 (CA)

SANKEY LJ: The Court can always exercise its discretion to decide whether a question as to credit is one which the witness should be compelled to answer, and in my view, . . . referring to the Indian Evidence Act, s 148, in the exercise of its discretion the Court should have regard to the following considerations: '(1.) Such questions are proper if they are of such a nature that the truth of the imputation conveyed by them would seriously affect the opinion of the Court as to the credibility of the witness on the matter to which he testifies. (2.) Such questions are improper if the imputation which they convey relates to matters so remote in time, or of such a character, that the truth of the imputation would not affect, or would affect in a slight degree, the opinion of the Court as to the credibility of the witness on the matter to which he testifies. (3.) Such questions are improper if there is a great disproportion between the importance of the imputation made against the witness's character and the importance of his evidence.'

And in *R v Sweet-Escott*, Lawton J said: 'Since the purpose of cross-examination as to credit is to show that the witness ought not to be believed on oath, the matters about which he is questioned must relate to his likely standing after cross-examination with the tribunal which is trying him or listening to his evidence.'[45]

The notion that cross-examination as to credit must be kept within proper limits finds expression in the requirement in the Australian Evidence Act 1995 that evidence elicited by such cross-examination must possess 'substantial probative value':

Extract 4.5.5

Evidence Act 1995 (Australia), ss 102, 103

102. The credibility rule
Evidence that is relevant only to a witness's credibility is not admissible.

[45] (1971) 55 Cr App R 316, 320.

103. Exception: cross-examination as to credibility
(1) The credibility rule does not apply to evidence adduced in cross-examination of a witness if the evidence has substantial probative value.
(2) Without limiting the matters to which the court may have regard in deciding whether the evidence has substantial probative value, it is to have regard to:
- (a) whether the evidence tends to prove that the witness knowingly or recklessly made a false representation when the witness was under an obligation to tell the truth; and
- (b) the period that has elapsed since the acts or events to which the evidence relates were done or occurred.

(c) The rule in *Browne v Dunn*

As a general rule, a party which fails to cross-examine a witness on a particular issue cannot later invite the jury to reject the witness's evidence-in-chief on that issue:

Extract 4.5.6

Wharf Properties Ltd v Eric Cumine Associates (1991)
29 Con LR 84, 97–8 (PC)

LORD OLIVER OF AYLMERTON: Their Lordships have been referred to a number of authorities relating to the need, where the court is invited to reject the testimony of a witness, and to accept evidence to a contrary effect, to put the conflicting evidence to the witness whose testimony is attacked. *Browne v Dunn* (1893) 6 R 67 reported only in an obscure series known as 'The Reports' in 1893 is cited as authority for proposition which is stated thus in the headnote:

'If in the course of a case it is intended to suggest that a witness is not speaking the truth upon a particular point, his attention must be directed to the fact by cross-examination showing that that imputation is intended to be made, so that he may have an opportunity of making any explanation which is open to him, unless it is otherwise perfectly clear that he has had full notice beforehand that there is an intention to impeach the credibility of his story, or (per Lord Morris) the story is of an incredible and romancing character.'

The principle, is of course, of particular importance in criminal cases (see *R v Hart* (1932) 23 Cr App R 202; *R v Fenlon* (1980) 71 Cr App R 307) ...

(d) The collateral-finality rule

(i) The rule

The *collateral-finality rule* provides that where cross-examination goes solely to a collateral matter (typically, the credit of a witness), then the witness's answers are to be treated as final. The cross-examining party may not adduce evidence to rebut these answers. It is only where cross-examination goes to a fact in issue that the cross-examining party may call rebuttal evidence. What is the rationale for this rule?

Extract 4.5.7

A-G v Hitchcock (1847) 1 Ex 91, 103–4; 154 ER 38, 44
(Exchequer Division)

ALDERSON B: The reason why a party is obliged to take the answer of a witness is, that if he were permitted to go into it, it is only justice to allow the witness to call other evidence in support of the testimony he has given, and as those witnesses might be cross-examined as to their conduct, such a course would be productive of endless collateral issues. . . . Then in the next place, in my opinion, when the question is not relevant, strictly speaking, to the issue, but tending to contradict the witness, his answer must be taken, although it tends to shew that he, in that particular instance, speaks falsely, and although it is not altogether immaterial to the matter in issue, for the sake of the general public convenience; for great inconvenience would follow from a continual course of those sorts of cross-examinations which would be let in in the case of a witness being called for the purposes of contradiction.

ROLFE B: The laws of evidence on this subject, as to what ought and what ought not to be received, must be considered as founded on a sort of comparative consideration of the time to be occupied in examinations of this nature, and the time which it is practicable to bestow upon them. If we lived for a thousand years instead of about sixty or seventy, and every case were of sufficient importance, it might be possible, and perhaps proper, to throw a light on matters in which every possible question might be suggested, for the purpose of seeing by such means whether the whole was unfounded, or what portion of it was not, and to raise every possible inquiry as to the truth of the statements made. But I do not see how that could be; in fact, mankind find it to be impossible. Therefore some line must be drawn . . .

The crucial issue, therefore, is to determine whether the cross-examination goes to facts in issue, with the result that the collateral-finality rule has no application. That determination is not, however, a straightforward one.

Extract 4.5.8

R v Busby (1981) 75 Cr App R 79, 82 (CA)

The appellant was alleged to have made very damaging remarks to the police when interviewed about his alleged offences. Two police officers were cross-examined to establish that one of them, in the presence of the other, had threatened a potential defence witness to prevent him from giving evidence.

Both officers denied threatening this witness. The issue arose as to whether this witness could be called to testify about the officers' visit to him.

EVELEIGH LJ: We are of the opinion that the learned judge was wrong to refuse to admit the evidence. If true, it would have shown that the police were prepared to go to improper lengths in order to secure the accused's conviction. It was the accused's case that the statement attributed to him had been fabricated, a suggestion which could not be accepted by the jury unless they thought that the officers concerned were prepared to go to improper lengths to secure a conviction.

... In the present case, the evidence, if true, would have indicated that the officers were prepared to cheat in furtherance of the prosecution.

As will be seen, there is considerable uncertainty about whether the true basis of the decision in *Busby* was that the cross-examination went to facts in issue, with the result that the collateral-finality rule was inapplicable. It has also been interpreted in the following ways:

(1) The cross-examination did go to credit, but the 'bias' exception to the collateral-finality rule (examined below) applied.[46]
(2) The cross-examination did go to credit, but there is a new exception to the collateral-finality rule which allows evidence showing the improper lengths to which the police are prepared to resort to secure a conviction.[47]

The law has recognised that injustice would result if the collateral-finality rule were to be applied rigidly in all circumstances. Accordingly, there are five established exceptions to the rule.

(ii) The exceptions

PRIOR INCONSISTENT STATEMENTS

Where a witness under cross-examination denies having made a prior inconsistent statement, it may be possible to adduce evidence that such a statement was in fact made:

Extract 4.5.9

Criminal Procedure Act 1865 ('Lord Denman's Act'), s 4

4. As to proof of contradictory statements of adverse witnesses
If a witness, upon cross-examination as to a former statement made by him relative to the subject matter of the indictment or proceeding, and inconsistent

---

[46] See *R v Edwards*, below.
[47] See *R v Funderburk*, below.

with his present testimony, does not distinctly admit that he has made such statement, proof may be given that he did in fact make it; but before such proof can be given the circumstances of the supposed statement, sufficient to designate the particular occasion, must be mentioned to the witness, and he must be asked whether or not he has made such statement.

Extract 4.5.10

Criminal Procedure Act 1865 ('Lord Denman's Act'), s 5

5. Cross-examinations as to previous statements in writing
A witness may be cross-examined as to previous statements made by him in writing, or reduced into writing, relative to the subject matter of the indictment or proceeding, without such writing being shown to him; but if it is intended to contradict such witness by the writing, his attention must, before such contradictory proof can be given, be called to those parts of the writing which are to be used for the purpose of so contradicting him: Provided always, that it shall be competent for the judge, at any time during the trial, to require the production of the writing for his inspection, and he may thereupon make such use of it for the purposes of the trial as he may think fit.

These provisions apply to both civil and criminal proceedings. Section 4 applies to statements made either orally or in writing, while s 5 applies only to statements made in writing.

The following case demonstrates that normal common-law considerations govern the question whether a witness may be cross-examined on a prior inconsistent statement with a view to discrediting that witness. It is only in relation to leading evidence of the statement in rebuttal that s 4 and, if applicable, s 5 of the Criminal Procedure Act 1865 would come into play. These sections require that the prior statement be 'relative to the subject matter of the indictment or proceeding'.

Extract 4.5.11

R v Funderburk [1990] 1 WLR 587, 591, 593–5, 597–9 (CA)

The appellant was accused of unlawful sexual intercourse with a 13-year-old girl. The girl described the first incident in terms which clearly amounted to an account of the loss of her virginity. The defence applied (a) to put to her that, prior to that incident, she had told a potential witness that she had had intercourse with two other men and, if she denied this, (b) to call that witness to testify to the contrary. The judge refused both applications, ruling that whether she was a virgin at the time of the first incident was immaterial to the issue of whether the appellant had had sexual intercourse with her.

HENRY J: Where questions go solely to the credibility of the witness or to collateral facts the general rule is that answers given to such questions are final and cannot be contradicted by rebutting evidence. . . .

The authorities show that the defence may call evidence contradicting that of the prosecution witnesses where their evidence: (a) goes to an issue in the case (that is obvious); (b) shows that the witness made a previous inconsistent statement relating to an issue in the case (Denman's Act, which we deal with below); (c) shows bias in the witness: *Rex v Phillips* (1936) 26 Cr App R 17; (d) shows that the police are prepared to go to improper lengths to secure a conviction; *Reg v Busby* (1981) 75 Cr App R 79; (e) in certain circumstances proves the witness's previous convictions; (f) shows that the witness has a general reputation for untruthfulness; (g) shows that medical causes would have affected the reliability of his testimony.

[Later in his judgment Henry J makes the following observation: 'It may be that the categories of exception [to the collateral-finality rule] we have already listed are not closed. It is impossible to tell the circumstances in which some problems may arise in the future.']

. . . two questions arise in this case. First, should the disputed questions have been permitted as questions either going to an issue or going to the credibility of the child? Second, if so, were her answers to such questions final or could evidence be given of previous inconsistent statements relating to previous sexual activities?

. . .

. . . though the limits on cross-examination as to credit imposed by [the Sexual Offences (Amendment) Act 1976] do not apply to this case, the court will not wish to see the mischief sought to be prevented by that Act perpetuated in this context and therefore will be astute to see that such cross-examination is not abused or extended unnecessarily. . . .

So far as concerns the general test as to the limits of cross-examination as to credit, the locus classicus of that is to be found in the judgment of Lawton J in *Reg v Sweet-Escott* (1971) 55 Cr App R 316, 320. . . .

. . .

Was the trial judge right to apply the test set out in section 4 of [Denman's] Act (dealing with the calling of evidence relating to the cross-examination) instead of the ordinary test set out in *Reg v Sweet-Escott* relating to allowing questions going to the credibility of a witness? We see nothing in section 4 which would prevent a witness's previous statement inconsistent with his testimony before the judge being put to him to challenge his credibility even where the section did not allow the evidence of the making of the inconsistent statement to be given. . . .

. . .

Accordingly we can see no basis either on the authorities or as a matter of principle for applying the Denman's Act test, relating to the calling of contradictory evidence, to the question of allowing cross-examination as to credit. To that problem it seems to us that the test suggested by Lawton J in *Reg v Sweet-Escott*, 55 Cr App R 316, is appropriate: how might the matters put to him affect his standing with the jury after cross-examination?

Applying that test it seems to us that the jury, having heard a graphic account from the child's evidence-in-chief as to how she had lost her virginity, might reasonably have wished to re-appraise her evidence and her credibility if they had heard that on other occasions she had spoken of experiences which, if true, would indicate that she could not have been a virgin at the time of the incident she so vividly described. Her standing as a witness might have been reduced.

Therefore, in our judgment, . . . the trial judge was wrong not to allow the disputed questions to be put in cross-examination.

. . . it is necessary for us to consider whether, on the likely scenario that the child had denied making the inconsistent statements, the disputed evidence could have been called.

. . .

We are disposed to agree with the editors of *Cross on Evidence*, 6th ed (1985), p 295 that where the disputed issue is a sexual one between two persons in private the difference between questions going to credit and questions going to the issue is reduced to vanishing point. I read from that work:

'It has also been remarked that sexual intercourse, whether or not consensual, most often takes place in private, and leaves few visible traces of having occurred. Evidence is often effectively limited to that of the parties, and much is likely to depend on the balance of credibility between them. This has important effects for the law of evidence since it is capable of reducing the difference between questions going to credit and questions going to the issue to vanishing point.'

Similar problems arise when considering what facts are collateral. Again, we cite from *Cross*, at p 283:

'As relevance is a matter of degree, it is impossible to devise an exhaustive means of determining when a question is collateral for the purpose of the rule under consideration; Pollock CB said in the leading case of *Attorney-General v Hitchcock* (1847) 1 Exch 91, 99: "The test whether the matter is collateral or not is this: if the answer of a witness is a matter which you would be allowed on your own part to prove in evidence – if it have such a connection with the issues, that you would be allowed to give it in evidence – then it is a matter on which you may contradict him."'

The difficulty we have in applying that celebrated test is that it seems to us to be circular. If a fact is not collateral then clearly you can call evidence to contradict it, but the so-called test is silent on how you decide whether that fact is collateral. The utility of the test may lie in the fact that the answer is an instinctive one based on the prosecutor's and the court's sense of fair play rather than any philosophic or analytic process. . . .

. . . It seems to us that on the way the prosecution presented the evidence the challenge to the loss of virginity was a challenge that not only did the jury deserve to know about on the basis that it might have affected their view on the central question of credit, but was sufficiently closely related to the subject matter of the indictment for justice to require investigation for the basis of such a challenge.

. . .

194

Accordingly it seems to us that the defence should have been allowed to put the disputed questions and, if met with a denial, to call the disputed evidence.

Where a prior inconsistent statement is given in evidence in *criminal* proceedings under s 4 or s 5 of the Criminal Procedure Act 1865, it may be used only to discredit the witness; the hearsay rule prevents it from being admitted as evidence of the facts contained in it. The Law Commission has recommended, however, that such a statement should be admissible as evidence of the facts contained in it.[48] In *civil* proceedings, the Civil Evidence Act 1995 permits such a statement to be admitted as evidence of the facts contained in it, so long as the requirements of the Act (see Chapter 7) are satisfied.

Since s 5 provides that it is open to the judge to 'make such use of that statement for the purposes of the trial as he may think fit', he or she is able, strictly speaking, to allow the entire statement to go before the jury. It may, however, be preferable in appropriate cases to permit the jury to see only that portion of the statement which relates to the matter on which the witness has been cross-examined.[49]

PRIOR CONVICTIONS

Extract 4.5.12

Clifford v Clifford [1961] 1 WLR 1274, 1276 (CA)

CAIRNS J: It has never, I think, been doubted that a conviction for any offence could be put to a witness by way of cross-examination as to credit, even though the offence was not one of dishonesty.

Section 6 of the Criminal Procedure Act 1865, which applies to both civil and criminal proceedings, provides that if, on being questioned as to whether he or she has any prior convictions, a witness 'either denies or does not admit the fact, or refuses to answer, it shall be lawful for the cross-examining party to prove such conviction'.

Section 4(1) of the Rehabilitation of Offenders Act 1974 provides that evidence of 'spent' convictions is inadmissible. Under s 7(3) of the same Act, however, such evidence is permissible where justice cannot be done in the case without the evidence being admitted. Section 4(1) has no application in

---

[48] Law Commission (Law Com No 245), *Evidence in Criminal Proceedings: Hearsay and Related Topics* (1997) 167.
[49] See *R v Beattie* (1989) 89 Cr App R 302, 306.

criminal proceedings,[50] but a *Practice Direction*[51] recommends that a spent conviction never be referred to in criminal proceedings 'when such reference can be reasonably avoided'. Further, 'no one should refer in open court to a spent conviction without the authority of the judge, which authority should not be given unless the interests of justice so require'. It is notable that the Law Commission's 'provisional view is that the Practice Direction (Crime: Spent Convictions) should be enacted in statutory form'. The Commission also

> provisionally propose[s] that in deciding whether to allow a party to refer to a 'spent' conviction within the meaning of the Rehabilitation of Offenders Act 1974, the court should take into account all factors relevant to the interests of all parties, including
> (a) the nature of the conviction and its relevance to any issue in the case;
> (b) the length of time that has elapsed since the date of the conviction; and
> (c) the age of the relevant witness at the time when the offence was committed.[52]

As will be seen in Chapter 6, however, s 1(f) of the Criminal Evidence Act 1898 places restrictions on the extent to which a *defendant* in a criminal case may be cross-examined on his or her previous convictions.

The admissibility in civil trials of evidence of spent convictions was considered by the Court of Appeal in the following case:

Extract 4.5.13

Thomas v Comr of Police [1997] 1 All ER 747, 761–5 (CA)

EVANS LJ: Until 1974 there was little restriction, if any, on the right to cross-examine a witness in civil proceedings as to his or her previous convictions. It was commonly accepted that such convictions could affect the creditworthiness of the witness, even when, as was often the case, the convictions themselves and the circumstances which gave rise to them had no direct relevance to any issue before the court. Sometimes the convictions were so insignificant or so obviously irrelevant, even to credit, that the questioner was discouraged, perhaps by a formal ruling but usually by some other expression of disapproval by the judge. And in a jury trial the judge would be reluctant to exclude evidence which a reasonable jury could take into account when deciding where the truth lay. So the scope for judicial intervention was limited.

The common law position was stated by Cairns J in *Clifford v Clifford* [1961] 3 All ER 231 at 232, [1961] 1 WLR 1274 at 1276 . . .

The 1974 Act introduced the concept of spent convictions. Depending on the gravity of the offence and the length of sentence imposed for it, after a certain period of up to ten years a defendant who is not further convicted

---

[50] Section 7(2)(a).
[51] [1975] 1 WLR 1065.
[52] Law Commission (Consultation Paper No 141), *Criminal Law – Evidence in Criminal Proceedings: Previous Misconduct of a Defendant – A Consultation Paper* (1996) 270.

becomes a rehabilitated person, and by s 4(1) the offence is expunged for all purposes from his record. No reference may be made to it, whether in or out of court, subject to the provisions of the 1974 Act. As Lord Denning MR said in *Reynolds v Phoenix Assurance Co Ltd* [1978] 2 Lloyd's Rep 22 at 24:

'The man has to be treated as if he had never been convicted at all . . . If he is asked whether he has been convicted, he need not answer. He can say "No".'

Section 4(1), however, is expressly made subject to s 7(3). The judicial authority . . . has a discretionary power to allow the previous convictions of a party to be adduced in evidence when the interests of justice so require. In *Reynolds'* case the spent conviction was relevant or potentially relevant (depending on the trial judge's findings as to 'materiality' for insurance purposes) to a liability issue in the case. In *Dickinson v Yates, Lettice v Chief Constable of the Lancashire Constabulary* [1986] CA Transcript 554 the Court of Appeal upheld the judge's ruling which excluded the evidence in a case where, if the evidence had been given, it could not have been regarded as relevant to any issue in the case and would have been admitted solely in relation to credit. I respectfully agree with Nourse LJ that s 7(3) has imposed a further (statutory) requirement in addition to the common law test, which he defined as 'materiality'.

. . .

. . . Section 7(3) is expressed as a qualification to the general rule of exclusion in s 4(1), and its terms demonstrate that the evidence must be excluded unless the judicial authority, ie the trial judge, is 'satisfied . . . that justice cannot be done . . . except by admitting [it]'. So there is a strong presumption against permitting cross-examination or admitting the evidence, but the section also emphasises that the discretion is a broad one. The judge may take into account 'any considerations which appear to [him] to be relevant' and the overriding requirement is that 'justice shall be done'. In the context of civil proceedings, this means taking account of the interests of both parties, and justice requires that there shall be a fair trial between them.

This marks a clear distinction from criminal cases, where the interests of the defendant tend to be pre-eminent. But it is in criminal cases that the concepts of relevance and admissibility of such evidence have been most often considered. Those authorities are now the subject of the Law Commission's meticulous and scholarly consultation paper, *Evidence in Criminal Proceedings: Previous Misconduct by a Defendant* (No 141) (1996). . . .

The criminal authorities
First, evidence of previous convictions may sometimes, although rarely, be admissible as relevant, ie logically probative of an issue in the particular case.

This test of relevance is satisfied in the 'similar facts' cases, most recently *R v P* [1991] 3 All ER 337, [1991] 2 AC 447. Relevance in this sense is a question of law, but the House of Lords also affirmed that the evidence may nevertheless be excluded by the trial judge, if its probative force is outweighed by its potential for prejudice to the defendant. The reason why the limits of admissibility were narrowly drawn was explained by Lord Devlin in his *Trial by Jury* (1956 Hamlyn Lectures p 114) as follows:

'Similarly, a knowledge of the accused's previous convictions might often help in determining whether or not he had committed the crime, but because with a jury the prejudice created might outweigh its value, the evidence, again except for limited purposes, is not allowed.'

This is one example of the judicial function in a jury trial. Lord Devlin continued (p 115):

'. . . so the judge determines relevancy by admitting categories of evidence according to the principles settled by precedent and admitting particular pieces of evidence according to his own judgment. In both cases the law is at work in the task of limitation and definition by the drawing of general and particular lines.'

Secondly, cross-examination of the defendant, if he gives evidence, is restricted by the well-known provisions of s 1(f) of the Criminal Evidence Act 1898, but it is clear that when cross-examination is allowed previous convictions may be referred to which are not relevant to any issue in the case, ie not logically probative in the sense referred to above. The underlying principle is that they may be taken into account by the jury when considering the creditworthiness of the defendant, or as it is sometimes put, they are regarded as 'relevant to credit', meaning that the jury can properly take them into account in deciding whether to believe the defendant when he gives evidence.

The assessment of credit is not exclusively a logical process. Juries invariably are directed to use their 'knowledge of human nature' when deciding whether a witness is telling the truth, and the law not only permits but requires them to form their subjective though collective view, taking such account of demeanour, motive, consistency and other characteristics of the person they have seen giving evidence as they think fit. In this broad sense, certain matters can be described as 'relevant to credit', but this is something different from relevance meaning logically probative of an issue.

Thirdly, the distinction is made between the defendant's *credibility*, which is said to be supported by evidence of previous good character and damaged by evidence of past convictions, and his *propensity* towards the kind of conduct which is charged against him. This may be negatived by evidence of good character but clearly it is enhanced if the previous convictions include any which the jury could regard as establishing such propensity, even where they are not admissible under the narrower confines of the 'similar facts' rule. When dishonesty is alleged, proof of previous dishonesty on an unrelated occasion could be regarded as such. This provides another degree of meaning for 'relevant', because a previous conviction which tends to establish 'propensity' could well be taken into account by a jury whether assessing credibility or guilt, although the jury is directed not to do so as regards guilt unless the evidence is 'logically probative' within the similar fact rule. It is when such evidence is admissible under that rule or when the previous convictions might properly be put to the defendant in cross-examination, which could be given disproportionate weight by the jury as regards relevance or propensity, that the judge is most likely to exercise his power to exclude it or them on grounds of undue prejudice to the defendant.

Civil cases

Though it is necessary to allow for the fact that in criminal cases the circumstances are different, nevertheless in my judgment these authorities are relevant to the exercise of the judge's discretion in civil cases to permit the introduction of past 'spent' convictions under s 7(3).

. . . Given that previous convictions can sometimes be 'relevant to credit' then it follows, in my judgment, that in such cases the interests of justice must require that such evidence should be admitted before the jury, rather than withheld from it, when credit is in issue. Moreover, a past conviction for dishonesty could be said to be directly relevant to credit, a fortiori if the conviction was for giving perjured evidence in court.

. . .

In my judgment, it would be wrong to restrict the scope of the judge's discretion under s 7(3) except by reference to the words of the statute – the interests of justice – and equally wrong to limit the facts which he may properly take into account – any considerations which appear to him to be relevant. The criminal authorities are useful because they have formulated a number of concepts which it may be helpful for him to identify and give such weight to as he considers appropriate in the circumstances of the particular case. But he should equally bear in mind, in my judgment, that the concepts are not independent of each other and they may often overlap. For example, the more 'relevant' the previous conviction is, the more likely it is to be prejudicial to the party giving evidence, because some degree of propensity will be shown in addition to any damage caused to his credibility as a witness. The fact is that any previous conviction is likely to be prejudicial to the party or witness to whom it is put, unless it is so obviously trivial and irrelevant that it must be disregarded by a reasonable jury (eg a minor motoring offence). These fail the test of relevance however it is formulated, and the need to exclude them probably will not arise, because only an over-enthusiastic cross-examiner would seek to rely upon them in any event.

Furthermore, when the question is whether the party is telling the truth on a central issue in the case, then his creditworthiness is bound up with the decision on that issue itself. . . .

Section 7(3) therefore calls, in my view, for a single exercise of judgment by the trial judge, and it follows that this court cannot interfere unless, in accordance with general principles, the judge misdirected himself as to the test he should apply or where his decision was obviously wrong. . . .

The question raised by s 7(3) has to be answered by the judge, although it is not a matter of law, nor can it be answered by logic or by any process of reasoning alone. A negative answer would be required, in my judgment, where the previous conviction was so obviously irrelevant both to the issues in the case and to the moral standing of the witness that a reasonable jury could not properly take it into account when deciding whether to believe him or not. But the interests of justice are synonymous with a search for the truth, and the judge has to recognise that a reasonable jury may take a wide range of factors into account when deciding which witnesses to believe and therefore where the truth lies. It is also his responsibility, in my judgment, to consider whether the likely significance of the fact of a previous conviction in the jury's eyes is such that they may be unfairly prejudiced against the witness in question, when deciding whether to accept his evidence, or not. The adverb 'unfairly' is a necessary qualification, because some prejudice is inevitable except in cases of total and obvious irrelevance where, as stated above, the evidence should be excluded in any event. When relevance and prejudice co-exist, then the judge can carry out a similar though not identical balancing exercise to that which is required in 'similar facts' (criminal) cases by virtue of *R v P*; he can decide whether the potential prejudice to one party outweighs the prima facie right of the other party to introduce evidence of previous convictions, even if they are 'relevant' only to credit, meaning that they could influence the decision of a reasonable jury whether to accept a witness's evidence, or not.

In summary: some degree of relevance, including relevance to credit, is a sine qua non requirement for admitting the evidence. If it has any relevance, then it has some potential for prejudice. The degree of relevance can be weighed against the amount of prejudice, and other factors may be taken into account. The judge must be satisfied that the parties will not have a fair trial, or that a witness's credit cannot be fairly assessed, unless the evidence is admitted. The statutory exclusion does not apply if, in his view, the interests of justice otherwise dictate.

. . .

Two footnotes. First, s 7(3) implies that the judicial authority is separate from the tribunal of fact, which is factually correct when . . . the s 7(3) decision is taken by a judge and the evidence then admitted, if it is admitted, before a jury. If the judge is himself the tribunal of fact then, if he rules that the evidence should not be admitted, he has to put it out of his mind and decide the case without reference to it. This is never an easy exercise, and in my judgment a considerable responsibility rests upon counsel, not to seek leave to refer to previous convictions except in a case where it is clearly arguable that they should be admitted under s 7(3). It would be wrong even to make an application which had no realistic prospect of success.

Secondly, the Law Commission's Paper contains details of research which was carried out using mock juries in order to assess the effects of admitting this kind of evidence in criminal cases. One factor which emerged was that knowledge of a previous conviction for a sexual offence was disproportion-ately likely to prejudice the jury against the defendant, regardless of the nature of the offence for which he was standing trial. This could mean that in a civil case where s 7(3) applies and there is no issue of a sexual nature the judge would more readily recognise that the potential for prejudice out-weighed any 'relevance to credit' which such a conviction might otherwise have. But by the same token if the previous sexual misconduct was potentially relevant, then although the prejudice would be greater the judge might decide that justice could not be done between the parties unless the evidence was admitted.

For a detailed discussion of *Thomas*, see C Manchester, 'Admissibility of Spent Convictions in Civil Cases: *Thomas v Commissioner of Police for the Metropolis*' (1997) 1(3) *International Journal of Evidence and Proof* 152.

Extract 4.5.14

R v Mendy (1976) 64 Cr App R 4, 6 (CA)

While a detective was giving evidence at the appellant's trial for assault, a constable observed that a man in the public gallery was taking notes. This man then left the court, and was seen by the constable and a court officer discussing the case with the appellant's husband. The appellant's husband then testified, and in cross-examination denied that the incident with the man had occurred. The issue arose as to whether the prosecution could call the constable and court officer to give evidence in rebuttal.

GEOFFREY LANE LJ: . . . no one seriously suggests that the issue in the present case was other than collateral. On the other hand, it seems strange, if it be the case, that the Court and jury have to be kept in ignorance of behaviour by a witness such as that in the present case. The suggestion which lay behind the evidence in question was that Mr Mendy was prepared to lend himself to a scheme designed to defeat the purpose of keeping prospective witnesses out of Court; that he allowed the messenger to give him details of what Detective Constable Price had been saying in the witness-box about the assault which the appellant was alleged to have committed. If the evidence of the Court officer and Constable Thatcher was to be believed, the jury could be in little doubt that the witness's object in receiving such instruction must have been to enable him the more convincingly to describe how he and not the appellant had caused the injuries to the policeman.

The truth of the matter is, as one would expect, that the rule is not all-embracing. It has always been permissible to call evidence to contradict a witness's denial of bias or partiality towards one of the parties and to show that he is prejudiced so far as the case being tried is concerned.

Pollock CB in *Attorney-General v Hitchcock* (1847) 1 Ex 9 puts the matter thus at p 101: 'It is no disparagement to a man that a bribe is offered to him; it may be a disparagement to the man who makes the offer. If therefore the witness is asked about the fact and denies it or if he is asked whether he said so and so and he denies it he cannot be contradicted as to what he has said. *Lord Stafford's Case* [(1680) 7 How St Tr 1400] was totally different. There the witness himself had been implicated in offering a bribe to some other person. That immediately affected him as proving that he had acted the part of a suborner for the purpose of preventing the truth. In that case the evidence was to show that the witness was offered a bribe in a particular case, and the object was to show that he was so far affected towards the party accused as to be willing to adopt any corrupt course in order to carry out his purposes.' In *Lord Stafford's Case*, (*supra*) the evidence was admitted.

Those words apply almost precisely to the facts in the present case. The witness was prepared to cheat in order to deceive the jury and help the defendant. The jury were entitled to be apprised of that fact.

Is the 'bias' exception applicable where what is at issue is cross-examination of police witnesses for the purpose of eliciting evidence of police malpractice?

Extract 4.5.15

R v Edwards [1991] 1 WLR 207, 215–7, 220 (CA)

LORD LANE CJ: It has been suggested – see *Reg v Funderburk* [1990] 1 WLR 587, 591 – that a further exception [to the collateral-finality rule] now exists, namely to show 'that the police are prepared to go to improper lengths to secure a conviction.' That proposition is drawn from the decision in *Reg v Busby* (1981) 75 Cr App R 79. . . .

. . . Eveleigh LJ delivering the judgment of the Court of Appeal held that the evidence should not have been excluded. It would have tended to support the defendant's case that the officers concerned were prepared to go to improper lengths to secure a conviction. It was therefore, it was said, relevant to an issue which had to be tried.

A close study of the decision in *Reg v Busby* seems to show however that its true basis may well have been the suggestion of bias against those particular defendants in that particular case. . . .

It follows that, had the suggested evidence been available, the present case would have raised these problems: first, what questions could properly be asked of the police witnesses in cross-examination, and secondly, whether evidence to contradict those answers would have been admissible.

. . . the police officers could certainly be cross-examined as to any relevant criminal offences or disciplinary charges found proved against them.

. . .

We do not consider that it would have been proper to suggest to the officer in the present case that he had committed perjury or any other criminal offence by putting to him that he had been charged but not yet tried. Nor do we think that complaints to the Police Complaints Authority which have not been adjudicated upon would properly be the subject of cross-examination. It would not be proper to direct questions to an officer about allegedly discreditable conduct of other officers, whether or not they happened to be serving in the same squad.

. . .

. . . The acquittal of a defendant in case A, where the prosecution case depended largely or entirely upon the evidence of a police officer, does not normally render that officer liable to cross-examination as to credit in case B. But where a police officer who has allegedly fabricated an admission in case B, has also given evidence of an admission in case A, where there was an acquittal by virtue of which his evidence is demonstrated to have been disbelieved, it is proper that the jury in case B should be made aware of that fact. However, where the acquittal in case A does not necessarily indicate that the jury disbelieved the officer, such cross-examination should not be allowed. In such a case the verdict of not guilty may mean no more than that the jury entertained some doubt about the prosecution case, not necessarily that they believed any witness was lying.

. . .

That leaves the second question, namely, whether it would have been proper to allow the defence to call evidence to contradict any answers given by the police officers in cross-examination, in the unlikely event of those officers giving answers unfavourable to the defence? In our judgment this questioning would have been as to credit alone, that is to say, on a collateral issue. It would not have fallen within any exception to the general rule.

For a thorough discussion of *Edwards*, see R Pattenden, 'Evidence of Previous Malpractice by Police Witnesses and R v Edwards' [1992] *Criminal Law Review* 549. Why, in the view of the Court of Appeal in *Edwards*, would no exception to the collateral-finality rule have been applicable? What about the 'bias' exception? Is *Edwards* consistent with *Busby*? See also *R v Meads*.[53]

INCAPACITY

Extract 4.5.16

Toohey v Metropolitan Police Commissioner [1965] AC 595, 608 (HL)

LORD PEARCE: If a witness purported to give evidence of something which he believed that he had seen at a distance of 50 yards, it must surely be possible to call the evidence of an oculist to the effect that the witness could not possibly see anything at a greater distance than 20 yards, or the evidence of a surgeon who had removed a cataract from which the witness was suffering at the material time and which would have prevented him from seeing what he thought he saw.

GENERAL REPUTATION FOR LACK OF VERACITY

Extract 4.5.17

R v Richardson [1969] 1 QB 299, 304–5 (CA)

EDMUND DAVIES LJ: The legal position may be thus summarised:
1. A witness may be asked whether he has knowledge of the impugned witness's general reputation for veracity and whether (from such knowledge) he would believe the impugned witness's sworn testimony.
2. The witness called to impeach the credibility of a previous witness may also express his individual opinion (based upon his personal knowledge) as

---

[53] [1996] Crim LR 519.

to whether the latter is to be believed on his oath and is *not* confined to giving evidence merely of general reputation.

3. But whether his opinion as to the impugned witness's credibility be based simply upon the latter's general reputation for veracity or upon his personal knowledge, the witness cannot be permitted to indicate during his examination-in-chief the particular facts, circumstances or incidents which formed the basis of his opinion, although he may be cross-examined as to them.

This method of attacking a witness's veracity, though ancient, is used with exceeding rarity.

Is this exception to the collateral-finality rule justifiable? Note the reservations about the exception expressed in the following extract:

Extract 4.5.18

Toohey v Metropolitan Police Commissioner [1965] AC 595, 605–6 (HL)

LORD PEARCE: From olden times it has been the practice to allow evidence of bad reputation to discredit a witness's testimony. It is perhaps not very logical and not very useful to allow such evidence founded on hearsay. None of your Lordships and none of the counsel before you could remember being concerned in a case where such evidence was called. But the rule has been sanctified through the centuries in legal examinations and textbooks and in some rare cases, and it does not create injustice.

(iii) An evaluation

The collateral-finality rule represents one of the most problematic areas of the law of evidence. For one thing, the distinction between relevance to a fact in issue and relevance to credit, upon which the entire rule is premised, is far from clear. We have seen, for example, that the precise basis of the decision in *Busby* (did the cross-examination go to facts in issue, or did an exception to the collateral-finality rule apply?) remains the subject of differing views. As Zuckerman has observed:

Extract 4.5.19

A A S Zuckerman, *The Principles of Criminal Evidence* (1989) 95–6

The fact that the witness says: 'The man who committed the offence was the accused' is relevant because it renders it more probable that the accused was the offender. However, *W*'s testimony could have this effect only if it has some credibility. If the testimony has no credibility at all, for example, because it is the blabber of a madman, it is irrelevant. It follows that the connecting link between *W*'s testimony and the conclusion based on it is credibility. In other words, the relevance of a witness's testimony is embedded in his credibility, actual or potential. Credibility is not something separate (a separate issue) which is somehow suspended between the witness's statement and the fact asserted therein.[54]

In a similar vein, it has been acknowledged judicially that 'the distinction between matters going directly to the primary issue and those going to the credit of those who give evidence on the issue is hard to operate in practice, and possibly unsound in theory'.[55]

A further difficulty with the current state of the law is suggested by the decision in *Edwards*: it may presently be impermissible to call rebuttal evidence in situations in which this should be permitted. It is strongly arguable, for example, that police officers' denials, under cross-examination, of allegations of malpractice should not be treated as final (as *Edwards* suggests they should be), but that the defence should be permitted to call rebuttal evidence.[56]

There are, essentially, three possible reform options.[57] First, given that the distinction between relevance to facts in issue and relevance to credit may in any event be illusory, a broad and functional approach to what constitutes relevance to facts in issue may be able to be taken. (This, as we have seen, was the approach which the Court of Appeal took in *Funderburk* in order to find that the prior inconsistent statement in question was 'relative to the subject matter of the indictment or proceeding' under s 4 of the Criminal Procedure Act 1865.) Secondly, it may be possible to treat the list of exceptions to the collateral-finality rule as not closed. This was an option mentioned in *Funderburk*. The third option acknowledges openly that, ultimately, the aim is to achieve a fair balance between the considerations of convenience and justice in the circumstances of the particular case:

Extract 4.5.20

M Newark, 'Opening Up the Collateral Issue Rule' (1992) 43 *Northern Ireland Legal Quarterly* 166, 176

The advantage of a discretionary approach would be that it calls for a more open balancing of the inconvenience and danger of opening up the collateral issue against the dangers of not doing so. Thus contradiction on trivial details

---

[54] See also J McEwan, 'The Law Commission Consultation Paper on Previous Misconduct: (2) Law Commission Dodges the Nettles in Consultation Paper No 141' [1997] *Criminal Law Review* 93, 99: 'Once the notion of credibility is extended to the credibility of a particular defence, we are dealing with the issue of guilt.'

[55] *R v Wright* (1989) 90 Cr App R 325, 333.

[56] See R Pattenden, 'Evidence of Previous Malpractice by Police Witnesses and R v Edwards' [1992] *Criminal Law Review* 549, 557.

[57] See generally M Newark, 'Opening Up the Collateral Issue Rule' (1992) 43 *Northern Ireland Legal Quarterly* 166, 176–7.

which are likely to be hotly contested, wasting much time, requiring adjournments in fairness to the other side, confusing or misleading the jury, could be prevented, while contradictions on matters vitally affecting the reliability of the witness's testimony which can be quickly and fairly resolved, can be allowed. Of course, there will be difficult cases in between; but the argument in favour of discretion is based on the assumption that all sensible, fair-minded judges, without being able to formulate any general rule on the matter, can intuitively recognize those side issues that ought to be explored and those that ought not. Greater latitude could be granted to an accused seeking to contradict a prosecution witness than to a prosecutor seeking to contradict a defence witness.

Would not this be a sensible way forward?

6. RE-EXAMINATION

The following Australian statutory provision reflects the law in England (see *Prince v Samo*[58]):

Extract 4.6.1

Evidence Act 1995 (Australia), s 39

39. Limits on re-examination
On re-examination:
- (a) a witness may be questioned about matters arising out of evidence given by the witness in cross-examination; and
- (b) other questions may not be put to the witness unless the court gives leave.

The same restrictions apply to re-examination as apply to examination-in-chief. Thus, for example, no leading questions may generally be asked.

---

[58] (1838) 7 Ad & E 627; 112 ER 606.

5

SIMILAR-FACT EVIDENCE

In this chapter and in the following chapter, we are concerned with the broad issue of evidence of the accused's character. In the present chapter, we examine the general prohibition on the adduction in chief by the prosecution of evidence showing the accused's involvement in misconduct on occasions other than that which is the subject of the present trial. Specifically, we identify the situations in which such evidence is considered admissible as 'similar-fact evidence'. The next chapter looks at the extent to which the prosecution may cross-examine the accused with a view to eliciting evidence of his or her bad character, or of his or her prior offences.

The law regards evidence of an accused's past misconduct as presumptively inadmissible because of the likely prejudicial effect of such evidence.[1] In very broad terms, the risk of prejudice may arise in one of two ways. First, the jury may overestimate the probative value of the evidence in question: they 'may reason that because the accused stole a bottle of whisky from a supermarket five years earlier he must also have been guilty of the theft of the car with which he is now charged'.[2] Secondly, even if not in fact satisfied beyond reasonable doubt of the accused's guilt, the jury may return a guilty verdict because he or she is thought to deserve punishment for the previous misconduct. This misconduct may not have led to a criminal prosecution, or a prosecution in respect of the conduct may have resulted either in an acquittal or in what the jury regard as unduly lenient punishment. The first type of prejudice may be termed 'reasoning prejudice' and the second 'moral prejudice'.[3] It is notable that, in answer to the question '[if] a defendant has any similar previous convictions, do you think the jury should always be told about them before they go to consider their verdict?', 58% of the jurors in the *Crown Court Study* said no, while 42% said yes.[4] The mock jury research

[1] See generally Law Commission (Consultation Paper No 141), *Criminal Law – Evidence in Criminal Proceedings: Previous Misconduct of a Defendant – A Consultation Paper* (1996) 122–33.
[2] A A S Zuckerman, *The Principles of Criminal Evidence* (1989) 222.
[3] A Palmer, 'The Scope of the Similar Fact Rule' (1994) 16 *Adelaide Law Review* 161, 169–72.
[4] M Zander and P Henderson, *The Royal Commission on Criminal Justice: Crown Court Study* (1993) 210.

conducted at Oxford revealed that[5] 'after deliberation, participants who were told of a recent similar conviction rated the defendant as significantly more likely to have committed the crime with which he was charged than when they were told that he had a dissimilar conviction or no convictions'. Interestingly, the mock jurors regarded the defendant as *less* likely to have committed the crime if they were told that he had a recent dissimilar conviction, than if they were told nothing about his criminal record. 'A possible explanation for this finding', according to the Law Commission, 'is that a previous conviction for a specific offence evokes a stereotype of a person who commits that type of offence *rather than* the different one charged. Another possible explanation . . . [is] that participants felt it was unfair on the defendant to introduce potentially prejudicial evidence of marginal relevance.' These results broadly followed the findings of the LSE Jury Project over 20 years previously.

1. THE MODERN LAW

There have been three landmark cases on similar-fact evidence. These are the 1894 decision of the Privy Council in *Makin v A-G for NSW*,[6] and the decisions of the House of Lords (in 1974 and 1991 respectively) in *R v Boardman*[7] and *DPP v P*.[8] A study of the development of the law on similar-fact evidence this century provides fascinating insights into the manner in which the law of criminal evidence has gradually adapted to keep up with changing social attitudes. In the contemporary context, the case of *P* is regarded as providing an authoritative discussion of the relevant principles which are to be applied in determining the admissibility of evidence adduced in chief of an accused's misconduct on other occasions. The House of Lords in *P* also subjected the earlier cases of *Makin*, and, in particular, *Boardman*, to scrutiny.

Extract 5.1.1

DPP v P [1991] 2 AC 447, 452–63 (HL)

LORD MACKAY OF CLASHFERN LC: The appellant, the Director of Public Prosecutions, applied for a certificate that a point of law of general public importance was involved in this decision and for leave to appeal to this House. The Court of Appeal granted these applications and certified the following questions for this House:

---

[5] Law Commission (Consultation Paper No 141), *Criminal Law – Evidence in Criminal Proceedings: Previous Misconduct of a Defendant – A Consultation Paper* (1996) 329 (emphasis in original).
[6] [1894] AC 57.
[7] [1975] AC 421.
[8] [1991] 2 AC 447.

'1. Where a father or stepfather is charged with sexually abusing a young daughter of the family, is evidence that he also similarly abused other young children of the family admissible (assuming there to be no collusion) in support of such charge in the absence of any other "striking similarities"? 2. Where a defendant is charged with sexual offences against more than one child or young person, is it necessary in the absence of "striking similarities" for the charges to be tried separately?'

. . .

Consideration of this matter has normally begun with *Makin v Attorney-General for New South Wales* [1894] AC 57. In that case evidence was led that several infants had been received by the accused from their mothers on representations that they were willing to adopt the children and upon a payment of a sum inadequate for the support of the children for more than a very limited period and that the bodies of these children had been found buried in a similar manner in the gardens of several houses occupied by the accused and the question was whether this was relevant where another child was shown to have been received by the accused from its mother on similar representations as to their willingness to adopt it and upon payment of a sum similarly inadequate for its support for more than a very limited period. In giving the judgment of the Board Lord Herschell LC said, at p 65:

'In their Lordships' opinion the principles which must govern the decision of the case are clear, though the application of them is by no means free from difficulty. It is undoubtedly not competent for the prosecution to adduce evidence tending to show that the accused has been guilty of criminal acts other than those covered by the indictment, for the purpose of leading to the conclusion that the accused is a person likely from his criminal conduct or character to have committed the offence for which he has been tried. On the other hand, the mere fact that the evidence adduced tends to show the commission of other crimes does not render it inadmissible if it be relevant to an issue before the jury, and it may be so relevant if it bears upon the question whether the acts alleged to constitute the crime charged in the indictment were designed or accidental, or to rebut a defence which would otherwise be open to the accused. The statement of these general principles is easy, but it is obvious that it may often be very difficult to draw the line and to decide whether a particular piece of evidence is on the one side or the other.'

This matter was very fully discussed in this House in *Reg v Boardman* [1975] AC 421. In that case the appellant was charged on an indictment with three counts. The first alleged that on a day between 1 October 1972 and 30 November 1972 the appellant had committed buggery with S who was a boy then aged 16. The second count charged the appellant with having on 14 January 1973 unlawfully incited H who was then aged 17 to commit buggery with him. The decision of the House of Lords was not concerned with the third count which concerned A. In order to appreciate the matters discussed in the House it is necessary to summarise the evidence given respectively by S and by H and by the appellant. S spoke of a number of incidents; the first occurred at Tehran before the autumn term of 1972 began. According to S there was an indecent assault in a Tehran hotel. The second incident was at Cambridge during the term when S said that the appellant had tried to touch him in the private parts but was repulsed. The third incident which was at the end of September or beginning of October occurred at about four or five o'clock in the morning when S was asleep in the school dormitory of the school of which the appellant was headmaster and was awakened and felt something touch his face and he was invited by the appellant to come to the sitting-room for five minutes, the appellant expressing an affection for S. The next incident, according to S, was when the appellant asked him to go alone with him to the sitting-room and offered him money; he knelt in front of him and made this specific request not only that buggery should take place but furthermore that S should play the active and the appellant the passive part. The next occasion was when the appellant said to S that he would tell the seniors not to go to the sitting-room that night and that S should come by himself. Then came the occasion when according to S the actual act of buggery took place. Some time after 10.45 pm the appellant had asked S to go to him and had threatened him with expulsion, 'if tonight you don't do it on me.' S later went to the appellant and in his evidence he described in some detail what he said had taken place. The appellant offered explanations in respect of some of these incidents and others he wholly denied.

H gave evidence of two incidents; the first of these began when one night the appellant, at some time between midnight and 2 am, woke H who was asleep in a dormitory and told him to get dressed. Together they went by taxi to a club and after some drinks there they returned to the school and sat drinking and talking in the sitting-room. Then, according to H, the appellant started to touch H's private parts through his trousers and asked H to sleep with him and made the specific suggestion that H should play the active part and the appellant the passive part. The second incident spoken of by H occurred on or about 14 January 1973 in the sitting-room where the appellant again asked H to sleep with him and then touched H's private parts.

The speeches in this House are rather lengthy. I begin by quoting the principal statements of principle to be found in them.

Lord Morris of Borth-y-Gest puts it thus, at p 441:

'But there may be cases where a judge, having both limbs of Lord Herschell LC's famous proposition [*Makin v Attorney-General for New South Wales* [1894] AC 57, 65] in mind, considers that the interests of justice (of which the interests of fairness form so fundamental a component) make it proper that he should permit a jury when considering the evidence on a charge concerning one fact or set of facts also to consider the evidence concerning another fact or set of facts if between the two there is such a close or striking similarity or such an underlying unity that probative force could fairly be yielded.'

Lord Wilberforce puts it thus, at p 442:

'Whether in the field of sexual conduct or otherwise, there is no general or automatic answer to be given to the question whether evidence of facts similar to those the subject of a particular charge ought to be admitted. In each case it is necessary to estimate (i) whether, and if so how strongly, the evidence as to other facts tends to support, ie, to make more credible, the evidence given as to the fact in question, (ii) whether such evidence, if given, is likely to be prejudicial to the accused. Both these elements involve questions of degree. It falls to the judge, in the first place by way of preliminary ruling, and indeed on an application for separate trials if such is made (see the opinion of my noble and learned friend Lord Cross of Chelsea), to estimate the respective and relative weight of these two factors and only to allow the evidence to be put before the jury if he is satisfied that the answer to the first question is clearly positive, and, on the assumption, which is likely, that the second question must be similarly answered, that on a combination of the two the interests of justice clearly require that the evidence be admitted. Questions of this kind arise in a number of different contexts and have, correspondingly, to be resolved in different ways.'

He went on to say, at p 444:

'The basic principle must be that the admission of similar fact evidence (of the kind now in question) is exceptional and requires a strong degree of probative force.'

Lord Hailsham of St Marylebone said, at pp 452–453:

'The truth is that a mere succession of facts is not normally enough (see *Moorov v HM Advocate*, 1930 JC 68 on "a course of criminal conduct"), whether the cases are many or limited to two as in *HM Advocate v AE*, 1937 JC 96. There must be something more than mere repetition. What there must be is variously described as "underlying unity" (*Moorov v HM Advocate*), "system" (see *per* Lord Reid in *Reg v Kilbourne*), "nexus", "unity of intent, project, campaign or adventure" (*Moorov v HM Advocate*), "part of the same criminal conduct," "striking resemblance" (*Rex v Sims* [1946] KB 531). These are all highly analogical not to say metaphorical expressions and should not be applied pedantically. It is true that the doctrine "must be applied with great caution" (see *Ogg v HM Advocate*, 1938 JC 152, *per* the Lord Justice-Clerk (Lord Aitchison), at p 158), but: "The test in each case, and in considering each particular charge, is, Was the evidence with regard to other charges relevant to that charge?" (*per* Lord Wark, at p 160). The test is (*per* Lord Simon of Glaisdale in *Reg v Kilbourne* [1973] AC 729, 759) whether there is ". . . such an underlying unity between the offences as to make coincidence an affront to common sense" or, to quote Hallett J in *Reg v Robinson*, 37 Cr App R 95, 106–107, in the passage cited by Professor Cross, *Evidence*, 3rd ed, p 316: "If a jury are precluded by some rule of law from taking the view that something is a coincidence which is against all the probabilities if the accused person is innocent, then it would seem to be a doctrine of law which prevents a jury from using what looks like ordinary common sense." '

Lord Cross of Chelsea put the matter thus, at p 457:

'The question must always be whether the similar fact evidence taken together with the other evidence would do no more than raise or strengthen a suspicion that the accused committed the offence with which he is charged or would point so strongly to his guilt that only an ultra-cautious jury, if they accepted it as true, would acquit in face of it. In the end – although the admissibility of such evidence is a question of law, not of discretion – the question as I see it must be one of degree.'

Lord Salmon after stating that he had no wish to add to the anthology of guidance concerning the special circumstances in which evidence is relevant or admissible against an accused, notwithstanding that it may disclose that he is a man of bad character with a disposition to commit the kind of crime with which he is charged, went on later to say, at p 462:

'The test must be: is the evidence capable of tending to persuade a reasonable jury of the accused's guilt on some ground other than his bad character and disposition to commit the sort of crime with which he is charged? In the case of an alleged homosexual offence, just as in the case of an alleged burglary, evidence which proves merely that the accused has committed crimes in the past and is therefore disposed to commit the crime charged is clearly inadmissible. It has, however, never been doubted that if the crime charged is committed in a uniquely or strikingly similar manner to other crimes committed by the accused the manner in which the other crimes were committed may be evidence upon which a jury could reasonably conclude that the accused was guilty of the crime charged. The similarity would have to be so unique or striking that common sense makes it inexplicable on the basis of coincidence.'

I now turn to examine the way in which their Lordships applied these statements of principle to the facts. Lord Morris of Borth-y-Gest said, at p 442:

'In dealing with the similarity of the kind of behaviour spoken to by S and by H the learned judge concentrated, and perhaps unduly so, on that feature of it which showed that the request and desire was that it was the youngster who was to play the active part and the appellant the passive part. But another feature of rather striking similarity lay in the evidence concerning the nocturnal dormitory visits of the appellant. The waking up of S during the night and all that was said during the "five minute incident" could legitimately be compared with the early morning waking up of H and of all that followed. The matter could perhaps also have been considered on a wider basis. The appellant stated that the S "five minute incident" only came about because he (the appellant) "was doing the rounds in the dormitory." The question is raised whether the visits at night merely marked the innocent activity of a zealous schoolmaster whose association with those in his charge and under his care made him solicitous for their welfare or whether the evidence negatived any such innocent explanation. In the course which he took the learned judge acted, in my view, within legal principle and in so far as the matter depended upon his exercise of his discretion I do not consider that his exercise of it was unjustified.'

Lord Wilberforce said, at p 445:

'The present case is, to my mind, right on the border-line. There were only two relevant witnesses, S and H. The striking similarity as presented to the jury was and was only the active character of the sexual performance to which the accused was said to have invited the complainants. In relation to the incident which was the subject of the second charge, the language used by the boy was not specific: the "similarity" was derived from an earlier incident in connection with which the boy used a verb connoting an active role. I agree with, I think, all your Lordships in thinking that all of this, relating not very specifically to the one striking element, common to two boys only, is, if sufficient, only just sufficient. Perhaps other similarities could have been found in the accused's approaches to the boys (I do not myself find them particularly striking), but the judge did not rest upon them or direct the jury as to their "similarity." I do not think that these ought now to be relied upon. The dilution of the "striking" fact by more prosaic details might have weakened the impact upon the jury rather than strengthened it. The judge dealt properly and fairly with the possibility of a conspiracy between the boys. These matters lie largely within the field of the judge's discretion, and of the jury's task; the Court of Appeal has reviewed the whole matter in a careful judgment. I do not think that there is anything which justifies the interference of this House. But I confess to some fear that the case, if regarded as an example, may be setting the standard of "striking similarity" too low.'

Lord Hailsham of St Marylebone, at p 447E, gave a more detailed account of the evidence of S and H and said, at p 455:

'It is fair to the appellant's argument to say that there is undoubted force in the criticism that, by fastening on the purely passive role said to have been adopted by the appellant towards the act of buggery suggested or performed as the sole element of "striking resemblance" between S's testimony and that of H, the trial judge was on dubious ground, partly because it might be said that, as between two witnesses only, the fact, although perhaps unusual, was perhaps not so unusual as to render the evidence admissible, and partly because over the sequence of all the evidence, including that of A, it was not perhaps so unambiguously and consistently displayed as to render it a kind of signature which would make it an "affront to common sense" [*Reg v Kilbourne* [1973] AC 729, 759] in the jury to disregard it as coincidental. But I hope that I have exposed enough of the evidence to indicate that, if the learned judge erred here, he erred by giving too little weight to the case for a conviction. There were other points of resemblance sufficiently striking to have their value as corroboration whether in conjunction with or without the "catamite" feature left to the jury and, in S's case, there was admittedly strong independent corroboration in the testimony of the police officer.'

Lord Cross of Chelsea said, at pp 460–461:

'It is by no means unheard of for a boy to accuse a schoolmaster falsely of having made homosexual advances to him. If two boys make accusations of that sort at about the same time independently of one another then no doubt the ordinary man would tend to think that there was "probably something in it." But it is just this instinctive reaction of the ordinary man which the general rule is intended to counter and I think that one needs to find very striking peculiarities common to the two stories to justify the admission of one to support the other. The feature in the two stories upon which attention was concentrated in the courts below is that both youths said that the appellant suggested not that he should bugger them but that they should bugger him. This was said to be an "unusual" suggestion. If I thought that the outcome of this appeal depended on whether such a suggestion was in fact "unusual" I would be in favour of allowing it. It is no doubt unusual for a middle-aged man to yield to the urge to commit buggery or to try to commit buggery with youths or young men but whether it is unusual for such a middle-aged man to wish to play the pathic rather than the active role I have no idea whatever and I am not prepared, in the absence of any evidence on the point, to make any assumption one way or the other. As I see it, however, the point is not whether what the appellant is said to have suggested would be, as coming from the middle-aged active homosexual, in itself particularly unusual but whether it would be unlikely that two youths who were saying untruly that the appellant had made homosexual advances to them would have put such a suggestion into his mouth. In one passage in his summing up the judge touched on this aspect of the matter and said that the jury might think it more likely that if their stories were untrue S and H would have said that the appellant wished to bugger or did bugger them than that he wished them to bugger or induced them to bugger him. There is, I think, force in that observation, but I do not think that this similarity standing alone would be sufficient to warrant the admission of the evidence. My noble and learned friends, Lord Morris of Borth-y-Gest, Lord Hailsham of St Marylebone and Lord Salmon, point, however, to other features common to the two stories which, it may be said, two liars concocting false stories independently of one another would have been unlikely to hit upon and, although I must say that I regard this as very much a borderline case, I am not prepared to dissent from their view that the "similar fact" evidence was admissible here and that the appeal should be dismissed.'

Lord Salmon said, at pp 463–464:

'Whenever these unnatural practices are indulged in, someone ex hypothesi is in the active and someone in the passive role. It may be that it is most unusual for the older man to be in the passive role. If it is so, then there is a striking similarity between the two cases. For all I know, however, the one may be as usual as the other, in which case there is not the striking similarity between the case of S and that of H upon which the learned trial judge relied. Nevertheless there was what seems to me to be another striking similarity between the two cases. According to the evidence of the two boys, the improper advances were made to each of them by the appellant in their respective dormitories at about midnight or in the early hours of the morning with an admonition not to wake up any of the other boys. The appellant, whilst denying any improper suggestions, admitted the admonitions and said that he roused H and then took him to a night club where he plied him with drink for a purpose to which reference has been made and which seems to me to be wholly incredible. He also admitted that he asked S to come to his room for five minutes. He says that he did so because he found him in bed with another boy, that S became angry and refused and that he then went away and left the boys in bed together. This is an equally incredible story. Any master who went his rounds at such odd hours and made such a discovery would have told the boys to go back to their own beds immediately and ordered each to come and see him after breakfast. He would not have left until each boy was in his own bed. He would probably also have gone round at least once later to make sure that each boy had remained in his own bed. The approach to S prior to the alleged impropriety was, to say the least, most unusual and strikingly similar to the approach to H. It strongly suggests that the appellant, in order to commit the crime charged, proceeded "according to a particular technique . . . [or] particular pattern," to quote Professor Cross in his book on *Evidence*, 3rd ed, p 319. . . . I would only add that, in my view, the fact that there was some corroboration of S's evidence other than that given by H is irrelevant in considering whether or not the judge erred in admitting H's evidence in respect of the count relating to S.'

As this matter has been left in *Reg v Boardman* I am of opinion that it is not appropriate to single out 'striking similarity' as an essential element in every case in allowing evidence of an offence against one victim to be heard in connection with an allegation against another. Obviously, in cases where the identity of the offender is in issue, evidence of a character sufficiently special reasonably to identify the perpetrator is required and the discussion which follows in Lord Salmon's speech on the passage which I have quoted indicates that he had that type of case in mind.

From all that was said by the House in *Reg v Boardman* I would deduce the essential feature of evidence which is to be admitted is that its probative force in support of the allegation that an accused person committed a crime is sufficiently great to make it just to admit the evidence, notwithstanding that it is prejudicial to the accused in tending to show that he was guilty of another crime. Such probative force may be derived from striking similarities in the evidence about the manner in which the crime was committed and the authorities provide illustrations of that of which *Reg v Straffen* [1952] 2 QB 911 and *Reg v Smith* (1915) 11 Cr App R 229, provide notable examples. But restricting the circumstances in which there is sufficient probative force to overcome prejudice of evidence relating to another crime to cases in which there is some striking similarity between them is to restrict the operation of the principle in a way which gives too much effect to a particular manner of stating it, and is not justified in principle. *Hume on Crimes*, 3rd ed (1844), vol II, p 384, said long ago:

'the aptitude and coherence of the several circumstances often as fully confirm the truth of the story, as if all the witnesses were deponing to the same facts.'

Once the principle is recognised, that what has to be assessed is the probative force of the evidence in question, the infinite variety of circumstances in which the question arises, demonstrates that there is no single manner in which this can be achieved. Whether the evidence has sufficient probative value to outweigh its prejudicial effect must in each case be a question of degree.

The view that some feature of similarity beyond what has been described as the paederast's or the incestuous father's stock in trade before one victim's evidence can be properly admitted upon the trial of another seems to have been stated for the first time in those terms in *Reg v Inder* (1977) 67 Cr App R 143. Although that case also contains a reference to a warning not to attach too much importance to Lord Salmon's vivid phrase 'uniquely or strikingly similar' I think in the context this is what has occurred. This trend has been followed in later cases, for example, *Reg v Clarke (Leslie)* (1977) 67 Cr App R 398, *Reg v Tudor* (unreported), 18 July 1988, and particularly *Reg v Brooks* (1990) 92 Cr App R 36. In so far as these decisions required, as an essential feature, a similarity beyond the stock in trade I consider they fall to be overruled.

In the present case the evidence of both girls describes a prolonged course of conduct in relation to each of them. In relation to each of them force was used. There was a general domination of the girls with threats against them unless they observed silence and a domination of the wife which inhibited her intervention. The defendant seemed to have an obsession for keeping the girls to himself, for himself. The younger took on the role of the elder daughter when the elder daughter left home. There was also evidence that the defendant was involved in regard to payment for the abortions in respect of both girls. In my view these circumstances taken together gave strong probative force to the evidence of each of the girls in relation to the incidents involving the other, and was certainly sufficient to make it just to admit that evidence, notwithstanding its prejudicial effect. This was clearly the view taken by the Court of Appeal and they would have given effect to it were it not for the line of authority in the Court of Appeal to which I have referred.

. . .

When a question of the kind raised in this case arises I consider that the judge must first decide whether there is material upon which the jury would be entitled to conclude that the evidence of one victim, about what occurred to that victim, is so related to the evidence given by another victim, about what happened to that other victim, that the evidence of the first victim provides strong enough support for the evidence of the second victim to make it just to admit it notwithstanding the prejudicial effect of admitting the evidence. This relationship, from which support is derived, may take many forms and while these forms may include 'striking similarity' in the manner in which the crime is committed, consisting of unusual characteristics in its execution the necessary relationship is by no means confined to such circumstances. Relationships in time and circumstances other than these may well be important relationships in this connection. Where the identity of the perpetrator is in issue, and evidence of this kind is important in that connection, obviously something in the nature of what has been called in the course of the argument a signature or other special feature will be necessary. To transpose this requirement to other situations where the question is whether a crime has been committed, rather than who did commit it, is to impose an unnecessary and improper restriction upon the application of the principle.

For the reasons which I have given, I am of opinion that there was sufficient connection between the circumstances spoken of by the two girls in the present case for their testimonies mutually to support each other, that the appeal should be allowed, and the conviction restored.

I would answer the first question posed by the Court of Appeal by saying that the evidence referred to is admissible if the similarity is sufficiently strong, or there is other sufficient relationship between the events described in the evidence of the other young children of the family, and the abuse charged, that the evidence if accepted, would so strongly support the truth of that charge that it is fair to admit it notwithstanding its prejudicial effect. It follows that the answer to the second question is no, provided there is a relationship between the offences of the kind I have just described.

These matters raise questions of law but also involve judgments on matters of degree. Judgments properly made in the light of the appropriate principles should not, I think, yield results which could properly be described as a lottery.

In a nutshell then, the fact that evidence of an accused's misconduct on other occasions sought to be adduced in chief can be shown to be relevant is, of itself, insufficient to render it admissible. Such evidence is admissible only if its probative value is sufficiently high to justify its admission, notwithstanding its prejudicial effect. Although a determination of whether such evidence is admissible is required as a matter of law, the 'probative value versus prejudicial effect' test is a 'discretionary' one in the sense that it is flexible and open-textured. Whether the test is satisfied must depend on the circumstances of the particular case. It is clear that the test may be satisfied where there is a 'striking similarity' between the offence charged and the offence of which evidence is sought to be adduced. The following are the two cases cited in *P* as providing illustrations of 'striking similarity':

Extract 5.1.2

R v Straffen [1952] 2 QB 911, 916–17 (CCA)

The accused was charged with the murder of Linda Bowyer, whose body was found in the village of Little Farley. At issue was the admissibility of evidence of two other murders, which the accused had confessed to committing.

SLADE J: The grounds on which the admissibility of the evidence was urged by the Solicitor-General in the court below was the similarity of the circumstances surrounding the murders in the case of the two Bath murders on the one hand and the Farley Village murder on the other. He stated the similarities to be, firstly, that each of the victims was a young girl; secondly, that each was killed by manual strangulation; thirdly, that in none of the cases was there any attempt at sexual interference or any apparent motive for the crime; fourthly, that in no case was there any evidence of a struggle; and fifthly, that in none of the three cases was any attempt made to conceal the body, though that could easily have been done.

Those similarities were fortified by the evidence of the doctor who examined the bodies of the two girls murdered at Bath and by the pathologist called in the case of Linda Bowyer, who had studied the depositions, the photographs and the post-mortem reports in the two cases at Bath. The evidence with regard to the Bath murders was tendered and admitted for the purpose of showing that the same person killed all three little girls; that is to say, that the person who strangled Brenda Goddard and Cicely Batstone, in the circumstances described, also manually strangled Linda Bowyer in similar circumstances as regards the method of death, the precision of the strangulation, and the other similar circumstances to which I have referred. In the opinion of the court that evidence was rightly admitted . . . for the purpose of identifying the murderer of Linda Bowyer as being the same individual as the person who had murdered the other two little girls in precisely the same way.

. . . I think one cannot distinguish abnormal propensities from identification. Abnormal propensity is a means of identification. . . . It is an abnormal propensity to strangle young girls and to do so without any apparent motive, without any attempt at sexual interference, and to leave their dead bodies where they can be seen and where, presumably, their deaths would be detected. In the judgment of the court, that evidence was admissible because it tended to identify the person who murdered Linda Bowyer with the person who confessed in his statements to having murdered the other two girls a year before, in exactly similar circumstances.

Extract 5.1.3

R v Smith (1915) 11 Cr App R 229, 236–8 (CCA)

This was the (in)famous case of the 'brides in the bath'. The accused was charged with the murder of Bessie Munday, with whom he had gone through a bigamous marriage, and who was found dead in her bath. At issue was the admissibility of evidence of the deaths of two other women, Alice Burnham and Margaret Lofty, on dates subsequent to the death of Munday. The accused had also gone through a bigamous marriage with each of these women, who also died in their baths in circumstances very similar to those surrounding the death of Munday. The trial judge directed the jury in the following terms: 'The jury have to take into account three things, the circumstances of the dead body, and the way in which it is found, and the evidence they have as to the way it died; the opportunity of the prisoner to cause the death or not; the motive of the prisoner for causing the death. It may be that even then they are not sure whether it is accident or design. And then comes in the purpose, and the only purpose, for which you are allowed to consider the evidence as to the other deaths. If you find an accident which benefits a person and you find that the person has been sufficiently fortunate to have that accident happen to him a number of times, benefiting him each time, you draw a very strong, frequently an irresistible inference, that the occurrence of so many accidents benefiting him is such a coincidence that it cannot have happened unless it was design.'

LORD READING CJ: The first question raised is that the judge was wrong in admitting evidence of the deaths of Alice Burnham and Margaret Lofty. . . . Viewing the case put forward with regard to Bessie Munday only, we are of opinion that there was a case which the judge was bound in strict law to put to the jury. The case was reinforced by the evidence admitted with reference to the other two cases for the purpose of shewing the design of the appellant. We think that that evidence was properly admitted, and the judge was very careful to point out to the jury the use they could properly make of the evidence. He directed them more than once that they must not allow their minds to be confused and think that they were deciding whether the murders of Burnham and Lofty had been committed; they were trying the appellant for the murder of Munday. We are of opinion therefore that the first point fails.

The second point taken is that even assuming that evidence of the death of the other two women was admissible, the prosecution ought only to have been allowed to prove that the women were found dead in their baths. For the reasons already given in dealing with the first point, it is apparent that to cut short the evidence there would have been of no assistance to the case. In our opinion it was open to the prosecution to give, and the judge was right in admitting, evidence of the facts surrounding the deaths of the two women.

As the House of Lords makes clear in *P*, however, a 'striking similarity' need not necessarily be demonstrated in every case as a prerequisite to admissibility. A distinction is to be drawn between, on the one hand, a situation in which what is at issue is the identity of the perpetrator, and, on the other hand, a situation in which what is at issue is whether an offence was committed (rather than who committed it). Because evidence of past misconduct would have 'more work . . . to do'[9] in the former situation, it must possess a higher probative value. Although a close examination of Lord Mackay's speech indicates that he was probably not prescribing a 'striking similarity' requirement for *all* cases in which identity is in issue,[10] it has generally been interpreted as imposing just such a requirement. For example, in *R v Johnson* the Court of Appeal held, applying *P*, that 'in cases where identity is the sole issue, it must always be a question of fact and degree as to whether the proposed evidence, when compared with the evidence of the complaint in the instant trial, fulfils the criterion of "a special similarity" so as to lead to the conclusion that each and every incident bears "the signature" of the accused. . . . In deciding that question, it is incumbent on the judge not only to look at those features, but at the nature and quality of any demonstrable disparities.'[11]

The existence of *dis*similarities, whilst a relevant consideration, is not of itself decisive:

The existence of dissimilarities cannot alone determine the question of admissibility (see for example *Morris* (1969) 54 Cr App R 69, 77 and 81; *Barrington* [1981] 1 All ER 1132; *Butler* (1986) 84 Cr App R 12; *Pfennig v R* (1995) 127 ALR 99 and *Simpson* (1993) 99 Cr App R 48). In our judgment, the existence of dissimilarities is simply a feature of the proposed evidence to which the judge must have regard

---

[9] Law Commission (Consultation Paper No 141), *Criminal Law – Evidence in Criminal Proceedings: Previous Misconduct of a Defendant – A Consultation Paper* (1996) 33.
[10] See R Pattenden, 'Similar Fact Evidence and Proof of Identity' (1996) 112 *Law Quarterly Review* 446, 468–9.
[11] [1995] 2 Cr App R 41, 46–7. See also *R v West* [1996] 2 Cr App R 374, 390; *R v Lee* [1996] Crim LR 825.

when assessing its probative force in the light of the purpose for which the prosecution seek to adduce it.[12]

It might be thought that, given the existence of a judicial discretion to exclude evidence whose probative value is outweighed by its prejudicial effect, the similar-facts doctrine is, in effect, otiose. This, however, overlooks the fundamental distinction between exclusionary rules, such as the similar-facts rule, and exclusionary discretions. This distinction relates to the fact that the situations in which an appeal court will overturn a decision reached in the exercise of discretion, rather than pursuant to the application of an exclusionary rule, are limited.

Is the test of balancing probative value against prejudicial effect, in any event, a workable one? Specifically, is it realistic to speak in terms of probative value *outweighing* prejudicial effect, when it may precisely be in those cases where high probative value derives from propensity to act in an unusual manner (as in *Straffen*) that prejudicial effect will correspondingly be high? McHugh J has remarked in the High Court of Australia:

> ... the proposition that the probative value of the evidence must outweigh its prejudicial effect is one that can be easily misunderstood. The use of the term 'outweigh' suggests an almost arithmetical computation. But prejudicial effect and probative value are incommensurables. They have no standard of comparison. The probative value of the evidence goes to proof of an issue, the prejudicial effect to the fairness of the trial. In criminal trials, the prejudicial effect of evidence is not concerned with the cogency of its proof but with the risk that the jury will use the evidence or be affected by it in a way that the law does not permit. In no sense does the probative value of evidence disclosing propensity, when admitted, outweigh its prejudicial effect. On the contrary, in many cases the probative value either creates or reinforces the prejudicial effect of the evidence.[13]

It has been argued that even to admit evidence of prior misconduct only in cases where its prejudicial effect is 'outweighed' by its probative value would not afford to accused persons sufficient protection against undue prejudice. 'Therefore, at least as important as the precise test for admissibility of similar fact evidence is the guidance the jury should be given in assessing the probative force of the evidence – in particular, the jury should be warned in no uncertain terms against undue prejudice.'[14] Even if such a warning would prove effective, the Court of Appeal has nonetheless held that

---

[12] *R v West* [1996] 2 Cr App R 374, 390–1.
[13] *Pfennig v R* (1995) 182 CLR 461, 528. See also P B Carter, 'Forbidden Reasoning Permissible: Similar Fact Evidence a Decade after *Boardman*' (1985) 48 *Modern Law Review* 29, 36–7 ('the judge must compare what are not altogether comparable. He must decide whether the true probative worth (a euphemism for judicial assessment of probative worth) of the evidence fully measures up to its prejudicial effect (*ie* the judge's conjecture as to what its effect is in the circumstances in fact likely to be upon the jury). Obviously this new approach will often impose a formidable task upon the judge'); J D Jackson, 'Judicial Responsibility in Criminal Proceedings' (1996) 49 *Current Legal Problems* 59, 80.
[14] R Nair, 'Weighing Similar Fact and Avoiding Prejudice' (1996) 112 *Law Quarterly Review* 262, 265. See also A A S Zuckerman, *The Principles of Criminal Evidence* (1989) Ch 12.

there is . . . no principle requiring a judge in all cases to warn the jury specifically about the dangers of convicting a person because evidence had been received showing him or her to have a propensity to commit a certain offence or to have been guilty of other gross misconduct. (See *Rance* (1975) 62 Cr App R 118, *Roy* (CA Transcript November 5, 1991 and [1992] Crim LR 185).) In some cases it will be desirable; in others no useful purpose will be served.[15]

The Law Commission has provisionally recommended little change to the existing law, stating that evidence of an accused's prior misconduct should be admissible in chief if

(1) it is relevant to a specific fact in issue; and
(2) on the assumption that the evidence is true, the *degree* to which it is relevant to that fact (in other words, its probative value) outweighs the risk that, if admitted, it might
   (a) result in prejudice;
   (b) mislead, confuse or distract the fact-finders; or
   (c) cause undue waste of time.[16]

The Commission also

provisionally propose[s] that the factors to be taken into account in balancing these considerations should be expressly set out, and should include
(1) in the case of the evidence's probative value,
   (a) the extent (if any) to which the evidence tends to suggest that the defendant has a *propensity* to act in the manner alleged;
   (b) any *similarities* between the facts revealed by the evidence and those now alleged;
   (c) the extent to which any such similarities may reasonably be attributed to coincidence; and
   (d) any *dis*similarities between the facts revealed by the evidence and those now alleged; and
(2) in the case of the evidence's likely prejudicial effect,
   (a) the risk of the fact-finders attaching undue significance to the evidence in question in determining whether the defendant is guilty as charged; and
   (b) the risk of their convicting the defendant on the basis of his or her conduct on some other occasion or occasions, rather than because they are satisfied that he or she is guilty as charged.[17]

The Commission's failure to recommend any substantial change to the present approach may be easily criticised: 'It is not clear why it is thought that placing what amounts to the common law principle into a statute is going to make any difference to judicial decisions. The application of such a clause would depend on the subjectivity of a court's perception of probative value, and that is the root cause of the present levels of unpredictability

---

[15] *R v West* [1996] 2 Cr App R 374, 395.
[16] Law Commission (Consultation Paper No 141), *Criminal Law – Evidence in Criminal Proceedings: Previous Misconduct of a Defendant – A Consultation Paper* (1996) 262 (emphasis in original).
[17] At 262–3 (emphasis in original).

in the similar facts case law.'[18] Perhaps a more appropriate solution would be to discard the 'probative value versus prejudicial effect' test altogether in favour of some other test, such as the Australian common law test of asking whether there is any reasonable explanation for the evidence other than that the defendant is guilty:

> ... the basis for the admission of similar fact evidence lies in its possessing a particular probative value or cogency such that, if accepted, it bears no reasonable explanation other than the inculpation of the accused in the offence charged. In other words, for propensity or similar fact evidence to be admissible, the objective improbability of its having some innocent explanation is such that there is no reasonable view of it other than as supporting an inference that the accused is guilty of the offence charged.[19]

> ... the trial judge ... must recognize that propensity evidence is circumstantial evidence and that, as such, it should not be used to draw an inference adverse to the accused unless it is the only reasonable inference in the circumstances. More than that, the evidence ought not to be admitted if the trial judge concludes that, viewed in the context of the prosecution case, there is a reasonable view of it which is consistent with innocence.[20]

An interesting development in the United States has been the recent introduction of Rules 413, 414 and 415 of the Federal Rules of Evidence. In essence, the effect of these rules is that, in sexual assault and child molestation cases, the similar-facts doctrine is abrogated and replaced with the orthodox test of relevance.

Extract 5.1.4

US Federal Rules of Evidence, Rule 413

Rule 413. Evidence of Similar Crimes in Sexual Assault Cases

(a) In a criminal case in which the defendant is accused of an offense of sexual assault, evidence of the defendant's commission of another offense or offenses of sexual assault is admissible, and may be considered for its bearing on any matter to which it is relevant.

(b) In a case in which the Government intends to offer evidence under this rule, the attorney for the Government shall disclose the evidence to the defendant, including statements of witnesses or a summary of the substance of any testimony that is expected to be offered, at least fifteen days before the scheduled date of trial or at such later time as the court may allow for good cause.

---

[18] J McEwan, 'The Law Commission Consultation Paper on Previous Misconduct: (2) Law Commission Dodges the Nettles in Consultation Paper No 141' [1997] *Criminal Law Review* 93, 94–5.
[19] *Pfennig v R* (1995) 182 CLR 461, 481–2.
[20] Ibid, 485.

(c) This rule shall not be construed to limit the admission or consideration of evidence under any other rule.

(d) For purposes of this rule and Rule 415, 'offense of sexual assault' means a crime under Federal law or the law of a State (as defined in section 513 of title 18, United States Code) that involved –

    (1) any conduct proscribed by chapter 109A of title 18, United States Code;

    (2) contact, without consent, between any part of the defendant's body or an object and the genitals or anus of another person;

    (3) contact, without consent, between the genitals or anus of the defendant and any part of another person's body;

    (4) deriving sexual pleasure or gratification from the infliction of death, bodily injury, or physical pain on another person; or

    (5) an attempt or conspiracy to engage in conduct described in paragraphs (1)–(4).

Analogous provision is made in Rule 414 for criminal cases concerning child molestation, and in Rule 415 for civil cases concerning sexual assault or child molestation.

These new provisions have been defended on the ground that sexual assault and child molestation are serious crimes which are often difficult to prosecute: such crimes typically take place in private and the prosecution may have little corroborative physical evidence at its disposal. As a consequence, trials often dissolve into situations where what is crucially at issue is 'the word of the complainant against the word of the defendant'. It is further argued that the probative value of evidence of prior involvement in offences of sexual assault and child molestation is especially high, given that research has generally demonstrated that those who commit such offences display a high recidivism rate. Are you persuaded that these arguments justify the introduction of the new provisions?[21]

2. THE PROBLEM OF POSSIBLE CONTAMINATION

In a case where multiple complainants have made similar allegations against the accused, there is potentially a danger that the evidence of the complainants may have become 'contaminated' in some way. Such contamination

---

[21] There is a wealth of literature on the new provisions, amongst which are K K Baker, 'Once a Rapist? Motivational Evidence and Relevancy in Rape Law' (1997) 110 *Harvard Law Review* 563; S S Beale, 'Prior Similar Acts in Prosecutions for Rape and Child Sex Abuse' (1993) 4 *Criminal Law Forum* 307; D P Bryden and R C Park, '"Other Crimes" Evidence in Sex Offense Cases' (1994) 78 *Minnesota Law Review* 529; D A Nance (ed), 'Symposium on the Admission of Prior Offense Evidence in Sexual Assault Cases' (1994) 70 *Chicago-Kent Law Review* 1; R C Park, 'Sexual Assault and the Rule against Character Reasoning' in J F Nijboer and J M Reijntjes (eds), *Proceedings of the First World Conference on New Trends in Criminal Investigation and Evidence* (1997); Law Commission (Consultation Paper No 141), *Criminal Law – Evidence in Criminal Proceedings: Previous Misconduct of a Defendant – A Consultation Paper* (1996) 144–8.

may well be the result of collusion between the complainants, who may have put their heads together to concoct a story against the accused. Alternatively, there may be a more innocent explanation for the contamination: distortions may have crept in over time as the complainants repeatedly discussed the incidents amongst themselves. And contamination 'may happen without the witnesses even communicating directly with each other, eg where the witnesses are inexpertly questioned by the same investigative team'.[22] The problem of possible contamination arose for consideration by the House of Lords in the following case. The essential question relates to the respective roles of judge and jury: is possible contamination to be taken into account by the trial judge in determining admissibility, or is it to be taken into account by the jury in assessing weight?

Extract 5.2.1

R v H [1995] 2 AC 596, 601–2, 612–14, 622, 625–7 (HL)

LORD MACKAY OF CLASHFERN LC: My Lords, the appellant in this case was tried and convicted on indictment of indecent assault on his adopted daughter whom I shall call S; of committing gross indecency with S and of having sexual intercourse with S when she was under 13 years of age. He was also tried and convicted of an offence of indecent assault on his step-daughter whom I shall call C. The appellant was sentenced to a total of nine years' imprisonment.

. . .

The three offences alleged to have been committed against S were said to have occurred on various occasions between 18 April 1987 and 20 April 1989. The fourth offence was alleged to have been committed against C on an occasion between 19 December 1987 and 31 December 1988. S was born on 19 April 1978 and was about nine at the start of the period over which the offences are alleged to have taken place. C was born on 20 December 1973 and was about 14 at the time of the alleged offence against her.

The allegations were first made to the police by the appellant's wife on 24 May 1992. She had been informed of their content for the first time on 24 May 1992 by S and had subsequently talked to C. S approached C and talked about the subject matter of the allegations for the first time on about 22 May 1992. C initially told S that nothing had happened to her but then later on made the allegations to which she was to depose. All the matters I have stated were apparent from the documents initially before the trial judge.

Prior to speaking to her mother, S had talked to her boyfriend and it was he who had prompted S to go to her mother. S's sexual relationship with her boyfriend started a month or two before the appellant's arrest on 24 May 1992. Two months after the appellant left the family home S's boyfriend moved in. It is accepted by both parties to this appeal that upon the facts of this case

[22] Law Commission (Consultation Paper No 141), *Criminal Law – Evidence in Criminal Proceedings: Previous Misconduct of a Defendant – A Consultation Paper* (1996), 184 n 105.

there must have existed a risk of collusion between C and S. In his directions to them, the judge made clear to the jury that they had to consider whether the girls had told a pack of lies by putting their heads together, collaborating and concocting a false story against their father; and also whether they might have fantasised about these matters. The judge continued, however, that it was for the prosecution to satisfy the jury that the girls were in fact telling the truth, and that the evidence of one girl could support the evidence of the other only if the jury was sure that the girls had not collaborated to concoct a false story against the defendant. The judge also pointed out that there was no support from C or anywhere else for the evidence of S that the appellant had had sexual intercourse with her.

. . .

Where there is an application to exclude evidence on the ground that it does not qualify as similar fact evidence and the submission raises a question of collusion (not only deliberate but including unconscious influence of one witness by another) the judge should approach the question of admissibility on the basis that the similar facts alleged are true and apply the test set out by this House in *Director of Public Prosecutions v P* [1991] 2 AC 447 accordingly. It follows that generally collusion is not relevant at this stage.

. . . if a submission is made raising a question of collusion in such a way as to cause the judge difficulty in applying the test referred to he may be compelled to hold a voire dire. The situations in which collusion is relevant in the consideration of admissibility would arise only in a very exceptional case of which no illustration was afforded in the argument on this appeal but I regard it as right to include this as a possibility since it is difficult to foresee all the circumstances that might arise. The present is certainly not a case in which the risk of collusion affects the application of the test.

. . . if evidence of similar facts has been admitted and circumstances are adduced in the course of the trial which indicate that no reasonable jury could accept the evidence as free from collusion the judge should direct the jury that it cannot be relied upon . . . for any . . . purpose adverse to the defence.

. . . where this is not so but the question of collusion has been raised the judge must clearly draw the importance of collusion to the attention of the jury and leave it to them to decide whether, notwithstanding such evidence of collusion as may have been put before them, they are satisfied that the evidence can be relied upon as free from collusion and tell them that if they are not so satisfied they cannot properly rely upon it . . . for any . . . purpose adverse to the defence.

. . .

I consider that in all the cases which might arise in this part of the law the statutory discretion provided by section 78 of the Police and Criminal Evidence Act 1984 and the common law discretion preserved by section 82(3) of that Act have to be kept in mind.

LORD GRIFFITHS: In the past when jurors were often uneducated and illiterate and the penal laws were of harsh severity, when children could be transported, and men were hanged for stealing a shilling and could not be heard in their own defence, the judges began to fashion rules of evidence to protect the accused from a conviction that they feared might be based on emotion or prejudice rather than a fair evaluation of the facts of the case against him. The judges did not trust the jury to evaluate all the relevant material and evolved many restrictive rules which they deemed necessary to ensure that the accused had a fair trial in the climate of those times. Today with better educated and more literate juries the value of those old restrictive rules of evidence is being re-evaluated and many are being discarded or modified. . . .

. . . The basic reason why criminal cases are heard by juries rather than by a judge alone is that our society prefers to trust the collective judgment of 12 men and women drawn from different backgrounds to decide the facts of the case rather than accept the view of a single professional judge. Deciding the facts requires the jury in all cases to decide whose evidence they find credible and what inferences they are prepared to draw from the facts as they find them. I would therefore resist any attempt to remove this essential role from the jury for to do so seems to me to strike root and branch at the very reason we have jury trial.

. . .

It is the function of the jury not the judge to decide whether a witness is to be believed. In every contested criminal trial the defence will put forward a number of arguments to persuade the jury not to accept the evidence given by the prosecution witnesses. Sometimes it will be suggested that they have wickedly conspired to give false evidence, sometimes that they have talked the matter over together so often that they have coloured each other's recollections, sometimes that they have persuaded themselves of events that never happened and so forth. It is because there is a consensus that 12 men and women from different walks of life are better able to evaluate such arguments and decide on the credibility of the witnesses that jury trial remains, with all its attendant expense, in preference to trial by a judge alone.

Of course the jury cannot rely on either sister's evidence to convict the stepfather, unless they are sure she is speaking the truth. But I can see no reason why they should not evaluate the attack on the credibility of the witnesses in this case, as they do in all other cases.

I would therefore say that it is the duty of the judge to rule upon the admissibility of evidence upon the assumption that the prosecution statements will be accepted by the jury as truthful and accurate. If the evidence is admitted it is for the jury then to determine its credibility and this applies to 'similar fact' evidence as it does to all other admissible evidence.

LORD MUSTILL: In these circumstances I am unable to accept that the rationale (in either version) of the reception of similar fact evidence in cases such as the present justifies either the proposition of law that the existence of a risk of 'collusion' between complainants makes the evidence inadmissible or the inauguration of a practice whereby the possibility of risk is explored on a voire dire. In my opinion it should continue in a case such as the present to be the practice, otherwise than in exceptional situations, that the trial judge rules upon the admissibility of the evidence of the witness who speaks to the fact alleged to be similar to the fact which forms the basis of the charge against the defendant by assuming that what is contained in her or his witness statement is unembroidered truth, leaving it to the jury to decide, in the light of whatever attack may be made on it in the course of the trial, what weight should be given to it.

My Lords I have qualified this opinion in two respects. First, it is limited to cases such as the present, where the occurrence of both the act which constitutes the offence and the act alleged to be similar are in issue and where the credibility or accuracy (or both) of the witnesses who speak to them is said to be compromised by 'collusion'. By no means all similar fact cases are of this kind. *Pfennig v The Queen*, 127 ALR 99 is an example of a quite different situation to which different reasoning may apply. The question has not been explored at all. I mention it only to emphasise that the views here expressed are confined to the immediate practical problems raised by the inconsistent decisions of the Court of Appeal (Criminal Division) of which this appeal is the outcome. Secondly, I have added the words 'otherwise than in exceptional situations' because it is impossible to predict with certainty all the manifold turns of event which may happen during criminal trials, and there is always a risk that an unqualified rule of procedure may later prove to be too rigid. Nevertheless, I find myself unable at present to envisage any situation where a voire dire of the kind proposed in argument would be appropriate.

LORD LLOYD OF BERWICK: In *Reg v Bedford*, 93 Cr App R 113, 116, Stuart-Smith LJ suggested that the evidence should be excluded if in the judge's view there is a 'real possibility' of concoction or collaboration. Lord Taylor of Gosforth CJ used similar language in *Reg v Ryder* [1994] 2 All ER 859, 878. Other courts have suggested 'serious risk' or 'real chance.' Ultimately it is a question of policy where the line is to be drawn: see *Phipson on Evidence*, 14th ed (1990), p 379. The House should, I think, be slow to differ from the Court of Appeal in formulating a practical test for admitting or excluding evidence. But there is a danger in choosing a particular formula to encapsulate policy, since it tends to become set in stone. This is the danger the House exposed in *Director of Public Prosecutions v P* [1991] 2 AC 447 when it released the law from the bondage of 'striking similarity,' useful though that expression must have been when it was first coined. Rather than choose a particular formulation, it therefore seems better to say that where a risk of collusion or contamination is apparent on the face of the documents, it will always be an element, and exceptionally a decisive element, in deciding whether the probative force of the similar fact evidence is sufficiently strong to justify admitting the evidence, notwithstanding its prejudicial effect.

It will no doubt be said that this leaves the test somewhat vague. It may be so. But at least it is flexible, and it is a natural and logical development of the approach adopted by the House in *Director of Public Prosecutions v P*.

LORD NICHOLLS OF BIRKENHEAD: In reaching their decision the jury will need to consider, where necessary, the possibility of collusion or unconscious influence of one witness by another. The appropriate course is for the judge to give the jury a clear direction that they should not accept the evidence unless they are satisfied that it is reliable and true and not tainted by collusion or other defects. If in the course of the trial the judge forms the view that no reasonable jury could be so satisfied, he should direct the jury that the evidence is not to be relied on ... for any ... prosecution purpose. That extreme case apart, the risk of collusion is one of the matters for the consideration of the jury.

The whole of the foregoing is subject to the judge's overriding discretion under section 78(1) of the Police and Criminal Evidence Act 1984 and the common law powers preserved by section 82(3).

Does *H* leave open the possibility that there may be situations in which contamination will be an issue for consideration by the judge in determining admissibility, rather than for consideration by the jury in assessing weight? If so, is it clear what precisely these situations are? What role, if any, might s 78(1) of the Police and Criminal Evidence Act 1984 (which gives trial judges a discretion to exclude evidence to ensure a fair trial), or the common law 'probative value versus prejudicial effect' discretion, play in this area? More generally, does the consideration of trust in, and respect for, the jury justify the decision in *H*? Or does this decision accord insufficient weight to the protection of the innocent from wrongful conviction? Consider the arguments advanced in the following extract:

Extract 5.2.2

S Doran, 'Similar Facts and the Shadow of Collusion: A Matter of Judicial Responsibility', *Archbold News*, 12 December 1995, 5, 7–8

There are at least three objections to the course which the House of Lords has taken in the *H* decision. First, by denying that the danger of contamination of evidence is generally a factor to be taken into account when gauging its probative force for the purposes of the similar fact rule, their Lordships assume a rather mechanical view of the judicial function in which assessment of the probative worth of evidence can be cleanly separated from the issue of its weight. It may be argued that it is impossible for a trial judge to conduct a meaningful assessment of the probative value of evidence, as measured against its potential prejudice, without making certain judgments on its reliability. Where there exists a danger of collusion or a threat to the independence of evidence, its probative value is diminished and potential prejudice increased in consequence. . . .

A particular concern voiced by Lord Mustill is that once a judge embarks on an examination of the prosecution witnesses in a *voire dire*, he or she will almost inevitably be drawn into a decision on whether they are telling the truth, thus merging the ultimate decision in the case with the decision on admissibility . . . Surely, however, the two can be kept distinct. A finding by the trial judge that the danger of collusion between witnesses deprives their evidence of the necessary degree of probative force to justify cross-admissibility does not entail a finding as to the veracity of their individual allegations. It may also be asked why the *voire dire* is generally regarded by their Lordships as such an undesirable course to adopt. The concern over putting vulnerable witnesses through an additional ordeal must be taken seriously; but the problem would arise relatively rarely. . . .

The second objection is that by confining so narrowly the judge's role in the filtering of evidence in such cases, their Lordships place too little emphasis on the trial judge's role in ensuring that the accused receives a fair trial. . . . The last few years have seen a generally more robust attitude to the exclusion, under section 78 of the Police and Criminal Evidence Act 1984, of evidence obtained in an unfair or improper manner; and an even more recent phenomenon has been the willingness of judges to halt trials because adverse media publicity has jeopardised the prospect of a fair trial. If these developments represent a trend towards enhanced judicial responsibility in the criminal process, then *H* is clearly out of line with that trend.

The response to this may be that prosecutions in cases of the kind involved here are notoriously difficult to pursue and involve considerable trauma for the victim witnesses. The force of this point cannot be underestimated. It does in my view, however, prompt the third objection to the *H* decision. This is that developments in the law of evidence and procedure have *already*, and properly, gone far to facilitate the reception and presentation of evidence in cases of this nature.

See also S Doran, 'Character Evidence and the Threat of Collusion: Free Evaluation or Judicial Responsibility?' in J F Nijboer and J M Reijntjes (eds), *Proceedings of the First World Conference on New Trends in Criminal Investigation and Evidence* (1997); P Mirfield, 'Proof and Prejudice in the House of Lords' (1996) 112 *Law Quarterly Review* 1; R Munday, 'Similar Fact Evidence and the Risk of Contaminated Testimony' [1995] *Cambridge Law Journal* 522.

The Law Commission

provisionally propose[s] that where a judge is satisfied, after hearing *all* the evidence, that a conviction would be unsafe because, in the light of the risk of contamination or collusion, the probative value of any evidence admitted is outweighed by its likely prejudicial effect and the risk that the jury may be misled, confused or distracted, the judge should discharge the jury and consider whether to order a retrial or to enter a verdict of not guilty.[23]

The following extract illustrates the approach taken in Australia:

Extract 5.2.3

Hoch v R (1988) 165 CLR 292, 297, 302 (HCA)

MASON CJ, WILSON and GAUDRON JJ: Thus, in our view, the admissibility of similar fact evidence in cases such as the present depends on that evidence having the quality that it is not reasonably explicable on the basis of concoction. That is a matter to be determined, as in all cases of circumstantial evidence, in the light of common sense and experience. It is not a matter that necessarily involves an examination on a voir dire. If the depositions of witnesses in committal proceedings or the statements of witnesses indicate that the witnesses had no relationship with each other prior to the making of

---

[23] Ibid, 263 (emphasis in original).

the various complaints, and that is unchallenged, then, assuming the requisite degree of similarity, common sense and experience will indicate that the evidence bears that probative force which renders it admissible. On the other hand, if the depositions or the statements indicate that the complainants have a sufficient relationship to each other and had opportunity and motive for concoction then, as a matter of common sense and experience, the evidence will lack the degree of probative value necessary to render it admissible. Of course there may be cases where an examination on the voir dire is necessary, but that will be for the purpose of ascertaining the facts relevant to the circumstances of the witnesses to permit an assessment of the probative value of the evidence by reference to the consideration whether, in the light of common sense and experience, it is capable of *reasonable* explanation on the basis of concoction. It will not be for the purpose of the trial judge making a preliminary finding whether there was or was not concoction.

BRENNAN and DAWSON JJ: If there is a real danger of the concoction of similar fact evidence it is consistent with the attitude which the law adopts toward evidence of that kind that it should exclude it upon the basis that its probative value is depreciated to an extent that a jury may be tempted to act upon prejudice rather than proof. That consideration is of special importance in cases where the fact to be proved is inferred not from similar facts which have been clearly established but from the concatenation of the testimony of a number of witnesses who depose to the occurrence of similar facts. The credibility of that testimony bears directly on the probative force of the evidence. Several witnesses all giving evidence to a similar effect are generally easier to believe than one witness. But if the witnesses have put their heads together that is not the case.

Should such an approach be adopted in England?

3. THE SIMILAR-FACTS RULE AND IDENTIFICATION EVIDENCE

Suppose that a defendant is charged with two offences which bore a number of similarities, and that there is disputed identification evidence in relation to both offences. Must the jury be satisfied of the defendant's guilt of each individual offence before it can use evidence of this offence as similar-fact evidence in determining whether the defendant also committed the other offence? Or is it appropriate to invite the jury to decide whether, in the light of the similarities between them, the offences were committed by the same person, and, if so satisfied, to use the identification evidence in relation to both offences *cumulatively* to determine whether the defendant was responsible for both offences? There has been a trio of Court of Appeal decisions in which the law in this area has been developed. Following is an extract from the latest of these cases, in which the two earlier decisions are discussed.

Extract 5.3.1

R v Barnes [1995] 2 Cr App R 491, 494–9 (CA)

LORD TAYLOR CJ: On this appeal the main ground is that the judge mis-directed the jury as to the correct approach to the identification evidence. Mr Cooke submits that the judge should have directed the jury first to consider a single count and in doing so to have regard to the identification evidence only of the victim on that count. Identification evidence by other victims must be disregarded at that stage. Only if the jury were sure of guilt on that count could they use the identification evidence on that count to support the identification evidence on the next count they proceeded to consider. Since the judge did not adopt that approach, it is said that his summing up was fatally flawed.

In support of his argument, Mr Cooke relied heavily on the judgment of this Court in *McGranaghan* (Note) [1995] 1 Cr App R 559. In that case there had been three separate incidents each involving aggravated burglary, a sexual offence and robbery. This Court accepted that the similarities between the three incidents was such as to render the evidence of one offence admissible in relation to the others. However, at p 572G of the judgment, Glidewell LJ pointed out that similar fact evidence may be adduced for different purposes. He went on:

'Here, the purpose was ... of supporting the identification of the appellant by each of the ladies as her assailant.

If it is sought to adduce similar fact evidence in order to prove that one of two or more offences was committed by the defendant, in our view such evidence may only be admitted if the jury are sure on evidence other than the similar fact evidence, that the defendant is guilty of the other offence. In other words, if a defendant is charged with two offences and the circum-stances and features of the offences are said to be so similar that evidence of one offence is admissible in support of the identification of the defendant as the perpetrator of the second offence, the jury should be directed to con-sider first whether, disregarding the similarity of the facts, the other evidence is sufficient to make them sure that the defendant committed offence number one. Only if they are so sure is evidence of similarity admissible to prove that the defendant committed offence number two. An identification about which the jury are not sure cannot support another identification of which they are also not sure however similar the facts of the two offences may be. The similar facts go to show that the same man committed both offences, not that the defendant was that man. There must be some evidence to make the jury sure that on at least one offence the defendant was that man.'

The Court then held that the trial judge's direction had been flawed where he said:

'In this case you might be entitled to look in general terms at the marked and obvious similarities which exist between the three groups of cases. That might help you, not to assist an original identification, but as some supportive evidence of the identification made in the individual cases or in any individual case ...'

Thus the Court in *McGranaghan* was considering whether similar fact evidence can be used 'as some support of evidence of the identification' so as to prove the accused guilty of offence A. If the similarity of the facts of offence B is to be used in that way as direct support for the guilt of the accused of offence A, the rationale being that the same man committed both A and B, then the jury would first have to be sure of the accused's guilt of B before the similarity of the facts could support the identification of him as guilty of A. Accordingly, we respectfully agree with the criticism of the trial judge's summing up in that case. We also agree with the last two sentences of the passage quoted from Glidewell LJ's judgment. However, the ante-penultimate sentence is more difficult.

It has been suggested that the judgment in *McGranaghan* 'may go too far'. The editors of *Archbold* ((1995) para 13–36), pose two situations as follows:

> 'Suppose there was only one charge of, for example, robbery and the prosecution case consisted of five identifying witnesses, all of whom were entirely independent of the events and of each other and all of whom identified the defendant on identification parades conducted exactly in accordance with the prescribed procedure. A jury, properly directed, would be entitled to reason that the chances of five people making the same mistake, without that mistake being revealed as a result of cross-examination was so remote that the explanation must be that the identifications are accurate. If the situation was that there were five separate offences against women and each victim identified the defendant without any possibility of contamination and in unimpeachable circumstances and there was other evidence which did not implicate the defendant but proved beyond reasonable doubt that all the offences were the work of the same man, why should the jury not start with the proposition that there is only one man involved and approach the issue of identity in the same way as the jury on the robbery charge?'

Mr Sells QC for the Crown submits that the answer to that rhetorical question is that if the evidence other than the visual identifications of the accused proves to the jury's satisfaction that one man committed all five offences, they can consider the identification evidence of all five victims in determining that that one man is the accused. Likewise, if there were a sixth victim who failed to identify the accused on a parade, the jury should take that into account as well. Mr Cooke in the course of argument, accepted the logic of this analysis.

Moreover, in *Downey* [1995] 1 Cr App R 547 Evans LJ, giving the judgment of the Court, considered *McGranaghan*, referred to the above passage in *Archbold* and at p 552 went on:

> 'There are indeed, in our judgment, two different aspects at least in this kind of situation. . . . The first is where in deciding the defendant committed offence A the jury can have regard to evidence that he also committed offence B. This involves proof not only of similarity, but that the defendant did in fact commit offence B.'

That was the situation described in the above passage from *McGranaghan*. Evans LJ went on:

'The second is where there is evidence that both offences A and B were committed by the same man, that the evidence falls short of proving that that man was the defendant in either case, regarded alone. If there is evidence which entitles the jury to reach the conclusion that it was the same man, even though the evidence in either case does not enable them to be sure who the man was then it follows that they can take account of evidence relating to both offences in deciding whether that man was the defendant.'

Later on the same page, the Court approved the judge's summing up in that case, saying:

'The jury was invited to consider whether the evidence established that both offences were committed by the same man, whoever that man might be, and if they were satisfied that that was the case, then they were entitled to take account of the evidence relating to both offences when reaching their decisions in respect of each.'

That passage was expressly approved by this Court in *Black* (unreported February 23, 1995).

Thus in *McGranaghan* the Court was considering the propriety of using similar fact evidence to support a doubtful identification. Here, the question is a different one, namely whether identifications of the appellant by several victims can be used cumulatively once the jury is satisfied that other evidence shows all the offences to have been committed by one man.

In this situation (*ie* the second of the 'two different aspects' identified in *Downey*) the analysis quoted from Evans LJ's judgment, which accords with the views expressed in *Archbold*, is in our view correct. The *McGranaghan* analysis is appropriate to the first aspect identified in *Downey* which was the situation predicated in the trial judge's summing up in *McGranaghan*. If the one sentence to which we have drawn attention in the passage quoted from *McGranaghan* sought to go further, as is claimed by Mr Cooke, we consider it to have been *obiter* and to have gone too far.

Mr Cooke's proposition would lead to an unreal exercise by a jury in seeking to compartmentalise the evidence properly put before them. Even if they were sure on the evidence other than the visual identifications that all the offences were committed by one man, they would then have to focus attention on one count wearing blinkers to shut out the visual identifications by any victim other than the victim on that one count. If they were not sure that the evidence on that count proved the guilt of the accused, they would then have to move to another count repeating the exercise, again wearing blinkers as to any evidence of visual identification save for that of the victim in this second count. There have been a number of situations in which the requirements of a jury have been said to involve mental gymnastics, but the gymnastics required in this exercise would need to be of Olympic standard. Nor would such an exercise accord with common sense. If the jury are satisfied by other evidence that one man committed all the offences then the victims at the identification parades are, *ex hypothesi*, all seeking to identify the same man and we can see no reason why their identifications should not be regarded as mutually supportive. The safeguards peculiar to identification evidence are provided by the regime laid down in *Turnbull* (1976) 63 Cr App R 132, [1977] QB 224. That involves warning the jury that a mistaken witness can be a convincing one and that a number of such witnesses can all be mistaken.

Having accepted the logic of the above analysis, Mr Cooke still complains that the learned judge did not sufficiently indicate to the jury that at the first stage when they were considering whether all the offences were committed by one man, they had to exclude the visual identifications. It is therefore necessary to look at the trial judge's directions.

He told the jury they had first to decide whether the offences were committed at all. As already observed, there was no dispute about this at the trial. The judge then went on:

'The next question to be answered is this: are the similarities between the separate incidents so telling that you are sure that the offences are committed by one and the same man? Because this is important, I will repeat it.' (and he did repeat it) 'In coming to grips with that question and, naturally, you will look at the time, the place, the manner and the descriptions. What may your answer be? It may be, "all of them, all seven." It may be, "yes, some of them". It may be "no, none. All of them are separate incidents in the sense that they were committed by seven separate people". It is your decision. It is your detailed answer to that question that I have posed and this necessary preliminary question that governs the next stage for your consideration. Therefore, your approach to a decision, to a verdict on any particular count will necessarily be along these lines. You will assess, first, the directly relevant evidence that is to say from the incidents referred to in that count itself, the incident, that time, that day, that place, the mode of approach and the detail of the incident itself. You will look at descriptions, physical appearance, clothing, identification at parade, what was said in interview and what witnesses said by way of alibi.

On any particular count, members of the jury, you may also take into consideration evidence under the same headings from similar incidents and, evidence from the other incidents whether one of the three on the indictment or those three named persons who are outside it.'

The learned judge then gave some examples. It is not necessary to lengthen this judgment by repeating them in full but in the course of giving them the judge made it clear that it was the evidence from the incidents themselves to which the jury should look on the question whether they were committed by one man and only when they had reached that conclusion could they look at the identification evidence from more than one of the victims. At the end of the very long summing up, the judge came back to this matter and at p 127 he said:

'When deciding about any one incident, you are entitled to take into account also any evidence pointing to identification of the defendant in respect of any one or more of the other incidents, provided of course that you are first satisfied so that you are sure that it is the same man in the incident being considered and in the other incident or incidents that you were turning to.'

It might have been better if the learned judge, having said what matters the jury should take into account on the issue of whether one man committed all the offences, had in a single sentence specifically excluded the identification evidence. However, taken together, the passages to which we have referred would in our judgment have conveyed clearly to the jury that evidence of visual identifications could only afford mutual support if the jury were first sure on the evidence of the incidents themselves that only one man was involved. Accordingly, this ground of appeal is rejected.

Whilst the decision in *Barnes* may be justifiable on pragmatic grounds,[24] it is not without its difficulties:

> The most recent decision of the Court of Appeal, *R v Barnes*, says that once the jury have decided that several counts were the work of the same person because of the similarities between them and/or because of other connecting features, the jury should consider the identity of the malefactor and for this purpose *all* relevant evidence, including disputed visual identification evidence, may be taken into account regardless of the count on the indictment to which it relates. . . . Since both the Court of Appeal and Appeal Committee of the House of Lords refused the defence leave to appeal to the House of Lords, the decision in *Barnes* settles the law for the time being, notwithstanding that it is out-of-step with a long line of cases and that the simultaneous endorsement and undermining of *R v McGranaghan* in *Barnes* is likely to cause confusion amongst those who have to apply the law.[25]

Barnes has been applied by the Court of Appeal in *R v Grant*[26] and *R v Brown*.[27]

4. JOINDER AND SEVERANCE

The relationship between the similar-facts rule and the rules relating to joinder of charges in the same indictment was considered recently by the House of Lords in the following case:

Extract 5.4.1

R v Christou [1996] 2 WLR 620, 622, 623, 629–30 (HL)

LORD TAYLOR OF GOSFORTH CJ: . . . the Court of Appeal certified a point of general public importance in the following terms:

> 'Where an accused is charged with sexual offences against more than one person and the evidence of one complainant is not so related to that of the other complainants as to render it admissible on the charges concerning

[24] R Pattenden, 'Similar Fact Evidence and Proof of Identity' (1996) 112 *Law Quarterly Review* 446, 462.
[25] At 470–1.
[26] [1996] 2 Cr App R 272.
[27] [1997] Crim LR 502.

those other complainants in accordance with the principle laid down in *Director of Public Prosecutions v P* [1991] 2 AC 447 has the trial judge a discretion to order that all charges should be tried together, having regard to the provisions of section 4 of the Indictments Act 1915 (as amended) and rule 9 of the Indictment Rules?'

Your Lordships' House gave leave to appeal . . .

. . .

Rule 9 of the Indictment Rules 1971 (made under the Indictments Act 1915) is in the following terms:

'Charges for any offences may be joined in the same indictment if those charges are founded on the same facts, or form or are a part of a series of offences of the same or a similar character.'

Section 5(3) of the Indictments Act 1915 provides:

'Where, before trial, or at any stage of a trial, the court is of opinion that a person accused may be prejudiced or embarrassed in his defence by reason of being charged with more than one offence in the same indictment, or that for any other reason it is desirable to direct that the person should be tried separately for any one or more offences charged in an indictment, the court may order a separate trial of any count or counts of such indictment.'

. . .

First, the statutory provisions undoubtedly give the trial judge a discretion. To hold that he must decide the question of severance in a particular way would be to fetter that statutory discretion.

Again, in what cases would the fetter apply? To all sexual offences? Or only . . . to sexual abuse of children? If so, children of what age? Would such a fetter apply only where children were giving evidence or equally . . . where mature adults were giving evidence of abuse during their childhood? No satisfactory answer of general application can be given to such questions.

. . .

. . . the factors a judge should consider . . . will vary from case to case, but the essential criterion is the achievement of a fair resolution of the issues. That requires fairness to the accused but also to the prosecution and those involved in it. Some, but by no means an exhaustive list, of the factors which may need to be considered are: – how discrete or inter-related are the facts giving rise to the counts; the impact of ordering two or more trials on the defendant and his family, on the victims and their families, on press publicity; and importantly, whether directions the judge can give to the jury will suffice to secure a fair trial if the counts are tried together. In regard to that last factor, jury trials are conducted on the basis that the judge's directions of law are to be applied faithfully. Experience shows . . . that juries, where counts are jointly tried, do follow the judge's directions and consider the counts separately.

Approaching the question of severance as indicated above, judges will often consider it right to order separate trials. But I reject the argument that either generally or in respect of any class of case, the judge must so order. Accordingly, I would answer the certified question, 'Yes' . . .

Inasmuch as s 5(3) of the Indictments Act 1915 gives the court a *discretion* as to whether to order separate trials, it is clearly right that the House of Lords has decided that this discretion cannot be fettered. Perhaps the appropriate solution lies, therefore, in amending the legislation so that

> where evidence of two complainants is inadmissible against each other, separate trials must be held, if the defence so apply. If this were to increase the number of trials, at a greater cost to the public, it would be an unfortunate but unavoidable result. Without this reform, however, the defendant is being cheated of the basic tenet of criminal evidence: prejudice caused by admitting evidence must never exceed its probative value.[28]

5. POSSESSION OF INCRIMINATING ARTICLES

Just as evidence of an accused's prior misconduct may be admissible in appropriate circumstances on the issue of the accused's guilt, so too, in a similar vein, may evidence that the accused was found in possession of incriminating articles. As the following case indicates, it is necessary once again, in determining admissibility, to have regard to the precise purpose for which it is sought to adduce the evidence.

Extract 5.5.1

R v B [1997] 2 Cr App R 88, 88–93 (CA)

ROSE LJ: On July 12, 1996, at Oxford Crown Court, this appellant was convicted by the jury before Judge Corrie of eight counts of indecent assault and was subsequently sentenced to three years' imprisonment concurrently. He appeals against conviction by leave of the single judge.

The charges related to indecent assaults on his two grandsons, aged approximately nine and 11 years old at the time of the offences. His defence was that no such indecent assaults had occurred.

The essence of the appeal before this Court, presented by Mr Wide QC, is that the judge was wrong to admit in evidence before the jury certain homosexual pornographic magazines, found in the appellant's possession, and that he was wrong, furthermore, in permitting questions and answers about the magazines and about the appellant's sexual propensities to go before the jury; those questions and answers occurred in the course of a lengthy interview of the appellant by police officers. There are further grounds of appeal to which it is unnecessary, as will emerge, to refer.

. . .

---

[28] C Mortimore, 'Severance Revisited' (1996) 140 *Solicitors Journal* 611, 611. See also R Munday, 'Vaguely Similar Facts and Severance of Counts' (1996) 160 *Justice of the Peace* 663.

When the appellant was arrested, his home was searched and there were found in his bedroom pornographic magazines of both a heterosexual and a homosexual kind relating, in the latter case, it has to be said, to men not boys. In interview the appellant denied, as we have already indicated, having behaved in any way indecently towards his two grandsons. He suggested that the boys had been put up by their mother to make up these allegations against him, and he in turn also made allegations about the sexual behaviour of the boys in relation to each other. In evidence the appellant denied the charges entirely and said he had a perfectly normal relationship with his grandsons. His wife also gave evidence before the jury.

We indicated at an earlier stage in this judgment the focus of this appeal. It was anticipated by submissions made in the course of the trial to the trial judge, by Mr Wide, who appeared in the Court below. He submitted that the evidence of the pornographic homosexual magazines found in the defendant's possession should not be admitted before the jury. The judge ruled against that submission. He did exclude from evidence certain mechanical devices of a sexual nature but he ruled that the magazines should be admitted in evidence. Somewhat curiously, that ruling having been made, the magazines were not actually seen by the jury, although the appellant, in the course of his evidence, was cross-examined about their content.

A submission was also made in the course of the trial that the interviews, in so far as they bore upon the appellant's alleged homosexual proclivities, should not have been adduced in evidence before the jury. It is to be noted that the decision of this court in *Wright* (1989) 90 Cr App R 325, where the reserved judgment of the court was given by Mustill LJ, as he then was, was not cited to the learned judge in the course of argument. Indeed, no reference to that authority was to be found, either in the written skeleton argument on behalf of the appellant, submitted by Mr Wide, or in the oral submissions of Mr Bright, until the court drew counsel's attention to that authority. To the significance of that authority we shall come in a moment.

The fact that it was not referred to either in the court below, or, initially, in this Court, may well be due to this. Although that authority is referred to, for example, in *Archbold*, (1997) para 13–32, it is not identified as bearing upon the issue with which this Court is presently concerned. It is an authority which, it seems to this Court, ought to be more widely known. Indeed, as recently as January 20, 1997 it was referred to in a case called *Sabouri*, unreported, where it had a significant impact upon the hearing of the appeal. It is convenient to cite from the judgment in *Wright* of Mustill LJ, at p 331. The facts in that case were in many, though not all, respects similar to those in the present case, and what was in issue in that case, amongst other things, was whether or not pornographic magazines, found in the possession of that appellant, and answers which he had given in interview with the police, in relation to his sexual proclivities, had properly been admitted before the jury. Mustill LJ said this:

'One must begin by asking whether, in a case where the issue is whether the act alleged by the complainant ever took place at all, evidence is admissible that the defendant had done similar acts in the past, or could be shown through the possession of incriminating articles or otherwise, to have a leaning towards such acts.

It is not hard to imagine legal systems in which such evidence would not only be admissible, but would be regarded as having high probative value. Nevertheless, this has never been the policy of the English criminal law, not so much on the grounds of logic, but because it is considered that to entrust it to a jury would be too great a risk. It is unnecessary to cite any more authority for this proposition than the oft-quoted opinion of Lord Herschell in *Makin v Attorney-General for New South Wales* [1894] AC 57, 65.

The principle is subject to exceptions, as Lord Herschell himself acknowledged. Thus if a person accused of indecently touching a child admits the contact but asserts that it was accidental, evidence of previous similar acts may be admitted, because it is relevant to the issue of accident or design: see *Makin* (*supra*) and *Bond* [1906] 2 KB 389. So also if there is a defence that acts prima facie attributable to guilt in fact had an innocent explanation. See *Gale* (1987) (unreported), where a defendant who had taken indecent photographs of his young step-daughter claimed that he had done so for artistic purposes at the instigation of his wife, and where it was held to have been proper to admit evidence that he had written pornographic fantasies to describe, in a manner which bore a close resemblance to the very type of incident which the girl had herself described, the sexual initiation of a young girl by her father.

Again such evidence may be permitted where it goes to disprove a defence that an association with the complainant bears an innocent explanation. Another exception exists where there is no doubt that an offence was committed by someone, but where the defendant denies that he was that person, and where the evidence is of acts done by the defendant which bear a striking similarity to those done by the offender on the occasion in question: *Thompson v DPP* (1918) 13 Cr App R 61 . . . *Reading* (1965) 50 Cr App R 98 . . . *Mustafa* (1976) 65 Cr App R 26. (Whether *Twiss* (1918) 13 Cr App R 177, . . . can now be justified on this ground may one day have to be discussed. We need not decide this here.)

Although these exceptions are well established, it is also quite clear that they are not brought into play simply through a denial that the acts in question ever happened at all. This is demonstrated by *Cole* (1941) 28 Cr App R 43, *Horwood* (1969) 53 Cr App R 619 . . . and perhaps most clearly by *Lewis* (1982) 76 Cr App R 33, where evidence of paedophiliac tendencies was held admissible in relation to counts where the touching was said to have been innocent or accidental, but not in relation to an incident which could have had no innocent explanation, but which the defendant denied had ever taken place.

Here it cannot be said that the appellant had raised any defence of the types we have mentioned: he did not admit the incidents whilst denying that they involved any criminality on his part. He asserted that the boys made them up. In argument at the trial counsel for the prosecution asserted, and the judge must be taken to have accepted, that the book was 'strong probative evidence that he was a homosexual'. The authorities show that this is not a permissible ground for admitting the evidence, any more than was the evidence of the questions about homosexuality in the police interviews, and of the visit to Paris, which were properly omitted pursuant to the agreement reached before the trial began.

In our judgment the evidence concerning the booklet should not have been admitted, and the booklet itself should not have been seen by the jury.'

On behalf of the appellant, Mr Wide submits that the magazines of a porno-graphic homosexual nature, and the questions and answers in interview, in relation to the possibility of the appellant having homosexual proclivities, went only to propensity, and the judge in concluding that they went to the extent and mode of expression of the defendant's sexual urges was effectively saying exactly that. He submits that this material should not have gone before the jury. That submission gained strength from the passage in the judgment of Mustill LJ which we have just read. On behalf of the prosecution, Mr Bright, who appeared at the trial, does not seek to suggest that *Wright* is other than good law, nor does he seek to suggest that it either was overruled or merits reconsideration in the light of the House of Lords' decision in *DPP v P* (1991) 93 Cr App R 267, [1991] 2 AC 447.

However, he submits that, so far as the evidence sought to be excluded is concerned, it was admissible because the appellant had sought to suggest that there was a plot or conspiracy against him, between the boys and their mother; he sought to suggest that any touching by him was accidental, or if it was deliberate, innocent, in particular, in connection with bathing the boys. He also relies upon the appellant's allegations made against the boys, in relation to their own sexual behaviour with each other. It is also pertinent, says Mr Bright, that the appellant claimed in interview that his sexual desires related to women only, and therefore that which was found of a pornographic nature in relation to homosexual activity between men was relevant to demon-strate that those answers in interview were dishonest.

So far as the contents of the interview are concerned, we have read the whole of it. It is right to say that, at one stage in the course of the interview, the appellant referred to 'washing the penis' of each of the boys in the course of bathing them. In certain circumstances that might give rise to an innocent explanation capable of being rebutted by the material upon which the pros-ecution rely. But that is not this case, because there is no allegation made by either of the boys based on indecency towards them in the bath. Having read, as we have said, the whole of the interview, we are entirely satisfied that the general thrust of the appellant's answers was to deny that there ever had been any sort of indecency. That which he said in relation to the plot which he claimed had been concocted against him amounted to no more than an underlining of that denial, as indeed Mr Bright himself was constrained to concede. In any event, as appears in part of the judgment of Mustill LJ which we have read, the fact that the appellant asserts that allegations have been made up against him is not a basis on which an exception can have been established to the general principle enunciated in *Makin*.

Mr Bright sought to submit that because, as he claimed, the appellant gave a dishonest answer in relation to his sexual proclivities, it was open to the prosecution to adduce evidence tending to show that he was a homosexual, because that went to credit. The difficulty with that submission is that, if it were correct, a person who habitually burgled houses who in interview denied that he ever burgled houses could have adduced before the jury evidence of his previous convictions. That situation would simply not arise because the answers given in relation to proclivities with regard to burgling people's houses would, as it seems to us, properly be excised from the evidence of that which had transpired in interview. So, in the present case, in our judgment, the questions and answers bearing upon the appellant's alleged homosexual proclivities should have been excised from the interview; and there should have been excluded from the evidence which was led before the jury the magazines relating to male adult sexual activity of a pornographic nature which were found in his possession. The reason for this is that neither the answers nor the magazines were probative of anything save propensity; and that, in the judgment of this Court, following the judgment of Mustill LJ in *Wright*, is not a proper basis to render them admissible. It follows that the convictions in this case cannot be regarded as safe. They are quashed and the appeal is allowed.

6. STATUTORY EXCEPTIONS TO THE GENERAL PROHIBITION

Statutory provisions may have the effect of rendering admissible, in specific circumstances, evidence of an accused's prior misconduct. Such evidence would remain capable, however, of being excluded in the exercise of the probative value versus prejudicial effect discretion.[29]

Extract 5.6.1

Official Secrets Act 1911, s 1(2)

1. Penalties for spying
    (2) On a prosecution under this section, it shall not be necessary to show that the accused person was guilty of any particular act tending to show a purpose prejudicial to the safety or interests of the State, and, notwithstanding that no such act is proved against him, he may be convicted if, from the circumstances of the case, or his conduct, or his known character as proved, it appears that his purpose was a purpose prejudicial to the safety or interests of the State; and if any sketch, plan, model, article, note, document, or information relating to or used in any prohibited place within the meaning of this Act, or anything in such a place or any secret official code word or pass word, is made, obtained, collected, recorded, published or communicated by any person other than a person acting under lawful authority, it shall be deemed to have been made, obtained, collected, recorded, published or communicated for a purpose prejudicial to the safety or interests of the State unless the contrary is proved.

---

[29] The availability of this discretion in the context of s 27(3) of the Theft Act 1968 was acknowledged by the House of Lords in *R v Hacker* [1994] 1 WLR 1659.

Extract 5.6.2

Theft Act 1968, s 27(3)

27. Evidence and procedure on charge of theft or handling stolen goods
(3) Where a person is being proceeded against for handling stolen goods (but not for any offence other than handling stolen goods), then at any stage of the proceedings, if evidence has been given of his having or arranging to have in his possession the goods the subject of the charge, or of his undertaking or assisting in, or arranging to undertake or assist in, their retention, removal, disposal or realisation, the following evidence shall be admissible for the purpose of proving that he knew or believed the goods to be stolen goods: –
   (a) evidence that he has had in his possession, or has undertaken or assisted in the retention, removal, disposal or realisation of, stolen goods from any theft taking place not earlier than twelve months before the offence charged; and
   (b) (provided that seven days' notice in writing has been given to him of the intention to prove the conviction) evidence that he has within the five years preceding the date of the offence charged been convicted of theft or of handling stolen goods.

The House of Lords has held in *R* v *Hacker*[30] that, under s 27(3)(b), it is permissible for the goods in question to be identified: the prosecution is not restricted to identifying the fact, date and place of conviction. This decision has been the subject of criticism,[31] as, indeed, has s 27(3) itself. There have been a number of calls for its repeal, with the Law Commission recently recommending provisionally 'that section 27(3) ... should be repealed, and that handling cases should be dealt with under the same rules as other cases'.[32]

7. CIVIL TRIALS

To what extent does the similar-facts rule apply in civil trials as it does in criminal trials?

Extract 5.7.1

Mood Music Publishing Co v *De Wolfe Ltd* [1976] Ch 119, 127 (CA)

LORD DENNING MR: The admissibility of evidence as to 'similar facts' has been much considered in the criminal law. Some of them have reached the highest tribunal, the latest of them being *Reg* v *Boardman* [1975] AC 421. The

[30] [1994] 1 WLR 1659.
[31] R Munday, 'Handling Convictions Admissible under S 27(3) of the Theft Act 1968: Part 1' (1995) 159 *Justice of the Peace* 223; R Munday, 'Handling Convictions Admissible under S 27(3) of the Theft Act 1968: Part 2' (1995) 159 *Justice of the Peace* 261.
[32] Law Commission (Consultation Paper No 141), *Criminal Law – Evidence in Criminal Proceedings: Previous Misconduct of a Defendant – A Consultation Paper* (1996) 270.

criminal courts have been very careful not to admit such evidence unless its probative value is so strong that it should be received in the interests of justice: and its admission will not operate unfairly to the accused. In civil cases the courts have followed a similar line but have not been so chary of admitting it. In civil cases the courts will admit evidence of similar facts if it is logically probative, that is, if it is logically relevant in determining the matter which is in issue: provided that it is not oppressive or unfair to the other side: and also that the other side has fair notice of it and is able to deal with it. Instances are *Brown v Eastern & Midlands Railway Co* (1889) 22 QBD 391; *Moore v Ransome's Dock Committee* (1898) 14 TLR 539 and *Hales v Kerr* [1908] 2 KB 601.

Why is a more liberal approach taken in civil cases than in criminal cases? Is it necessary to distinguish between different types of civil proceedings?

Extract 5.7.2

***Thorpe v Chief Constable, Manchester* [1989] 1 WLR 665, 670 (CA)**

DILLON LJ: . . . I apprehend that Lord Denning MR was thinking of civil cases tried by a judge alone. Where there is a jury the court must be more careful about admitting evidence which is in truth merely prejudicial, than is necessary where there is a trial by a judge alone who is trained to distinguish between what is probative and what is not.

Further reading

The following is a selection of the vast literature on this topic:

A E Acorn, 'Similar Fact Evidence and the Principle of Inductive Reasoning: Makin Sense' (1991) 11 *Oxford Journal of Legal Studies* 63

T R S Allan, 'Similar Fact Evidence and Disposition: Law, Discretion and Admissibility' (1985) 48 *Modern Law Review* 253

— 'Some Favourite Fallacies about Similar Facts' (1988) 8 *Legal Studies* 35

A J Ashworth, 'Evidence of Previous Misconduct' [1996] *Criminal Law Review* 681

P B Carter, 'Forbidden Reasoning Permissible: Similar Fact Evidence a Decade after *Boardman*' (1985) 48 *Modern Law Review* 29

L H Hoffmann, 'Similar Facts after *Boardman*' (1975) 91 *Law Quarterly Review* 193

Law Commission (Consultation Paper No 141), *Criminal Law – Evidence in Criminal Proceedings: Previous Misconduct of a Defendant – A Consultation Paper* (1996)

P Mirfield, 'Similar Facts – *Makin* Out?' [1987] *Cambridge Law Journal* 83

R Nair, 'Weighing Similar Fact and Avoiding Prejudice' (1996) 112 *Law Quarterly Review* 262

A Palmer, 'The Scope of the Similar Fact Rule' (1994) 16 *Adelaide Law Review* 161

R Pattenden, 'Similar Fact Evidence and Proof of Identity' (1996) 112 *Law Quarterly Review* 446

J Stone, 'The Rule of Exclusion of Similar Fact Evidence: England' (1933) 46 *Harvard Law Review* 954

A A S Zuckerman, *The Principles of Criminal Evidence* (1989) Ch 12

6

CROSS-EXAMINATION OF THE ACCUSED

1. INTRODUCTION

When the legislature made accused persons competent to give evidence in their own defence in 1898, a decision had to be taken about what questions an accused person should be able to be asked in cross-examination. A compromise was reached between, on the one hand, treating the accused like any other defence witness, and, on the other hand, protecting accused persons from all cross-examination in relation to matters such as previous offences or bad character. This compromise is reflected in provisos (e) and (f) to s 1 of the Criminal Evidence Act 1898:

Extract 6.1.1

Criminal Evidence Act 1898, s 1

1. Competency of witnesses in criminal cases

Every person charged with an offence shall be a competent witness for the defence at every stage of the proceedings, whether the person so charged is charged solely or jointly with any other person. Provided as follows:

...

(e) A person charged and being a witness in pursuance of this Act may be asked any question in cross-examination notwithstanding that it would tend to criminate him as to the offence charged;

(f) A person charged and called as a witness in pursuance of this Act shall not be asked, and if asked shall not be required to answer, any question tending to show that he has committed or been convicted of or been charged with any offence other than that wherewith he is then charged, or is of bad character, unless –

(i) the proof that he has committed or been convicted of such other offence is admissible evidence to show that he is guilty of the offence wherewith he is then charged; or

(ii) he has personally or by his advocate asked questions of the witnesses for the prosecution with a view to establish his own good character, or has given evidence of his good character, or

---

the nature or conduct of the defence is such as to involve imputations on the character of the prosecutor or the witnesses for the prosecution or the deceased victim of the alleged crime; or
(iii) he has given evidence against any other person charged in the same proceedings.

...

In essence, then, the position is as follows. Proviso (e) permits an accused person to be cross-examined even if this 'would tend to criminate him as to the offence charged'. This is subject to proviso (f), which provides the accused with a 'shield' against cross-examination as to matters such as previous offences or bad character. The exceptions to proviso (f) provide, however, for loss of this shield in four situations:

(1) Where evidence of previous offences elicited by the cross-examination would be admissible evidence of guilt: exception (i) to proviso (f).
(2) Where the accused has put his or her character in issue: first limb of exception (ii) to proviso (f).
(3) Where the accused has cast imputations on the character of the prosecutor, or of prosecution witnesses, or of the deceased victim of the alleged crime: second limb of exception (ii) to proviso (f).
(4) Where the accused has given evidence against a co-accused: exception (iii) to proviso (f).

(a) The relationship between provisos (e) and (f)

In the following case, the House of Lords split 3:2 on the issue of the relationship between provisos (e) and (f). The two speeches from which extracts are provided below are illustrative, respectively, of the majority and minority views.

Extract 6.1.2

Jones v DPP [1962] AC 635, 662–8, 670 (HL)

Jones was accused of the murder of a young girl guide. He had earlier been convicted of the rape of another young girl guide. When questioned by the police about the murder he advanced a false alibi. He later admitted that this alibi was false, and put forward another alibi. There were significant similarities between this second alibi and an alibi which he had advanced at his rape trial. At his trial for murder, Jones testified in examination-in-chief that he had initially given a false alibi because he had been 'in trouble' with the police before and did not want to be in trouble again. The prosecution sought to cross-examine him with a view to showing that the similarities between the alibi which he was now advancing and that advanced at his rape trial were such that his present alibi must be false.

LORD REID: This raises at once the question what is the proper construction of the words in proviso (e) 'tend to criminate him, as to the offence charged.' Those words could mean 'tend to convince or persuade the jury that he is guilty,' or they could have the narrower meaning – 'tend to connect him with the commission of the offence charged.' If they have the former meaning, there is at once an insoluble conflict between provisos (e) and (f). No line of questioning could be relevant unless it (or the answers to it) might tend to persuade the jury of the guilt of the accused. It is only permissible to bring in previous convictions or bad character if they are so relevant, so, unless proviso (f) is to be deprived of all content, it must prohibit some questions which would tend to criminate the accused of the offence charged if those words are used in the wider sense. But if they have the narrower meaning, there is no such conflict. So the structure of the Act shows that they must have the narrower meaning.

So I turn to consider proviso (f). . . .

The questions prohibited are those which 'tend to show' certain things. Does this mean tend to prove or tend to suggest? Here I cannot accept the argument of the Attorney-General. What matters is the effect of the questions on the jury. A veiled suggestion of a previous offence may be just as damaging as a definite statement. In my judgment, 'tends to show' means tends to suggest to the jury. But the crucial point in the present case is whether the questions are to be considered in isolation or whether they are to be considered in the light of all that had gone before them at the trial. If the questions or line of questioning has to be considered in isolation I think that the questions with which this appeal is concerned would tend to show at least that the accused had previously been charged with an offence. The jury would be likely to jump to that conclusion, if this was the first they had heard of this matter. But I do not think that the questions ought to be considered in isolation. If the test is the effect the questions would be likely to have on the minds of the jury that necessarily implies that one must have regard to what the jury had already heard. If the jury already knew that the accused had been charged with an offence, a question inferring that he had been charged would add nothing and it would be absurd to prohibit it. If the obvious purpose of this provision is to protect the accused from possible prejudice, as I think it is, then 'show' must mean 'reveal,' because it is only a revelation of something new which could cause such prejudice.

. . .

. . . I am of opinion that this appeal should be dismissed on the ground that these questions were not prohibited because they did not 'tend to show' any of the matters specified in proviso (f).

. . .

It is said that the views which I have expressed involve overruling two decisions of the Court of Criminal Appeal, *Rex v Chitson* [1909] 2 KB 945 and *Rex v Kennaway* [1917] 1 KB 25. I do not think so. I think the decisions were right but the reasons given for them were not. In the former case the accused was charged with having had carnal knowledge of a girl aged 14. Giving evidence, she said that the accused told her that he had previously done the same thing to another girl, who, she said, was under 16. No objection was taken to this evidence, I assume rightly. So before the accused gave evidence

247

the jury already knew that he was alleged to have committed another offence. If the views which I have already expressed are right, cross-examining the accused about this matter disclosed nothing new to them and therefore did not offend against the prohibition in proviso (*f*). But the judgment of the court was not based on that ground: it was said that although the questions tended to prove that the accused was of bad character they also tended to show that he was guilty of the offence with which he was charged. For the reasons which I have given I do not think that that is sufficient to avoid the prohibition in proviso (*f*).

Rex v Kennaway was a prosecution for forgery. Accomplices giving evidence for the prosecution described the fraudulent scheme of which the forgery was a part and related a conversation with the accused in which he stated to them that some years earlier he had forged another will in pursuance of a similar scheme. Then in cross-examination the accused was asked a number of questions about this other forgery. Those questions were held to have been properly put to him. Here, again, these questions disclosed nothing new to the jury and I can see no valid objection to them. But again that was not the ground of the court's decision. Their ground of decision was similar to that in *Chitson's* case, and I need not repeat what I have said about that case.

LORD DENNING: My Lords, much of the discussion before your Lordships was directed to the effect of section 1(*f*) of the Criminal Evidence Act, 1898: and, if that were the sole paragraph for consideration, I should have thought that counsel for the Crown ought not to have asked the questions he did. My reasons are these:

First: The questions *tended* to show that Jones had previously been charged in a court of law with another offence. True it is that they did not point definitely to that conclusion, but they conveyed that impression, and that is enough. Counsel may not have intended it, but that does not matter. What matters is the impression the questions would have on the jury. . . . I do not think that it is open to the prosecution to throw out prejudicial hints and insinuations – from which a jury might infer that the man had been charged before – and then escape censure under the cloak of ambiguity.

Second: I think that the questions tended to *show* that Jones had been charged with an offence, even though he had himself brought out the fact that he had been 'in trouble' before. It is one thing to confess to having been in trouble before. It is quite another to have it emphasised against you with devastating detail. Before these questions were asked by the Crown, all that the jury knew was that at some unspecified time in the near or distant past, this man had been in trouble with the police. After the questions were asked, the jury knew, in addition, that he had been very recently in trouble for an offence on a Friday night which was of so sensational a character that it featured in a newspaper on the following Sunday – in these respects closely similar to the present offence – and that he had been charged in a court of law with that very offence. It seems to me that questions which tend to reveal an offence, thus particularised, are directly within the prohibition in section 1(*f*) and are not rendered admissible by his own vague disclosure of some other offence. I do not believe that the mere fact that he said he had been in trouble before with the police – referring as he did to an entirely different matter many years past – let in this very damaging cross-examination as to recent events.

Third: The questions do not come within the exception (i) to section 1(*f*). . . . If the case rested solely on section 1(*f*), I would therefore have held that these questions were inadmissible. But I do not think it rests on section 1(*f*). In my judgment, the questions were admissible under section 1(*e*), which says that a person charged 'may be asked any question in cross-examination notwithstanding that it would tend to criminate him as to the offence charged.' As to this subsection, Viscount Sankey LC, speaking for all in this House in *Maxwell's* case, said that under section 1(*e*) 'a witness may be cross-examined in respect of the offence charged, and cannot refuse to answer questions directly relevant to the offence on the ground that they tend to incriminate him: thus if he denies the offence, he may be cross-examined to refute the denial.' I would add that, if he gives an explanation in an attempt to exculpate himself, he may be cross-examined to refute his explanation. And nonetheless so because it tends incidentally to show that he had previously been charged with another offence.

Let me first say why I think in this case the questions were directly relevant to the offence charged. They were directly relevant because they tended to refute an explanation which the accused man had given. He had given a detailed explanation of his movements on the crucial weekend, and so forth, all in an attempt to exculpate himself. The prosecution sought to show that this explanation was false: and I think it was of direct relevance for them to do so. . . .

Such is the law as it is, and always has been, as to the evidence which can be called for the prosecution. They can, in the first place, give evidence of any explanation given by the accused of his movements and they can, in the second place, give evidence that his explanation is false, even though it tends incidentally to show the commission by him of some other offence. Now, when Parliament in 1898 enabled an accused man to give evidence on his own behalf, they did not cut down evidence of this kind for the prosecution. And when the prosecution gives such evidence, it must be open to the accused man himself to answer it. He must be able to give evidence about it and to be cross-examined upon it. He can be cross-examined as to any explanation he has given and as to its truth or falsity: and he can be cross-examined upon it nonetheless because incidentally it may tend to show that he has been guilty of some other offence.

The approach of Lord Reid is, therefore, as follows. Section 1(e) permits only such questioning in cross-examination as would tend to connect the accused with the commission of the offence charged. Section 1(f) *prohibits* all other cross-examination in relation to other offences or charges, or bad character, *unless* one of the three exceptions applies. The prohibition in section 1(f) applies, however, only if the fact that the accused has committed or been charged with the other offence, or is of bad character, has not already been revealed to the jury. Which do you find preferable – the approach of Lord Reid or that of Lord Denning?

The majority approach in *Jones* was applied by the Court of Appeal in the following case:

Extract 6.1.3

R v Anderson [1988] QB 678, 685–9 (CA)

Anderson was charged with conspiracy to cause explosions. She denied her involvement in the conspiracy and, without the prosecution having been fore-warned, explained the evidence against her on the basis that she had been involved in a conspiracy to smuggle IRA members, who had escaped from prison in Ireland, through Scotland to Denmark. To rebut this, the prosecution sought to cross-examine her to establish that she had been 'wanted' by the police prior to her arrest. The prosecution wished to show that it was unlikely that, as a wanted person, she would have chosen, or have been chosen, to assist escaped prisoners.

LORD LANE CJ: The way in which the problem can be put is this: a defend-ant is faced with prosecution evidence which prima facie incriminates her of the offence charged. She puts forward in evidence an explanation of that prosecution case which is consistent with her innocence of the offence charged. The prosecution wish to cross-examine her about that explanation. Cross-examination necessarily involves questions which tend to show that she, the defendant, has committed a criminal offence, the nature of which the prosecution neither require nor intend to reveal. Are they allowed, by the terms of section 1 of the Criminal Evidence Act 1898 to ask those ques-tions? I have no doubt the immediate reaction of the practitioner would be 'Of course they are allowed to ask the questions. If not it would be giving the dishonest defendant an unjust and ludicrous advantage.' The same practitioner would no doubt add 'In any event, the judge has an overriding discretion to reject the submission and disallow the questions if he thinks that they are going to produce unfairness to the defendant in the particular circumstances.'
. . .
Section 1 of the Criminal Evidence Act 1898 is a nightmare of construction. No doubt the reasons for its difficulty may be found in its Parliamentary his-tory, but we are not allowed and nor do we wish to embark upon that sort of research. . . . Section 1(*e*) allows the accused person to be asked any ques-tion in cross-examination notwithstanding that it would tend to incriminate him as to the offence charged. Paragraph (*f*), however, provides that he shall not be asked 'any question tending to show that he has committed or been convicted of or been charged with any offence' subject to certain exceptions. Those two provisions are mutually contradictory, at least on the face of them, as has been said more than once by courts over the last 90 years. The reason for that is this: a question which tends to incriminate the defendant as to the offence charged, and so is relevant and admissible under paragraph (*e*), may very well tend to show, and often does, that the defendant has committed another offence and so is inadmissible under paragraph (*f*). This problem has been the subject of differing views, and those differing views are exemplified by the opinions of five of their Lordships in *Jones v Director of Public Pro-secutions* [1962] AC 635.
. . .

In the present case there was, in the question, a clear tendency to show that Martina Anderson had committed an offence other than that with which she was charged – obviously so because otherwise she would not be 'wanted' by the police. So in the light of the decision in *Jones* the question would be admissible in any of the following circumstances, that is applying the reasoning which we have attempted to set out as explained by the House of Lords: first of all, if there was no tendency to reveal the commission of an offence as in *Jones*, for example, because the commission of an offence had already (properly) been made known to the jury. Secondly, if the proof of the commission tended to connect the appellant with the offence charged. Thirdly, if the appellant had given evidence of her own good character.

The third matter can be dealt with very shortly. Mr Mansfield on the appellant's behalf did persuade the prosecution to concede that the appellant was of good character, apart from being 'wanted' by the police, but that concession was only made after the judge had ruled upon the submission and consequently that would not, we are prepared to assume, be a ground for admitting the evidence under section 1(*f*) of the Act.

As to the tendency to reveal, the appellant had already revealed that it was likely that she had committed a number of offences in respect of any one of which she might well have been 'wanted' by the police. There was probably a conspiracy to assist the escape of a prisoner; probably forgery of documents; probably conspiracy to forge; possession of firearms and so on, as already set out when we detailed the evidence which she gave before the jury. Thus it was already revealed that she had committed offences, although it might be that she was not yet 'wanted' by the police in respect of them. The jury already knew, therefore, that she had committed a number of offences, and the fact that she was 'wanted' by the police in respect of an unspecified offence, and therefore was probably guilty of committing an unspecified offence was not, on the reasoning in *Jones*, in the view of this court, a revelation to the jury.

As to the second point, 'does evidence which tends to destroy the defendant's innocent explanation of prima facie damning circumstances, connect the defendant with the crime so as to come within Lord Reid's analysis of the meaning of paragraph (*e*)?' We are inclined to think that it may, but we prefer to base our conclusion primarily on the fact that the appellant had already revealed that she had committed crimes.

There is however a different approach which is perhaps less artificial than the reasoning in *Jones*, if we may say so.

Section 1 of the Act of 1898 did nothing to alter the pre-existing law as to what evidence the prosecution were entitled to adduce in order to prove their case. . . . The extent of that pre-existing law had been examined only four years previously in *Makin v Attorney-General for New South Wales* [1894] AC 57. . . .

Thus, if the prosecution know that a particular defence is going to be advanced, they may (subject to the judge's discretion) call evidence to rebut it as part of their own substantive case even if that tends to show the commission of other crimes. The defendant can plainly then be cross-examined about the matter. If the prosecution do not know of the defence in advance, then they may call evidence to rebut it and the defendant can then be recalled, if that is desired, to deal with the rebutting evidence. The judge in the present case – wisely, the evidence not being in dispute – allowed that somewhat laborious process to be short-circuited. The result however was just as much in accordance with authority and the Act of 1898 as if the procedure had been carried out in extenso.

These considerations strengthen our view that the judge's decision in the present case was correct.

There only remains to deal with the question of discretion. We take the view that there is ample authority that the judge could exercise his discretion in the way that he did. Obviously he examined the matter very closely and we, in our judgment, feel he was not only entitled to exercise his discretion as he did, but was correct in doing so.

The application in *Anderson* of the reasoning in *Jones* is questionable. As has been observed: 'It should . . . be noted that in *Anderson*, in critical distinction from *Jones*, not even the most imperceptive juror could have supposed the accused to be "wanted" at the relevant time in respect of crimes which had then been undiscovered, or even uncommitted.'[1]

(b) Proviso (f): some general issues

The shield in proviso (f) protects the accused from questioning tending to show any of the following:

(1) *commission* of another offence;
(2) *conviction* of another offence;
(3) the fact that the accused has been *charged* with another offence;
(4) the fact that the accused is of *bad character*.

The third and fourth of these merit further examination.

(i) '. . . been charged with any offence . . .'

The meaning of being 'charged' with an offence is explained in the following extract:

Extract 6.1.4

Stirland v DPP [1944] AC 315, 323 (HL)

VISCOUNT SIMON LC: It is necessary . . . to guard against a possible confusion in the use of the word 'charged.' In para (*f*) of s 1 of the Act of 1898 the word appears five times and it is plain that its meaning in the section

---

[1] C F H Tapper, *Cross and Tapper on Evidence* (8th ed 1995) 425.

is 'accused before a court' and not merely 'suspected or accused without prosecution.'

As the following extract indicates, care must be exercised in determining whether questioning tending to show that the accused has been charged with another offence will be permitted under the exceptions to proviso (f):

Extract 6.1.5

Maxwell v DPP [1935] AC 309, 319–21 (HL)

VISCOUNT SANKEY LC: . . . it seems clear that the mere fact of a charge cannot in general be evidence of bad character or be regarded otherwise than as a misfortune. . . . The mere fact that a man has been charged with an offence is no proof that he committed the offence. Such a fact is, therefore, irrelevant; it neither goes to show that the prisoner did the acts for which he is actually being tried nor does it go to his credibility as a witness. Such questions must, therefore, be excluded on the principle which is fundamental in the law of evidence as conceived in this country, especially in criminal cases, because, if allowed, they are likely to lead the minds of the jury astray into false issues; not merely do they tend to introduce suspicion as if it were evidence, but they tend to distract the jury from the true issue – namely, whether the prisoner in fact committed the offence on which he is actually standing his trial. It is of the utmost importance for a fair trial that the evidence should be prima facie limited to matters relating to the transaction which forms the subject of the indictment and that any departure from these matters should be strictly confined.

It does not result from this conclusion that the word 'charged' in proviso (f) is otiose: it is clearly not so as regards the prohibition; and when the exceptions come into play there may still be cases in which a prisoner may be asked about a charge as a step in cross-examination leading to a question whether he was convicted on the charge, or in order to elicit some evidence as to statements made or evidence given by the prisoner in the course of the trial on a charge which failed, which tend to throw doubt on the evidence which he is actually giving, though cases of this last class must be rare and the cross-examination permissible only with great safeguards.

Again, a man charged with an offence against the person may perhaps be asked whether he had uttered threats against the person attacked because he was angry with him for bringing a charge which turned out to be unfounded. Other probabilities may be imagined. Thus, if a prisoner has been acquitted on the plea of autrefois convict such an acquittal might be relevant to his credit, though it would seem that what was in truth relevant to his credit was the previous conviction and not the fact that he was erroneously again charged with the same offence; again, it may be, though it is perhaps a remote supposition, that an acquittal of a prisoner charged with rape on the plea of consent may possibly be relevant to a prisoner's credit.

But these instances all involve the crucial test of relevance.

(ii) '... is of bad character ...'

The meaning of 'bad character' is discussed in the following extract:

Extract 6.1.6

R v Carter (1996) 161 JPR 207, 211–12, 216 (CA)

SEDLEY J: ... the prohibition in the statute is not confined to cross-examination which shows the accused to have a criminal record. It includes cross-examination which tends to show him to be of bad character, and it has been established since the early days of the Act that character here encompasses both reputation and disposition, not merely criminal record: see *R v Dunkley* (1926) 90 JP 75; [1927] 1 KB 323 and *Cross on Evidence* (8th edn) pp 432–433.

...

... Any cross-examination of an accused designed to show that he is unworthy of belief, and which does not arise from evidence relating to the indictment before the jury, relates to character in the sense of disposition and so falls within s 1, proviso (f), of the Criminal Evidence Act 1898.

---

2. REQUIREMENT OF LEAVE

Where it is sought to cross-examine an accused person on the basis that one of the exceptions to proviso (f) applies, leave to do so must be obtained from the trial judge. The requirement of leave would appear to be taken seriously: the Court of Appeal has held that 'this court will not countenance a submission that where leave to cross-examine as to character has not been sought, an irregular cross-examination can be overlooked on the ground that leave would have been given had it been sought. The point of the procedure is that a defendant should know why it is proposed to put his character in and should have a chance to submit either why it should not go in or why its exposure should be limited by the Judge.'[2]

3. SECTION 1(f)(i)

A thorough discussion of the history of s 1(f)(i) is to be found in C F H Tapper, 'The Meaning of Section 1(f)(i) of the Criminal Evidence Act 1898' in C F H Tapper (ed), *Crime, Proof and Punishment: Essays in Memory of Sir Rupert Cross* (1981). It is to be noted that all that is permitted by s 1(f)(i) is questioning conducted with a view to proving the *commission* or *conviction* of another offence. As the following case illustrates, this is construed strictly by the courts.

---

[2] *R v Carter* (1996) 161 JPR 207, 212.

Extract 6.3.1

R v Cokar [1960] 2 QB 207, 210 (CCA)

LORD PARKER CJ: It is to be observed that the exception deals only with the case where proof that the accused has 'committed or been convicted' of another offence is admissible evidence. There is no reference in the exception to being 'charged' and, accordingly, it seems to this court that the prohibition against any of the matters in the first part of proviso (*f*) is only lifted when it is sought to prove that the accused has committed or been convicted of the other offence. Provided that proof of that other offence is admissible evidence, it would be clearly proper as leading up to proof of conviction to say to the prisoner: 'Were you charged?' and, if the answer is 'Yes,' 'Were you convicted?'; but it seems to this court quite impossible, under exception (i), to question a man in regard to a charge in respect of which he was acquitted.

Is it anomalous that there is no reference in exception (i) to proof that the accused has been *charged* with another offence or is of *bad character*, in view of the prohibition in the first part of proviso (f) of questions tending to show these matters? Should exception (i) be amended in order that all four matters covered by the prohibition – commission, conviction, charge and bad character – are covered by the exception? See generally Tapper, ibid.

Section 1(f)(i) allows evidence of previous offences to be elicited in cross-examination of the accused if it would constitute admissible evidence if adduced in chief. As we saw in the previous chapter, evidence of previous offences adduced in chief is admissible if the test in *DPP v P* is satisfied, or if rendered admissible by statute. As we have also seen, the Court of Appeal in *Anderson* suggests that, if the prosecution failed to adduce such evidence in chief owing to lack of awareness of a defence which would later be raised, it may elicit such evidence through cross-examination of the accused under s 1(f)(i). This would save the prosecution the trouble of re-opening its case in order to adduce the evidence in chief.

4. SECTION 1(f)(ii): FIRST LIMB

An accused may put his character in issue either by cross-examining prosecution witnesses with a view to establishing his good character, or by adducing good-character evidence in chief (in the form of evidence given by the accused himself or by other defence witnesses). Where an accused has put his or her character in issue, two consequences follow. First, the prosecution has a common-law right to rebut the good-character evidence by questioning witnesses other than the accused to elicit evidence of the accused's bad character. Secondly, the accused is exposed to cross-examination under the first limb of s 1(f)(ii).

The following cases provide illustrations of actions which have been held to amount to putting character in issue:

- *R v Ferguson:* Even though 'he never intended to put his character in issue', the defendant effectively did so by introducing evidence that 'he had attended mass and service for over thirty-six years' and 'was a member of several religious societies'.[3]
- *R v Baker:* 'He gave evidence that for four years he had been earning an honest living, and in our opinion this was evidence of good character . . .'.[4]
- *R v Coulman:* 'If you ask a man whether he is a married man with a family, in regular work, and has a wife and three children, you are setting up his character . . .'.[5]

Extract 6.4.1

R v Samuel (1956) 40 Cr App R 8, 10–11 (CCA)

LORD GODDARD CJ: At the beginning of his examination-in-chief, Mr Titheridge asked him: 'Have you ever found on a previous occasion property belonging to another person? (A) Yes, Sir. (Q) When was the first time you ever found property belonging to somebody else? (A) In Dartford. (Q) Is that a hospital? (A) Yes, Sir. (Q) What did you find there? (A) £28. (Q) When was that? (A) In 1945. (Q) What did you do with that £28? (A) I handed it to the superintendent. (Q) Have you found other property? (A) Yes, Sir. (Q) What property was that? (A) I found a parcel in a 'phone box at the beginning of this year. (Q) What was in that parcel, do you know? (A) A pair of shoes, I believe. (Q) What did you do with that property? (A) Handed it to a policeman at the Elephant and Castle. (Q) At the Elephant and Castle Police Station? (A) Yes.'
. . . the only object of those questions could be to induce the jury to say: 'This man is one of those people who, if he finds property, gives it up; in other words, he is an honest man.' That was obviously the purpose of the questions . . . In the opinion of the court, it is clear that those questions did put the appellant's character in issue. He was asking the jury to assume that he was a man who dealt honestly with property which he found.

In the following cases, however, the accused was held not to have put his character in issue:

Extract 6.4.2

R v Ellis [1910] 2 KB 746, 762–3 (CCA)

The defendant was accused of obtaining cheques from a Mr Dickins by false pretences. It was alleged that the defendant sold certain articles to Mr Dickins under an agreement whereby he was to charge Mr Dickins the cost price plus 10% profit; that he represented to Mr Dickins that the cost was much in

---

[3] (1909) 2 Cr App R 250, 251.
[4] (1912) 7 Cr App R 252, 253.
[5] (1927) 20 Cr App R 106, 108.

excess of the real cost; and that he thereby obtained from Mr Dickins much larger sums than he was entitled to.

BRAY J: It was said that in the examination-in-chief of the appellant Mr Elliott had asked questions relating to his purchase of this business, to his general relations with Mr Dickins, and to other transactions under the cost plus 10 per cent agreement. In our opinion it would not be correct to say that the appellant had given evidence of his own good character. It may or may not have been relevant to go into other sales on the cost price plus 10 per cent basis. Mr Bodkin thought it was not and objected, and Mr Elliott did not further pursue that line of examination, but its object was not to set up the appellant's good character, it was to negative fraud. In our opinion, if we were to give the slightest colour to the idea that a general examination as to the surrounding circumstances was such evidence of good character as to entitle the prosecution to prove or to cross-examine as to other offences or convictions, we should deprive the prisoner of the protection which the statute has given him. Sub-clause (ii.) of s 1, clause (f), of the Criminal Evidence Act, 1898, was not intended to apply to a case like this. . . . the statute refers . . . not to mere assertions of innocence or repudiation of guilt on the part of the prisoner, nor to reasons given by him for such assertion or repudiation.

Extract 6.4.3

R v Lee (Paul) [1976] 1 WLR 71, 73 (CA)

ORR LJ: . . . this court finds it impossible to hold that the questions which were put to the prosecution witness, Mr Robert Ludlain, as to the convictions of the other men, were with a view to establishing the defendant's own good character. The questions were put with a view to establishing the bad character of the two other men and nothing else and the answer 'Yes' to the question 'Had they previous convictions?' had nothing whatever to do with the character of the defendant. As MacKenna J put in argument, and in our view this is entirely right, it is not implicit in an accusation of dishonesty that the accuser himself is an honest man.

And in *R v Redd* it was held that the appellant 'was not endeavouring to establish a good character merely because a witness whom he called, voluntarily and probably against the appellant's own desire, made a statement as to the appellant's good character . . .'.[6]

(a) What is the relevance of evidence of good character?

What precisely is the relevance of evidence of the accused's good character? What directions does the trial judge need to give the jury where such evidence is introduced?

[6] [1923] 1 KB 104, 107.

Extract 6.4.4

R v Vye [1993] 1 WLR 471, 474–9 (CA)

LORD TAYLOR OF GOSFORTH CJ: Before considering the authorities, it is helpful to say something of the historical background. The defendant was entitled to adduce evidence of his good character long before the law treated him as a competent witness in his own defence. Such evidence was allowed 'to be submitted to the jury, to induce them to say whether they think it likely that a person with such a character would have committed the offence:' *Rex v Stannard* (1837) 7 C & P 673, 675, *per* Williams J.

Once the defendant became able to give evidence, a further consideration in regard to good character was introduced. Thus in *Reg v Bellis* [1966] 1 WLR 234 that consideration was encapsulated by Widgery J at p 236:

> 'Although there is . . . no formal or standard direction in these terms, this court does take the view that possession of a good character is a matter which primarily goes to credibility . . .'

In *Reg v Bryant* [1979] QB 108, the defendant, a man of good character, elected not to give evidence. In his direction to the jury, the judge appeared to suggest that good character was relevant only to credibility. In this court, that approach was said to be 'too restrictive.' Good character was relevant 'primarily to the issue of credibility.' Nevertheless, juries 'should' be directed that it was capable of general significance of the kind suggested in the passage quoted from *Rex v Stannard*, 7 C & P 673, 675. However, notwithstanding the omission of a *Stannard* direction, the verdict was found neither unsafe nor unsatisfactory.

In February 1989, in *Reg v Berrada (Note)* (1989) 91 Cr App R 131, this court considered among other grounds, an alleged misdirection about good character. The defendant had given evidence. Waterhouse J, giving the judgment of the court, said, at p 134:

> 'In the judgment of this court, the appellant was entitled to have put to the jury from the judge herself a correct direction about the relevance of his previous good character to his credibility. That is a conventional direction and it is regrettable that it did not appear in the summing up in this case. It would have been proper also (but was not obligatory) for the judge to refer to the fact that the previous good character of the appellant might be thought by them to be one relevant factor when they were considering whether he was the kind of man who was likely to have behaved in the way that the prosecution alleged. . . . We have no doubt, however, that the modern practice is that, if good character is raised by a defendant, it should be dealt with in the summing up. Moreover, when it is dealt with, the direction should be fair and balanced, stressing its relevance primarily to a defendant's credibility.'

That decision therefore confirmed that, whatever the position may have been previously, it is now an established principle that, where a defendant of good character has given evidence, it is no longer sufficient for the judge to comment in general terms. He is required to direct the jury about the relevance of good character to the credibility of the defendant. Conventionally this has come to be described as the 'first limb' of a character direction. The passage quoted also stated that the judge was entitled, but not obliged, to refer to the possible relevance of good character to the question whether the defendant was likely to have behaved as alleged by the Crown. That, in effect the *Stannard* direction, is the 'second limb.'

Leaving aside cases involving more than one defendant where one is of good character and one is not, virtually all the numerous decisions since *Reg v Berrada (Note)*, 91 Cr App R 131 have reiterated that the first limb direction is necessary wherever the defendant has given evidence. This has been held to be so even when, on his own admission, he has told lies in interview with the police: *Reg v Kabariti* (1990) 92 Cr App R 362.

Accordingly, we turn to the three problems which seem presently to be unresolved on the authorities. They are (a) whether a 'first limb' direction needs to be given in a case where the defendant does not give evidence but has made statements to the police or others; (b) whether the 'second limb' direction should now be regarded as discretionary or obligatory; and (c) what course the judge should take in a joint trial where one defendant is of good character but another is not.

(a) Defendant of good character not giving evidence
. . .

In our judgment, when the defendant has not given evidence at trial but relies on exculpatory statements made to the police or others, the judge should direct the jury to have regard to the defendant's good character when considering the credibility of those statements. He will, of course, be entitled to make observations about the way the jury should approach such exculpatory statements in contrast to evidence given on oath (see *Reg v Duncan* (1981) 73 Cr App R 359); but, when the jury is considering the truthfulness of any such statements, it would be logical for them to take good character into account, just as they would in regard to a defendant's evidence.

Clearly, if a defendant of good character does not give evidence and has given no pre-trial answers or statements, no issue as to his credibility arises and a first limb direction is not required.

(b) 'Second limb' direction
. . .

We have considered the whole spectrum of the situations likely to face the trial judge. At one extreme there is the case of an employee who has been entrusted with large sums of money over many years by his employer and having carried out his duties impeccably, is finally charged with stealing from the till. There, a second limb direction is obviously relevant and necessary. At the other extreme, is a case such as *Reg v Richens*, The Times, 25 November 1992 where the defendant, charged with murder, admits manslaughter. It might be thought that in such a case a 'second limb' direction would be little help to the jury. The defendant's argument that he has never stooped to murder before would be countered by the fact that he had never stooped to manslaughter before either. Nevertheless, there might well be a residual argument that what was in issue was intent and he had never shown any intent to use murderous violence in the past.

We have reached the conclusion that the time has come to give some clear guidance to trial judges as to how they should approach this matter. It cannot be satisfactory for uncertainty to persist so that judges do not know whether this court, proceeding on a case by case basis, will hold that a 'second limb' direction should or need not have been given. Our conclusion is that such a direction should be given where a defendant is of good character.

Does the need for a second limb direction still exist when the defendant has not given evidence? . . .

We can see no logical ground for distinguishing in regard to a 'second limb' direction between cases where the defendant has given evidence and cases where he has not.

Having stated the general rule, however, we recognise it must be for the trial judge in each case to decide how he tailors his direction to the particular circumstances. He would probably wish to indicate, as is commonly done, that good character cannot amount to a defence. In cases such as that of the long serving employee exemplified above, he may wish to emphasise the 'second limb' direction more than in the average case. By contrast, he may wish in a case such as the murder/manslaughter example (*Reg v Richens*, The Times, 25 November 1992), to stress the very limited help the jury may feel they can get from the absence of any propensity to violence in the defendant's history. Provided that the judge indicates to the jury the two respects in which good character may be relevant, ie, credibility and propensity, this court will be slow to criticise any qualifying remarks he may make based on the facts of the individual case.

(c) Two or more defendants of good and bad character

. . .

. . . In our judgment, a defendant A of good character is entitled to have the judge direct the jury as to its relevance in his case even if he is jointly tried with a defendant B of bad character. This leaves the question as to what, if anything, the judge should say about the latter. In some cases the judge may think it best to grasp the nettle in his summing up and tell the jury they must try the case on the evidence, there has been no evidence about B's character, they must not speculate and must not take the absence of information as to B's character as any evidence against B. In other cases, the judge may however think it best to say nothing about the absence of evidence as to B's character. What course he takes must depend upon the circumstances of the individual case, for example, how great an issue has been made of character during the evidence and speeches.

The question has been raised, eg, in *Reg v Shaw*, The Times, 31 December 1992 whether defendants of disparate characters might require separate trials. However, in our judgment, the possibility of separate trials is a matter for the judge and is to be decided in accordance with well-established principles. Problems such as statements of one defendant being inadmissible against another, the possibility of cross-examination of one defendant adversely on behalf of another and disparate characters are to be considered and weighed on a case by case basis. There can certainly be no rule in favour of separate trials for defendants of good and bad character. Generally, those jointly indicted should be jointly tried.

To summarise, in our judgment the following principles are to be applied. (1) A direction as to the relevance of his good character to a defendant's credibility is to be given where he has testified or made pre-trial answers or statements. (2) A direction as to the relevance of his good character to the likelihood of his having committed the offence charged is to be given, whether or not he has testified, or made pre-trial answers or statements. (3) Where defendant A of good character is jointly tried with defendant B of bad character, (1) and (2) still apply.

The Court of Appeal has also emphasised that 'what is mandatory is to give both limbs of the direction, not to use any particular form of words'.[7]

What of the situation where there is positive evidence before the jury that a co-defendant is of bad character?

Extract 6.4.5

R v Cain [1994] 1 WLR 1449, 1453–4 (CA)

JUDGE J: ... the observations in *Reg v Vye* as to the co-defendant of 'bad character' did not extend to cases where there was positive evidence on the subject, and in particular did not suggest that the defendant whose previous convictions were put before the jury should be treated in the same way as the defendant about whose character there was no evidence either way. In other words it was not dealing with the problem which arises in the present case, where there was positive evidence before the jury that the co-defendant had previous criminal convictions.

The decision in *Reg v Vye* underlines that in a joint trial the defendant of good character is 'entitled' to the benefit of a direction 'as to its relevance,' both to credibility and to propensity. In the absence of directions about the possible relevance of evidence of the co-defendant's previous convictions, the jury may assume that they are relevant to the same issues and, in particular, to propensity to commit crime and, therefore, to guilt.

In our judgment that risk should be avoided by directions about the limited relevance of the evidence of previous convictions and the way in which it should be approached. The requirement for appropriate directions about character therefore applies equally to the defendant with previous convictions as it does to the defendant of good character. The precise terms of the directions will be decided by the judge on his analysis of the issues in the individual case.

The issue of whether there is a discretion not to give *Vye* directions in appropriate circumstances was considered by the House of Lords in the following case:

[7] *R v Miah* [1997] 2 Cr App R 12, 22.

Extract 6.4.6

R v Aziz [1995] 3 WLR 53, 62 (HL)

The following point of general public importance was certified by the Court of Appeal: 'Whether directions in accordance with *Reg v Vye* [1993] 1 WLR 471 must be given in all cases in which a defendant has adduced evidence of previous good character, and if not, in what circumstances must such directions be given?'

LORD STEYN: A good starting point is that a judge should never be compelled to give meaningless or absurd directions. And cases occur from time to time where a defendant, who has no previous convictions, is shown beyond doubt to have been guilty of serious criminal behaviour similar to the offence charged in the indictment. A sensible criminal justice system should not compel a judge to go through the charade of giving directions in accordance with *Vye* in a case where the defendant's claim to good character is spurious. I would therefore hold that a trial judge has a residual discretion to decline to give any character directions in the case of a defendant without previous convictions if the judge considers it an insult to common sense to give directions in accordance with *Vye*. I am reinforced in thinking that this is the right conclusion by the fact that after *Vye* the Court of Appeal in two separate cases ruled that such a residual discretion exists: *Reg v H* [1994] Crim LR 205 and *Reg v Zoppola-Barraza* [1994] Crim LR 833.

That brings me to the nature of the discretion. Discretions range from the open-textured discretionary powers to narrowly circumscribed discretionary powers. The residual discretion of a trial judge to dispense with character directions in respect of a defendant of good character is of the more limited variety. Prima facie the directions must be given. And the judge will often be able to place a fair and balanced picture before the jury by giving directions in accordance with *Vye* [1993] 1 WLR 471 and then adding words of qualification concerning other proved or possible criminal conduct of the defendant which emerged during the trial. On the other hand, if it would make no sense to give character directions in accordance with *Vye*, the judge may in his discretion dispense with them.

Subject to these views, I do not believe that it is desirable to generalise about this essentially practical subject which must be left to the good sense of trial judges. It is worth adding, however, that whenever a trial judge proposes to give a direction, which is not likely to be anticipated by counsel, the judge should follow the commendable practice of inviting submissions on his proposed directions.

Do you consider that the House of Lords was right in recognising the existence of a discretion not to give *Vye* directions in appropriate circumstances? Is it sufficiently clear what these circumstances might be?

The extent to which *Vye* directions are required in the case of defendants with 'blemishes' on their characters was considered by the Court of Appeal in the following case:

Extract 6.4.7

R v Durbin [1995] 2 Cr App R 84, 91–2 (CA)

EVANS LJ: In our judgment, the law now is as follows:

(1) Where the defendant is of previous good character, then he is entitled to the good character direction (both limbs if his credibility is in issue, the second limb only if it is not), notwithstanding that he may have admitted telling lies in interview (*Kabariti*) and may have admitted other offences or disreputable conduct in relation to the subject matter of the charge, as we hold here (contrast *Zoppola-Barraza* and *Buzalek and Schiffer* [[1991] Crim LR 116]). In such cases, however, the terms of the direction should be modified to take account of the circumstances of the case, including all facts known to the jury, either as regards credibility or propensity, or both.

(2) Where the defendant is not of absolutely good character, the trial judge has a discretion as to whether or not to give a 'good character' direction, and if so in what terms, but he cannot properly decide not to do so, and in unqualified terms, if the blemishes can only be regarded as irrelevant, or of no significance, in relation to the offence charged (*Herrox* [CA, 5 October 1993], and contrast *Zoppola-Barraza*).

(3) By the same token, there will be cases where the defendant is not of absolutely good character but where the only proper course is to give a qualified direction in suitably modified terms, assuming of course that the fact of the previous conviction or other character blemish is known to the jury. This is likely to mean that careful consideration will have to be given to the distinction between the two limbs of credibility and propensity.

(4) Character, bad or good, is not simply a matter of the presence or absence of previous convictions, nor is it the same as reputation, though the one may be evidence of the other.

(5) In all cases where the qualified direction is given, we consider it essential that it should be in realistic terms, taking account of all the facts as they are known to the jury. The jury should not be directed to approach the case on a basis which, to their knowledge, is artificial or untrue.

See generally R Munday, 'What Constitutes a Good Character?' [1997] *Criminal Law Review* 247.

(b) What is meant by 'good character'?

Extract 6.4.8

Stirland v DPP [1944] AC 315, 324–5 (HL)

VISCOUNT SIMON LC: There is perhaps some vagueness in the use of the term 'good character' in this connexion. Does it refer to the good reputation which a man may bear in his own circle, or does it refer to the man's real disposition as distinct from what his friends and neighbours may think of him? In *Reg v Rowton* (1865) 10 Cox CC 25, on a re-hearing before the full court, it was held by the majority that evidence for or against a prisoner's good character must be confined to the prisoner's general reputation, but Erle C J and Willes J thought that the meaning of the phrase extended to include actual moral disposition as known to an individual witness, though no evidence could be given of concrete examples of conduct. In the later case of *Rex v Dunkley* [1927] 1 KB 323, the question was further discussed in the light of the language of the section, but not explicitly decided. I am disposed to think that in para (*f*) (where the word 'character' occurs four times) both conceptions are combined.

(c) Cross-examination under the first limb of s 1(f)(ii)

The law regards an accused's character as 'indivisible'. Thus, an accused who claims to be of good character in certain respects may have rebuttal evidence led of his or her bad character in other respects, or may be cross-examined, under the first limb of s 1(f)(ii), as to his or her bad character in other respects.

Extract 6.4.9

R v Winfield [1939] 4 All ER 164, 165 (CCA)

HUMPHREYS J: . . . there is no such thing known to our procedure as putting half your character in issue and leaving out the other half. A man is not entitled to say, 'Well, I may have a bad character as a dishonest rogue, but at all events nobody has ever said that I have acted indecently towards women.' That cannot be done. If a man who is accused chooses to put his character in issue, he must take the consequences.

Extract 6.4.10

Stirland v DPP [1944] AC 315, 326–7 (HL)

VISCOUNT SIMON LC: An accused who 'puts his character in issue' must be regarded as putting the whole of his past record in issue. He cannot assert his good conduct in certain respects without exposing himself to inquiry about the rest of his record so far as this tends to disprove a claim for good character.

The Law Commission has provisionally recommended that the 'indivisibility' principle be abandoned, and 'that the defendant should be open to cross-examination only on *that part* of his or her character or truthfulness about which an assertion of good character has been made'.[8]

Given that, as we have seen, evidence of an accused's good character is to be treated as relevant both to the issue of guilt or innocence as well as to the issue of credit, it may be argued that cross-examination under the first limb of s 1(f)(ii) should go to both guilt and credit. However, despite some hints that this should be the case,[9] the generally accepted view appears to be that such cross-examination goes solely to credit.[10] Recognising the difficulties with this principle, the Law Commission has 'provisionally propose[d] that where the assertion of good character, and the evidence adduced to rebut that assertion, are directly relevant to the accused's propensities, the fact-finders should not be directed to treat the evidence as bearing solely on the accused's credibility'.[11]

5. SECTION 1(f)(ii): SECOND LIMB

(a) The law

The question of who are 'witnesses for the prosecution' for the purposes of the second limb of s 1(f)(ii) was considered by the Court of Appeal in the following case. Is the broad interpretation given to the phrase justifiable?

Extract 6.5.1

R v Miller (1996) 161 JPR 158, 167–8 (CA)

ROSE LJ: A witness within s 1(f)(ii) of the Criminal Evidence Act 1898 is a person with material evidence to give. Such evidence may be given in a variety of ways. It may be in a deposition before justices, which can subsequently be read at trial, in accordance with s 13(3) of the Criminal Justice Act 1925 [see now Criminal Procedure and Investigations Act 1996, Sched 2, para 2], or in accordance with s 23 of the Criminal Justice Act 1988. It may be given in a statement in accordance with s 9 of the Criminal Justice Act 1967, which can be the subject of either a conditional witness order or a notice of additional evidence and which thereafter, likewise, may be read at trial. It may be given orally before the jury.

---

[8] Law Commission (Consultation Paper No 141), *Criminal Law – Evidence in Criminal Proceedings: Previous Misconduct of a Defendant – A Consultation Paper* (1996) 266 (emphasis in original).
[9] See *Maxwell v DPP* [1935] AC 309, 319 per Viscount Sankey; *R v Samuel* (1956) 40 Cr App R 8, 12 per Lord Goddard C J.
[10] C Tapper, *Cross and Tapper on Evidence* (8th ed 1995) 434–5.
[11] Law Commission (Consultation Paper No 141), *Criminal Law – Evidence in Criminal Proceedings: Previous Misconduct of a Defendant – A Consultation Paper* (1996) 266.

In all three cases, as it seems to us, there is placed before the jury, as indeed Judges direct juries every day of the week, evidence for their consideration. It is the evidence of a witness. A witness, it seems to us, is nonetheless a witness if dead, or beyond the seas, or unfit to attend court or not required to attend court or, indeed, unwilling, through fear, to attend court. Such a view was clearly taken by Parliament when enacting s 13(3) of the 1925 Act [see now Criminal Procedure and Investigations Act 1996, Sched 2, para 2] . . .

Indeed, it is an approach of even greater historical respectability. In a decision of this court in *R v Thompson* (1981) 74 Cr App R 315, at p 321, the judgment of Dunn, LJ contains a reference to Hale's 1694 *Pleas of the Crown*, which, accepted that a witness unable to travel through illness might have his or her deposition read.

So far as sch 2 of the 1988 Act is concerned, this, in our judgment, affords no sustenance for the submission that a person making a statement, who is not called, is not a witness. It merely makes provision for the admissibility and effect of statements admissible under Part II of the Act, where their maker is not called, without in any way defining or seeking to define who is or is not a witness. The fact that sch 2 distinguishes between a statement and testimony, in our judgment, says nothing about whether the maker of a statement is or is not a witness.

It is to be observed that any other construction would be a charter for interference with witnesses. Once a witness could be discouraged from attending trial, he could then be attacked with impunity by or on behalf of a defendant with a record. That, in our judgment, cannot have been Parliament's intention in 1898 or subsequently.

For details of the provisions of the Criminal Justice Act 1967, the Criminal Justice Act 1988 and the Criminal Procedure and Investigations Act 1996 mentioned above, see Chapter 7.

It is strongly arguable that it is inappropriate to have extended the meaning of 'witnesses for the prosecution' in s 1(f)(ii) to include those not actually testifying at the trial. An examination of all other references to witnesses in s 1(e) and (f) demonstrates clearly that they can mean only those people testifying in court. For example, the first limb of s 1(f)(ii), as we have seen, provides for loss of the shield where the accused asks questions of 'witnesses for the prosecution' with a view to establishing his or her own good character. This clearly refers only to people testifying in court for the prosecution.[12]

Furthermore, Rose LJ's fear that, if it was held that only those actually testifying could count as 'witnesses', defendants with records would intimidate potential witnesses into not attending trial, so as to be able to cast imputations on their characters with impunity, is based purely on speculation.[13]

---

[12] See the commentary on *Miller* by D J Birch [1997] *Criminal Law Review* 218–20, and R Munday, 'Who Qualifies as a "Witness" for the Purpose of Imputations Made under Section 1(f)(ii) of the Criminal Evidence Act 1898' (1997) 161 *Justice of the Peace* 379, 379–80.

[13] See Munday, above, at 380.

It would appear that it is open to the trial judge to initiate a defence application to cross-examine the accused under the second limb of s 1(f)(ii) where the relevant imputations have been cast. The Court of Appeal has observed that, 'although it is the experience of all the members of this court . . . that applications of this sort are commonly initiated by prosecuting counsel, we do not see why, as a matter of principle, the trial Judge should not raise the matter if prosecuting counsel does not do so. . . . The Judge must, of course, take care not to descend into the arena . . .'.[14]

As the following case illustrates, the second limb of s 1(f)(ii) has no application where the accused makes imputations against prosecution witnesses but does not testify:[15]

Extract 6.5.2

***R v Butterwasser* [1948] 1 KB 4, 7 (CCA)**

LORD GODDARD CJ: But it is admitted that there is no authority, and I do not see on what principle it could be said, that if a man does not go into the box and put his own character in issue, he can have evidence given against him of previous bad character when all that he has done is to attack the witnesses for the prosecution. The reason is that by attacking the witnesses for the prosecution and suggesting they are unreliable, he is not putting his character in issue; he is putting their character in issue. And the reason why, if he gives evidence, he can be cross-examined if he has attacked the witnesses for the prosecution is that the statute says he can.

The Runciman Royal Commission recommended that the effect of *Butterwasser* be reversed:

34. The present rules on revealing the previous criminal convictions of the defendant only apply where the defendant gives evidence. This has the unfortunate effect of enabling an accused who does not go into the witness box to attack, through his or her advocate, the credibility of the prosecution's witnesses . . . while avoiding any counter-attack. The reasoning seems to be that the purpose of bringing in previous convictions in these circumstances is to impugn a person's credibility as a witness: if, however, a person does not go into the witness box, he or she is not a witness and therefore the question of his or her credibility does not arise. A better approach seems to us to be that, since the defendant, through his or her advocate, is seeking to undermine the credibility of the prosecution evidence, it should be open to the prosecution to suggest, by bringing in the defendant's

---

[14] *R v Chinn* (1996) 160 JPR 765, 768–9. Criticised by R Munday, 'Section 1(f)(ii) of the Criminal Evidence Act 1898: When should a Judge Stiffen a Prosecutor's Fibre?' (1997) 161 *Justice of the Peace* 155.

[15] See generally G J Durston, 'Character Evidence Going to Credit: Recent Developments with Reference to Section 1(f)(ii) (the Second Limb) of the Criminal Evidence Act 1898' (1996) 160 *Justice of the Peace* 439.

CROSS-EXAMINATION OF THE ACCUSED

criminal record, that the person who has cast doubt on the credibility of the prosecution's evidence is a person of bad character. It does not seem to us to be reasonable that a defendant can avoid the consequences of the present rule by the simple expedient of staying out of the witness box. If, therefore, a defendant attacks the credibility of a prosecution witness, or a victim in a case of murder, we believe that it must be possible for the prosecution, after the conclusion of the defence case, to lead, with the leave of the court, evidence of the defendant's previous convictions even if the defendant has not given evidence.[16]

As the Law Commission has noted, however, 'it is likely that the apparent unfairness of *Butterwasser* will arise less often in the future than it has in the past, because, as a consequence of section 35 of the Criminal Justice and Public Order Act 1994, it will be less common for defendants to exercise their right not to testify'.[17] (Section 35, as was seen in Chapter 3, allows adverse inferences to be drawn from an accused's silence at trial in appropriate circumstances.)

Cross-examination under the second limb of s 1(f)(ii) is of great practical importance. The *Crown Court Study* revealed that previous convictions emerged much more frequently pursuant to the second limb of s 1(f)(ii) than pursuant to the first limb, s 1(f)(i) or s 1(f)(iii).[18] Cross-examination under the second limb of s 1(f)(ii), as under the first limb, goes to credit rather than to guilt. Below are extracts from three leading cases on the second limb. The last of these contains numerous references to other cases. When reviewing these extracts, the following issues and questions should be borne in mind:

- What do the courts regard as the precise rationale underlying the second limb of s 1(f)(ii)?
- How precisely is it to be determined whether 'the nature or conduct of the defence . . . involve[s] imputations on the character of the prosecutor or the witnesses for the prosecution or the deceased victim of the alleged crime'? Does it matter that the casting of the imputations is necessary to enable the accused to establish his or her defence?
- Are the factors on which the judicial discretion to prevent cross-examination under the second limb of s 1(f)(ii) is to be exercised sufficiently clear? What is the significance of the fact that the accused's previous offences were (or were not) offences of dishonesty? To what extent is cross-examination in relation to offences which are similar to the offence charged permissible? How deeply should the prosecution be permitted to probe into the facts underlying an accused's previous convictions?
- Does the case law on the second limb of s 1(f)(ii) afford sufficient weight to the consideration of the protection of the innocent from wrongful conviction?

---

[16] Royal Commission on Criminal Justice, *Report* (Cm 2263) (1993) 127.
[17] Law Commission (Consultation Paper No 141), *Criminal Law – Evidence in Criminal Proceedings: Previous Misconduct of a Defendant – A Consultation Paper* (1996) 228.
[18] M Zander and P Henderson, *The Royal Commission on Criminal Justice: Crown Court Study* (1993) 119.

Extract 6.5.3

Selvey v DPP **[1970] AC 304, 339–42 (HL)**

VISCOUNT DILHORNE: The cases to which I have referred, some of which it is not possible to reconcile, in my opinion finally establish the following propositions:
(1) The words of the statute must be given their ordinary natural meaning (*R v Hudson* [1912] 2 KB 464; *R v Jenkins* (1945) 31 Cr App R 1; *R v Cook* [1959] 2 QB 340).
(2) The section permits cross-examination of the accused as to character both when imputations on the character of the prosecutor and his witness are cast to show their unreliability as witnesses independently of the evidence given by them and also when the casting of such imputations is necessary to enable the accused to establish his defence (*Hudson*; *Jenkins*; *Cook*).
(3) In rape cases the accused can allege consent without placing himself in peril of such cross-examination (*R v Sheean* (1908) 21 Cox CC 561; *R v Turner* [1944] KB 463). This may be because such cases are sui generis (*per* Devlin J in *R v Cook* [1959] 2 QB 340, 347), or on the ground that the issue is one raised by the prosecution.
(4) If what is said amounts in reality to no more than a denial of the charge, expressed, it may be, in emphatic language, it should not be regarded as coming within the section (*R v Rouse* [1904] 1 KB 184; *R v Grout* (1909) 3 Cr App R 64; *R v Jones* (1923) 17 Cr App R 117; *R v Clark* [1955] 2 QB 469).
. . .
I now turn to the question whether a judge has discretion to refuse to permit such cross-examination of the accused even when it is permissible under the section. . . .
. . .
In the light of what was said in all these cases by judges of great eminence, one is tempted to say . . . that it is far too late in the day even to consider the argument that a judge has no such discretion. Let it suffice for me to say that in my opinion the existence of such a discretion is now clearly established.
. . .
It is desirable that a warning should be given when it becomes apparent that the defence is taking a course which may expose the accused to such cross-examination.

Is the special position of rape cases justifiable? It is indeed true that an allegation of consent is simply a denial that the prosecution has proved an essential element of its case, but what is significant is that it is only in the context of rape trials that such a denial is automatically treated as not constituting an imputation.[19] The favoured treatment accorded to defendants in rape cases in the context of the second limb of s 1(f)(ii) is perhaps unsurprising, however, when viewed alongside the generous latitude accorded to the defence in rape trials to introduce sexual history evidence.

[19] See *R v Lasseur* [1991] Crim LR 53.

Mirfield has written persuasively of *Selvey*:

... the decision in *Selvey* is indefensible as a matter of consistency as well as because of its stark unfairness. The essence of the argument is that there is an established common law principle, described here as the 'no stymie principle', that the prosecution must not be prevented from cross-examining the accused in a way which tends to show him to have lied on oath in his present testimony. This principle exists despite the fact that such cross-examination is, as a matter of strict interpretation, forbidden by section 1(f) of the 1898 Act. The reason why the law acknowledges the 'no stymie principle' is that the prosecution ought not to be prevented from properly presenting its own case. Therefore, it is inconsistent for *Selvey* to announce that the accused with a record *may* be blocked by an equivalent stymie, one which prevents him, or, at the least, very actively discourages him, from putting his defence to the jury.

Extract 6.5.4

R v Britzman [1983] 1 WLR 350, 353, 355 (CA)

LAWTON LJ: A defence to a criminal charge which suggests that prosecution witnesses have deliberately made up false evidence in order to secure a conviction must involve imputations on the characters of those witnesses with the consequence that the trial judge may, in the exercise of his discretion, allow prosecuting counsel to cross-examine the defendant about offences of which he has been convicted. In our judgment this is what Parliament intended should happen in most cases. When allegations of the fabrication of evidence are made against prosecution witnesses, as they often are these days, juries are entitled to know about the characters of those making them.
...
We hope that it will be helpful for both judges and counsel if we set out some guidelines for the exercise of discretion in favour of defendants. First, it should be used if there is nothing more than a denial, however emphatic or offensively made, of an act or even a short series of acts amounting to one incident or in what was said to have been a short interview. Examples are provided by the kind of evidence given in pickpocket cases and where the defendant is alleged to have said: 'Who grassed on me this time?' The position would be different however if there were a denial of evidence of a long period of detailed observation extending over hours and just as in this case and in *Reg v Tanner* (1977) 66 Cr App R 56 where there were denials of long conversations.
    Second, cross-examination should only be allowed if the judge is sure that there is no possibility of mistake, misunderstanding or confusion and that the jury will inevitably have to decide whether the prosecution witnesses have fabricated evidence. Defendants sometimes make wild allegations when giving evidence. Allowance should be made for the strain of being in the witness-box and the exaggerated use of language which sometimes results from such strain or lack of education or mental instability. Particular care should be used when a defendant is led into making allegations during cross-examination.

The defendant who, during cross-examination, is driven to explaining away the evidence by saying it has been made up or planted on him usually convicts himself without having his previous convictions brought out. Finally, there is no need for the prosecution to rely upon section 1(*f*)(ii) if the evidence against a defendant is overwhelming.

In the light of what was said by the Court of Appeal in *Britzman*, would not the second limb of s 1(f)(ii) provide a significant stumbling block for accused persons seeking to dispute confessions attributed to them, or seeking to argue that evidence was planted on them? Why should the length of the interview in which the confessions were allegedly made matter?

Extract 6.5.5

R v McLeod [1994] 1 WLR 1500, 1505–13 (CA)

STUART-SMITH LJ: If an accused man who has attacked prosecution witnesses has many previous convictions for similar offences, it may be necessary that the jury should understand the character of the person making the allegations; at the same time it is difficult to pretend that such a history does not show a propensity to commit the instant offence. Take the case of a drugs dealer: a very common defence is that drugs were planted by the police and, any admission alleged to have been made, fabricated. If he had a number of previous convictions for supplying or possession with intent to supply drugs, the jury cannot judge the substance of the defence without knowing this, and perhaps also, if it be the case that the defence advanced on previous occasions was that the drugs were planted. Yet the more the convictions, the worse the character, the greater the propensity to commit the offence.

In *Reg v Selvey* [1970] AC 304 the appellant was charged with buggery of a young man. His defence involved an attack on the character of the complainant and the judge permitted cross-examination as to his previous convictions. The appellant had been convicted of indecent assault on two boys aged 8 and 6 in 1956. In 1960 he had been convicted of an indecent assault on boys of 8 and 11. In 1961 he was convicted of soliciting for an immoral purpose and in 1964 for persistently importuning male persons. Three things are plain from these facts. First, that at least some of the underlying facts must have been elicited in relation to the offences of indecent assault, since the ages of the boys would not normally appear in the record of convictions. Secondly, the convictions showed a propensity to homosexual acts with boys and young men. Thirdly, it might be thought that the offences were of a scandalous nature. For present purposes it is sufficient to note that the House of Lords held that the trial judge had a discretion which should be exercised depending on the circumstances of the particular case and his overriding duty to ensure that the trial is fair. They approved the dictum of Singleton J in *Rex v Jenkins* (1945) 31 Cr App R 1, 15:

'[The judge] may feel that even though the position is established in law, still the putting of such questions as to the character of the accused person may be fraught with results which immeasurably outweigh the result of questions put by the defence and which make a fair trial of the accused person almost impossible. On the other hand, in the ordinary and normal case he may feel that if the credit of the prosecutor or his witnesses has been attacked, it is only fair that the jury should have before them material on which they can form their judgment whether the accused person is any more worthy to be believed than those he has attacked.'

The House also held that this court should not interfere with the exercise of discretion of the trial judge unless he has erred in principle or there was no material on which he could properly exercise his discretion. They upheld the exercise of discretion by the judge in that case.

The next case is *Reg v Vickers* [1972] Crim LR 101. Vickers was charged with unlawful wounding. The victim was a prison officer. His defence exposed him to cross-examination on his character. He had a number of convictions for dishonesty, and at least five for violence, including assaults on the police. The attack in cross-examination was plainly directed to the fact that he had a propensity to violence, not that his evidence was not worthy of belief. Moreover, the summing up was quite inadequate in that it gave the jury no guidance as to what use they should make of the evidence relating to his previous convictions, including five for violence. The conviction was quashed on these grounds. The case is no authority for the proposition that an accused cannot be cross-examined as to convictions for similar offences and does not assist on the extent to which cross-examination as to underlying facts is permissible.

In *Reg v France and France* [1979] Crim LR 48, the appellants were charged with theft from a jeweller's shop. The Crown's case was that while the female appellant and the accomplice M distracted the jeweller's attention, the male appellant stole from the display. M gave evidence for the Crown. The defence attacked him; they said the whole case was a conspiracy between him and the police; the appellants had been nowhere near the jeweller's shop. The male appellant was cross-examined on his previous convictions. In respect of one of these, for which the female appellant was also convicted, the jeweller's attention had been distracted in a somewhat similar manner to that in the instant case, but the evidence did not amount to similar fact evidence. It is clear that the cross-examination must have gone to some extent into the underlying facts to show the similarity of offences. In giving the judgment of the court, Swanwick J said (see the transcript):

'Suffice it to say that in this case, taking an overall view of the matter, we regard these questions, directed as they were specifically to previous convictions which bore some similarity to the charges before the court, was ill-directed in that respect and should have been excluded by the judge – quite apart from the question of admissibility as being prejudicial rather than probative. It must have been highly prejudicial and we feel that the extent to which the cross-examination went was beyond the bounds of legitimate cross-examination as to credibility, the bounds of which we are not prepared to define more precisely than to say obviously it may be relevant on an issue of credibility to test or bring out the sort of scale of the previous offences or something of that sort. However, we do not propose to lay down hard and fast rules or indeed guidelines for that evidence. We consider this individual case and we consider in this case those questions were wrongly allowed and we think they must have prejudiced the jury.'

The text of the transcript is unsatisfactory in several ways and it has not been corrected by the judge. It does not appear that *Reg v Selvey* [1970] AC 304 was referred to, nor was there any consideration of the court's power to interfere with the exercise of the judge's discretion.

In *Reg v Duncalf* [1979] 1 WLR 918; 69 Cr App R 206 the appellants were charged with conspiracy to steal. The Crown's case was that they were seen to enter 11 shops within a period of 45 minutes, their objective being to see what they could steal. The defence was that they were 'window shopping' and they attacked the police evidence. Cross-examination showed that they had been convicted on a previous occasion of doing a very similar thing. It was contended that the cross-examination in relation to the underlying facts which disclosed the similarity of offence should not have been permitted. This court rejected this submission. Roskill LJ said [1979] 1 WLR 918, 924:

'The offending evidence in *Reg v France* was not relevant to any question of intent – indeed the judgment of this court given by Swanwick J shows that if that evidence had been directed to the intent, the position would have been different. The appellants in *Reg v France* had denied being present at all at the scene of the alleged theft. In the present case the appellants' presence was admitted and the sole issue was one of their intent. We do not see why this evidence was not admissible on this issue within proviso (*f*)(i) to section 1 of the Criminal Evidence Act 1898, subject, of course, in such a case to the judge's right to exclude such evidence if invited so to do on the ground that it is prejudicial rather than probative: see also the speech of Viscount Sankey LC in *Maxwell v Director of Public Prosecutions* [1935] AC 309, 319, 320.'

There is an important discrepancy between the two reports of this case. In the Weekly Law Reports the reference is to section 1(*f*)(i), whereas in the Criminal Appeal Reports it is to section 1(*f*)(ii) both in the headnote and the judgment. We think that the Weekly Law Report is probably correct, although the reference to the judge's discretion and to the dictum of Viscount Sankey LC might seem more appropriate to proviso (ii).

The court was not referred to *Reg v Selvey* [1970] AC 304 and appears to have followed the reasoning in *Reg v France and France* [1979] Crim LR 48, while distinguishing it on the facts.

In *Reg v Watts* [1983] 3 All ER 101 the appellant, a man of low intelligence, was charged with indecent assault on a young woman. He made an admission to the police which he alleged was fabricated. He was cross-examined on his previous convictions for indecently assaulting his two nieces aged five and three. This court allowed the appeal. It was referred to *Reg v Duncalf* [1979] 1 WLR 918 and *Reg v France and France* [1979] Crim LR 48 and said of the latter case that the transcript was corrupt and the decision should be viewed with considerable suspicion. The court relied upon the dictum of Viscount Sankey LC in *Maxwell v Director of Public Prosecutions* [1935] AC 309, 321. It was not referred to *Reg v Selvey* [1970] AC 304.

The next case is *Reg v Braithwaite; Reg v John* (unreported), 24 November 1983. The appellants were convicted of theft. The Crown's case was that they had taken a purse from a woman's open shoulder bag in Oxford Street and run off. The police gave chase. The loser could not be found and did not give evidence. The defence involved an attack on the police evidence and the appellants were cross-examined on their previous convictions. In the case of John, these included theft of a purse, three offences of theft from the person and theft of a handbag. In the case of Braithwaite they included five offences of theft of a purse and one of theft from the person. It is reasonably clear that some of the facts underlying the convictions must have been put in cross-examination, since the convictions were not simply put as theft. The court allowed the appeal following *Reg v Watts* [1983] 3 All ER 101.

In *Reg v Burke* (1985) 82 Cr App R 156 there had been two raids on the appellant's premises, one in March 1983 when the police seized 4.35 grams of cannabis, and one in November 1983 when the police found 47.45 grams, £1,343 in cash and the paraphernalia of supply. At his trial he was charged with three counts. The first alleged possession of the cannabis found in March, to which he pleaded guilty. Count 2 charged him with supplying cannabis and count 4 with the possession of the 47.45 grams with intent to supply, to which he pleaded not guilty. At the trial of these counts his defence was that the police had concocted the evidence against him. He was cross-examined as to his plea of guilty on count 1 and also to a previous conviction in 1981 for possessing cannabis with intent to supply, though apparently the cross-examination was conducted in such a way that it was not a necessary inference that he was supplying drugs. Nevertheless, it is plain that the conviction was for a similar type of offence to that charged. The court dismissed the appeal. At p 161, Ackner LJ summarised the principles applicable to the exercise of the judge's discretion in relation to section 1(*f*)(ii) of the Criminal Evidence Act 1898; we shall return to this later. The court also referred to *Reg v Selvey* [1970] AC 304. *Reg v Watts* [1983] 3 All ER 101 was distinguished on the facts while reservations were expressed about *Reg v Braithwaite; Reg v John*.

The next case is *Reg v Powell* [1985] 1 WLR 1364. Lord Lane CJ, who had been a member of the court in *Reg v Watts* [1983] 3 All ER 101 and *Reg v Braithwaite*, 24 November 1983, delivered the considered judgment of the court. The appellant was charged with living wholly or in part on earnings from prostitution. The evidence against him came from police officers who had kept observation on him and his premises for a considerable period of time. The defence was that the evidence was a fabrication. He was cross-examined on his previous convictions. These were two offences of allowing his premises to be used for prostitution in 1969 and a similar conviction in 1984. In dismissing the appeal, Lord Lane CJ, after referring to *Reg v Watts* [1983] 3 All ER 101, *Reg v Braithwaite*, 24 November 1983 and *Reg v Selvey* [1970] AC 304, said [1985] 1 WLR 1364, 1369–1370:

'The results of their Lordships' opinions in *Reg v Selvey* in so far as they are relevant to the instant case were analysed by another division of the Court of Appeal in *Reg v Burke* (unreported), 21 June 1985. We respectfully agree with the judgment in that case delivered by Ackner LJ, and cannot improve upon his analysis, which was as follows: "1. The trial judge must weigh the prejudicial effect of the questions against the damage done by the attack on the prosecution's witnesses, and must generally exercise his discretion so as to secure a trial that is fair both to the prosecution and the defence (thus approving the observations of Devlin J, when giving the judgment of the full court (five judges) of the Court of Criminal Appeal in *Reg v Cook* [1959] 2 QB 340, 345). 2. Cases must occur in which it would be unjust to admit evidence of a character gravely prejudicial to the accused, even though there may be some tenuous grounds for holding it technically admissible (thus approving the observation made by Lord du Parcq, giving the opinion of the Privy Council in *Noor Mohamed v The King* [1949] AC 182, 192). Thus, although the position is established in law, still the putting of the questions as to character of the accused person may be fraught with results which immeasurably outweigh the results of questions put by the defence and which make a fair trial of the accused almost impossible (thus approving the observations of Singleton J in *Rex v Jenkins* (1945) 31 Cr App R 1, 15). 3. In the ordinary and normal case the trial judge may feel that if the credit of the prosecutor or his witnesses has been attacked, it is only fair that the jury should have before them material on which they can form their judgment whether the accused person is any more worthy to be believed than those he has attacked. It is obviously unfair that the jury should be left in the dark about an accused person's character if the conduct of his defence has attacked the character of the prosecutor or the witnesses for the prosecution within the meaning of the section (thus approving the observations of Singleton J in *Rex v Jenkins*, at p 15). 4. In order to see if the conviction should be quashed, it is not enough that the court thinks it would have exercised its discretion differently. The court will not interfere with the exercise of a discretion by a judge below unless he has erred in principle, or there is no material on which he could properly have arrived at his decision (see Viscount Dilhorne in *Reg v Selvey* [1970] AC 304, 342, quoting Pickford J in *Rex v Watson* (1913) 8 Cr App R 249, 254 and Devlin J in *Reg v Cook* [1959] 2 QB 340, 348)." It may be helpful to make particular reference to a passage in the judgment of Devlin J in *Reg v Cook* [1959] 2 QB 340, 347–348: "The cases on this subject-matter . . . indicate the factors to be borne in mind and the sort of question that a judge should ask himself. Is a deliberate attack being made upon the conduct of the police officer calculated to discredit him wholly as a witness? If there is, a judge might well feel that he must withdraw the protection which he would desire to extend as far as possible to an accused who was endeavouring only to develop a line of defence. If there is a real issue about the conduct of an important witness which the jury will inevitably have to settle in order to arrive at their verdict, . . . the jury is entitled to know the credit of the man on whose word the witness's character is being impugned." In the light of all these considerations, it is clear that in *Reg v Braithwaite* (unreported), 24 November 1983, and possibly to a lesser extent in *Reg v Watts* [1983] 3 All ER 101, the court fell into error. First of all, we interfered too lightly with the exercise of the judge's discretion, thereby overlooking the observations of Viscount Dilhorne in *Reg v Selvey* [1970] AC 304, 342 already mentioned. Secondly, we overlooked the "tit for tat" principle as enunciated by Devlin J in *Reg v Cook* [1959]

2 QB 340 and by Lord Pearce in *Reg v Selvey* [1970] AC 304, 353, at the same time paying too much attention, at least in *Reg v Watts* [1983] 3 All ER 101, to the question whether the previous offences did or did not involve dishonesty in the ordinary sense of that word. We further suggested that care should be taken to conceal from the jury that the previous convictions of the prisoner were of a similar nature to the offence being charged. We have said enough about the speeches of their Lordships in *Reg v Selvey* [1970] AC 304 and the facts of that case to show that those views were wrong. Moreover, the words used by Viscount Sankey LC in *Maxwell v Director of Public Prosecutions* [1935] AC 309, 321 cited above, which were largely the foundation of the judgment in *Reg v Watts* [1983] 3 All ER 101 cannot in the light of *Selvey's* case [1970] AC 304, be interpreted as meaning that convictions for the same or kindred offences can never be admitted. A defendant with previous convictions for similar offences may indeed have a very great incentive to make false allegations against prosecution witnesses for fear of greater punishment on conviction. It does however require careful direction from the judge to the effect that the previous convictions should not be taken as indications that the accused has committed the offence. In short, if there is a deliberate attack being made upon the conduct of a prosecution witness calculated to discredit him wholly, if there is a real issue about the conduct of an important witness which the jury will have to settle in order to reach their verdict, the judge is entitled to let the jury know the previous convictions of the man who is making the attack. The fact that the defendant's convictions are not for offences of dishonesty, the fact that they are for offences bearing a close resemblance to the offences charged, are matters for the judge to take into consideration when exercising his discretion, but they certainly do not oblige the judge to disallow the proposed cross-examination.'

What is important in the present context is the fact that *Reg v Braithwaite; Reg v John*, 24 November 1983, which necessarily involved elucidation of the underlying facts which showed similarity between the previous offences and those the subject of the trial, was said to have been wrongly decided.

In *Reg v Owen* (1985) 83 Cr App R 100 the court in a reserved judgment followed *Reg v Burke* (1985) 82 Cr App R 156 and *Reg v Powell* [1985] 1 WLR 1364. Neill LJ again summarised, 83 Cr App R 100, 104–105, the considerations which it is necessary to be borne in mind on this topic. It is unnecessary to repeat them; for the most part they follow what was said by Ackner LJ in *Reg v Burke*, 82 Cr App R 156. There is one significant addition, 83 Cr App R 100, 105:

'(6) The fact that the accused's convictions are not for offences of dishonesty, but may be for offences bearing a close resemblance to the offences charged, are matters for the judge to take into consideration when exercising his discretion, but they certainly do not oblige the judge to disallow the proposed cross-examination: see *Reg v Powell* [1985] 1 WLR 1364.'

In *Reg v Khan* (unreported), 9 August 1990, the appellant was convicted of affray and common assault. His defence involved an attack on the prosecution witnesses and he said he had been assaulted by the police officers at the time of or after his arrest. He was cross-examined on his previous offences, one of which was for assault on the police. It is clear that prosecuting counsel went into the facts of that conviction in great detail. Watkins LJ, who gave the judgment of the court, described it thus:

'Step by step, allegation by allegation as made in the present case, Mr Sapsford tackled the appellant with his denial of the allegations and with the obvious similarity between what he was contending for now and what had been stated in a previous case were the facts upon which the prosecution relied and his reaction to those allegations. That was an attempt obviously to demonstrate to the jury that the way in which he behaved on this occasion was almost precisely similar to the way he had behaved previously.'

The court was referred to *Reg v Vickers* [1972] Crim LR 101, but no other authorities were expressly referred to. Watkins LJ said:

'In our judgment the line of cross-examination adopted here of the appellant by counsel for the prosecution, though no doubt it was not his intention, was such as to show unmistakably that this appellant was predisposed to using violence, bad language and other misbehaviour of the kind which was alleged against him in the indictment. On the authority of *Reg v Vickers* [1972] Crim LR 101 and other cases which have been decided more recently there can be no doubt that evidence of this kind is related, and must only relate, to the matter of credibility. So any evidence which is introduced no matter in what manner which tends to go beyond that and into the territory of disposition is inadmissible.'

With great respect, we consider that the second paragraph goes too far. It is plain from the cases we have cited it is permissible to cross-examine in respect of convictions both of a similar kind and in some circumstances where the offences may tend to show a disposition to commit offences of this sort. Section 1(f) of the Act of 1898 specifically states he may be asked about other offences and his bad character if the provisos are satisfied. The purpose of the cross-examination is to attack his credit worthiness as a witness and not to seek to show that he has a disposition to commit the offence in question, though in some cases it may have that incidental effect. It is not to be excluded for that reason alone.

Furthermore, it is not clear whether the court considered that the judge had erred in principle in the exercise of his discretion, or as they seem to have thought on the basis that the evidence was inadmissible. It is difficult to see, with respect, how the evidence was inadmissible, though it should perhaps have been excluded as a matter of discretion.

In *Reg v Khan*, 9 August 1990, the judge also failed to give the jury a proper direction as to how they should consider the cross-examination as to previous offences.

The last case to which we were referred . . . was *Reg v Barsoum* (unreported), 12 October 1993. The appellant was convicted of three offences involving supply or possession with intent to supply Class A drugs. His defence involved an attack on prosecution witnesses. He was cross-examined in great detail relating to the substance of the cases leading to previous convictions, one for drug trafficking in Venice for which he was sentenced to three years' imprisonment, and one for conspiracy to supply cocaine. It was submitted by the appellant's counsel that cross-examination should go no further than to establish what is necessary in order to enable the jury to consider how far the convictions bear upon the defendant's credibility. It should not extend to attempting to show that the defendant had done on other occasions precisely what he is alleged to be doing in the instant case. The court was referred to *Reg v Khan*, 9 August 1990. Prosecuting counsel conceded that the cross-examination went too far. There was an added complication in that case in that there was a co-accused who the appellant said was responsible for the possession of the drugs and not him. The co-accused was of good character. There was therefore a marked contrast between the two accused. The court did not adopt the appellant counsel's formulation but accepted that the cross-examination had gone too far.

For the general principles upon which the discretion should be exercised we cannot improve upon the analysis contained in the judgment of Ackner LJ in *Reg v Burke*, 82 Cr App R 156, as supplemented by the observations of Neill LJ in *Reg v Owen*, 83 Cr App R 100, 104–105 to which we have referred. As to the nature of the questions that may properly be put, we consider that the following propositions should be borne in mind.

1. The primary purpose of the cross-examination as to previous convictions and bad character of the accused is to show that he is not worthy of belief. It is not, and should not be, to show that he has a disposition to commit the type of offence with which he is charged: see *Reg v Vickers* [1972] Crim LR 101, *Reg v Khan* and *Reg v Barsoum*. But the mere fact that the offences are of a similar type to that charged or because of their number and type have the incidental effect of suggesting a tendency or disposition to commit the offence charged will not make them improper: see *Reg v Powell* [1985] 1 WLR 1364; *Reg v Owen*, 83 Cr App R 100 and *Reg v Selvey* [1970] AC 304.

2. It is undesirable that there should be prolonged or extensive cross-examination in relation to previous offences. This is because it will divert the jury from the principal issues in the case, which is the guilt of the accused on the instant offence, and not the details of earlier ones. Unless the earlier ones are admissible as similar fact evidence, prosecuting counsel should not seek to probe or emphasise similarities between the underlying facts of previous offences and the instant offence.

3. Similarities of defences which have been rejected by juries on previous occasions, for example false alibis or the defence that the incriminating substance has been planted and whether or not the accused pleaded guilty or was disbelieved having given evidence on oath, may be a legitimate matter for questions. These matters do not show a disposition to commit the offence in question; but they are clearly relevant to credibility.

4. Underlying facts that show particularly bad character over and above the bare facts of the case are not necessarily to be excluded. But the judge should be careful to balance the gravity of the attack on the prosecution with the degree of prejudice to the defendant which will result from the disclosure of the facts in question. Details of sexual offences against children are likely to be regarded by the jury as particularly prejudicial to an accused and may well be the reason why in *Reg v Watts* [1983] 3 All ER 101 the court thought the questions impermissible.

5. If objection is to be taken to a particular line of cross-examination about the underlying facts of a previous offence, it should be taken as soon as it is apparent to defence counsel that it is in danger of going too far. There is little point in taking it subsequently, since it will not normally be a ground for discharging the jury.

6. While it is the duty of the judge to keep cross-examination within proper bounds, if no objection is taken at the time it will be difficult thereafter to contend that the judge has wrongly exercised his discretion. In any event, this court will not interfere with the exercise of the judge's discretion save on well established principles.

7. In every case where the accused has been cross-examined as to his character and previous offences, the judge must in the summing up tell the jury that the purpose of the questioning goes only to credit and they should not consider that it shows a propensity to commit the offence they are considering.

Applying these principles to the present case we are quite satisfied that the questions were perfectly proper. They were by no means unduly prolonged or extensive. With regard to the first offence, there was nothing wrong in asking the appellant about his plea and defence of alibi that was rejected, particularly where, as here, the appellant giving evidence in chief persisted in his denial of guilt. There is no substance in the suggestion that he should not have been asked about the victim of the second offence being locked under the stairs; even if he had accepted that he had done it, which he did not, it merely showed that this offence was somewhat more ruthless than may normally be the case in a robbery where by definition violence, or the threat of violence, is used. The circumstances were in any event quite different from the instant case. In our judgment, it is fanciful to contend that the facts elicited in respect of the third and fourth offences, which occurred more than nine and four years before the instant offence, were designed to show a tendency or propensity to commit armed robbery, merely because the use of stolen vehicles with false registration plates is the stock in trade of armed robbery.

(b) Practical implications

The following extract provides an instructive account of the difficulties caused to defence solicitors in magistrates' courts by the second limb of s 1(f)(ii):

Extract 6.5.6

M McConville, J Hodgson, L Bridges and A Pavlovic, *Standing Accused: The Organisation and Practices of Criminal Defence Lawyers in Britain* (1994) 216–20

As a general rule, defence solicitors conducted cross-examinations so that they avoided casting imputations on the character of prosecution witnesses. This was an understandable tactic given the fact that 70 per cent of defendants had a prior criminal record of some kind, albeit not serious in many cases and sometimes for offences wholly unrelated to the kind of offence charged.

Solicitors were fully aware of the dangers involved as were, in some cases, 'experienced' defendants. Thus, in *MCT-41* the solicitor spoke to the client just before going into court, telling him that the line of defence would be confined to suggesting that the police were mistaken:

> SOLICITOR: If we say they're lying, they can call in your character and then there will be only one result.
>
> CLIENT: Guilty!
>
> SOLICITOR: Yes.

It would be wrong, however, to minimise the constraining effect that the 'character' rule can have upon the defence. In some cases, it can induce the solicitor to actively encourage suppression of what the defendant claims to be the true version of events. An example of this occurred in *MCT-23* in which it was alleged that the defendant had threatened another with violence in the course of a pub fight. The evidence against the client was his own statement given in police custody in which he said that he had picked up a bar stool. On the day of the trial, he repeated to his solicitor his story, given at earlier office interviews with other staff, that this was inaccurate ('I didn't even do that') and had been made because of threats by a named officer to hold him in custody. The pre-trial discussion continued:

> SOLICITOR: If I suggest [the police] acted improperly, you see, they can put your record in. There are two ways to do this. The magistrates are not entitled to know about your record, but we lose that shield if we challenge the police. So you can either say you had the stool, as you said in interview, or we can challenge that. It's a difficult decision because once your convictions go in, it's hard when you have a lot [of previous convictions].
>
> CO-DEFENDANT (interrupting): But he hasn't any for violence. Neither of us have. (To client) *Did* you pick a stool up?
>
> CLIENT: No.
>
> CO-DEFENDANT: Well, that's it then.
>
> SOLICITOR: Anyway, think about it and I'll come back to it in a minute.
>
> . . .
>
> SOLICITOR: What have you decided to do? I think you should just go with what you said in the interview because there's nothing damaging there really, so it's a shame to put your record in.
>
> CLIENT: Yeah, okay.

. . .

And in other cases, the 'bad' character of the defendant was a factor in the advice of solicitors not to contest the veracity of statements made in custody which the defendant alleged were, in some measure, the product of police malpractice.

In the usual case, where police evidence was seriously disputed, the strategy of the solicitor was to suggest that the officer was mistaken rather than lying, or to simply put to the officer the defendant's version as an accurate account of what really happened. Thus, in *MCT-07* there was a serious dispute as to the circumstances leading to the arrest of the defendant. According to the defendant, the police became angry because he had kicked their car in his stockinged feet in the course of a domestic argument. In the police version, the defendant was abusive and violent and had to be arrested to restore order.

MCT-07

SOLICITOR: I put it to you that one of you said 'get lost' . . . and I put it to you that he may have been told to 'piss off' – is that correct?

OFFICER: That is *in*correct.

SOLICITOR: And he was told 'you are under arrest because you kicked our car'.

OFFICER: No – he was told he was being arrested under the Public Order Act.

SOLICITOR: And at no time prior to the arrest did he use bad language.

OFFICER: That is incorrect.

SOLICITOR: And at no time did he punch anyone.

OFFICER: *In*correct (original emphasis).

Whilst this approach was almost universally ineffective in persuading the witness to adopt the account suggested, it was successful in keeping out defendants' prior criminal records.

In this context, it is worth noting that, for their part, prosecutors made no serious efforts to induce the defendant to attack the character of prosecution witnesses and risk dropping the shield which protected their own character. In *MCT-14*, for example, on an offensive weapon charge, the issue was whether the defendant, as the police alleged, had a stick in his hand, or whether, as he said, he did not. The defendant had not been coached by his solicitor or warned of the risk of attacking prosecution witnesses, being told simply: 'Just answer the questions and don't get ruffled.' Although the defendant had a prior criminal record and might easily have been goaded into saying that the police were 'lying', the prosecutor made no effort to rile the defendant who, for his part, answered impeccably:

MCT-14

PROSECUTOR: When the police came, you were out in the road with a stick heading for [Dave] – going to attack him?

DEFENDANT: No. I didn't have a stick.

PROSECUTOR: So the police officer is wrong?

DEFENDANT: I didn't have a stick.

In a few cases, however, the defence involved an outright attack on the integrity of prosecution witnesses. In most of these, there was a sharp contrast between the approach of the solicitor, who generally was moderate and restrained, and suggested an 'alternative account' to the witness, and that of the defendant who openly contradicted the witnesses. Thus, in *MCT-20*, on an assault police charge where the defendant was of previous good character, the defence solicitor sought to suggest that the officer rather than the defendant had been abusive and aggressive:

SOLICITOR: You were fairly unpleasant to him from the time you stopped his car?

OFFICER: I deny that.

SOLICITOR: And snatched the [breathalyser] meter from him?

OFFICER: I deny that.

SOLICITOR: And threw him in the back of the police car.

OFFICER: I deny that.

SOLICITOR: And he says 'no need for that' and you struck him across the face.

OFFICER: I deny that.

By contrast, the defendant gave evidence in forthright terms saying that the officers had 'concocted a story' and that they were 'telling lies'.

In only one case did we see a defence solicitor launch an all-out attack on prosecution witnesses, impugning their honesty and integrity. The case involved a 'status' client, a man with a substantial criminal record though much of it involving offences of a non-serious nature. It became clear that the attack on the police was made in this way because the solicitor knew that the client expected this (in commenting upon his closing speech, for example, the solicitor told the researcher that it was made 'for [the client's] benefit not for the magistrates') and because the solicitor felt that occasional attacks of this sort helped create a reputation among other potential clients in an 'outside' town where the firm was actively seeking to increase its client-base. The solicitor made no attempt to engage in 'skilful' cross-examination, laying a foundation for questioning the reliability or consistency of the witnesses. Instead, each police witness was subjected in turn to a confrontational attack, the flavour of which can be gathered from the following excerpts:

MCT-05

SOLICITOR: It became apparent to you that your initial conclusions were wrong and [the defendant] was wrongfully arrested.

OFFICER A: No.

SOLICITOR: You made up your notes to suit yourself.

OFFICER A: No, sir.

SOLICITOR: I'm suggesting that the notebook entries are *lies*, not mistaken. What do you say to that?

OFFICER A: No, sir.

SOLICITOR: All lies, made up to cover yourself having drawn wrong conclusions. . . .

SOLICITOR: I'm going to suggest that, because of a deliberate assault by your colleagues [on the defendant] you made your notes up to cover. Let's make no mistake – I'm alleging that you have perjured yourself today and conspired to pervert the course of justice.

OFFICER B: I totally refute that.

SOLICITOR: You and your colleagues exacted instant justice.

OFFICER B: Really, Mr [Thomas], we don't need to blacken someone's character – this is [Midshire].

SOLICITOR: Exactly! This is [Midshire]! These remarks are the icing on the cake – another bit of falsehood.

Other police witnesses were similarly accused of 'falsehoods', of 'committing perjury', and of telling 'lies'. When the defendant was called to give evidence, his solicitor immediately introduced his previous convictions emphasizing the fact that, although his record was lengthy, he had 'never appeared for anything like this involving the police'.

This case was, however, exceptional and defence solicitors generally avoided attacking the character of police officers even in cases where the defendant was of previous good character.

(c) Reform

In the view of the Runciman Royal Commission:

Where the main purpose of the attack by the defence on a witness for the prosecution is to shake his or her credibility as a witness, the defendant must expect to be subject to cross-examination in his or her turn. But where the attack is central to the defence, it should not of itself expose the accused to cross-examination on his or her previous convictions.[20]

Would such reform be desirable? Does the solution lie, as has been suggested,[21] in adopting a principle that the cross-examination must be proportionate to the breadth of the attack launched by the accused on the prosecution witnesses? According to this view, it is only in the rare case where the accused has embarked on a general moral campaign aimed at destroying the moral standing of the prosecution witnesses that an uninhibited attack on the accused's character should be permitted. This may be the case where, for example, an accused not only disputes a confession, but also seeks to expose the general corruption of the police officers involved, their perjury and their susceptibility to bribery.

The solution provisionally proposed by the Law Commission is 'that imputations should result in the loss of the shield only if they do not relate to the witness' conduct in the incident or investigation in question'.[22] As will be seen below, this concept of imputations which do not relate to the witness's conduct in the incident or investigation in question is one which has been borrowed from the Australian Evidence Act 1995. It should be noted, however, that 'the Commission's preferred formulation of the test may be too narrow. Asking whether the imputation "relate[s] to the witness's conduct in the incident or investigation" almost certainly leaves out of account what might be termed "reverse similar fact evidence," ie evidence of a prosecution witness's disposition or conduct on another occasion adduced by the defence to show that the witness behaved in a particular way in relation to the subject matter of the current charge. One example would be defence evidence that police officers have fabricated confessions in previous cases adduced to prove that the officers have followed their usual practice by fabricating the defendant's alleged confession in the instant trial.'[23]

Perhaps the most appropriate solution would be to adopt not a single narrow 'test', but rather an approach based upon a weighing up of all relevant factors. Whether the imputations relate to the witness's conduct in the incident or investigation in question is obviously one factor to be taken into

[20] Royal Commission on Criminal Justice, *Report* (Cm 2263) (1993) 127.
[21] A A S Zuckerman, *The Principles of Criminal Evidence* (1989) Ch 13.
[22] Law Commission (Consultation Paper No 141), *Criminal Law – Evidence in Criminal Proceedings: Previous Misconduct of a Defendant – A Consultation Paper* (1996) 266.
[23] P Roberts, 'The Law Commission Consultation Paper on Previous Misconduct: (1) All the Usual Suspects: A Critical Appraisal of Law Commission Consultation Paper No 141' [1997] *Criminal Law Review* 75, 88.

account. However, other factors which should be considered include: To what extent were the imputations necessary? Were they, for example, central to the defence? Is the proposed cross-examination proportionate to the breadth of the attack launched by the accused on the prosecution witnesses?

6. SECTION 1(f)(iii)

If an accused, A, gives evidence against a co-accused, B, then B, or any other party, may cross-examine A as to his or her previous offences or bad character. Such cross-examination goes to credit. What, then, is meant by 'giving evidence against' a co-accused?

Extract 6.6.1

R v Varley [1982] 2 All ER 519, 522 (CA)

KILNER BROWN J: Now, putting all the reported cases together, are there established principles which might serve as guidance to trial judges when called on to give rulings in this very difficult area of the law? We venture to think that they are these and, if they are borne in mind, it may not be necessary to investigate all the relevant authorities. (1) If it is established that a person jointly charged has given evidence against the co-defendant that defendant has a right to cross-examine the other as to previous convictions and the trial judge has no discretion to refuse an application. (2) Such evidence may be given either in chief or during cross-examination. (3) It has to be objectively decided whether the evidence either supports the prosecution case in a material respect or undermines the defence of the co-accused. A hostile intent is irrelevant. (4) If consideration has to be given to the undermining of the other's defence care must be taken to see that the evidence clearly undermines the defence. Inconvenience to or inconsistency with the other's defence is not of itself sufficient. (5) Mere denial of participation in a joint venture is not of itself sufficient to rank as evidence against the co-defendant. For the proviso to apply, such denial must lead to the conclusion that if the witness did not participate then it must have been the other who did. (6) Where the one defendant asserts or in due course would assert one view of the joint venture which is directly contradicted by the other such contradiction may be evidence against the co-defendant.

We apply these principles to the facts of this case and particularly the latter two. Here was Dibble going to say, as he did, that he took part in the joint venture because he was forced to do so by Varley. The appellant, Varley, was saying that he was not a participant and had not gone with Dibble and had not forced Dibble to go. His evidence therefore was against Dibble because it amounted to saying that not only was Dibble telling lies but that Dibble would be left as a participant on his own and not acting under duress. In our view, the judge was right to rule that cross-examination as to previous convictions was permissible. . . .

The other ground put forward was that the judge wrongly exercised his discretion by refusing to order separate trials. We recognise that there may well be occasions where there has been a successful application to cross-examine a co-defendant on his convictions and the trial judge, in his duty to ensure a fair trial, may properly exercise a discretion to order separate trials. We have in mind the situation where the effect of such cross-examination is such as to create such undue prejudice that a fair trial is impossible. But that is not this case. The truth of the matter is that this was a case where two experienced criminals metaphorically cut each other's throats in the course of their respective defences. If separate trials had been ordered, one or other or both might have succeeded in preventing a just result.

The Court of Appeal has held recently in *R v Crawford (Charisse)*[24] that the phrase 'it must have been the other who did' in point (5) above is inappropriate to cases where more than two persons are concerned, and that it would therefore be more appropriate if 'must' were substituted by 'may'. The court in *Crawford* considered that the essential question to be asked is: 'Did the evidence given by the defendant in the witness box, if accepted, damage in a significant way the defence of the co-defendant?'

As the extract from *Varley* indicates, there is no judicial discretion to prevent a co-accused, against whom evidence has been given by an accused, from cross-examining the accused under s 1(f)(iii). The reason for this is explained by Lord Donovan in the following case. Lord Pearce dissented on the issue of discretion.

Extract 6.6.2

Murdoch v Taylor **[1965] AC 574, 592–3, 587–8 (HL)**

LORD DONOVAN: On the question of discretion, I agree with the Court of Criminal Appeal that a trial judge has no discretion whether to allow an accused person to be cross-examined as to his past criminal offences once he has given evidence against his co-accused. Proviso (f)(iii) in terms confers no such discretion and, in my opinion, none can be implied. It is true that in relation to proviso (f)(ii) such a discretion does exist; that is to say, in the cases where the accused has attempted to establish his own good character or where the nature and conduct of the defence is such as to involve imputations on the character of the prosecutor or of a witness for the prosecution.

But in these cases it will normally, if not invariably, be the prosecution which will want to bring out the accused's bad character – not some co-accused; and in such cases it seems to me quite proper that the court should retain some control of the matter. For its duty is to secure a fair trial and the prejudicial value of evidence establishing the accused's bad character may at times wholly outweigh the value of such evidence as tending to show that he was guilty of the crime alleged.

[24] (1997) *The Times*, 10 June.

These considerations lead me to the view that if, in any given case (which I think would be rare), the prosecution sought to avail itself of the provisions of proviso (f)(iii) then here, again, the court should keep control of the matter in the like way. Otherwise, if two accused gave evidence one against the other, but neither wished to cross-examine as to character, the prosecution could step in as of right and reveal the criminal records of both, if both possessed them. I cannot think that Parliament in the Act of 1898 ever intended such an unfair procedure. So far as concerns the prosecution, therefore, the matter should be one for the exercise of the judge's discretion, as it is in the case of proviso (f)(ii). But when it is the co-accused who seeks to exercise the right conferred by proviso (f)(iii) different considerations come into play. He seeks to defend himself; to say to the jury that the man who is giving evidence against him is unworthy of belief; and to support that assertion by proof of bad character. The right to do this cannot, in my opinion, be fettered in any way.

LORD PEARCE: Admittedly the situation arising under section 1(f)(ii) differs from that arising under section 1(f)(iii). Under the former, an exercise of discretion could only deprive the prosecution of a right which they would otherwise have had; and the courts have always been ready to do that when fairness seemed to demand it. Under section 1(f)(iii), however, the judge, in using a discretion to refuse the introduction of a defendant's bad record, could only do so at the expense of a co-defendant. And how, it is argued, can he properly do this?

It is certainly not an easy problem. But the difficult burden of holding the scales fairly, not only as between the prosecution and defendants, but also as between the defendants themselves, and of doing his best thereby to secure a fair trial for all concerned, falls inevitably on the trial judge and is generally achieved in practice with considerable success. The use of a judicial discretion under section 1(f)(iii) as between co-defendants would be but an addition to the judge's existing burden.

The exercise of such a discretion would be within fairly narrow limits and the prima facie right could only be withheld for good judicial reasons. Two obvious examples occur to one of situations in which the judge ought to use a discretion to refuse a defendant's request to introduce a co-defendant's bad character. The first is where that defendant's counsel has deliberately led a co-defendant into the trap, or has, for the purpose of bringing in his bad record, put questions to him in cross-examination which will compel him, for the sake of his own innocence, to give answers that will clash with the story of the other defendant, or compel him to bring to the forefront implications which would otherwise have been unnoticed or immaterial. The second type of situation is where the clash between the two stories is both inevitable and trivial, and yet the damage by the introduction of a bad record (perhaps many years previous) will in the circumstances be unfairly prejudicial. Any attempt to deal with such a situation by means of the maxim de minimis is really to import some sort of discretion in disguise. For if a defendant is entitled to an absolute right, he can claim it on any technical ground that exists, whether it be large or small, fair or unfair: and however unfair or technical the ground may be, the right will be equally valuable to a defendant who can make his escape over the (perhaps innocent) body of a co-defendant.

In such a difficult matter which may not infrequently arise in borderline cases, the judge, who sees the general run of the case as it unfolds before him, can produce a fairer result by the exercise of a judicial discretion than by the strict and fettered application of an arbitrary rule of law.

Which view do you find more persuasive – that of Lord Donovan (which represents the prevailing view), or that of Lord Pearce?[25] See also the discussion in Chapter 1 of the desirability of recognising the existence of a judicial discretion to exclude admissible defence evidence.

The Law Commission has provisionally made a number of recommendations about reform of the law on s 1(f)(iii):

We provisionally propose . . . that, where a defendant, in the course of his or her evidence, or through his or her witness or representative, undermines the defence of a co-accused charged in the same proceedings,

(1) if the challenge to the co-accused's account concerns the co-accused's conduct in the incident in question or the investigation of it, the shield should not be lost; but

(2) if this is not the case, any party to the proceedings should be entitled to apply to the court for leave to adduce evidence of the defendant's character.

We provisionally propose that

(1) where the party making the application for leave is the co-accused whose defence has been undermined, leave should be granted unless the court considers that it would be contrary to the interests of justice to grant leave;

(2) where the party making the application for leave is not the co-accused whose defence has been undermined, leave should not be granted unless the court considers that it would be in the interests of justice for leave to be granted; and

(3) in deciding whether to grant leave a court should have regard, amongst any other relevant considerations, to

(a) the degree to which the co-accused's defence has been undermined;

(b) how unavoidable it is for the defendant to undermine the co-accused's defence;

(c) the nature, number and age of the matters of bad character which it is sought to adduce; and

(d) the relative characters of all the accused as they would appear to the fact-finders if the evidence of bad character were allowed.

We provisionally propose that, where an application could have been made for leave to cross-examine a defendant about his or her previous misconduct on the ground that he or she has undermined the defence of a co-accused, but the defendant does not testify, any other party should be able to apply for leave to adduce evidence of the defendant's previous misconduct if the nature of the defence is such as to put the defendant's own credibility in issue; and the criteria for determining the application should be the same as where the defendant does testify.

---

[25] See generally I H Dennis, 'Evidence against a Co-Accused' (1983) 36 *Current Legal Problems* 177. See also A Stein, 'The Refoundation of Evidence Law' (1996) 9 *Canadian Journal of Law and Jurisprudence* 279, 330.

We provisionally propose the abolition of the common law rule that, where evidence of an accused's bad character is admitted under section 1(f)(iii), it is directly relevant only to the accused's credibility.[26]

Would adoption of these provisional proposals represent the right way forward?

7. A GENERAL EVALUATION

We have seen that cross-examination under both limbs of s 1(f)(ii), and s 1(f)(iii), goes only to credit and should not be treated as being of relevance to guilt. As Munday points out, however, 'any direction to a jury, that they may only use their knowledge of the defendant's criminal record to help gauge his credibility and that they are forbidden to treat it as evidence that the defendant is the kind of person who commits offences generally or any particular type of offence, demands unusual analytical temerity'.[27] After all, the distinction between the question whether the evidence shows the defendant to be guilty, and the question whether the evidence shows the defendant to be lying when he says he is not guilty, is far from clear.[28] Empirical research has confirmed that scepticism about the ability of juries to follow limiting instructions may be justified.[29] Furthermore, one of the main assumptions underlying this area of the law – that bad character provides a good indication that a witness is not worthy of belief – 'contrasts sharply with the tentative judgements of the psychologists in the matter of credibility assessment'.[30] As the Law Commission notes, psychological research has failed generally to demonstrate a significant link between bad-character evidence and lack of veracity as a witness.[31] This is supported by the finding of the Oxford mock jury research that a defendant with a prior conviction (even one for an offence of dishonesty) was not rated as a less credible witness. Only a prior conviction for an indecent assault (especially an indecent assault on a child) adversely affected his credibility as a witness in the eyes of the participants.[32] In the light of such considerations, Munday makes the following general observations:

---

[26] Law Commission (Consultation Paper No 141), *Criminal Law – Evidence in Criminal Proceedings: Previous Misconduct of a Defendant – A Consultation Paper* (1996) 268–9.

[27] R Munday, 'The Paradox of Cross-Examination to Credit – Simply too Close for Comfort' [1994] *Cambridge Law Journal* 303, 305–6.

[28] *State v Schwab* 409 NW 2d 876, 882 (1987) per Randall J.

[29] See generally A N Doob and H M Kirshenbaum, 'Some Empirical Evidence on the Effect of S 12 of the Canada Evidence Act upon an Accused' (1972) 15 *Criminal Law Quarterly* 88; V P Hans and A N Doob, 'Section 12 of the Canada Evidence Act and the Deliberations of Simulated Juries' (1976) 18 *Criminal Law Quarterly* 235; M A Myers, 'Rule Departures and Making Law: Juries and their Verdicts' (1979) 13 *Law and Society Review* 781; P M Tiersma, 'Reforming the Language of Jury Instructions' (1993) 22 *Hofstra Law Review* 37; R L Wissler and M J Saks, 'On the Inefficacy of Limiting Instructions: When Jurors Use Prior Conviction Evidence to Decide on Guilt' (1985) 9 *Law and Human Behavior* 37; H Kalven, Jr and H Zeisel, *The American Jury* (1966).

[30] R Munday, 'The Paradox of Cross-Examination to Credit – Simply Too Close for Comfort' [1994] *Cambridge Law Journal* 303, 308.

[31] Law Commission (Consultation Paper No 141), *Criminal Law – Evidence in Criminal Proceedings: Previous Misconduct of a Defendant – A Consultation Paper* (1996) 99–100.

[32] At Appendix D.

7. A GENERAL EVALUATION

If distrust of an impressionable jury, for example, was thought at the root of the problem, jury procedures might be modified, possibly along the lines of some European jurisdictions, to allow judges to retire to deliberate with the jury. Judicial control could thereby be exerted over the manner in which evidence of bad character is actually employed by the tribunal of fact, some variety of reasoned judgments might be handed down, and in these circumstances one might feel less uneasy in allowing the court to learn more of a defendant's criminal history. Alternatively, it might be productive to review portions of the Criminal Evidence Act 1898. In particular, if sub-proviso (ii) were reshaped so as to focus on defendants who adduce evidence of their good character, separating them from the tit-for-tat provision which controls defendants who attack the character of the prosecutor and the witnesses for the prosecution – a far more problematic class of cases, there might be grounds for allowing the Crown to adduce evidence of bad character in the form of evidence of propensity, fighting fire with fire. The present position, in which D claims a good character for himself and, upon being cross-examined on his record, the jury is solemnly told that D's previous record (particularly, if for broadly similar offences) reflects only on his credit, makes comparatively little sense. Again, there looks to be a case for re-examining the most basic notions in this area of law, and more specifically the accuracy of legal concepts like defendant- or witness- credibility.[33]

What is notable about reform proposals relating to cross-examination of accused persons, including the provisional recommendations of the Law Commission, is that they are typically premised on the assumption that the basic structure of the provisions in the 1898 Act should be maintained.[34] Most suggestions for reform focus upon two matters: first, what changes might be made to the manner in which particular provisions are judicially interpreted, and, secondly, what minor amendments might be made to the current statutory provisions. It is surely time that serious consideration be given to the issue of how the current statutory provisions might be overhauled in a more fundamental manner. The following, for example, is the approach taken in the Australian Evidence Act 1995:

Extract 6.7.1

Evidence Act 1995 (Australia), s 104

104. Further protections: cross-examination of accused

(1) . . .

(2) A defendant must not be cross-examined about a matter that is relevant only because it is relevant to the defendant's credibility, unless the court gives leave.

---

[33] R Munday, 'The Paradox of Cross-Examination to Credit – Simply too Close for Comfort' [1994] *Cambridge Law Journal* 303, 324.

[34] See generally J McEwan, 'The Law Commission Consultation Paper on Previous Misconduct: (2) Law Commission Dodges the Nettles in Consultation Paper No 141' [1997] *Criminal Law Review* 93; P Roberts, 'The Law Commission Consultation Paper on Previous Misconduct: (1) All the Usual Suspects: A Critical Appraisal of Law Commission Consultation Paper No 141' [1997] *Criminal Law Review* 75.

289

(3) Despite subsection (2), leave is not required for cross-examination by the prosecutor about whether the defendant:
  (a) is biased or has a motive to be untruthful; or
  (b) is, or was, unable to be aware of or recall matters to which his or her evidence relates; or
  (c) has made a prior inconsistent statement.
(4) Leave must not be given for cross-examination by the prosecutor about any matter that is relevant only because it is relevant to the defendant's credibility unless:
  (a) evidence has been adduced by the defendant that tends to prove that the defendant is, either generally or in a particular respect, a person of good character; or
  (b) evidence adduced by the defendant has been admitted that tends to prove that a witness called by the prosecutor has a tendency to be untruthful, and that is relevant solely or mainly to the witness's credibility.
(5) A reference in paragraph (4)(b) to evidence does not include a reference to evidence of conduct in relation to:
  (a) the events in relation to which the defendant is being prosecuted; or
  (b) the investigation of the offence for which the defendant is being prosecuted.
(6) Leave is not to be given for cross-examination by another defendant unless:
  (a) the evidence that the defendant to be cross-examined has given includes evidence adverse to the defendant seeking leave to cross-examine; and
  (b) that evidence has been admitted.

Further reading

I H Dennis, 'Evidence against a Co-Accused' (1983) 36 *Current Legal Problems* 177

D W Elliott, 'Cut Throat Tactics: The Freedom of an Accused to Prejudice a Co-Accused' [1991] *Criminal Law Review* 5

J McEwan, 'The Law Commission Consultation Paper on Previous Misconduct: (2) Law Commission Dodges the Nettles in Consultation Paper No 141' [1997] *Criminal Law Review* 93

P Mirfield, 'The Argument from Consistency for Overruling *Selvey*' [1991] *Cambridge Law Journal* 490

R Munday, 'Comparative Law and English Law's Character Evidence Rules' (1993) 13 *Oxford Journal of Legal Studies* 589

— 'The Paradox of Cross-Examination to Credit – Simply too Close for Comfort' [1994] *Cambridge Law Journal* 303

R Pattenden, 'The Purpose of Cross-Examination under Section 1(f) of the Criminal Evidence Act 1898' [1982] *Criminal Law Review* 707

P Roberts, 'The Law Commission Consultation Paper on Previous Misconduct: (1) All the Usual Suspects: A Critical Appraisal of Law Commission Consultation Paper No 141' [1997] *Criminal Law Review* 75

C F H Tapper, 'The Meaning of Section 1(f)(i) of the Criminal Evidence Act 1898' in C F H Tapper (ed), *Crime, Proof and Punishment: Essays in Memory of Sir Rupert Cross* (1981)

7

HEARSAY EVIDENCE

1. INTRODUCTION

Hearsay is any 'statement made otherwise than by a person while giving oral evidence in the proceedings which is tendered as evidence of the matters stated'.[1] All hearsay evidence is presumptively inadmissible by virtue of the rule against hearsay. In order to be admissible, hearsay evidence must either fall within a common law exception to the hearsay rule, or be rendered admissible by a statutory provision. In the following case, the House of Lords confirmed that the list of common law exceptions to the hearsay rule is closed, and that this list does not include a residual discretion to admit hearsay evidence in the interests of justice. Thus, new exceptions to the hearsay rule may only be created by the legislature.

Extract 7.1.1

Myers v DPP [1965] AC 1001, 1024 (HL)

LORD REID: In argument the Solicitor-General maintained that, although the general rule may be against the admission of private records to prove the truth of entries in them, the trial judge has a discretion to admit a record in a particular case if satisfied that it is trustworthy and that justice requires its admission. That appears to me to be contrary to the whole framework of the existing law. It is true that a judge has a discretion to exclude legally admissible evidence if justice so requires, but it is a very different thing to say that he has a discretion to admit legally inadmissible evidence. The whole development of the exceptions to the hearsay rule is based on the determination of certain classes of evidence as admissible or inadmissible and not on the apparent credibility of particular evidence tendered. No matter how cogent particular evidence may seem to be, unless it comes within a class which is admissible, it is excluded. Half a dozen witnesses may offer to prove that they heard two men of high character who cannot now be found discuss in detail the fact now in issue and agree on a credible account of it, but that evidence would not be admitted although it might be by far the best evidence available.

---

[1] Civil Evidence Act 1995, s 1(2)(a).

Lord Morris of Borth-y-Gest and Lord Hodson delivered concurring speeches. Lords Pearce and Donovan dissented.

The perceived unreliability of hearsay evidence constitutes the main justification for the hearsay rule:

> [Hearsay evidence] is not the best evidence and it is not delivered on oath. The truthfulness and accuracy of the person whose words are spoken to by another witness cannot be tested by cross-examination, and the light which his demeanour would throw on his testimony is lost.[2]

Any statement may be unreliable because of defects in the *perception, memory, sincerity*, or *ability to narrate clearly*, of the maker of the statement. Suppose that a witness, W, states in his or her testimony that 'The car I saw driving away was red'. This statement may be unreliable because (1) W may have perceived the car to be red when it was in reality of some other colour; (2) W may have genuinely forgotten that the car was of some other colour; (3) W may be lying; or (4) W may be trying to say that the car was of some other colour, but be lacking in the ability to narrate this clearly. In this situation, because the statement has been made in court by the person who witnessed the event, his or her demeanour at the time of making the statement will have been able to be observed. Further, the statement is likely to have been a sworn statement. Finally, he or she would be able to be subjected to 'contemporaneous' cross-examination in relation to the statement. Such cross-examination would, it is said, assist in exposing any defects in the witness's perception, memory, sincerity or clarity of narration. Suppose, however, that the situation is one in which W is reporting an out-of-court statement: '*X said* that the car she saw driving away was red.' In such a situation, cross-examination of W would be of limited efficacy in exposing possible defects in the perception, memory, sincerity, or ability to narrate clearly, of X. It is for this reason, it is said, that the hearsay rule exists.

These arguments are, however, far from insurmountable, for the following reasons:

(1) As mentioned in Chapter 4, the extent to which observation of a witness's demeanour actually provides a good indication of the reliability of his or her testimony is a matter of considerable speculation.

(2) It is uncertain whether, in modern times, the taking of an oath (or the making of a solemn affirmation) necessarily guarantees the reliability of testimony.

(3) The utility of contemporaneous cross-examination in ensuring the reliability of evidence is also uncertain. Cross-examination may well be of little use in exposing insincerity,[3] and it is also possible that the efficacy

---

[2] *Teper v R* [1952] AC 480, 486 per Lord Normand.

[3] T Finman, 'Implied Assertions as Hearsay: Some Criticisms of the Uniform Rules of Evidence' (1962) 14 *Stanford Law Review* 682, 690; R C Park, 'A Subject Matter Approach to Hearsay Reform' (1987) 86 *Michigan Law Review* 51, 96; E Swift, 'A Foundation Fact

of cross-examination in exposing faulty perception may not be as high as may be assumed.[4] Additionally, it should be noted that suggesting facts to a witness in cross-examination may actually distort, rather than assist, his or her memory.[5]

(4) Empirical evidence conducted in the United States has revealed that the assumption that juries are incapable of assessing the reliability of hearsay evidence competently may well be questionable.[6]

Excellent aids to understanding the reliability rationale for the hearsay rule are provided by L H Tribe, 'Triangulating Hearsay' (1974) 87 *Harvard Law Review* 957 and M H Graham, ' "Stickperson Hearsay": A Simplified Approach to Understanding the Rule against Hearsay' [1982] *University of Illinois Law Review* 887.

Additionally, the hearsay rule as applied to prosecution evidence in criminal proceedings may be justified by reference to considerations of extrinsic policy.[7] It may be argued that a legal system where, for example, observers of events testify directly to what they saw would be perceived as procedurally fairer than one where hearsay evidence is adduced. Further, the hearsay rule may be regarded as protecting the value of individual dignity in criminal proceedings. Unlike its civil counterpart, a criminal trial has a special moral dimension, with the weight of the State ranged against an individual, whose conviction and punishment are being sought. An important feature of criminal justice is, therefore, the notion that human dignity must be respected when the power of the State is ranged against an individual, as in a criminal prosecution.[8] The ability of an accused person to confront and cross-examine the maker of a statement against him or her, and not just a person reporting the statement, is consistent with the right of accused persons to be treated with dignity. Moreover, the dignity of witnesses other than the accused is also respected by the hearsay rule: the phenomenon of witnesses testifying in court and being subject to cross-examination reinforces the moral significance

Approach to Hearsay' (1987) 75 *California Law Review* 1339, 1357 n 50. See also J Allan, 'The Working and Rationale of the Hearsay Rule and the Implications of Modern Psychological Knowledge' (1991) 44 *Current Legal Problems* 217.

[4] E A Scallen, 'Constitutional Dimensions of Hearsay Reform: Toward a Three-Dimensional Confrontation Clause' (1992) 76 *Minnesota Law Review* 623, 627 n 15.

[5] Australian Law Reform Commission, *Evidence (Vol 1)* (Report No 26: Interim) (1985) 362; Scottish Law Commission, *Evidence: Report on Hearsay Evidence in Criminal Proceedings* (Scot Law Com No 149) (1995) 16.

[6] S Landsman and R F Rakos, 'Research Essay: A Preliminary Empirical Enquiry Concerning the Prohibition of Hearsay Evidence in American Courts' (1991) 15 *Law and Psychology Review* 65; R F Rakos and S Landsman, 'Researching the Hearsay Rule: Emerging Findings, General Issues, and Future Directions' (1992) 76 *Minnesota Law Review* 655; P Miene, R C Park and E Borgida, 'Juror Decision Making and the Evaluation of Hearsay Evidence' (1992) 76 *Minnesota Law Review* 683; M B Kovera, R C Park and S D Penrod, 'Jurors' Perceptions of Eyewitness and Hearsay Evidence' (1992) 76 *Minnesota Law Review* 703.

[7] For a much fuller discussion, see A L-T Choo, *Hearsay and Confrontation in Criminal Trials* (1996) 37–42.

[8] See generally H Gross, *A Theory of Criminal Justice* (1979) 32–3; P Stein and J Shand, *Legal Values in Western Society* (1974) 130 ff.

of the role of witnesses in the trial process.[9] This is particularly true in the case of a witness who is also the alleged victim, since the phenomenon of a victim 'accusing' the defendant in person, in the formal setting of a court-room, is of considerable symbolic importance.[10]

2. THE RULE AGAINST HEARSAY IN CIVIL PROCEEDINGS

The admissibility of hearsay evidence in civil proceedings is governed by the Civil Evidence Act 1995, the salient provisions of which are reproduced below:

Extract 7.2.1

Civil Evidence Act 1995, ss 1, 2, 3, 4, 5, 7, 10(1), 14(3)

1. Admissibility of hearsay evidence
(1) In civil proceedings evidence shall not be excluded on the ground that it is hearsay.
(2) In this Act –
  (a) 'hearsay' means a statement made otherwise than by a person while giving oral evidence in the proceedings which is tendered as evidence of the matters stated; and
  (b) references to hearsay include hearsay of whatever degree.
(3) Nothing in this Act affects the admissibility of evidence admissible apart from this section.
(4) The provisions of sections 2 to 6 (safeguards and supplementary provisions relating to hearsay evidence) do not apply in relation to hearsay evidence admissible apart from this section, notwithstanding that it may also be admissible by virtue of this section.

2. Notice of proposal to adduce hearsay evidence
(1) A party proposing to adduce hearsay evidence in civil proceedings shall, subject to the following provisions of this section, give to the other party or parties to the proceedings –
  (a) such notice (if any) of that fact, and
  (b) on request, such particulars of or relating to the evidence,
as is reasonable and practicable in the circumstances for the purpose of enabling him or them to deal with any matters arising from its being hearsay.

---

[9] K W Graham, Jr, 'The Right of Confrontation and the Hearsay Rule: Sir Walter Raleigh Loses Another One' (1972) 8 *Criminal Law Bulletin* 99, 133: 'The idea that one who accuses another of wrong ought to do so in a forum where he assumes the consequences of his statement has sufficient power that no amount of cynical sneering about the utility of the oath, incidence of perjury prosecutions, or the value of cross-examination will suffice to overcome it as an important symbol of fairness.'
[10] E Swift, 'Smoke and Mirrors: The Failure of the Supreme Court's Accuracy Rationale in *White v Illinois* Requires a New Look at Confrontation' (1993) 22 *Capital University Law Review* 145, 172–3.

(2) Provision may be made by rules of court –

(a) specifying classes of proceedings or evidence in relation to which subsection (1) does not apply, and

(b) as to the manner in which (including the time within which) the duties imposed by that subsection are to be complied with in the cases where it does apply.

(3) Subsection (1) may also be excluded by agreement of the parties; and compliance with the duty to give notice may in any case be waived by the person to whom notice is required to be given.

(4) A failure to comply with subsection (1), or with rules under subsection (2)(b), does not affect the admissibility of the evidence but may be taken into account by the court –

(a) in considering the exercise of its powers with respect to the course of proceedings and costs, and

(b) as a matter adversely affecting the weight to be given to the evidence in accordance with section 4.

3. Power to call witness for cross-examination on hearsay statement

Rules of court may provide that where a party to civil proceedings adduces hearsay evidence of a statement made by a person and does not call that person as a witness, any other party to the proceedings may, with the leave of the court, call that person as a witness and cross-examine him on the statement as if he had been called by the first-mentioned party and as if the hearsay statement were his evidence in chief.

4. Considerations relevant to weighing of hearsay evidence

(1) In estimating the weight (if any) to be given to hearsay evidence in civil proceedings the court shall have regard to any circumstances from which any inference can reasonably be drawn as to the reliability or otherwise of the evidence.

(2) Regard may be had, in particular, to the following –

(a) whether it would have been reasonable and practicable for the party by whom the evidence was adduced to have produced the maker of the original statement as a witness;

(b) whether the original statement was made contemporaneously with the occurrence or existence of the matters stated;

(c) whether the evidence involves multiple hearsay;

(d) whether any person involved had any motive to conceal or misrepresent matters;

(e) whether the original statement was an edited account, or was made in collaboration with another or for a particular purpose;

(f) whether the circumstances in which the evidence is adduced as hearsay are such as to suggest an attempt to prevent proper evaluation of its weight.

5. Competence and credibility

(1) Hearsay evidence shall not be admitted in civil proceedings if or to the extent that it is shown to consist of, or to be proved by means of, a statement made by a person who at the time he made the statement was not competent as a witness.

For this purpose 'not competent as a witness' means suffering from such mental or physical infirmity, or lack of understanding, as would render a person incompetent as a witness in civil proceedings; but a child shall be treated as competent as a witness if he satisfies the requirements of section 96(2)(a) and (b) of the Children Act 1989 (conditions for reception of unsworn evidence of child).

(2) Where in civil proceedings hearsay evidence is adduced and the maker of the original statement, or of any statement relied upon to prove another statement, is not called as a witness –

(a) evidence which if he had been so called would be admissible for the purpose of attacking or supporting his credibility as a witness is admissible for that purpose in the proceedings; and

(b) evidence tending to prove that, whether before or after he made the statement, he made any other statement inconsistent with it is admissible for the purpose of showing that he had contradicted himself.

Provided that evidence may not be given of any matter of which, if he had been called as a witness and had denied that matter in cross-examination, evidence could not have been adduced by the cross-examining party.

7. Evidence formerly admissible at common law

(1) The common law rule effectively preserved by section 9(1) and (2)(a) of the Civil Evidence Act 1968 (admissibility of admissions adverse to a party) is superseded by the provisions of this Act.

(2) The common law rules effectively preserved by section 9(1) and (2)(b) to (d) of the Civil Evidence Act 1968, that is, any rule of law whereby in civil proceedings –

(a) published works dealing with matters of a public nature (for example, histories, scientific works, dictionaries and maps) are admissible as evidence of facts of a public nature stated in them,

(b) public documents (for example, public registers, and returns made under public authority with respect to matters of public interest) are admissible as evidence of facts stated in them, or

(c) records (for example, the records of certain courts, treaties, Crown grants, pardons and commissions) are admissible as evidence of facts stated in them,

shall continue to have effect.

(3) The common law rules effectively preserved by section 9(3) and (4) of the Civil Evidence Act 1968, that is, any rule of law whereby in civil proceedings –

(a) evidence of a person's reputation is admissible for the purpose of proving his good or bad character, or

(b) evidence of reputation or family tradition is admissible –

(i) for the purpose of proving or disproving pedigree or the existence of a marriage, or

(ii) for the purpose of proving or disproving the existence of any public or general right or of identifying any person or thing,

shall continue to have effect in so far as they authorise the court to treat such evidence as proving or disproving that matter.

Where any such rule applies, reputation or family tradition shall be treated for the purposes of this Act as a fact and not as a statement or multiplicity of statements about the matter in question.

(4) The words in which a rule of law mentioned in this section is described are intended only to identify the rule and shall not be construed as altering it in any way.

10. Admissibility and proof of Ogden Tables

(1) The actuarial tables (together with explanatory notes) for use in personal injury and fatal accident cases issued from time to time by the Government Actuary's Department are admissible in evidence for the purpose of assessing, in an action for personal injury, the sum to be awarded as general damages for future pecuniary loss.

14. Savings

(3) Nothing in this Act affects the operation of the following enactments –
- (a) section 2 of the Documentary Evidence Act 1868 (mode of proving certain official documents);
- (b) section 2 of the Documentary Evidence Act 1882 (documents printed under the superintendence of Stationery Office);
- (c) section 1 of the Evidence (Colonial Statutes) Act 1907 (proof of statutes of certain legislatures);
- (d) section 1 of the Evidence (Foreign, Dominion and Colonial Documents) Act 1933 (proof and effect of registers and official certificates of certain countries);
- (e) section 5 of the Oaths and Evidence (Overseas Authorities and Countries) Act 1963 (provision in respect of public registers of other countries).

The position, in short, is therefore as follows:

(1) Certain common law exceptions to the hearsay rule are preserved by s 7 of the Act. Sections 2–5 of the Act do not apply in relation to evidence admissible under these exceptions, or to evidence admissible by virtue of s 10 or s 14.

(2) Other hearsay evidence (including, as seen in Chapter 4, evidence of prior consistent statements and prior inconsistent statements) is admissible, subject to the provisions of ss 2–5. Thus, for example, notice of intention to adduce the evidence is to be given.

The provisions of the Act are buttressed by Rules of the Supreme Court and by County Court Rules.

Extract 7.2.2

Rules of the Supreme Court 1965, Ord 38, rr 21, 22, 23

21. Hearsay notices

(1) A hearsay notice must
- (a) state that it is a hearsay notice;
- (b) identify the hearsay evidence;

(c) identify the person who made the statement which is to be given in evidence;

(d) state why that person will (or may) not be called to give oral evidence; and

(e) if the hearsay evidence is contained in a witness statement, refer to the part of the witness statement where it is set out.

(2) A single hearsay notice may deal with the hearsay evidence of more than one witness.

(3) The requirement to give a hearsay notice does not apply to

(a) evidence which is authorised to be given by or in an affidavit; or

(b) a statement which a party to a probate action desires to give in evidence and which is alleged to have been made by the person whose estate is the subject of the action.

(4) Subject to paragraph (5), a party who desires to give in evidence at the trial or hearing of a cause or matter hearsay evidence shall

(a) in the case of a cause or matter which is required to be set down for trial or hearing or adjourned into Court, within 28 days after it is set down or so adjourned or within such other period as the Court may specify, and

(b) in any other case, within 28 days after the date on which an appointment for the first hearing of the cause or matter is obtained, or within such other period as the Court may specify,

serve a hearsay notice on every party to the cause or matter.

(5) Where witness statements are served under rule 2A of this Order, any hearsay notice served under this rule shall be served at the same time as the witness statements.

22. Power to call witness for cross-examination on hearsay evidence

(1) Where a party tenders as hearsay evidence a statement made by a person but does not propose to call the person who made the statement to give evidence, the court may, on application, allow another party to call and cross-examine the person who made the statement on its contents.

(2) An application under paragraph (1) shall be made on notice to all other parties not later than 28 days after service of the hearsay notice.

(3) Where the court allows another party to call and cross-examine the person who made the statement, it may give such directions as it thinks fit to secure the attendance of that person and as to the procedure to be followed.

23. Credibility

(1) If

(a) a party tenders as hearsay evidence a statement made by a person but does not call the person who made the statement to give oral evidence, and

(b) another party wishes to attack the credibility of the person who made the statement;

that other party shall notify the party tendering the hearsay evidence of his intention.

(2) A notice under paragraph (1) shall be given not later than 28 days after service of the hearsay notice.

The above rules correspond, respectively, with Ord 20, rr 15, 16 and 17 of the County Court Rules 1981.

See generally 'The Civil Evidence Act 1995' (1996) 160 *Justice of the Peace* 82; I Grainger, 'Hearsay Evidence Admissible' (1996) 140 *Solicitors Journal* 536; I Grainger, 'New Rules on Hearsay Notices' (1997) 141 *Solicitors Journal* 112; A Hogan, 'The Civil Evidence Act 1995' (1997) 147 *New Law Journal* 226; D O'Brien, 'The Rule against Hearsay RIP' (1996) 146 *New Law Journal* 153.

3. THE RULE AGAINST HEARSAY IN CRIMINAL PROCEEDINGS

In criminal proceedings, there is no wide-ranging legislation akin to the Civil Evidence Act 1995. Thus, the position in criminal trials is that hearsay evidence remains inadmissible, subject to the common law exceptions and to a number of specific statutory provisions.

(a) Applications of the rule

The extracts in this section provide some illustrations of the application of the hearsay rule in criminal proceedings. The first three extracts illustrate the principle that the rule applies only to out-of-court statements sought to be introduced in evidence to establish the truth of matters asserted in them.[11] Is, however, the determination of whether a statement is sought to be adduced in evidence to establish the truth of a matter asserted in it a straightforward one?

Extract 7.3.1

***Subramaniam v Public Prosecutor* [1956] 1 WLR 965, 970 (PC)**

Subramaniam was charged with being in possession of ammunition contrary to the Emergency Regulations 1951 of Malaya. He argued that he had been acting under duress, having been captured by terrorists, one of whom pointed a gun and said to him, 'I am a communist'. The trial judge, however, held that evidence of the conversation between Subramaniam and the terrorists was inadmissible as hearsay.

MR L M D DE SILVA: Evidence of a statement made to a witness by a person who is not himself called as a witness may or may not be hearsay. It is hearsay and inadmissible when the object of the evidence is to establish the truth of what is contained in the statement. It is not hearsay and is admissible when it is proposed to establish by the evidence, not the truth of the

---

[11] See generally G J Durston, 'Is it Hearsay?' (1996) 160 *Justice of the Peace* 535.

statement, but the fact that it was made. The fact that the statement was made, quite apart from its truth, is frequently relevant in considering the mental state and conduct thereafter of the witness or of some other person in whose presence the statement was made. In the case before their Lordships statements could have been made to the appellant by the terrorists, which, whether true or not, if they had been believed by the appellant, might reasonably have induced in him an apprehension of instant death if he failed to conform to their wishes.

Extract 7.3.2

Woodhouse v Hall (1980) 72 Cr App R 39, 42 (DC)

In order to prove that certain premises were being used as a brothel, the prosecution sought to adduce evidence of conversations between police officers and women employed at the premises concerning the availability and cost of sexual services.

DONALDSON LJ: I suspect that the justices were misled by *Subramaniam's* case . . . and thought that this was a hearsay case, because they may have thought that they had to be satisfied as to the truth of what the ladies said or were alleged to have said in the sense they had to satisfy themselves that the words were not a joke but were meant seriously and something of that sort. But this is not a matter of truth or falsity. It is a matter of what was really said – the quality of the words, the message being transmitted.

That arises in every case where the words themselves are a relevant fact. The quality of the words has to be assessed, but that is quite different from the situation where the words are evidence of some other matter. Then their truth and accuracy has to be assessed and they are hearsay.

There is no question here of the hearsay rule arising at all. The relevant issue was did these ladies make these offers? The offers were oral and the police officers were entitled to give evidence of them.

Extract 7.3.3

R v Lydon (1986) 85 Cr App R 221, 224–5 (CA)

At issue was the admissibility of evidence of two pieces of paper on which were written, in ink, 'Sean rules' and 'Sean rules 85'. These pieces of paper were found in the immediate vicinity of a gun which was alleged to have been used in a robbery. Similar ink to that on the pieces of paper was found on the gun.

WOOLF LJ: The reference to Sean could be regarded as no more than a statement of fact involving no assertion as to the truth of the contents of the document.

. . .

In dealing with the distinction between writing which is admissible and which is not admissible in these circumstances, *Cross on Evidence* (6th ed at p 464) states:

> 'In these cases it seems that the writing when properly admissible at all, is relevant not as an assertion of the state of facts but as itself a fact which affords circumstantial evidence upon the basis of which the jury may draw an inference as it may from any other relevant circumstance of the case.'

The inference that the jury could draw from the words written on the piece of paper is that the paper had been in the possession of someone who wished to write 'Sean rules,' and that person would presumably either be named Sean himself or at least be associated with such a person, and thus it creates an inferential link with the appellant. By itself it could not possibly satisfy the jury that the appellant was the other robber, but it could be circumstantial evidence which could help to satisfy the jury that the Crown's case was correct.

In effect, therefore, the hearsay rule was held to be inapplicable because what was written on the pieces of paper was not being adduced in evidence to prove that Sean ruled anything.

The hearsay rule has on occasion led courts to conclusions which they would rather not have reached:

Extract 7.3.4

R v McLean (1967) 52 Cr App R 80, 83–4 (CA)

The victim of an attack and robbery, Gomery, dictated a few minutes later to Cope the registration number of a car which had allegedly been involved in the attack. Cope wrote down the number but Gomery did not see what Cope wrote. (Had Gomery verified what Cope wrote, Gomery would presumably have been permitted at trial to refresh his memory from the note.) By the time of trial Gomery could no longer remember the number, of which Cope gave evidence.

EDMUND DAVIES LJ: With the utmost reluctance, which is shared by all three members of this Court, this appeal against conviction is allowed.

. . .

The crucial defect in this case arises in relation to the evidence given by Mr Cope, Mr Cope being called to say (in effect): 'I wrote down on a piece of paper – here is the paper – what Mr Gomery told me was the number of the car. It was HKB138D.' We confess that we have strained to find some means whereby the testimony of Mr Cope might be regarded as properly admitted in this case, for it is difficult to see that justice is done by its exclusion. But we are bound to apply the law as we find it, and by reference to such cases as *Jones v Metcalfe* [1967] 3 All ER 205. . . . it seems to us that for Mr Cope to be allowed to say that what he was told by Mr Gomery was that the car involved was HKB138D is a contravention of the hearsay rule when that remark is adduced as evidence that the car involved in the robbery was in fact HKB138D, and we so hold.

The hearsay rule applies to the defence as it does to the prosecution:

Extract 7.3.5

Sparks v R [1964] AC 964, 978 (PC)

Sparks, a white man, was accused of indecent assault on a child. The defence sought to call the victim's mother to give evidence that the victim (who was not called as a witness in the trial) had told her that 'it was a coloured boy'.

LORD MORRIS OF BORTH-Y-GEST: The mother would clearly be giving hearsay evidence if she were permitted to state what her girl had said to her. It becomes necessary, therefore, to examine the contentions which have been advanced in support of the admissibility of the evidence. It was said that 'it was manifestly unjust for the jury to be left throughout the whole trial with the impression that the child could not give any clue to the identity of her assailant.' The cause of justice is, however, best served by adherence to rules which have long been recognised and settled. If the girl had made a remark to her mother (not in the presence of the appellant) to the effect that it was the appellant who had assaulted her and if the girl was not to be a witness at the trial, evidence as to what she had said would be the merest hearsay. In such circumstances it would be the defence who would wish to challenge a contention, if advanced, that it would be 'manifestly unjust' for the jury not to know that the girl had given a clue to the identity of her assailant. If it is said that hearsay evidence should freely be admitted and that there should be concentration in any particular case upon deciding as to its value or weight it is sufficient to say that our law has not been evolved upon such lines but is firmly based upon the view that it is wiser and better that hearsay should be excluded save in certain well defined and rather exceptional circumstances.

Do you agree with Lord Morris that, because such evidence would be excluded if adduced by the prosecution, it must also be excluded where adduced by the defence? In the interests of protecting the innocent from conviction, should the defence be accorded more liberal rights than the prosecution to adduce hearsay evidence?

Hearsay statements can be used in evidence 'not for the purpose of establishing the truth of the assertions contained therein, but for the purpose of asking the jury to hold the assertions false and to draw inferences from their falsity'.[12]

---

[12] *Mawaz Khan v R* [1967] 1 AC 454, 462.

(b) Evasions of the rule

The cases discussed in this section provide illustrations of situations in which the implications of the hearsay rule have apparently either been simply over-looked, or been deliberately evaded in order to achieve a particular result.

See generally A Ashworth and R Pattenden, 'Reliability, Hearsay Evidence and the English Criminal Trial' (1986) 102 *Law Quarterly Review* 292; D J Birch, 'Hearsay-Logic and Hearsay-Fiddles: *Blastland* Revisited' in P Smith (ed), *Criminal Law: Essays in Honour of J C Smith* (1987).

(i) *The problem of* Rice

There has been much debate about the decision of the Court of Criminal Appeal in *R v Rice*.[13] This decision pre-dated *Myers v DPP* and was relied upon both in the decision of the Court of Criminal Appeal in *Myers* (which was later to be overturned by the House of Lords), as well as in Lord Pearce's dissenting speech in the House of Lords. The majority of the House of Lords, however, made no mention of the case. At issue in *Rice* was the admissibility in evidence of a used airline ticket which bore two names, Rice and Moore, to prove that either of them had taken particular flights. The ticket was produced by an airline representative whose duty was to deal with tickets returned after use. The Court of Criminal Appeal had

> no doubt that the ticket and the fact of the presence of that ticket in the file or other place where tickets used by passengers would in the ordinary course be found, were facts which were in logic relevant to the issue whether or not there flew on those flights two men either of whom was a Mr Rice or a Mr Moore. The relevance of that ticket in logic and its legal admissibility as a piece of real evidence both stem from the same root, viz, the balance of probability recognised by common sense and common knowledge that an air ticket which has been used on a flight and which has a name upon it has more likely than not been used by a man of that name or by one of two men whose names are upon it.[14]

The court emphasised that what was prohibited by the hearsay rule was the use of the air ticket to prove that the booking had been made by a person by the name of Rice: this would be a use of the ticket to prove the truth of the factual assertion that 'I was issued to Rice'. Instead, the court effectively treated the ticket as containing the factual assertion that 'I was used by Rice', and held that this did not infringe the hearsay rule. Yet why should this not infringe the hearsay rule when the court expressly recognised that the assertion 'I was issued to Rice' would do so?[15] *Rice* is probably most appropriately regarded as a case in which the hearsay rule was sidestepped, and which was impliedly overruled by the House of Lords in *Myers v DPP*.

[13] [1963] 1 QB 857.
[14] At 871.
[15] R Cross, 'The Periphery of Hearsay' (1969) 7 *Melbourne University Law Review* 1, 10; Law Commission (Consultation Paper No 138), *Criminal Law – Evidence in Criminal Proceedings: Hearsay and Related Topics – A Consultation Paper* (1995) 17.

(ii) Identification and photofit evidence

Extract 7.3.6

R v Osbourne [1973] QB 678, 690 (CA)

Osbourne and Virtue were picked out at an identification parade by Mrs Brookes and Mrs Head respectively. At the trial seven-and-a-half months later, Mrs Brookes said that she could not remember picking anyone out at a parade. Mrs Head first said that she thought that one of the accused was a man she had picked out at a parade, but later said that she did not think that the man she had picked out was in court. The police officer in charge of the parade was then called to give evidence of the out-of-court identifications.

LAWTON LJ: All that the prosecution were seeking to do was to establish the fact of identification at the identification parades held on November 20. This court can see no reason why that evidence should not have been admitted.

It is to be noted that there was no mention at all of the hearsay rule in this case. Is not the decision in this case inconsistent with that in *McLean*? Surely the evidence of the police officer in *Osbourne* is analogous to that of Cope in *McLean*, and should, if the orthodox approach taken in *McLean* had been applied, have been excluded as hearsay. Perhaps the best explanation of *Osbourne*, therefore, is that it effectively creates an exception to the hearsay rule in the case of identification evidence, in contravention of the decision of the House of Lords in *Myers*.

See generally D F Libling, 'Evidence of Past Identification' [1977] *Criminal Law Review* 268.

The evidential status of photofit evidence was clarified by the Court of Appeal in the following case:

Extract 7.3.7

R v Cook [1987] QB 417, 424–5 (CA)

A victim described her attacker to a police officer, who put together a photofit picture. The issue arose as to whether this picture was inadmissible in evidence as hearsay.

WATKINS LJ: There is no doubt that a photograph taken, for example, of a suspect during the commission of an offence is admissible. In a bigamy case, namely, *Reg v Tolson* (1864) 4 F & F 103, 104 Willes J said:

'The photograph was admissible because it is only a visible representation of the image or impression made upon the minds of the witnesses by the sight of the person or the object it represents; and, it therefore is, in reality, only another species of the evidence which persons give of identity, when they speak merely from memory.'

That ruling has never since been doubted and is applied with regularity to photographs, including those taken nowadays automatically in banks during a robbery. Such photographs are invaluable aids to identification of criminals. It has never been suggested of them that they are subject to the rule against hearsay.

We regard the production of the sketch or photofit by a police officer making a graphic representation of a witness's memory as another form of the camera at work, albeit imperfectly and not produced contemporaneously with the material incident but soon or fairly soon afterwards. As we perceive it the photofit is not a statement in writing made in the absence of a defendant or anything resembling it in the sense that this very old rule against hearsay has ever been expressed to embrace. It is we think sui generis, that is to say, the only one of its kind. It is a thing apart, the admissibility to evidence of which would not be in breach of the hearsay rule.

To draw an analogy between photofits and photographs is surely unconvincing. A photofit is based on out-of-court assertions of the victim, whereas a photograph is not based on out-of-court assertions but is rather a direct reproduction of events. To adduce photofit evidence is effectively to adduce in evidence the victim's out-of-court statements (made to the compiler of the photofit) to prove the truth of facts asserted in these statements.[16]

See also *R v Constantinou*.[17]

(iii) Confessions by third parties and co-defendants

In *R v Turner (Bryan James)*, the Court of Appeal stated that there did not exist

> any authority for the proposition advanced in this case that hearsay evidence is admissible in a criminal case to show that a third party who has not been called as a witness in the case has admitted committing the offence charged. The idea, which may be gaining prevalence in some quarters, that in a criminal trial the defence is entitled to adduce hearsay evidence to establish facts, which if proved would be relevant and would assist the defence, is wholly erroneous.[18]

This strict application of the hearsay rule has been affirmed in the House of Lords, Lord Bridge of Harwich remarking in *R v Blastland* that 'to admit in criminal trials statements confessing to the crime for which the defendant is being tried made by third parties not called as witnesses would be to create a very significant and, many might think, a dangerous new exception'.[19]

---

[16] See generally P B Carter, *Cases and Statutes on Evidence* (2nd ed 1990) 306–7; C Tapper, *Cross and Tapper on Evidence* (8th ed 1995) 590.
[17] (1989) 91 Cr App R 74.
[18] (1975) 61 Cr App R 67, 88 per Lawton LJ.
[19] [1986] AC 41, 52–3.

Evidence of confessions by a co-defendant, as opposed to a third party, was considered recently by the House of Lords in the following case:

Extract 7.3.8

R v Myers [1997] 3 WLR 552, 555–8, 560–4 (HL)

Myers appealed against her conviction on the basis that the trial judge had erred in permitting evidence of her confessions to be adduced by her co-accused. The appellant had been convicted of murder and her co-accused, Quartey, of manslaughter, after a trial in which each blamed the other for the killing. After being charged with murder, the appellant had allegedly made confessions to police officers which supported Quartey's version of events (and which, in fact, went a long way towards supporting his denial of murder). Because these confessions had been obtained by the police officers in breach of the Codes of Practice issued under the Police and Criminal Evidence Act 1984, the prosecution declined to adduce them in evidence. (As will be seen in Chapter 8, such breaches can lead to confession evidence, even if admissible under s 76(2) of the Police and Criminal Evidence Act 1984, being excluded in the discretion of the trial judge.)

The trial judge rejected an application for separate trials and permitted Quartey's counsel to adduce the confessions in evidence. Myers's appeal was dismissed by the Court of Appeal. The following question was certified for consideration by the House of Lords: 'In a joint trial of two defendants, A and B, is an out of court confession by A which exculpates B but which is ruled, or is conceded to be, inadmissible as evidence for the Crown nevertheless admissible at the instigation of B in support of B's defence, or does such a confession in all circumstances offend the rule against hearsay?'

LORD SLYNN OF HADLEY: In considering whether the statements should be admitted the judge found that there was a direct conflict between two Court of Appeal decisions *Reg v Campbell and Williams* [1993] Crim LR 448 and *Reg v Beckford and Daley* [1991] Crim LR 833. Following the course that he thought right, he ruled: 'a statement against interest by one party is provable against that party by another so long as both remain parties to the particular action.' The confessions were relevant to Quartey's case and, since sections 76 and 78 did not apply, there was no fetter on counsel for Quartey adducing this evidence 'either by way of cross-examination of the officers if they are called by the Crown or by calling them as part of his case.'

. . .

In *Reg v Beckford and Daley* three men were charged with murder. One of them, Correia, admitted in an interview with the police that he had stabbed a man near a door in a bar. His confession was not admitted by the judge because of a breach of the Code of Practice to which I have referred. Counsel for Daley applied to cross-examine the police witnesses about Correia's confession. Auld J ruled that this confession could only be introduced through cross-examination of Correia. To allow it through cross-examination of the police would breach the hearsay rule as stated in *Phipson on Evidence*, 14th ed (1990), p 557, para 21–02:

'Former statements of any person whether or not he is a witness in the proceedings, may not be given in evidence if the purpose is to tender them as evidence of the truth of the matters asserted in them. The rule at common law applies strictly to all classes of proceedings, and there is no special dispensation for the defendant in a criminal case.'

Auld J with whom the Court of Appeal, in a judgment given by Watkins LJ agreed, said:

'[Counsel for Daley's] application, to succeed as to relevance, must be that the statement made by Correia to the police officer is not only adverse to Correia but favourable to Daley but the exception to the hearsay rule does not permit the admission of confessions of one person in relation to the case against another, whether they are for or against that other.'

He could not create a new exception to the hearsay rule to cover that case since on the basis of *Myers v Director of Public Prosecutions* [1965] AC 1001 and *Reg v Blastland* [1986] AC 41 the category of exceptions to the hearsay rule is now closed and could only be extended by the legislature.

He further ruled that section 76 of the Act of 1984 applied only as between the prosecution and the defendant whose confession was sought to be given against him and added:

'In my view section 76 does not touch the general rule of which the cases of *Turner* and *Blastland* are examples and that the same principle applies whether or not the statement of confession sought to be adduced is made by a third party to the proceedings or by a co-defendant.'

It is, however, not without interest that the Court of Appeal felt that had Correia's confession been admitted, the jury might have taken a different view as to the cogency of evidence that it was Daley and not Correia who had struck the fatal blow and convicted Correia, acquitting Daley. They said 'As we have said, the hearsay rule, sound though it is when usually applied is capable sometimes of obscuring − shielding even − the truth. It may have done so here.' In the result, although the court held that the judge was right not to allow Correia's confession to be introduced through cross-examination of the police witnesses, the conviction of both men was quashed.

In *Reg v Campbell and Williams* [1993] Crim LR 448 one of three defendants ('A') had recorded a conversation which clearly implicated him and another defendant ('B') but which supported the defence of a third defendant ('C'). The prosecution had not known of this evidence but did not object to the evidence being given on behalf of C. A and B objected on the ground that this was inadmissible evidence though no suggestion was made that it would have been excluded under the Act of 1984 if the prosecution had sought to adduce it. The trial judge ruled that the evidence could be led; it was a confession admissible against A and its admission did not adversely affect the fairness of the trial. A in evidence adopted what he had said in the tape. The jury was told that the taped conversation was not evidence against B.

On appeal A and B contended that the judge was wrong to admit the evidence of the tape and that this was a material irregularity in the trial. The Court of Appeal, in a judgment given by Hobhouse J, rejected these contentions and dismissed the appeal. Hobhouse J distinguished (a) 'straightforward hearsay statements' which are not admissible unless falling within one of the recognised exceptions when they become evidence for all purposes; (b) previous inconsistent statements admissible to challenge a witness and usable only to discredit him and (c) a confession only admissible against the party who made it and then subject to special safeguards in criminal cases.

He distinguished the decision in *Reg v Beckford and Daley* from *Reg v Campbell and Williams* on the basis that the former was a case where the confession of one defendant had been ruled inadmissible under the Act of 1984 so that another defendant could not get it in as part of his cross-examination of a police witness. In *Reg v Campbell and Williams* on the other hand the question raised was as to 'whether it is permissible for a defendant to adduce confession evidence against a co-defendant when the prosecution has not adduced that evidence, although there would have been no objection to its doing so.' Recognising the conflicts which can arise in a joint trial he said:

'Thus it is commonplace that in criminal trials one defendant's interest may be that the prosecution's case against a co-defendant should be strengthened and should succeed. A defendant is therefore entitled to lead admissible evidence which is relevant to the proof of the case against the co-defendant if in so doing the defendant is advancing his own case.

[To say] that the proof against one defendant that he has confessed to the crime with which a co-defendant is also charged is not relevant to the case of the co-defendant in the same trial, that would, in our judgment, be contrary both to common sense and to the cases we have earlier referred to.'

The problem in *Reg v Beckford and Daley* was not relevance; it was that evidence of the confession had already been ruled inadmissible as against Correia and therefore it could only be put in evidence at the trial if it was admissible on some other basis. As the judge and the Court of Appeal held, it was not, 'it is implicit in the decision in *Beckford* that a co-defendant cannot be in a better position than the prosecution in relation to the proof of an inadmissible confession.' He went on:

'[the *Beckford* case] is clearly distinguishable on the ground that the confession was not admissible as a confession and the question raised was whether the appellant could independently adduce the out-of-court statement. Here the question is whether the proof of a confession which was admissible against the appellant was a material irregularity in the trial of the appellant because the evidence by which it was proved was led by a co-defendant not the prosecution. Accordingly we consider that the decision in *Beckford* does not preclude us from reaching a conclusion in the present case that admission of the confession did not amount to an irregularity during the trial material to the conviction of either appellant.'

The situations in the *Beckford* and *Campbell* cases were, I agree, different. The *Beckford* case was concerned with the admissibility of a confession which the prosecution could not put in because of breaches of the police

Code of Practice whereas in the *Campbell* case there was no suggestion of any such breach, the issue being whether there was some other irregularity in the trial because of the admission of the tape which it was sought to put in as a confession by one defendant to be used against and only against that defendant.

Yet it seems to me, as it did to the Court of Appeal in the present case, that on the issue crucial to the present case the two decisions of the Court of Appeal are in conflict. In the *Beckford* case Auld J and the Court of Appeal rejected the submission that in a joint trial a defendant could rely on another defendant's confession to support his own case albeit it was not evidence against the maker of the statement. In the *Campbell* case the Court of Appeal held the statement of one defendant to be admissible as a confession furthering the case of the co-defendant. In both cases the evidence was clearly relevant.

Since the specific grounds of exclusion of a confession in section 76(2) of the Act of 1984 relate to confessions which the prosecution proposes to put in evidence that section does not apply to the present case where it is the co-accused seeking to put in the confession. Section 78 of the Act of 1984 provides for the exclusion of 'evidence on which the prosecution proposes to rely' where the judge thinks that the admission of the evidence would lead to unfairness. That again does not apply to the present case.

It is therefore necessary to consider whether other authorities indicate that the decision in *Reg v Campbell and Williams* or that in *Reg v Beckford and Daley* is the one which ought to be followed.

. . .

In [*R v Turner (Bryan James)* and *R v Blastland*] it was the statement of a third party which was held to be inadmissible. These are clearly hearsay. On the other hand there are decisions where it has been held that one defendant is entitled to cross-examine a co-defendant as to the latter's confession which is inconsistent with his evidence at the trial.

Thus in *Reg v Miller* [1952] 2 All ER 667 where counsel for one alleged conspirator to import goods unlawfully sought to ask a prosecution witness whether another conspirator was not in prison at a time when no illegal importations took place, Devlin J, said that questions as to previous character and convictions were not normally admissible 'not primarily for the reason that they are prejudicial, but because they are irrelevant.' The judge may exclude questions of that sort if the prosecution seeks to ask them even if they are relevant in circumstances where the prejudice outweighs the relevance. Devlin J added however, at p 669:

'No such limitation applies to a question asked by counsel for the defence. His duty is to adduce any evidence which is relevant to his own case and assists his client, whether or not it prejudices anyone else.'

A similar principle was stated in *Reg v Bracewell* (1978) 68 Cr App R 44 where Ormrod LJ giving the judgment of the Court of Appeal said, at p 50:

'The problem generally arises in connection with evidence tendered by the Crown, so that marginal cases can be dealt with by the exercise of discretion. "When in doubt, exclude," is a good working rule in such cases. But when the evidence is tendered by a co-accused, the test of relevance must be applied, and applied strictly, for if irrelevant, and therefore inadmissible evidence is admitted, the other accused is likely to be seriously prejudiced, and grave injustice may result.'

On the basis of this decision it seems that relevance is the appropriate test even if the admission of relevant evidence at the suit of one defendant will cause prejudice to the other accused.

To similar effect is a statement in *Lowery v The Queen* [1974] AC 85 in the Privy Council. In that case evidence by a psychiatrist of one defendant's aggressiveness was admitted to rebut his statement that he was not the sort of person who would have committed the murder. It was evidence which could be relied on by the co-accused to show that his version of the facts was more probable than that of the other. Lord Morris of Borth-y-Gest approved a statement in the judgment of the Supreme Court of Victoria from which the appeal came, to the following effect, at p 102:

'It is, however, established by the highest authority that in criminal cases the Crown is precluded from leading evidence that does no more than show that the accused has a disposition or propensity or is the sort of person likely to commit the crime charged . . . It is, we think, one thing to say such evidence is excluded when tendered by the Crown in proof of guilt, but quite another to say it is excluded when tendered by the accused in disproof of his own guilt. We see no reason of policy or fairness which justifies or requires the exclusion of evidence relevant to prove the innocence of an accused person.'

See also *Reg v Reid* [1989] Crim LR 719 where it was held that it was proper for one co-defendant to seek to undermine the appellant's defence in so far as that consisted in blaming the co-defendant.

An analogous point arose in *Murdoch v Taylor* [1965] AC 574 in relation to section 1(*f*)(iii) of the Criminal Evidence Act 1898 which provides that a person charged with an offence, and giving evidence on his own behalf, may not be asked questions tending to show that he has committed or been convicted of or charged with some other offence unless 'he has given evidence against any other person charged with the same offence.' If the prosecution sought to avail themselves of the proviso then the judge had a discretion as to whether in the interests of a fair trial the prosecution should be allowed to cross-examine as to character or previous convictions.

'But when it is the co-accused who seeks to exercise the right conferred by proviso (*f*)(iii) different considerations come into play. He seeks to defend himself; to say to the jury that the man who is giving evidence against him is unworthy of belief; and to support that assertion by proof of bad character. The right to do this cannot in my opinion, be fettered in any way:' *per* Lord Donovan, at p 593, with whom Lord Reid and Lord Evershed agreed.

Lord Donovan's speech was relied on by the Court of Appeal in *Reg v Rowson* [1986] QB 174 although the case was not concerned with section 1(*f*) of the Act of 1898. There three men were charged with assault causing grievous bodily harm with intent. The Court of Appeal in a judgment delivered by Robert Goff LJ held, at p 180, that one defendant (Keating) who had made a previous inconsistent statement that he had had a piece of wood with which he had hit the person injured could be cross-examined as to that statement by the other defendants. This was a matter, it was said, which was material to the defence of the two Rowsons because:

'since there was an issue whether the injury to Williamson was caused by a blow from the piece of wood, it was relevant for the Rowsons to establish that at no time did any of them have the piece of wood in his possession. That being so, we know of no principle of law which justified the judge in limiting the cross-examination by [Rowsons' counsel] on this matter, thereby inhibiting two of the defendants in pursuing it as part of their defence.'

The court distinguished *Rex v Treacy* [1944] 2 All ER 229 and *Reg v Rice* [1963] 1 QB 857 as being cases where the prosecution was not allowed to cross-examine on the basis of a statement which had been ruled, or conceded, to be inadmissible against the accused person because it was involuntary or obtained in breach of the judges' rules.

The judgment in *Rowson* was approved by the Privy Council in *Lui Mei Lin v The Queen* [1989] AC 288 and found to be consistent with the principles annunciated in *Murdoch v Taylor* [1965] AC 574 and *Reg v Miller* [1952] 2 All ER 667. In *Lui Mei Lin v The Queen* a defendant was not allowed to cross-examine a co-defendant on a statement incriminating the defendant which the judge had ruled inadmissible as part of the prosecution case because it was not made voluntarily. Having referred to section 5 of the Criminal Procedure Act 1865, the Privy Council in the opinion of Lord Roskill said, at p 297:

'The only limit on the right of a co-accused to cross-examine another co-accused in these circumstances is, in their Lordships' opinion, relevancy. If one co-accused has given evidence incriminating another it must be relevant for the latter to show, if he can, that the former has on some other occasion given inconsistent evidence and thus is unworthy of belief.'

He stressed, at p 298, however, that the judge must warn the jury:

'that they must not use the statement in any way as evidence in support of the prosecution's case and that its only relevance is to test the credibility of the evidence which the maker of the statement has given against his co-accused.'

It is to be noted that in *Perrie v HM Advocate*, 1991 JC 27 the Court of Session in the opinion given by the Lord Justice-Clerk, Lord Ross, accepted the view of Lord Bridge in *Reg v Blastland* [1986] AC 41, 53 that a statement by a third party not called as a witness could not be admitted, but considered that an exception to the hearsay rule existed for statements by an accused person, at p 31:

'This exception is allowed because an accused is a party to proceedings and an admission is a statement against interest, and is thus more likely to be true than false. . . . An accused is a party to proceedings in a way in which an incriminee is not; he is entitled to the full protection which the law gives to accused persons.'

That opinion however has to be read subject to the view of the Court of Session that, contrary to what was said in *Reg v Turner*, 61 Cr App R 67 and in *Reg v Blastland* [1986] AC 41, in the law of Scotland the categories of hearsay evidence are not closed.

It is, however, clear that in the cases referred to a distinction has been drawn between statements by parties to the proceedings and by third parties, the former, if relevant and voluntary, being admissible the latter not being admissible.

On the other hand it is to be noted that in 'Evidence in Criminal Proceedings: Hearsay and Related Topics,' Law Commission consultation paper No 138 (1995), at para 7.44 it is stated:

'The fact that someone else has confessed to the offence is logically relevant to the issue of whether the defendant committed it or not: this is so whether the other person is a co-defendant who gives evidence, a co-defendant who exercises his right not to give evidence, a co-defendant who is tried separately, or a person who is never caught or never prosecuted.'

It seems to me that there is force in that comment despite Lord Bridge's anxiety that if confessions by third parties were admitted it would only be too easy for fabricated confessions to produce unjustified acquittals. Accepting Lord Bridge's view in *Reg v Blastland* that statements by third persons are not admissible there is a long line of authority showing that a defendant must be allowed to cross-examine a co-defendant as to a previous inconsistent confession so long as the material is relevant to the defendant's own defence. In my opinion a defendant should also be allowed to put a co-defendant's confession to witnesses to whom the confession was made so long as the confession is relevant to the defendant's defence and so long as it appears that the confession was not obtained in a manner which would have made it inadmissible at the instance of the Crown under section 76(2) of the Act of 1984. There may be doubt as to whether the co-defendant will be called (so that it may not be possible to put the confession to the co-defendant directly) and not to allow the defendant to introduce it by way of cross-examination of prosecution witnesses could lead to great unfairness.

This seems to me to be consistent with the opinion of the Privy Council in *Lobban v The Queen* [1995] 1 WLR 877, 888–889. There it was said, at p 889:

'The principled objection to the discretion envisaged by counsel' – ie of the judge at the request of one defendant to exclude evidence tending to support the defence of another defendant – 'is that it conflicts with a defendant's absolute right, subject to considerations of relevance, to deploy his case asserting his evidence as he thinks fit.'

This seems to me the position whether or not the judge and the Court of Appeal in *Reg v Beckford and Daley* [1991] Crim LR 833 were right to hold that section 76(1) of the Act of 1984 only applies to evidence which the prosecution seeks to adduce, a question which is still subject to debate and on which it is not necessary to rule in this case, particularly since the Law Commission has recommended that 'the admissibility of a confession by one co-accused at the instance of another should be governed by provisions similar to section 76 of the Police and Criminal Evidence Act, but taking into account the standard of proof applicable to a defendant.' (Recommendation 19 of the 'Evidence in Criminal Proceedings: Hearsay and Related Topics,' Law Com No 245) (1997) (Cm 3670.)

In *Reg v Rowson* [1986] QB 174, 180E, the evidence was said to be relevant 'in the sense that it went to the credibility to be attached to evidence given by Keating on a material issue' and in *Lui Mei Lin v The Queen* [1989] AC 288, 298D–E, it was said that the judge should warn the jury 'that its only relevance is to test the credibility of the evidence which the maker of the statement has given against his co-accused.' The previous statement by Keating in *Reg v Rowson* was, however, regarded as not only relevant to Keating's credibility but it was also material to the Rowsons' defence that they did not at any time have any wood in their possession.

A confession may be relevant both as to credibility and as to the facts in issue and it does not cease to be admissible because it does so. Indeed so long as it is relevant to establish his defence or to undermine the prosecution case against him a defendant should in my view be allowed to cross-examine a co-defendant as to his confession which goes to the facts in issue rather than only to the credibility of the maker of the statement. He should not less be allowed to cross-examine the person to whom a statement is made as to the terms of the confession even though, since the defendant has not given evidence, the question of credibility has not arisen.

In *Reg v Rowson* and *Lui Mei Lin v The Queen* the Court of Appeal and the Privy Council respectively stressed that the judge must tell the jury that weight should not be placed on such statement in considering the prosecution case against the maker of the statement; it was considered that the jury would be able to understand the difference and give effect to the judge's direction. On the other hand for a jury to make this distinction may not always be easy as has been fully recognised by the trial judge in the present case, by Lord Lane CJ in *Reg v O'Boyle* (1990) 92 Cr App R 202 and by academic commentators. But even allowing for a risk of prejudice to the maker of the statement in the mind of the jury, the authorities to which reference has been made make it plain that a defendant must be allowed to cross-examine a co-defendant as to, and in appropriate circumstances to introduce, relevant evidence of a previous confession made by the co-defendant.

In the present case Myers's previous confessions to the police officers were relevant to the question whether her assertion that it was Quartey who had murdered the cab driver was to be believed and therefore was clearly relevant to Quartey's defence that it was not he who had killed. It was obviously either one or the other who had killed the driver and justice required that Quartey should be allowed to bring out the earlier confession in his defence as casting doubt on Myers's denial. For Myers to deny the confession in evidence would have allowed the police officers to be called by Quartey pursuant to section 4 of Lord Denman's Act. It seems to me that it was also relevant and admissible for the police officers who were not called, but were tendered, by the prosecution to be asked about the confession on behalf of Quartey. It was not suggested that the confessions were obtained in the circumstances referred to in section 76(2) of the Act of 1984, and the fact that the prosecution was not able to introduce the evidence because of breaches of the police Code did not preclude Quartey's counsel from doing so.

The question certified goes much wider than the facts of the present case and it is neither necessary not desirable to answer it further than in the present context.

Myers's appeal should accordingly be dismissed.

The reasoning of the House of Lords would appear, therefore, to be as follows. It is a well-established principle that a defendant may, with a view to discrediting a co-defendant's testimony, cross-examine him on a previous inconsistent confession. In the light of this, there is no reason why a defendant should not also be entitled to introduce a co-defendant's confession in evidence *for its truth*, by way of cross-examination either of the co-defendant himself or of prosecution witnesses to whom the confession was made. A confession may be utilised in this way only if it would be admissible in evidence for the prosecution under s 76(2). The fact that, though technically admissible, the confession evidence may be liable to exclusion in the exercise of discretion (for example, because of breaches of the Codes of Practice) is immaterial. It is clear that, in reaching its conclusion, the House of Lords was heavily influenced by the importance of giving defendants an adequate opportunity to present a defence. Be that as it may, it is difficult to avoid the impression that the House of Lords was endorsing an entirely new exception to the hearsay rule which had effectively been created by the Court of Appeal in *Campbell*, in complete contravention of the principle that new exceptions may be created only by Parliament. Furthermore, to treat evidence of a third-party confession as inadmissible whatever the circumstances, while treating evidence of a confession by a co-accused as admissible so long as the test in s 76(2) is satisfied, is anomalous. Underlying both categories of cases, surely, is the same fundamental consideration: that the law should enable accused persons to defend themselves adequately, in the interests of protecting the innocent from wrongful conviction. It is noteworthy that had Myers and Quartey been tried in separate trials, evidence of Myers's confessions would have been inadmissible at the behest of Quartey.

See generally, on the decision of the Court of Appeal in this case, A L-T Choo, 'The Hearsay Rule and Confessions Relied upon by the Defence: *R v Myers*' (1997) 1(3) *International Journal of Evidence and Proof* 158.

(iv) Further illustrations

Further possible examples of situations in which the hearsay rule has been either evaded or overlooked are provided by:

(1) The principle that, if the inculpatory part of a mixed statement is admissible in evidence as a confession, the exculpatory part will also be admissible as evidence of the matters asserted in it (see Chapter 8).

(2) The principle that an expert witness may draw upon the work of others in reaching his or her conclusion (see Chapter 11).

(c) Implied assertions

The hearsay rule applies to express assertions made orally or in writing. Equally, the rule applies to express assertions made by conduct.[20] However, where there has been no express assertion of a particular matter (either by words or by conduct), but where it is possible to *infer* an assertion of that matter from words or conduct, is evidence of the words or conduct inadmissible under the hearsay rule to establish the relevant matter in the same way that it would be had the assertion been express?

Extract 7.3.9

R v Kearley [1992] 2 AC 228, 245–7, 251, 238, 242 (HL)

The following point of law of general public importance was certified for consideration by the House of Lords: 'Whether evidence may be adduced at a trial of words spoken (namely a request for drugs to be supplied by the defendant), not spoken in the presence or hearing of the defendant, by a person not called as a witness, for the purpose not of establishing the truth of any fact narrated by the words, but of inviting the jury to draw an inference from the fact that the words were spoken (namely that the defendant was a supplier of drugs).'

The House of Lords split 3:2, with Lord Bridge of Harwich, Lord Ackner and Lord Oliver of Aylmerton answering the question in the negative, and Lords Griffiths and Browne-Wilkinson answering it in the affirmative. The following are extracts from the speeches of Lords Bridge and Griffiths.

LORD BRIDGE OF HARWICH: ... evidence of words spoken by a person not called as a witness which are said to assert a relevant fact by necessary implication are inadmissible as hearsay just as evidence of an express statement made by the speaker asserting the same fact would be.

...

... words spoken involving an implied assertion of a relevant fact, certainly if they are not otherwise relevant, are excluded by the hearsay rule unless they can be brought within some established exception to the rule. . . .

... here the mere fact of the calls being made to the defendant's house was by itself of no relevance whatever, so we are back to the bare issue as to whether the implied assertion involved in the request for drugs should be excluded as hearsay. As English law presently stands, I am clearly of the opinion that it should.

The next question is whether, if evidence from a police officer that he heard one person, in the absence of the defendant, requesting a supply of drugs from the defendant is inadmissible to prove the defendant's intent to supply on the ground that it is hearsay, the evidence becomes admissible if the

---

[20] *Chandrasekera v R* [1937] AC 220.

prosecution are in a position to tender evidence relating to a plurality of such requests made at the same place and on the same day. I know of no principle which can be applied to render evidence of many such requests admissible, if the evidence of each one, considered separately, would not be. Of course I appreciate the probative force of a plurality of requests. But the probative force of hearsay evidence in particular circumstances has never afforded a ground for disregarding the hearsay rule, as *Myers v Director of Public Prosecutions* [1965] AC 1001 . . . amply demonstrates. I have never heard it suggested that a plurality of statements by persons who could not be called as witnesses, all known to be persons of the highest integrity and all describing the crime they witnessed in similar terms, afforded such overwhelming proof of the truth of the facts stated that this would be a ground for admitting the statements in evidence.

. . .

. . . However strong the temptation to legislate judicially in favour of what is seen as a 'common sense' result and however tardy Parliament may appear to be in reforming an area of the law which is seen to be in need of radical reform, the uncertainty and confusion to which well intentioned attempts at judicial legislation can lead have been clearly demonstrated by recent decisions of your Lordships' House. The operation of the hearsay rule in modern conditions is in many respects unsatisfactory. But Lord Reid's warning that in this field of the law a judicial 'policy of make do and mend is no longer adequate' is as true today as it was in 1964. However long overdue we may feel an overhaul of the hearsay rule in criminal cases to be, we should not be deluded into thinking that we can achieve it piecemeal.

LORD GRIFFITHS: It is of course true that it is almost certain that the customers did believe that they could obtain drugs from the appellant, otherwise they would not have telephoned or visited his premises. But why did all these people believe they could obtain drugs from the appellant? The obvious inference is that the appellant had established a market as a drug dealer by supplying or offering to supply drugs and was thus attracting customers. There are of course other possible explanations such as a mistaken belief or even a deliberate attempt to frame the appellant, but there are very few factual situations from which different inferences cannot be drawn and it is for the jury to decide which inference they believe they can safely draw.

The evidence is offered not for the purpose of inviting the jury to draw the inference that the customers believed they could obtain drugs but to prove as a fact that the telephone callers and visitors were acting as customers or potential customers which was a circumstance from which the jury could if so minded draw the inference that the appellant was trading as a drug dealer; or to put it in the language of the indictment that he was in possession of drugs with intent to supply them to others.

. . .

I would be prepared to answer the certified question in the affirmative. It is true that the question as drafted refers to only one customer and the strength of the evidence lies in the fact that there were so many customers. But in order to be able to establish so many customers as to constitute a market in the drugs created by the dealer it is necessary to introduce evidence of the number of individual customers which collectively can be regarded as a market. If the evidence of each individual customer is held to be inadmissible it is obviously impossible ever to give evidence of a market. If there had been only one or two calls made to the premises offering to buy drugs they would carry little weight; they might be the result of mistake or even malice, but as the number of calls increases so these possibilities recede till the point is reached when any man of sense will be confident that any inference other than that the accused was a dealer can be safely rejected. A judge always has power to refuse to admit any evidence whose prejudicial value outweighs its probative value and if in the circumstances of this case it had been wished to adduce no more than one or possibly two calls I feel confident that a judge would have exercised his discretion to exclude such evidence.

The following case was approved by the House of Lords in *Kearley*:

Extract 7.3.10

Wright v Doe d Tatham (1837) 7 Ad & E 313, 388–9; 112 ER 488, 516–17 (Exchequer Chamber)

On the issue of whether one Marsden had testamentary capacity, the question arose as to whether three old letters to him, written in such a manner as to suggest that the writers (who were long dead) believed that they were dealing with a person of reasonable understanding, were admissible in evidence to prove competency.

PARKE B: Many other instances of a similar nature, by way of illustration, were suggested by the learned counsel for the defendant in error, which, on the most cursory consideration, any one would at once declare to be inadmissible in evidence. Others were supposed on the part of the plaintiff in error, which, at first sight, have the appearance of being mere facts, and therefore admissible, though on further consideration they are open to precisely the same objection. Of the first description are the supposed cases of a letter by a third person to any one demanding a debt, which may be said to be a treatment of him as a debtor, being offered as proof that the debt was really due; a note, congratulating him on his high state of bodily vigour, being proposed as evidence of his being in good health; both of which are manifestly at first sight objectionable. To the latter class belong the supposed conduct of the family or relations of a testator, taking the same precautions in his absence as if he were a lunatic; his election, in his absence, to some high and responsible office; the conduct of a physician who permitted a will to be executed by a sick testator; the conduct of a deceased captain on a question of seaworthiness, who, after examining every part of the vessel, embarked in it with his family; all these, when deliberately considered, are, with reference to the matter in issue in each case, mere instances of hearsay evidence, mere statements, not on oath, but implied in or vouched by the actual conduct of persons by whose acts the litigant parties are not to be bound.

The conclusion at which I have arrived is, that proof of a particular fact, which is not of itself a matter in issue, but which is relevant only as implying a statement or opinion of a third person on the matter in issue, is inadmissible in all cases where such a statement or opinion not on oath would be of itself inadmissible; and, therefore, in this case the letters which are offered only to prove the competence of the testator, that is the truth of the implied statements therein contained, were properly rejected, as the mere statement or opinion of the writer would certainly have been inadmissible.

It has been persuasively argued that to regard implied assertions inferred from *conduct* as automatically being subject to the hearsay rule is particularly problematic, since it is potentially possible for countless assertions to be inferred from a piece of conduct. Thus, in the absence of guidance as to where the line should be drawn, *all* evidence of out-of-court conduct will constitute hearsay.[21]

The Law Commission has recommended that the hearsay rule apply only where it appears that one of the purposes of the maker of the statement was to cause another person to believe the matter stated, or to cause another person to act or a machine to operate on the basis that the matter is as stated.[22] In a similar vein, s 59(1) of the Australian Evidence Act 1995 and rule 801(a) of the US Federal Rules of Evidence take the approach of including only intended assertions within the definition of hearsay.[23] A clear-cut application of rule 801(a), in factual circumstances similar to those of *Kearley*, is to be found in the decision of the US Federal Court of Appeals for the District of Columbia Circuit in *US v Long*.[24] The defendant appealed against his conviction of drug offences on the basis, inter alia, that evidence about a telephone call received at the apartment of his co-defendant, Mayfield, while arrests were being made, was hearsay and therefore incorrectly admitted. The evidence related to the fact that an unidentified caller had asked to speak to the defendant, and whether the defendant 'still had any stuff'. When asked what she meant, the caller replied 'a fifty', this apparently being a reference to a bag of crack worth $50. The caller then asked whether someone could come round to collect the 'fifty'. The defendant's contention was that the evidence should have been excluded because, although the caller had not expressly asserted that the defendant was involved in drug distribution, she had, through her questions, impliedly asserted that the defendant 'has crack and sells it out of Mayfield's apartment'. In England, this is, of course, precisely the argument that would have been accepted, on the basis

---

[21] A Rein, 'The Scope of Hearsay' (1994) 110 *Law Quarterly Review* 431, 437; J R Spencer, 'Hearsay, Relevance and Implied Assertions' [1993] *Cambridge Law Journal* 40, 41.

[22] Law Commission (Law Com No 245), *Evidence in Criminal Proceedings: Hearsay and Related Topics* (1997) 90.

[23] See the criticisms by D Ormerod, 'Reform of Implied Assertions' (1996) 60 *Journal of Criminal Law* 201. See also Symposium on Hearsay and Implied Assertions: How Would (or Should) the Supreme Court Decide the *Kearley* Case? (1995) 16 *Mississippi College Law Review* 1.

[24] 905 F 2d 1572 (DC Cir 1990).

of *Kearley*. However, the court in *Long*, applying rule 801(a), held that the evidence in question did not constitute hearsay, since the defendant had not produced any evidence to suggest that the caller had intended to assert that the defendant was involved in drug dealing 'The caller may indeed have conveyed messages about Long through her questions, but any such messages were merely incidental and not intentional.'[25]

The rationale for such an approach was explained succinctly by the court in *Long*:

> One of the principal goals of the hearsay rule is to exclude declarations when their veracity cannot be tested through cross-examination. When a declarant does not intend to communicate anything, however, his sincerity is not in question and the need for cross-examination is sharply diminished. Thus, an unintentional message is presumptively more reliable.[26]

In other words, absence of intent to assert or communicate the fact that is sought to be established is considered to negate the danger of insincerity.

This approach may be subjected to criticism. First, it may be argued that to focus on one hearsay danger, insincerity, to the exclusion of the dangers of faulty perception, erroneous memory, and lack of clarity in narration, is unduly narrow. Secondly, difficulties are likely to be encountered in determining whether the declarant intended to assert or communicate the fact in question. What courts may effectively be forced to do in determining the issue is to apply objective tests. Milich has argued, for example, that because the rationale of the 'intent' test is to identify situations where it seems unlikely that the statement or conduct was being used to lie about the fact in question, the determination of 'intent' should be made with this in mind. Thus Milich argues that what should be determined is whether the statement or conduct was a good choice for a person who intended to lie about the implied proposition in question. If so, then he or she will be deemed to have intended to assert that proposition.[27] Another objective test is propounded by Schaitkin:

> Intent to communicate exists when a reasonable person in the position of the actor at the time and place under consideration would intend his conduct to be communicative. A subjective standard, based on the actual intent of the actor, seems unworkable since the primary source of establishing that intent, the testimony of the actor, is unavailable.[28]

---

[25] At 1580. See also *US v Zenni* 492 F Supp 464 (ED Ky 1980); *US v Giraldo* 822 F 2d 205 (2nd Cir 1987).

[26] 905 F 2d 1572, 1580 (DC Cir 1990).

[27] P S Milich, 'Re-Examining Hearsay under the Federal Rules: Some Method for the Madness' (1991) 39 *University of Kansas Law Review* 893, 909 ff.

[28] K A Schaitkin, '"Negative Hearsay" – The Sounds of Silence' (1980) 84 *Dickinson Law Review* 605, 612. See also P S Milich, 'Hearsay Antinomies: The Case for Abolishing the Rule and Starting Over' (1992) 71 *Oregon Law Review* 723, 729; D E Seidelson, 'Implied Assertions and Federal Rule of Evidence 801: A Quandary for Federal Courts' (1986) 24 *Duquesne Law Review* 741, 761 ff. See the criticisms of such an objective approach in O G Wellborn III, 'The Definition of Hearsay in the Federal Rules of Evidence' (1982) 61 *Texas Law Review* 49, 76–7.

Ultimately, therefore, 'intent' (or 'purpose') becomes a fiction and a mere tool in what is essentially an objective test. But if what one should be concerned with is 'objectively manifested intent'[29] rather than actual intent, there seems little point in pretending that one is trying to determine the latter. If the rationale of the 'intent' test is to expose insincerity, perhaps the preferable approach would be simply to focus squarely upon the issue of whether the danger of insincerity in the particular case is sufficiently grave to justify withholding the evidence from the jury, than to use the (fictional) vehicle of 'intent'. And if we are isolating insincerity as a hearsay danger deserving of such treatment, should we not, for the sake of consistency, subject all hearsay dangers to the same type of analysis?

(d) Common law exceptions to the rule

Following is an examination of a number of common law exceptions to the hearsay rule which are likely to be of relevance to criminal trials.

(i) *Statements of deceased persons*

This category of exceptions concerns statements made by a person now deceased.

DECLARATIONS AGAINST PECUNIARY OR
PROPRIETARY INTEREST

Extract 7.3.11

R v Rogers (1994) 158 JPR 909, 913–14 (CA)

STUART SMITH LJ: In order for the exception to apply, four conditions have to be satisfied. First of all, that the deceased must have had a peculiar means of knowing the facts stated in the declaration. . . . Secondly, the interest against which his declaration is made must be either proprietary or pecuniary. In the *Sussex Peerage* case (1844) 11 Cl & Finley 85, 105, Lord Brougham said this:

> 'The law in *Higham v Ridgway* (1808) 10 East 109 has been carried far enough, although not too far. The rule, as understood now, is that the only declarations of deceased persons receivable in evidence, are those made against the proprietary or pecuniary interests of the party making them, when the subject-matter of such declarations is within the peculiar knowledge of the party so making them.'

---

[29] E W Cleary (ed), *McCormick on Evidence* (3rd ed 1984) 732 n 2.

Thirdly, it must be against the interest of the deceased at the time that the statement was made, in other words, it must be a present obligation and not one arising in the future. Fourthly, the declarant must know that the declaration is against his interests.

The non-applicability of this exception to declarations against penal interest means that a confession of guilt by a person who is now deceased is effectively unable to be adduced in evidence on behalf of a defendant as a declaration against interest. This principle was colourfully described by Wigmore as 'a barbarous doctrine, which would refuse to let an innocent accused vindicate himself even by producing to the tribunal a perfectly authenticated written confession, made on the very gallows, by the true culprit now beyond the reach of justice'.[30] Thus, the Canadian Supreme Court has taken the view that the limitation of the exception to declarations against pecuniary or proprietary interest is unjustified:

> There is little or no reason why declarations against penal interest and those against pecuniary or proprietary interest should not stand on the same footing. A person is as likely to speak the truth in a matter affecting his liberty as in a matter affecting his pocketbook. For these reasons and the ever-present possibility that a rule of absolute prohibition could lead to grave injustice I would hold that, in a proper case, a declaration against penal interest is admissible according to the law of Canada; the rule as to absolute exclusion of declarations against penal interest, established in *The Sussex Peerage* case, should not be followed.[31]

See generally D J Birch, 'Hearsay-Logic and Hearsay-Fiddles: *Blastland* Revisited' in P Smith (ed), *Criminal Law: Essays in Honour of J C Smith* (1987) 28–9.

DECLARATIONS IN THE COURSE OF DUTY

A declaration by a deceased person, made in the course of discharging a duty owed to another[32] to perform and record an act,[33] is admissible in evidence to prove the precise facts (but not opinions[34]) which the declarant was under a duty to record,[35] so long as:

---

[30] J H Wigmore (rev J H Chadbourn), *Evidence in Trials at Common Law (Vol 5)* (1974) 360.
[31] *R v O'Brien* (1977) 76 DLR (3d) 513, 518–19. See also *Demeter v R* (1977) 75 DLR (3d) 251.
[32] *Mills v Mills* (1920) 36 TLR 772; *Simon v Simon* [1936] P 17.
[33] *Smith v Blakey* (1867) LR 2 QB 326; *Mercer v Denne* [1905] 2 Ch 538.
[34] *R v McGuire* (1985) 81 Cr App R 323.
[35] *Chambers v Bernasconi* (1834) 1 C M & R 347; 149 ER 1114; *Smith v Blakey* (1867) LR 2 QB 326, 332–3.

- the act was performed by the declarant;[36]
- the declaration was made immediately[37] after[38] the performance of the act; and
- the declarant had no motive to misrepresent the facts.[39]

This exception is now of little practical importance in the light of s 24 of the Criminal Justice Act 1988, examined below.

DYING DECLARATIONS

In *Mills v R*, the Privy Council explained this exception in the following terms:

> The rule is usually stated to be that a statement of a deceased is admissible as evidence of the cause of his death at a trial for his murder or manslaughter if the deceased was under a settled hopeless expectation of death when he made the statement: *Nembhard v The Queen* [1981] 1 WLR 1515.[40]

The rationale for this exception was stated in an oft-quoted passage in the 1789 case of *R v Woodcock*:

> The general principle on which this species of evidence is admitted is, that they are declarations made in extremity, when the party is at the point of death, and when every hope of this world is gone: when every motive to falsehood is silenced, and the mind is induced by the most powerful considerations to speak the truth; a situation so solemn, and so awful, is considered by the law as creating an obligation equal to that which is imposed by a positive oath administered in a Court of Justice.[41]

Whatever may have been the position in 1789, the validity of this rationale – that a settled hopeless expectation of death would induce sincerity – may now be seriously questioned. In an increasingly secular society, fear of after-life 'punishment' for making a false accusation has become a far less significant consideration (if it was ever truly significant). Nevertheless, the assumption remains that one would not wish to die with a lie on one's lips. Even this 'modern' justification for the rule, however, is questionable. The making of the declaration may have been motivated by spite, a feeling of hatred, a desire for revenge or a desire to protect the real perpetrator. Thus the danger of insincerity may be greater than is commonly imagined.[42]

---

[36] *The Henry Coxon* (1878) 3 PD 156.
[37] *Champneys v Peck* (1816) 1 Stark 404; 171 ER 511; *The Henry Coxon* (1878) 3 PD 156.
[38] *Rowlands v De Vecchi* (1882) Cab & El 10.
[39] *Marks v Lahee* (1837) 3 Bing (NC) 408; 132 ER 467; *The Henry Coxon* (1878) 3 PD 156.
[40] [1995] 1 WLR 511, 521.
[41] (1789) 1 Leach 500, 502; 168 ER 352, 353.
[42] S A Goldman, 'Not So "Firmly Rooted": Exceptions to the Confrontation Clause' (1987) 66 *North Carolina Law Review* 1, 24.

The exception applies only in prosecutions for murder and manslaughter. Attempts to have the exception extended to prosecutions for using an instrument with intent to procure a miscarriage,[43] perjury,[44] robbery[45] and rape,[46] where the deaths of the victims resulted, have all failed. Restriction of the exception to cases of homicide (if this in fact represents the law) is anomalous. If it is the declarant's fear of the consequences of lying, induced by an expectation of death, that gives the evidence its stamp of reliability, why should it matter what offence the accused is actually charged with?[47] In Canada the dying declarations exception has been held to be applicable in a prosecution for causing death by criminal negligence in the operation of a motor vehicle.[48]

The requirement that the statement have been made with a settled hopeless expectation of death is interpreted strictly. In *R v Jenkins*[49] a magistrates' clerk attended the victim at her death-bed to take her statement, writing that it was made 'with no hope of my recovery'. She required this to be amended to 'with no hope at present of my recovery' before signing the statement. It was held that

> the declaration . . . must be made under a belief and a belief without hope, that the declarant is about to die. . . . It must be made when every hope of this world is gone . . . Any hope of recovery, however slight, will exclude the declaration. . . . The burden of proof . . . is on the prosecution . . . We must be perfectly satisfied beyond a reasonable doubt that the declaration in question was made by the deceased while under the belief that there was no hope of recovery.[50]

The statement was held to be inadmissible in evidence on the basis that the victim's objection to signing it without the addition of the words 'at present' suggested that she entertained some faint hope of recovery.

Although there is no requirement that evidence of dying declarations be corroborated, the trial judge has a general duty to leave the jury with a clear consciousness of the need to take care in assessing the significance of such a declaration,[51] and, it would seem, an obligation to point out to the jury that the declaration was not subject to cross-examination.[52] Dying declarations are admissible in evidence even if they are partly adverse to the declarant. An example is provided by *R v Scaife*,[53] where the deceased's statement that the

---

[43] *R v Hutchinson* (1822) 2 B & C 608n; 107 ER 510n. See also *R v Hind* (1860) 8 Cox CC 300.

[44] *R v Mead* (1824) 2 B & C 605; 107 ER 509.

[45] *R v Lloyd* (1830) 4 Car & P 233; 172 ER 684.

[46] *R v Newton and Carpenter* (1859) 1 F & F 641; 175 ER 887.

[47] Law Commission (Consultation Paper No 138), *Criminal Law – Evidence in Criminal Proceedings: Hearsay and Related Topics – A Consultation Paper* (1995) 32.

[48] *R v Jurtyn* (1958) 28 CR 295.

[49] (1869) 20 LT 372.

[50] At 375 per Kelly CB.

[51] *Nembhard v R* [1981] 1 WLR 1515, 1520 per Sir Owen Woodhouse.

[52] *Waugh v R* [1950] AC 203.

[53] (1836) 2 Lewin 150; 168 ER 1110.

accused 'would not have struck me but that I provoked him to it' was held to be admissible in evidence.

Interestingly, the Privy Council hinted recently in *Mills v R* that the time may well be ripe for a reassessment, and possible liberalisation, of the law on dying declarations.[54]

See generally R Munday, 'Musings on the Dying Declaration' (1993) 22 *Anglo-American Law Review* 42.

(ii) Statements forming part of the res gestae

Literally, the term res gestae means 'the transaction'. In essence, evidence of facts may be admissible as part of the res gestae if these facts are so closely connected in time, place and circumstances with some transaction which is at issue that they can be said to form a part of that transaction. There are three main contexts in which hearsay statements may be admissible in evidence as part of the res gestae, and each of these will now be examined separately.

SPONTANEOUS STATEMENTS

Extract 7.3.12

R v Andrews (Donald) [1987] AC 281, 295, 300–2 (HL)

Two men entered the victim's flat and attacked him, seriously wounding him. When the police arrived soon afterwards, the victim identified Andrews as one of his attackers. The victim died two months later.

LORD ACKNER: Mr Worsley sought to have the statement of the deceased admitted as evidence of the truth of the facts that he had asserted, namely that he had been attacked by both O'Neill and the appellant. Since evidence of this statement could only be given by a witness who had merely heard it, such evidence was clearly hearsay evidence. It was not being tendered as evidence limited to the fact that an assertion had been made, without reference to the truth of anything alleged in the assertion. The evidence merely of the fact that such an assertion was made would not have related to any issue in the trial and therefore would not have been admissible. Had, for example, the deceased's state of mind been in issue and had his exclamation been relevant to his state of mind, then evidence of *the fact* that such an assertion was made, would not have been hearsay evidence since it would have been tendered without reference to the truth of anything alleged in the assertion. Such evidence is often classified as 'original' evidence.
. . .

---

[54] [1995] 1 WLR 511, 521–2.

Mr Worsley based his submission that this hearsay evidence was admissible upon the so-called doctrine of 'res gestae.' He could not submit that the statement was a 'dying declaration' since there was no evidence to suggest that at the time when the deceased made the statement (two months before his ultimate death), he was aware that he had been mortally injured. . . .

. . .

My Lords, may I therefore summarise the position which confronts the trial judge when faced in a criminal case with an application under the res gestae doctrine to admit evidence of statements, with a view to establishing the truth of some fact thus narrated, such evidence being truly categorised as 'hearsay evidence?'

1. The primary question which the judge must ask himself is – can the possibility of concoction or distortion be disregarded?

2. To answer that question the judge must first consider the circumstances in which the particular statement was made, in order to satisfy himself that the event was so unusual or startling or dramatic as to dominate the thoughts of the victim, so that his utterance was an instinctive reaction to that event, thus giving no real opportunity for reasoned reflection. In such a situation the judge would be entitled to conclude that the involvement or the pressure of the event would exclude the possibility of concoction or distortion, providing that the statement was made in conditions of approximate but not exact contemporaneity.

3. In order for the statement to be sufficiently 'spontaneous' it must be so closely associated with the event which has excited the statement, that it can be fairly stated that the mind of the declarant was still dominated by the event. Thus the judge must be satisfied that the event, which provided the trigger mechanism for the statement, was still operative. The fact that the statement was made in answer to a question is but one factor to consider under this heading.

4. Quite apart from the time factor, there may be special features in the case, which relate to the possibility of concoction or distortion. In the instant appeal the defence relied upon evidence to support the contention that the deceased had a motive of his own to fabricate or concoct, namely, a malice which resided in him against O'Neill and the appellant because, so he believed, O'Neill had attacked and damaged his house and was accompanied by the appellant, who ran away on a previous occasion. The judge must be satisfied that the circumstances were such that having regard to the special feature of malice, there was no possibility of any concoction or distortion to the advantage of the maker or the disadvantage of the accused.

5. As to the possibility of error in the facts narrated in the statement, if only the ordinary fallibility of human recollection is relied upon, this goes to the weight to be attached to and not to the admissibility of the statement and is therefore a matter for the jury. However, here again there may be special features that may give rise to the possibility of error. In the instant case there was evidence that the deceased had drunk to excess, well over double the permitted limit for driving a motor car. Another example would be where the identification was made in circumstances of particular difficulty or where the declarant suffered from defective eyesight. In such circumstances the trial judge must consider whether he can exclude the possibility of error.

Croom-Johnson LJ, in giving the judgment of the Court of Appeal (Criminal Division) dismissing the appeal, stated, in my respectful view quite correctly, that the Common Serjeant had directed himself impeccably in his approach to the evidence that he had heard. It is perhaps helpful to set out verbatim how the judge stated his conclusions:

'I am satisfied that soon after receiving very serious stab wounds the deceased went downstairs for help unassisted and received some assistance. He was able to talk for a few minutes before he became unconscious. I am satisfied on the evidence – and not only the primary evidence but the inference of fact to which I am irresistibly driven – that the deceased only sustained the injuries a few minutes before the police arrived and subsequently, of course, the ambulance took him to hospital. Even if the period were longer than a few minutes, I am satisfied that there was no possibility in the circumstances of any concoction or fabrication of identification. I think that the injuries which the deceased sustained were of such a nature that it would drive out of his mind any possibility of him being activated by malice and I cannot overlook as far as the identification was concerned, he was right over Mr O'Neill who was a former co-defendant with the accused.'

... Of course, having ruled the statement admissible the judge must, as the Common Serjeant most certainly did, make it clear to the jury that it is for them to decide what was said and to be sure that the witnesses were not mistaken in what they believed had been said to them. Further, they must be satisfied that the declarant did not concoct or distort to his advantage or the disadvantage of the accused the statement relied upon and where there is material to raise the issue, that he was not activated by any malice or ill-will. Further, where there are special features that bear on the possibility of mistake then the juries' attention must be invited to those matters.

... I wholly accept that the doctrine [of res gestae] admits the hearsay statements, not only where the declarant is dead or otherwise not available but when he is called as a witness. Whatever may be the position in civil proceedings, I would, however, strongly deprecate any attempt in criminal prosecutions to use the doctrine as a device to avoid calling, when he is available, the maker of the statement. Thus to deprive the defence of the opportunity to cross-examine him, would not be consistent with the fundamental duty of the prosecution to place all the relevant material facts before the court, so as to ensure that justice is done.

My Lords, I would accordingly dismiss this appeal.

See also *Ratten v R*[55] and *Mills v R.*[56]

STATEMENTS ACCOMPANYING AND EXPLAINING A RELEVANT ACT

In *R v Kearley*, Lord Bridge of Harwich 'accept[ed] the proposition that, if an action is *of itself* relevant to an issue, the words which accompany and

---

[55] [1972] AC 378.
[56] [1995] 1 WLR 511.

explain the action may be given in evidence, whether or not they would be relevant independently'.[57] Thus, a statement made at the time of performing an act which would be relevant in the absence of the statement is admissible in evidence so long as the statement explains the act,[58] and was made more or less contemporaneously with the act by the person performing the act. The fact 'that the declaration was by one person, and the accompanying act by another', would not suffice.[59] If the relevant act was a continuing one, it is immaterial that a considerable period of time elapsed before the making of the statement; what is crucial is that it must have been made during the continuance of the act.[60]

STATEMENTS CONCERNING CONTEMPORANEOUS STATE OF MIND

To what extent is evidence of hearsay statements suggesting knowledge of particular facts admissible?

Extract 7.3.13

R v Blastland [1986] AC 41, 54 (HL)

The defendant was charged with murdering a young boy, Karl Fletcher, and argued in his defence that the crime had been committed by one Mark, who had been in the area at the time. The defence wished to call a number of witnesses to testify that Mark had said, before the discovery of the body, that a young boy had been murdered. One of the points of law certified by the Court of Appeal for consideration by the House of Lords was 'whether evidence of words spoken by a third party who is not called as a witness is hearsay evidence if it is advanced as evidence of the fact that the words were spoken and so as to indicate the state of knowledge of the person speaking the words if the inference to be drawn from such words is that the person speaking them is or may be guilty of the offence with which the defendant is charged'.

LORD BRIDGE OF HARWICH: It is, of course, elementary that statements made to a witness by a third party are not excluded by the hearsay rule when they are put in evidence solely to prove the state of mind either of the maker of the statement or of the person to whom it was made. What a person said or heard said may well be the best and most direct evidence of that person's state of mind. This principle can only apply, however, when the state of mind evidenced by the statement is either itself directly in issue at the trial or of direct and immediate relevance to an issue which arises at the trial. It is at this

---

[57] [1992] 2 AC 228, 246 (emphasis added).
[58] *R v Bliss* (1837) 7 Ad & E 550; 112 ER 577.
[59] *Howe v Malkin* (1878) 40 LT 196, 196.
[60] *Rawson v Haigh* (1824) 2 Bing 99; 130 ER 242; *Homes v Newman* [1931] 2 Ch 112.

point, as it seems to me, that the argument for the appellant breaks down. The issue at the trial of the appellant was whether it was proved that the appellant had buggered and murdered Karl Fletcher. Mark's knowledge that Karl had been murdered was neither itself in issue, nor was it, per se, of any relevance to the issue. What was relevant was not the fact of Mark's knowledge but how he had come by that knowledge. He might have done so in a number of ways, but the two most obvious possibilities were either that he had witnessed the commission of the murder by the appellant or that he had committed it himself. The statements which it was sought to prove that Mark made, indicating his knowledge of the murder, provided no rational basis whatever on which the jury could be invited to draw an inference as to the source of that knowledge. To do so would have been mere speculation.

It will be seen that what Lord Bridge required was a degree of probative value substantially above the bare minimum, or, in his own words, 'direct and immediate relevance'. But why should this heightened probative value have been necessary in *Blastland*, where it was, after all, the defence, rather than the prosecution, which was seeking to have the evidence admitted? Should not the right of the innocent to be protected from wrongful conviction have been a paramount consideration in determining the admissibility of the evidence? See generally P B Carter, 'Hearsay, Relevance and Admissibility: Declarations as to State of Mind and Declarations against Penal Interest' (1987) 103 *Law Quarterly Review* 106.

There appear to be conflicting authorities on whether evidence suggesting an intent to perform a particular act is admissible to establish that the intent was in fact carried out (that is, that the act in question was performed). The main authority cited for the view that such evidence is admissible is *R v Buckley*.[61] The accused was charged with murdering a police officer on a certain night. The deceased's superior officer was permitted to testify that, that morning, the deceased had told him that he intended to watch the movements of the accused that night. The superior officer had then said, 'I will send a man to assist you about nine o'clock', to which the deceased had responded, 'That will be too late, I will go about dusk, myself'. No reference was made to the hearsay rule, and it should be noted that the decision might well have been influenced by the fact that there was evidence that the victim was seen shortly after dark, possibly travelling in the direction of the accused's cottage. More recently, in *R v Moghal*,[62] the accused was charged with a murder which could have been committed only by him, his mistress, or both. The mistress had earlier been acquitted. To support his defence that the mistress had alone been responsible for the murder, the accused sought to adduce in evidence a tape recording by her in which she declared her intention to kill the victim. The Court of Appeal thought that, had the trial judge been asked to rule on the issue, this evidence should have been held admissible.

[61] (1873) 13 Cox CC 293.
[62] (1977) 65 Cr App R 56.

The main authority cited for the view that such evidence is inadmissible is *R v Wainwright*.[63] This was a murder case in which the prosecution sought to adduce evidence that the victim had said, on leaving her home, that she was going to the accused's premises. The evidence was held to be inadmissible on the basis that 'it was only a statement of intention which might or might not have been carried out'.[64] To a similar effect are *R v Pook*[65] and *R v Thomson*.[66] In *Thomson*, the accused was charged with using an instrument on a woman for the purpose of procuring an abortion. In support of his defence that the woman (who had later died from an unrelated cause) had operated on herself, the accused sought to ask a prosecution witness in cross-examination whether the woman had stated, some weeks before the operation, that she intended to operate on herself. The Court of Criminal Appeal held that this evidence had been correctly excluded, expressly rejecting the argument that cases such as this, where it was the defence which was seeking to adduce the evidence of intent, should be distinguished from cases where such evidence was sought to be adduced by the prosecution. Finally, it should be noted that Lord Bridge expressed doubts in *Blastland* about what the Court of Appeal had said in *Moghal*, remarking that 'I cannot see how a threat by Sadiga against Rashid's life, made six months before the murder, however virulently the threat was expressed, was of any relevance to the issue whether Moghal was a willing accomplice or an unwilling spectator when the murder was committed'.[67]

How, in your view, should this apparent conflict be resolved? Do you agree with the view expressed by Mason CJ in the Australian High Court case of *Walton v R* that 'out-of-court statements which tend to prove a plan or intention of the author [should be admissible in evidence], subject to remoteness in time and indications of unreliability or lack of probative value'?[68]

See generally C F H Tapper, '*Hillmon* Rediscovered and Lord St Leonards Resurrected' (1990) 106 *Law Quarterly Review* 441.

STATEMENTS CONCERNING CONTEMPORANEOUS PHYSICAL STATE

Extract 7.3.14

Gilbey v Great Western Railway Co (1910) 102 LT 202, 203 (CA)

COZENS-HARDY MR: ... statements made by a workman to his wife of his sensations at the time, about the pain in the side or head, or what not – whether the statements were made by groans or by actions or were verbal statements – would be admissible to prove the existence of those sensations.

---

[63] (1875) 13 Cox CC 171.
[64] At 172 per Lord Cockburn CJ.
[65] (1871) 13 Cox CC 172n.
[66] [1912] 3 KB 19.
[67] [1986] AC 41, 60.
[68] (1989) 166 CLR 283, 290.

Extract 7.3.15

R v Nicholas (1846) 2 Car & K 246, 248; 175 ER 102, 102 (Assizes)

POLLOCK CB: If a man says to his surgeon, 'I have a pain in the head,' or a pain in such a part of the body, that is evidence; but, if he says to his surgeon, 'I have a wound'; and was to add, 'I met John Thomas, who had a sword, and ran me through the body with it,' that would be no evidence against John Thomas . . .

Note also the following statement of Charles J in *R v Gloster*: 'the statements must be confined to contemporaneous symptoms, and nothing in the nature of a narrative is admissible as to who caused them, or how they were caused'.[69] Note, however, the flexible approach taken in relation to another issue:

Extract 7.3.16

Tickle v Tickle [1968] 1 WLR 937, 942 (P, D & A)

SIR JOCELYN SIMON P: If what a patient says about her state of health to a doctor is admissible as part of the res gestae notwithstanding the hearsay rule, it seems to me that what the doctor says to the patient is no less admissible when its adduction is required in order that justice should be done.

(iii) Statements in public documents

A public document is admissible as evidence of the truth of its contents if the following conditions are satisfied:

(1) The document must have been prepared by a public officer 'for the purpose of the public making use of it, and being able to refer to it'.[70]
(2) The statement in the document must have been made pursuant to a duty to inquire into the fact stated and to record it. However, it is no longer material that the officer who made the record pursuant to a duty to do so had not conducted the inquiry him- or herself, and had no personal knowledge of the truth of the facts that he or she recorded. It is sufficient that the inquiry was conducted by another officer whose duty it was to do so.[71]
(3) The document must have been prepared as a permanent record, rather than merely for temporary purposes[72] or as a draft document.[73]

---

[69] (1888) 16 Cox CC 471, 473.
[70] *Sturla v Freccia* (1880) 5 App Cas 623, 643 per Lord Blackburn. See also *Lilley v Pettit* [1946] KB 401; *R v Sealby* [1965] 1 All ER 701. See also *Ioannou v Demetriou* [1952] AC 84.
[71] See *R v Halpin* [1975] QB 907, 915. See also *R v Sealby* [1965] 1 All ER 701, 703. Cf *White v Taylor* [1969] 1 Ch 150.
[72] *Mercer v Denne* [1905] 2 Ch 538; *Heyne v Fischel & Co* (1913) 30 TLR 190.
[73] *White v Taylor* [1969] 1 Ch 150.

It should be noted that this exception has diminished substantially in import-ance owing to the existence of s 24 of the Criminal Justice Act 1988, exam-ined below.

(iv) Statements in works of reference

Published works dealing with matters of a public nature are admissible as evidence of facts of a public nature stated in them.[74]

(v) Statements made in former proceedings

The main area of application of this exception is in relation to transcripts of evidence. Such transcripts are admissible in evidence on the same (or substantially the same) issue in subsequent proceedings between the same parties (or those in privity with them), provided that:

• the transcripts are appropriately authenticated;[75]
• the witness in question was subject to cross-examination; and
• he or she is now dead or too ill[76] to attend the subsequent proceedings, or has been kept out of the way by the other party.

Even where admissible in evidence, however, transcripts of previous testi-mony may be excluded in the discretion of the trial judge if it would be unfair to the accused to admit the evidence.[77]

(e) Statutory exceptions to the rule

A number of the main statutory exceptions to the hearsay rule in criminal proceedings will now be examined.

(i) Criminal Justice Act 1988, Part II

FIRST-HAND DOCUMENTARY HEARSAY (S 23)

Section 23 deals with situations in which a statement has been made in a document by a person with first-hand knowledge of the relevant facts. In essence, such a statement will be admissible in evidence so long as its maker is unavailable *either* by virtue of the fact that one of the three paragraphs of subs (2) is satisfied; *or* by virtue of the fact that both paragraphs of subs (3) are satisfied.

---

[74] See, eg, *Read v Bishop of Lincoln* [1892] AC 644; *McCarthy v The Melita (Owners)* (1923) 16 BWCC 222; *R v Minister of Agriculture and Fisheries, ex p Graham* [1955] 2 QB 140.
[75] *R v Hall* [1973] QB 496, 504 per Forbes J.
[76] *R v Thompson* [1982] QB 647.
[77] *R v Hall* [1973] QB 496, 504–5 per Forbes J.

Extract 7.3.17

Criminal Justice Act 1988, s 23

23. First-hand hearsay

(1) Subject –
(a) to subsection (4) below;
(b) to paragraph 1A of Schedule 2 to the Criminal Appeal Act 1968 (evidence given orally at original trial to be given orally at retrial); and
(c) to section 69 of the Police and Criminal Evidence Act 1984 (evidence from computer records),

a statement made by a person in a document shall be admissible in criminal proceedings as evidence of any fact of which direct oral evidence by him would be admissible if –

    (i) the requirements of one of the paragraphs of subsection (2) below are satisfied; or
    (ii) the requirements of subsection (3) below are satisfied.

(2) The requirements mentioned in subsection (1)(i) above are –
(a) that the person who made the statement is dead or by reason of his bodily or mental condition unfit to attend as a witness;
(b) that –
    (i) the person who made the statement is outside the United Kingdom; and
    (ii) it is not reasonably practicable to secure his attendance; or
(c) that all reasonable steps have been taken to find the person who made the statement, but that he cannot be found.

(3) The requirements mentioned in subsection (1)(ii) above are –
(a) that the statement was made to a police officer or some other person charged with the duty of investigating offences or charging offenders; and
(b) that the person who made it does not give oral evidence through fear or because he is kept out of the way.

(4) Subsection (1) above does not render admissible a confession made by an accused person that would not be admissible under section 76 of the Police and Criminal Evidence Act 1984.

(5) This section shall not apply to proceedings before a magistrates' court inquiring into an offence as examining justices.

'the person who made the statement':

Extract 7.3.18

R v McGillivray (1992) 97 Cr App R 232, 237 (CA)

Some days prior to his death, a murder victim made a statement in hospital to police officers, one of whom took down what he said and then read it back to him. He agreed that what had been taken down was accurate, but was unable to sign the record because he was heavily bandaged.

WATKINS LJ: In our judgment where, as here, a person who has been injured and some time later, but before the trial of the defendant, dies after having made a statement to police officers which is recorded contemporaneously by one of them, and the deceased has signed the record as accurate, that is in law a statement made by that person in a document and is accordingly admissible in law. Likewise, if that person clearly indicates by speech, or otherwise, that the record of what he said made by the police officer is accurate he being at the time unable to sign the record because of some physical disability: in this instance the deceased was too badly burnt to sign, as has been said, he was heavily bandaged, his hands and arms especially.

Do you agree with the Court of Appeal in *McGillivray*? Whilst it is true that it should not matter in such a case that the acknowledgement of accuracy was made orally rather than in writing, is it not arguable that it should have mattered that the victim *did not actually read the record himself*, but simply relied upon what was read back to him?[78]

'by reason of his bodily or mental condition unfit to attend as a witness':

Extract 7.3.19

R v Setz-Dempsey (1993) 98 Cr App R 23, 27 (CA)

BELDAM LJ: In our view it is obvious that the words of the section, which include unfitness by reason of bodily or mental condition, are not intended merely to apply to the physical act of getting to court but to the capacity of the witness when there to give evidence in accordance with the statements which will become admissible if the conditions specified are fulfilled.

'it is not reasonably practicable to secure his attendance':

Extract 7.3.20

R v Hurst [1995] 1 Cr App R 82, 92 (CA)

BELDAM LJ: The requirements of the subsection may have to be examined either before the trial, or at the trial. In the former case where an application is made that a statement of a witness should be admitted in evidence without calling the maker, the court obviously would have to look to the future to see whether it would be practicable for the witness's attendance to be secured at the date of the trial.

---

[78] See the commentary by D J Birch [1993] *Criminal Law Review* 532.

The words 'reasonably practicable' involve a consideration of the normal steps which would be taken to secure the attendance of a witness, and the qualification of reasonableness includes other circumstances such as the cost and the steps which may be available to secure attendance. Obviously, however, circumstances may occur at short notice which render it impracticable to secure the attendance of the witness on the day when he is required to testify and when practicable arrangements have already been made for him to attend. Faced with an application at the trial when a witness does not attend the court has to rule taking account of all the circumstances; for example, if it were shown that no steps whatever had been taken to secure the attendance of the witness, the court could not be satisfied that it was not reasonably practicable to secure his attendance.

Similarly, if the court is satisfied that all reasonable steps have in the past been taken, it does not follow that circumstances may not have arisen which have made it impracticable to secure his attendance on the day of the trial. Thus, the mere fact that means have been assured to the witness and that the witness has stated an intention to attend does not necessarily determine the question.

Extract 7.3.21

R v Castillo [1996] 1 Cr App R 438, 442-3 (CA)

STUART-SMITH LJ: Mr Paul's submission, stripped to its bare essentials, is that if the witness says that he can come, then it is reasonably practicable for him to come, notwithstanding that there may be other good or powerful reasons why he should not do so. . . .

. . . in our judgment, the mere fact that it is possible for the witness to come does not answer the question. The judge has to consider a number of factors. First, he has to consider the importance of the evidence that the witness can give and whether or not it was prejudicial, and how prejudicial it would be to the defence that the witness did not attend. . . .

Secondly, we have to consider the expense and inconvenience of securing the witness's attendance . . . It may well be that if a witness is part of the prosecution team, so to speak, that should not be a major consideration, but it is a matter of considerable expense to bring a witness all the way from Venezuela simply to give evidence on a matter which it seems to this Court could not seriously be challenged in cross-examination.

Thirdly, the judge has to consider the reasons put forward as to why it is not convenient or reasonably practicable for the officer to come. This is a question of fact, and this Court does not lightly interfere with findings of fact by the trial judge.

See also *R v Bray*;[79] *R v Gonzales de Arango*;[80] *R v Jiminez-Paez*.[81]

---

[79] (1988) 88 Cr App R 354 (discussing the forerunner to s 23(2)(b)).
[80] (1991) 96 Cr App R 399 (discussing the forerunner to s 23(2)(b)).
[81] (1993) 98 Cr App R 239.

'fear':

R v Acton JJ, ex p Mcmullen (1990) 92 Cr App R 98, 105–6 (CA)

WATKINS LJ: It is not helpful in this context to speak of the objective or subjective approach and wholly inappropriate in my view to introduce the concept of reasonable grounds. It will be sufficient that the court on the evidence is sure that the witness is in fear as a consequence of the commission of the material offence or of something said or done subsequently in relation to that offence and the possibility of the witness testifying as to it.

See also *R v Martin*.[82]

'The fact of the witness being absent through fear must be proved by admissible evidence': *Neill v North Antrim Magistrates' Court*.[83] A person who attends court and enters the witness box but fails to say a word because of fear obviously satisfies subs (3)(b). So does a person who, having started to give oral evidence, does not continue because of fear. Subsection (3)(b) will be satisfied irrespective of how much evidence he or she has already given.

R v Waters (1997) 161 JPR 249, 252 (CA)

KENNEDY LJ: When this case was before the full court and leave was granted, attention was drawn to the words 'does not give oral evidence' because in *R v Ashford Magistrates' Court, ex parte Hilden* (1992) 156 JP 869; 96 Cr App R 92, the judgments of the Divisional Court disclosed some difference of judicial opinion as to the full import of those words.

In the present case, it will be recalled, Mr Dixon did give some evidence before an application was made, and acceded to, that his earlier statement should be placed before the jury. It could, therefore, be contended that on one reading of the provisions of s 23(3)(b), that section could not be invoked because he did not satisfy the requirement of not having given oral evidence.

That was not an interpretation of the words of the section which commended itself to Popplewell, J in the case of *Ex parte Hilden* and we respectfully agree with his approach.

In our judgment, what matters is whether or not there is, at the time when the section is invoked, any relevant evidence which the witness is still expected to give, because if there is such evidence, then it can properly be said that the witness is in the position where he does not give oral evidence. If it is shown, to a criminal standard of proof, that he or she does not give that oral evidence through fear, then the requirement of s 23(3)(b) is, in our judgment, satisfied.

---

[82] [1996] Crim LR 589.
[83] (1992) 97 Cr App R 121, 129.

For a discussion of the previous uncertainty, generated by *Hilden*, about the proper interpretation of subs (3)(b), see generally R Munday, 'The Proof of Fear: Part 1' (1993) 143 *New Law Journal* 542; R Munday, 'The Proof of Fear: Part 2' (1993) 143 *New Law Journal* 587.

Considerable public controversy was caused in 1996 when the victim of a serious assault and a witness to the incident were sentenced for contempt of court following their refusal, out of fear, to testify at the trial of the alleged attacker. Quashing the sentences, the Court of Appeal advocated the use of s 23 in such situations.

Extract 7.3.24

R v Bird (1996) 161 JPR 96, 102–4, 105 (CA)

ROCH LJ: Counsel, Mr Alun Jones, QC, for the appellants, has brought to our attention a policy document published by the Crown Prosecution Service in August 1995 entitled 'CPS Policy for Prosecuting Cases of Domestic Violence'. In that document there is a heading, 'What happens when the victim changes his or her mind about giving evidence?' These paragraphs appear under that heading:

'Sometimes the victim will change his or her mind and will ask to withdraw the complaint. This may happen if the victim allows the abuser back into their shared home.

If this happens, the Crown Prosecutor must find out why the victim has decided not to give evidence. This may involve putting off the court hearing to investigate the facts and decide the best course of action.

We will take the following steps:

– We will ask a prosecutor of at least Principal Crown Prosecutor (PCP) level to supervise the case.

– If the information about the victim's decision not to give evidence has come from the abuser, the Crown Prosecutor will ask the victim to confirm it in writing.

– We will ask the police to find out whether the victim wants to withdraw support for the prosecution, and if so, why. If the victim withdraws the complaint, the police will take a written statement explaining why.

– We will ask the police what they think about the case and the victim, as well as for any other relevant information.'

The next paragraph is:

'If we suspect that the victim has been frightened into withdrawing the complaint, we will put off the case for the police to investigate further.'

Then, a little later this appears:

'If the victim confirms that the complaint is true but wants to withdraw support, the Crown Prosecutor will consider the following to find out whether it is still possible to continue with the prosecution:

– Is it necessary to call the victim as a witness in order to prove the case? If not, the case may continue if a prosecution is needed in the public interest.

– Should the victim be forced to give evidence in court?

– Could the victim's statement be used as evidence under s 23 of the Criminal Justice Act 1988?

We will explore all these possibilities fully before we abandon a prosecution.'

Then, under the heading 'Forcing a victim to go to court', the policy document says:

'We always use our powers sensitively if we have to force a witness to go to court.'

This procedure was not followed despite the fact that the appellants had, in the week preceding September 16, indicated their wish to withdraw the complaint and not to give evidence.

. . .

. . . despite indications by the appellants in the week before the trial that they wished to withdraw their statements, the Crown Prosecution Service's sensible procedure did not operate. Had it done so it might have resulted in the trial proceeding, following a successful prosecution application under s 23(3)(b) of the Criminal Justice Act 1988 for the witnesses' . . . statements to be used as evidence because the appellants were witnesses who did not give oral evidence through fear. We would draw attention to this provision and express the hope that greater use will be made in future of it in cases like the case from which these proceedings emerge. It is a provision in which Parliament has recognised, and tried to combat, the growing ruthlessness of some criminals and their associates.

BUSINESS AND OTHER DOCUMENTS (S 24)

In essence, s 24 provides for the admissibility in evidence of a statement in a document where two conditions are satisfied: first, the document must have been created or received by a person in the course of a job, and secondly, the information contained in the document must have been supplied by a person who had, or may reasonably be supposed to have had, personal knowledge of the matters dealt with.

Extract 7.3.25

Police and Criminal Justice Act 1988, s 24

24. Business etc documents

(1) Subject –

(a) to subsections (3) and (4) below;

(b) to paragraph 1A of Schedule 2 to the Criminal Appeal Act 1968; and

(c) to section 69 of the Police and Criminal Evidence Act 1984, a statement in a document shall be admissible in criminal proceedings as evidence of any fact of which direct oral evidence would be admissible, if the following conditions are satisfied –

    (i) the document was created or received by a person in the course of a trade, business, profession or other occupation, or as the holder of a paid or unpaid office; and

    (ii) the information contained in the document was supplied by a person (whether or not the maker of the statement) who had, or may reasonably be supposed to have had, personal knowledge of the matters dealt with.

(2) Subsection (1) above applies whether the information contained in the document was supplied directly or indirectly but, if it was supplied indirectly, only if each person through whom it was supplied received it –

    (a) in the course of a trade, business, profession or other occupation; or

    (b) as the holder of a paid or unpaid office.

(3) Subsection (1) above does not render admissible a confession made by an accused person that would not be admissible under section 76 of the Police and Criminal Evidence Act 1984.

(4) A statement prepared otherwise than in accordance with section 3 of the Criminal Justice (International Co-operation) Act 1990 or an order under paragraph 6 of Schedule 13 to this Act or under section 30 or 31 below for the purposes –

    (a) of pending or contemplated criminal proceedings; or

    (b) of a criminal investigation,

shall not be admissible by virtue of subsection (1) above unless –

    (i) the requirements of one of the paragraphs of subsection (2) of section 23 above are satisfied; or

    (ii) the requirements of subsection (3) of that section are satisfied; or

    (iii) the person who made the statement cannot reasonably be expected (having regard to the time which has elapsed since he made the statement and to all the circumstances) to have any recollection of the matters dealt with in the statement.

(5) This section shall not apply to proceedings before a magistrates' court inquiring into an offence as examining justices.

Extract 7.3.26

R v Carrington (1993) 99 Cr App R 376, 379–81 (CA)

WAITE LJ: On July 30, 1991 a Mr Roger Thompson had his wallet stolen. The contents included a National Westminster switch card in the name of R Thompson. At 4.55 pm on Wednesday August 28, 1991 a man came to one of the check-out points in Sainsbury's in High Road Tottenham, North London ... The man offered to make ... payment with a switch card, tendering for that purpose a card which was later identified as Mr Thompson's. When the cashier ran the card through the magnetic tape reader, the machine showed her the warning signal designed to alert cashiers to the fact that the card is listed in the central database of stolen credit cards.

She called out to a supervisor, Mrs Bond . . . Mrs Bond came to the till . . . She called for a fellow supervisor, Mrs Sivell, to come and join them . . . Mrs Bond said to the customer that she was going to run the card through an electronic device elsewhere in the premises which would 'highlight the scratches'. She then went upstairs, and telephoned the National Westminster Bank on the store's external telephone line. Mrs Sivell, who was going off duty, left the store at that point to collect her car from the store car park and drive home.

The customer remained at the check-out for a few moments, and then – making a remark to the cashier about having to collect something from his car – he went out from the store to the car park. He did not return.

Meanwhile Mrs Sivell, out in the car park, was on the point of getting into her own car, when her attention was caught by the sight of a car being driven past her towards the exit at a very high speed. She recognised the driver as being the same customer she had seen a few minutes earlier tendering the suspect credit card. She was able to note the model of the vehicle he was driving and its registration number, which she wrote down on the cover of a magazine. She immediately went back into the store and reported what she had seen to Lyn Hill, who was the operator of the store's internal telephone system. Lyn Hill buzzed Mrs Bond on the internal line and passed on to her at Mrs Sivell's dictation the particulars which were being reported by Mrs Sivell. Mrs Bond wrote those particulars down on her memo pad. The relevant fly-leaf from the pad became Exhibit MB1 at the trial. . . .

. . .

Mr Beck, counsel for the appellant, concedes that certain elements of section 24 are satisfied in this case, namely:

(1) MB1 was a document created by Mrs Bond in the course of a trade or occupation for the purposes of section 24(1)(i).

(2) The information contained in MB1 was supplied to the maker of the statement (Mrs Bond) indirectly through the message passed via the telephonist Lyn Hill, who herself received it and supplied it in the course of a trade or occupation for the purposes of section 24(2)(a).

Mr Khamisa, counsel for the Crown, for his part concedes:

(1) that the contents of MB1 constitute a statement which was prepared for the purposes of pending or contemplated criminal proceedings; and

(2) that this is not a case in which the requirements of (i) and (ii) of subsection (4) are satisfied; and that accordingly,

(3) MB1 was not admissible unless the requirement in subsection (4)(iii) is satisfied.

. . .

Some commentators have questioned whether it can really have been the intention of Parliament to concentrate in this subsection upon the recollective power of the maker of the statement (ie the person with clerical responsibility for maintaining the business record) as opposed to that of the eye witness whose observations supplies the subject-matter of the record – see *Cross on Evidence*, 7th ed, at p 633. Nevertheless there is no dispute between Mr Beck and Mr Khamisa as to the individual to whom the requirement applies for the purposes of this appeal. They are agreed that it applies solely to Mrs Bond as the 'person who made' MB1.

. . .

... Certainly it may be artificial, in a case where it is sought to introduce under section 24(4) a document in relation to which the maker has a clear recollection both of the circumstances in which it was made and of some (though not all) of the details contained in it, to select particular words or passages from the document and treat them as independent 'statements' which then pass muster under subsection (iii). Nevertheless the definition in the 1988 Act of a 'statement' in terms so wide as to include 'any representation of fact, whether made in words or otherwise' necessarily entitles the prosecution, in our judgment, to adopt precisely that approach. Indeed it scarcely makes sense to construe section 24 in any other way. Some very capricious results might follow if the admissibility under section 24(4) of a statement of which the maker did not retain (or could not reasonably be expected to retain) a recollection depended upon whether the statement concerned was an independent record isolated in context from other matters of which the record maker retained or might be expected to retain some memory (in which case it would be admissible); or was found in the company of other more memorable statements within the same document of which the maker retained, or might be expected to retain, some recollection (in which case it would not).

The prosecution was accordingly entitled, in our judgment, to treat the part of MB1 which contained particulars of the car's registration number as an independent 'statement' for the purposes of sub-rule (4)(iii) in relation to which Mrs Bond could not reasonably be expected (having regard to the time which had elapsed since she made that particular statement and to all the circumstances) to have any recollection of the matters dealt with in it. The judge had jurisdiction to grant the application to admit evidence of those particulars on that basis.

It will be noted that the court recognised the illogicality of interpreting 'the person who made the statement' in s 24(4)(iii) as meaning the creator of the document rather than the supplier of the information. A preferable approach would clearly be to treat the reference to the maker of the statement in s 24(4)(iii) as a reference to the supplier of the information. This would, however, render the words 'whether or not the maker of the statement' in s 24(1)(ii) otiose. These words would, therefore, have to be amended to read 'whether or not the creator of the document'.[84]

<hr>

Extract 7.3.27

<hr>

R v Lockley [1995] 2 Cr App R 554, 559 (CA)

PILL LJ: We construe the expression 'statement prepared for the purposes of contemplated criminal proceedings' as including a statement made in the

---

[84] See generally D J Birch, 'The Criminal Justice Act 1988: (2) Documentary Evidence' [1989] *Criminal Law Review* 15, 25–6; J C Smith, 'Sections 23 and 24 of the Criminal Justice Act 1988: (1) Some Problems' [1994] *Criminal Law Review* 426, 427–8; J A Andrews and M Hirst, *Criminal Evidence* (2nd ed 1992) 529; J D Heydon and M Ockelton, *Evidence: Cases and Materials* (4th ed 1996) 347; Law Commission (Consultation Paper No 138), *Criminal Law – Evidence in Criminal Proceedings: Hearsay and Related Topics – A Consultation Paper* (1995) 108–9.

course of criminal proceedings. One of the purposes of recording criminal proceedings is in any event to make available a record for use upon any appeal to a higher court. The transcript is admissible as a 'business, etc, document' under section 24.

Extract 7.3.28

R v Foxley [1995] 2 Cr App R 523, 536–7 (CA)

ROCH LJ: Section 24 deals with the statements in a document and makes such statements admissible of any fact of which direct oral evidence would be admissible if two conditions are satisfied. The wording of condition (ii) demonstrates that Parliament anticipated that courts would draw inferences as to the personal knowledge of the person supplying the information of the matters dealt with. The purpose of section 24 is to enable the document to speak for itself; the safeguard being the two conditions and the other statutory provisions applicable, for example in the case of a statement made for the purpose of a criminal investigation, one of the requirements of section 23(2) or the requirements of section 23(3) have to be fulfilled. . . .

With regard to section 24, we would suggest that Parliament's intention would be defeated if oral evidence was to be required in every case from a person who was either the creator or keeper of the document, or the supplier of the information contained in the document.

See also *R v Ilyas*[85] and *R v Hogan*.[86]

JUDICIAL DISCRETION

Section 25 vests an exclusionary discretion in the court.

Extract 7.3.29

Criminal Justice Act 1988, s 25

25. Principles to be followed by court
    (1) If, having regard to all the circumstances –
        (a) the Crown Court –
            (i) on a trial on indictment;
            (ii) on an appeal from a magistrates' court;
            (iii) on the hearing of an application under section 6 of the Criminal Justice Act 1987 (applications for dismissal of charges of fraud transferred from magistrates' court to Crown Court); or

---

[85] [1996] Crim LR 810.
[86] [1997] Crim LR 349.

        (iv) on the hearing of an application under paragraph 5 of Schedule
            6 to the Criminal Justice Act 1991 (applications for dismissal of
            charges in certain cases involving children transferred from mag-
            istrates' court to Crown Court); or
    (b) the criminal division of the Court of Appeal; or
    (c) a magistrates' court on a trial of an information,
is of the opinion that in the interests of justice a statement which is admissible
by virtue of section 23 or 24 above nevertheless ought not to be admitted, it
may direct that the statement shall not be admitted.

    (2) Without prejudice to the generality of subsection (1) above, it shall be
the duty of the court to have regard –
    (a) to the nature and source of the document containing the statement
        and to whether or not, having regard to its nature and source and to
        any other circumstances that appear to the court to be relevant, it is
        likely that the document is authentic;
    (b) to the extent to which the statement appears to supply evidence
        which would otherwise not be readily available;
    (c) to the relevance of the evidence that it appears to supply to any issue
        which is likely to have to be determined in the proceedings; and
    (d) to any risk, having regard in particular to whether it is likely to be
        possible to controvert the statement if the person making it does not
        attend to give oral evidence in the proceedings, that its admission or
        exclusion will result in unfairness to the accused or, if there is more
        than one, to any of them.

The effect of s 26 is as follows. Statements which would otherwise be
admissible in evidence by virtue of s 23 or s 24, but which appear to have
been prepared for the purposes of criminal proceedings or a criminal investigation, are rendered presumptively inadmissible in evidence, albeit subject
to be admitted in evidence in the exercise of an inclusionary discretion.

Extract 7.3.30

Criminal Justice Act 1988, s 26

**26. Statements in documents that appear to have been prepared for
purposes of criminal proceedings or investigations**
Where a statement which is admissible in criminal proceedings by virtue of
section 23 or 24 above appears to the court to have been prepared, otherwise than in accordance with section 3 of the Criminal Justice (International
Co-operation) Act 1990 or an order under paragraph 6 of Schedule 13 to this
Act or under section 30 or 31 below, for the purposes –
    (a) of pending or contemplated criminal proceedings; or
    (b) of a criminal investigation,
the statement shall not be given in evidence in any criminal proceedings
without the leave of the court, and the court shall not give leave unless it is
of the opinion that the statement ought to be admitted in the interests of

343

justice; and in considering whether its admission would be in the interests of justice, it shall be the duty of the court to have regard –

    (i)   to the contents of the statement;

    (ii) to any risk, having regard in particular to whether it is likely to be possible to controvert the statement if the person making it does not attend to give oral evidence in the proceedings, that its admission or exclusion will result in unfairness to the accused or, if there is more than one, to any of them; and

    (iii) to any other circumstances that appear to the court to be relevant.

This section shall not apply to proceedings before a magistrates' court inquiring into an offence as examining justices.

Extract 7.3.31

R v Cole [1990] 1 WLR 866, 875–7 (CA)

RALPH GIBSON LJ: The nature of the discretion to be exercised by the court under sections 25 and 26 of the Act of 1988, and the matters to which in exercising that discretion the court is required to have regard, have been laid down by Parliament and, in the view of this court, are clearly expressed. There will be difficulty in applying those provisions to the facts of particular cases.

The overall purpose of the provisions was to widen the power of the court to admit documentary hearsay evidence while ensuring that the accused receives a fair trial. In judging how to achieve the fairness of the trial a balance must on occasions be struck between the interests of the public in enabling the prosecution case to be properly presented and the interest of a particular defendant in not being put in a disadvantageous position, for example by the death or illness of a witness. The public of course also has a direct interest in the proper protection of the individual accused. The point of balance, as directed by Parliament, is set out in the sections.

It is not of course the case that these provisions are available only to enable the prosecution to put evidence before the court. A defendant also may wish to make use of the provisions, in order to get before the jury documentary evidence which would not otherwise be admissible.

Next, some comment on the structure of these sections is necessary. By section 25, if, having regard to all the circumstances, the court is of the opinion that a statement, admissible by virtue of section 23 or section 24, 'in the interests of justice ought not to be admitted,' it may direct that it be not admitted. The court is then, in considering that question, directed to have regard to the list of matters set out in section 25(2). They include 'any risk' of unfairness caused by admission or exclusion of the statement 'having regard in particular to whether it is likely to be possible to controvert the statement if the person making it does not attend.' In short the court must be made to hold the opinion that the statement ought not to be admitted.

By contrast under section 26, which deals with documents prepared for purpose of criminal proceedings or investigations, when a statement is admissible in criminal proceedings by virtue of section 23 or section 24, and was prepared for the purposes of criminal proceedings, the statement shall not be given in evidence unless the court is of opinion that the statement *'ought to be admitted in the interests of justice.'* The matters to which the court must have regard . . . include, again, 'any risk' of unfairness caused by admission or exclusion having regard to the possibility of controverting the statement. Again, in short, the court is not to admit the statement unless made to hold the opinion that in the interests of justice it *ought to be admitted.* The emphasis is the other way round.

. . .

. . . The meaning of 'controvert' includes that of 'dispute' or 'contradict.' The court is entitled, in our judgment, to have regard to such information as it has at the time that the application is made which shows 'whether it is likely to be possible to controvert the statement' in the absence of the ability to cross-examine the maker. The court cannot require to be told whether the accused intends to give evidence or to call witnesses, but the court is not required, in our judgment, to assess the possibility of controverting the statement upon the basis that the accused will not give evidence or call witnesses known to be available to him. The decision by an accused whether or not to give evidence or to call witnesses is to be made by him by reference to the admissible evidence put before the court; and the accused has no right, as we think, for the purposes of this provision, to be treated as having no possibility of controverting the statement because of his right not to give evidence or to call witnesses. If Parliament had intended the question to be considered on that basis, express words would, we think, have been used to make the intention clear.

This question however is only one part of a complex balancing exercise which the court must perform. For example the fact that the court concludes that it is likely to be possible for the accused to controvert the statement if the person making it cannot be cross-examined does not mean that the court will therefore necessarily be of opinion that admission of the statement will not result in unfairness to the accused or that the statement ought not to be admitted in the interests of justice.

. . .

. . . the weight to be attached to the inability to cross-examine and the magnitude of any consequential risk that admission of the statement will result in unfairness to the accused, will depend in part upon the court's assessment of the quality of the evidence shown by the contents of the statement. Each case, as is obvious, must turn upon its own facts. The court should, we accept, consider whether . . . the inability to probe a statement by cross-examination of the maker of it must be regarded as having such consequences, having regard to the terms and substance of the statement in the light of the issues in the case, that for that reason the statement should be excluded.

In considering a submission to that effect the court is entitled, and in our view required, to consider how far any potential unfairness, arising from the inability to cross-examine on the particular statement, may be effectively counter-balanced by [a] warning and explanation in the summing up . . . The court will also, for example, consider whether, having regard to other evidence available to the prosecution, the interests of justice will be properly served by excluding the statement.

Extract 7.3.32

R v Setz-Dempsey (1993) 98 Cr App R 23, 29 (CA)

BELDAM LJ: The mere fact that the statements sought to be given in evidence go to prove matters which are vital or of great significance in the case is not, in our judgment, a ground of exclusion. The interests of justice are not generally served by refusing to admit admissible evidence which is of importance to the issues a jury have to consider any more than they are served by admitting evidence of poor quality or evidence which could substantially be weakened by cross-examination.

See also *R v French*[87] and *R v Dragic*, in which the Court of Appeal stated that

the fact that there is no ability to cross-examine, that the witness who is absent is the only evidence against the accused and that his evidence is identification evidence is not sufficient to render the admission of written evidence from that witness contrary to the interests of justice or unfair to the defendant, *per se*. What matters, in our judgment, is the content of the statement and the circumstances of the particular case, bearing in mind the considerations which section 26 require the judge to have in mind.[88]

Extract 7.3.33

R v Lockley [1995] 2 Cr App R 554, 560–1 (CA)

PILL LJ: We cannot accept that the character of the witness is an overriding factor in considering whether the admission of her evidence is in the interests of justice. It may in some situations be in the interests of justice to admit the evidence of a person of bad character, particularly when the bad character can readily be demonstrated. Mrs Freestone's evidence was, if believed, important evidence in this case. The evidence was however about a cell confession made in the absence of any other witnesses. Such evidence is always treated with caution by the courts. Further, while it can be said that it is a big step from being a persistent shoplifter to inventing a confession to murder, the witness has demonstrated and indeed boasted a remarkable ability to deceive. Her claim is that her dishonesty is confined to a particular activity and she has indignantly denied other suggestions made against her. In these circumstances it was of great importance in this case that the members of the jury should have the opportunity to assess the witness for themselves, including her demeanour and the manner in which she gave her evidence. The potential unfairness to the accused in the jury not having that opportunity was in the view of the Court such as to require the exclusion of the transcript in the interests of justice.

---

[87] (1993) 97 Cr App R 421, 428.
[88] [1996] 2 Cr App R 232, 239.

CREDIBILITY AND WEIGHT

Extract 7.3.34

Criminal Justice Act 1988, Sched 2, paras 1, 3

1. Where a statement is admitted as evidence in criminal proceedings by virtue of Part II of this Act –
   (a) any evidence which, if the person making the statement had been called as a witness, would have been admissible as relevant to his credibility as a witness shall be admissible for that purpose in those proceedings;
   (b) evidence may, with the leave of the court, be given of any matter which, if that person had been called as a witness, could have been put to him in cross-examination as relevant to his credibility as a witness but of which evidence could not have been adduced by the cross-examining party; and
   (c) evidence tending to prove that that person, whether before or after making the statement, made (whether orally or not) some other statement which is inconsistent with it shall be admissible for the purpose of showing that he has contradicted himself.

3. In estimating the weight, if any, to be attached to such a statement regard shall be had to all the circumstances from which any inference can reasonably be drawn as to its accuracy or otherwise.

(ii) Computer-produced documents

A document produced by a computer will be admissible as real evidence if it has been produced 'without the input of information provided by the human mind'.[89] Where a computer-produced document constitutes hearsay because there has been such input, it may nevertheless be admissible in evidence under s 23 or s 24 of the Criminal Justice Act 1988. However, *any* document produced by a computer, whether constituting hearsay or real evidence, must, in order to be admissible in evidence, satisfy the requirements of s 69 of the Police and Criminal Evidence Act 1984.[90]

Extract 7.3.35

Police and Criminal Evidence Act 1984, s 69(1)

69. Evidence from computer records
   (1) In any proceedings, a statement in a document produced by a computer shall not be admissible as evidence of any fact stated therein unless it is shown –

---

[89] *R v Shephard* [1993] AC 380, 384 per Lord Griffiths, with whom Lords Emslie, Roskill, Ackner and Lowry agreed. See also *R v Governor of Brixton Prison, ex p Levin* [1997] 3 WLR 117.
[90] Ibid.

(a) that there are no reasonable grounds for believing that the statement is inaccurate because of improper use of the computer;
(b) that at all material times the computer was operating properly, or if not, that any respect in which it was not operating properly or was out of operation was not such as to affect the production of the document or the accuracy of its contents; and
(c) that any relevant conditions specified in rules of court under subsection (2) below are satisfied.

Extract 7.3.36

Police and Criminal Evidence Act 1984, Sched 3, Part II, paras 8, 9, 11, 12

8. In any proceedings where it is desired to give a statement in evidence in accordance with section 69 above, a certificate –
(a) identifying the document containing the statement and describing the manner in which it was produced;
(b) giving such particulars of any device involved in the production of that document as may be appropriate for the purpose of showing that the document was produced by a computer;
(c) dealing with any of the matters mentioned in subsection (1) of section 69 above; and
(d) purporting to be signed by a person occupying a responsible position in relation to the operation of the computer,
shall be evidence of anything stated in it; and for the purposes of this paragraph it shall be sufficient for a matter to be stated to the best of the knowledge and belief of the person stating it.

9. Notwithstanding paragraph 8 above, a court may require oral evidence to be given of anything of which evidence could be given by a certificate under that paragraph; but the preceding provisions of this paragraph shall not apply where the court is a magistrates' court inquiring into an offence as examining justices.

11. In estimating the weight, if any, to be attached to a statement regard shall be had to all the circumstances from which any inference can reasonably be drawn as to the accuracy or otherwise of the statement and, in particular –
(a) to the question whether or not the information which the information contained in the statement reproduces or is derived from was supplied to the relevant computer, or recorded for the purpose of being supplied to it, contemporaneously with the occurrence or existence of the facts dealt with in that information; and
(b) to the question whether or not any person concerned with the supply of information to that computer, or with the operation of that computer or any equipment by means of which the document containing the statement was produced by it, had any incentive to conceal or misrepresent the facts.

12. For the purposes of paragraph 11 above information shall be taken to be supplied to a computer whether it is supplied directly or (with or without human intervention) by means of any appropriate equipment.

Extract 7.3.37

R v Shephard [1993] AC 380, 382, 386–7 (HL)

LORD GRIFFITHS: My Lords, the Court of Appeal has certified the following point of law of general public importance:

'Whether a party seeking to rely on computer evidence can discharge the burden under section 69(1)(*b*) of the Police and Criminal Evidence Act 1984 without calling a computer expert, and if so how?'

. . .

The defendant's argument requires one to read into section 69(1) after the words 'unless it is shown' the following words lifted from paragraph 8 of Schedule 3 'by [the oral evidence of] a person occupying a responsible position in relation to the operation of the computer.'

These words do not appear in the section. They are, for the reasons I have given, contained in Schedule 3 as a necessary qualification to sign a certificate but I can see no reason to read them into section 69(1) when oral evidence will be open to challenge by cross-examination.

Documents produced by computers are an increasingly common feature of all business and more and more people are becoming familiar with their uses and operation. Computers vary immensely in their complexity and in the operations they perform. The nature of the evidence to discharge the burden of showing that there has been no improper use of the computer and that it was operating properly will inevitably vary from case to case. The evidence must be tailored to suit the needs of the case. I suspect that it will very rarely be necessary to call an expert and that in the vast majority of cases it will be possible to discharge the burden by calling a witness who is familiar with the operation of the computer in the sense of knowing what the computer is required to do and who can say that it is doing it properly.

. . .

I therefore answer the certified question by saying that section 69(1) of the Police and Criminal Evidence Act 1984 can be satisfied by the oral evidence of a person familiar with the operation of the computer who can give evidence of its reliability and such a person need not be a computer expert.

Extract 7.3.38

DPP v McKeown [1997] 1 WLR 295, 297–304 (HL)

LORD HOFFMANN: My Lords, these two appeals concerning convictions under the Road Traffic Act 1988, one for driving with an excessive proportion of alcohol in the breath and the other for failing without reasonable excuse to provide a specimen of breath, both arise out of the fact that in late July 1992 the computer clock in the Lion Intoximeter 3000 in use at Widnes Police Station was displaying a time about an hour and a quarter slow. In neither case was there any dispute about the correct time at which the Intoximeter was used; in fact, the precise time was not a matter of any importance. In the one case the Intoximeter recorded that the motorist had twice the prescribed limit of alcohol in both specimens of her breath; in the other, the first specimen was more than four times the prescribed limit, after which the motorist deliberately refused to provide a second. Nevertheless the Divisional Court accepted that the inaccuracy of the clock reading vitiated both convictions and against that decision the Director of Public Prosecutions appeals to your Lordships' House.

By section 5(1) of the Act of 1988 it is an offence to drive a motor vehicle on a road after consuming so much alcohol that the proportion in his breath exceeds the prescribed limit of 35 microgrammes of alcohol in 100 millilitres of breath. By section 7(1), a constable investigating whether a person has committed an offence under section 5 may require him to provide two specimens of breath for analysis by means of a device of a type approved by the Secretary of State and by section 7(6) a person who without reasonable excuse fails to provide a specimen when required to do so pursuant to subsection (1) is guilty of an offence.

The Lion Intoximeter 3000 is a device approved by the Secretary of State for the purposes of section 7(1). It consists of an analyser which measures the alcohol content of the breath by means of an electrical signal; a computer which converts the signal into digital form with a visual display on which the result of the test is shown and a printer on which it can be printed out; and a breath simulator which provides air containing a measured quantity of alcohol so that the constable operating the machine may check whether it is calibrating correctly. The standard procedure is for the machine to be tested before and after the analysis of the two specimens provided by the motorist.

The usual way in which evidence of the proportion of alcohol in the breath is proved in court is by certificate under section 16 of the Road Traffic Offenders Act 1988. This provides:

'(1) Evidence of the proportion of alcohol . . . in a specimen of breath . . . may, subject to subsections (3) and (4) below . . . be given by the production of a document or documents purporting to be . . . (a) a statement automatically produced by the device by which the proportion of alcohol in a specimen of breath was measured and a certificate signed by a constable (which may but need not be contained in the same document as the statement) that the statement relates to a specimen provided by the accused at the date and time shown in the statement . . . (3) Subject to subsection (4) below – (a) a document purporting to be such a statement or such a certificate (or both such a statement and such a certificate) as is mentioned in subsection (1)(a) above is admissible in evidence on behalf of the prosecution in pursuance of this section only if a copy of it either has been handed to the accused when the document was produced or has been served on him not later than seven days before the hearing . . . (4) A document purporting to be a certificate (or so much of a document as purports to be a certificate) is not so admissible if the accused, not later than three days before the hearing or within such further time as the court may in special circumstances allow, has served notice on the prosecutor requiring the attendance at the hearing of the person by whom the document purports to be signed.'

The section is a specialised exception to the hearsay rule which, on compliance with its conditions, enables evidence which the constable could have given orally to be given instead by a certificate admissible on mere production. But the requirement that the certificate and statement be served on the accused and that they should not be admissible if the accused gives notice that he requires the constable who signed the certificate to attend the hearing means that the procedure is for practical purposes consensual. If such notice is given, or the prosecution is unable to comply with the conditions, the prosecution must prove its case by other admissible evidence.

This will in practice mean calling the officer who operated that Intoximeter to testify to the results of the test by reference to what he saw on the visual display and what the machine printed out. Such first-hand evidence of what was displayed or recorded on a mechanical measuring device is real evidence admissible at common law: see *Castle v Cross* [1984] 1 WLR 1372, applying *The Statue of Liberty* [1968] 1 WLR 739. But when the measuring device, as in this case, includes a computer, the evidence is not admissible unless it satisfies the requirements of section 69 of the Police and Criminal Evidence Act 1984 . . .

. . .

Late on 21 July 1992 Ms McKeown was observed to be driving erratically in Liverpool Road, Widnes, arrested on suspicion of being over the limit and taken to Widnes Police Station. There she was required to provide specimens of breath for analysis. The Lion Intoximeter 3000 was operated by Sergeant O'Dell. He tested the machine and it calibrated correctly. By this time it was about a quarter after midnight; the sergeant's watch said 00.13 am. But the time display on the machine read 23:00. Part of the discrepancy was explained by the fact that, as the printout made plain, the machine was set to GMT. But there was no explanation of the balance. Ms McKeown provided the required two specimens, both of which registered 78; well in excess of the prescribed limit of 35. Afterwards Sergeant O'Dell tested the machine again and once more it calibrated correctly. He filled in the standard form of witness statement for use in such cases, attaching the printout from the Intoximeter but noting on his statement 'Time shown on printout is 1 hr 13 mins slow.'

Ms McKeown was charged under section 5(1). She was served with the statement of Sergeant O'Dell and also a statement of Dr Paul Williams, a director of Lion Laboratories Ltd, which supplies the Intoximeter to the police. It said that the alcohol analytical system and breath sampling system were separate from the circuitry which controlled the accuracy of the clock. Inaccuracy in the time display could have absolutely no effect on the accuracy of the readings obtained on breath samples.

. . .

As the time inaccuracy meant that Sergeant O'Dell was unable to certify, in accordance with section 16 of the Road Traffic Offenders Act 1988, that the statement automatically produced by the Intoximeter related to 'a specimen provided by the accused at the date and time shown in the statement,' he was called to give evidence and testified to the conduct of the test and the readings on the visual display and printout which I have described. Dr Williams also gave evidence. He said that he was not an electronics expert and did not understand the circuitry of the Intoximeter clock but that the clock had no bearing on the accuracy of the breath readings. The justices accepted this evidence and found, as later recorded in the case stated, that the Intoximeter was not affected by the clock and that the statements as to the breath readings it produced were accurate.

. . .

The second question is whether, given Dr Williams's lack of expertise in electronics, his expert evidence was admissible on the question of the reliability of the device. In my view Dr Williams was entitled to give this evidence by reason of his familiarity with the working of the Lion Intoximeter 3000. It is notorious that one needs no expertise in electronics to be able to know whether a computer is working properly. Dr Williams was qualified to say that he was familiar with Intoximeters which displayed the time incorrectly but nevertheless produced correct breath analyses. Sergeant O'Dell, who tested his Intoximeter to see whether it was calibrating correctly, was able to give evidence to the same effect. This was evidence on which the justices were entitled to make their finding that the statements produced by the device were accurate.

This brings me to the chief question in Ms McKeown's case, which is whether the evidence of the Intoximeter's breath analysis satisfied the requirements of section 69(1) of the Police and Criminal Evidence Act 1984. If it did not, there was no other evidence of the alcohol content in her breath and her conviction cannot stand. It will be recalled that section 69(1) deals with the admissibility of 'a statement in a document produced by a computer' as evidence of 'any fact stated therein.' In order for the statement to be admissible, it must be shown, in accordance with subsection (1)(b):

> 'that at all material times the computer was operating properly, or if not, that any respect in which it was not operating properly or was out of operation was not such as to affect the production of the document or the accuracy of its contents; . . . '

A 'statement' has the same meaning as in section 10(1)(c) of Part I of the Civil Evidence Act 1968, where it includes 'any . . . device in which . . . data . . . are embodied so as to be capable . . . of being reproduced therefrom.' This would include the memory of a computer.

I shall for the moment assume that the inaccuracy in the time display meant that 'the computer . . . was not operating properly.' The question is therefore whether that was 'such as to affect the production of the document or the accuracy of its contents.' If the words are read literally, it did. The document said that the first test had occurred at 23.00 GMT when it was in fact 00.13 BST. As to one hour, the discrepancy is merely as to the way in which the time was expressed. 23.00 GMT is the same time as 00.00 BST. But the remaining 13 minutes cannot, I think, be dismissed as de minimis. The inaccuracy of the time reading therefore affected the accuracy of a part of the contents of the document.

In my view, however, the paragraph was not intended to be read in such a literal fashion. '[T]he production of the document or the accuracy of its contents' are very wide words. What if there was a software fault which caused the document to be printed in lower case when it was meant to be in upper case? The fault has certainly affected the production of the document. But a rule which excluded an otherwise accurate document on this ground would be quite irrational. To discover the legislative intent, it is necessary to consider the purpose of the rule.

The first thing to notice is that section 69 is concerned solely with the proper operation and functioning of a computer. A computer is a device for storing, processing and retrieving information. It receives information from, for example, signals down a telephone line, strokes on a keyboard or (in this case) a device for chemical analysis of gas, and it stores and processes that information. If the information received by the computer was inaccurate (for example, if the operator keyed in the wrong name) then the information retrieved from the computer in the form of a statement will likewise be inaccurate. Computer experts have colourful phrases in which to express this axiom. But section 69 is not in the least concerned with the accuracy of the information supplied to the computer. If the gas analyser of the Intoximeter is not functioning properly and gives an inaccurate signal which the computer faithfully reproduces, section 69 does not affect the admissibility of the statement. The same is true if the operator keys in the wrong name. Neither of these errors is concerned with the proper operation or functioning of the computer.

The purpose of section 69, therefore, is a relatively modest one. It does not require the prosecution to show that the statement is likely to be true. Whether it is likely to be true or not is a question of weight for the justices or jury. All that section 69 requires as a condition of the admissibility of a computer-generated statement is positive evidence that the computer has properly processed, stored and reproduced whatever information it received. It is concerned with the way in which the computer has dealt with the information to generate the statement which is being tendered as evidence of a fact which it states.

The language of section 69(1) recognises that a computer may be malfunctioning in a way which is not relevant to the purpose of the exclusionary rule. It cannot therefore be argued that any malfunction is sufficient to cast doubt upon the capacity of the computer to process information correctly. The legislature clearly refused to accept so extreme a proposition. What, then, was contemplated as the distinction between a relevant and an irrelevant malfunction? It seems to me that there is only one possible answer to that question. A malfunction is relevant if it affects the way in which the computer processes, stores or retrieves the information used to generate the statement tendered in evidence. Other malfunctions do not matter. It follows that the words 'not such as to affect the production of the document or the accuracy of its contents' must be read subject to the overall qualification that the paragraph is referring to those aspects of the document or its contents which are material to the accuracy of the statement tendered in evidence.

Paragraph (a) of section 69(1), which deals with improper use of the computer, clearly has this meaning. The statement is inadmissible only if there are reasonable grounds for believing that the improper use has caused the statement tendered in evidence to be inaccurate. It was argued that because paragraph (b) uses different language and speaks of the 'production of the document or the accuracy of its contents' rather than being concerned, as in paragraph (a), with the accuracy of 'the statement,' it must have a different meaning. I shall not speculate on the reasons why the draftsman thought it necessary to deal with improper use of the computer separately from the question of whether it was in proper working order. But there cannot have been any difference in the purpose of the two paragraphs: in both cases the legislature was concerned with the reliability of the statement tendered in evidence as a properly processed and reproduced piece of information. On the point now in issue I think it would be quite irrational if the effect of the two paragraphs was not the same.

The justices had before them a certificate signed by Sergeant O'Dell under paragraph 8 of Schedule 3 stating that to the best of his knowledge and belief the requirements of section 69(1) had been complied with. In the absence of contrary evidence, they were entitled to accept this certificate as sufficient to satisfy section 69(1). The question is then whether they were obliged to regard the inaccuracy of the clock display as contrary evidence. The justices also had evidence from Dr Williams and Sergeant O'Dell, which they were entitled to accept, that the clock display was not affecting the proper functioning of the computer in processing the information from the breath analyser. Having accepted this evidence, there was in my view nothing to displace the effect of Sergeant O'Dell's certificate.

I have considered the matter on the assumption that the error in the clock display showed that the computer was not operating properly. I should say, however, that I am not satisfied that this conclusion should have been drawn. Computer clocks, like any others, have to be set to the correct time and the most obvious explanation for the 13-minute discrepancy was that someone had made a mistake when he last set the clock. This would not have anything to do with the computer not operating properly. Furthermore, if the error lay in the clock mechanism itself, I doubt whether it would constitute part of 'the computer' for the purposes of section 69(1). The section, as I have said, is concerned with the processing and storage of information and not with the accuracy of the information supplied. The clock, although no doubt physically in the same box as the computer, is something which supplies information to the computer rather than being part of the processing mechanism. But I do not explore this question any further because there was no evidence about why the time was inaccurate and I prefer to base my decision on the construction of section 69(1). In my view, there was admissible evidence upon which the justices were entitled to convict Ms McKeown and the Director's appeal in her case should be allowed.

Mr Christopher Jones was brought into Widnes Police Station about a week after Ms McKeown. He had driven his car onto a roundabout and appeared to be very drunk indeed. He provided one specimen of breath which registered 148; more than four times the prescribed limit. He then did not blow hard enough to provide a second specimen. The visual display and print out indicated that the test had aborted. The officer who operated the machine and gave evidence at the trial was Sergeant Draycott. Like Sergeant O'Dell, he noted that the time display was inaccurate by his watch; in his case, by an hour and 15 minutes, but the discrepancy of two minutes from the evidence in the earlier case is as likely to have been in the policemen's watches as an indication that the computer clock had fallen further behind.

Mr Jones was charged under section 7(6) with failing without reasonable excuse to provide a specimen of breath when required to do so in pursuance of section 7(1). At the trial he gave evidence that he had tried his best but was overcome by a fit of coughing. The justices rejected his explanation, found that he had deliberately refused to blow into the machine as instructed and convicted.

. . .

Finally, it was submitted for Mr Jones that the only admissible evidence that his second breath specimen was inadequate was the computer reading showing that the test had aborted. If this was inadmissible for failure to comply with section 69(1), he could not be convicted. The arguments against the admissibility of the computer evidence were the same as those which I have already rejected in the case of Ms McKeown. It follows that in my view this point also fails and the Director's appeal in Mr Jones's case should also be allowed.

See J S W Black, 'Breath Testing Devices and Computer Evidence' (1997) 141 *Solicitors Journal* 236.

The Law Commission has recommended that s 69 be repealed without replacement,[91] pointing out persuasively that an anomaly arises from the fact that s 69 applies only where the document is tendered in evidence, and has no application where it is used by an expert in reaching his or her conclusions, or where a witness uses it to refresh his or her memory. Further, it is in any event questionable whether there is any need for a provision like s 69 at all: developments in computer technology and the complexity of modern-day computer systems are making compliance with s 69 increasingly difficult, and the provision fails to address the main problem with computer evidence, which is caused by incorrect data being fed into computers rather than by defects in the software.[92]

(iii) Use at trial of written statements and depositions admitted in evidence in committal proceedings

Extract 7.3.39

Criminal Procedure and Investigations Act 1996, Sched 2, paras 1, 2

1. Statements
(1) Sub-paragraph (2) applies if –
  (a) a written statement has been admitted in evidence in proceedings before a magistrates' court inquiring into an offence as examining justices,

---

[91] Law Commission (Law Com No 245), *Evidence in Criminal Proceedings: Hearsay and Related Topics* (1997) 193.
[92] At 188–9.

(b) in those proceedings a person has been committed for trial,

(c) for the purposes of section 5A of the Magistrates' Courts Act 1980 the statement complied with section 5B of that Act prior to the committal for trial,

(d) the statement purports to be signed by a justice of the peace, and

(e) sub-paragraph (3) does not prevent sub-paragraph (2) applying.

(2) Where this sub-paragraph applies the statement may without further proof be read as evidence on the trial of the accused, whether for the offence for which he was committed for trial or for any other offence arising out of the same transaction or set of circumstances.

(3) Sub-paragraph (2) does not apply if –

(a) it is proved that the statement was not signed by the justice by whom it purports to have been signed,

(b) the court of trial at its discretion orders that sub-paragraph (2) shall not apply, or

(c) a party to the proceedings objects to sub-paragraph (2) applying.

(4) If a party to the proceedings objects to sub-paragraph (2) applying the court of trial may order that the objection shall have no effect if the court considers it to be in the interests of justice so to order.

2. Depositions

(1) Sub-paragraph (2) applies if –

(a) in pursuance of section 97A of the Magistrates' Courts Act 1980 (summons or warrant to have evidence taken as a deposition etc) a person has had his evidence taken as a deposition for the purposes of proceedings before a magistrates' court inquiring into an offence as examining justices,

(b) the deposition has been admitted in evidence in those proceedings,

(c) in those proceedings a person has been committed for trial,

(d) for the purposes of section 5A of the Magistrates' Courts Act 1980 the deposition complied with section 5C of that Act prior to the committal for trial,

(e) the deposition purports to be signed by the justice before whom it purports to have been taken, and

(f) sub-paragraph (3) does not prevent sub-paragraph (2) applying.

(2) Where this sub-paragraph applies the deposition may without further proof be read as evidence on the trial of the accused, whether for the offence for which he was committed for trial or for any other offence arising out of the same transaction or set of circumstances.

(3) Sub-paragraph (2) does not apply if –

(a) it is proved that the deposition was not signed by the justice by whom it purports to have been signed,

(b) the court of trial at its discretion orders that sub-paragraph (2) shall not apply, or

(c) a party to the proceedings objects to sub-paragraph (2) applying.

(4) If a party to the proceedings objects to sub-paragraph (2) applying the court of trial may order that the objection shall have no effect if the court considers it to be in the interests of justice so to order.

(iv) Proof by written statement

Extract 7.3.40

Criminal Justice Act 1967, s 9(1)–(4)

9. Proof by written statement

(1) In any criminal proceedings, other than committal proceedings, a written statement by any person shall, if such of the conditions mentioned in the next following subsection as are applicable are satisfied, be admissible as evidence to the like extent as oral evidence to the like effect by that person.

(2) The said conditions are –

    (a) the statement purports to be signed by the person who made it;

    (b) the statement contains a declaration by that person to the effect that it is true to the best of his knowledge and belief and that he made the statement knowing that, if it were tendered in evidence, he would be liable to prosecution if he wilfully stated in it anything which he knew to be false or did not believe to be true;

    (c) before the hearing at which the statement is tendered in evidence, a copy of the statement is served, by or on behalf of the party proposing to tender it, on each of the other parties to the proceedings; and

    (d) none of the other parties or their solicitors, within seven days from the service of the copy of the statement, serves a notice on the party so proposing objecting to the statement being tendered in evidence under this section:

Provided that the conditions mentioned in paragraphs (c) and (d) of this subsection shall not apply if the parties agree before or during the hearing that the statement shall be so tendered.

(3) The following provisions shall also have effect in relation to any written statement tendered in evidence under this section, that is to say –

    (a) if the statement is made by a person under the age of eighteen, it shall give his age;

    (b) if it is made by a person who cannot read it, it shall be read to him before he signs it and shall be accompanied by a declaration by the person who so read the statement to the effect that it was so read; and

    (c) if it refers to any other document as an exhibit, the copy served on any other party to the proceedings under paragraph (c) of the last foregoing subsection shall be accompanied by a copy of that document or by such information as may be necessary in order to enable the party on whom it is served to inspect that document or a copy thereof.

(4) Notwithstanding that a written statement made by any person may be admissible as evidence by virtue of this section –

    (a) the party by whom or on whose behalf a copy of the statement was served may call that person to give evidence; and

(b) the court may, of its own motion or on the application of any party to the proceedings, require that person to attend before the court and give evidence.

(v) Further exceptions

Section 30 of the Criminal Justice Act 1988 (relating to expert reports) and s 32A of the Criminal Justice Act 1988 (relating to video recordings of testimony from child witnesses) may also be regarded as having created statutory exceptions to the hearsay rule in criminal proceedings. These provisions are discussed in Chapters 11 and 3 respectively.

(f) The Implications of the European Convention on Human Rights

Brief consideration should be given to the issue of the extent to which the admission in evidence for the prosecution of out-of-court statements may fall foul of the European Convention on Human Rights. Article 6(3)(d) of the Convention provides, inter alia, that everyone charged with a criminal offence has the right 'to examine or have examined witnesses against him . . .'. There have been a number of decisions of the European Court of Human Rights interpreting this provision,[93] but there is little predictive value, and not a great deal of consistency, in these pronouncements. The only general principle which seems to have emerged is that the admissibility of evidence is to be regarded primarily as a matter for regulation by national law, with the role of the European Court being not to express a view on whether the evidence in question was correctly admitted, 'but rather to ascertain whether the proceedings considered as a whole, including the way in which evidence was taken, were fair'.[94] Further, it has frequently been stated that what art 6(3)(d) requires is that an accused be given an 'adequate and proper opportunity' to challenge and question a person whose statements are being used as prosecution evidence, either at the time of the making of the statement or at some later stage in the proceedings.[95]

---

[93] See generally D J Birch, 'Hearsay-Logic and Hearsay-Fiddles: *Blastland* Revisited' in P Smith (ed), *Criminal Law: Essays in Honour of J C Smith* (1987) 35–6; C Osborne, 'Hearsay and the European Court of Human Rights' [1993] *Criminal Law Review* 255; H Reiter, 'Hearsay Evidence and Criminal Process in Germany and Australia' (1984) 10 *Monash University Law Review* 51, 70–1; Law Commission (Law Com No 245), *Evidence in Criminal Proceedings: Hearsay and Related Topics* (1997) Part V.

[94] *Kostovski v Netherlands* (1989) 12 EHRR 434, 447. See also *Windisch v Austria* (1990) 13 EHRR 281, 286; *Delta v France* (1990) 16 EHRR 574, 586; *Isgrò v Italy* (1/1990/192/252); *Asch v Austria* (1991) 15 EHRR 597, 606; *Lüdi v Switzerland* (1992) 15 EHRR 173, 200; *Saïdi v France* (1993) 17 EHRR 251, 269; *Doorson v Netherlands* (1996) 22 EHRR 330, 357–8.

[95] *Kostovski v Netherlands* (1989) 12 EHRR 434, 448. See also *Windisch v Austria* (1990) 13 EHRR 281, 286; *Delta v France* (1990) 16 EHRR 574, 587; *Isgrò v Italy* (1/1990/192/252); *Asch v Austria* (1991) 15 EHRR 597, 606; *Lüdi v Switzerland* (1992) 15 EHRR 173, 200; *Saïdi v France* (1993) 17 EHRR 251, 269.

In *Unterpertinger v Austria*,[96] *Kostovski v Netherlands*,[97] *Windisch v Austria*,[98] *Delta v France*,[99] *Lüdi v Switzerland*[100] and *Saïdi v France*,[101] the European Court upheld the applicants' arguments that they had been denied fair trials on the basis of violations of art 6(3)(d). In all of these cases, the out-of-court statements constituted the only evidence, or an important part of the evidence, against the applicant. Illustrative is *Windisch v Austria*,[102] in which the applicant argued that his conviction had to a large extent been based upon statements by two anonymous persons who had been heard only by the police (in the absence of the defence), and not by the trial court. Referring approvingly to its earlier decision in *Kostovski v Netherlands*,[103] the European Court held that the defence, being unaware of the identity of the two persons, had 'an almost insurmountable handicap' as it was deprived of the necessary information for testing their veracity. Additionally, the trial court had been deprived of the opportunity of observing their demeanour under questioning and thus of forming its own impression of their reliability. The European Court was careful to point out that 'the Convention does not preclude reliance, at the investigation stage, on sources such as anonymous informants. However, the subsequent use of their statements by the trial court to found a conviction is another matter.'[104] The present case was one in which there were no eyewitnesses to the offence, the statements of the two people constituting the only evidence which indicated the applicant's presence at the scene of the crime. And this evidence was relied upon to a large extent by the trial court in convicting the applicant.[105]

In *Isgrò v Italy*,[106] *Asch v Austria*,[107] *Artner v Austria*[108] and *Doorson v Netherlands*,[109] however, the applicants' arguments failed in the European Court. In all three cases, there was other substantial prosecution evidence implicating the applicants. Illustrative is *Isgrò v Italy*, in which the applicant's conviction was based partially upon statements made before an investigating judge and read out at the trial on the basis that their maker, Mr D, was 'untraceable'. The European Court provided a number of reasons for rejecting the applicant's argument that he had been denied a fair trial. First, the maker of the statements was not anonymous: his identity was known to the defence and investigating judge, as well as to the first instance and appeal

---

[96] (1986) 13 EHRR 175.
[97] (1989) 12 EHRR 434.
[98] (1990) 13 EHRR 281.
[99] (1990) 16 EHRR 574.
[100] (1992) 15 EHRR 173.
[101] (1993) 17 EHRR 251.
[102] (1990) 13 EHRR 281.
[103] (1989) 12 EHRR 434.
[104] (1990) 13 EHRR 281, 287.
[105] At 287–8.
[106] 1/1990/192/252.
[107] (1991) 15 EHRR 597.
[108] 39/1991/291/362.
[109] (1996) 22 EHRR 330.

courts. This meant that the applicant's lawyer was able during the trial to challenge the accuracy of Mr D's allegations and the credibility of Mr D himself. Secondly, a confrontation organised by the investigating judge enabled the applicant to put questions directly to Mr D and to discuss his statements, thus providing the investigating judge with all the information capable of casting doubt upon Mr D's credibility. Thirdly, the first instance and appeal courts had, in reaching their decisions, considered other evidence apart from that of the statements in question.

From the preceding discussions, it would appear that there are two factors which are likely to lead to a decision by the European Court that an applicant has been denied a fair trial because of a violation of art 6(3)(d). The first is that the identity of the maker of the out-of-court statement is unknown, and the second that the statement constitutes at least an important part of the evidence against the applicant. Beyond this, however, little guidance is provided by the cases on the interpretation of art 6(3)(d).

(g) Reform

The following represent some possible options for reform of criminal hearsay doctrine. What are the merits and demerits of each of these options?

Option 1: Preserve existing exceptions, but recognise a residual inclusionary discretion

One option for reform would be to keep the existing list of specific exceptions to the rule largely intact (perhaps with some modifications to some of these exceptions), but to add to this list a residual discretion to admit hearsay evidence in appropriate circumstances. Rule 807 of the US Federal Rules of Evidence, for example, may facilitate the admission of hearsay evidence not already rendered admissible by the specific exceptions listed in Rules 803 and 804:

Extract 7.3.41

US Federal Rules of Evidence, rule 807

Rule 807. Residual Exception
A statement not specifically covered by Rule 803 or 804 but having equivalent circumstantial guarantees of trustworthiness, is not excluded by the hearsay rule, if the court determines that (A) the statement is offered as evidence of a material fact; (B) the statement is more probative on the point for which it is offered than any other evidence which the proponent can procure through reasonable efforts; and (C) the general purposes of these rules and the interests of justice will best be served by admission of the statement into evidence.

However, a statement may not be admitted under this exception unless the proponent of it makes known to the adverse party sufficiently in advance of the trial or hearing to provide the adverse party with a fair opportunity to prepare to meet it, the proponent's intention to offer the statement and the particulars of it, including the name and address of the declarant.

Option 2: Recognise broader categories of exception

This is the approach recommended by the Law Commission:

Extract 7.3.42

Law Commission (Law Com No 245), *Evidence in Criminal Proceedings: Hearsay and Related Topics* (1997) 207–15 Draft Criminal Evidence Bill, clauses 1, 2, 3, 4, 5, 6, 9, 14, 15

1. The hearsay rule

(1) In criminal proceedings a statement not made in oral evidence in the proceedings is not admissible as evidence of any matter stated unless –
    (a) this Act or any other statutory provision makes it admissible,
    (b) any rule of law preserved by section 6 makes it admissible, or
    (c) all parties to the proceedings agree to it being admissible.

(2) The common law rules governing the admissibility of hearsay evidence in criminal proceedings are abolished (except for the rules preserved by section 6).

2. Statements and matters stated

(1) In this Act references to a statement or to a matter stated are to be read as follows.

(2) A statement is any representation of fact or opinion made by a person by whatever means; and it includes a representation made in a sketch, photofit or other pictorial form.

(3) A matter stated is one to which this Act applies if (and only if) the purpose, or one of the purposes, of the person making the statement appears to the court to have been –
    (a) to cause another person to believe the matter, or
    (b) to cause another person to act or a machine to operate on the basis that the matter is as stated.

3. Cases where a witness is unavailable

In criminal proceedings a statement not made in oral evidence in the proceedings is admissible as evidence of any matter stated if –
    (a) oral evidence given in the proceedings by the person who made the statement would be admissible as evidence of that matter,
    (b) the person who made the statement (the relevant person) is identified to the court's satisfaction, and
    (c) any of the five conditions mentioned in section 5 is satisfied (absence of relevant person etc).

4. Business and other documents

(1) In criminal proceedings a statement contained in a document is admissible as evidence of any matter stated if –

  (a) oral evidence given in the proceedings would be admissible as evidence of that matter,

  (b) the requirements of subsection (2) are satisfied, and

  (c) the requirements of subsection (5) are satisfied, in a case where subsection (4) requires them to be.

(2) The requirements of this subsection are satisfied if –

  (a) the document or the part containing the statement was created or received by a person in the course of a trade, business, profession or other occupation, or as the holder of a paid or unpaid office,

  (b) the person who supplied the information contained in the statement (the relevant person) had or may reasonably be supposed to have had personal knowledge of the matters dealt with, and

  (c) each person (if any) through whom the information was supplied from the relevant person to the person mentioned in paragraph (a) received the information in the course of a trade, business, profession or other occupation, or as the holder of a paid or unpaid office.

(3) The persons mentioned in paragraphs (a) and (b) of subsection (2) may be the same person.

(4) The additional requirements of subsection (5) must be satisfied if the statement –

  (a) was prepared for the purposes of pending or contemplated criminal proceedings, or for a criminal investigation, but

  (b) was not prepared in accordance with section 3 of the Criminal Justice (International Co-operation) Act 1990 or an order under paragraph 6 of Schedule 13 to the Criminal Justice Act 1988 (which relate to overseas evidence).

(5) The requirements of this subsection are satisfied if –

  (a) any of the five conditions mentioned in section 5 is satisfied (absence of relevant person etc), or

  (b) the relevant person cannot reasonably be expected to have any recollection of the matters dealt with in the statement (having regard to the length of time since he supplied the information and all other circumstances).

(6) A statement is not admissible under this section if the court makes a direction to that effect under subsection (7).

(7) The court may make a direction under this subsection if satisfied that the statement's reliability as evidence for the purpose for which it is tendered is doubtful in view of –

  (a) its contents,

  (b) the source of the information contained in it,

  (c) the way in which or the circumstances in which the information was supplied or received, or

  (d) the way in which or the circumstances in which the document concerned was created or received.

5. The five conditions

(1) Here are the five conditions referred to in sections 3 and 4.

(2) The first condition is that the relevant person is dead.

(3) The second condition is that the relevant person is unfit to be a witness because of his bodily or mental condition.

(4) The third condition is that the relevant person is outside the United Kingdom and it is not reasonably practicable to secure his attendance.

(5) The fourth condition is that the relevant person cannot be found although such steps as it is reasonably practicable to take to find him have been taken.

(6) The fifth condition is that through fear the relevant person does not give (or does not continue to give) oral evidence in the proceedings –

    (a) at all, or

    (b) in connection with the subject matter of the statement,

and the court gives leave for the statement to be given in evidence.

(7) For the purposes of subsection (6) 'fear' must be widely construed and (for example) includes fear of the death or injury of another person or of financial loss.

(8) Leave may be given under subsection (6) only if the court considers that the statement ought to be admitted in the interests of justice, having regard –

    (a) to the statement's contents,

    (b) to any risk that its admission or exclusion will result in unfairness to any party to the proceedings (and in particular to how likely it is that the statement can be controverted if the relevant person does not give oral evidence),

    (c) in appropriate cases, to the fact that special arrangements could be made for the relevant person to give evidence (for example, through a television link or from behind a screen), and

    (d) to any other relevant circumstances.

(9) A condition which is in fact satisfied is to be treated as not satisfied if it is shown that the circumstances described in it are caused –

    (a) by the person in support of whose case it is sought to give the statement in evidence, or

    (b) by a person acting on his behalf,

in order to prevent the relevant person giving oral evidence in the proceedings (whether at all or in connection with the subject matter of the statement).

6. Common law exceptions

(1) The rules of law to which this section applies are preserved.

(2) This section applies to any rule of law under which in criminal proceedings –

    (a) published works dealing with matters of a public nature (such as histories, scientific works, dictionaries and maps) are admissible as evidence of facts of a public nature stated in them,

    (b) public documents (such as public registers, and returns made under public authority with respect to matters of public interest) are admissible as evidence of facts stated in them,

(c) records (such as the records of certain courts, treaties, Crown grants, pardons and commissions) are admissible as evidence of facts stated in them, or

(d) evidence relating to a person's age or date or place of birth may be given by a person without personal knowledge of the matter.

(3) This section also applies to any rule of law under which in criminal proceedings evidence of a person's reputation is admissible for the purpose of proving his good or bad character; but the rule is preserved only so far as it allows the court to treat such evidence as proving the matter concerned.

(4) This section also applies to any rule of law under which in criminal proceedings evidence of reputation or family tradition is admissible for the purpose of proving or disproving –

(a) pedigree or the existence of a marriage,

(b) the existence of any public or general right, or

(c) the identity of any person or thing;

but the rule is preserved only so far as it allows the court to treat such evidence as proving or disproving the matter concerned.

(5) This section also applies to any rule of law under which in criminal proceedings a statement is admissible as evidence of any matter stated if –

(a) the statement was made by a person so emotionally overpowered by an event that the possibility of concoction or distortion can be disregarded,

(b) the statement accompanied an act which can be properly evaluated as evidence only if considered in conjunction with the statement, or

(c) the statement relates to a physical sensation or a mental state (such as intention or emotion).

(6) This section also applies to any rule of law relating to the admissibility of confessions or mixed statements in criminal proceedings.

(7) This section also applies to any rule of law under which in criminal proceedings –

(a) an admission made by an agent of an accused person is admissible against the accused as evidence of any matter stated, or

(b) a statement made by a person to whom an accused person refers a person for information is admissible against the accused as evidence of any matter stated.

(8) This section also applies to any rule of law under which in criminal proceedings a statement made by a party to a common enterprise is admissible against another party to the enterprise as evidence of any matter stated.

(9) This section also applies to any rule of law under which in criminal proceedings an expert witness may draw on the body of expertise relevant to his field.

9. Discretion to admit hearsay

In criminal proceedings a statement not made in oral evidence in the proceedings is admissible as evidence of any matter stated if the court is satisfied that, despite the difficulties there may be in challenging the statement, its probative value is such that the interests of justice require it to be admissible.

14. Court's duty where evidence is unconvincing

(1) If on a person's trial on indictment for an offence the court is satisfied at any time after the close of the case for the prosecution that –

    (a) the case against the accused is based wholly or partly on a statement not made in oral evidence in the proceedings, and

    (b) the evidence provided by the statement is so unconvincing that, considering its importance to the case against the accused, his conviction of the offence would be unsafe,

    the court must direct the jury to acquit him of that offence.

(2) If on a person's trial on indictment for an offence –

    (a) the circumstances are such that (under the common law or a statutory provision) he may if acquitted of that offence be found guilty of another offence, and

    (b) the court is satisfied as mentioned in subsection (1) in respect of that other offence,

the court must direct the jury to acquit him of that other offence.

(3) If –

    (a) a jury is required to determine under section 4A(2) of the Criminal Procedure (Insanity) Act 1964 whether a person being tried on indictment for an offence did the act or made the omission charged against him as the offence, and

    (b) the court is satisfied as mentioned in subsection (1) above in respect of that offence,

the court must direct the jury to return a verdict of acquittal of that offence.

(4) If on the summary trial of an information for an offence the court is satisfied as mentioned in subsection (1) in respect of –

    (a) that offence, and

    (b) any other offence of which the court may (under the common law or a statutory provision) find the accused guilty on that information,

the court must dismiss the information.

(5) Subsections (1) to (3) apply to an indictment containing more than one count as if each count were a separate indictment.

(6) This section does not prejudice any other power a court may have to direct a jury to acquit a person of an offence or to dismiss an information.

15. Court's general discretion to exclude evidence

(1) In criminal proceedings the court may refuse to admit a statement as evidence of a matter stated if –

    (a) the statement was made otherwise than in oral evidence in the proceedings, and

    (b) the court is satisfied that the statement's probative value is substantially outweighed by the danger that to admit it would result in undue waste of time.

(2) Nothing in this Act prejudices –

    (a) any power of a court to exclude evidence under section 78 of the Police and Criminal Evidence Act 1984 (exclusion of unfair evidence), or

    (b) any other power of a court to exclude evidence at its discretion (whether by preventing questions from being put or otherwise).

In essence, therefore, the Commission's recommendation is that the exceptions to the hearsay rule should consist of:

(1) categories of automatic admissibility where the declarant's testimony is, for one of a number of specified reasons, unavailable;
(2) an exception allowing statements made by witnesses who are in fear to be admitted in evidence with the leave of the court;
(3) a business documents exception; and
(4) certain preserved common-law and statutory exceptions.

To cater, however, for hearsay that is inadmissible on each of the above bases, the Commission recommends the recognition of an inclusionary discretion. In addition, courts would have a general discretion to exclude hearsay evidence, and a duty to direct an acquittal where the prosecution case is based wholly or partly on unconvincing hearsay evidence.

Option 3: A discretionary approach

Such an approach has evolved in Canada:

Extract 7.3.43

R v Hawkins (1996) 141 DLR (4th) 193, 219 (SCC)

LAMER CJC AND IACOBUCCI J: In *Khan* [[1990] 2 SCR 531] and *Smith* [[1992] 2 SCR 915], this Court signalled the beginning of a modern principled framework for defining exceptions to the hearsay rule. The Court rejected the traditional approach of the common law premised on rigid, categorical exceptions to the hearsay rule in favour of a more flexible approach which seeks to give effect to the underlying purposes of the rule. As Lamer CJC said in *Smith*, at p 932:

> . . . *Khan* should [. . .] not be understood as turning on its particular facts, but, instead, must be seen as a particular expression of the fundamental principles that underlie the hearsay rule and the exceptions to it. What is important, in my view, is the departure signalled by *Khan* from a view of hearsay characterized by a general prohibition on the reception of such evidence, subject to a limited number of categorical exceptions, and a movement towards an approach governed by the principles which underlie the rule and its exceptions alike.

With this Court's subsequent holdings in *B (KG)* [[1993] 1 SCR 740], and, most recently, in *R v U (FJ)*, [1995] 3 SCR 764, 101 CCC (3d) 97, 128 DLR (4th) 121 (SCC), this new approach has become firmly entrenched in our jurisprudence.

Under this reformed framework, a hearsay statement will be admissible for the truth of its contents if it meets the separate requirements of 'necessity' and 'reliability'. These two requirements serve to minimize the evidentiary dangers normally associated with the evidence of an out-of-court declarant, namely the absence of an oath or affirmation, the inability of the trier of fact to assess the demeanour of the declarant, and the lack of contemporaneous cross-examination.

Consistent with the spirit of this modern approach, the twin requirements of 'necessity' and 'reliability' must always be applied in a flexible manner. As Lamer CJC stressed in *U (FJ)*, at p 787:

> *Khan* and *Smith* establish that hearsay evidence will be substantively admissible when it is necessary and sufficiently reliable. Those cases state that both necessity and reliability must be interpreted flexibly, taking account of the circumstances of the case and ensuring that our new approach to hearsay does not itself become a rigid pigeon-holing analysis.

If a hearsay statement satisfies these two requirements, the trial judge may put the statement to the trier of fact, subject to appropriate safeguards and to cautions regarding weight.

On the Canadian approach to hearsay, see generally R Prithipaul, 'Observations on the Current Status of the Hearsay Rule' (1996) 39 *Criminal Law Quarterly* 84.

Further reading

P B Carter, 'Hearsay: Whether and Whither?' (1993) 109 *Law Quarterly Review* 573

A L-T Choo, 'Reform of the Hearsay Rule: Developments in Commonwealth Jurisdictions' in J F Nijboer and J M Reijntjes (eds), *Proceedings of the First World Conference on New Trends in Criminal Investigation and Evidence* (1997)

— *Hearsay and Confrontation in Criminal Trials* (1996)

S Guest, 'Hearsay Revisited' (1988) 41 *Current Legal Problems* 33

— 'The Scope of the Hearsay Rule' (1985) 101 *Law Quarterly Review* 385

P Murphy, 'Hearsay: The Road to Reform' (1997) 1(2) *International Journal of Evidence and Proof* 107

— 'Practising Safe Hearsay: Surrender may be Inevitable, but Shouldn't We Take Precautions?' (1997) 1(3) *International Journal of Evidence and Proof* 105

D C Ormerod, 'Law Commission Consultation Paper No 138 on Hearsay: (2) The Hearsay Exceptions' [1996] *Criminal Law Review* 16

— 'Reform of Implied Assertions' (1996) 60 *Journal of Criminal Law* 201

R Pattenden, 'Conceptual versus Pragmatic Approaches to Hearsay' (1993) 56 *Modern Law Review* 138

A Rein, 'The Scope of Hearsay' (1994) 110 *Law Quarterly Review* 431

J N Spencer, 'The Current Hearsay Rule and Proposals for Reform' (1996) 60 *Journal of Criminal Law* 77

J R Spencer, 'Law Commission Consultation Paper No 138 on Hearsay: (3) Hearsay Reform: A Bridge Not Far Enough?' [1996] *Criminal Law Review* 29

— 'Orality and the Evidence of Absent Witnesses' [1994] *Criminal Law Review* 628

A A S Zuckerman, 'Law Commission Consultation Paper No 138 on Hearsay: (1) The Futility of Hearsay' [1996] *Criminal Law Review* 4

8

CONFESSION EVIDENCE AND RELATED MATTERS

1. INTRODUCTION

One of the most important exceptions to the hearsay rule is that which permits evidence of a confession to be adduced by the prosecution in a criminal trial in certain circumstances. A confession is defined in s 82(1) of the Police and Criminal Evidence Act 1984 as *including* 'any statement wholly or partly adverse to the person who made it, whether made to a person in authority or not and whether made in words or otherwise'. This definition clearly contemplates that a voluntary re-enactment of the crime by the accused amounts to a confession:

Extract 8.1.1

Li Shu-Ling v R [1989] 1 AC 270, 279–80 (PC)

LORD GRIFFITHS: The truth is that if an accused has himself voluntarily agreed to demonstrate how he committed a crime it is very much more difficult for him to escape from the visual record of his confession than it is to challenge an oral confession with the familiar suggestions that he was misunderstood or misrecorded or had words put into his mouth. Provided an accused is given a proper warning that he need not take part in the video recording and agrees to do so voluntarily the video film is in principle admissible in evidence as a confession and will in some cases prove to be most valuable evidence of guilt.

To meet the suggestion that lack of acting skill may result in serious distortion of a fair demonstration by the accused the video recording should be shown to the accused as soon as practicable after it has been completed and he should be given the opportunity to make and have recorded any comments he wishes about the film. If the accused says the film does not show what he meant to demonstrate there will then be a contemporary record of his criticism which the judge and jury can take into account when assessing the value of the film as evidence of his confession.

Confession evidence represents one of the most powerful and compelling types of evidence which the prosecution may have at its disposal:

Confessions potentially carry very strong emotional weight. Their persuasiveness is reflected in the superficially attractive rationale used to explain the probative value of confessions: that only a person who truly believed that he or she was guilty would confess to a crime.[1]

One need, however, only state this traditional justification for the admissibility of confession evidence (viz, that only a guilty person would make a statement which is against his or her self-interest) to see the flaws inherent in it. Cases such as those of the Guildford Four, Birmingham Six, Judith Ward[2] and Bridgewater Three have brought dramatically to public attention the sorts of miscarriages of justice which can occur as a result of the admission of confession evidence. Broadly speaking, three possible problems with confession evidence may be identified. First, the confession may have been totally *fabricated* by the police; it may never have been made at all by the person to whom it is attributed. This practice of, in effect, putting confessions into the mouths of accused persons who never made them is sometimes termed 'verballing'. Secondly, whilst the suspect may indeed have confessed, he or she may have made a *false confession*. There are a number of possible reasons why false confessions are sometimes made:

> ... there is now a substantial body of research which shows that there are four distinct categories of false confession:
> (i) people may make confessions entirely voluntarily as a result of a morbid desire for publicity or notoriety; or to relieve feelings of guilt about a real or imagined previous transgression; or because they cannot distinguish between reality and fantasy;
> (ii) a suspect may confess from a desire to protect someone else from interrogation and prosecution;
> (iii) people may see a prospect of immediate advantage from confessing (eg an end to questioning or release from the police station), even though the long-term consequences are far worse (the resulting confessions are termed 'coerced-compliant' confessions); and
> (iv) people may be persuaded temporarily by the interrogators that they really have done the act in question (the resulting confessions are termed 'coerced-internalised' confessions).[3]

Thirdly, even if the confession in question was in fact made, and even if it is true, there may be considerations of *extrinsic policy* which dictate that it is still inappropriate to use the confession in evidence, because of the unacceptable methods by which it was extracted.

---

[1] J Hunter, 'Unreliable Memoirs and the Accused: Bending and Stretching Hearsay – Part One' (1994) 18 *Criminal Law Journal* 8, 8.
[2] For a good account of the three preceding cases, see I Dennis, 'Miscarriages of Justice and the Law of Confessions: Evidentiary Issues and Solutions' [1993] *Public Law* 291.
[3] Royal Commission on Criminal Justice, *Report* (Cm 2263) (1993) 57.

As we shall see, exclusion remains the primary mechanism utilised by English law to deal with the problem of confession evidence. Despite many exhortations that confession evidence should be inadmissible unless corroborated, or at least supported, by other evidence, it remains extremely unlikely that a requirement for supporting evidence will be introduced into English law.

2. NO REQUIREMENT FOR SUPPORTING EVIDENCE

The Runciman Royal Commission on Criminal Justice, set up in the aftermath of the release of the Birmingham Six, addressed the issue of supporting evidence in Chapter 4 of its *Report*:

67. . . . Those who argue for a requirement for supporting evidence say that failure to impose such a requirement will continue to result in confessions being seen as the end of the investigation and that the prospect of a warning by the judge will not make any significant difference to the way in which the police conduct their enquiries. They also doubt whether even a strong warning by the judge will carry sufficient weight with juries to remove the risk of further miscarriages of justice in respect of unsupported confessions. They further argue that a judicial warning is by its nature contradictory. In their view, to tell a jury that it is dangerous to convict on the basis of an unsupported confession but then invite them to convict if they so choose does nothing to help them to decide whether the confession is true or false; the jury have nothing against which to measure it and therefore no means of distinguishing between a valid confession and a false one. Those who take this view accept that supporting evidence can be fabricated and that the requirement for supporting evidence will not eliminate the risk of miscarriages of justice in the future. But they believe that such a requirement would significantly reduce that risk.

68. The main argument against a requirement for supporting evidence is the likely effect on the numbers of people who are properly convicted on the basis of genuine confessions alone. A significant number of people plead guilty after a confession who might be strongly advised by their lawyers not to do so if the confession were the only evidence against them. There is no reason to believe that most of them are not in fact guilty. If they were to walk free, not only would justice not have been done in the individual case but there would be a cumulative adverse effect on the public's perception of the effectiveness of the criminal justice system. Furthermore, if there were a requirement of corroboration or supporting evidence, some prosecutions that are properly brought now could not be brought at all for lack of such evidence.
. . .
70. Taken together these studies [two empirical studies commissioned by the Royal Commission] suggest that a supporting evidence requirement would affect only a very small percentage of cases. But the absolute numbers would nevertheless be quite high, since over 100,000 cases a year are tried in the Crown Court and between 1 million and 1 1/2 million in the magistrates' courts.
. . .

86. Three of us think that a conviction should never be based on a confession alone. They believe that there should be a requirement for supporting evidence in the *Turnbull* sense. . . .

87. The majority of us, however, recommend that, where a confession is credible and has passed the tests laid down in PACE, the jury should be able to consider it even in the absence of other evidence. Where a confession is not credible we would expect the case to be dropped before it reaches the jury; either the police will not pursue it, or the prosecution review will screen it out, or the judge will direct an acquittal following the reversal of *Galbraith*[4] or exclude the confession under section 76 or 78 of PACE. We think that a confession which passes all these tests should be left to the jury to consider it. We do, however, recommend that the judge should in all such cases give a strong warning . . . , and that the other evidence which the jury should be advised to look for should be supporting evidence in the *Turnbull* sense.[5]

Are you persuaded by the arguments of the majority of the Royal Commission? Does the fact that a supporting evidence requirement may mean that a *numerically* large number of confession cases would collapse justify not introducing such a requirement, even though these cases would constitute only a very small *percentage* of all confession cases? Is it fair to suggest, as some have done, that a Royal Commission set up in the aftermath of the exposure of a spectacular miscarriage of justice should have been far more sensitive to the dangers of confession evidence, and been less influenced by crime control considerations?[6]

The warning requirement advocated by the majority of the Royal Commission may be compared with the mandatory warning requirement laid down by the High Court of Australia in *McKinney v R*[7] for certain classes of confession cases.

It should be noted that even if a corroboration, or supporting evidence, requirement were to be introduced, careful consideration would need to be given to the issue of what exactly should constitute sufficient corroborative or supporting evidence. The experience of some jurisdictions suggests that, if the requirement were too easy to satisfy, its protective value might simply be illusory.[8]

---

[4] As mentioned in Chapter 4, the Commission recommended that the decision of the Court of Appeal in *Galbraith* be reversed so that a case can be stopped if the judge takes the view that the prosecution evidence is demonstrably unsafe or unsatisfactory or too weak to be allowed to go to the jury.

[5] Royal Commission on Criminal Justice, *Report* (Cm 2263) (1993) 64–8.

[6] See generally S Greer, 'The Right to Silence, Defence Disclosure, and Confession Evidence' (1994) 21 *Journal of Law and Society* 102; A Sanders and R Young, *Criminal Justice* (1994) 187–91.

[7] (1991) 171 CLR 468. See generally A L-T Choo, 'Corroboration of Disputed Confessions' (1991) 107 *Law Quarterly Review* 544.

[8] See generally A L-T Choo, 'Confessions and Corroboration: A Comparative Perspective' [1991] *Criminal Law Review* 867; R Pattenden, 'Should Confessions be Corroborated?' (1991) 107 *Law Quarterly Review* 317; M McConville, *Corroboration and Confessions: The Impact of a Rule Requiring that no Conviction Can be Sustained on the Basis of Confession Evidence Alone* (Royal Commission on Criminal Justice Research Study No 13) (1993).

3. MANDATORY EXCLUSION

At common law, an involuntary confession had to be excluded from evidence. A confession was regarded as involuntary if it had been induced 'by fear of prejudice or hope of advantage exercised or held out by a person in authority',[9] or if it had been obtained by oppression.[10] The common law position has been superseded by s 76 of the Police and Criminal Evidence Act 1984, which lays down two grounds for the mandatory exclusion of confession evidence.

Extract 8.3.1

Police and Criminal Evidence Act 1984, s 76(1), (2), (3), (9)

76. Confessions

(1) In any proceedings a confession made by an accused person may be given in evidence against him in so far as it is relevant to any matter in issue in the proceedings and is not excluded by the court in pursuance of this section.

(2) If, in any proceedings where the prosecution proposes to give in evidence a confession made by an accused person, it is represented to the court that the confession was or may have been obtained –

   (a) by oppression of the person who made it; or

   (b) in consequence of anything said or done which was likely, in the circumstances existing at the time, to render unreliable any confession which might be made by him in consequence thereof,

the court shall not allow the confession to be given in evidence against him except in so far as the prosecution proves to the court beyond reasonable doubt that the confession (notwithstanding that it may be true) was not obtained as aforesaid.

(3) In any proceedings where the prosecution proposes to give in evidence a confession made by an accused person, the court may of its own motion require the prosecution, as a condition of allowing it to do so, to prove that the confession was not obtained as mentioned in subsection (2) above.

(9) Where the proceedings mentioned in subsection (1) above are proceedings before a magistrates' court inquiring into an offence as examining justices this section shall have effect with the omission of –

   (a) in subsection (1) the words 'and is not excluded by the court in pursuance of this section', and

   (b) subsections (2) to (6) and (8).

There are, therefore, two possible grounds for the mandatory exclusion of confession evidence: (1) oppression (s 76(2)(a)); (2) the use of words or

---

[9] *Ibrahim v R* [1914] AC 599, 609 per Lord Sumner. Note, however, *DPP v Ping Lin* [1976] AC 574, 597–8 per Lord Hailsham of St Marylebone: '... the word "exercised" ... though repeatedly reproduced, is, I believe, meaningless and corrupt in the report. I believe that Lord Sumner really said "excited" ...'.

[10] *Callis v Gunn* [1964] 1 QB 495, 501; *R v Prager* [1972] 1 WLR 260, 266.

conduct conducive to unreliability (s 76(2)(b)). Each of these grounds will be considered in turn.

(a) Oppression

'Oppression' is defined in s 76(8) of the Police and Criminal Evidence Act 1984 as *including* 'torture, inhuman or degrading treatment, and the use or threat of violence (whether or not amounting to torture)'.

Extract 8.3.2

R v Fulling [1987] QB 426, 432–3 (CA)

While the appellant, Ruth Fulling, was being interviewed, one of the police officers, Detective Constable Ronald Holliday, told her, quite truthfully, that, for the last three years or so, her lover had been having an affair with another woman, Christine, and that Christine was in the next cell. According to the appellant, these revelations distressed her so much that she could not bear to remain in the cells any longer. She said in her evidence: 'As soon as the matter about Christine came out, Detective Constable Holliday left the room and my head was swimming. I felt numb and after a while I said to Detective Sergeant Beech, "Is it true?" and he said, "Ronnie shouldn't have said that, he gets a bit carried away. Look Ruth, why don't you make a statement?"' The appellant then confessed. She argued in the Court of Appeal that the police had acted oppressively by giving her the information about Christine, and that, accordingly, the confession should have been excluded from evidence under s 76(2)(a).

LORD LANE CJ: . . . 'oppression' in section 76(2)(*a*) should be given its ordinary dictionary meaning. The *Oxford English Dictionary* as its third definition of the word runs as follows: 'Exercise of authority or power in a burdensome, harsh, or wrongful manner; unjust or cruel treatment of subjects, inferiors, etc; the imposition of unreasonable or unjust burdens.' One of the quotations given under that paragraph runs as follows: 'There is not a word in our language which expresses more detestable wickedness than oppression.'

We find it hard to envisage any circumstances in which such oppression would not entail some impropriety on the part of the interrogator. We do not think that the judge was wrong in using that test. What, however, is abundantly clear is that a confession may be invalidated under section 76(2)(*b*) where there is no suspicion of impropriety. No reliance was placed on the words of section 76(2)(*b*) either before the judge at trial or before this court. Even if there had been such reliance, we do not consider that the policeman's remark was likely to make unreliable any confession of the appellant's own criminal activities, and she expressly exonerated – or tried to exonerate – her unfaithful lover.

In those circumstances, in the judgment of this court, the judge was correct to reject the submission made to him under section 76 of the Act of 1984.

Extract 8.3.3

R v Paris **(1992) 97 Cr App R 99, 103–4 (CA)**

LORD TAYLOR CJ: We are bound to say that on hearing tape 7, each member of this Court was horrified. Miller [one of Paris' co-accused] was bullied and hectored. The officers, particularly Detective Constable Greenwood, were not questioning him so much as shouting at him what they wanted him to say. Short of physical violence, it is hard to conceive of a more hostile and intimidating approach by officers to a suspect. It is impossible to convey on the printed page the pace, force and menace of the officer's delivery, but a short passage may give something of the flavour:

Stephen Wayne Miller:	'I wasn't there.'
DC Greenwood:	'How you can ever . . .?'
Stephen Wayne Miller:	'I wasn't there.'
DC Greenwood:	'How you . . . I just don't know how you can sit there, I . . .'
Stephen Wayne Miller:	'I wasn't . . .'
DC Greenwood:	'Really don't.'
Stephen Wayne Miller:	'I was not there, I was not there.'
DC Greenwood:	'Seeing that girl, your girlfriend, in that room that night like she was. I just don't know how you can sit there and say it.'
Stephen Wayne Miller:	'I wasn't there.'
DC Greenwood:	'You were there that night.'
Stephen Wayne Miller:	'I was not there.'
DC Greenwood:	'Together with all the others, you were there that night.'
Stephen Wayne Miller:	'I was not there. I'll tell you already . . .'
DC Greenwood:	'And you sit there and say that.'
Stephen Wayne Miller:	'They can lock me up for 50 billion years, I said I was not there.'
DC Greenwood:	''Cause you don't wanna be there.'
Stephen Wayne Miller:	'I was not there.'
DC Greenwood:	'You don't wanna be there because if . . .'
Stephen Wayne Miller:	'I was not there.'
DC Greenwood:	'As soon as you say that you're there you know you're involved.'
Stephen Wayne Miller:	'I was not there.'
DC Greenwood:	'You know you were involved in it.'
Stephen Wayne Miller:	'I was not involved and I wasn't there.'
DC Greenwood:	'Yes you were there.'
Stephen Wayne Miller:	'I was not there.'
DC Greenwood:	'You were there, that's why Leanne is come up now . . .'
Stephen Wayne Miller:	'No.'
DC Greenwood:	''Cause her conscience is . . .'
Stephen Wayne Miller:	'I was not there.'
DC Greenwood:	'She can't sleep at night . . .'

Stephen Wayne Miller:	'No. I was not there.'
DC Greenwood:	'To say you were there that night...'
Stephen Wayne Miller:	'I was not there.'
DC Greenwood:	'Looking over her body seeing what she was like...'
Stephen Wayne Miller:	'I was not there.'
DC Greenwood:	'With her head like she had and you have got the audacity to sit there and say nothing at all about it.'
Stephen Wayne Miller:	'I was not there.'
DC Greenwood:	'You know damn well you were there.'
Stephen Wayne Miller:	'I was not there.'

and so on for many pages.

We have no doubt that this was oppression within the meaning of section 76(2).

Extract 8.3.4

Mohd Ali bin Burut v Public Prosecutor **[1995] 2 AC 579, 593 (PC)**

At issue here was the 'special procedure' applicable in cases of suspected firearms offences in Brunei, and involving suspects being manacled and hooded during interrogation.

LORD STEYN: The first question is whether the 'special procedure' to which the appellants were subjected was inherently oppressive. . . . It is unnecessary to examine the decided cases. For the police to interview an arrested person while he is manacled and hooded is plainly oppressive conduct calculated to sap the will of the person being interviewed.

The question then arises whether the statements were *obtained* by oppression. The statements were not obtained in interviews conducted while the appellants were subjected to the 'special procedure.' In the case of the first appellant it was conceded that the special procedure was applied to him on 15 December. On the next day he was questioned for five hours. On 17 December he signed a written statement. Eight days later he signed a formal statement confirming the first statement. In the case of the second appellant the 'special procedure' took place on 15 December and he signed detailed statements on 18 and 26 December. In the case of the third appellant the 'special procedure' was applied on 16 December, and he signed written statements on 17 and 25 December.

In the gaps between the application of the 'special procedure' and the signing of the written statements the appellants were questioned by police officers. As their Lordships have observed virtually nothing is known about those interviews. Moreover, during those gaps the appellants remained deprived of visits of relatives. Nothing had happened to remove the implied threat of further sessions subject to the 'special procedure.' The trial court misdirected itself by finding that in the absence of oral evidence from the appellants on the voire dire there was no evidence that the statements were obtained by oppression. Even without evidence from the appellants the very nature of the 'special procedure,' and the relatively short gaps between the application of the 'special procedure' and the taking of the statements, inferentially suggested that the statements were, or may have been, obtained by oppression. In these circumstances their Lordships are free to depart from the findings of fact of the trial court. The correct conclusion is that, against the background of the 'special procedure,' the prosecution upon whom the burden rested failed to prove to the requisite standard that the statements were not obtained by oppression. It follows that the trial court should have ruled all the written statements inadmissible.

In *R v Emmerson*, by contrast, the allegation of oppression was based on the fact that 'about three-quarters of the way through the interview . . . one of the officers raised his voice and used some bad language. He was saying in effect that it was plain that the appellant had committed the offences and why was he wasting their time. The impression given is one of impatience and irritation. The judge found it rude and discourteous.' The Court of Appeal held that 'the conduct of the police officer was not in any sense oppressive'.[11]

It is clear from the cases, therefore, that the word 'oppression' in s 76(2)(a) connotes rather harsh treatment of the suspect. Consequently, the number of occasions on which confession evidence is excluded under s 76(2)(a) may be expected to be somewhat limited.

Further assistance on the meaning of 'oppression' in s 76(2)(a) may be provided by decisions on art 3 of the European Convention on Human Rights, which prohibits both torture and 'inhuman or degrading treatment'. As seen above, s 76(8) makes it clear that either torture or 'inhuman or degrading treatment' will constitute oppression. In *Ireland v UK*, the European Court of Human Rights held that conduct which 'caused, if not actual bodily injury, at least intense physical and mental suffering to the persons subjected thereto and also led to acute psychiatric disturbances during interrogation . . . fell into the category of inhuman treatment within the meaning of Article 3. The techniques were also degrading since they were such as to arouse in their victims feelings of fear, anguish and inferiority capable of humiliating and debasing them and possibly breaking their physical or moral resistance.' The European Court also expressed the view that the distinction between inhuman or degrading treatment on the one hand, and torture on the other, 'derives principally from a difference in the intensity of the suffering inflicted': the use of the term 'torture' 'attach[es] a special stigma to deliberate inhuman treatment causing very serious and cruel suffering'.[12]

[11] (1990) 92 Cr App R 284, 287.
[12] (1978) 2 EHRR 25, 79–80.

(b) Words or conduct conducive to unreliability

R v Goldenberg (1988) 88 Cr App R 285, 289–90 (CA)

NEILL LJ: It was submitted on behalf of the appellant that the words 'said or done' in the phrase 'in consequence of anything said or done' could include what was said or done by the appellant himself.

He had requested the interview and his motive, it was said, was to obtain bail or alternatively, as one of the police officers said in the course of the trial, to obtain credit for helping the police. . . .

. . .

In the present case it is clear that no reliance was placed at the trial on anything said or done by Detective Sergeant Leader at the start of the interview. The argument was based on what was said or done by the appellant himself and on his state of mind. It is in that context that the judge's ruling has to be considered. It is also to be noted that on the *voire dire* the appellant himself did not give evidence.

It was submitted on behalf of the appellant that in a case to which section 76(2)(*b*) of the 1984 Act applied, the Court was concerned with the objective reliability of the confession and not merely with the conduct of any police officer or other person to whom the confession was made. Accordingly the Court might have to look at what was said or done by the person making the confession, because the confession might have been made 'in consequence' of what he himself had said or done and his words or actions might indicate that this confession was or might be unreliable.

In our judgment the words 'said or done' in section 76(2)(*b*) of the 1984 Act do not extend so as to include anything said or done by the person making the confession. It is clear from the wording of the section and the use of the words 'in consequence' that a causal link must be shown between what was said or done and the subsequent confession.

In our view it necessarily follows that 'anything said or done' is limited to something external to the person making the confession and to something which is likely to have some influence on him.

Is it not unduly narrow to confine the operation of s 76(2)(b) to situations where the words or actions in question were those of someone other than the person making the confession? This interpretation of s 76(2)(b) in *Goldenberg* would seem, however, to have gained general acceptance.

R v Crampton (1990) 92 Cr App R 369, 372–4 (CA)

STUART-SMITH LJ: The Court has considered the case of *Goldenberg* (1988) 88 Cr App R 285, in which questions of admissibility of confessions where a drug addict may have been suffering symptoms of withdrawal was considered. In that case it is plain that it was the appellant himself who requested the interview with the police. The Court held that there was nothing said or done other than by the appellant himself and that the case therefore did not fall within section 76(2)(*b*) at all.

Mr Batcup submits that case is distinguishable from the present because in this case it was the police who conducted the interview at their own convenience and not at the request of the appellant. That is perfectly true; but nevertheless it seems to us that it is in fact doubtful whether the mere holding of an interview at a time when the appellant is withdrawing from the symptoms of heroin addiction is something which is done within the meaning of section 76(2). However, for the purpose of this appeal we are content to assume that it is. The reason why we say it is doubtful is because the words of the subsection seem to postulate some words spoken by the police or acts done by them which were likely to induce unreliable confessions. The word 'unreliable,' in our judgment, means 'cannot be relied upon as being the truth.' What the provision of subsection 2(*b*) is concerned with is the nature and quality of the words spoken or the things done by the police which are likely to, in the circumstances existing at the time, render the confession unreliable in the sense that it is not true. It is quite plain that if those acts and words are of such a quality, whether or not the confession is in fact true, it is inadmissible. That becomes clear when one reads the following words of subsection (3). It is the likelihood of the confession being unreliable in the sense of being untrue that is being considered in subsection (3).

In our judgment, the learned judge was right to reject the submission that was made to him. It is plain that the experienced officers, who dealt with drug addicts, considered that he was fit to be interviewed. More important perhaps, Dr Koppell said that when he saw the appellant he considered that he was then fit to be interviewed. It follows *a fortiori* that the appellant would have been fit at the time of his interview, which occurred earlier. Mr Batcup makes the point that that answer given by Dr Koppell was some eight months after the event. He was not asked about it at the time and therefore that answer is not reliable. In our judgment, the learned judge was perfectly entitled to accept that evidence, as he plainly did. He accepted the doctor's evidence as reliable, based upon the symptoms that the doctor saw when he examined the appellant after the interview. It is clear from the evidence that when Dr Koppell did examine the appellant there were no serious symptoms at all. Indeed there were no symptoms other than a raised pulse, which may have been attributable to stress or excitement at being in the police station.

The medical opinion is to be found at p 35G of the summing-up. It was said:

'A patient suffering from withdrawal symptoms can be manipulative and tell lies; he can do anything to get more drugs or to get rid of the symptoms. At the same time, he can be perfectly lucid.

When he is manipulative, he might pretend his symptoms are worse than they are to get more drugs or substitute medication. He might say that he is suffering from a pain he has not really got, but normally there is no mental confusion and the addict's intelligence is working normally during the withdrawal – they know that they are telling lies.'

The appellant's own evidence about why he confessed is of interest. He was reminded that he had said he was feeling all right at the beginning of the interview. At p 42A he said this:

'In fact, I was feeling a bit sick. I'd been in custody for 14 or 15 hours and I was withdrawing from heroin, but I thought I might as well get it over and out of the way. I understood what I was saying and I understood what was going on.'

A little later he said that his answers were designed to protect Joe, that is Mr Vieira. He said: 'Joe was selling gear; I knew it later. I was trying to protect him. I knew that he had a little bit of form. That is a previous record.'
Finally, he said this:

'I understood all the questions. The answers I gave I intended to give. Withdrawal makes you confused. My answers were confused at the interview. I wanted to get on the streets again. When I gave the answers in the interview I understood how serious my admissions were, how serious was the charge I was being charged with, but I wanted to get out and to help Joe. Mainly I wanted to get out.'

In re-examination he said in the interview:

'I gave all the answers, I understood what I was saying. So far as my answers were concerned about dealing, the answers were not true. I was sick and I was slightly confused. I was concerned about the flat.'

There is no mention there of any desire to get the interview over quickly because he required another fix, which, as I understand it, is the basis upon which it is suggested that he might have been motivated to tell lies.
The high-watermark of the appellant's case if I can put it like that, is that the police themselves said that they would not have interviewed the appellant if they had known he was withdrawing. Mr Batcup submits that that view should take precedence; yet at the same time, and in the same breath, he says that the police were not medically qualified and were not therefore competent to make the judgment they did that he was fit to be interviewed.
In our judgment, the position is this. Whether or not someone who is a drug addict is fit to be interviewed, in the sense that his answers can be relied upon as being truthful, is a matter for judgment of those present at the time. It is interesting to observe what a note to the Code of Practice says on this point. I am reading the note C: 9B of the Code of Practice where it says this:

'It is important to remember that a person who appears to be drunk or behaving abnormally may be suffering from illness or the effect of drugs or may have sustained injury (particularly head injury) which is not apparent, and that someone needing or addicted to certain drugs may experience harmful effects within a short time of being deprived of their supply. Police should therefore always call the police surgeon when in any doubt, and act with all due speed.'

That of course is concerned mainly with the condition of the defendant in the police station and the need to call a doctor in the event that the police are in doubt as to whether or not he is well. Nevertheless, it has relevance, in our judgment, in relation to the question of interview. The position here, as it seems to us, is this. If the police had summoned the doctor, Dr Koppell, and he had seen the appellant before the interview, the doctor would have certified that he was fit to be interviewed. That is the evidence that he effectively gave and the evidence that the judge accepted. It is then for the judge at the trial within the trial to decide whether the assessment of those present at the time was correct. The mere fact that someone is withdrawing, and may have a motive for making a confession, does not mean the confession is necessarily unreliable. In the case of *Rennie* (1981) 74 Cr App R 207, a case which was before the Police and Criminal Evidence Act 1984 – nevertheless the observations of the Lord Chief Justice at p 212 are, in our judgment, relevant – the learned judge said this:

> 'Very few confessions are inspired solely by remorse. Often the motives of an accused are mixed and include a hope that an early admission may lead to an earlier release or a lighter sentence. If it were the law that the mere presence of such a motive, even if prompted by something said or done by a person in authority, led inexorably to the exclusion of a confession, nearly every confession would be rendered inadmissible. This is not the law. In some cases the hope may be self-generated. If so, it is irrelevant, even if it provides the dominant motive for making the confession. In such a case the confession will not have been obtained by anything said or done by a person in authority. More commonly the presence of such a hope will, in part at least, owe its origin to something said or done by such a person. There can be few prisoners who are being firmly but fairly questioned in a police station to whom it does not occur that they might be able to bring both their interrogation and their detention to an earlier end by confession.'

In our judgment, those words are in point here. We can see no reason upon the evidence in this case to conclude that the learned judge came to the wrong conclusion on the facts before him, either on the application under section 76(2), if indeed it was applicable, or in the exercise of his discretion under section 78.

In the following case, by contrast, s 76(2)(b) was successfully invoked:

Extract 8.3.7

R v McGovern (1990) 92 Cr App R 228, 231–4 (CA)

FARQUHARSON LJ: Whilst she was at the police station, two interviews took place. One was at 3.20 pm on November 17, when she was on her own and the second was in the morning of the following day, but on this occasion in the presence of the solicitor who had been summoned on her behalf. The contents of both those interviews amounted to confessions on the part of the appellant and of her complicity in the homicide. . . . Before us, Mr Clegg submits that the learned judge was wrong to admit the evidence of that first interview. His submission is based on the admitted facts that the police officers responsible for the custody of the appellant and for the conduct of the interviews were in breach of section 58 of the Police and Criminal Evidence Act 1984 and certain of the Codes of Conduct made thereunder. Section 58(1) provides that a person who is in police detention 'shall be entitled, if he so requests, to consult a solicitor privately at any time.' On her arrival at the police station the appellant had requested access to a solicitor, but this was unlawfully refused. It is not suggested that the police had any grounds for delaying access. The refusal was unlawful, as I have stated, and is agreed by the Crown to be unlawful. So far as the first interview was concerned, no contemporaneous note was taken and when a note of the interview was made subsequently it was not thereafter given to the appellant to read and to sign. Furthermore, no record was made in the interviewing officer's notebook of the reason why no contemporaneous note was taken. These omissions were in breach of Code C . . . We assume for the purposes of this appeal that the police were not, at any stage, acting in bad faith.

These breaches are, of course, important features of the case. . . . Mr Clegg submits in the present appeal that the effect of these admitted breaches should have caused the trial judge to have excluded the evidence of the first interview either under the provisions of section 76(2) of the Act or of section 78. Section 76(2) provides:

. . .

It will be observed that unless the prosecution prove to the necessary standard that the confession was not so obtained, the court has a mandatory duty to exclude it. Before the trial judge, Mr Clegg submitted that the prosecution had failed to prove the absence of oppression, but the learned judge rejected that submission. He ruled that there was no evidence of oppression before him. Mr Clegg, before us, tacitly accepts that ruling of the learned judge and he has not sought to renew his argument under the provisions of paragraph (a) of subsection (2). He does, however, rely, primarily now, on the provisions of paragraph (b). He submits that there are four grounds for saying that the confession was made in consequence of things said or done which are likely in the circumstances existing at the time to render the confession unreliable. These grounds are, first, the fact that the appellant was unlawfully denied access to a solicitor; secondly the breach of the Code of Conduct by the police in relation to the notes of the interview; thirdly, the appellant was peculiarly vulnerable; and, fourthly, the physical condition of the appellant at the time of the interview. While it appears that grounds three and four, thus described, are hardly within the rubric of 'anything said or done,' they do form the background upon which the submission is made that the confession was unreliable. It is really the absence of the solicitor which is Mr Clegg's main ground of criticism. The importance of this feature is underlined by the course the interview took. The appellant, when reminded of the caution, said she did not understand what the officer was saying. The words of the caution were then spelt out in the usual form and the appellant then said she did understand it. At the interview which took place the following day when those same words were recited, she denied comprehension and the caution had to be explained to her again in ordinary language. Returning now to the first interview, the police asked her to account for her movements on November 16.

She proceeded to tell lies to them, saying that she had been with her mother all day until she was taken home in the evening. She was told that she had been seen by a neighbour at Charlton Avenue and to that she replied that she was confused. It is apparent from the following questions that were being put that the police were anxious to establish the whereabouts of Helen and whether she was alive or dead.

Under repeated questions designed to get an answer to that inquiry the appellant began to cry, saying that she did not know where Helen was. As more questions were asked, she began weeping heavily and gradually admitted that she was present at the house at the time Helen was assaulted, that there had been a fight but, as she put it, 'it was an accident.' After further questions, she finally admitted to stabbing Helen. The interviewing officer, Detective Sergeant Snow, who was apparently unaware that the appellant had been denied the services of a solicitor, then made enquiries about one being summoned. By that time – and to use his words – 'the appellant was weeping uncontrollably.' Mr Clegg submits that if a solicitor had been present he or she would never have allowed the appellant to be questioned when she was in such an emotional state. Indeed, when a solicitor arrived at the police station later that evening it was agreed that the appellant was in no fit state to be further questioned. Mr Clegg further points out that the appellant, who was six months pregnant at the time, had been vomiting in her cell before the interview took place. At the trial a psychologist had described her as borderline subnormal with an IQ of 73. The psychologist compared her mentally with a child of 10.

Mr Bevan, on behalf of the Crown, submits that the prosecution has satisfied the burden laid upon it by section 76. He submits that one has to look at the effect of the admitted breaches upon the girl and then determine whether her response to questions demonstrated that the confession was unreliable. When she was asked to explain her movements on the day of Helen's death, the appellant gave an account in some detail which in substance was quite untrue. The judge, having heard the psychologist's evidence and looking at the evidence of the girl's own statements, described the appellant as streetwise.

In the more formal second interview, when her solicitor was present, she gave a long and coherent account of what she said was her part in the attack upon Helen. It was a much more detailed and comprehensive description than she had given at the interview the day before. Counsel claims that the judge can properly take those factors into account when considering the effect upon the appellant of the breaches which are complained of and which are admitted. It must be remembered that while the psychologist had rated her as nearly subnormal she was, in fact, a woman at that time of 19 years of age, the mother of a child, carrying another, and has lived as the wife of Watkinson for some years.

Having considered these conflicting arguments and submissions, this Court is clearly of the view that even if the confession given at the first interview was true, as it was later admitted to be, it was made in consequence of her being denied access to a solicitor and is for that reason in the circumstances likely to be unreliable. It follows that the prosecution has not in our judgment proved otherwise. We think Mr Clegg is right, that if a solicitor had been present at the time this mentally backward and emotionally upset young woman was being questioned, the interview would have been halted on the very basis that her responses would be unreliable. It seems that the interview was held quickly and without the formalities prescribed by the Code of Conduct because the police were anxious to discover the missing girl, but this heightened the risk of the confession being unreliable.

This view of the Court is underlined by the evidence of Detective Sergeant Snow given to the learned judge at the trial on the voire dire. Amongst other answers he gave to the questions put to him were these:

'I conduct most of my interviews with a solicitor present. That is because it is not fair without a solicitor. . . . If we had used or made contemporary notes we would have got nowhere. That's my experience. . . . The appellant was questioned as a suspect for murder.'

The officer went on to say that he did not believe that they had done anything outside the spirit of the Police and Criminal Evidence Act 1984. He said that a contemporary note would have slowed the interview down or prevented them from recovering the body. He said that she had been at the prison – meaning the police station – for eight hours before he had spoken to her. He did not think that anyone had spoken to her before. He could not say why he did not take a contemporaneous note but said that he chose not to. In a later section of his evidence he made these observations: 'The lady' – meaning the prisoner – 'didn't understand all the questions. She didn't even know why she was in the police station. In the last part of the interview she was crying; she was clearly upset; she was crying heavily. Yes, I carried on questioning her. She was not offered a break to compose herself, not even a glass of water. I never offered her a solicitor until she confessed.' I say at once, in fairness to the officer, that he was unaware that she had been refused one. Finally, he said that the appellant seemed confused and he did not ask her to sign anything. Later she did, in fact, ask for a solicitor.

The second interview, to which I have already made reference, took place the following day in compliance with the provisions of the Code. The appellant, in the presence of her solicitor, made a full confession. Mr Bevan seeks to rely upon that second interview on the grounds that it was not tarnished by the shortcomings of the first. He submitted that the interview was entirely voluntary and that in no sense throughout the interview had the appellant been overborne. She had the advantage of a solicitor to advise her whom she previously consulted for a period of about half an hour before that second interview had taken place. She was in no sense under stress emotionally and there had, of course, been the delay between the two interviews so that she could compose herself.

Mr Clegg, however, argues, correctly in our view, that if the first interview is inadmissible where the appellant has made admissions she may not otherwise have done, then the subsequent confession was a direct consequence of the first. Moreover, the appellant's solicitor was not informed, as he tells us, that the appellant had been wrongfully denied access when she was brought to the police station. If the solicitor had known that she would have realised immediately that the first confession was suspect and in all probability would not have allowed the second interview to have taken place.

We are of the view that the earlier breaches of the Act and of the Code renders the contents of the second interview inadmissible also. One cannot refrain from emphasising that when an accused person has made a series of admissions as to his or her complicity in a crime at a first interview, the very fact that those admissions have been made are likely to have an effect upon her during the course of the second interview. If, accordingly, it be held, as it is held here, that the first interview was in breach of the rules and in breach of section 58, it seems to us that the subsequent interview must be similarly tainted.

In the circumstances of this case, it is difficult to determine what additional effect the breaches of the Code on their own may have had on the reliability of the confession that the girl made. The fact that the confession was in substance true is expressly excluded by the Act as being a relevant factor. In any case at the time he made his ruling the learned judge was not aware of whether the confession was admitted to be true or not. As already observed, the anxiety of the police at the time of the first interview was to establish the whereabouts of Helen, dead or alive, and whilst in no way wishing to detract from the importance of these rules being observed, it is not perhaps necessary for us to decide whether the breach of the rules in this case materially affected the reliability of the confession made by the appellant.

In our judgment, had a solicitor been called at the time the appellant requested one should be made available to her, the first interview would be most unlikely to have taken place – certainly in the form that it did. The girl was ill at the time, and it was apparent at the outset of the interview that she failed to understand the meaning of the caution. During the course of the interview questions were asked by the Detective Sergeant in the form which I have already described which would immediately, I would suggest, have caused protest on the part of a solicitor advising the girl. Certainly, when it was observed what condition she was in emotionally, it would, as Mr Clegg submits, inevitably have followed that the solicitor would have prevented the interview being continued further. In those circumstances, the learned judge should have found that the prosecution had failed to discharge the burden of proof which was laid upon it with regard to the admissibility of that interview.

On the issue, discussed in *McGovern*, of the 'tainting' of subsequent interviews by a previous impropriety, see generally P Mirfield, 'Successive Confessions and the Poisonous Tree' [1996] *Criminal Law Review* 554.

What s 76(2)(b) requires, therefore, is that the judge focus on the hypothetical question of whether what was said or done (by someone other than the suspect) was likely in the circumstances to have rendered any resulting confession unreliable. The provision does not require the judge to assess the actual reliability of the confession; it is considered that for a judge to do so would be to usurp the function of the jury.

4. DISCRETIONARY EXCLUSION

Even if a confession cannot be excluded from evidence under s 76, it may still be possible for it to be excluded in the exercise of discretion on the ground that it was improperly obtained.

CONFESSION EVIDENCE AND RELATED MATTERS

Extract 8.4.1

Police and Criminal Evidence Act 1984, s 78

---

78. Exclusion of unfair evidence

(1) In any proceedings the court may refuse to allow evidence on which the prosecution proposes to rely to be given if it appears to the court that, having regard to all the circumstances, including the circumstances in which the evidence was obtained, the admission of the evidence would have such an adverse effect on the fairness of the proceedings that the court ought not to admit it.

(2) Nothing in this section shall prejudice any rule of law requiring a court to exclude evidence.

(3) This section shall not apply in the case of proceedings before a magistrates' court inquiring into an offence as examining justices.

Extract 8.4.2

Police and Criminal Evidence Act 1984, s 82(3)

---

82. Part VIII – interpretation

(3) Nothing in this Part of this Act shall prejudice any power of a court to exclude evidence (whether by preventing questions from being put or otherwise) at its discretion.

The common law discretion to exclude improperly obtained evidence where this is necessary to ensure a fair trial[13] is effectively preserved by s 82(3). This discretion is, however, a narrow one, and it has been expressly acknowledged by the House of Lords that 'the power conferred by s 78 to exclude evidence in the interests of a fair trial is at least as wide as that conferred by the common law'.[14] To all intents and purposes, therefore, the common law may be regarded as having been rendered otiose by s 78(1): at least the same range of improperly obtained evidence may be excluded under s 78(1) as could be excluded at common law. As stated by the Court of Appeal:

The judge held that the discretion under section 78 may be wider than the common law discretion identified in *Reg v Sang* [1980] AC 402, the latter relating solely to evidence obtained from the defendant after the offence is complete, the statutory discretion not being so restricted. However, he held that the criteria of unfairness are the same whether the trial judge is exercising his discretion at common law or under the statute. We agree. What is unfair cannot sensibly be subject to different standards depending on the source of the discretion to exclude it.[15]

---

[13] *R v Sang* [1980] AC 402.
[14] *R v Khan (Sultan)* [1996] 3 All ER 289, 298.
[15] *R v Christou* [1992] 1 QB 979, 988.

There is one situation, however, in which it would be necessary, in order to secure the exclusion of confession evidence, to have recourse to the common law discretion. This is where s 76 and s 78(1) are inapplicable because the confession has already been given in evidence.[16] The Court of Appeal stated in *R v Sat-Bhambra*:

> The words of section 76 are crucial: 'proposes to give in evidence' and 'shall not allow the confession to be given' are not, in our judgment, appropriate to describe something which has happened in the past. They are directed solely to the situation before the statement goes before the jury. Once the judge has ruled that it should do so, section 76 (and section 78, for the same reasons) ceases to have effect.[17]

Thus, where the trial judge decides to exclude confession evidence which has already been heard by the jury, the common law discretion would be able to be invoked to achieve such exclusion, with the jury being directed to disregard the evidence.

(a) Police lies

The exclusion of confession evidence under s 78(1) was considered by the Court of Appeal in the following case not long after the provision came into force:

Extract 8.4.3

R v Mason [1988] 1 WLR 139, 142–3, 144 (CA)

WATKINS LJ: Before arrest one or more police officers decided to invent evidence and to acquaint the appellant of that so-called evidence as though it was genuinely possessed. What they decided to do was to tell the appellant that a fingerprint of his had been found in a very telling place. . . .

Having been told by these police officers, falsely, that a fingerprint of his had been found on a fragment of glass from the bottle, the appellant saw his solicitor and told him his version of what had happened. The solicitor asked DC Gunton to confirm the fact, as the police were asserting, that they had found a fingerprint upon a fragment of glass at the scene of the crime. He confirmed to the solicitor that that was so. That was a deliberate falsehood. . . .

The solicitor, influenced by what he had been told by the police as to the fingerprint, advised the appellant to answer their questions and to give his explanation of any involvement he had had in the incident. . . .

---

[16] See generally D J Birch, 'The Pace Hots up: Confessions and Confusions under the 1984 Act' [1989] *Criminal Law Review* 95, 99.

[17] (1988) 88 Cr App R 55, 62.

... The judge heard argument in the absence of the jury and heard some evidence from the police as to how the confession had been obtained. He decided that the confession was, in his discretion, admissible. He was referred in the course of argument to sections 76 and 78 of the Police and Criminal Evidence Act 1984. He gave a ruling at the conclusion of argument and then said he would allow the prosecution to adduce that evidence. He dealt with what he believed to be the effects of sections 76 and 78, and went on to say, with the provisions of section 78 in mind:

'I have no doubt that this defendant was well aware of his right to remain silent and could have remained silent, with his solicitor being present, had he so chosen that alternative. But he did not choose that alternative; he chose to give the interview, listen to the questions and decide individually which questions he was going to answer. In fact he answered all of them. I see nothing in his doing that which adversely affects the fairness of the proceedings.'

. . .

It is obvious from the undisputed evidence that the police practised a deceit not only upon the appellant, which is bad enough, but also upon the solicitor whose duty it was to advise him. In effect, they hoodwinked both solicitor and client. That was a most reprehensible thing to do. It is not however because we regard as misbehaviour of a serious kind conduct of that nature that we have come to the decision soon to be made plain. This is not the place to discipline the police. That has been made clear here on a number of previous occasions. We are concerned with the application of the proper law. The law is, as I have already said, that a trial judge has a discretion to be exercised of course upon right principles to reject admissible evidence in the interests of a defendant having a fair trial. The judge in the present case appreciated that, as the quotation from his ruling shows. So the only question to be answered by this court is whether, having regard to the way the police behaved, the judge exercised that discretion correctly. In our judgment he did not. He omitted a vital factor from his consideration, namely, the deceit practised upon the appellant's solicitor. If he had included that in his consideration of the matter we have not the slightest doubt that he would have been driven to an opposite conclusion, namely, that the confession be ruled out and the jury not permitted therefore to hear of it. If that had been done, an acquittal would have followed for there was no other evidence in the possession of the prosecution.

For those reasons we have no alternative but to quash this conviction.

Before parting with this case, despite what I have said about the role of the court in relation to disciplining the police, we think we ought to say that we hope never again to hear of deceit such as this being practised upon an accused person, and more particularly possibly on a solicitor whose duty it is to advise him unfettered by false information from the police.

Do you think the result in *Mason* would have been the same if the police had deceived the accused only, rather than both the accused *and his solicitor*?

(b) Denial of access to legal advice

Section 58 of the Police and Criminal Evidence Act 1984 makes provision for access to legal advice for persons arrested and held in custody. This is supported by detailed provisions in Code C of the Codes of Practice issued pursuant to s 66. The question has arisen whether a breach of s 58, or the provisions of Code C which relate to access to legal advice, should lead to the exclusion of confession evidence under s 78(1). As will be seen below, the cases suggest that such breaches are regarded by the courts as providing a good justification for exclusion.

Extract 8.4.4

Police and Criminal Evidence Act 1984, s 58(1)-(11)

58. Access to legal advice

(1) A person arrested and held in custody in a police station or other premises shall be entitled, if he so requests, to consult a solicitor privately at any time.

(2) Subject to subsection (3) below, a request under subsection (1) above and the time at which it was made shall be recorded in the custody record.

(3) Such a request need not be recorded in the custody record of a person who makes it at a time while he is at a court after being charged with an offence.

(4) If a person makes such a request, he must be permitted to consult a solicitor as soon as is practicable except to the extent that delay is permitted by this section.

(5) In any case he must be permitted to consult a solicitor within 36 hours from the relevant time, as defined in section 41(2) above.

(6) Delay in compliance with a request is only permitted –

    (a) in the case of a person who is in police detention for a serious arrestable offence; and

    (b) if an officer of at least the rank of superintendent authorises it.

(7) An officer may give an authorisation under subsection (6) above orally or in writing but, if he gives it orally, he shall confirm it in writing as soon as is practicable.

(8) Subject to subsection (8A) below an officer may only authorise delay where he has reasonable grounds for believing that the exercise of the right conferred by subsection (1) above at the time when the person detained desires to exercise it –

    (a) will lead to interference with or harm to evidence connected with a serious arrestable offence or interference with or physical injury to other persons; or

    (b) will lead to the alerting of other persons suspected of having committed such an offence but not yet arrested for it; or

    (c) will hinder the recovery of any property obtained as a result of such an offence.

(8A) An officer may also authorise delay where the serious arrestable offence is a drug trafficking offence or an offence to which Part VI of the Criminal Justice Act 1988 applies and the officer has reasonable grounds for believing –

    (a) where the offence is a drug trafficking offence, that the detained person has benefited from drug trafficking and that the recovery of the value of that person's proceeds of drug trafficking will be hindered by the exercise of the right conferred by subsection (1) above; and

    (b) where the offence is one to which Part VI of the Criminal Justice Act 1988 applies, that the detained person has benefited from the offence and that the recovery of the value of the property obtained by that person from or in connection with the offence or of the pecuniary advantage derived by him from or in connection with it will be hindered by the exercise of the right conferred by subsection (1) above.

(9) If delay is authorised –

    (a) the detained person shall be told the reason for it; and

    (b) the reason shall be noted on his custody record.

(10) The duties imposed by subsection (9) above shall be performed as soon as is practicable.

(11) There may be no further delay in permitting the exercise of the right conferred by subsection (1) above once the reason for authorising delay ceases to subsist.

Extract 8.4.5

Police and Criminal Evidence Act 1984
Code C: Code of Practice for the Detention, Treatment and Questioning of Persons by Police Officers

. . .

6 Right to legal advice

(a) Action

6.1 Subject to the provisos in Annex B all people in police detention must be informed that they may at any time consult and communicate privately, whether in person, in writing or by telephone with a solicitor, and that independent legal advice is available free of charge from the duty solicitor. . . .

6.2 [Not Used]

6.3 A poster advertising the right to have legal advice must be prominently displayed in the charging area of every police station. . . .

6.4 No police officer shall at any time do or say anything with the intention of dissuading a person in detention from obtaining legal advice.

6.5 The exercise of the right of access to legal advice may be delayed only in accordance with *Annex B* to this code. Whenever legal advice is requested (and unless *Annex B* applies) the custody officer must act without delay to secure the provision of such advice to the person concerned. If, on being informed or reminded of the right to legal advice, the person declines to speak to a solicitor in person, the officer shall point out that the right to legal advice includes the right to speak with a solicitor on the telephone and ask him if he wishes to do so. If the person continues to waive his right to legal advice the officer shall ask him the reasons for doing so, and any reasons shall be recorded on the custody record or the interview record as appropriate. . . . Once it is clear that a person neither wishes to speak to a solicitor in person nor by telephone he should cease to be asked his reasons. . . .

6.6 A person who wants legal advice may not be interviewed or continue to be interviewed until he has received it unless:

(a) *Annex B* applies; or

(b) an officer of the rank of superintendent or above has reasonable grounds for believing that:

    (i) delay will involve an immediate risk of harm to persons or serious loss of, or damage to, property; or

    (ii) where a solicitor, including a duty solicitor, has been contacted and has agreed to attend, awaiting his arrival would cause unreasonable delay to the process of investigation; or

(c) the solicitor nominated by the person, or selected by him from a list:

    (i) cannot be contacted; or

    (ii) has previously indicated that he does not wish to be contacted; or

    (iii) having been contacted, has declined to attend;

and the person has been advised of the Duty Solicitor Scheme but has declined to ask for the duty solicitor, or the duty solicitor is unavailable. (In these circumstances the interview may be started or continued without further delay provided that an officer of the rank of Inspector or above has given agreement for the interview to proceed in those circumstances . . .).

(d) the person who wanted legal advice changes his mind.

In these circumstances the interview may be started or continued without further delay provided that the person has given his agreement in writing or on tape to being interviewed without receiving legal advice and that an officer of the rank of Inspector or above, having inquired into the person's reasons for .his change of mind, has given authority for the interview to proceed. Confirmation of the person's agreement, his change of mind, his reasons where given and the name of the authorising officer shall be recorded in the taped or written interview record at the beginning or re-commencement of interview. . . .

6.7 Where 6.6(b)(i) applies, once sufficient information to avert the risk has been obtained, questioning must cease until the person has received legal advice unless 6.6(a), (b)(ii), (c) or (d) apply.

6.8 Where a person has been permitted to consult a solicitor and the solicitor is available (ie present at the station or on his way to the station or easily contactable by telephone) at the time the interview begins or is in progress, the solicitor must be allowed to be present while he is interviewed.

6.9 The solicitor may only be required to leave the interview if his conduct is such that the investigating officer is unable properly to put questions to the suspect. . . .

. . .

6.15 If a solicitor arrives at the station to see a particular person, that person must (unless *Annex B* applies) be informed of the solicitor's arrival whether or not he is being interviewed and asked whether he would like to see him. This applies even if the person concerned has already declined legal advice or having requested it, subsequently agreed to be interviewed without having received advice. The solicitor's attendance and the detained person's decision must be noted in the custody record.

. . .

ANNEX B DELAY IN NOTIFYING ARREST OR ALLOWING ACCESS TO LEGAL ADVICE

A. Persons detained under the Police and Criminal Evidence Act 1984

(a) Action
1. The rights set out in sections 5 or 6 of the code or both may be delayed if the person is in police detention in connection with a serious arrestable offence, has not yet been charged with an offence and an officer of the rank of superintendent or above has reasonable grounds for believing that the exercise of either right:

(i) will lead to interference with or harm to evidence connected with a serious arrestable offence or interference with or physical injury to other people; or

(ii) will lead to the alerting of other people suspected of having committed such an offence but not yet arrested for it; or

(iii) will hinder the recovery of property obtained as a result of such an offence.

. . .

2. These rights may also be delayed where the serious arrestable offence is either:

(i) a drug trafficking offence and the officer has reasonable grounds for believing that the detained person has benefited from drug trafficking, and that the recovery of the value of that person's proceeds of drug trafficking will be hindered by the exercise of either right or;

(ii) an offence to which Part VI of the Criminal Justice Act 1988 (covering confiscation orders) applies and the officer has reasonable grounds for believing that the detained person has benefited from the offence, and that the recovery of the value of the property obtained by that person from or in connection with the offence, or if the pecuniary advantage derived by him from or in connection with it, will be hindered by the exercise of either right.

3. Access to a solicitor may not be delayed on the grounds that he might advise the person not to answer any questions or that the solicitor was initially asked to attend the police station by someone else, provided that the person himself then wishes to see the solicitor. In the latter case the detained person must be told that the solicitor has come to the police station at another person's request, and must be asked to sign the custody record to signify whether or not he wishes to see the solicitor.

4. These rights may be delayed only for as long as is necessary and, subject to paragraph 9 below, in no case beyond 36 hours after the relevant time as defined in section 41 of the Police and Criminal Evidence Act 1984. If the above grounds cease to apply within this time, the person must as soon as practicable be asked if he wishes to exercise either right, the custody record

must be noted accordingly, and action must be taken in accordance with the relevant section of the code.

5. A detained person must be permitted to consult a solicitor for a reasonable time before any court hearing.

Extract 8.4.6

R v Alladice (1988) 87 Cr App R 380, 386–7 (CA)

THE LORD CHIEF JUSTICE: If the police have acted in bad faith, the court will have little difficulty in ruling any confession inadmissible under section 78, if not under section 76. If the police, albeit in good faith, have nevertheless fallen foul of section 58, it is still necessary for the Court to decide whether to admit the evidence would adversely affect the fairness of the proceedings, and would do so to such an extent that the confession ought to be excluded. No doubt in many cases it will, and it behoves the police to use their powers of delaying access to a solicitor only with great circumspection. It is not possible to say in advance what would or would not be fair.

In *Samuel* [[1988] QB 615] for instance, the solicitor in question gave evidence. He said it was not his policy always to advise a client not to answer questions put to him by the police. He took the view that it was in many cases of advantage to a detainee to answer proper questions put to him. In that particular case, however, he knew that his client had already been interviewed on four occasions on all of which he had strenuously denied being involved in the crime and had already been charged with two serious offences. He took the view that in those circumstances he would probably have advised his client to refuse to answer any further questions. The Court came to the conclusion that the judge, had he arrived at a correct conclusion on the two points argued before him, might well have decided that the refusal of access to a solicitor compelled him to find that the admission of the evidence would have had 'such an adverse effect on the fairness of the proceedings' that he ought not to have admitted it.

. . .

What the appellant himself said in evidence was that he was well able to cope with the interviews; that he had been given the appropriate caution before each of them; that he had understood the caution and was aware of his rights. Indeed he asserted that he had said nothing at all after the first four (innocuous) questions, and what had been written down by the interviewing officer was nothing that he said but had been invented by the writer. His reason for wanting a solicitor was to have some sort of check on the conduct of the police during the interview.

. . .

It may seldom happen that a defendant is so forthcoming about his attitude towards the presence of a legal adviser. That candour does however simplify the task of deciding whether the admission of the evidence 'would have such an adverse effect on the fairness of the proceedings' that it should not have been admitted. Had the solicitor been present, his advice would have added nothing to the knowledge of his rights which the appellant already had. The police, as the judge found, had acted with propriety at the interviews and therefore the solicitor's presence would not have improved the appellant's case in that respect.

This is therefore a case where a clear breach of section 58 nevertheless does not require the Court to rule inadmissible subsequent statements made by the defendant.

See also *R v Dunford*.[18]

Extract 8.4.7

R v Walsh (1989) 91 Cr App R 161, 162–4 (CA)

SAVILLE J: It is common ground that there was a breach of section 58 of the Act. The appellant had therefore been arrested and was being held in custody at the police station. He requested a solicitor, but was denied access to one on grounds that the Crown do not seek to suggest fell within the exceptions set out in that section. It is also common ground that in breach of Code C the police conducted the interview with a person who had asked for but not received legal advice . . . , that they failed to make contemporaneous notes . . . , that they failed to record in the officers' pocket books the reasons for not keeping a record in the course of the interview . . . , that they failed to give the appellant a chance to read and sign an interview record . . .

. . .

The main object of section 58 of the Act and indeed of the Codes of Practice is to achieve fairness – to an accused or suspected person so as, among other things, to preserve and protect his legal rights; but also fairness for the Crown and its officers so that again, among other things, there might be reduced the incidence or effectiveness of unfounded allegations of malpractice.

To our minds it follows that if there are significant and substantial breaches of section 58 or the provisions of the Code, then prima facie at least the standards of fairness set by Parliament have not been met. So far as a defendant is concerned, it seems to us also to follow that to admit evidence against him which has been obtained in circumstances where these standards have not been met, cannot but have an adverse effect on the fairness of the proceedings. This does not mean, of course, that in every case of a significant or substantial breach of section 58 or the Code of Practice the evidence concerned will automatically be excluded. Section 78 does not so provide. The task of the court is not merely to consider whether there would be an adverse effect on the fairness of the proceedings, but such an adverse effect that justice requires the evidence to be excluded.

In the present case, we have no material which would lead us to suppose that the judge erred in concluding that the police officers were acting in good faith. However, although bad faith may make substantial or significant that which might not otherwise be so, the contrary does not follow. Breaches which are in themselves significant and substantial are not rendered otherwise by the good faith of the officers concerned.

[18] (1990) 91 Cr App R 150.

In our judgment, . . . it seems to us that the breaches in this case were both significant and substantial. For no good reason the officers concerned failed to follow the proper proceedings, denying the appellant legal advice and neither protecting nor preserving his right in the way laid down in the Code.

The trial judge expressed the view that even if a solicitor had been present he did not feel that this would have made any difference. . . .

Having considered the matter, we can see nothing in this case which could properly lead the court to the conclusion that the breach of section 58 made no difference; or in other words that it was likely that the appellant would have made the admissions in any event. The very highest it could be put, to our minds, was that it was perhaps uncertain whether or not the presence of a solicitor would have made any difference. Added to this, of course, is the fact that it appeared through the cross-examination of the officers during the *voire dire* that the appellant was challenging root and branch that he had made any admissions at all. Accordingly, it seems to us that a major, if not the major, premise on which the learned judge exercised his discretion was a false premise. . . .

In these circumstances, coupled with the failure of the police officers to comply with the Code in the respects that we have categorised as significant and substantial, we consider that to admit the evidence would have such an adverse effect on the proceedings that the judge should have excluded it.

See also *R v Samuel*[19] and *R v Parris*.[20]

As has been seen, the courts have generally refrained from providing clear guidelines as to the circumstances in which confession evidence should be excluded under s 78(1) by reason of a breach of s 58 or the provisions of Code C which relate to access to legal advice. The closest we have to a clear principle is that a 'significant and substantial' breach will weigh heavily in favour of exclusion, but will not lead automatically to exclusion. For example, a confession will not be excluded from evidence if it is determined that the presence of a legal adviser would have 'made no difference' since the defendant would have made the confession in any event. It is clear that such a determination can involve courts in a certain amount of *post hoc* rationalisation of events. The desirability of this may be questioned.

More fundamentally, what constitutes a 'significant and substantial' breach is not entirely clear. It would seem that a breach may be significant and substantial even if the police acted in good faith, and that bad faith can convert a breach which is not otherwise significant and substantial into one which is, but little guidance beyond this is provided by the cases.

If, as the courts have acknowledged, s 78(1) is not to be used to discipline the police, what is the actual rationale for the exclusion of confession evidence under this provision? Are the courts primarily concerned with safeguarding the reliability of evidence, or are they equally concerned with upholding values and protecting the moral integrity of the criminal justice system? These are also questions the answers to which do not emerge clearly from the cases.

---

[19] [1988] QB 615.
[20] (1988) 89 Cr App R 68.

Given that (as will be seen below) the Criminal Justice and Public Order Act 1994 now permits adverse inferences to be drawn, in appropriate circumstances, from silence in the face of police questioning, access to legal advice would seem to assume particular importance.

(c) Recording requirements

Breaches of the requirements governing the recording of confessions may also constitute a good ground for the exclusion of confession evidence under s 78(1).

Extract 8.4.8

Police and Criminal Evidence Act 1984
Code C: Code of Practice for the Detention, Treatment and Questioning of Persons by Police Officers

---

. . .

11 Interviews: general

. . .

(b) Interview records

11.5 (a) An accurate record must be made of each interview with a person suspected of an offence, whether or not the interview takes place at a police station.

(b) The record must state the place of the interview, the time it begins and ends, the time the record is made (if different), any breaks in the interview and the names of all those present; and must be made on the forms provided for this purpose or in the officer's pocket book or in accordance with the code of practice for the tape-recording of police interviews with suspects (Code E).

(c) The record must be made during the course of the interview, unless in the investigating officer's view this would not be practicable or would interfere with conduct of the interview, and must constitute either a verbatim record of what has been said or, failing this, an account of the interview which adequately and accurately summarises it.

11.6 The requirement to record the names of all those present at any interview does not apply to police officers interviewing people detained under the Prevention of Terrorism (Temporary Provisions) Act 1989. Instead the record shall state the warrant or other identification number and duty station of such officers.

11.7 If an interview record is not made during the course of the interview it must be made as soon as practicable after its completion.

11.8 Written interview records must be timed and signed by the maker.

11.9 If an interview record is not completed in the course of the interview the reason must be recorded in the officer's pocket book.

11.10 Unless it is impracticable the person interviewed shall be given the opportunity to read the interview record and to sign it as correct or to indicate the respects in which he considers it inaccurate. If the interview is tape-recorded the arrangements set out in Code E apply. If the person concerned cannot read or refuses to read the record or to sign it, the senior police officer present shall read it to him and ask him whether he would like to sign it as correct (or make his mark) or to indicate the respects in which he considers it inaccurate. The police officer shall then certify on the interview record itself what has occurred. . . .

11.11 If the appropriate adult or the person's solicitor is present during the interview, he shall also be given an opportunity to read and sign the interview record (or any written statement taken down by a police officer).

11.12 Any refusal by a person to sign an interview record when asked to do so in accordance with the provisions of the code must itself be recorded.

11.13 A written record shall also be made of any comments made by a suspected person, including unsolicited comments, which are outside the context of an interview but which might be relevant to the offence. Any such record must be timed and signed by the maker. Where practicable the person shall be given the opportunity to read that record and to sign it as correct or to indicate the respects in which he considers it inaccurate. Any refusal to sign shall be recorded. . . .

. . .

Extract 8.4.9

R v Keenan [1990] 2 QB 54, 59, 60, 63, 66, 68–70 (CA)

The appellant was driving a car when he was stopped and arrested by police officers for motoring offences. He was also charged with possession of an offensive weapon which had apparently been found in the car, and was committed for trial on that offence alone. It was argued on appeal that evidence of certain questions and answers in a police station interview should have been excluded on the ground that provisions of Code C had been breached.

HODGSON J: There was no reason recorded in the pocket book as to why the interview had not been contemporaneously recorded nor had the appellant been given the opportunity to read the note. . . .

. . . Time and again when Miss Hammond put the relevant provisions of the code to the officers, they said not only that they had not known of the provisions at the time but that they still did not know of them. Indeed in respect of two paragraphs Edwards said he knew of none of his colleagues who were aware of them. If that statement is correct, such a degree of ignorance some 18 months after the Act of 1984 came into force (1 January 1986) is appalling, particularly on the part of officers in the Metropolitan Police, which force, as this court knows, conducted a 'trial run' of the Act's provisions for many months before the Act came into force.

. . .

It is not easy to deduce from the argument what the assistant recorder's reasoning was, but we think that, looking at the whole argument, his main reason for permitting the evidence to be adduced was that, given that he had no reason to think that the appellant was challenging the fact that the interview took place at all, any unfairness could be disposed of by the appellant going into the witness box and giving whatever was his version of the interview.

. . .

Code C, in extension of the provisions of Part III (arrest), Part IV (detention) and Part V (questioning and treatment of persons by police) of the Act of 1984, addresses two main concerns. First, it provides safeguards for detained persons and provides for their proper treatment with the object of ensuring that they are not subjected to undue pressure or oppression. Equally importantly, these code provisions are designed to make it difficult for a detained person to make unfounded allegations against the police which might otherwise appear credible. Second, it provides safeguards against the police inaccurately recording or inventing the words used in questioning a detained person. These practices are compendiously described by the slang terms 'to verbal' and 'the verbals.'

Again, equally importantly, the provisions, if complied with, are designed to make it very much more difficult for a defendant to make unfounded allegations that he has been 'verballed' which appear credible. (It is to be hoped that the general introduction of tape recording will make it even more difficult.)

. . .

In this case we are concerned with the provisions of Code C aimed at preventing verballing and the credible allegation of verballing. In such cases evidence from the defendant at the stage where admissibility is in issue is most unlikely to be needed by the defence. If the proper procedures have, on the face of the record, been observed, then the defendant's contentions, eg that the apparently properly conducted and contemporaneously recorded interviews were inaccurate or did not happen, might possibly succeed with a jury but would be most unlikely to succeed before a judge alone.

But where, as in the instant case, the breaches are obvious, a different situation inevitably arises. The trial judge has no means of knowing what will ensue after he has made his ruling. If he rules against admissibility, it may be that where, as here, the other evidence is not strong, the defendant will exercise his right not to give evidence. To permit the evidence of the interviews to be given may therefore effectively deprive the defendant of a right he would otherwise have had. And if the evidence is admitted, the judge does not know what the response to it will be. Clear possibilities are first, that the defendant will give evidence that the interviews never took place at all or that, although they took place, the questions and answers were fabricated; second, he may say that the interview took place but that the questions and answers were inaccurately recorded or, third, he might accept the fact that the interview took place and the accuracy of the record.

Even more obviously the judge has no means at that stage of deciding what the truth of the matter is. If he admits the evidence, that task will fall to the jury, not to him. If he rules against admitting the evidence, there will never be a decision.

. . .

... where there have been substantial breaches of the 'verballing' provisions, this court has not been slow to hold that the trial judge was wrong to admit the interview evidence....

...

It is clear ... that there has been a number of different ways in which the courts have approached the problems which arise when objection is taken to admissibility on the ground that there have been breaches of the Codes of Practice. Additionally the situations in which the cases have reached this court have varied. Apart from the main difference between cases where a judge has erroneously ruled that there has been no breach, and cases where he has correctly found a breach but exercised his discretion to permit the evidence to be given, the way in which the voire dire has been conducted by the judge and counsel has varied widely. Sometimes counsel has called the defendant, sometimes not. Sometimes he has revealed to the judge, whether in cross-examination or submission, what the eventual response to the evidence will be, or may be, if it is admitted; sometimes, as here, he has not.

A difficulty perceived by the judge and counsel in this case was that, at the stage when objection was taken, the trial judge was not apprised of all the facts. In such cases he cannot know what will happen if he admits the evidence, nor what will happen if he excludes it (will the defendant then go into the witness box?).

At first sight it seems unjust that evidence, otherwise admissible, should be excluded under section 78 when, if all the facts, and particularly what the defence's response is going to be, were known, it would be clear that admission of the evidence would not have 'an adverse effect on the fairness of the proceedings.'

We have given this problem anxious consideration but, within the confines of our present rules of criminal procedure, we can see no way in which this difficulty can be avoided. The decision has to be made at a stage when the judge does not know the full facts....

...

We think that in cases where there have been 'significant and substantial' breaches of the 'verballing' provisions of the code, the evidence so obtained will frequently be excluded. We do not think that any injustice will be caused by this. It is clear that not every breach or combination of breaches of the codes will justify the exclusion of interview evidence under section 76 or section 78 ... They must be significant and substantial....

But if the breaches are 'significant and substantial,' we think it makes good sense to exclude them. At the voire dire stage a judge can foresee that a number of different situations may arise which the 'verballing' provisions are specifically designed to prevent. If the rest of the evidence is strong, then it may make no difference to the eventual result if he excludes the evidence. In cases where the rest of the evidence is weak or non-existent, that is just the situation where the temptation to do what the provisions are aimed to prevent is greatest, and the protection of the rules is most needed.

As we have said before, this case was tried at a time when Bench and Bar were struggling to understand and properly apply new and complicated provisions, and it is entirely understandable if the assistant recorder got it wrong. We think he did. He was wrong to assume that any unfairness could be cured by the appellant going into the witness box. If the appellant intended not to give evidence if the officers' evidence was excluded, then admitting it unfairly robbed him of his right to remain silent . . . If the defence case was to be (as it turned out to be in fact) that the evidence was concocted, then it was unfair to admit it, because by doing so the defendant was not only forced to give evidence but also, by attacking the police, to put his character in issue. If the defence was to be that the interview was inaccurately recorded, then it was plainly unfair to admit it, because it placed the appellant at a substantial disadvantage in that he had been given no contemporaneous opportunity to correct any inaccuracies nor would he have his own contemporaneous note of what he had said.

Without the evidence of the interview the case against the appellant would have been very much weaker . . . Accordingly the conviction must be quashed.

See also *R v Canale*.[21]

In spite of the strong statements made in *Keenan* (and in *Canale*), however, it seems clear that serious breaches of the recording requirements of Code C will not lead invariably to the exclusion of confession evidence. As in the context of breaches of s 58 and the provisions of Code C relating to access to legal advice, the courts appear willing to engage in assessments of whether the defendant was likely to have been actually prejudiced by the breaches. This is illustrated by the following case.

Extract 8.4.10

R v Dunn (1990) 91 Cr App R 237, 241, 243 (CA)

LLOYD LJ: . . . there were serious breaches of the code by the police . . . First, there was no contemporaneous note of the disputed conversation. Secondly, the reason for the absence of a contemporaneous record was not recorded in the police officer's notebook. Thirdly, and most important, the appellant was not given the opportunity to read the subsequent record said to have been made within a few minutes of the completion of the interview, so that he could either sign it as correct or indicate the respects in which he considered it inaccurate. . . . It was submitted in the court below that those breaches justified the exclusion of the evidence under section 78(1) of the Police and Criminal Evidence Act 1984.

. . .

. . . it would seem contrary to commonsense to regard the presence of the solicitor during the disputed conversation as irrelevant. The judge's reason for admitting the evidence was that Mrs Hemmings was there 'to protect the appellant's interests.' We agree with that line of reasoning. In the first place Mrs Hemmings could have intervened during the conversation, before the relevant answers were given. Secondly, her mere presence would inhibit the

[21] [1990] 2 All ER 187.

police from fabricating the conversation which did not in fact take place. Thirdly, if they were to fabricate a conversation despite the inhibition, then it would not simply be a question of their evidence against the evidence of the appellant. The appellant's solicitor would be there to give evidence, as she did, in support of the appellant's case. So the presence of the solicitor's clerk was, in our view, a factor which the judge was entitled to take into account in the exercise of his discretion. We are not persuaded that he gave that factor excessive or unreasonable weight. Nor is there any other ground on which we should interfere with his discretion. . . .

Before leaving the case we stress yet again the importance of the police complying strictly with the Codes of Practice. There were serious breaches in this case. The presence of the solicitor's clerk during the disputed conversation did not excuse those breaches. But it tipped the balance in favour of admitting the evidence. Had it not been for Mrs Hemmings' presence, the evidence would have been rightly excluded.

Should the presence of Mrs Hemmings really have been regarded as crucial?

It is to be noted that, in the light of Code E, the recording requirements of Code C now assume far less importance.

Extract 8.4.11

Police and Criminal Evidence Act 1984
Code E: Code of Practice on Tape Recording of Interviews with Suspects

. . .

3 Interviews to be tape recorded

3.1 Subject to paragraph 3.2 below, tape recording shall be used at police stations for any interview:

(a) with a person who has been cautioned in accordance with section 10 of Code C in respect of an indictable offence (including an offence triable either way) . . . ;

(b) which takes place as a result of a police officer exceptionally putting further questions to a suspect about an offence described in sub-paragraph (a) above after he has been charged with, or informed he may be prosecuted for, that offence . . . ; or

(c) in which a police officer wishes to bring to the notice of a person, after he has been charged with, or informed he may be prosecuted for an offence described in sub-paragraph (a) above, any written statement made by another person, or the content of an interview with another person . . .

3.2 Tape recording is not required in respect of the following:

(a) an interview with a person arrested under section 14(1)(a) or Schedule 5 paragraph 6 of the Prevention of Terrorism (Temporary Provisions) Act 1989 or an interview with a person being questioned in respect of an offence where there are reasonable grounds for suspecting that it is connected to terrorism or was committed in furtherance of the objectives of an organisation engaged in terrorism. This sub-paragraph applies only where the terrorism is connected with the affairs of Northern Ireland or is terrorism of any other description except terrorism connected solely with the affairs of the United Kingdom or any part of the United Kingdom other than Northern Ireland. 'Terrorism' has the meaning given by section 20(1) of the Prevention of Terrorism (Temporary Provisions) Act 1989 . . . ;

(b) an interview with a person suspected on reasonable grounds of an offence under section 1 of the Official Secrets Act 1911 . . .

3.3 The custody officer may authorise the interviewing officer not to tape record the interview:

(a) where it is not reasonably practicable to do so because of failure of the equipment or the non-availability of a suitable interview room or recorder and the authorising officer considers on reasonable grounds that the interview should not be delayed until the failure has been rectified or a suitable room or recorder becomes available . . . ; or

(b) where it is clear from the outset that no prosecution will ensue.

In such cases the interview shall be recorded in writing and in accordance with section 11 of Code C. In all cases the custody officer shall make a note in specific terms of the reasons for not tape recording. . . .

3.4 Where an interview takes place with a person voluntarily attending the police station and the police officer has grounds to believe that person has become a suspect (ie the point at which he should be cautioned in accordance with paragraph 10.1 of Code C) the continuation of the interview shall be tape recorded, unless the custody officer gives authority in accordance with the provisions of paragraph 3.3 above for the continuation of the interview not to be recorded.

3.5 The whole of each interview shall be tape recorded, including the taking and reading back of any statement.

Although the issue does not appear as yet to have given rise to any reported appellate case law, it is reasonable, in the light of the case law on Code C breaches, to expect confession evidence to be excluded under s 78(1) in appropriate circumstances where the requirements of Code E have been violated.

(d) The limitations of discretionary exclusion

As the preceding pages have demonstrated, the courts have not been slow in advocating the use of s 78(1) to exclude confession evidence in appropriate circumstances. In particular, an accused who can point to significant and substantial breaches of PACE and/or the Codes of Practice will be well placed to argue that confession evidence tainted by the breaches should be excluded. The Court of Appeal has made it clear, however, that even where there has been flagrant abuse by the police of their powers in breach of PACE, a trial judge does not have a duty to exclude evidence of his or her motion under s 78(1):

Extract 8.4.12

R v Raphaie [1996] Crim LR 812; LEXIS transcript (CA)

STEPHENS J: Mr Fitzgerald contends that where . . . there is, in his words, flagrant abuse by the police of their powers in breach of PACE, the judge has a duty to intervene and should exclude it of his own motion. We do not accept that submission. Where the defendant is represented by an advocate who is, on the face of it, competent, and where a particular part of the evidence may be the subject of a tactical or strategic plan on the part of the defence, it is no part of a judge's duty to take it on himself to exclude evidence. That does not mean that if he feels it appropriate the judge should not make a pertinent enquiry of the advocate in the jury's absence in certain circumstances, but beyond that he need not go.

There is also the question of whether an exclusionary discretion is sufficient where fundamental issues like access to legal advice and the tape-recording of interviews are concerned. It is certainly arguable that an absolute rule rendering inadmissible in evidence any confession made in the absence of a legal adviser, or any confession that is not tape-recorded, should be introduced. Such a rule would go some considerable way further in ensuring that unreliable confessions are not given in evidence. The counter-argument, which found favour with the Runciman Royal Commission, is that such a rule would be undesirable as it would lead to the exclusion of reliable evidence: confessions made in the absence of legal advice, or which are not tape-recorded, will in some circumstances be perfectly reliable.[22] This seems to miss the point. An inevitable consequence of any rule designed to ensure that unreliable evidence is inadmissible is the exclusion of *some* reliable evidence. And the more rigid and absolute the rule, the more likely this is to happen. The issue, surely, is whether the introduction of an absolute rule is justified in the special context of confession evidence, the admission of which has resulted in so many major miscarriages of justice.

5. THE RESPECTIVE FUNCTIONS OF JUDGE AND JURY

An argument that confession evidence should be excluded under s 76 or in the exercise of discretion raises, of course, a question of law to be decided by the trial judge. An argument that confession evidence was fabricated, however, is a question of fact, and is therefore to be decided, in a trial on indictment, by the jury. As is made clear in the following case (which was decided under the common law and not under the Police and Criminal Evidence

---

[22] Royal Commission on Criminal Justice, *Report* (Cm 2263) (1993) 60–2.

Act 1984), it is quite permissible for both arguments to be raised in the alternative:

Extract 8.5.1

Ajodha v The State **[1982] AC 204, 220 (PC)**

LORD BRIDGE OF HARWICH: The fallacy, in their Lordships' respectful opinion, which underlies the reasoning of the judgments in the cases considered above which have arrived at a contrary conclusion, is to suppose that a challenge by an accused person to a statement tendered in evidence against him on the ground that he never made it and a challenge on the ground that the statement was not voluntary are mutually exclusive, so as to force upon the judge a choice between leaving an issue of fact to the jury and deciding an issue of admissibility himself. In all cases where the accused denies authorship of the contents of a written statement but complains that the signature or signatures on the document which he admits to be his own were improperly obtained from him by threat or inducement, he is challenging the prosecution's evidence on both grounds and there is nothing in the least illogical or inconsistent in his doing so.

The precise extent to which statements made by a defendant in a 'trial within a trial' can be utilised by the prosecution in the trial proper is unclear. At common law,[23] the position was as follows:

(1) Regardless of whether the confession evidence had been admitted or excluded, the prosecution could not adduce as part of its case in chief evidence of statements made by the defendant in the 'trial within a trial'.
(2) If, however, the 'trial within a trial' had resulted in the defendant's confession being *admitted* in evidence, then the prosecution could cross-examine the defendant on any inconsistencies between his statements in the 'trial within a trial' and his testimony in the trial proper, with a view to discrediting that testimony.

It is arguable that the common law position has been reversed by s 76 of the Police and Criminal Evidence Act 1984. The argument is that any incriminating statements made by the defendant in the 'trial within a trial' would themselves constitute confessions which may be given in evidence by the prosecution so long as they were obtained in a manner consistent with s 76(2) (as would presumably be the case). If this argument is correct, it is surely in the interests of justice that the trial judge's exclusionary discretion (either at common law or under s 78) be invoked in order to exclude such statements from evidence.

---

[23] *Wong Kam-Ming v R* [1980] AC 247; *R v Brophy* [1982] AC 476.

6. POLICE AND CRIMINAL EVIDENCE ACT 1984, S 77

Extract 8.6.1

Police and Criminal Evidence Act 1984, s 77

77. Confessions by mentally handicapped persons

(1) Without prejudice to the general duty of the court at a trial on indictment to direct the jury on any matter on which it appears to the court appropriate to do so, where at such a trial –

    (a) the case against the accused depends wholly or substantially on a confession by him; and

    (b) the court is satisfied –

        (i) that he is mentally handicapped; and

        (ii) that the confession was not made in the presence of an independent person,

the court shall warn the jury that there is special need for caution before convicting the accused in reliance on the confession, and shall explain that the need arises because of the circumstances mentioned in paragraphs (a) and (b) above.

(2) In any case where at the summary trial of a person for an offence it appears to the court that a warning under subsection (1) above would be required if the trial were on indictment, the court shall treat the case as one in which there is a special need for caution before convicting the accused on his confession.

(3) In this section –

'independent person' does not include a police officer or a person employed for, or engaged on, police purposes;

'mentally handicapped', in relation to a person, means that he is in a state of arrested or incomplete development of mind which includes significant impairment of intelligence and social functioning; and

'police purposes' has the meaning assigned to it by section 101(2) of the Police Act 1996.

In *R v Campbell*[24] the Court of Appeal noted, perhaps somewhat unhelpfully, that a case depends 'substantially on a confession' if it would be substantially less strong without that confession. In determining whether a person is 'mentally handicapped' for the purposes of s 77, a court must not place undue weight on figures produced by intelligence tests. Thus it does not automatically follow, from the fact that someone who has achieved certain scores has been held to be mentally handicapped in one case, that another person who has achieved similar scores must also be held to be mentally handicapped. Each case must be decided on its own facts.[25] The 'independent

---

[24] [1995] 1 Cr App R 522, 535.
[25] *R v Kenny* (1993) *The Times*, 27 July.

person' must be a person who was independent of the person to whom the confession was made; they cannot have been the same person.[26] An illustration of the application of s 77 is provided by *R v Lamont*.[27] The defendant was mentally subnormal, with a reading and comprehension ability of a child of eight and an IQ of 73. The trial judge failed to issue a s 77 warning. The defendant's conviction for attempted murder was quashed by the Court of Appeal on the basis that such a warning should have been given. The dearth of reported case law on s 77 is probably attributable to the fact that in many cases where s 77 was potentially applicable, s 76 or s 78 might have been utilised instead to exclude the confession evidence altogether. The relationship between the exclusion of confession evidence and the use of s 77 warnings was discussed briefly in *R v Moss*.[28] The trial judge in this case had treated the defendant as mentally handicapped and given the jury a direction in accordance with s 77. On the defendant's appeal against conviction, Taylor LJ, giving the judgment of the Court of Appeal, stated:

> Section 77 simply deals with 'a confession,' and in the simplest case a confession may well be obtained from a defendant in one interview during a comparatively short period of custody; that situation is clearly to be distinguished from one such as existed in the present case where there were in all some nine interviews. It was not until the fifth interview that any admission was made and all those interviews where admissions were made, were made in the absence of a solicitor or any other independent person.
>
> We appreciate that this was one of those cases which presents a trial judge with a very difficult decision as to whether to allow the case to go forward or not. This trial judge approached the case most sympathetically. His summing up was a model of fairness and fully warned the jury of the dangers arising from the appellant's mental state and the prolonged police interrogation process. Nevertheless, the real question is whether he ought to have allowed the evidence to go before the jury. . . .
>
> We can only say that each member of this Court, reading the papers independently, felt troubled about the confession evidence in this case going to the jury and having heard the argument each member of this court is of the opinion that the verdict here would be unsafe and unsatisfactory if allowed to stand. These cases are very much a matter of impression, but where the impression of all three judges of this court is unanimous as I have indicated, we feel that the only proper course must be to allow this appeal and we do so.[29]

See also *R v Cox*.[30]

It should be noted that, ultimately, s 77 is of only limited value in addressing the problems associated with confession evidence. Most notably, the provision applies only to the mentally *handicapped*, and does not cover the mentally ill. The reason given for this was that the mentally ill, unlike the mentally

---

[26] *R v Bailey* [1995] 2 Cr App R 262.
[27] [1989] Crim LR 813.
[28] (1990) 91 Cr App R 371.
[29] At 377–8.
[30] [1991] Crim LR 276.

handicapped, are not a readily identifiable group. Even if this reasoning were to be accepted, it fails to explain why juveniles, who clearly constitute a readily identifiable group, are also excluded from the operation of s 77. The exclusion of juveniles creates the anomaly that s 77 applies to an adult with a mental age of 10, but not to a 10-year-old.[31]

7. WITHDRAWAL OF CASE FROM JURY

Extract 8.7.1

R v McKenzie [1993] 1 WLR 453, 455 (CA)

LORD TAYLOR OF GOSFORTH CJ: . . . applying the guidance given by this court in *Reg v Galbraith* [1981] 1 WLR 1039, we consider that where (1) the prosecution case depends wholly upon confessions; (2) the defendant suffers from a significant degree of mental handicap; and (3) the confessions are unconvincing to a point where a jury properly directed could not properly convict upon them, then the judge, assuming he has not excluded the confessions earlier, should withdraw the case from the jury. The confessions may be unconvincing, for example, because they lack the incriminating details to be expected of a guilty and willing confessor, or because they are inconsistent with other evidence, or because they are otherwise inherently improbable. Cases depending solely or mainly on confessions, like cases depending upon identification evidence, have given rise to miscarriages of justice. We are therefore of opinion that when the three conditions tabulated above apply at any stage of the case, the judge should, in the interests of justice, take the initiative and withdraw the case from the jury.

See also *R v Wood*.[32] Is there any reason for confining this judicial power to cases of mental handicap? Should not the power to withdraw the case from the jury be exercised wherever the prosecution case depends wholly on confessions which are so unconvincing that no properly directed jury could properly convict on them, *regardless* of whether the unreliability of the confessions is attributable to mental handicap or to some other factor?

8. PARTLY ADVERSE STATEMENTS

Statements made by accused persons may contain both exculpatory and inculpatory remarks. Such statements are known as partly adverse statements or mixed statements. Assuming that the inculpatory part of the statement

---

[31] See A L-T Choo, 'Confessions and Corroboration: A Comparative Perspective' [1991] *Criminal Law Review* 867, 869; P Mirfield, *Confessions* (1985) 166.
[32] [1994] Crim LR 222.

is admissible in evidence as a confession, what of the exculpatory part? It has been held that, in such a situation, the exculpatory part would also be admissible as evidence of the facts contained in it. In *R v Sharp*,[33] the House of Lords approved the following statement of Lord Lane CJ in *R v Duncan*:

> Where a 'mixed' statement is under consideration by the jury in a case where the defendant has not given evidence, it seems to us that the simplest, and, therefore, the method most likely to produce a just result, is for the jury to be told that the whole statement, both the incriminating parts and the excuses or explanations, must be considered by them in deciding where the truth lies. It is, to say the least, not helpful to try to explain to the jury that the exculpatory parts of the statement are something less than evidence of the facts they state. Equally, where appropriate, as it usually will be, the judge may, and should, point out that the incriminating parts are likely to be true (otherwise why say them?), whereas the excuses do not have the same weight.[34]

This principle applies to oral statements as well as to written ones.[35] It has also been observed by the House of Lords that, 'as was emphasised in *Duncan* and *Sharp*, a judge is entitled to comment adversely on the quality of the exculpatory parts of a mixed statement which has not been tested by cross-examination' because of the accused's failure to testify.[36]

9. 'FRUIT OF THE POISONOUS TREE'

Suppose that non-confession evidence has been discovered by the police as a result of a confession that is inadmissible in evidence under s 76(2). Does this 'fruit of the poisonous tree' constitute admissible evidence? If so, is the prosecution permitted to adduce evidence that it was discovered as a result of the inadmissible confession?

Extract 8.9.1

Police and Criminal Evidence Act 1984, s 76(4), (5), (6)

76. Confessions

(4) The fact that a confession is wholly or party excluded in pursuance of this section shall not affect the admissibility in evidence –
  (a) of any facts discovered as a result of the confession; or
  (b) where the confession is relevant as showing that the accused speaks, writes or expresses himself in a particular way, of so much of the confession as is necessary to show that he does so.

---

[33] [1988] 1 All ER 65. See also *R v Grayson* [1993] Crim LR 864 and *R v Downes and Rawlinson* (1993) *The Times*, 10 December.
[34] (1981) 73 Cr App R 359, 365.
[35] *R v Polin* [1991] Crim LR 293.
[36] *R v Aziz* [1995] 3 WLR 53, 59.

(5) Evidence that a fact to which this subsection applies was discovered as a result of a statement made by an accused person shall not be admissible unless evidence of how it was discovered is given by him or on his behalf.

(6) Subsection (5) above applies –

    (a) to any fact discovered as a result of a confession which is wholly excluded in pursuance of this section; and

    (b) to any fact discovered as a result of a confession which is partly so excluded, if the fact is discovered as a result of the excluded part of the confession.

This legislative strategy is consistent with a number of judicial decisions at common law. In the old case of *R v Warickshall*,[37] Jane Warickshall confessed to receiving stolen property, and as a result of this confession the stolen property was found concealed in her bed in her lodgings. It was held that the confession was inadmissible in evidence, but that this did not affect the admissibility of the evidence of the discovery of the stolen property. However, no reference could be made to the fact that the stolen property was discovered as a result of the inadmissible confession.

In *Lam Chi-ming v R*,[38] the three defendants were charged with murder. The prosecution case was that they had stabbed the deceased to death with a knife which they had then thrown into the sea. The trial judge held that the defendants' confessions were inadmissible in evidence. However, he admitted evidence of a video recording which showed the first defendant directing the police to the water front, where each of the defendants in turn made gestures indicating the throwing of the knife into the water. The judge also admitted police evidence describing these actions of the defendants which led to the recovery of the knife. On appeal to the Privy Council, it was held that the evidence of the video recording, and the police evidence, had been incorrectly admitted.

The prohibition of adducing evidence that the non-confession evidence was discovered as a result of an inadmissible confession can have important practical implications, and prove a substantial impediment for the prosecution. In cases where the non-confession evidence was discovered in a 'neutral' place unconnected with the defendant, such evidence will be of little relevance or value in the absence of evidence of what led the police to its discovery. As the Privy Council in *Lam Chi-ming* noted:

> Of course in the case of Jane Warickshall the fact that the stolen property was found hidden in her bed implicated her as the receiver without introducing any part of her confession in evidence, whereas in the present appeal the mere finding of the knife in the sea in no way implicated the defendants. What implicated them was their admission that they had thrown it into the sea.[39]

---

[37] (1783) 1 Leach 263.
[38] [1991] 2 AC 212.
[39] At 217.

10. EROSION OF THE RIGHT TO SILENCE IN THE FACE OF POLICE QUESTIONING

So far in this chapter we have been concerned with the evidential significance of inculpatory out-of-court *statements* by accused persons. A related issue pertains to the evidential significance of the accused's *silence* in the face of police questioning. For many years, debate raged as to whether the law should be reformed to permit the trier of fact to draw adverse inferences from the accused's failure to mention facts when questioned or charged. The issue was addressed in Chapter 4 of the report of the Runciman Royal Commission:

> 19. The research evidence may be summarised as follows. The right of silence is exercised only in a minority of cases. It may tend to be exercised more often in the more serious cases and where legal advice is given. There is no evidence which shows conclusively that silence is used disproportionately by professional criminals. Nor is there evidence to support the belief that silence in the police station leads to improved chances of an acquittal. Most of those who are silent in the police station either plead guilty later or are subsequently found guilty. Nevertheless it is possible that some defendants who are silent and who are now acquitted might rightly or wrongly be convicted if the prosecution and the judge were permitted to suggest to the jury that silence can amount to supporting evidence of guilt.
>
> . . .
>
> 20. In the light of all the evidence put before us, we have had to weigh against each other two conflicting considerations. One is the prospect, if adverse comment at trial were to be permissible, of an increase in the number of convictions of guilty defendants who have refused to answer police questions. The other is the risk of an increase in the number of innocent defendants who are convicted because they have made admissions prejudicial to themselves through the fear of adverse comment at trial or whose silence has been taken by the jury to add sufficient weight to the prosecution case to turn a not guilty verdict into one of guilty.
>
> 21. Two of us take the view that it would be right for adverse comment . . . to be permitted at the trial and for a consequential amendment . . . to be made to the wording of the caution. In the appropriate case the jury could thus be invited to draw its own conclusions as to whether the silence in the case in question supported the evidence pointing to guilt. . . .
>
> 22. The majority of us, however, believe that the possibility of an increase in the convictions of the guilty is outweighed by the risk that the extra pressure on suspects to talk in the police station and the adverse inferences invited if they do, not may result in more convictions of the innocent. They recommend retaining the present caution and trial direction unamended. In taking this view, the majority acknowledge the frustration which many police officers feel when confronted with suspects who refuse to offer any explanation whatever of strong *prima facie* evidence that they have committed an offence. But they doubt whether the possibility of adverse comment at trial would make the difference which the police suppose. The experienced professional criminals who wish to remain silent are likely to continue to do so and will justify their silence by stating at trial that their solicitors have advised them to say nothing at least until the allegations against them have been fully disclosed. It may be that some more defendants would be

convicted whose refusal to answer police questions had been the subject of adverse comment; but the majority believe that their number would not be nearly as great as is popularly imagined.

23. It is the less experienced and more vulnerable suspects against whom the threat of adverse comment would be likely to be more damaging. . . .

The government did not, however, accept this recommendation, and instead legislated to permit adverse inferences to be drawn in appropriate circumstances from the exercise of the right to silence in the face of police questioning:

Extract 8.10.1

Criminal Justice and Public Order Act 1994, s 34

34. Effect of accused's failure to mention facts when questioned or charged

(1) Where, in any proceedings against a person for an offence, evidence is given that the accused –
- (a) at any time before he was charged with the offence, on being questioned under caution by a constable trying to discover whether or by whom the offence had been committed, failed to mention any fact relied on in his defence in those proceedings; or
- (b) on being charged with the offence or officially informed that he might be prosecuted for it, failed to mention any such fact,
  being a fact which in the circumstances existing at the time the accused could reasonably have been expected to mention when so questioned, charged or informed, as the case may be, subsection (2) below applies.

(2) Where this subsection applies –
- (a) a magistrates' court inquiring into the offence as examining justices;
- (b) a judge, in deciding whether to grant an application made by the accused under –
  - (i) section 6 of the Criminal Justice Act 1987 (application for dismissal of charge of serious fraud in respect of which notice of transfer has been given under section 4 of that Act); or
  - (ii) paragraph 5 of Schedule 6 to the Criminal Justice Act 1991 (application for dismissal of charge of violent or sexual offence involving child in respect of which notice of transfer has been given under section 53 of that Act);
- (c) the court, in determining whether there is a case to answer; and
- (d) the court or jury, in determining whether the accused is guilty of the offence charged,

may draw such inferences from the failure as appear proper.

(3) Subject to any directions by the court, evidence tending to establish the failure may be given before or after evidence tending to establish the fact which the accused is alleged to have failed to mention.

(4) This section applies in relation to questioning by persons (other than constables) charged with the duty of investigating offences or charging offenders as it applies in relation to questioning by constables; and in subsection (1) above 'officially informed' means informed by a constable or any such person.

(5) This section does not –

    (a) prejudice the admissibility in evidence of the silence or other reaction of the accused in the face of anything said in his presence relating to the conduct in respect of which he is charged, in so far as evidence thereof would be admissible apart from this section; or

    (b) preclude the drawing of any inference from any such silence or other reaction of the accused which could properly be drawn apart from this section.

(6) This section does not apply in relation to a failure to mention a fact if the failure occurred before the commencement of this section.

The common law principles preserved by s 34(5) may be illustrated by the following cases:

Extract 8.10.2

R v Norton [1910] 2 KB 496, 499–501 (CCA)

PICKFORD J: As a general rule, statements as to the facts of a case under investigation are not evidence unless made by witnesses in the ordinary way, but to this rule there are exceptions. One is that statements made in the presence of a prisoner upon an occasion on which he might reasonably be expected to make some observation, explanation, or denial are admissible under certain circumstances. We think it is not strictly accurate, and may be misleading, to say that they are admissible in evidence against the prisoner, as such an expression may seem to imply that they are evidence of the facts stated in them and must be considered upon the footing of other evidence. Such statements are, however, never evidence of the facts stated in them; they are admissible only as introductory to, or explanatory of, the answer given to them by the person in whose presence they are made. Such answer may, of course, be given either by words or by conduct, eg, by remaining silent on an occasion which demanded an answer.

If the answer given amount to an admission of the statements or some part of them, they or that part become relevant as shewing what facts are admitted; if the answer be not such an admission, the statements are irrelevant to the matter under consideration and should be disregarded. This seems to us to be correctly and shortly stated in Taylor on Evidence, s 814, p 574: 'The statements only become evidence when by such acceptance he makes them his own statements.'

. . . We think that the contents of such statements should not be given in evidence unless the judge is satisfied that there is evidence fit to be submitted to the jury that the prisoner by his answer to them, whether given by word or conduct, acknowledged the truth of the whole or part of them. If there be no such evidence, then the contents of the statement should be excluded; if there be such evidence, then they should be admitted, and the question whether the prisoner's answer, by words or conduct, did or did not in fact amount to an acknowledgment of them left to the jury.

In trials of prisoners on indictment, in which the most numerous and important of these cases arise, there is, as a rule, no difficulty in deciding whether there be such evidence or not, as the prisoner's answer appears upon the depositions, and the chance that the evidence with regard to it may be different on the trial is so small that it may be disregarded. When, however, the evidence of the prisoner's answer does not appear, there does not seem to be any practical difficulty in applying the rule above stated. The fact of a statement having been made in the prisoner's presence may be given in evidence, but not the contents, and the question asked, what the prisoner said or did on such a statement being made. If his answer, given either by words or conduct, be such as to be evidence from which an acknowledgment may be inferred, then the contents of the statement may be given and the question of admission or not in fact left to the jury; if it be not evidence from which such an acknowledgment may be inferred, then the contents of the statement should be excluded. To allow the contents of such statements to be given before it is ascertained that there is evidence of their being acknowledged to be true must be most prejudicial to the prisoner, as, whatever directions be given to the jury, it is almost impossible for them to dismiss such evidence entirely from their minds. It is perhaps too wide to say that in no case can the statements be given in evidence when they are denied by the prisoner, as it is possible that a denial may be given under such circumstances and in such a manner as to constitute evidence from which an acknowledgment may be inferred, but, as above stated, we think they should be rejected unless there is some evidence of an acknowledgment of the truth. Where they are admitted we think the following is the proper direction to be given to the jury: – That if they come to the conclusion that the prisoner had acknowledged the truth of the whole or any part of the facts stated they might take the statement, or so much of it as was acknowledged to be true (but no more), into consideration as evidence in the case generally, not because the statement standing alone afforded any evidence of the matter contained in it, but solely because of the prisoner's acknowledgment of its truth; but unless they found as a fact that there was such an acknowledgment they ought to disregard the statement altogether.

Extract 8.10.3

Parkes v R [1976] 1 WLR 1251, 1252–5 (PC)

LORD DIPLOCK: The defendant was convicted of murdering a young woman, Daphne Graham. He was tried in the circuit court for the parish of Kingston before Smith CJ and a jury. The evidence against him was circumstantial and given mainly by Mrs Graham, the mother of the deceased. The defendant and the deceased lived in separate rooms of a house owned by Mrs Graham. She lived in the adjoining house. According to her evidence Mrs Graham left her house on the morning of September 14, 1971, at about 7.30 am in order to go to work. She then saw the deceased standing at her room door. Before she left she had seen the defendant standing on the verandah on to which the deceased's room opened. As soon as she had got on to the road outside the house she was told something which caused her to return. She found her daughter in her room bleeding from two stab wounds from which she died three days later. She was assisted to her bed and said something to her mother as a result of which Mrs Graham went out of the room to the yard which was common to the two houses. There she found the defendant with a ratchet knife in his hand. The knife was at that time closed. Mrs Graham said to the defendant 'What she do you – why you stab her?' The defendant made no reply nor did he reply when she repeated the question. Mrs Graham then boxed him twice and seized him by the waist-band of his trousers saying she would keep him there until the police came. The defendant then opened the knife and made to strike Mrs Graham with it. She noticed that it had blood stains on the blade. She put up her arm to defend herself and her finger was cut requiring five stitches. A Mr Jarrett, the uncle-in-law of the defendant, who had by then arrived upon the scene told the defendant to hand over the knife to him. The defendant did so, and Mr Jarrett subsequently handed over the knife to the police.

...

In support of the argument that the defendant's failure to answer Mrs Graham's accusation that he had stabbed her daughter was not a matter from which the jury were entitled to draw any inference that the defendant accepted the truth of the accusation the defendant relied on the following passage in the judgment of this Board in *Hall v The Queen* [1971] 1 WLR 298, 301:

'It is a clear and widely known principle of the common law in Jamaica, as in England, that a person is entitled to refrain from answering a question put to him for the purpose of discovering whether he has committed a criminal offence. A fortiori he is under no obligation to comment when he is informed that someone else has accused him of an offence. It may be that in very exceptional circumstances an inference may be drawn from a failure to give an explanation or a disclaimer, but in their Lordships' view silence alone on being informed by a police officer that someone else has made an accusation against him cannot give rise to an inference that the person to whom this information is communicated accepts the truth of the accusation.'

As appears from this passage itself, it was concerned with a case where the person by whom the accusation was communicated to the accused was a police constable whom he knew was engaged in investigating a drug offence. There was no evidence of the defendant's demeanour or conduct when the accusation was made other than the mere fact that he failed to reply to the constable. The passage cited had been preceded by a quotation from a speech of Lord Atkinson in *Rex v Christie* [1914] AC 545, 554, in which it was said that when a statement is made in the presence of an accused person:

'He may accept the statement by word or conduct, action or demeanour, and it is the function of the jury which tries the case to determine whether his words, action, conduct or demeanour at the time when the statement was made amount to an acceptance of it in whole or in part.'

In the instant case, there is no question of an accusation being made by or in the presence of a police officer or any other person in authority or charged with the investigation of the crime. It was a spontaneous charge made by a mother about an injury done to her daughter. In circumstances such as these, their Lordships agree with the Court of Appeal of Jamaica that the direction given by Cave J in *Reg v Mitchell* (1892) 17 Cox CC 503, 508 (to which their Lordships have supplied the emphasis) is applicable:

> 'Now the whole admissibility of statements of this kind rests upon the consideration that if a charge is made against a person in that person's presence it is reasonable to expect that he or she will immediately deny it, and that the absence of such a denial is some evidence of an admission on the part of the person charged, and of the truth of the charge. *Undoubtedly, when persons are speaking on even terms*, and a charge is made, and the person charged says nothing, and expresses no indignation, and does nothing to repel the charge, that is some evidence to show that he admits the charge to be true.'

Here Mrs Graham and the defendant were speaking on even terms. Furthermore, as the Chief Justice pointed out to the jury, the defendant's reaction to the twice-repeated accusation was not one of mere silence. He drew a knife and attempted to stab Mrs Graham in order to escape when she threatened to detain him while the police were sent for. In their Lordships' view, the Chief Justice was perfectly entitled to instruct the jury that the defendant's reactions to the accusations including his silence were matters which they could take into account along with other evidence in deciding whether the defendant in fact committed the act with which he was charged. For these reasons their Lordships have humbly advised Her Majesty that the appeal be dismissed.

Section 34 has now been the subject of consideration by the Court of Appeal:

Extract 8.10.4

R v Condron (1996) 161 JPR 1, 9–10, 11–14 (CA)

STUART-SMITH LJ: . . . the current specimen direction suggested by the Judicial Studies Board . . . is in these terms:

> 'If he failed to mention . . . when he was questioned, decide whether, in the circumstances which existed at the time, it was a fact which he could reasonably have been expected then to mention.
>
> The law is that you may draw such inferences as appear proper from his failure to mention it at that time. You do not have to hold it against him. It is for you to decide whether it is proper to do so. Failure to mention such a fact at that time cannot, on its own, prove guilt, but depending on the circumstances, you may hold that failure against him when deciding whether he is guilty, that is, take it into account as some additional support for the prosecution's case. It is for you to decide whether it is fair to do so.'

. . .

The question of what adverse inference can be drawn from an accused's failure to give evidence is obviously similar to the questions which arise under s 34. . . . We consider . . . that the specimen direction on s 34, coupled with the usual direction on burden and standard of proof and the fact that the jury will inevitably understand from the form of caution itself that the accused was entitled to remain silent at interview, covers the matters dealt with in paras 1–4 [of the passage in *R v Cowan* [1995] 3 WLR 818 in which the Court of Appeal provided guidelines on the directions which may be given to the jury pursuant to s 35 of the Criminal Justice and Public Order Act 1994: see Chapter 3]. Paragraph 5 goes somewhat further than the specimen direction . . . Having regard to the views of this court in *Cowan*, we consider that it is desirable that a direction on the lines indicated [in para 5 of the relevant passage in *Cowan*] should be given. There is as much a need to remind the jury of the circumstances in which a proper inference may be drawn under s 34 as under s 35. There is no basis for distinguishing between the sections in that respect. . . .

. . .

Issues arising under s 34
In the course of their submissions, counsel dealt with two problems that are likely to arise for consideration in relation to s 34. The first related to the procedure to be adopted if a challenge is to be mounted to the admissibility of a 'no-comment' interview, and the second related to the question of legal professional privilege if the defendant asserts . . . that they refused to answer on their solicitor's advice. Both counsel invited the court to give some guidance on these matters.

Procedure
Two questions arise. First, how should the prosecution deal with a 'no-comment' interview and, secondly, at what stage should the defence raise objection to the admissibility of the 'no-comment' interview or make submissions as to the drawing of adverse inferences. We would wish to make it plain that no hard-and-fast procedure should be laid down; each case will depend upon its own particular facts. Section 34(3) makes it plain that, subject to the direction of the court, evidence tending to establish the failure may be given before or after evidence tending to establish the fact which the accused is alleged to have failed to mention. This is no doubt partly because the court can consider the matter when deciding whether there is a case to answer (s 34(2)(c)). In the ordinary way, therefore, it would seem appropriate for prosecuting counsel to adduce evidence limited to the fact that after the appropriate caution the accused did not answer questions or made no comment. Unless the relevance of a particular point has been revealed in cross-examination, it would not seem appropriate to spend time at this stage going through the questions asked at interview.

If and when the accused gives evidence and mentions facts which, in the view of prosecuting counsel, he can reasonably have been expected to mention in interview, he can be asked why he did not mention them. The accused's attention will then no doubt be drawn to any relevant and pertinent questions asked at interview. The accused's explanation for his failure can then be tested in cross-examination. It will not generally be necessary to call evidence in rebuttal, unless there is a dispute as to the relevant contents of the interview.

If the explanation is that the accused was advised by his solicitor not to answer, then we consider hereafter to what extent this waives his privilege, and to what extent the matter can be explored by prosecuting counsel.

At what stage should objection to the admissibility of no-comment interviews or submissions to the effect that the jury should not be invited to draw adverse inferences be made? There may, of course, be objections to the admissibility of an interview based on breaches of the relevant Code, and s 76 or 78 of the Police and Criminal Evidence Act 1984, in which case such objection will be taken before any reference is made to the interview and the Judge must rule, if necessary, following a *voir dire*. But if the objection is simply that the jury should not be invited to draw any adverse inference, it will seldom be appropriate to invite the Judge to rule on this before the conclusion of all the evidence. . . . First, it will not be apparent until the accused gives evidence what are the material facts that were not disclosed or the reason why he did not disclose them. Only in the most exceptional case, for example, where the accused is of very low intelligence and understanding and has been advised by his solicitor to say nothing, could it be appropriate to make such a submission before the introduction of the evidence by the Crown. If defence counsel wishes to object to the prosecuting counsel cross-examining on the failure to mention the matters in interview, then it will be a matter for the Judge to rule upon, if necessary, after a *voir dire*. But, except in clear cases, where, in effect, it would be perverse for the jury to draw an adverse inference, we do not think this is an appropriate course, since the Judge is likely to consider that the question why the accused did not answer is one for the jury. In the ordinary way, therefore, we would expect, if defence counsel wishes to submit that the Judge should not invite the jury to consider drawing adverse inferences, that the submission should be made in the absence of the jury at the conclusion of the evidence.

Legal professional privilege

Communications between an accused person and his solicitor prior to interviews by the police are subject to legal professional privilege. But the privilege can be waived by the client, though not the solicitor. If an accused person gives as a reason for not answering questions, that he has been advised by his solicitor not to do so, that advice, in our judgment, does not amount to a waiver of privilege. But, equally, for reasons which we have already given, that bare assertion is unlikely by itself to be regarded as a sufficient reason for not mentioning matters relevant to the defence. So it will be necessary, if the accused wishes to invite the court not to draw an adverse inference, to go further and state the basis or reason for the advice. Although the matter was not fully argued, it seems to us that, once this is done, it may well amount to a waiver of privilege so that the accused, or if his solicitor is also called, the solicitor, can be asked whether there were any other reasons for the advice, and the nature of the advice given, so as to explore whether the advice may also have been given for tactical reasons.

However, it should be borne in mind that the inference which the prosecution seek to draw from failure to mention facts in interview is that they have been subsequently fabricated. It is always open to a party to attempt to rebut this inference by showing that the relevant facts were communicated to a third person, usually the solicitor, at about the time of the interview (see *R v Wilmot* (1988) 89 Cr App R 341). This does not involve waiver of privilege if it is the solicitor to whom the fact is communicated; the solicitor is, for this purpose, in the same position as anyone else.

In the unlikely event, therefore, that the solicitor advised his client to say nothing, even though the client has given him information which amounts to a defence, or affords an innocent explanation of otherwise incriminating evidence, the solicitor can be called to say that he was given that information and this, if accepted, will rebut the inference of subsequent fabrication. Moreover, it is always open to an accused person who has failed to mention some important fact at interview, to communicate it to the police at any time before trial; but unless it is done promptly, it is unlikely to rebut any adverse inference which might otherwise be drawn. . . .

It is probably desirable that the Judge should warn counsel, or the accused, that the privilege may be taken to have been waived if the accused gives evidence of the nature of the advice.

It is clear that the decision in *Condron* places an accused person in an unenviable position. In order to prevent an adverse inference from being drawn, he or she may have to state the basis or reason for legal advice which he or she has received to refrain from answering questions. Not only may the pressure to adduce such evidence be considered unfair in itself, but, by doing so, an accused person may also effectively be waiving legal professional privilege. See generally J N Spencer, 'The Right of Silence, Legal Privilege and the Decision in *Condron*' (1996) 160 *Justice of the Peace* 1167. Legal professional privilege is examined in detail in Chapter 13.

Extract 8.10.5

R v Argent (1996) 161 JPR 190, 191–200 (CA)

LORD BINGHAM OF CORNHILL CJ: The facts giving rise to this appeal are in brief as follows. A gentleman named Tony Sullivan was stabbed to death with a knife in the early hours of August 19, 1995 outside an East London nightclub, the Lotus Club. The appellant was arrested following an anonymous telephone call to the police which named him as the attacker. The prosecution case was that the appellant became aware that the deceased (who was unknown to him) had asked the appellant's wife to dance in the club and had later attacked him outside. At the time of the attack the deceased was, as the evidence showed, very drunk.

There were eye-witnesses to the fight between the deceased and another man. One witness who knew the appellant named him and two others picked him out on an identity parade.

The defence case was that there had been no contact between the deceased and the appellant or his wife in the club. They had left the nightclub before the deceased was attacked.

. . .

On August 19, at about midday, the appellant was arrested and was first interviewed by the police. On that occasion he was in receipt of legal advice and declined to answer questions. There was during the trial a *voir dire* to determine the admissibility of the evidence of that interview. The Judge held that the arrest had been lawful, but nonetheless excluded the police officer's evidence of the interview. He gave his reasons at p 3F of the transcript of that ruling when he said:

'I do not myself take the view that at that stage on one anonymous telephone call there were any circumstances existing at the time which required the accused to mention anything. I think Mr Mackintosh [the solicitor] gave the right advice.

Nothing transpired in the course of the interview, except an assertion of not guilty, and if the Crown seek to rely upon the negative answers or absence of answers to other questions I, as at present advised, would tell the jury that no inference should be drawn.'

It appears to us that in that brief ruling the Judge may have overstepped the bounds of his judicial function, but it is plain that the ruling was not unfavourable to the defence and it gives rise to no complaint.

A second interview conducted by Detective Constable Armstrong took place on November 16, 1995 after an identification parade at which the appellant had been identified. The appellant was accompanied by an experienced solicitor, Mr Ryan, who gave the appellant certain advice. The advice had essentially three limbs: first, that in all the circumstances the appellant was well-advised to remain silent; secondly, that if he declined to answer questions there was a risk that inferences adverse to him might be drawn at the trial; and thirdly, that the decision whether or not to answer any questions was that of the appellant. In the light of this advice the appellant elected to say nothing and he accordingly replied, 'No comment' to a series of questions put to him by the officer.

At the *voir dire* a challenge was raised to the admissibility of this evidence also, the defence seeking a ruling that evidence of the questions asked and of the appellant's negative response to them should be excluded from consideration by the jury. In relation to this interview the Judge ruled as follows:

'The situation is quite different in regard to the second interview. This was preceded by an identification parade with a positive identification and Mr Ryan knew that. He was concerned that the police on this occasion were not showing the usual co-operative attitude and were not disclosing to him such evidence as they had, as would normally be the case. As far as he was concerned there was a [feeling] of tension at the police station and that seems to have affected his own attitude to the problem of advice. In the situation which existed at that time the accused could reasonably have been expected to mention facts which were relevant or might be relevant. I cannot at this stage say what those facts are because I do not at this stage know precisely what the defence is. But I think the Act provides that

I do not need to know at this point and if a fact were to arise upon which the defendant wished to rely, his failure to mention it at the second interview does seem to me something upon which comment can properly be made and something from which inferences can properly be drawn. I do not think I can go further at this point. I can only indicate that [this] is my preliminary view. I do not make a ruling until a ruling is required to a fact.'

The trial proceeded and Detective Constable Armstrong gave evidence on May 8. In the course of his evidence, he testified to the second interview which took place on November 16 and detailed certain of the questions which he had asked and the appellant's negative responses to them.

The appellant himself gave evidence at the trial and a very brief summary of the effect of that evidence was given by the trial Judge to the jury in the course of his summing-up at p 15A, where he said:

'Yesterday he gave you his account of what had happened on August 19. He said that he, like others in the case, had had a good drink that evening but was not drunk. He did dance with his wife and believed that no one else did so. He was unaware that any other man sought to dance with her.

By about three o'clock in the morning his wife had agreed with him that they should leave and try to get a meal at the local Cantonese restaurant. They duly left. They went to that restaurant but were too late to be served. On the way he was concerned in no act of violence. They passed Walter Lee by the bus stop, and you can see on the plan where that is. They had a word with him. They then walked home – a distance of about a mile. They saw their babysitter and the [appellant] returned to bed. He said he knew nothing about injury to or death of anyone at the Lotus club until the police arrived at his house at about one o'clock that afternoon.'

That takes us to ground 1 of the perfected grounds of appeal which is that:

'The learned trial Judge erred in law and/or in the exercise of his discretion in failing to exclude the evidence of the appellant's interview with the police on November 16, 1995.'

That challenge is made under s 78 of the Police and Criminal Evidence Act 1984, which entitles a Judge to exclude evidence which has an unfair effect on the conduct of a trial. In this instance, the interview itself was properly conducted; the appellant's solicitor was present and in a position to advise him; he was duly cautioned on two occasions; and the appellant chose to act on the solicitor's advice.

We can readily accept that there will be some situations in which a Judge should rule against the admissibility of evidence such as this. For example (and only by way of example), the Judge might so rule in the case of an unlawful arrest where a breach of the Codes had occurred, or if the situation were one in which a jury properly directed could not properly draw an inference adverse to a defendant. Again such a situation might arise if, in application of s 78, the Judge concluded that the prejudicial effect of evidence outweighed any probative value it might reasonably have. However, save in a case of such a kind the proper course in our judgment is ordinarily for a trial Judge to allow evidence to be given and direct a jury carefully concerning the drawing of inferences. In our judgment, the ruling which the learned Judge gave in this case was not wrong and it is relevant to note that at the time when he gave the ruling he did not know what the facts were upon which the appellant might rely in his defence.

We therefore turn to the second ground, which is closely linked with the first, and which is in these terms:

'The learned trial Judge erred in law and/or in the exercise of his discretion in directing the jury that it was open to them to draw an inference from the appellant's silence in interview in accordance with s 34 of the Criminal Justice and Public Order Act 1994.'

It is in our judgment important to bear in mind the detailed terms of s 34. It is convenient to begin by considering subs (2)(d) which reads:

'Where this subsection applies – (d) the court or jury, in determining whether the accused is guilty of the offence charged, may draw such inferences from the failure as appear proper.'

The failure there referred to is a failure to mention at an earlier stage a fact relied on by the appellant in his defence, as is made plain by subs (1)(a).

Subsection (2)(d) empowers a jury in prescribed circumstances to draw such inferences as appear proper. That must mean as appear proper to a jury because the jury is the tribunal of fact and the drawing of appropriate inferences from the facts is the task of the tribunal of fact. The trial Judge is of course responsible for the overall fairness of the trial and it is open to him to give the jury guidance on the approach to the evidence. There will undoubtedly be circumstances in which a Judge should warn a jury against drawing inferences, but the Judge must always bear in mind that the jury is the tribunal of fact and that Parliament in its wisdom has seen fit to enact this section.

What then are the formal conditions to be met before the jury may draw such an inference? In our judgment, there are six such conditions. The first is that there must be proceedings against a person for an offence; that condition must necessarily be satisfied before s 34(2)(d) can bite and plainly it was satisfied here. The second condition is that the alleged failure must occur before a defendant is charged. That condition also was satisfied here. The third condition is that the alleged failure must occur during questioning under caution by a constable. The requirement that the questioning should be by a constable is not strictly a condition, as is evident from s 34(4), but here the alleged failure did occur during questioning by a constable, DC Armstrong, and the appellant had been properly cautioned. The fourth condition is that the constable's questioning must be directed to trying to discover whether or by whom the alleged offence had been committed. Here it is not in doubt that Mr Sullivan was killed by someone. The detective constable was trying to discover who inflicted the fatal wound and whether the killing was murder or manslaughter, it being fairly clear that the offence must have been one or the other (unless the killer struck the fatal blow in the course of defending himself). The fifth condition is that the alleged failure by the defendant must be to mention any fact relied on in his defence in those proceedings. That raises two questions of fact: first, is there some fact which the defendant has relied on in his defence; and second, did the defendant fail to mention it to the constable when he was being questioned in accordance with the section? Being questions of fact these questions are for the jury as the tribunal of fact to resolve. Here it would seem fairly clear that there were matters which the appellant relied on in his defence which he had not mentioned. These included the fact that he had had no quarrel with Mr Sullivan in the club; that he and his wife had left the club before the rest of the party; that he had not at any stage of the evening carried a knife; that he had not been involved in any altercation in the street in which Mr Sullivan was stabbed; that he saw and was a witness of no such altercation; that he saw Mr Lee in the street waiting for a cab; that he went to a restaurant for a meal but found that he was too late and that the restaurant was closed; and that he returned home and saw his babysitter. The sixth condition is that the appellant failed to mention a fact which in the circumstances existing at the time the accused could reasonably have been expected to mention when so questioned. The time referred to is the time of questioning, and account must be taken of all the relevant circumstances existing at that time. The courts should not construe the expression 'in the circumstances' restrictively: matters such as time of day, the defendant's age, experience, mental capacity, state of health, sobriety, tiredness, knowledge, personality and legal advice are all part of the relevant circumstances; and those are only examples of things which may be relevant. When reference is made to 'the accused' attention is directed not to some hypothetical, reasonable accused of ordinary phlegm and fortitude but to the actual accused with such qualities, apprehensions, knowledge and advice as he is shown to have had at the time. It is for the jury to decide whether the fact (or facts) which the defendant has relied on in his defence in the criminal trial, but which he had not mentioned when questioned under caution before charge by the constable investigating the alleged offence for which the defendant is being tried, is (or are) a fact (or facts) which in the circumstances as they actually existed the actual defendant could reasonably have been expected to mention.

Like so many other questions in criminal trials this is a question to be resolved by the jury in the exercise of their collective common sense, experience and understanding of human nature. Sometimes they may conclude that it was reasonable for the defendant to have held his peace for a host of reasons, such as that he was tired, ill, frightened, drunk, drugged, unable to understand what was going on, suspicious of the police, afraid that his answer would not be fairly recorded, worried at committing himself without legal advice, acting on legal advice, or some other reason accepted by the jury.

In other cases the jury may conclude, after hearing all that the defendant and his witnesses may have to say about the reasons for failing to mention the fact or facts in issue, that he could reasonably have been expected to do so. This is an issue on which the Judge may, and usually should, give appropriate directions. But he should ordinarily leave the issue to the jury to decide. Only rarely would it be right for the Judge to direct the jury that they should, or should not, draw the appropriate inference.

In this particular case the trial Judge directed the jury in the course of his summing-up in these terms, beginning at p 16D of the transcript:

'There is, however, another matter of law to which I must now turn. As you may be aware there has been a change which came into effect last year.

It is not a change which requires the defendant to say anything which he does not wish to say. He is still entitled to do what this defendant did and to decline to answer questions put to him by the police in interview but now if he chooses that course certain consequences may follow. When he was cautioned before the interview he was warned about this and you may be satisfied that he understood that warning which was repeated more than once in the course of the interview.

In this case as part of his defence the defendant relies upon certain facts, namely that when he left the Lotus club he did not encounter Tony Sullivan, he did not have a knife in his possession and did not inflict any knife wound upon Mr Sullivan and that he had no blood on his hands, that he met a friend Walter Lee on the way home who was able to confirm some of his account, there was a babysitter at his home who can give further confirmation and throughout his journey from the club to his home he was accompanied by his wife who can support the entirety of his account.

There is no dispute that when he was questioned under caution before he was charged he failed to mention any of those facts. That he failed to do so cannot by itself prove guilt. However, if you are sure that the defendant did fail to mention those facts and that in all the circumstances existing at the time he could reasonably have been expected to mention them, you are entitled to draw such inferences from this failure as you think proper. In judging this matter, as indeed throughout your consideration of the evidence, you apply your ordinary common sense. Always remembering that any conclusion you draw from the defendant's failure to mention facts must be a conclusion about which you are sure before you can act upon it.

You are entitled to consider whether the reason for failure was because the defendant had not thought out all the facts by November 16 or that he then had no innocent explanation to offer or none which he believed would then stand up to scrutiny and that may cast doubt upon the truthfulness of his account now, but you are not obliged to draw any inference against a defendant. He has told you why he chose to be silent. That was the advice he received at the time from his solicitor. You will consider whether or not he is able to decide for himself what he should do or whether having asked for a solicitor to advise him he would not challenge that advice.

Was this a situation where you are sure that it is proper to draw an inference against the defendant for his failure to mention the facts on which he now relies? The law in these circumstances permits you to do so but does not for a moment oblige you to do so.

The inference which the prosecution invite you to draw is that the account put forward in the defendant's evidence has been tailored to meet the case which the prosecution has supported by evidence and had not been thought out on November 16.

Let me add this, which I hope simplifies this aspect: if you are satisfied that the evidence called by the prosecution has proved to your satisfaction that it was the [appellant] who stabbed Tony Sullivan, in reaching that conclusion you will inevitably have rejected the evidence put forward for the defence and no inferences will be necessary. If, on the other hand, you consider that the prosecution evidence does not make you sure of the identity of the stabber, you must not draw any inferences of guilt from the [appellant's] failure to answer questions on November 16. If there was no case to answer the [appellant] cannot be blamed for not answering it.'

The appellant's criticism of the Judge's ruling in this case rests on two main grounds. First, it is said that the police had failed to make such full disclosure of the case against the appellant as they could and should have made; and secondly, that in the absence of such full disclosure the appellant's solicitor was right to advise him not to answer questions and that advice was in strict compliance with guidance given by the Law Society to solicitors acting in such a situation. As counsel succinctly summarized his submission, the crucial question is whether the police gave sufficient information to enable the solicitor to advise his client. If not, the solicitor was entitled to advise his client to say nothing and the Judge should have excluded evidence of the interview on the *voir dire*.

As to the first of the points made, it appears to us that the police may have made more limited disclosure than is normal in such circumstances. Under the Codes they had no obligation to make disclosure and they may well have had reasons for limiting the disclosure which they made. It is, however, relevant to note that by November 16 the firm to which the appellant's solicitor belonged had been advising him for a period of three months. The material given to the appellant and his solicitor made it plain that several witnesses had identified the appellant as having been present in the Lotus club on the night of the killing, that the fatal stabbing had occurred at about 3.25 am on August 19 outside the Lotus club, that persons at the club had identified the appellant as the person responsible for the stabbing and that a description communicated to the appellant and his solicitor had been given.

This was not, on any showing, a very complex case to which to respond. There is an obvious contrast with cases perhaps of fraud or conspiracy which depend on a complex web of interlocking facts. It would, one might think, have been very easy to say, if it were true, that the appellant had left the club before there was any trouble and that he never was involved in or even saw any violence of any kind.

The second observation we would make is that, under s 34, the jury is not concerned with the correctness of the solicitor's advice, nor with whether it complies with the Law Society guidelines, but with the reasonableness of the appellant's conduct in all the circumstances which the jury have found to exist. One of those circumstances, and a very relevant one, is the advice given to a defendant. There is no reason to doubt that the advice given to the appellant is a matter for the jury to consider. But neither the Law Society by its guidance, nor the solicitor by his advice can preclude consideration by the jury of the issue which Parliament has left to the jury to determine. The Judge's direction to the jury on this point, which we have recited, was as we think a model of succinctness and also, as it seems to us, of comprehensiveness. We see no ground for criticizing it in any way. Even if there were grounds for criticism, such criticism would be largely academic since the Judge concluded the passage by indicating that inferences would be unlikely to assist the jury in their task.

The guidance issued by the Criminal Law Committee of the Law Society, referred to by the Court of Appeal in *Argent*, is described in the following extract:

Extract 8.10.6

D Wolchover and A Heaton-Armstrong, *Wolchover and Heaton-Armstrong on Confession Evidence* (1996) 698

The Committee advise [in the circular *Changes in the Law Relating to Silence*] that where a suspect admits guilt to a solicitor who is unsure whether the police have sufficient and strong evidence on which the Crown Prosecution Service would decide to prosecute or a court would convict, the safest advice remains unchanged: the client should remain silent. The Committee go on to suggest that answering police questions may pose a greater risk of wrongful conviction than in the case of silence if the client: – (a) is in an emotional, highly compliant and highly suggestible state of mind at the time of the interview; (b) is confused and liable to make mistakes which could be subsequently interpreted incorrectly as deliberate lies; (c) has forgotten important details and distrusts his or her memory; (d) responds inappropriately to negative feedback by the police and may tend to go along with their suggestive questioning; (e) uses loose expressions and is unaware of the possible adverse interpretations which can be placed on them; (f) for some psychological reason may perform badly during interview and not do justice to his or her case. In addition, the Committee acknowledges as legitimate a decision to advise silence based on previous experience of the police using unfair pressure during questioning.

The change in the law introduced by s 34 has meant that the caution given to suspects has also had to be altered. Previously, suspects were cautioned as follows: 'You do not have to say anything unless you wish to do so, but what you say may be given in evidence.' The new caution is considerably more complicated: 'You do not have to say anything. But it may harm your defence if you do not mention when questioned something which you later rely on in court. Anything you do say may be given in evidence.'[40] Given that even the old caution was misunderstood by many suspects,[41] there seems little prospect of the new one being properly understood.

Note also ss 36 and 37 of the Criminal Justice and Public Order Act 1994:

Extract 8.10.7

Criminal Justice and Public Order Act 1994, s 36

36. Effect of accused's failure or refusal to account for objects, substances or marks

(1) Where –
    (a) a person is arrested by a constable, and there is –
        (i) on his person; or
        (ii) in or on his clothing or footwear; or

---

[40] Police and Criminal Evidence Act 1984, Code of Practice C, 10.4.
[41] M Zander, *Cases and Materials on the English Legal System* (7th ed 1996) 122.

(iii) otherwise in his possession; or

(iv) in any place in which he is at the time of his arrest,

any object, substance or mark, or there is any mark on any such object; and

(b) that or another constable investigating the case reasonably believes that the presence of the object, substance or mark may be attributable to the participation of the person arrested in the commission of an offence specified by the constable; and

(c) the constable informs the person arrested that he so believes, and requests him to account for the presence of the object, substance or mark; and

(d) the person fails or refuses to do so,

then if, in any proceedings against the person for the offence so specified, evidence of those matters is given, subsection (2) below applies.

(2) Where this subsection applies –

(a) a magistrates' court inquiring into the offence as examining justices;

(b) a judge, in deciding whether to grant an application made by the accused under –

(i) section 6 of the Criminal Justice Act 1987 (application for dismissal of charge of serious fraud in respect of which notice of transfer has been given under section 4 of that Act); or

(ii) paragraph 5 of Schedule 6 to the Criminal Justice Act 1991 (application for dismissal of charge of violent or sexual offence involving child in respect of which notice of transfer has been given under section 53 of that Act);

(c) the court, in determining whether there is a case to answer; and

(d) the court or jury, in determining whether the accused is guilty of the offence charged,

may draw such adverse inferences from the failure or refusal as appear proper.

(3) Subsections (1) and (2) above apply to the condition of clothing or footwear as they apply to a substance or mark thereon.

(4) Subsections (1) and (2) above do not apply unless the accused was told in ordinary language by the constable when making the request mentioned in subsection (1)(c) above what the effect of this section would be if he failed or refused to comply with the request.

(5) This section applies in relation to officers of customs and excise as it applies in relation to constables.

(6) This section does not preclude the drawing of any inference from a failure or refusal of the accused to account for the presence of an object, substance or mark or from the condition of clothing or footwear which could properly be drawn apart from this section.

(7) This section does not apply in relation to a failure or refusal which occurred before the commencement of this section.

Extract 8.10.8

Criminal Justice and Public Order Act 1994, s 37

37. Effect of accused's failure or refusal to account for presence at a particular place

(1) Where –

    (a) a person arrested by a constable was found by him at a place at or about the time the offence for which he was arrested is alleged to have been committed; and

    (b) that or another constable investigating the offence reasonably believes that the presence of the person at that place and at that time may be attributable to his participation in the commission of the offence; and

    (c) the constable informs the person that he so believes, and requests him to account for that presence; and

    (d) the person fails or refuses to do so,

then if, in any proceedings against the person for the offence, evidence of those matters is given, subsection (2) below applies.

(2) Where this subsection applies –

    (a) a magistrates' court inquiring into the offence as examining justices;

    (b) a judge, in deciding whether to grant an application made by the accused under –

        (i) section 6 of the Criminal Justice Act 1987 (application for dismissal of charge of serious fraud in respect of which notice of transfer has been given under section 4 of that Act); or

        (ii) paragraph 5 of Schedule 6 to the Criminal Justice Act 1991 (application for dismissal of charge of violent or sexual offence involving child in respect of which notice of transfer has been given under section 53 of that Act);

    (c) the court, in determining whether there is a case to answer; and

    (d) the court or jury, in determining whether the accused is guilty of the offence charged,

may draw such inferences from the failure or refusal as appear proper.

(3) Subsections (1) and (2) do not apply unless the accused was told in ordinary language by the constable when making the request mentioned in subsection (1)(c) above what the effect of this section would be if he failed or refused to comply with the request.

(4) This section applies in relation to officers of customs and excise as it applies in relation to constables.

(5) This section does not preclude the drawing of any inference from a failure or refusal of the accused to account for his presence at a place which could properly be drawn apart from this section.

(6) This section does not apply in relation to a failure or refusal which occurred before the commencement of this section.

It is important also not to lose sight of the following provisions:

Extract 8.10.9

Criminal Justice and Public Order Act 1994, s 38(3), (6)

38. Interpretation and savings for sections 34, 35, 36 and 37

(3) A person shall not have the proceedings against him transferred to the Crown Court for trial, have a case to answer or be convicted of an offence

solely on an inference drawn from such a failure or refusal as is mentioned in section 34(2), 35(3), 36(2) or 37(2).

(6) Nothing in sections 34, 35, 36 or 37 prejudices any power of a court, in any proceedings, to exclude evidence (whether by preventing questions being put or otherwise) at its discretion.

The European Court of Human Rights held recently in the following case (by a majority of 14 to 5) that the drawing of adverse inferences under arts 4 and 6 of the Criminal Evidence (Northern Ireland) Order 1988 (the equivalent of ss 35 and 37 of the Criminal Justice and Public Order Act 1994) did not infringe the right to a fair trial guaranteed by art 6(1) of the European Convention on Human Rights, or the principle of the presumption of innocence enshrined in art 6(2) of that Convention.

Extract 8.10.10

Murray v UK (1996) 22 EHRR 29, 61–2, 64 (ECHR)

47. . . .

Whether the drawing of adverse inferences from an accused's silence infringes Article 6 is a matter to be determined in the light of all the circumstances of the case, having particular regard to the situations where inferences may be drawn, the weight attached to them by the national courts in their assessment of the evidence and the degree of compulsion inherent in the situation.

48. As regards the degree of compulsion involved in the present case, it is recalled that the applicant was in fact able to remain silent. Notwithstanding the repeated warnings as to the possibility that inferences might be drawn from his silence, he did not make any statements to the police and did not give evidence during his trial. Moreover under Article 4(5) of the Order he remained a non-compellable witness . . . Thus his insistence in maintaining silence throughout the proceedings did not amount to a criminal offence or contempt of court. Furthermore, as has been stressed in national court decisions, silence, in itself, cannot be regarded as an indication of guilt.

. . .

50. Admittedly a system which warns the accused – who is possibly without legal assistance (as in the applicant's case) – that adverse inferences may be drawn from a refusal to provide an explanation to the police for his presence at the scene of a crime or to testify during his trial, when taken in conjunction with the weight of the case against him, involves a certain level of indirect compulsion. However, since the applicant could not be compelled to speak or to testify, as indicated above, this factor on its own cannot be decisive. The Court must rather concentrate its attention on the role played by the inferences in the proceedings against the applicant and especially in his conviction.

51. In this context, it is recalled that these were proceedings without a jury, the trier of fact being an experienced judge. Furthermore, the drawing of inferences under the Order is subject to an important series of safeguards

designed to respect the rights of the defence and to limit the extent to which reliance can be placed on inferences.

In the first place, before inferences can be drawn under Article 4 and 6 of the Order appropriate warnings must have been given to the accused as to the legal effects of maintaining silence. Moreover, . . . the prosecutor must first establish a prima facie case against the accused, *ie* a case consisting of direct evidence which, if believed and combined with legitimate inferences based upon it, could lead a properly directed jury to be satisfied beyond reasonable doubt that each of the essential elements of the offence is proved.

The question in each particular case is whether the evidence adduced by the prosecution is sufficiently strong to require an answer. The national court cannot conclude that the accused is guilty merely because he chooses to remain silent. . . . it is only common sense inferences which the judge considers proper, in the light of the evidence against the accused, that can be drawn under the Order.

In addition, the trial judge has a discretion whether, on the facts of the particular case, an inference should be drawn. As indicated by the Court of Appeal in the present case, if a judge accepted that an accused did not understand the warning given or if he had doubts about it, 'we are confident that he would not activate Article 6 against him'. Furthermore in Northern Ireland, where trial judges sit without a jury, the judge must explain the reasons for the decision to draw inferences and the weight attached to them. The exercise of discretion in this regard is subject to review by the appellate courts.

. . .

57. Against the above background, and taking into account the role played by inferences under the Order during the trial and their impact on the rights of the defence, the Court does not consider that the criminal proceedings were unfair or that there had been an infringement of the presumption of innocence.

58. Accordingly, there has been no violation of Article 6(1) and (2) of the Convention.

See generally R Munday, 'Inferences from Silence and European Human Rights Law' [1996] *Criminal Law Review* 370; S Nash and M Furse, '*Murray* and the Right to Silence' (1996) 146 *New Law Journal* 261.

It will be noted that considerable emphasis was placed by the European Court of Human Rights on the fact that the proceedings in question took place without a jury, in circumstances where the trier of fact was an experienced judge who was obliged to explain the reasons for the decision to draw inferences and the weight attached to them. This decision would also be subject to review by appellate courts. May not, therefore, the equivalent English legislation, which operates in a system where trials of serious offences take place before a judge and jury, be more likely to fall foul of arts 6(1) and 6(2) of the European Convention?

Notably, the European Court of Human Rights held in the following case that art 6(1) had been infringed where use was made at his trial of statements which the defendant had been obliged to provide in circumstances where failure so to do could have led to a determination that he was in contempt, and to the imposition of a fine or prison sentence.

Extract 8.10.11

Saunders v UK (1996) 23 EHRR 313, 333, 337–40 (ECHR)

59. The applicant contended that he was denied a fair trial in breach of Article 6(1) of the Convention which, in so far as relevant, states: 'In the determination of . . . any criminal charge against him, everyone is entitled to a fair . . . hearing . . . by an independent and impartial tribunal . . .'.
. . .

68. The Court recalls that, although not specifically mentioned in Article 6 of the Convention, the right to silence and the right not to incriminate oneself, are generally recognised international standards which lie at the heart of the notion of a fair procedure under Article 6. Their rationale lies, *inter alia*, in the protection of the accused against improper compulsion by the authorities thereby contributing to the avoidance of miscarriages of justice and to the fulfilment of the aims of Article 6. The right not to incriminate oneself, in particular, presupposes that the prosecution in a criminal case seek to prove their case against the accused without resort to evidence obtained through methods of coercion or oppression in defiance of the will of the accused. In this sense the right is closely linked to the presumption of innocence contained in Article 6(2) of the Convention.

69. The right not to incriminate oneself is primarily concerned, however, with respecting the will of an accused person to remain silent. As commonly understood in the legal systems of the Contracting Parties to the Convention and elsewhere, it does not extend to the use in criminal proceedings of material which may be obtained from the accused through the use of compulsory powers but which has an existence independent of the will of the suspect such as, *inter alia*, documents acquired pursuant to a warrant, breath, blood and urine samples and bodily tissue for the purpose of DNA testing.

In the present case the Court is only called upon to decide whether the use made by the prosecution of the statements obtained from the applicant by the Inspectors amounted to an unjustifiable infringement of the right. This question must be examined by the Court in the light of all the circumstances of the case. In particular, it must be determined whether the applicant has been subject to compulsion to give evidence and whether the use made of the resulting testimony at his trial offended the basic principles of a fair procedure inherent in Article 6(1) of which the right not to incriminate oneself is a constituent element.

70. It has not been disputed by the Government that the applicant was subject to legal compulsion to give evidence to the Inspectors. He was obliged under sections 434 and 436 of the Companies Act 1985 to answer the questions put to him by the Inspectors in the course of nine lengthy interviews of which seven were admissible as evidence at his trial. A refusal by the applicant to answer the questions put to him could have led to a finding of contempt of court and the imposition of a fine or committal to prison for up to two years and it was no defence to such refusal that the questions were of an incriminating nature.

However, the Government have emphasised, before the Court, that nothing said by the applicant in the course of the interviews was self-incriminating and that he had merely given exculpatory answers or answers which, if true, would serve to confirm his defence. In their submission only statements which are self-incriminating could fall within the privilege against self-incrimination.

71. The Court does not accept the Government's premise on this point since some of the applicant's answers were in fact of an incriminating nature in the sense that they contained admissions to knowledge of information which tended to incriminate him. In any event, bearing in mind the concept of fairness in Article 6, the right not to incriminate oneself cannot reasonably be confined to statements of admission of wrongdoing or to remarks which are directly incriminating. Testimony obtained under compulsion which appears on its face to be of a non-incriminating nature – such as exculpatory remarks or mere information on questions of fact – may later be deployed in criminal proceedings in support of the prosecution case, for example to contradict or cast doubt upon other statements of the accused or evidence given by him during the trial or to otherwise undermine his credibility. Where the credibility of an accused must be assessed by a jury the use of such testimony may be especially harmful. It follows that what is of the essence in this context is the use to which evidence obtained under compulsion is made in the course of the criminal trial.

72. In this regard, the Court observes that part of the transcript of answers given by the applicant was read to the jury by counsel for the prosecution over a three-day period despite objections by the applicant. The fact that such extensive use was made of the interviews strongly suggests that the prosecution must have believed that the reading of the transcripts assisted their case in establishing the applicant's dishonesty. This interpretation of the intended impact of the material is supported by the remarks made by the trial judge in the course of the *voir dire* concerning the eighth and ninth interviews to the effect that each of the applicant's statements was capable of being a 'confession' for the purposes of section 82(1) of the Police and Criminal Evidence Act 1984. Similarly, the Court of Appeal considered that the interviews formed 'a significant part' of the prosecution's case against the applicant. Moreover, there were clearly instances where the statements were used by the prosecution to incriminating effect in order to establish the applicant's knowledge of payments to persons involved in the share support operation and to call into question his honesty. They were also used by counsel for the applicant's co-accused to cast doubt on the applicant's version of events.

In sum, the evidence available to the Court supports the claim that the transcripts of the applicant's answers, whether directly self-incriminating or not, were used in the course of the proceedings in a manner which sought to incriminate the applicant.

. . .

74. . . .

[The Court] does not accept the Government's argument that the complexity of corporate fraud and the vital public interest in the investigation of such fraud and the punishment of those responsible could justify such a marked departure as that which occurred in the present case from one of the basic principles of a fair procedure. Like the Commission, it considers that the general requirements of fairness contained in Article 6, including the right not to incriminate oneself, apply to criminal proceedings in respect of all types of criminal offences without distinction, from the most simple to the most complex. The public interest cannot be invoked to justify the use of answers compulsorily obtained in a non-judicial investigation to incriminate the accused during the trial proceedings. It is noteworthy in this respect that under the relevant legislation statements obtained under compulsory powers by the Serious Fraud Office cannot, as a general rule, be adduced in evidence at the subsequent trial of the person concerned. Moreover the fact that statements were made by the applicant prior to his being charged does not prevent their later use in criminal proceedings from constituting an infringement of the right.

75. It follows from the above analysis and from the fact that section 434(5) of the Companies Act 1985 authorises, as noted by both the trial judge and the Court of Appeal, the subsequent use in criminal proceedings of statements obtained by the Inspectors that the various procedural safeguards to which reference has been made by the respondent Government cannot provide a defence in the present case since they did not operate to prevent the use of the statements in the subsequent criminal proceedings.

76. Accordingly, there has been an infringement in the present case of the right not to incriminate oneself.

What was regarded by the European Court of Human Rights as crucial, therefore, was the legal compulsion to answer questions created by s 436 of the Companies Act 1985. It is this direct compulsion which distinguishes s 436 from ss 34, 36 and 37 of the Criminal Justice and Public Order Act 1994.

For further discussion of the erosion of the right to silence in the face of police questioning, see K Browne, 'An Inference of Guilt?' (1997) 141 *Solicitors Journal* 202; G J Durston, 'A Brief Recap on the Implications of the Abolition of the Right to Silence in the Criminal Justice and Public Order Act 1994' (1996) 160 *Justice of the Peace* 62; S Easton, 'The Right to Silence and the Pursuit of Truth' in E Attwooll and D Goldberg (eds), *Criminal Justice: United Kingdom Association for Legal and Social Philosophy – Twentieth Annual Conference at Glasgow. 24–26 March, 1994* (1995); S Greer, 'The Right to Silence, Defence Disclosure, and Confession Evidence' (1994) 21 *Journal of Law and Society* 102; A F Jennings, 'Resounding Silence' (1996) 146 *New Law Journal* 725; A F Jennings, 'Resounding Silence – 2' (1996) 146 *New Law Journal* 764; A F Jennings, 'Resounding Silence – 3' (1996) 146 *New Law Journal* 821; J Michael and B Emmerson, 'Current Topic: The Right to Silence' [1995] *European Human Rights Law Review* 4; P Mirfield, 'Two Side-Effects of Sections 34 to 37 of the Criminal Justice and Public Order Act 1994' [1995] *Criminal Law Review* 612; S Nash, 'Silence as Evidence: Inquisitorial Developments in England and Wales' [1996] *Scots Law Times* 69; S Nash and S Solley, 'Limitations on the Right to Silence and Abuse of Process' (1997) 61 *Journal of Criminal Law* 95; R Pattenden, 'Inferences from Silence' [1995] *Criminal Law Review* 602; A Sanders and R Young, *Criminal Justice* (1994) 191–8.

9

IMPROPERLY OBTAINED
NON-CONFESSION EVIDENCE

The various situations in which confession evidence must, or may, be excluded have been examined in the previous chapter. In the case of non-confession evidence, the position is broadly as follows. Non-confession evidence is admissible as a matter of law even if it has been obtained improperly. Such evidence may, however, be excluded in the exercise of discretion either under the general common law duty to ensure a fair trial (*R v Sang*[1]), or pursuant to s 78(1) of the Police and Criminal Evidence Act 1984. This provision, which has been judicially described as one which 'is by now known almost by heart by most people who have anything to do with the law',[2] provides:

> In any proceedings the court may refuse to allow evidence on which the prosecution proposes to rely to be given if it appears to the court that, having regard to all the circumstances, including the circumstances in which the evidence was obtained, the admission of the evidence would have such an adverse effect on the fairness of the proceedings that the court ought not to admit it.

Section 78(1) began life as an amendment to the Police and Criminal Evidence Bill which was moved in the House of Lords by Lord Scarman and agreed to by the House. This amendment read:

> If it appears to the court in any proceedings that any evidence (other than a confession) proposed to be given by the prosecution may have been obtained improperly, the court shall not allow the evidence to be given unless –
>   (a) the prosecution proves to the court beyond reasonable doubt that it was obtained lawfully and in accordance with a code of practice (where applicable) issued, approved, and in force, under Part VI of this Act; or
>   (b) the court is satisfied that anything improperly done in obtaining it was of no material significance in all the circumstances of the case and ought, therefore, to be disregarded; or
>   (c) the court is satisfied that the probative value of the evidence, the gravity of the offence charged, and the circumstances in which the evidence was obtained are such that the public interest in the fair administration of the

[1] [1980] AC 402.
[2] *Hudson v DPP* [1992] RTR 27, 34 per Hodgson J.

criminal law requires the evidence to be given, notwithstanding that it was obtained improperly.

It is to be noted that this amendment placed the onus of proof upon the prosecution: improperly obtained evidence would be excluded unless the prosecution could justify inclusion. When the Bill returned to the Commons, however, an amendment to replace the Lords' amendment was proposed by the Home Secretary. This was agreed to and now appears as s 78(1). The Home Secretary opined that it was inappropriate for improperly obtained evidence to be excluded to mark society's disapproval of the improper police conduct or for disciplinary reasons.[3] Rather, the sole purpose of exclusion should be to avert an unfair trial.[4] A further objection to the Lords' amendment related to the heavy onus of proof which it placed upon the prosecution.[5] Finally, the criteria laid down in the Lords' amendment were considered to be too complex for a court to have to address in the course of ordinary criminal proceedings.[6]

By contrast, what has now become s 78(1) was described as 'simple and clear in form, yet suitably flexible'.[7] 'The provision of a simple requirement based on the fundamental requirement of fairness gives the court a more flexible approach that better meets the case and goes less far in a direction that we would be wise to avoid.'[8] Do you prefer the Lords' amendment or s 78(1) as we know it? Why?

In this chapter, we shall consider the main contexts in which submissions have been made for the exclusion of non-confession evidence (apart from identification evidence, which will be discussed in the next chapter) on the ground that it was improperly obtained. This will be followed by an exploration of whether English law has evolved a coherent rationale for the exclusion of improperly obtained evidence.

1. THE ROAD TRAFFIC CASES

Since s 78(1) of the Police and Criminal Evidence Act 1984 came into force, there have been a number of cases involving road traffic prosecutions in which submissions for the exclusion of evidence on the ground that it was obtained improperly have been made. Following are extracts from a selection of these cases. What, if anything, do these cases suggest about the principles which are to be applied in determining whether improperly obtained evidence should be excluded?

---

[3] See generally *Parliamentary Debates (Hansard): House of Commons (Vol 65)* (1984) col 1012.
[4] At col 1012.
[5] At col 1013.
[6] At col 1014.
[7] Ibid.
[8] At col 1029.

Extract 9.1.1

Thomas v DPP **[1991] RTR 292, 295-6 (DC)**

The defendant was driving a motor vehicle when he was stopped by a uniformed police inspector. The inspector did have reasonable cause to suspect that the defendant was driving under the influence of alcohol. The inspector required the defendant to submit to a breath test, and explained to the defendant that he would have to wait for the testing kit to be brought to the scene. At that stage the defendant gave no indication either that he was prepared to take the test, or that he refused. A sergeant arrived a short time later, and, misunderstanding the situation, proceeded to arrest the defendant without either administering a breath test or being informed by the defendant that he refused to take the test. The defendant was taken to a police station, where he was required to provide two breath specimens but refused to do so. He was convicted for failing to provide the specimens, and appealed on the basis that the evidence of what happened in the police station should have been excluded under s 78, because his arrest had been unlawful.

TUDOR EVANS J: But a discretion to exclude the procedures at the police station was open to the justices on a finding of mala fides. This follows from the decision of this court in *Matto v Wolverhampton Crown Court* [1987] RTR 337. In that case, a Crown Court had found that the police had acted mala fide and in excess of their statutory powers in arresting the defendant when they knew that their implied licence to be on the defendant's premises had been withdrawn by the defendant, but the Crown Court nevertheless held that the defendant had voluntarily provided a specimen of breath and dismissed his appeal. This court concluded that the fairness of the procedure at the police station was so affected by the previous oppressive conduct of the police as to give rise to an argument of admissibility of the evidence about the breath analysis under section 78 of the Police and Criminal Evidence Act 1984. It was then held that the Crown Court had adopted a wrong approach to the exercise of its discretion to exclude the evidence relating to the taking of a breath analysis and this court allowed the defendant's appeal.

It follows, in my view, that in principle and upon authority, it is open to a defendant to argue that the procedures at the police station were so tainted by the previous conduct of the police at the roadside that there was a discretion to exclude the evidence of what happened at the police station. But, speaking for myself, the defendant is confronted by an insuperable difficulty. There is an express finding by the justices that the sergeant misunderstood what may or may not have happened before he arrived. It follows that the justices did not accept that the sergeant was told and understood that the defendant had not indicated whether or not he would refuse to take a test. There was a misunderstanding as to what may or may not have happened. Moreover, here is an express finding which negatives misconduct at any time. The justices directed their minds to the question of whether there was mala fides and found that there had been a misunderstanding.

In view of these findings, it seems to me that it is not open to the defendant to argue that there was mala fides on the part of the sergeant. As I have already said, Mr Leigh-Morgan contended that the justices did not exercise their discretion at all whether or not to exclude the evidence. That they did not exercise a discretion is true but their failure to do so cannot be criticised for, on their finding of fact, no discretion for them to exercise arose. They negatived mala fides. That was the end of the matter.

In subsequent cases, however, the courts appear to have changed their tune in relation to the issue of mala fides (bad faith).

Extract 9.1.2

DPP v McGladrigan [1991] RTR 297, 301, 302–3 (DC)

The defendant stalled his car while manoeuvring out of a parking place, restarted the engine, and continued to drive for some 40 to 50 feet. He was stopped by a police constable and required to provide a specimen of breath for a breath test. He was later charged with driving with excess alcohol. This charge was dismissed on the ground that the constable had had no reasonable grounds to suspect that the defendant had alcohol in his body, and thus the requirement to provide a specimen, and the arrest of the defendant when the test proved positive, had been unlawful. The prosecutor appealed, mounting an argument based on *Thomas* – that an unlawful arrest, in itself, was insufficient to lead to the exclusion of the evidence; there must also be evidence of mala fides on the part of the police.

HODGSON J: An argument that before a court could exercise its discretion under section 78 there had to be established some mala fides was advanced in terms in *Reg v Samuel* [1988] QB 615. In its judgment in that case the Court of Appeal (Criminal Division) emphatically rejected that argument. . . .
. . .
There is no suggestion that *Reg v Samuel* [1988] QB 615 was cited to the court in *Thomas v Director of Public Prosecutions (Note)* [1991] RTR 292. Indeed it seems to me impossible to believe that, had it been cited, Tudor Evans J could have expressed himself in that way.
Despite the careful argument of counsel in this case I am clearly of the view that it would not be right to remit this case to the justices with a direction to find the defendant guilty only on the basis that there was, as I accept there was, no finding of mala fides on behalf of the police.
However, the second argument put forward on behalf of the prosecutor in this case is much more cogent in my view. He submits that on the findings of fact actually made by the justices the defendant's arrest was not unlawful, and upon the findings themselves the justices had no alternative but to find that the arrest was lawful.
. . .
In this case it is submitted that the justices were wrong in restricting their consideration to the belief of the constable as to the manner of driving of the defendant. What is submitted is that the time when the constable had reasonable cause to suspect was after the car had been stopped and after the

defendant had himself confirmed that he had consumed alcohol. That was a firm, and indeed complete, basis for the constable to have the necessary reasonable cause and to require the defendant to provide a specimen, and thereafter to arrest him if the test was a positive one. It seems to me that that argument is well founded, that the justices were wrong on their own findings of fact in restricting their consideration to the reasonable cause the constable had whilst the car was being driven, and on the finding of fact the defendant had himself confirmed that he had consumed alcohol. The constable was clearly entitled, indeed driven, to have reasonable cause to suspect that the defendant had alcohol in his body.

In those circumstances I would remit the case to the justices with a direction to convict.

The statements of Hodgson J on the s 78(1) discretion are therefore strictly obiter, given his finding that the arrest was not unlawful in the first place.

Extract 9.1.3

DPP v Godwin [1991] RTR 303, 308 (DC)

The defendant was driving on a road when he was stopped by a police constable carrying out traffic stop checks. The constable asked the defendant whether he had been drinking, and he replied in the negative. He failed to produce a specimen of breath for a breath test, and was arrested for failure to do so contrary to s 6 of the Road Traffic Act 1988. He was taken to a police station where he provided specimens of breath for analysis on being required to do so, and was charged with driving with excess alcohol under s 5 of the Act. The justices held that the defendant's arrest had been unlawful because the constable had had no reasonable cause to suspect alcohol in his body before requesting him to take a breath test. The justices exercised their discretion under s 78 to exclude evidence of what happened at the police station, with the result that the excess alcohol charge was dismissed. The prosecutor appealed.

BINGHAM LJ: Thirdly, it is argued on behalf of the prosecutor that the justices should not have exercised their discretion to exclude the evidence in the absence of bad faith on behalf of the police or the prosecuting authorities or oppressive conduct. For reasons which Hodgson J has just given in *Director of Public Prosecutions v McGladrigan* [1991] RTR 297, it is not necessary for justices to be satisfied that the police or the prosecuting authorities have acted in bad faith or oppressively for the discretion under section 78 to be exercised. Hodgson J has rehearsed the reasons for that ruling, and it is quite unnecessary for me to repeat them. It is enough to say that the discretion in section 78 is phrased in general terms, that section 78 has been so construed in what is now a series of cases and that the need to show mala fides was emphatically rejected in the well known case of *Reg v Samuel* [1988] QB 615.

The prosecutor's argument here has to be that on the facts found no justices properly directing themselves could reasonably have decided to exclude this evidence. I am not, for my part, prepared to accept that argument. The justices were entitled to conclude that the substantial breach by the constable of the protection afforded to members of the public by section 6 was denied to the defendant, that as a result the prosecutor obtained evidence which he would not otherwise have obtained, and that as a result the defendant was prejudiced in a significant manner in resisting the charge against him.

Accordingly, the justices were entitled to exclude the evidence. Some justices and other tribunals might no doubt have made the opposite decision without acting unreasonably. It could well be thought that the defendant in this case was fortunate. None the less this is a discretion invested in the trial court, and so invested in this case in the justices.

This court is entitled to intervene only if it is shown that that discretion has been exercised in a manner which is legally challengeable. On the facts here the justices have directed themselves accurately and correctly so far as the law is concerned. There is in my judgment no ground for impugning their decision.

I would accordingly dismiss this appeal.

In *Daniels v DPP*,[9] the Divisional Court has also endorsed the *McGladrigan* view in preference to the *Thomas* one: the presence or otherwise of mala fides, it was said, was only one factor for consideration in deciding whether to exclude evidence under s 78(1). The cases suggest, therefore, that the courts have moved towards the view that proof of mala fides is not a prerequisite to the exclusion of improperly obtained evidence under s 78(1). An impropriety may be considered 'significant and substantial' (and, hence, grounds for exclusion under s 78(1)) in the absence of mala fides on the part of the police, and simply because it constitutes a breach of an important right of the accused. At the same time proof of mala fides remains, of course, an important factor weighing in favour of exclusion.

2. VIOLATIONS OF THE POLICE AND CRIMINAL EVIDENCE ACT 1984 (OR THE CODES OF PRACTICE)

It was seen in the previous chapter that breaches of provisions of the Police and Criminal Evidence Act 1984 and/or the Codes of Practice have led on occasion to the exclusion of confession evidence under s 78(1). The courts are sometimes confronted, too, with the argument that non-confession evidence should be excluded under s 78(1) on account of such breaches.

Extract 9.2.1

R v Cooke [1995] 1 Cr App R 318, 328–9 (CA)

GLIDEWELL LJ: Until the Police and Criminal Evidence Act 1984 came into force, the discretion of the court not to admit evidence which, though improperly

[9] (1991) 156 JPR 543.

obtained, was nevertheless relevant to and admissible in the proceedings was strictly circumscribed. (See the decision of the House of Lords in *R v Sang* (1979) 69 Cr App R 282, [1980] AC 402, following the decision of the Privy Council in *Kuruma v R* [1955] AC 197.)

However, despite some expressions of opinion to the contrary, it is now clear that section 78 has given the courts a substantially wider discretion to refuse to admit evidence improperly obtained. We agree in this respect with the views expressed by Professor Zander in his *Commentary on the Police and Criminal Evidence Act 1984* (2nd ed) at p 200 and the following pages.

Adopting this approach, the Court has in a series of appeals since the passage of the Police and Criminal Evidence Act 1984 ruled inadmissible evidence which it considered improperly obtained under section 78, quite apart from rulings relating to section 76 of the Police and Criminal Evidence Act. However, so far as we are aware the vast majority of cases in which the court has ruled such evidence inadmissible have been cases in which what was challenged was an alleged confession obtained from the defendant in breach of one of the Police and Criminal Evidence Act Codes of Practice.

It must be remembered that the fairness of proceedings involves both fairness to the accused person and fairness to the public good, as represented by the Crown. In this case the evidence which was sought to be adduced of the DNA profile obtained from the hair roots and sheaths plucked from the appellant's head on August 19, 1991, was very strong evidence that the appellant had had sexual intercourse with Miss K on the night of April 14, 1990. If section 63 and section 65 of the Police and Criminal Evidence Act did not authorise the taking of the sample upon which this evidence was based, then in law there had been an assault on the appellant. Nevertheless in our view this did not in any way cast doubt upon the accuracy or strength of the evidence. In this way evidence of this kind differs from, for example, a disputed confession, where the truth of the confession may well itself be in issue.

Thus we wholly agree with Mantell J that even if the sample of August 19, 1991 was not authorised to be obtained by section 63 and section 65 of the Police and Criminal Evidence Act 1984, nevertheless the evidence which it provided and which resulted from it should properly have been admitted in evidence on the trial of the appellant for the rape and kidnapping of Miss K.

Similar sentiments were expressed in the following case:

Extract 9.2.2

R v McCarthy [1996] Crim LR 818; LEXIS transcript (CA)

AULD LJ: McCarthy's appeal against conviction concerns the evidence of the police officers who stopped her and Murray when they were driving from Brighton to London on 13 September with the package containing over £50,000 in cash. Mr Houston on behalf of McCarthy at the trial sought to exclude that evidence on the ground of unfairness provided by s 78 of the Police and Criminal Evidence Act 1984. He maintained that the officers' pretence that they were stopping the car for a routine stop and search instead of telling the truth that they suspected it would contain drugs was a breach of s 2(2) and (3) of the 1984 Act, and of the corresponding provision of the Code of Practice A2 para 4. Sections 2(2) and (3) of the 1984 Act, so far as material, read:

'(2) If a constable contemplates a search, other than a search of an unattended vehicle, in the exercise –
   (a) of the power conferred by section 1 above; or
   (b) of any other power . . .
it shall be his duty . . . to take reasonable steps before he commences the search to bring to the attention of the appropriate person –
      (i) . . .
      (ii) . . . the matters specified in sub-section (3) below;
and the constable shall not commence the search until he has performed that duty.'

Sub-section (3) reads:

'(3) The matters referred to in sub-section 2(ii) above are –
   (a) the constable's name and the name of the police station to which he is attached;
   (b) the object of the proposed search;
   (c) the constable's grounds for proposing to make it.'

Paragraph 4 of the code of practice A2 is in corresponding terms.

Mr Houston submitted that the officer's deception was a clear and substantial breach of that provision, and that the Judge should, in the exercise of his discretion, exclude the evidence as unfair. He suggested that the unfairness of it to McCarthy was that, because they did not tell her that they suspected drug trafficking, she had no occasion to disassociate herself from Murray's activities. The Judge rejected the submission saying that he did not consider that there had been any significant or substantial breach of the Act – the test of this Court in *R v Keenan* [1990] 2 QB 54, (1989) 90 Cr App Rep 1. He also said that he was sure that the admission of such evidence would not be unfair, thereby clearly exercising his discretion in the matter in any event.
. . .

Mr Houston has repeated and elaborated on this appeal his submission to the judge that the police evidence about the stopping of the car on 13 September should have been excluded. He has described the police conduct as flagrant and a deliberate breach of the provisions of the 1984 Act and the relevant provision of the code and an arbitrary use of their powers.

As to the unfairness of the evidence, he said that the case against McCarthy rested entirely on her association with Murray. He maintained that the evidence of her knowledge of the existence of the substantial amount of cash in the car was the only, as he described it, hard evidence going to her state of mind. He submitted that the apparent (and deliberately misleading) acceptance by the police of Murray's explanation of the cash may well have influenced her, if she was innocent, not to disassociate herself from him. He said also that the decision of the police to allow them both to go on their way lulled her into a false sense of security. He did not elaborate what the effect of that might have had on the fairness of the trial – lull her into a false sense of security to do what thereafter? He concluded his submissions by saying that

it was not enough for the prosecution to say that the police could not tell McCarthy and Murray the true purposes of the search because it would prejudice their investigation. The law required them to tell the truth.
. . .

The essential question for the Judge was whether the admission of the evidence could have so affected the fairness of the trial as to require him to exclude it, whether or not there had been some breach of the 1984 Act or other provision on the way. . . .

The only recorded instance of a court excluding evidence of this sort is the first instance decision in R v Fenelley [1989] CLR 142 in which the Judge excluded evidence of a finding of drugs because the arresting officer had breached his stop and search powers. However, as Miss D J Birch in her useful commentary on the case at 143–144, pointed out, it is hard to see why the evidence was excluded. It was highly probative. Fenelley did not dispute that he had drugs on him. The officers would have discovered them anyway, whether or not they complied with the terms of their powers. There does not appear to have been anything unfair about the evidence.

Different considerations may apply in cases of confessions, whether at common law as indicated by Lord Diplock in R v Sang [1980] AC 402, [1979] 2 All ER 1222 at p 437 D to E of the former report, or under s 78, where there has been bad faith or a flagrant and deliberate breach of a code under the 1984 Act. See, for example, R v Alladice 87 Cr App Rep 380, [1988] Crim LR 608 and R v Canale [1990] 2 All ER 187, 91 Cr App Rep 1, both decisions of this Court, and Lam Chi-Ming v R [1991] 2 AC 212, [1991] 3 All ER 172 a decision of the Privy Council, per Lord Griffiths giving judgment of the Board at 220.

It is difficult to see what possible unfairness there was in this evidence such as to require its exclusion. The incident in question was not the only hard evidence going to McCarthy's state of mind. As Mr Coleman for the respondents submitted, there was no dispute that there was a package containing a large amount of cash in the car. It was there for all to see. Its presence was consistent with drug trafficking or some other criminal conduct.
. . .

We agree with the Judge that there could have been no unfairness in admitting the evidence of the police stop. If there was anything about what had occurred with which McCarthy might have wished to disassociate herself from Murray – and there was plenty – she had an opportunity to do so at the time of the stop or at any time before or afterwards, prior to her and Murray's arrest.

We cannot see the police's stopping of the car as an act of bad faith by them. They were investigating very serious drug trafficking. Their concern must have been for the long term success of their operation, which was to find the drugs and arrest the main conspirators. Nor, in those circumstances, do we regard it as a significant or substantial or flagrant breach of the code.

Finally, we observe . . . that this Court does not interfere lightly with the exercise by a Judge of his discretion under s 78 not to exclude evidence. That is effectively the Wednesbury (Associated Provincial Picture Houses Ltd v Wednesbury Corporation ([1948] 1 KB 223, [1947] 2 All ER 680)) test as applied by the High Court when exercising its jurisdiction on judicial review. Here, as we have made plain, we do not consider that the Judge's decision not to exclude the evidence was unreasonable, *Wednesbury* or otherwise. We agree with it. Accordingly we dismiss the appeal by McCarthy against conviction.

Even if the actual decisions of the Court of Appeal in *Cooke* and *McCarthy* are justifiable, the court's reasoning in these cases is far from satisfactory. It can be seen that the court regarded the undoubted reliability of the evidence in each case as a crucial consideration in reaching its conclusion. Evidence of the type in question was distinguished from confession evidence (the reliability of which, as was seen in the previous chapter, may well be in doubt). Is the court suggesting, in effect, that highly reliable evidence should practically never be excluded on the ground that it was improperly obtained, especially where the offence charged is serious? If so, this would seem to fly completely in the face of the recent trend (illustrated by the road traffic cases discussed above) towards taking into account not only considerations of intrinsic policy, but also considerations of extrinsic policy, in determining whether to exclude evidence. More will be said about this issue at the end of this chapter.

3. ENTRAPMENT SITUATIONS, UNDERCOVER POLICE ACTIVITY GENERALLY AND ELECTRONIC LISTENING DEVICES

In very broad terms, entrapment may be regarded as the enticement of a person, by an agent provocateur, to commit an offence which he or she would not otherwise have committed. To what extent can evidence be excluded on the ground that it was obtained by entrapment, or (more generally) during an undercover police operation?

Extract 9.3.1

***R v Smurthwaite* [1994] 1 All ER 898, 902–3 (CA)**

LORD TAYLOR CJ: In our judgment, s 78 has not altered the substantive rule of law that entrapment or the use of an agent provocateur does not per se afford a defence in law to a criminal charge. A purely evidential provision in a statute, which does not even mention entrapment or agent provocateur, cannot, in our view, have altered a substantive rule of law enunciated so recently by the House of Lords. Had Parliament intended to alter the substantive law, it would have done so in clear terms.

However, that is not to say that entrapment, agent provocateur or the use of a trick are irrelevant to the application of s 78. The right approach to the 1984 Act, a codifying Act, is that stated in *R v Fulling* [1987] 2 All ER 65, [1987] QB 426 following the principles laid down in *Bank of England v Vagliano*

Bros [1891] AC 107 at 144, [1891–4] All ER Rep 93 at 113. That is simply to examine the language of the relevant provision in its natural meaning and not to strain for an interpretation which either reasserts or alters the pre-existing law. Viewed in that way, the phrase emphasised by Mr Worsley clearly permits the court to have regard to 'the circumstances in which the evidence was obtained' and to exclude it, but only if it 'would have such an adverse effect on the fairness of the proceedings that the court ought not to admit it'. Thus, the fact that the evidence has been obtained by entrapment, or by agent provocateur, or by a trick, does not of itself require the judge to exclude it. If, however, he considers that in all the circumstances the obtaining of the evidence in that way would have the adverse effect described in the statute, then he will exclude it. (See also *R v Governor of Pentonville Prison, ex p Chinoy* [1992] 1 All ER 317 at 331–332 to the same effect.) 'Fairness of the proceedings' involves a consideration not only of fairness to the accused but also, as has been said before, of fairness to the public (see for example *R v Sang* [1979] 2 All ER 1222 at 1246–1247, [1980] AC 402 at 456 per Lord Scarman).

In exercising his discretion whether to admit the evidence of an undercover officer, some, but not an exhaustive list, of the factors that the judge may take into account are as follows. Was the officer acting as an agent provocateur in the sense that he was enticing the defendant to commit an offence he would not otherwise have committed? What was the nature of any entrapment? Does the evidence consist of admissions to a completed offence, or does it consist of the actual commission of an offence? How active or passive was the officer's role in obtaining the evidence? Is there an unassailable record of what occurred, or is it strongly corroborated? In *R v Christou* [1992] 4 All ER 559, [1992] QB 979 this court held that discussions between suspects and undercover officers, not overtly acting as police officers, were not within the ambit of the codes under the 1984 Act. However, officers should not use their undercover pose to question suspects so as to circumvent the code. In *R v Bryce* [1992] 4 All ER 567 the court held that the undercover officer had done just that. Accordingly, a further consideration for the judge in deciding whether to admit an undercover officer's evidence is whether he has abused his role to ask questions which ought properly to have been asked as a police officer and in accordance with the codes.

Beyond mentioning the considerations set out above, it is not possible to give more general guidance as to how a judge should exercise his discretion under s 78 in this field, since each case must be determined on its own facts (see *R v Samuel* [1988] 2 All ER 135 at 146, [1988] QB 615 at 630, *R v Parris* (1988) 89 Cr App R 68 at 72 and *R v Jelen, R v Katz* (1989) 90 Cr App R 456 at 465 and other cases cited in *Archbold's Pleading Evidence and Practice in Criminal Cases* (44th edn, 1993) para 15–364.)

See generally D Birch, 'Excluding Evidence from Entrapment: What is a "Fair Cop"?' (1994) 47 *Current Legal Problems* 73; A L-T Choo and M Mellors, 'Undercover Police Operations and What the Suspect Said (or Didn't Say)' in M Allen (ed), *Web Journal of Current Legal Issues Yearbook 1995* (1996); G Robertson, 'Entrapment Evidence: Manna from Heaven, or Fruit of the Poisoned Tree?' [1994] *Criminal Law Review* 805; S Sharpe, 'Covert Police Operations and the Discretionary Exclusion of Evidence' [1994] *Criminal Law Review* 793; S Sharpe, 'Covert Policing: A Comparative View' (1996) 25 *Anglo-American Law Review* 163.

It is unfortunate that the factors listed in *Smurthwaite* were not accompanied by more detailed explanation. For example, it would have been extremely helpful to have been given some guidance on the important issue of what *weight* should be attached to the first factor. Would the presence of entrapment weigh heavily in favour of exclusion, or is it a factor carrying no special weight? The second factor implies that some types of entrapment may be more acceptable than others, but again, no assistance is provided on this issue. The fourth factor implies that to play an active role in an undercover operation may be less justifiable than playing a passive role, and thus the more active the officer's role, the more likely exclusion would be. But no guidance is provided as to what may constitute an active role, and what may constitute a passive role.

It would appear, however, that the exclusion of evidence does not constitute the only 'remedy' to which an accused person may be entitled in this area. The House of Lords has recently held that it may be possible, in appropriate circumstances, for the court to stay the proceedings altogether as an abuse of process.

Extract 9.3.2

***R v Latif* [1996] 1 WLR 104, 111–13 (HL)**

LORD STEYN:

The abuse of process issue

. . .

. . . First, [counsel for Shahzad, whose appeal was conjoined with that of Latif,] submitted that the customs officers encouraged Shahzad to commit the offence. Secondly, he argued that the customs officer, who brought the drugs to England, himself committed the offence of which Shahzad was convicted. It is necessary to examine these arguments. As to the first, I approach the matter on the basis that Shahzad took the initiative at the critical meeting between him and Honi. He was 37 years of age. He was not a vulnerable and unwilling person. He was an organizer in the heroin trade. He made clear from the start that he was ready and willing to arrange the export of heroin from Pakistan. But I also accept . . . that the particular importation would not have taken place when and how it did without the assistance of Honi and the customs and excise. The highest that the argument for Shahzad can be put is that Honi gave him the opportunity to commit or to attempt to commit the crime of importing heroin into the United Kingdom if he was so minded. And he was so minded. That is not necessarily a decisive factor, but it is an important point against the claim of abuse of process.

That brings me to the second matter, ie the question whether the customs officer, who brought the heroin to England, was himself guilty of criminal behaviour. Section 50(3) of the [Customs and Excise Management Act 1979] reads:

'If any person imports or is concerned in importing any goods contrary to any prohibition or restriction for the time being in force under or by virtue of any enactment with respect to those goods . . . and does so with intent to evade the prohibition or restriction, he shall be guilty of an offence under this subsection . . .'

It was common ground in argument before your Lordships that the customs officer had committed an offence under this statutory provision. Despite the requirement of 'intent to evade,' I incline to the view that this concession was rightly made. . . .

. . . I am prepared to assume, without deciding, that the customs officer was [also] guilty of [the] offence [of being knowingly concerned in the fraudulent evasion of the prohibition on importation of a controlled drug] under section 170(2).

It is now necessary to consider the legal framework in which the issue of abuse of process must be considered. The starting point is that entrapment is not a defence under English law. That is, however, not the end of the matter. Given that Shahzad would probably not have committed the particular offence of which he was convicted, but for the conduct of Honi and customs officers, which included criminal conduct, how should the matter be approached? This poses the perennial dilemma: see W G Roser, 'Entrapment: Have the Courts Found a Solution to this Fundamental Dilemma to the Criminal Justice System?' (1993) 67 ALJ 722 and Andrew L-T Choo, 'Halting Criminal Prosecutions: The Abuse of Process Doctrine Revisited' [1995] Crim LR 864. If the court always refuses to stay such proceedings, the perception will be that the court condones criminal conduct and malpractice by law enforcement agencies. That would undermine public confidence in the criminal justice system and bring it into disrepute. On the other hand, if the court were always to stay proceedings in such cases, it would incur the reproach that it is failing to protect the public from serious crime. The weaknesses of both extreme positions leaves only one principled solution. The court has a discretion: it has to perform a balancing exercise. If the court concludes that a fair trial is not possible, it will stay the proceedings. That is not what the present case is concerned with. It is plain that a fair trial was possible and that such a trial took place. In this case the issue is whether, despite the fact that a fair trial was possible, the judge ought to have stayed the criminal proceedings on broader considerations of the integrity of the criminal justice system. The law is settled. Weighing countervailing considerations of policy and justice, it is for the judge in the exercise of his discretion to decide whether there has been an abuse of process, which amounts to an affront to the public conscience and requires the criminal proceedings to be stayed: *Reg v Horseferry Road Magistrates' Court, Ex parte Bennett* [1994] 1 AC 42. *Ex parte Bennett* was a case where a stay was appropriate because a defendant had been forcibly abducted and brought to this country to face trial in disregard of extradition laws. The speeches in *Ex parte Bennett* conclusively establish that proceedings may be stayed in the exercise of the judge's discretion not only where a fair trial is impossible but also where it would be contrary to the public interest in the integrity of the criminal justice system that a trial should take place. An infinite variety of cases could arise. General guidance as to how the discretion should be exercised in particular circumstances will not be useful. But it is possible to say that in a case such as the present the judge must weigh in the balance the public interest in ensuring that those that are charged with grave crimes should be tried and the competing public interest in not conveying the impression that the court will adopt the approach that the end justified any means.

In my view the judge took into consideration the relevant considerations placed before him. He performed the balancing exercise. He was entitled to take the view that Shahzad was an organiser in the heroin trade, who took the initiative in proposing the importation. It is true that he did not deal with arguments about the criminal behaviour of the customs officer. That was understandable since that was not argued before him. If such arguments had been put before him, I am satisfied that he would still have come to the same conclusion. And I think he would have been right. The conduct of the customs officer was not so unworthy or shameful that it was an affront to the public conscience to allow the prosecution to proceed. Realistically, any criminal behaviour of the customs officer was venial compared to that of Shahzad.

In these circumstances I would reject the submission that the judge erred in refusing to stay the proceedings.

Section 78(1) of the Act of 1984

By way of alternative submission, counsel for Shahzad argued that the judge erred in not excluding the evidence of Honi and the customs officers under section 78(1) of the Act of 1984. Exclusion under section 76, which deals with confessions, does not arise. . . .

. . .

The judge found as a fact that Shahzad was not in any way prejudiced in the presentation of his defence. Counsel found it impossible to challenge that finding. Given that conclusion counsel accepted that if his submissions on abuse of process failed his separate argument based on section 78(1) of the Act of 1984 must inevitably also fail. I need say no more about this aspect of the case.

See generally K Grevling, 'Undercover Operations: Balancing the Public Interest?' (1996) 112 *Law Quarterly Review* 401; S Sharpe, 'Judicial Discretion and Investigative Impropriety' (1997) 1(2) *International Journal of Evidence and Proof* 149.

It would seem, therefore, that in this area, either the exclusion of evidence (*Smurthwaite*) or a stay of the proceedings as a whole (*Latif*) may be able to be obtained by the defence. Unfortunately, the relationship between these alternative 'remedies' has not been clarified. It has not, for example, been made clear how precisely, if at all, the factors to be taken into account in determining whether to stay the proceedings as a whole differ from those to be taken into account in determining whether to exclude evidence under s 78(1). It would clearly be in the interests of the defence to seek to obtain a stay rather than mere exclusion. Exclusion may of course lead to the proceedings being effectively stayed, but this can happen only where the evidence constitutes the only, or the main, prosecution evidence in the case.

The following case on evidence obtained by means of an electronic listening device presented the House of Lords with its first real opportunity to address the issue of exclusion under s 78(1).

<hr>

Extract 9.3.3

<hr>

R v Khan (Sultan) [1996] 3 All ER 289, 292–303 (HL)

LORD NOLAN: My Lords, on 17 September 1992 the appellant arrived at Manchester airport on a flight from Pakistan. On the same flight was his cousin, Farooq Nawab. Both men were stopped and searched by customs officials. Nawab was found to be in possession of heroin with a street value of almost £100,000. He was interviewed and then arrested and charged. No drugs were found on the appellant. He too was interviewed, but made no admissions. He was released without charge.

On 26 January 1993 the appellant went to an address in Sheffield, the home of a man named Bashforth, on the outside of which a listening device had been installed by the South Yorkshire Police. Neither the appellant nor Mr Bashforth were aware of its presence. By means of that device, the police obtained a tape recording of a conversation which took place between Mr Bashforth, the appellant and others. In the course of the conversation the appellant made statements which amounted to an admission that he was a party to the importation of drugs by Nawab on 17 September 1992.

As a result, the appellant was arrested on 11 February 1993. Again he made no admissions when interviewed, but subsequently he and Nawab were jointly charged with offences under the Customs and Excise Management Act 1979 and the Misuse of Drugs Act 1971. They were committed for trial in the Crown Court at Sheffield.

At the trial it was admitted on behalf of the appellant that he had been present at the Sheffield address and that his voice was one of those recorded on the tape. It was admitted on behalf of the Crown that the attachment of the listening device had involved a civil trespass, and had occasioned some damage to the property. Thereupon, the judge conducted a hearing on the voire dire as to the admissibility in evidence of the conversation recorded on the tape. The Crown accepted that without it there was no case against the appellant.

The judge ruled that the evidence was admissible. Following an amendment to the indictment, the appellant was rearraigned and pleaded guilty to being knowingly concerned in the fraudulent evasion of the prohibition on the importation of heroin. He was sentenced to three years' imprisonment. It was made clear that his plea of guilty was tendered only on the basis of the judge's ruling, and that he reserved the right to challenge that ruling.

His appeal to the Court of Appeal was dismissed on 27 May 1994, but the court certified the following question as being one of general public importance:

447

'... whether in a criminal trial evidence as to the terms of tape recorded conversations obtained by means of an electronic listening device attached by the police to a private house without the knowledge of the owners or occupiers was admissible against the defendant.'

It became clear in the course of argument, however, that this question raised two separate issues, the first being whether the evidence was admissible at all, and the second whether, if admissible, it should none the less have been excluded by the judge in the exercise of his discretion at common law or under the powers conferred upon him by s 78 of the Police and Criminal Evidence Act 1984 (PACE). That is how the matter had been approached both by the judge and by the Court of Appeal ([1994] 4 All ER 426, [1995] QB 27). But although the issues are separate, the focal point of the appellant's case upon each of them was the fact that there is no legal framework regulating the installation and use by the police of covert listening devices. This is in contrast to the use of such devices by the security service which has been regulated by statute since 1989 under the Security Service Act of that year.

That is a matter to which I shall return. It should not be assumed, however, that the use by the police of such devices is wholly arbitrary and undisciplined. They are the subject of guidelines which were issued to police authorities by the Home Office in 1984, entitled 'Guidelines on the use of equipment in police surveillance operations'. They are also dealt with in standing orders issued by the South Yorkshire Police, but it is unnecessary to refer to these since they do not differ materially from the Home Office guidelines.

The guidelines amount to a detailed and comprehensive code restricting the authorised use of the devices in question. For present purposes it is, I think, sufficient to quote paras 4, 5 and 6, which read as follows:

'4. In each case in which the covert use of a listening device is requested the authorising officer should satisfy himself that the following criteria are met ... a) the investigation concerns serious crime; b) normal methods of investigation must have been tried and failed, or must, from the nature of things, be unlikely to succeed if tried; c) there must be good reason to think that use of the equipment would be likely to lead to an arrest and a conviction, or where appropriate, to the prevention of acts of terrorism; d) use of equipment must be operationally feasible.
5. In judging how far the seriousness of the crime under investigation justifies the use of particular surveillance techniques, authorising officers should satisfy themselves that the degree of intrusion into the privacy of those affected by the surveillance is commensurate with the seriousness of the offence. Where the targets of surveillance might reasonably assume a high degree of privacy, for instance in their homes, listening devices should be used only for the investigation of major organised conspiracies and of other particularly serious offences, especially crimes of violence.
6. The covert use in operations of listening, recording and transmitting equipment (for example microphones, tape recorders and tracking equipment) requires the personal authority of the chief officer.'

In certain circumstances, which do not exist in the present case, this authority may be delegated to an assistant chief constable. As appears from the facts found by the judge, after the hearing on the voire dire, the installation of the listening device in Mr Bashforth's premises was authorised by the Chief Constable of South Yorkshire on the grounds that there was good reason to suppose that Mr Bashforth was dealing in heroin, but that conventional methods of surveillance were unlikely to provide proof that he was doing so. No suggestion was made in your Lordships' House that the South Yorkshire Police had operated otherwise than in accordance with the Home Office guidelines.

Even so, it was argued for the appellant, the evidence was unacceptable in principle and should not be admitted. Private conversations on private property of a kind which could not be overheard save by means of listening devices should be inviolate save where intrusion upon them was authorised by law. The procedure adopted in the present case should not be accepted as a means of obtaining evidence, the more so in a case, such as the present, where it involved trespass and, at least arguably, criminal damage to property.

Mr Muller QC, representing the appellant, likened the case of a private conversation conducted in a private house to that of a private telephone conversation by means of the public telecommunications system. The interception of the latter was strictly regulated by the provisions of the Interception of Communications Act 1985. This Act had been passed as a result of the decision of the European Court of Human Rights in *Malone v UK* (1984) 7 EHRR 14. In that case, the applicant's telephone calls and correspondence had been intercepted by the police. The interception had been carried out pursuant to a warrant issued by the Home Secretary, but there was no authority in statute or common law for such a warrant. The applicant had brought civil proceedings against the police in the High Court, but without success. Megarry V-C concluded, after an extensive review of the authorities, that the applicant had no right of action against the police under English law (*Malone v Comr of Police of the Metropolis (No 2)* [1979] 2 All ER 620, [1979] Ch 344). In the course of his judgment, however, Megarry V-C commented that telephone tapping was a subject which cried out for legislation, and that the requirements of the European Convention on Human Rights (Convention for the Protection of Human Rights and Fundamental Freedoms (Rome, 4 November 1950; TS 71 (1953); Cmd 8969) should provide a spur to action (see [1979] 2 All ER 620 at 649, [1979] Ch 344 at 380)).

These comments were resoundingly echoed by the European Court of Human Rights. The court held that the tapping of the applicant's telephone amounted to a breach of his rights under art 8 of the convention. That article provides as follows:

'1. Everyone has the right to respect for his private and family life, his home and his correspondence.
2. There shall be no interference by a public authority with the exercise of this right except such as is in accordance with the law and is necessary in a democratic society in the interests of national security, public safety or the economic well-being of the country, for the prevention of disorder or crime, for the protection of health or morals, or for the protection of the rights and freedoms of others.'

The Court held, in its judgment, that art 8.2 imposed requirements over and above compliance with the domestic law (see (1984) 7 EHRR 14 at 39–40 (para 66)). These included the requirement that the law must be adequately accessible. The court added that –

'the law must be sufficiently clear in its terms to give citizens an adequate indication as to the circumstances in which and the conditions on which public authorities are empowered to resort to this secret and potentially dangerous interference with the right to respect for private life and correspondence.' (See 7 EHRR 14 at 40–41 (para 67).)

Mr Muller contended that in the present case there had been interception which was not in accordance with the law and further, that there had been a breach of the requirement of accessibility to information about the conditions in which it took place. The Home Office circular was placed in the library of the House of Commons, but knowledge of its terms was not available to the general public.

Reverting to the 1985 Act, Mr Muller pointed out that the use in evidence of material obtained by the interception of communications was expressly forbidden by s 9. He added that there had evidently been a similar restriction on material obtained by the use of surveillance devices in the years prior to 1984. He referred us in this connection to a Home Office letter dated 1 July 1977, addressed to chief constables, which appears to have been the precursor to the 1984 guidelines, and which stated that –

'the primary purpose of using equipment for aural or visual surveillance should be to help confirm or dispel a suspicion of serious crime, and not to collect evidence (except where, as in blackmail, the spoken word is the kernel of the offence) . . .'

This is to be contrasted with the opening sentence of para 10 of the 1984 guidelines, which reads

'It is accepted that there may be circumstances in which material obtained through the use of equipment by the police for surveillance as a necessary part of a criminal investigation could appropriately be used in evidence at subsequent court proceedings . . .'

In *R v Preston* [1993] 4 All ER 638 at 650, [1994] 2 AC 130 at 148 Lord Mustill, referring to para 10, had said that this departure from previous practice was itself contradicted a few weeks later by the Home Office White Paper, *The Interception of Communications in the United Kingdom* (Cmnd 9438 (1985)) designed to lay the ground for the Bill which became the 1985 Act. Paragraph 12(f) of the White Paper had stated:

'The Bill will provide for controls over the use of intercepted material. By making such material generally inadmissible in legal proceedings it will ensure that interception can be used only as an aspect of investigation, not of prosecution.'

It is true that the Home Office guidelines were concerned with aural and visual surveillance devices, whereas the 1985 Act is concerned with telephone tapping and the interception of postal communications, but it is difficult to see why different rules should apply to the admissibility of evidence gained from these sources. The difficulty is compounded by the provisions of the Intelligence Services Act 1994, which govern the activities of the secret intelligence service, the government communications headquarters and the security service. One of the effects of ss 2(2)(a) and 5(4) of the 1994 Act is that information obtained by the secret intelligence service or the security service through the use of listening devices may be disclosed, not only for the purpose of preventing or detecting serious crime, but also for the purpose of any criminal proceedings.

Finally, Mr Muller turned to the decision of your Lordships' House in *R v Sang* [1979] 2 All ER 1222, [1980] AC 402. That decision is, of course, authority for the proposition that a judge has no discretion to refuse to admit relevant evidence on the ground that it was obtained by improper or unfair means. Lord Diplock said ([1979] 2 All ER 1222 at 1231, [1980] AC 402 at 437):

'(1) A trial judge in a criminal trial has always a discretion to refuse to admit evidence if in his opinion its prejudicial effect outweighs its probative value. (2) Save with regard to admissions and confessions and generally with regard to evidence obtained from the accused after commission of the offence, he has no discretion to refuse to admit relevant admissible evidence on the ground that it was obtained by improper or unfair means. The court is not concerned with how it was obtained.'

As to this, Mr Muller submitted firstly that the general rule in *R v Sang* did not apply to the evidence with which the present case was concerned, because that evidence fell within the category of admissions, confessions, and other evidence obtained from the accused after commission of the offence. In my judgment, this submission has no force. It is clear from an earlier passage in the speech of Lord Diplock that the exceptional category which he had in mind consisted of –

'evidence tantamount to a self-incriminatory admission which was obtained from the defendant, after the offence had been committed, by means which would justify a judge in excluding an actual confession which had the like self-incriminating effect.' (See [1979] 2 All ER 1222 at 1229–1230, [1980] AC 402 at 436.)

He continued ([1979] 2 All ER 1222 at 1230, [1980] AC 402 at 436):

'My Lords, I propose to exclude, as the certified question does, detailed consideration of the role of the trial judge in relation to confessions and evidence obtained from the defendant after commission of the offence that is tantamount to a confession. It has a long history dating back to the days before the existence of a disciplined police force, when a prisoner on a charge of felony could not be represented by counsel and was not entitled to give evidence in his own defence either to deny that he had made the confession, which was generally oral, or to deny that its contents were true. The underlying rationale of this branch of the criminal law, though it may originally have been based upon ensuring the reliability of confessions is, in my view, now to be found in the maxim, nemo debet prodere se ipsum, no one can be required to be his own betrayer, or in its popular English mistranslation "the right to silence". That is why there is no discretion to exclude evidence discovered as the result of an illegal search but there is discretion to exclude evidence which the accused has been induced to produce voluntarily if the method of inducement was unfair.'

In the present case, I would regard it as a misuse of language to describe the appellant as having been 'induced' to make the admissions which were recorded on the tape. He was under no inducement to do so. But if this be too narrow a view, the only result would be to bring into play the judge's discretion as to whether or not the evidence should in fairness be admitted. It would not make the evidence intrinsically inadmissible.

Secondly, Mr Muller submitted that the rule in R v Sang must be taken to have been modified by the enactment of s 9 of the 1985 Act, prohibiting the admission of what would otherwise be admissible evidence. This too appears to me to be, with respect, a wholly unsustainable submission. If we were to have regard to the provisions of the 1985 Act which prohibit the admission of evidence obtained by comparable means to those used in the present case, why should we not also have regard to the provisions of the 1994 Act which authorise the admission of evidence obtained by identical means? I am satisfied, for my part, that neither of these statutes should be regarded as affecting the common law principles laid down by your Lordships' House in R v Sang.

In truth, in the light of R v Sang, the argument that the evidence of the taped conversation is inadmissible could only be sustained if two wholly new principles were formulated in our law. The first would be that the appellant enjoyed a right of privacy, in terms similar to those of art 8 of the convention, in respect of the taped conversation. The second, which is different though related, is that evidence of the conversation obtained in breach of that right is inadmissible. The objection to the first of these propositions is that there is no such right of privacy in English law. The objection to the second is that even if there were such a right, the decision of your Lordships' House in R v Sang and the many decisions which have followed it make it plain that, as a matter of English law, evidence which is obtained improperly or even unlawfully remains admissible, subject to the power of the trial judge to exclude it in the exercise of his common law discretion or under the provisions of s 78 of PACE.

If evidence obtained by way of entrapment is admissible, then a fortiori there can hardly be a fundamental objection to the admission of evidence obtained in breach of privacy. In R v Sang itself, Lord Diplock noted that if evidence obtained by entrapment were inadmissible, this would have the effect of establishing entrapment as a defence to a criminal charge (see [1979] 2 All ER 1222 at 1224–1225, [1980] AC 402 at 429–430). By parity of reasoning, if evidence obtained by a breach of privacy were inadmissible, then privacy too would become a defence to a criminal charge where the substance of the charge consisted of acts done or words spoken in private. Such a proposition does not bear serious examination.

I conclude, therefore, that the appellant fails upon the first issue. The evidence of the taped conversation was clearly admissible as a matter of law.

I turn, then, to the second issue, namely whether the judge should nevertheless have excluded it in the exercise of his common law discretion or under the powers conferred upon him by s 78 of PACE. The only element of the common law discretion which is relevant for present purposes is that part of it which authorises the judge 'to exclude admissible evidence if it is necessary in order to secure a fair trial for the accused', as Lord Griffiths put it in *Scott v R, Barnes v R* [1989] 2 All ER 305 at 310, [1989] AC 1242 at 1256. It is, therefore, unnecessary to consider the common law position separately from that which arises under s 78. I would respectfully agree with Lord Taylor of Gosforth CJ that the power conferred by s 78 to exclude evidence in the interests of a fair trial is at least as wide as that conferred by the common law (see [1994] 4 All ER 426 at 435, [1995] QB 27 at 38).

I hope that I do not unduly condense the case put forward by Mr Muller if I say that, whereas his submissions upon the first issue placed indirect reliance upon art 8 of the convention, his submissions upon the second issue were based directly and almost exclusively upon the terms of that article read with s 78. In considering the second issue I have been much assisted by the written submission, put forward with the consent of your Lordships' House and of the parties, by the National Council for Civil Liberties (Liberty). As Liberty has observed, this case raises for the first time the question whether a criminal court, in considering its power under s 78 of PACE, is required to have regard to the convention and the jurisprudence of the European Court of Human Rights, and if so, whether a violation of the convention is to be regarded per se as a ground for excluding otherwise admissible evidence.

I take first the submissions on this question which were put forward by Mr Muller on behalf of the appellant. He referred to the full terms of s 78(1) ...

The appellant contends that these words plainly require the court, in considering whether or not to allow the relevant evidence, to have regard to 'all the circumstances, including the circumstances in which the evidence was obtained'. If the circumstances in which the evidence was obtained amounted to an apparent invasion of the appellant's rights of privacy under art 8, that is accordingly something to which the court must have regard. The only remaining question is whether the evidence which was obtained in such circumstances would have such an adverse effect on the fairness of the proceedings that the court ought not to admit it. As to that, the appellant submits that since the proceedings themselves are only possible because of the improper conduct of the executive, the court should conclude that the admission of evidence obtained in these circumstances would have such an adverse effect on the fairness of the proceedings that the court ought not to admit it.

The argument put forward by Liberty similarly started from the premise that the duty of the court under s 78 to have regard to the circumstances in which the evidence was obtained, necessarily included a duty to have regard to the fact that the evidence was apparently obtained in circumstances which amounted to a breach of the provisions of art 8. As a result, the appellant was entitled to invoke art 13 of the convention, which provides: 'Everyone whose rights and freedoms as set forth in this Convention are violated shall have an effective remedy before a national authority ...'

In *Brind v Secretary of State for the Home Dept* [1991] 1 All ER 720 at 722, [1991] 1 AC 696 at 747 Lord Bridge of Harwich had accepted that 'The obligations of the United Kingdom ... are to secure ... the rights which the convention defines, including ... the right under art 13 to "an effective remedy before a national authority" for any violation'. But the remedy which art 13 required, according to the submissions of Liberty, need not go so far as to exclude evidence obtained in breach of art 8. It is sufficient if the national law provides an effective means of reviewing the admissibility of the evidence in the light of the provisions of art 8. Section 78 provides for just such a review, and therefore satisfies the requirements of art 13.

In the present case, the trial judge had substantially followed the view of the law advocated by Liberty. He had accepted that there was at any rate an arguable breach of art 8, but had concluded that neither this nor any of the other circumstances of the case required the exclusion of the taped evidence. In the Court of Appeal, however, Lord Taylor of Gosforth CJ had expressed himself somewhat differently. He said ([1994] 4 All ER 426 at 437, [1995] QB 27 at 40):

'As to the argument based on art 8 of the [European Convention on Human Rights], counsel for the Crown rightly pointed out that it is not (as yet) part of the law of the United Kingdom since it has not been enacted into our statutory law. He referred to *Chundawadra v Immigration Appeal Tribunal* [1988] Imm AR 161 and *Pan-American World Airways Inc v Dept of Trade* [1976] 1 Lloyd's Rep 257. From these authorities it is clear that it is permissible to have regard to the convention, which is of persuasive assistance, in cases of ambiguity or doubt. In the circumstances of the present case the position is neither ambiguous nor doubtful: nor is it incumbent on us to consider whether there was a breach of art 8, and we do not propose to do so.'

Both Liberty and the Crown have taken these words as amounting to an assertion that art 8 is irrelevant to a court's exercise of its powers under s 78. On that basis, say Liberty, Lord Taylor CJ has fallen into error. If art 8 were irrelevant to the exercise of the s 78 power, then that power could not amount to an effective remedy for the purposes of art 13. The Crown, on the other hand, argues that Lord Taylor CJ was quite right to regard the convention as irrelevant. In my judgment, both of these arguments proceed on a fallacious assumption. Lord Taylor CJ did not describe art 8 as 'irrelevant'. On the contrary, he referred to it twice in the paragraph of his judgment immediately following that which I have quoted, and in which he sets out the ratio of the decision of the Court of Appeal. In the passage which I have quoted, Lord Taylor CJ, as I understand him, was saying simply that art 8 forms no part of our law, that this was not a case of ambiguity or doubt in which it could be invoked as an aid to construction, and that it was no part of the function of the Court of Appeal to consider whether there was a breach of the article. The question whether there was a breach, and if so what the consequences should be, is solely one for the European Court of Human Rights.

That is not to say that the principles reflected in the convention are irrelevant to the exercise of the s 78 power. They could hardly be irrelevant, because they embody so many of the familiar principles of our own law and of our concept of justice. In particular, of course, they assert the right of the individual to a fair trial, that is to say, in the words of art 6.1 'a fair and public hearing within a reasonable time by an independent and impartial tribunal established by law'.

My Lords, I think it is of interest in the present case that the appellant makes no complaint of an infringement of his rights under art 6.1. I also note with interest the decision of the European Court of Human Rights in *Schenk v Switzerland* (1988) 13 EHRR 242. In that case the applicant had complained that the making and use as evidence against him of an unlawfully obtained recording of a telephone conversation violated his right to a fair trial under art 6 and his right to confidentiality of telephone communications under art 8. Rejecting the complaint under art 6, the court said this (at 265–266 (paras 46, 47)):

'46. While article 6 of the Convention guarantees the right to a fair trial, it does not lay down any rules on the admissibility of evidence as such, which is therefore primarily a matter for regulation under national law. The Court therefore cannot exclude [sic] as a matter of principle and in the abstract that unlawfully obtained evidence of the present kind may be admissible. It has only to ascertain whether Mr Schenk's trial as a whole was fair.
47. Like the Commission it notes first of all that the rights of the defence were not disregarded. The applicant was not unaware that the recording complained of was unlawful because it had not been ordered by the competent judge. He had the opportunity – which he took – of challenging its authenticity and opposing its use, having initially agreed that it should be heard. The fact that his attempts were unsuccessful makes no difference.'

The court went on to hold that it was not necessary to consider the complaint under art 8 'as the issue is subsumed under the question (already dealt with from the point of view of Article 6) of the use made of the cassette during the judicial investigation and the trial' (see (1988) 13 EHRR 242 at 268 (para 53)).

The submission put forward on behalf of Liberty suggests that the European Court of Human Rights would not necessarily have reached the same conclusion under art 6 in the circumstances of the present case, firstly because in the present case (unlike *Schenk*) there was no evidence against the accused other than the tape-recorded conversation and secondly because, whilst the interception in *Schenk* was conceded by the Swiss government to have been in breach of domestic law safeguards, in the present case there are no domestic law safeguards and for that reason the breach is arguably of a more fundamental character. I would, for my part, find it difficult to attach very great significance to either of these distinguishing features, but in any event we are not concerned with the view which the European Court of Human Rights might have taken of the facts of the present case. Its decision is no more a part of our law than the convention itself. What is significant to my mind is the court's acceptance of the proposition that the admissibility of evidence is primarily a matter for regulation under national law, and its rejection of the proposition that unlawfully obtained evidence is necessarily inadmissible.

Further, it is to be noted in this connection that, although the recording of the relevant conversation in the present case was achieved by means of a civil trespass and, on the face of it, criminal damage to property, Mr Muller accepted at the outset that these matters were not fundamental to his argument. His submissions would have been essentially the same if the surveillance device had been lawfully positioned outside the premises, or, for that matter, if the conversation had been overheard by a police officer with exceptionally acute hearing listening from outside the window.

This brings one back to the fact that, under English law, there is, in general, nothing unlawful about a breach of privacy. The appellant's case rests wholly upon the lack of statutory authorisation for the particular breach of privacy which occurred in the present case, and the consequent infringement, as the appellant submits, of art 8.

My Lords, I am satisfied, for my part, that in these circumstances the appellant can no more succeed upon the second issue than upon the first. I am prepared to accept that if evidence has been obtained in circumstances which involve an apparent breach of art 8, or, for that matter an apparent breach of the law of a foreign country, that is a matter which may be relevant to the exercise of the s 78 power. This does not mean that the trial judge is obliged to decide whether or not there has been a breach of the convention or of the foreign law. That is not his function, and it would be inappropriate for him to do so. By the same token, it would have been inappropriate for the judge in the present case to have decided whether the admitted damage caused by the police to Mr Bashforth's property amounted to a criminal offence under s 1 of the Criminal Damage Act 1971. But if the behaviour of the police in the particular case amounts to an apparent or probable breach of some relevant law or convention, common sense dictates that this is a consideration which may be taken into account for what it is worth. Its significance, however, will normally be determined not so much by its apparent unlawfulness or irregularity, as upon its effect, taken as a whole, upon the fairness or unfairness of the proceedings. The fact that the behaviour in question constitutes a breach of the convention or of a foreign law can plainly be of no greater significance per se than if it constituted a breach of English law. Upon the facts of the present case, in agreement with the Court of Appeal, I consider that the judge was fully entitled to hold that the circumstances in which the relevant evidence was obtained, even if they constituted a breach of art 8, were not such as to require the exclusion of the evidence.

I confess that I have reached this conclusion not only quite firmly as a matter of law, but also with relief. It would be a strange reflection on our law if a man who has admitted his participation in the illegal importation of a large quantity of heroin should have his conviction set aside on the grounds that his privacy has been invaded.

There is only one further word which I would add. The sole cause of this case coming to your Lordships' House is the lack of a statutory system regulating the use of surveillance devices by the police. The absence of such a system seems astonishing, the more so in view of the statutory framework which has governed the use of such devices by the security service since 1989, and the interception of communications by the police as well as by other agencies since 1985. I would refrain, however, from further comment, because counsel for the Crown was able to inform us, on instructions, that the government proposes to introduce legislation covering the matter in the next session of Parliament.

My Lords, I would dismiss the appeal.

456

LORD NICHOLLS OF BIRKENHEAD: My Lords, I have had the opportunity to read in advance a draft of the speech of my noble and learned friend Lord Nolan. I agree that this appeal should be dismissed. I add only two observations of my own. First, the appellant contended for a right of privacy in respect of private conversations in private houses. I prefer to express no view, either way, on the existence of such a right. This right, if it exists, can only do so as part of a larger and wider right of privacy. The difficulties attendant on this controversial subject are well known. Equally well known is the continuing, widespread concern at the apparent failure of the law to give individuals a reasonable degree of protection from unwarranted intrusion in many situations. I prefer to leave open for another occasion the important question whether the present, piecemeal protection of privacy has now developed to the extent that a more comprehensive principle can be seen to exist. It is not necessary to pursue this question on this appeal. Even if the right for which the appellant contended does exist, this would not lead to the consequence that obtaining evidence for the purpose of detecting or preventing serious crime was an infringement of the right or, even if it were, that the evidence was inadmissible at the trial.

Secondly, the discretionary powers of the trial judge to exclude evidence march hand in hand with art 6.1 of the European Convention on Human Rights (Convention for the Protection of Human Rights and Fundamental Freedoms (Rome, 4 November 1950; TS 71 (1953); Cmd 8969)). Both are concerned to ensure that those facing criminal charges receive a fair hearing. Accordingly, when considering the common law and statutory discretionary powers under English law, the jurisprudence on art 6 can have a valuable role to play. English law relating to the ingredients of a fair trial is highly developed. But every system of law stands to benefit by an awareness of the answers given by other courts and tribunals to similar problems. In the present case the decision of the European Court of Human Rights in *Schenk v Switzerland* (1988) 13 EHRR 242 confirms that the use at a criminal trial of material obtained in breach of the rights of privacy enshrined in art 8 does not of itself mean that the trial is unfair. Thus, the European Court of Human Rights case law on this issue leads to the same conclusion as English law.

See generally S Sharpe, 'Electronic Eavesdropping: A Chance for Accountability?' (1996) 146 *New Law Journal* 1088; J R Spencer, 'Bugging and Burglary by the Police' [1997] *Cambridge Law Journal* 6; P Tain, 'Covert Surveillance, *R v Khan* and the European Convention' (1996) 140 *Solicitors Journal* 785; C F H Tapper, 'Overhearing and Oversight' (1997) 1(2) *International Journal of Evidence and Proof* 162.

Anyone consulting *Khan* for a definitive account of the views of the House of Lords on the exclusion of improperly obtained evidence under s 78(1) could be forgiven for being very disappointed. The House of Lords reiterates the obvious proposition that improperly obtained evidence remains admissible in English law, but fails to address in any detail the more important question of what considerations should govern the determination of whether improperly obtained evidence should be excluded under s 78(1). The only English case on the exclusion of improperly obtained evidence which is cited in *Khan* is that of *Sang*, decided a number of years before s 78(1) came into force. There is no discussion at all in *Khan* of the large body of recent case law from the Court of Appeal on the exclusion of improperly obtained confession evidence under s 78(1).

The new statutory framework governing the use of surveillance devices by the police, mentioned by Lord Nolan, is contained in Part III of the Police Act 1997. In essence, such action must normally be authorised by an authorising officer. Authorisation may be given 'where the authorising officer believes – (a) that it is necessary for the action specified to be taken on the ground that it is likely to be of substantial value in the prevention or detection of serious crime, and (b) that what the action seeks to achieve cannot reasonably be achieved by other means'.[10]

4. EVIDENCE OBTAINED IMPROPERLY OUTSIDE THE JURISDICTION

It would seem that evidence obtained improperly in a foreign jurisdiction in contravention of the laws of that jurisdiction may be excluded under the s 78(1) discretion in appropriate circumstances: *R v Governor of Pentonville Prison, ex p Chinoy*.[11]

5. IS THERE A CLEAR RATIONALE FOR THE EXCLUSION OF IMPROPERLY OBTAINED EVIDENCE?

It is probably no accident that confession evidence and identification evidence are the two categories of evidence that have generated the bulk of the case law on improperly obtained evidence. In relation to both these types of evidence, the issue of illegality or impropriety is often inextricably linked with the issue of possible unreliability. Yet the crucial question is the extent to which evidence should be excluded *solely* on the ground that it was improperly obtained, and regardless of considerations of reliability. As we have seen, the extent to which English law has addressed this question remains surprisingly disappointing despite the existence of the s 78(1) discretion. While the road traffic cases suggest an increasingly liberal approach on the part of the courts, cases such as *Cooke* and *McCarthy* suggest the reverse.

The courts appear reluctant to go beyond stating that what is required by s 78(1) is a determination of whether the admission of the improperly obtained evidence would render the proceedings so unfair that it ought not to be admitted. Little guidance is provided on *how* such a determination is to be made, and Lord Nicholls's statement in *Khan* that 'English law relating

[10] Section 93(2).
[11] [1992] 1 All ER 317.

to the ingredients of a fair trial is highly developed' appears wildly optimistic. Empirical evidence suggests that trial judges regard 'trial fairness' as a concept that requires no elaboration.[12] Yet it is, in reality, a highly nebulous concept. At one extreme, a trial may be regarded as 'fair' so long as it protects the innocent from wrongful conviction. On this view, the admission of improperly obtained, but reliable, evidence could never render a trial 'unfair'. This would, however, defeat the whole purpose of s 78(1), and in particular its exhortation to courts to consider 'the circumstances in which the evidence was obtained'. Given that s 78(1) is clearly concerned with more than just reliability, detailed guidance from the courts on what precisely is to be taken into account in considering the exercise of the discretion is badly needed.

In contrast with the failure of English law to articulate guidelines governing the admission or exclusion of improperly obtained evidence, a number of other jurisdictions have adopted far more innovative approaches:

Extract 9.5.1

Evidence Act 1995 (Australia), s 138

138. Discretion to exclude improperly or illegally obtained evidence
(1) Evidence that was obtained:
  (a) improperly or in contravention of an Australian law; or
  (b) in consequence of an impropriety or of a contravention of an Australian law;
is not to be admitted unless the desirability of admitting the evidence outweighs the undesirability of admitting evidence that has been obtained in the way in which the evidence was obtained.
(2) ...
(3) Without limiting the matters that the court may take into account under subsection (1), it is to take into account:
  (a) the probative value of the evidence; and
  (b) the importance of the evidence in the proceeding; and
  (c) the nature of the relevant offence, cause of action or defence and the nature of the subject-matter of the proceeding; and
  (d) the gravity of the impropriety or contravention; and
  (e) whether the impropriety or contravention was deliberate or reckless; and
  (f) whether the impropriety or contravention was contrary to or inconsistent with a right of a person recognised by the International Covenant on Civil and Political Rights; and
  (g) whether any other proceeding (whether or not in a court) has been or is likely to be taken in relation to the impropriety or contravention; and
  (h) the difficulty (if any) of obtaining the evidence without impropriety or contravention of an Australian law.

---

[12] M Hunter, 'Judicial Discretion: Section 78 in Practice' [1994] *Criminal Law Review* 558.

It can be seen that there are a number of similarities between this provision and the 'Lords' amendment' to the Police and Criminal Evidence Bill, discussed at the beginning of this chapter.

A somewhat similar approach is prescribed for Canada by s 24(2) of the Canadian Charter of Rights and Freedoms, which provides: 'Where . . . a court concludes that evidence was obtained in a manner that infringed or denied any rights or freedoms guaranteed by this Charter, the evidence shall be excluded if it is established that, having regard to all the circumstances, the admission of it in the proceedings would bring the administration of justice into disrepute.' Of the numerous cases in which this provision has been considered by the Supreme Court of Canada, the following remains the most important:

Extract 9.5.2

Collins v R (1987) 38 DLR (4th) 508, 523–5 (SCC)

LAMER J: It is whether *the admission of the evidence* would bring the administration of justice into disrepute that is the applicable test. Misconduct by the police in the investigatory process often has some effect on the repute of the administration of justice, but s 24(2) is not a remedy for police misconduct, requiring the exclusion of the evidence if, because of this misconduct, the administration of justice was brought into disrepute. Section 24(2) could well have been drafted in that way, but it was not. Rather, the drafters of the Charter decided to focus on the admission of the evidence in the proceedings, and the purpose of s 24(2) is to prevent having the administration of justice brought into *further disrepute* by the admission of the evidence in the proceedings. This further disrepute will result from the admission of evidence that would deprive the accused of a fair hearing, or from judicial condonation of unacceptable conduct by the investigatory and prosecutorial agencies. It will also be necessary to consider any disrepute that may result from the exclusion of the evidence. It would be inconsistent with the purpose of s 24(2) to exclude evidence if its exclusion would bring the administration of justice into greater disrepute than would its admission. Finally, it must be emphasized that even though the inquiry under s 24(2) will necessarily focus on the specific prosecution, it is the long-term consequences of regular admission or exclusion of this type of evidence on the repute of the administration of justice which must be considered . . .

The concept of disrepute necessarily involves some element of community views, and the determination of disrepute thus requires the judge to refer to what he conceives to be the views of the community at large. This does not mean that evidence of the public's perception of the repute of the administration of justice . . . will be determinative of the issue . . . Members of the public generally become conscious of the importance of protecting the rights and freedoms of accused only when they are in some way brought closer to the system either personally or through the experience of friends or family. . . . The Charter is designed to protect the accused from the majority, so the enforcement of the Charter must not be left to that majority.

The approach I adopt may be put figuratively in terms of the reasonable person test proposed by Professor Yves-Marie Morissette in his article 'The Exclusion of Evidence under the Canadian Charter of Rights and Freedoms: What to Do and What Not to Do', 29 McGill LJ 521 at p 538 (1984). In applying s 24(2), he suggested that the relevant question is: 'Would the admission of the evidence bring the administration of justice into disrepute in the eyes of the reasonable man, dispassionate and fully apprised of the circumstances of the case?' The reasonable person is usually the average person in the community, but only when that community's current mood is reasonable.

... In practice, as Professor Morissette wrote, the reasonable person test is there to require of judges that they 'concentrate on what they do best: finding within themselves, with cautiousness and impartiality, a basis for their own decisions, articulating their reasons carefully and accepting review by a higher court where it occurs.' It serves as a reminder to each individual judge that his discretion is grounded in community values, and, in particular, long-term community values. He should not render a decision that would be unacceptable to the community when that community is not being wrought with passion or otherwise under passing stress due to current events. ...

In determining whether the admission of evidence would bring the administration of justice into disrepute, the judge is directed by s 24(2) to consider 'all the circumstances'. . . . The factors that the courts have most frequently considered include:
– what kind of evidence was obtained?
– what Charter right was infringed?
– was the Charter violation serious or was it of a merely technical nature?
– was it deliberate, wilful or flagrant, or was it inadvertent or committed in good faith?
– did it occur in circumstances of urgency or necessity?
– were there other investigatory techniques available?
– would the evidence have been obtained in any event?
– is the offence serious?
– is the evidence essential to substantiate the charge?
– are other remedies available?
I do not wish to be seen as approving this as an exhaustive list of the relevant factors . . .

The US Supreme Court has expressly adopted a deterrent rationale for the exclusion of improperly obtained evidence:

Extract 9.5.3

Arizona v Evans **115 S Ct 1185, 1191 (1995) (US Supreme Court)**

REHNQUIST CJ: The Fourth Amendment states that '[t]he right of the people to be secure in their persons, houses, papers, and effects, against unreasonable searches and seizures, shall not be violated, and no Warrants shall issue, but upon probable cause, supported by Oath or affirmation, and particularly describing the place to be searched, and the persons or things to be seized.' US Const. We have recognized, however, that the Fourth Amendment contains no provision expressly precluding the use of evidence obtained in violation of its commands. . . .

. . . The exclusionary rule operates as a judicially created remedy designed to safeguard against future violations of Fourth Amendment rights through the rule's general deterrent effect. . . . As with any remedial device, the rule's application has been restricted to those instances where its remedial objectives are thought most efficaciously served. . . .

See also *US v Leon*;[13] *Massachusetts v Sheppard*;[14] *Illinois v Krull*.[15]

This approach of regarding the exclusion of improperly obtained evidence as a mechanism aimed primarily at deterring the police from future impropriety has not generally found favour in jurisdictions such as England and Canada.

It has been persuasively argued that adoption of the type of approach encapsulated in s 24(2) of the Canadian Charter represents the right way forward:

Extract 9.5.4

**A A S Zuckerman, *The Principles of Criminal Evidence* (1989)
343, 345–50, 352**

THE PERENNIAL DILEMMA

. . . Should a court give judgment on the basis of evidence that has been procured by illegal or immoral means? Although the question often comes up the courts find it difficult to confront it, except in relation to confessions. This is due to two principal factors: first, a failure to come to terms with the nature of the problem, and, secondly, a reluctance on the part of the courts to look beyond the immediate confines of the law of evidence.

. . .

There is an uncanny symmetry between the consequences of an admissibility and an inadmissibility rule. If applied consistently, each of these rules will undermine public confidence in the criminal process. If the court always admits illegally obtained evidence, it will be seen to condone the malpractice of the law-enforcement agencies. If it always excludes it, it will be seen to abandon its duty to protect us from crime. The first thing that we must therefore accept is that the criminal trial presents a dilemma which cannot be solved by an inflexible rule. . . .

---

[13] 104 S Ct 3405 (1984).
[14] 104 S Ct 3424 (1984).
[15] 107 S Ct 1160 (1987).

THE SHORTCOMINGS OF THE EXCLUSIONARY PRINCIPLE

An exclusionary jurisdiction is clearly necessary and two theoretical bases for the jurisdiction are current. The first is the vindication or remedial theory, which holds that the object of an exclusionary rule is to vindicate the accused for the infringement of his rights. The second is the deterrent theory, which suggests that the object of exclusion is to deter the law-enforcement agencies from future abuses. I shall deal with each of these in turn.

A person has a right not to have his person and premises illegally searched, not to have his possessions illegally seized, and not to be unlawfully arrested. It is suggested that by imposing these restrictions the state has staked out the boundaries for lawful access to evidence and has indicated that beyond these limits it is willing to forego evidence of crime in deference to individual freedom. Consequently, it is said, exclusion of evidence secured through illegal search, seizure, and arrest puts the prosecution in the position where the constitution, or the legislature, meant to put it when it imposed those restrictions: without the evidence.

This argument ignores a crucial factor in the situation that we are considering: the evidence has been obtained, is now available, and does tend to prove the accused's guilt. In devising the powers of search and seizure the lawmaker laid down that an individual, who must be presumed innocent, should not be disturbed without probable cause. Here, whether we like it or not, we are no longer concerned with the question of whether we should disturb an individual against whom there is no probable cause but with the question of whether a person, in relation to whom evidence of guilt is now available, should be treated as if there were no increased probability of his guilt. The increased probability of guilt creates the need to protect the public from the crime, which makes a return to the *status quo ante* rather awkward.

The perception of the problem as purely one of admissibility of evidence at the trial has diverted attention from other areas in which a similar conflict of interests and rights takes place. If we look beyond the confines of the law of evidence we discover that the situation of *ex post facto* calculation is quite normal in relation to civil liberties. Section 24(5) of the Police and Criminal Evidence Act 1984 lays down: 'Where an arrestable offence has been committed, any person may arrest without warrant – (a) anyone who is guilty of the offence; (b) anyone whom he has reasonable grounds for suspecting to be guilty of it.'

This means that an otherwise groundless arrest is excused, if it turns out that the arrested person has in fact committed an arrestable offence. This constitutes a choice of policy about the protection of civil liberties. A similar choice was made in relation to seizure when Horridge J held that 'the interests of the State must excuse the seizure of documents, which seizure would otherwise be unlawful, if it appears in fact that such documents were evidence of a crime committed by anyone . . .' [*Elias v Pasmore* [1934] 2 KB 164, 173.]

Moreover, in the fight against crime our institutions are prepared at times to forgive a lesser crime in order to punish a more serious one, as the practice of immunity given to state witnesses shows.

Turning to the law of tort, we find that here too the tension between legality and just deserts has been resolved, to some extent, in favour of the latter. Under the American Civil Rights Act a person may sue for damages for infringement of his constitutional rights. However, if as a result of an infringement of rights, evidence is found that leads to the aggrieved person's conviction, that person loses his claim. The reason given is that immunity from action will encourage bolder and more efficient police action in combating crime. While there is no direct English authority on the point, it is difficult to believe that, in practice, the guilty would secure any better remedies under English tort law.

It would be odd if the consideration of the *ex post facto* realization that the infringement of the suspect's rights resulted in the discovery of his guilt were completely absent from the law of evidence, when it is so potent in the law of arrest, in the rules of search and seizure, and in the law of tort. It is, however, claimed that we need to remedy infringements of rights by the exclusion of evidence precisely because tort remedies are not taken seriously by the civil courts, where convicted plaintiffs find little sympathy. This line of reasoning is unlikely to persuade the courts because the practical preferences that prevent an effective civil remedy cannot be neutralized simply by saying that we are dealing with a question of exclusion of evidence rather than with one of damages.

Furthermore, the vindication theory runs up against the difficulty of maintaining a satisfactory balance between illegality and its remedy. In a criminal trial exclusion of evidence of guilt amounts to a contribution towards the acquittal of a person who may be guilty. It is by no means self-evident that acquittal of the guilty is an appropriate response to earlier police transgressions. Nor is a blanket exclusion capable of achieving a balance between the seriousness of the infringement and the benefit to the accused.

Given these difficulties, the justification for the exclusion of illegally obtained evidence shifts to the second theory: the argument that exclusion is necessary not so much to vindicate the accused as to deter the police from unauthorized searches and thus protect the peace and privacy of individuals against whom there is no probable cause. This theory flies in the face of the general willingness, just described, to detract from constitutional liberties in order to further crime control. In the absence of widespread resentment of the police, citizens are unlikely to feel that they require protection from the police by means which let guilty persons go free.

From a practical point of view there are a number of reasons for doubting whether a general exclusionary rule would have significant deterrent effects. First, police officers are subject to influences that may well outweigh the sanction of exclusion; for example, the expectations of peers and supervisors, and public pressure to apprehend offenders. Secondly, the violation of search rules would involve, at most, exclusion at some distant date and is therefore unlikely to constitute a serious brake on illegal searches. Thirdly, even if officers were inclined to comply, it may be that the provisions of the search and seizure rules are not communicated to them effectively enough to secure compliance. Finally, if objections to unauthorized search turn out to be rare, or if police officers stand a good chance of concealing the breaches, the efficacy of an exclusion rule as a deterrent will be limited.

464

LEGITIMACY: A BALANCING EXERCISE

The manifest weaknesses of a pure vindication theory and of a pure deterrent one in justifying a rule of exclusion, and the shortcomings of an inclusionary rule, leave us with only one possible policy to pursue, that of avoiding the undesirable consequences of an absolute commitment to either exclusion or inclusion. We may refer to this as the principle of judicial integrity or the principle of legitimacy. This principle has been criticized for lack of clarity. It is, however, a mistake to assume that because individual decisions cannot be easily derived from a principle, the principle has no guiding force. The social need to balance two conflicting constitutional requirements is in itself a powerful consideration. Indeed, it is important that the courts should be seen to exercise a balancing jurisdiction, for this will inform the public of the difficulty of choosing between admissibility and inadmissibility and will secure support even from those who might have preferred a different result in an individual case.

. . .

The legitimacy principle has found its clearest statement in [s 24(2) of] the new Canadian Constitution . . .

What is notable is that this 'balancing' approach is precisely that which found favour with the House of Lords in *Latif*, in the context of the abuse of process doctrine. It is unfortunate that in English law this approach has so far been confined to determinations of whether proceedings should be stayed on account of pre-trial police or prosecutorial misconduct, and has not been extended to determinations of whether evidence should be excluded on account of such misconduct. Surely consistency requires that the same approach be adopted in both contexts.[16]

Further reading

C J W Allen, 'Discretion and Security: Excluding Evidence under Section 78(1) of the Police and Criminal Evidence Act 1984' [1990] *Cambridge Law Journal* 80

A J Ashworth, 'Excluding Evidence as Protecting Rights' [1977] *Criminal Law Review* 723

T Carmody, 'Recent and Proposed Statutory Reforms to the Common Law Exclusionary Discretions' (1997) 71 *Australian Law Journal* 119

A L-T Choo, 'Halting Criminal Prosecutions: The Abuse of Process Doctrine Revisited' [1995] *Criminal Law Review* 864

— *Abuse of Process and Judicial Stays of Criminal Proceedings* (1993)

I H Dennis, 'Reconstructing the Law of Criminal Evidence' (1989) 42 *Current Legal Problems* 21

---

[16] See generally J Hunter, '"Tainted" Proceedings: Censuring Police Illegalities' (1985) 59 *Australian Law Journal* 709.

M A Gelowitz, 'Section 78 of the Police and Criminal Evidence Act 1984: Middle Ground or No Man's Land?' (1990) 106 *Law Quarterly Review* 327

D M Paciocco, 'The Judicial Repeal of S 24(2) and the Development of the Canadian Exclusionary Rule' (1990) 32 *Criminal Law Quarterly* 326

R Stone, 'Exclusion of Evidence under Section 78 of the Police and Criminal Evidence Act: Practice and Principles' in M J Allen (ed), *Web Journal of Current Legal Issues Yearbook 1995* (1996)

A A S Zuckerman, *The Principles of Criminal Evidence* (1989) Ch 16

IO

IDENTIFICATION EVIDENCE

1. THE PROBLEM

Extract 10.1.1

J Hunter and K Cronin, *Evidence, Advocacy and Ethical Practice: A Criminal Trial Commentary* (1995) 394–5

Glaring miscarriages of justice have occurred when witnesses have misidentified the accused. One notable English case concerned Adolf Beck who in 1895 was identified by a dozen women as the man who had inveigled each of them into an intimate relationship and then persuaded them to hand over various valuables before disappearing. In the late 1870s, when Beck was in South America, a John Smith had been convicted and imprisoned in England for a series of similar frauds. At Beck's trial the prosecution case was founded on the assumption that Beck and Smith were one and the same. Two police officers from Smith's 1877 case testified that Beck was Smith. As a result of the identification evidence of the women and the police officers, Beck was convicted of the frauds. Beck's prison records assumed that he was the John Smith convicted and imprisoned in the 1870s. The Crown case against Beck also included circumstantial evidence. Beck was unable to prove any alibis, and he had in his possession pawn tickets for women's jewellery, although none of the pawned jewellery belonged to the women victims. The Crown case against Beck also contained certain inconsistencies. The witnesses described the culprit as well-dressed, as speaking with a foreign accent and as writing fluently. Beck wore shabby clothes and was not a fluent writer. One of the victims had been certain that Beck was not the culprit. Despite these inconsistencies, the cumulative strength of the circumstantial evidence, when combined with the identification evidence, convinced the jury. Beck was convicted and imprisoned for seven years. He petitioned the Home Office on the ground that he had been wrongly identified, arguing that as he had been in South America when the frauds first occurred in the 1870s, the Crown case was defective. A Home Office minute described this argument as a 'clever ruse' because it presented an alibi that the Crown could not answer.

After Beck's release from gaol similar frauds were reported. In 1904 Beck was again charged and convicted. This time four women identified him as the person who had tricked them into intimacy and into parting with their possessions. Whilst Beck was in custody awaiting sentencing John Smith was caught red-handed. Smith fitted the descriptions given by his various victims, including their information that the fraudster was circumcised. This information accorded with Smith's prison records relating to the 1877 conviction. Beck was not circumcised. Beck received a pardon and £5,000 compensation.

The possible causes of misidentification are many and varied. Broadly, these may be classified as 'witness' factors, 'event' factors or 'post-event' factors. Witness factors include:

Matters associated with the witness's vision. Obviously, perceptual ability would be affected by a visual handicap such as shortsightedness or colour blindness. An individual's perceptual ability would also be affected by the fact that he or she has recently arrived in a dark environment from a bright one: dark adaptation, 'a function of differences in the chemical activity of the rods and cones of the retina', is said to take approximately 30 minutes.[1] In a similar vein, a move from a darker to a brighter environment would require 'light adaptation'.[2]

The witness's biases and prejudices. One may 'perceive' what one expects to perceive. A person's capacity for accurate perception may be seriously impaired, therefore, by his or her biases and prejudices (for example, the expectation that the perpetrator of an offence would be a person of a particular ethnic origin or gender).[3]

Expectations from past experience. The following hypothetical example provided by Williams, Loftus and Deffenbacher illustrates this issue well:

> Suppose, for instance, that a gang of four young males are often seen together by members of a small community. They are easy to spot because of their distinctive clothing. One night, four young males dressed in this distinctive clothing are seen robbing a liquor store. An eyewitness clearly sees three of the four boys and recognizes them as the gang members. The fourth boy is not seen well, but the eyewitness *assumes* it is the same boy that has been seen before with that gang, and modifies her memory in such a way to recall seeing that boy. In fact, the fourth boy did not participate in the robbery, and another had taken his place. But, because of prior expectations of the eyewitness, she recalls seeing the boy she had seen in the past.[4]

Momentary or temporary expectations. Our capacity for accurate perception may be affected by what we expect, at that particular moment, to perceive.

---

[1] A D Yarmey, *The Psychology of Eyewitness Testimony* (1979) 39.
[2] Ibid.
[3] See, eg, the classic experiments conducted in the 1940s by Allport and Postman: G W Allport and L Postman, *The Psychology of Rumor* (1947) (reprinted 1965) 111. See also E F Loftus, *Eyewitness Testimony* (1979) 40.
[4] K D Williams, E F Loftus and K A Deffenbacher, 'Eyewitness Evidence and Testimony' in D K Kagehiro and W S Laufer (eds), *Handbook of Psychology and Law* (1992) 144 (emphasis in original).

Thus, as Loftus points out, a party of hunters scanning the landscape eagerly for deer may mistakenly perceive a moving object as a deer even if it is in reality a person.[5]

Perceptual activity. The ability to perceive accurately may be dependent upon the activity in which the witness is engaged whilst 'perceiving': 'for example, an eyewitness to a robbery could spend a good deal of time examining the individual features of the face, or he could spend most of his time staring in the direction of the face but might actually be trying to figure out how to escape from an unpleasant situation'.[6]

The following is a discussion of possible 'event' factors:

Extract 10.1.2

B L Cutler and S D Penrod, *Mistaken Identification: The Eyewitness, Psychology, and the Law* (1995) 101–4

1. Exposure duration. Common sense tells us that the amount of time available for viewing a perpetrator is positively associated with the witness's ability to subsequently identify him. But common sense does not tell us much about the nature of this relationship. Some investigations show a linear increase in face recognition accuracy with exposure time . . . Others show a logarithmic relationship . . . ; that is, as exposure duration increases, face recognition accuracy improves, but the improvements become smaller as duration increases. . . .

2. The presence of a weapon. Several investigators . . . have posited that the presence of a weapon during a crime attracts the attention of the witness to the weapon, leaving less attention to the perpetrator's facial and physical characteristics. This phenomenon is often referred to as 'weapon focus.' The notion is that when confronted with a handgun, a knife, or another weapon, there is a tendency to attend primarily to the weapon. . . .

One result of weapon focus is that because less attention is paid to the perpetrator, identifications are less likely to be correct. . . .

3. Crime seriousness. Crime seriousness can be operationalized in a variety of ways. It can refer to the amount of danger in a crime situation, the monetary worth of objects that are stolen or damaged, or the personal stake one has in the object of the crime. Leippe, Wells, and Ostrom . . . staged a theft for their subjects. . . . When witnesses believed the stolen item to be expensive, they correctly identified the thief more frequently than if the stolen item was believed to be inexpensive.

Hosch and his colleagues . . . examined whether being a victim, or merely a bystander-witness, influences eyewitness identifications. In these studies subjects were exposed to an elaborate staged theft. Either a laboratory calculator or the subject's own wristwatch was stolen. It is reasonable to assume that a crime is viewed as more serious by the victim of the crime than by an

---

[5] E F Loftus, *Eyewitness Testimony* (1979) 36–7.
[6] At 48.

uninvolved witness. Were victims more likely to make correct identifications than bystander eyewitnesses? In the experiments by Hosch and his colleagues victimization had no clear-cut effect on identification accuracy. . . .

Crime seriousness, as operationalized by monetary worth of the item, has shown some ability to influence identification accuracy, but as operationalized by personal involvement, has shown no direct relationship with identification accuracy. Caution must be exercised in the interpretation of the findings discussed here, however. First, there are obvious ethical limitations on the type of experiments that can be performed. Second, the studies bearing on the question of crime seriousness are few . . .

4. Stress, arousal, and violence. The issue of arousal and its effect on identification accuracy is controversial. On the one hand, it is of strong interest to the legal community because violence and threat of violence are present in many crimes. Such threats are likely to affect the ability to encode information and subsequently make accurate identifications. But adequate laboratory research on the effects of such stress is lacking because of obvious ethical constraints. Despite the importance of knowledge in this area, one cannot simulate violent crimes and pose a threat to the well-being of naive experimental subjects. Researchers have therefore resorted to a variety of manipulations including the use of violent versus nonviolent videotaped crimes. Increased violence in videotaped reenactments of crimes have been shown to lead to decrements in both identification accuracy and eyewitness recall . . . , but this finding is not universally obtained . . .

Deffenbacher . . . appealed to the 'Yerkes-Dodson Law' when explaining the effects of arousal on identification. Stress or arousal demonstrates an inverted U-shaped relationship with identification accuracy. Low levels of arousal, such as when waking up, produce low attentiveness; moderate levels of arousal, such as that felt by an athlete preparing to compete, serve to heighten perceptual and attentiveness skills; and, higher levels, such as that felt by an individual under extreme danger or duress, debilitates perceptual skills. Some critics . . . argue that the Yerkes-Dodson law is not relevant to the eyewitness situation and the research is too inconclusive to advance any conclusions regarding the effects of stress on identification accuracy. Further complaints are raised because no objective measure exists to allow between-study comparisons of subjects' arousal levels.
. . .

5. Cross-race identification. . . . neither the race of the witness nor the race of the perpetrator, if considered alone, is strongly associated with identification accuracy. But considered together, an interesting finding emerges. Own-race recognitions are more accurate than other-race identifications. . . .

6. Cross-gender identification. Like race, gender of witness and gender of target, when considered independently, have little effect on identification accuracy. In Shapiro and Penrod's meta-analysis, there was a small but significant tendency for subjects to identify correctly persons of their own gender . . . more often than persons of the opposite gender. No significant difference was observed for false identifications . . .

An important post-event factor is the lapse of time between the crime and the identification:

Extract 10.1.3

B L Cutler and S D Penrod, *Mistaken Identification: The Eyewitness,*
Psychology, and the Law (1995) 105–6

Common sense tells us that memory declines over time. Can we expect eyewitness identification accuracy to decline as the time between the crime and the identification test increases? Shepherd . . . reported the results of three experiments that included time delay as a factor. . . . Shepherd concluded that delays of less than 4 months have little influence on correct identification rate, but identification accuracy declines after 4 months. Shepherd also concluded that the false identification rate is relatively stable across time.

Though the research by Shepherd and colleagues is extensive, it is not entirely corroborated by other findings. Malpass and Devine . . . , for instance, found that a time delay influences *both* correct identifications and false identifications. Subjects in their experiment attempted identifications of a vandal (from a staged incident) within 3 days of the incident or 5 months after the incident. The 5-month delay caused an increase in false identifications (0% vs 35%) as well as a decrease in correct identifications (83% vs 36%).

With respect to shorter retention intervals, in Krafka and Penrod's . . . field experiment, convenience store clerks attempted identifications of customers from photoarrays after either 2 hours or after 24 hours. The time delay resulted in a significant and large increase in false identifications from 15% to 52%, and a small decrease in percentage of correct identifications, from 43% to 39%. Davies, Ellis, and Shepherd . . . tested recognition accuracy after a period of 48 hours or 3 weeks and found recognition performance to be superior in the shorter interval condition.

In an attempt to shed some light on these disparate results for retention interval, Shapiro and Penrod included retention interval in their meta-analysis. When studies that manipulated retention interval were grouped into long versus short time delays, longer delays led to fewer correct identifications . . . and more false identifications . . . Across experimental cells in all the studies examined in the meta-analysis (including those that did not directly manipulate retention interval) retention interval also proved to be an important determinant of correct identifications . . . , although there was no significant relationship with false identifications.

2. THE SOLUTION

Over the past two decades, two main mechanisms for dealing with the issue of evidence of identification of the accused have evolved in English law. First, there is a requirement that warnings about identification evidence be given to the jury in certain circumstances. Secondly, Code D of the Codes of Practice issued under the Police and Criminal Evidence Act 1984 makes provision in relation to different methods of obtaining identification evidence, and breaches of this Code may lead to the discretionary exclusion of identification evidence under s 78(1). Each of these mechanisms will now be considered in turn.

(a) Warnings to the jury

The following is an extract from the 1976 decision in which the famous '*Turnbull* guidelines' on judicial warnings to the jury about identification evidence were laid down by the Court of Appeal.

Extract 10.2.1

R v Turnbull [1977] QB 224, 228–31 (CA)

LORD WIDGERY CJ: . . . evidence of visual identification in criminal cases . . . can bring about miscarriages of justice and has done so in a few cases in recent years. The number of such cases, although small compared with the number in which evidence of visual identification is known to be satisfactory, necessitates steps being taken by the courts, including this court, to reduce that number as far as is possible. In our judgment the danger of miscarriages of justice occurring can be much reduced if trial judges sum up to juries in the way indicated in this judgment.

First, whenever the case against an accused depends wholly or substantially on the correctness of one or more identifications of the accused which the defence alleges to be mistaken, the judge should warn the jury of the special need for caution before convicting the accused in reliance on the correctness of the identification or identifications. In addition he should instruct them as to the reason for the need for such a warning and should make some reference to the possibility that a mistaken witness can be a convincing one and that a number of such witnesses can all be mistaken. Provided this is done in clear terms the judge need not use any particular form of words.

Secondly, the judge should direct the jury to examine closely the circumstances in which the identification by each witness came to be made. How long did the witness have the accused under observation? At what distance? In what light? Was the observation impeded in any way, as for example by passing traffic or a press of people? Had the witness ever seen the accused before? How often? If only occasionally, had he any special reason for remembering the accused? How long elapsed between the original observation and the subsequent identification to the police? Was there any material discrepancy between the description of the accused given to the police by the witness when first seen by them and his actual appearance? If in any case, whether it is being dealt with summarily or on indictment, the prosecution have reason to believe that there is such a material discrepancy they should supply the accused or his legal advisers with particulars of the description the police were first given. In all cases if the accused asks to be given particulars of such descriptions, the prosecution should supply them. Finally, he should remind the jury of any specific weaknesses which had appeared in the identification evidence.

Recognition may be more reliable than identification of a stranger; but even when the witness is purporting to recognise someone whom he knows, the jury should be reminded that mistakes in recognition of close relatives and friends are sometimes made.

All these matters go to the quality of the identification evidence. If the quality is good and remains good at the close of the accused's case, the danger of a mistaken identification is lessened; but the poorer the quality, the greater the danger.

In our judgment when the quality is good, as for example when the identification is made after a long period of observation, or in satisfactory conditions by a relative, a neighbour, a close friend, a workmate and the like, the jury can safely be left to assess the value of the identifying evidence even though there is no other evidence to support it: provided always, however, that an adequate warning has been given about the special need for caution. Were the courts to adjudge otherwise, affronts to justice would frequently occur. . . .

. . .

When, in the judgment of the trial judge, the quality of the identifying evidence is poor, as for example when it depends solely on a fleeting glance or on a longer observation made in difficult conditions, the situation is very different. The judge should then withdraw the case from the jury and direct an acquittal unless there is other evidence which goes to support the correctness of the identification. This may be corroboration in the sense lawyers use that word; but it need not be so if its effect is to make the jury sure that there has been no mistaken identification . . .

The trial judge should identify to the jury the evidence which he adjudges is capable of supporting the evidence of identification. If there is any evidence or circumstances which the jury might think was supporting when it did not have this quality, the judge should say so. . . .

Care should be taken by the judge when directing the jury about the support for an identification which may be derived from the fact that they have rejected an alibi. False alibis may be put forward for many reasons: an accused, for example, who has only his own truthful evidence to rely on may stupidly fabricate an alibi and get lying witnesses to support it out of fear that his own evidence will not be enough. Further, alibi witnesses can make genuine mistakes about dates and occasions like any other witnesses can. It is only when the jury is satisfied that the sole reason for the fabrication was to deceive them and there is no other explanation for its being put forward can fabrication provide any support for identification evidence. The jury should be reminded that proving the accused has told lies about where he was at the material time does not by itself prove that he was where the identifying witness says he was.

The *Crown Court Study* found that there was 'fairly important' or 'very important' identification evidence in close to about 25% of contested cases. Interestingly, *Turnbull* warnings were given in just over 50% of those cases in which there was 'fairly important' or 'very important' identification evidence.[7]

(i) Is a full warning necessary?

In spite of the detailed nature of the guidelines, it would appear that a considerable amount of latitude remains invested in trial judges. This has

---

[7] M Zander and P Henderson, *The Royal Commission on Criminal Justice: Crown Court Study* (1993) 92–3.

the potential to lead to considerable uncertainty about what exactly may be required of a judge in the circumstances of a particular case. In some situations, of course, warnings are considered of vital importance:

Extract 10.2.2

Scott v R [1989] 1 AC 1242, 1260 (PC)

LORD GRIFFITHS: Never can the importance of such a warning be greater than in a case such as the present where the sole evidence of identity is contained in the deposition of a deceased witness and where the quality of the identification may have been of the.fleeting glance type for in cross-examination the witness said he saw the men's faces as they ran from the bar. It is possible that he may have recognised the men as he passed them earlier in the street but he does not say so in the deposition and there will of course be no opportunity for investigating the matter at trial.

It has been held that in some circumstances something less than a full warning may suffice, or no warning may be required at all. For example, the distinction has been drawn between a 'fleeting-glance identification', in relation to which a full warning would be required, and the purported recognition of a familiar face which has taken place over a considerable period of time in perfectly good conditions, in relation to which a full warning would be unnecessary.[8] Equally, a distinction has been drawn between the paradigmatic case where the challenge is to the *accuracy* of the identification (that is, where the allegation is that the identifying witness was mistaken), and the case where what the defence is challenging is the *credibility* of the identifying witness. 'In cases where the defence challenges the credibility of the identifying witnesses as the principal or sole means of defence, there may be exceptional cases where a *Turnbull* direction is unnecessary or where it is sufficient to give it more briefly than in a case where the accuracy of identification is challenged.'[9] However, 'the cases in which the warning can be entirely dispensed with must be wholly exceptional, even where credibility is the sole line of defence. In the latter type of case the judge should normally, and even in the exceptional case would be wise to, tell the jury in an appropriate form to consider whether they are satisfied that the witness was not mistaken in view of the danger of mistake . . .'.[10] It has been emphasised that it will be very unusual to encounter cases in which credibility is genuinely the sole cause for concern: 'If, for example, the witness's identification evidence is that the accused was his workmate whom he has known for 20 years and that he was conversing with him for half an hour face to face in the same

---

[8] *R v Bentley* [1991] Crim LR 620.
[9] *Shand v R* [1996] 1 WLR 67, 72. See also *Daley v R* [1994] 1 AC 117 and *R v Cape* [1996] 1 Cr App R 191 on the accuracy/credibility distinction.
[10] *Shand v R* [1996] 1 WLR 67, 72.

room and the witness is sane and sober, then, if credibility is the issue, it will be the only issue. But cases like that will constitute a very rare exception . . .'.[11]

What if the defendant's presence at or near the scene of the crime is admitted?

Extract 10.2.3

R v Slater [1995] 1 Cr App R 584, 589–90 (CA)

ROSE LJ: In the judgment of this Court, the need for a *Turnbull* direction arises where there is the possibility of mistaken identification. Such a possibility will generally arise when the issue is whether the defendant was present and a witness claims to identify him on the basis of a previous sighting or sightings. In such a case, it is essential that the jury examine each of the relevant sightings with care and that they be directed to do so in accordance with *Turnbull*. Where, however, there is no issue as to the defendant's presence at or near the scene of the offence, but the issue is as to what he was doing, it does not automatically follow, in the judgment of this Court, that a *Turnbull* direction must be given. Whether such a direction is necessary will depend on the circumstances of the particular case. It will be necessary where, on the evidence, the possibility exists that a witness may have mistaken one person for another, for example, because of similarities in face, build, or clothing between two or more people present.

Thornton [1995] 1 Cr App R 578 . . . was such a case, as is apparent from . . . the judgment of the Court given by Beldam LJ where, in ruling that in that case a *Turnbull* direction should have been given, the learned Lord Justice said this:

> 'There were others similarly dressed to the appellant at the reception, and the possibility of mistake was clearly there' (p 583, *ante*).

. . .

But where there is no possibility of such a mistake, there is, in our judgment, no need to give a *Turnbull* direction. We do not accept that the Court in *Thornton* was seeking to say that it is mandatory for such a direction to be given in every case where the defendant admits presence but denies criminal conduct.

It is true that the Court posed a question in that form at p 582, *ante*. But the answer which the Court gave contained the passage which we have already cited from p 583, *ante*.

Indeed, it seems to us that a mandatory requirement for a *Turnbull* direction in all such cases would be contrary to the decision of another Division of this Court in *Hope and Others* [1994] Crim LR 118, a transcript of which is before the Court.

In the course of giving the judgment of the Court, Douglas Brown J said in relation to the circumstances of that case:

---

[11] *Beckford v R* (1993) 97 Cr App R 409, 415.

'There was in reality no disputed identification. . . . There was no dispute that Mr Hope was the first man. The question of whether Mr Ducker was right in saying the same man had attacked him a few seconds later was essentially a matter for the jury, having assessed Mr Ducker's reliability, and the appellant's evidence if he gave it.'

We respectfully agree with the comment of Beldam LJ at pp 582–583, *ante* in *Thornton's* case that the issue in *Hope* was slightly different, namely, whether there had been a breach of the Code of Practice in relation to holding an identification parade. But the crucial question in relation to the Code was whether there was a disputed identification and it seems to this Court that in many, if not most, cases similar considerations will arise when considering whether the possibility of mistake was such as to require a *Turnbull* direction.

Furthermore, it would, as it seems to us, be contrary to common sense to require a *Turnbull* direction in all cases where presence is admitted but conduct disputed. Purely by way of example, such a direction would not, in our view, generally be necessary if the defendant admitted he was the only person present when the complainant received his injuries, or if a woman and a man were present and the complainant said the man caused his injuries, or if a black man and a white man were present and the complainant said the white man caused the injuries, or if four men were present, three dressed in black and one in white, and the complainant said the man in white caused his injuries. Of course, in all but the first of those examples, an appropriate warning would need to be given if in a particular case, for example, the lighting was bad or there were other circumstances giving rise to the possibility of mistake. But, in our judgment, the possibility of mistake is a necessary prerequisite for an identification issue to arise such as to require a *Turnbull* direction.

(ii) The content of a warning

Extract 10.2.4

R v Fergus (1993) 98 Cr App R 313, 318 (CA)

STEYN LJ: *Turnbull* requires the judge to warn the jury of the special need for caution before convicting the accused in reliance on visual identification and to explain that a mistaken witness may be a convincing one. That means that the jury ought to be told that honesty as such is no guarantee against a false impression being so indelibly imprinted on the mind as to convince an honest witness that it was wholly reliable: *Reid v R* (1989) 90 Cr App R 121, [1990] 1 AC 363, 380F–381C. We do not, of course, say that these particular words must be used but the risk must be clearly conveyed to the jury. . . . *Turnbull* requires the judge to direct the jury to examine the circumstances in which the identification was made. This requirement has in practice led to trial judges posing a series of general questions to the jury: At what distance was the identification made? In what light? and so forth. While we do not wish in any way to decry the value of such general guidance to the jury, it seems to us that there is in the interests of justice a more important requirement. In *Turnbull*, the Court stated (at p 137 and p 228G):

'Finally, he should remind the jury of any specific weaknesses which had appeared in the identification evidence.'

Generally, it has often been said that it is not essential that a trial judge should rehearse all the arguments of defence counsel: *McGreevy v Director of Public Prosecutions* (1973) 57 Cr App R 424, 430, [1973] 1 All ER 503, 507. That is so. But in a case dependent on visual identification, and particularly where that is the only evidence, *Turnbull* makes it clear that it is incumbent on a trial judge to place before the jury any specific weaknesses which can arguably be said to have been exposed in the evidence. And it is not sufficient for the judge to invite the jury to take into account what counsel for the defence said about the specific weaknesses. Needless to say, the judge must deal with the specific weaknesses in a coherent manner so that the cumulative impact of those specific weaknesses is fairly placed before the jury.

Is there an obligation on the trial judge to summarise the specific weaknesses of the identification evidence to the jury?

Extract 10.2.5

R v Pattinson [1996] 1 Cr App R 51, 56 (CA)

HENRY LJ: In *Fergus* at 321, Steyn LJ said:

'It is not good enough for a trial judge simply to refer the jury to counsel's submissions about specific weaknesses in the identification. Under *Turnbull*, he must fairly and properly summarise for the jury such specific weaknesses as arguably are exposed by the evidence. The judge never came near to doing so.'

. . .

. . . We have been assisted in our evaluation of *Fergus* by the decision of another division of this Court in *Mussell* (unreported, February 27, 1995). There the Court made the following points:
(i)   There is nothing in *Fergus* which purports to supersede or to amplify *Turnbull*.
(ii)   That any such summary could not be limited to the defence case alone.
(iii)   That if the trial judge is under any duty to summarise, it must be a summary of the whole case on identification: that is to say the points made both by the prosecution and the defence.
(iv)   That there could not be a mandatory requirement to have such a summary in every case:

'The question is whether the summing-up, taken overall, did justice to the facts of the particular case. It seems to us that two general considerations should be borne in mind. Any summary, at whatever stage of the summing-up it occurs, carries with it a risk of omission of or a suggestion of possible lack of emphasis upon particular items which would go some way to defeat the objects of fairness upon which this submission is based. Secondly, it may well be more convenient, especially in the course of a lengthy summing-up where the evidence is reviewed in some detail (as it was here), to give specific reminders in relation to specific parts of the evidence as they are dealt with in the course of the summing-up, rather than to attempt any form of summary or shorthand which might itself be misleading either at the beginning or the end of that detailed review.'

We respectfully agree with those qualifications on the apparent principle expressed in *Fergus*. The summing-up must be tailored to the evidence in each case, and it is dangerous to make rules in relation to it.

(iii) *When should the case be withdrawn from the jury?*

The precise relationship between *Turnbull* warnings and the complete withdrawal of the case from the jury (or the outright exclusion of the identification evidence) also remains unclear. We have seen that the court in *Turnbull* said that the case should be withdrawn from the jury, and an acquittal directed, if the identification evidence is poor and there is no supporting evidence. The suggestion, therefore, is that 'at some point the adverse conditions for observation cannot be cured by a caution'.[12] Evidence which depends solely on a fleeting glance, or on a longer observation made in difficult conditions, is given by the court in *Turnbull* as an example of poor identification evidence. As has been noted, however, by Wilson J in the Canadian Supreme Court case of *Mezzo v R*:

> No one would take issue with the 'fleeting glance' test; it represents the extreme of frailty which cannot be cured by a caution. The real difficulty is with 'a longer observation made in difficult conditions'. In this sense *Turnbull* is more significant for what it does not lay down. If it sets out any principle with regard to the test for a directed verdict, it is the principle that the quality of a witness' identification is directly related to the extent of the witness' opportunity for observation. However, *Turnbull* offers no workable criteria for determining when conditions are so difficult that an eyewitness' testimony should not be relied on ...[13]

(iv) *Appeals*

What are the consequences on appeal of the failure to give an adequate *Turnbull* warning? A difference seems to have emerged between the views of the Privy Council and the High Court of Australia on this matter. The Privy Council appears to take the view that a conviction can stand so long as the

---

[12] *Mezzo v R* (1986) 30 DLR (4th) 161, 194 per Wilson J.
[13] Ibid.

appeal court considers the quality of the identification evidence in question to be 'exceptionally good'.[14] The Australian High Court, on the other hand, would appear to require that the appeal be allowed unless the appeal court concludes that the jury must inevitably have convicted the accused on the basis of the *other* prosecution evidence in the case.[15] Which view do you prefer?

(b) Discretionary exclusion of identification evidence

The issue of the discretionary exclusion of identification evidence for violations of Code D of the Codes of Practice issued under the Police and Criminal Evidence Act 1984 will now be examined.

Extract 10.2.6

Police and Criminal Evidence Act 1984
Code D: Code of Practice for the Identification of Persons by Police Officers

1 General
. . .

2 Identification by witnesses

2.0 A record shall be made of the description of the suspect as first given by a potential witness. This must be done before the witness takes part in the forms of identification listed in paragraph 2.1 or *Annex D* of this code. The record may be made or kept in any form provided that details of the description as first given by the witness can accurately be produced from it in a written form which can be provided to the suspect or his solicitor in accordance with this code. A copy shall be provided to the suspect or his solicitor before any procedures under paragraph 2.1 of this code are carried out. . . .

(a) Cases where the suspect is known

2.1 In a case which involves disputed identification evidence, and where the identity of the suspect is known to the police and he is available . . . , the methods of identification by witnesses which may be used are:
- (i) a parade;
- (ii) a group identification;
- (iii) a video film;
- (iv) a confrontation.

2.2 The arrangements for, and conduct of, these types of identification shall be the responsibility of an officer in uniform not below the rank of inspector

---

[14] *Freemantle v R* [1994] 1 WLR 1437; *Shand v R* [1996] 1 WLR 67.
[15] *Domican v R* (1992) 173 CLR 555.

who is not involved with the investigation ('the identification officer'). No officer involved with the investigation of the case against the suspect may take any part in these procedures.

Identification Parade

2.3 Whenever a suspect disputes an identification, an identification parade shall be held if the suspect consents unless paragraphs 2.4 or 2.7 or 2.10 apply. A parade may also be held if the officer in charge of the investigation considers that it would be useful, and the suspect consents.

2.4 A parade need not be held if the identification officer considers that, whether by reason of the unusual appearance of the suspect or for some other reason, it would not be practicable to assemble sufficient people who resembled him to make a parade fair.

2.5 Any parade must be carried out in accordance with *Annex A*. A video recording or colour photograph shall be taken of the parade.

2.6 If a suspect refuses or, having agreed, fails to attend an identification parade or the holding of a parade is impracticable, arrangements must if practicable be made to allow the witnesses an opportunity of seeing him in a group identification, a video identification, or a confrontation (see below).

Group Identification

2.7 A group identification takes place where the suspect is viewed by a witness amongst an informal group of people. The procedure may take place with the consent and co-operation of a suspect or covertly where a suspect has refused to co-operate with an identification parade or a group identification or has failed to attend. A group identification may also be arranged if the officer in charge of the investigation considers, whether because of fear on the part of the witness or for some other reason, that it is, in the circumstances, more satisfactory than a parade.

2.8 The suspect should be asked for his consent to a group identification and advised in accordance with paragraphs 2.15 and 2.16 of this code. However, where consent is refused the identification officer has the discretion to proceed with a group identification if it is practicable to do so.

2.9 A group identification shall be carried out in accordance with *Annex E*. A video recording or colour photograph shall be taken of the group identification in accordance with *Annex E*.

Video Film Identification

2.10 The identification officer may show a witness a video film of a suspect if the investigating officer considers, whether because of the refusal of the suspect to take part in an identification parade or group identification or other reasons, that this would in the circumstances be the most satisfactory course of action.

2.11 The suspect should be asked for his consent to a video identification and advised in accordance with paragraphs 2.15 and 2.16. However, where such consent is refused the identification officer has the discretion to proceed with a video identification if it is practicable to do so.

2.12 A video identification must be carried out in accordance with *Annex B*.

Confrontation

2.13 If neither a parade, a group identification nor a video identification procedure is arranged, the suspect may be confronted by the witness. Such a confrontation does not require the suspect's consent, but may not take place unless none of the other procedures are practicable.

2.14 A confrontation must be carried out in accordance with *Annex C.*

Notice to Suspect

2.15 Before a parade takes place or a group identification or video identification is arranged, the identification officer shall explain to the suspect:

(i)   the purposes of the parade or group identification or video identification;

(ii)   that he is entitled to free legal advice . . . ;

(iii)   the procedures for holding it (including his right to have a solicitor or friend present);

(iv)   where appropriate the special arrangements for juveniles;

(v)   where appropriate the special arrangements for mentally disordered and mentally handicapped people;

(vi)   that he does not have to take part in a parade, or co-operate in a group identification, or with the making of a video film and, if it is proposed to hold a group identification or video identification, his entitlement to a parade if this can practicably be arranged;

(vii)   if he does not consent to take part in a parade or co-operate in a group identification or with the making of a video film, his refusal may be given in evidence in any subsequent trial and police may proceed covertly without his consent or make other arrangements to test whether a witness identifies him;

(vii)a that if he should significantly alter his appearance between the taking of any photograph at the time of his arrest or after charge and any attempt to hold an identification procedure, this may be given in evidence if the case comes to trial; and the officer may then consider other forms of identification;

(vii)b that a video or photograph may be taken of him when he attends for any identification procedure;

(viii)   whether the witness had been shown photographs, photofit, identikit or similar pictures by the police during the investigation before the identity of the suspect became known; . . .

(ix)   that if he changes his appearance before a parade it may not be practicable to arrange one on the day in question or subsequently and, because of his change of appearance, the identification officer may then consider alternative methods of identification;

(x)   that he or his solicitor will be provided with details of the description of the suspect as first given by any witnesses who are to attend the parade, group identification, video identification or confrontation.

2.16 This information must also be contained in a written notice which must be handed to the suspect. The identification officer shall give the suspect a reasonable opportunity to read the notice, after which he shall be asked to sign a second copy of the notice to indicate whether or not he is willing to take part in the parade or group identification or co-operate with the making of a video film. The signed copy shall be retained by the identification officer.

(b) Cases where the identity of the suspect is not known
2.17 A police officer may take a witness to a particular neighbourhood or place to see whether he can identify the person whom he said he saw on the relevant occasion. Before doing so, where practicable a record shall be made of any description given by the witness of the suspect. Care should be taken not to direct the witness's attention to any individual.
2.18 A witness must not be shown photographs, photofit, identikit or similar pictures if the identity of the suspect is known to the police and he is available to stand on an identification parade. If the identity of the suspect is not known, the showing of such pictures to a witness must be done in accordance with *Annex D.* . . .

(c) Documentation
2.19 The identification officer shall make a record of the parade, group identification or video identification on the forms provided.
2.20 If the identification officer considers that it is not practicable to hold a parade, he shall tell the suspect why and record the reason.
2.21 A record shall be made of a person's refusal to co-operate in a parade, group identification or video identification.

(d) Showing films and photographs of incidents
2.21A Nothing in this code inhibits an investigating officer from showing a video film or photographs of an incident to the public at large through the national, or local media, or to police officers, for the purposes of recognition and tracing suspects. However when such material is shown to potential witnesses . . . for the purpose of obtaining identification evidence, it shall be shown on an individual basis so as to avoid any possibility of collusion, and the showing shall, as far as possible, follow the principles for Video Film Identification (see paragraph 2.10) or Identification by Photographs (see paragraph 2.18) as appropriate.
2.21B Where such a broadcast or publication is made a copy of the material released by the police to the media for the purposes of recognising or tracing the suspect shall be kept and the suspect or his solicitor should be allowed to view such material before any procedures under paragraph 2.1 of this Code are carried out . . . provided it is practicable to do so and would not unreasonably delay the investigation. Each witness who is involved in the procedure shall be asked by the investigating officer after they have taken part whether they have seen any broadcast or published films or photographs relating to the offence and their replies shall be recorded.

There has been a steady stream of cases in which applications have been made for the exclusion of identification evidence on the ground that it was obtained in contravention of Code D. It would appear that failure without good reason to hold an identification parade, in contravention of Code D, may lead to the exclusion of identification evidence under s 78(1).[16] As the following case demonstrates, however, exclusion is considered unnecessary

[16] *R v Conway* (1990) 91 Cr App R 143; *R v Nagah* (1990) 155 JPR 229.

where there is no suggestion of bad faith, and the accused is not regarded as having actually been prejudiced by the failure to hold a parade.

Extract 10.2.7

R v Tiplady (1995) 159 JPR 548, 548–54 (CA)

LORD TAYLOR OF GOSFORTH CJ: On July 28, 1994 at Snaresbrook Crown Court, this appellant was convicted on two counts of applying a false trade description to goods contrary to s 1(1)(b) of the Trade Descriptions Act 1968. . . .

The offences concerned the supply of defective concrete on August 28, 1992. . . .

It was common ground that at the material time the appellant lived with his girlfriend and their two children at the address, given in the advertisement, from which the company providing the concrete operated. That was a company which called itself First Call Readymix. The advertisement appeared in the Yellow Pages of the telephone directory. On August 25, 1992, a Mr Robinson telephoned First Call Readymix. He said that he needed some concrete to form the base of a single story extension he was building. The telephone was answered by a man who simply said, 'First Call Readymix'. Mr Robinson gave very specific instructions as to the concrete he wanted, and it was agreed it would be supplied on August 28. It was delivered on that day. The work was done by three men, one of whom was referred to by the others as 'Gary'. Gary seemed to be in charge and seemed to be the person to whom Mr Robinson had spoken on the telephone. He is the person to whom Mr Robinson subsequently complained about the quality of the work. Mr Robinson paid Gary £310 and received a receipt which Gary wrote out personally.

Mr Robinson, in his witness statement, described Gary as between six feet and six feet two inches tall, aged between 25 and 30 with tattoos on his arm. He gave a somewhat similar description of Gary in his evidence at the trial, save that he appeared to have only a tattoo on one upper arm.

Mrs Robinson had been upstairs in her home when the lorry arrived with the three men. She saw them get out by looking through her first floor window. She then went downstairs to the kitchen and saw the men working from time to time. When they finished they came into the house, she made them tea and sandwiches and she stood with them whilst they consumed the tea and sandwiches. Over a period of a quarter of an hour at that time, and perhaps half an hour in all, she had a good opportunity to observe the men, in particular Gary. She gave a description of him as having tattoos on both upper arms. She said he was about six feet tall and quite stocky. She did not notice a limp, although she did notice a limp when she came to identify a man later. That was at the Romford magistrates' court some 14 months after the delivery of the concrete, on November 1, 1993.

On that occasion the appellant had to turn up at the court in connection with his bail. Anticipating this, the trading standards officers arranged for the Robinsons to be at the court so that a group identification might take place. Mrs Robinson picked out the appellant as the man Gary, who had carried out the work at the house, and said that she was sure it was him. The appellant's first name is in fact Gary.

Other evidence was called at the trial from the trading standards officers. Mr Davenport said that he was not familiar with the codes of practice annexed to the Police and Criminal Evidence Act 1984. He was not aware that those codes applied to trading standards officers. He gave his account of the scene when the group identification took place. He estimated that about 50 per cent of the people who had entered the magistrates' court were between 30 and 40 years old and were male.

Another trading standards officer, Mr Baker, said that the age band was quite young, between 20 and 30, and there were a considerable number of people in the appellant's general age group.

A handwriting expert gave evidence that the receipt which Gary had given to the Robinsons and which they had retained was probably – although he could not be definite about the matter – in the appellant's handwriting, although he was unable to make any comment about the signature.

The appellant did not give evidence at his trial, but he called his solicitor on his behalf, the solicitor having been present when the group identification took place. He also called Dr Navarathan, who testified that the appellant had suffered a serious injury in 1980 which had left him with one leg permanently shorter than the other. The doctor did however say that by having a raised heel the effect of the shortening might very well have been much reduced.

Having heard the evidence, speeches and summing-up, the jury retired for only 20 minutes and returned unanimous verdicts of guilty on both charges.

Before the trial began, there was a submission on behalf of the defence that the evidence of Mrs Robinson concerning the group identification of the appellant should not be admitted; it should be excluded pursuant to s 78 of the 1984 Act. The learned Judge accordingly heard evidence as to the circumstances of the identification on a *voir dire*. The trading standards officers were called, as was Mrs Robinson. It was conceded that the officers were bound by the provisions of the Codes of Practice – Code D, which related to identification – a fact of which they had been totally unaware.

There were a number of breaches of the Code which were highlighted and the learned Judge accepted that those breaches had taken place. Nevertheless, directing himself as to whether within the express terms of s 78 the admission of the evidence of the identification would have such an adverse effect on the fairness of the proceedings that he ought to exclude it, he decided that the evidence should be admitted.

This appeal is based upon the contention that the learned Judge's ruling was wrong in that respect. Mr Janner has pointed out to the court the various breaches of the Code which were established before the trial Judge. It is necessary to mention them. First of all, para D2.6 and 2.7 of the Code were breached, in that no consideration was given to the practicability of holding an identification parade. Paragraph D2.8 was also breached; that paragraph requires that the suspect should be asked for his consent to a group identification and should be advised in accordance with other paragraphs of the Code. It is correct that the appellant here was not specifically and personally asked for his consent. However, his solicitor was informed of what was to take place the day before the confrontation. Although he expressed an unhappiness about the arrangement he did not ask for an identification parade, he did not say that the group identification should not take place or that he would so advise his client. Moreover, on the day, the trading officers saw the solicitor who attended on the appellant's behalf, and invited him, if he thought it right, to say that the Robinsons should be asked to leave – in other words, he gave him the opportunity of aborting the proposed group identification procedure. Asked whether he wished that to happen, the solicitor said no. He had the opportunity and took it of consulting the appellant before the appellant came into the foyer of the magistrates' court, and indeed it seems the solicitor advised the appellant not to go in straightaway, or not to go in with him, the solicitor, but to follow a little later on his own so that it would not be so easy for anyone expecting to have an opportunity of making an identification to do so.

Next, there was a breach of para D2.9, and its annexure at Annex A [see now Annex E], because a record was not kept of the circumstances of the group identification. Finally, para D2.15 was not observed. That requires notice to be given to the suspect, and an explanation to be given to him of various matters such as the purpose of the group identification, his entitlement to free legal advice and so on, including whether the witness had been shown photographs. In fact, Mrs Robinson had been shown a photograph of the appellant. That had happened shortly after the original incident when the concrete was delivered, and Mr Janner realistically accepts that having regard to the lapse of time, the learned Judge's finding that the showing of the photograph so long before the group identification could not really be thought to be prejudicial to the witness's free choice as to whether to identify or not at the magistrates' court.

Those breaches having been established, it was for the learned Judge to decide whether in the terms of s 78 he ought to exclude the identification evidence. As to that, Mr Janner has addressed his submissions under two heads, although they really complement one another. First, he submits that Mrs Robinson's identification was wholly unreliable, and secondly, he submits that its admission would have contravened s 78.

As to the unreliability, he relies, first of all, on the breaches of the Code, and in particular the lapse of time. He points out that 14 months after the incident at the Robinsons' home was a very long time to elapse before the witness was asked to make an identification. The suggestion was put by Mr Janner that at the time of the delivery of the concrete there were some limitations on Mrs Robinson's ability to observe Gary and form a clear picture in her mind so that she could recall his appearance. He pointed out that she was going about her business in the house, that the man was working outside and so on. However, there was clear evidence that she had had a quarter of an hour in her kitchen in good light at close quarters to observe those who were doing the work, in particular Gary who seemed to be in charge, as well as the opportunity that she had had to see him through the window when he first arrived and when the work was in progress. In our view, this was a case in which the original opportunities for recognition and for identification of the person concerned were very good compared with very many cases where less favourable circumstances obtain and a shorter period of time is available.

However, Mr Janner points out that in two respects the identification by Mrs Robinson may be thought to be flawed. First, she said that there were tattoos on both the upper arms of the man who was Gary, whereas this appellant has apparently tattoo marks only on one of his upper arms. He also points out that Mrs Robinson noticed no limp on the occasion when the concrete was delivered, although she did notice a limp when she identified the appellant at court.

As to that, the medical evidence suggests that the limp may not have been all that obvious if the appellant had taken steps to wear footwear which assisted him. In our view those two alleged flaws are not of great significance. What is more important than whether the tattoo was on both arms was that Mrs Robinson did notice tattoos on a man called Gary who she later said she could identify surely.

Mr Janner points out that the foyer of the magistrates' court may not be the ideal place at which to conduct a group identification. He sought to equate it with an identification attempted at a police station which is expressly disapproved in para D2.9 of the Code [see now Annex E, para 36]. However, we see a distinction between an identification made at a police station and one made in a magistrates' court. In the latter situation there is much more likely to be a greater coming and going of a greater variety of people than in a police station.

Mr Janner referred to *Martin v Nicholls* [1994] Crim LR 218, where a group identification was held to have been wrongly permitted on appeal. But that was a case in which there were rather striking limitations on the choice open to the witness making the identification. The persons who had committed the original offence were boys, and were said to have been wearing dreadlocks. The number of boys with dreadlocks at the magistrates' court was obviously very restricted. In the present case there was evidence that at any one time between 20 and 30 people were in the foyer of the court coming and going, young men mostly of an age equivalent to that of the appellant, and we do not consider that the venue was inappropriate if a group identification was to be attempted at all.

The learned Judge considered the circumstances of the identification, having recognized the breaches of the Code. He came to the conclusion, for various reasons which he gave, that the identification could properly be admitted without any unfairness. He drew attention to the fact that the appellant's solicitor was present throughout. In the respects already mentioned, that fact, to an extent limited the adverse result from the breaches of the Code, and the appellant's solicitor was able to see that fairness was observed in the mix of people at the court and by warning his client in advance that the procedure was to take place and the nature of it.

There was no evidence before the judge on the *voir dire* to suggest that the circumstances involved any unfairness. Again, the Judge drew attention to the fact that between Mrs Robinson being informed that the appellant was likely to be present and her making the identification, a considerable period had elapsed during which people had been milling about – something between 15 and 20 minutes – so that she did not purport to identify anyone readily, but only did so after that period of time and when the appellant appeared.

The Judge took into account that a picture had been shown to Mrs Robinson of the appellant a long time earlier, some 12 months earlier, but his view was (and this has been accepted by Mr Janner) that the lapse of time between the showing of the photograph and the group identification was such that the effect of the photograph would not have influenced the witness.

The learned Judge also said that he took into account the fact that those in charge of the investigation were not police officers. It is accepted that the Codes apply to the trading standards officers in just the same way they apply to police officers, even though s 67 deals with this matter in two separate subparagraphs and implies a stronger sanction in regard to police officers than in relation to others. The point of the Judge's observation was that the question of good faith is a relevant consideration. It would be much less credible that police officers would ignore or flout the Code in good faith than the trading officers who had not appreciated the application of the Code to their activities.

In our judgment, the identification of the appellant by Mrs Robinson could not be described as Mr Janner sought to describe it, as weak and wholly unreliable. Nevertheless, we have to consider his second submission as to whether the admission of that evidence would have an adverse effect upon the fairness of the trial.

In that regard, apart from considerations that have already been mentioned, there were a number of other sources of evidence which went to confirm, in greater or lesser degree, the identification of the appellant as the offender. First of all, he lived at the address which was given in the advert. Whilst that would not be conclusive, it is a striking factor. It is accepted that there was only one man living at that address, and when Mr Robinson telephoned it was to a man that he spoke. Secondly, the other two workmen of the three who arrived at the Robinsons' house referred to their leader as 'Gary' and this appellant's name is Gary. Thirdly, a handwriting expert, whilst he could not be adamant about the matter, said that the receipt had probably been written by this appellant. Finally, although Mrs Robinson referred to the tattoos on both arms whereas there is only a tattoo on one, she did identify a tattoo on the man Gary at her house, and indeed the appellant does have a tattoo on his upper arm.

Putting all those matters together with the circumstances of the identification, in our judgment the learned Judge was entitled to the view that the identification could properly be admitted without it having an adverse effect on the fairness of the proceedings. Since that is the only ground of appeal which is pursued, and we consider that it fails, this appeal must be dismissed.

It would seem that, even if breaches of Code D may not justify the exclusion of identification evidence in the circumstances of a particular case, they may require appropriate warnings to be given to the jury.

Extract 10.2.8

R v Quinn [1995] 1 Cr App R 480, 490 (CA)

LORD TAYLOR CJ: What is said by Mr Dein is that the learned judge at the very least, having decided to admit the identification evidence notwithstanding the breaches of the Code, ought to have drawn the jury's attention to the fact that there were breaches and invited the jury to consider the reasons why the

Code existed and whether in their estimation the breaches were such as to cause them to have doubts about the safety of the identifications they were asked to rely on.

We think there is force in the submissions made in this regard. We think that, although the learned judge was entitled to form the view he did about admitting the evidence, in view of the centrality of that evidence to the prosecution case – indeed it was the only real direct evidence in the case – and in view of the criticisms that have been properly made about the breaches of the Code, the learned judge ought to have made a specific reference to those breaches and left it to the jury to consider what their approach should be in the light of those proved breaches. This was particularly important in view of the discrepancies between the descriptions of the robber (dark brown eyes, fair hair) and the features of the appellant.

The relationship, in the context of Code D violations, between exclusion and warnings now requires to be clarified. It is to be hoped in particular that warnings will not be regarded as an adequate judicial response where nothing less than outright exclusion is warranted in the circumstances of the case.

In contrast to the position in England, where, as has been seen, the courts are invested with a great deal of latitude in determining whether identification evidence should be excluded, a rather more structured approach may be found in the Australian Evidence Act 1995:

Extract 10.2.9

Evidence Act 1995 (Australia), s 114

114. Exclusion of visual identification evidence
(1) In this section:
'**visual identification evidence**' means identification evidence relating to an identification based wholly or partly on what a person saw but does not include picture identification evidence.
(2) Visual identification evidence adduced by the prosecutor is not admissible unless:
    (a) an identification parade that included the defendant was held before the identification was made; or
    (b) it would not have been reasonable to have held such a parade; or
    (c) the defendant refused to take part in such a parade;
and the identification was made without the person who made it having been intentionally influenced to identify the defendant.
(3) Without limiting the matters that may be taken into account by the court in determining whether it was reasonable to hold an identification parade, it is to take into account:
    (a) the kind of offence, and the gravity of the offence, concerned; and
    (b) the importance of the evidence; and
    (c) the practicality of holding an identification parade having regard, among other things:

(i) if the defendant failed to cooperate in the conduct of the parade – to the manner and extent of, and the reason (if any) for, the failure; and

(ii) in any case – to whether the identification was made at or about the time of the commission of the offence; and

(d) the appropriateness of holding an identification parade having regard, among other things, to the relationship (if any) between the defendant and the person who made the identification.

(4) It is presumed that it would not have been reasonable to have held an identification parade if it would have been unfair to the defendant for such a parade to have been held.

(5) If:

(a) the defendant refused to take part in an identification parade unless a lawyer acting for the defendant, or another person chosen by the defendant, was present while it was being held; and

(b) there were, at the time when the parade was to have been conducted, reasonable grounds to believe that it was not reasonably practicable for such a lawyer or person to be present;

it is presumed that it would not have been reasonable to have held an identification parade at that time.

(6) In determining whether it was reasonable to have held an identification parade, the court is not to take into account the availability of pictures or photographs that could be used in making identifications.

11

EXPERT OPINION EVIDENCE

The admissibility in certain circumstances of expert opinion evidence constitutes an important exception to the general rule which prohibits the admission of evidence of a witness's opinion and allows only the admission of evidence of facts perceived by a witness. Expert opinion evidence has had a high profile in recent years owing to its role in contributing to a number of major miscarriages of justice. Pre-eminent amongst these was the case of Judith Ward, whose conviction was quashed by the Court of Appeal in 1992. The following is an extract from the judgment of the Court of Appeal:

Extract 11.0.1

R v Ward [1993] 2 All ER 577, 628 (CA)

GLIDEWELL LJ: What are the lessons to be learnt from this miscarriage of justice? The law is of necessity concerned with practical affairs, and it cannot effectively guard against all the failings of those who play a part in the criminal justice system. But that sombre realism does not relieve us, as judges, from persevering in the task to ensure that the law, practice and methods of trial should be developed so as to reduce the risk of conviction of the innocent to an absolute minimum. At the same time we are very much alive to the fact that, although the avoidance of the conviction of the innocent must unquestionably be the primary consideration, the public interest would not be served by a multiplicity of rules which merely impede effective law enforcement. Recognising that the Royal Commission on Criminal Justice will no doubt consider the subject of scientific evidence in criminal trials in depth, we propose to limit our observations about the lessons to be learnt to two matters which we regard as of critical importance. First, we have identified the cause of the injustice done to the appellant on the scientific side of the case as stemming from the fact that three senior forensic scientists at RARDE regarded their task as being to help the police. They became partisan. It is the clear duty of government forensic scientists to assist in a neutral and impartial way in criminal investigations. They must act in the cause of justice. That duty should be spelt out to all engaged or to be engaged in forensic services in the clearest terms. . . . Secondly, we believe that the surest way of preventing the misuse of scientific evidence is by ensuring that there is a proper understanding of the nature and scope of the prosecution's duty of disclosure. In our view there was an imperfect understanding of the position in 1974. Mr Langdale suggested to us that the problem was solved by the Crown Court (Advance Notice of Expert Evidence) Rules 1987, SI 1987/716, which came into force on 15 July 1987. Those rules enable the legal representatives of a defendant in a Crown Court criminal case to require the prosecution by notice in writing to provide in respect of scientific evidence a copy of (or an opportunity to inspect) 'the record of any observation, test, calculation or other procedure on which [any] finding or opinion is based' . . . The new rules are helpful. But it is a misconception to regard them as exhaustive: they do not in any way supplant or detract from the prosecution's general duty of disclosure in respect of scientific evidence. That duty exists irrespective of any request by the defence. It is also not limited to documentation on which the opinion or findings of an expert is based. It extends to anything which may arguably assist the defence. It is therefore wider in scope than the rule. Moreover, it is a positive duty, which in the context of scientific evidence obliges the prosecution to make full and proper inquiries from forensic scientists in order to ascertain whether there is discoverable material. Given the undoubted inequality as between prosecution and defence in access to forensic scientists, we regard it as of paramount importance that the common law duty of disclosure, as we have explained it, should be appreciated by those who prosecute and defend in criminal cases. And, if difficulties arise in a particular case, the court must be the final judge.

The comments in *Ward* on prosecutorial disclosure should now be read in the light of the Criminal Procedure and Investigations Act 1996 which (as seen in Chapter 4) replaces the common law on disclosure with a new statutory régime.

The *Crown Court Study* found that there was probably prosecution scientific evidence in around a third of contested cases. In only around a quarter of cases in which there was such evidence was it challenged by the defence. Overall, therefore, there was a challenge by the defence to prosecution scientific evidence in under a tenth of all contested cases.[1] According to prosecution barristers, defence barristers and the CPS respectively, the types of scientific evidence involved, in order of frequency, were as follows:

---

[1] M Zander and P Henderson, *The Royal Commission on Criminal Justice: Crown Court Study* (1993) 83–4, 86.

Extract 11.0.2

M Zander and P Henderson, *The Royal Commission on Criminal Justice: Crown Court Study* (1993) 85

Types of scientific evidence

	Pb%	Db%	CPS%
Medical	47	52	44
Drugs	22	18	24
Fingerprints	12	12	10
Blood samples (person)	9	10	8
Handwriting (documents)	7	7	6
Contact evidence (person)	7	(not listed)	6
Blood samples (alcohol/drugs)	6	5	4
Firearms/ballistics	5	4	7
Contact evidence (property)	4	2	6
Other	13	17	11
Total	132	127	126
	(N=249)	(N=269)	(N=197)

'Other' scientific evidence included DNA samples; footprints; evidence of cause of fire or impact of vehicle; evidence of speed of vehicle; facial mapping; meteorological evidence re weather on the day.

It is noteworthy that, although treated in the law of evidence as fundamental, the distinction between 'fact' and 'opinion' may not withstand close scrutiny. Thayer wrote that 'in a sense all testimony to matter of fact is opinion evidence; *ie*, it is a conclusion formed from phenomena and mental impressions'.[2] In a similar vein, Wigmore observed:

If... our notion of the supposed firm distinction between 'opinion' and 'fact' is that the one is certain and sure, the other not, surely a just view of their psychological relations serves to demonstrate that in strict truth nothing is certain. Or if we prefer the suggestion of Sir G C Lewis that the test is whether 'doubt can reasonably exist,' then certainly it must be perceived that the multiple doubts which ought to exist would exclude vast masses of indubitably admissible testimony. Or if we prefer the idea that 'opinion' is inference and fact is 'original perception,' then it may be understood that no such distinction can scientifically be made, since the processes of knowledge and the sources of illusion are the same for both. It is impossible, then (supposing it were desirable), to confine witnesses to some fancied realm of 'knowledge' or 'fact' and to forbid them to enter the domain of 'opinions' or inferences. There are no such contrasted groups of certain and uncertain testimony, and there never can be.[3]

[2] J B Thayer, *A Preliminary Treatise on Evidence at the Common Law* (1898) 524.
[3] J H Wigmore, *Evidence in Trials at Common Law (Vol 7)* (rev by J H Chadbourn, 1978) 16. See also C A G Jones, *Expert Witnesses: Science, Medicine, and the Practice of Law* (1994) 103: 'All statements of fact are, to some degree, statements of conclusion and judgement.'

I. ADMISSIBILITY

Although not often well articulated in the cases, there are clearly two fundamental issues which underlie considerations of the admissibility of expert opinion evidence. These may be referred to, in short, as the issues of necessity and reliability. The role of expert witnesses is 'to furnish the Judge or jury with the necessary scientific criteria for testing the accuracy of their conclusions, so as to enable the Judge or jury to form their own independent judgment by the application of these criteria to the facts proved in evidence'.[4] Thus expert opinion evidence is considered unnecessary where the trier of fact may be expected to have the ability to form its opinion on the issue in question without assistance. To treat the trier of fact to expert opinion evidence in such a situation would not only usurp the role of the trier of fact, but would also create the danger that the trier of fact would be too readily influenced by that evidence and thus accord it undue weight.[5] The potentially strong influence on a jury in a criminal trial of apparently cogent expert evidence adduced by the prosecution is undeniable.[6] It is, therefore, only in those situations where the trier of fact may be expected to require the assistance of an expert that such evidence should be admissible. Secondly, the evidence should be demonstrated to be sufficiently reliable to be admitted. As has been stated by the Court of Appeal: 'In each case it must be for the judge to decide whether the issue is one on which the jury could be assisted by expert evidence, and whether the expert tendered has the expertise to provide such evidence.'[7] In the remainder of this section, consider whether the twin issues of necessity and reliability are adequately accounted for in the law on the admissibility of expert opinion evidence.

---

[4] *Davie* v *Edinburgh Magistrates* [1953] SC 34, 40. See also *R* v *Stockwell* (1993) 97 Cr App R 260, 266 (where it was stressed that 'the judge should make clear to the jury that they are not bound by the expert's opinion, and that the issue is for them to decide') and *Dover District Council v Sherred* (1997) *The Times*, 11 February; LEXIS transcript (where the Court of Appeal observed that a county court judge 'is not bound to accept the evidence even of an expert witness, if there is a proper basis for rejecting it in the other evidence which he has heard, or the expert evidence is such that he does not believe it or for whatever reason is not convinced by it. This is the effect of the judgment of Donaldson LJ in *Patel v Mehtab* (1980) 5 HLR 78, to which we were referred, and it is wholly consistent with leading authorities such as *McLoughlin v O'Brien* [1983] 1 AC 410, [1982] 2 All ER 298 (per Lord Bridge at 423/3 of the former report)').

[5] It should be noted, however, that empirical evidence has suggested that the tendency of juries to accord undue weight to expert evidence may not be as strong as is popularly thought: E J Imwinkelried, 'The Next Step in Conceptualizing the Presentation of Expert Evidence as Education: The Case for Didactic Trial Procedures' (1997) 1(2) *International Journal of Evidence and Proof* 128, 134–6.

[6] Notably, 90% of jurors in the *Crown Court Study* found scientific evidence presented by expert witnesses either 'not at all difficult' (56%) or 'not very difficult' (34%) to understand, with only 9% finding it 'fairly difficult' and 1% 'very difficult': M Zander and P Henderson, *The Royal Commission on Criminal Justice: Crown Court Study* (1993) 206.

[7] *R* v *Stockwell* (1993) 97 Cr App R 260, 264.

(a) Express statutory provisions

Provision on the admissibility of expert opinion evidence is on occasion made expressly by Parliament:

Extract 11.1.1

Criminal Procedure (Insanity and Unfitness to Plead) Act 1991, s 1(1)

1. Acquittals on grounds of insanity

(1) A jury shall not return a special verdict under section 2 of the Trial of Lunatics Act 1833 (acquittal on ground of insanity) except on the written or oral evidence of two or more registered medical practitioners at least one of whom is duly approved.

In a similar vein, s 4(6) of the Criminal Procedure (Insanity) Act 1964 provides that a jury is not to make a finding of unfitness to plead 'except on the written or oral evidence of two or more registered medical practitioners at least one of whom is duly approved'.

Extract 11.1.2

Obscene Publications Act 1959, s 4

4. Defence of public good

(1) Subject to subsection (1A) of this section a person shall not be convicted of an offence . . . if it is proved that publication of the article in question is justified as being for the public good on the ground that it is in the interests of science, literature, art or learning, or of other objects of general concern.
. . .

(2) It is hereby declared that the opinion of experts as to the literary, artistic, scientific or other merits of an article may be admitted in any proceedings under this Act either to establish or to negative the said ground.
. . .

(b) Mens rea, defences and credibility

To what extent is expert opinion evidence admissible on the issues of the mens rea of the accused, defences raised by the accused, and the credibility of witnesses?

Extract 11.1.3

***R v Chard* (1971) 56 Cr App R 268, 270–1 (CA)**

ROSKILL LJ: . . . one purpose of jury trials is to bring into the jury box a body of men and women who are able to judge ordinary day-to-day questions by their own standards, that is, the standards in the eyes of the law of theoretically ordinary reasonable men and women. That is something which they are well able by their ordinary experience to judge for themselves. Where the matters in issue go outside that experience and they are invited to deal with someone supposedly abnormal, for example, supposedly suffering from insanity or diminished responsibility, then plainly in such a case they are entitled to the benefit of expert evidence. But where, as in the present case, they are dealing with someone who by concession was on the medical evidence entirely normal, it seems to this Court abundantly plain, on first principles of the admissibility of expert evidence, that it is not permissible to call a witness, whatever his personal experience, merely to tell the jury how he thinks an accused man's mind – assumedly a normal mind – operated at the time of the alleged crime with reference to the crucial question of what that man's intention was.

Extract 11.1.4

R v Toner (1991) 93 Cr App R 382, 387 (CA)

RUSSELL LJ: The problem with which we are confronted is that we do not know what, if any, effect mild hypoglycemia can have upon a man's ability to form an intent, and without that expert evidence the jury were deprived of assistance in a field where their ordinary experience did not enable them to judge for themselves.

. . . In principle we can see no distinction between medical evidence which relates to hypoglycemia and its possible effect upon intent and medical evidence as to the effect of a drug upon intent. These are matters outside the ordinary experience of jurors. They cannot bring to bear their own judgment without the assistance of expert evidence, and upon this ground we distinguish the instant case from that of *Chard*.

See also *R v Coles*.[8] In *R v Masih*,[9] the Court of Appeal considered that expert evidence would generally be admissible on the issue of mens rea in the case of defendants coming into the class of mental defective with an IQ of 69 and below. This was to enable the jury to be enlightened on a matter which was presumably outside their experience. The Court of Appeal in *R v Reynolds*[10] took a similar view.

The following decision of the Privy Council has proved somewhat troubling:

Extract 11.1.5

Lowery v R [1974] AC 85, 101 (PC)

LORD MORRIS OF BORTH-Y-GEST: As was pointed out in the Court of Criminal Appeal the very nature of the killing showed that it was 'a sadistic

[8] [1995] 1 Cr App R 157.
[9] [1986] Crim LR 395.
[10] [1989] Crim LR 220.

and otherwise motiveless killing.' Any prospect of the acquittal of either of the two accused could only have been on the basis that one alone was the killer and that the other took no part whatsoever. That was what Lowery alleged when he said that King alone was the killer and that he (Lowery) was power-less to save the girl. . . . The case for King was that Lowery had alone been the killer and that King had been heavily under the influence of drugs and had been powerless to stop Lowery. It was furthermore the evidence of each of them, in spite of what they said in their statements, that the idea or suggestion of seeing 'what it would be like to kill a chick' emanated from the other. In all these circumstances it was necessary on behalf of King to call all relevant and admissible evidence which would exonerate King and throw responsibility entirely on Lowery. If in imaginary circumstances similar to those of this case it was apparent that one of the accused was a man of great physical strength whereas the other was a weakling it could hardly be doubted that in forming an opinion as to the probabilities it would be relevant to have the disparity between the two in mind. . . . The evidence of Professor Cox was not related to crime or criminal tendencies: it was scientific evidence as to the respective personalities of the two accused as, and to the extent, revealed by certain well known tests. Whether it assisted the jury is not a matter that can be known. All that is known is that the jury convicted both the accused. But in so far as it might help in considering the probabilities as to what happened at the spot to which the girl was taken it was not only relevant to and indeed necessary for the case advanced by King but it was made relevant and admissible in view of the case advanced by Lowery and in view of Lowery's assertions against King.

Extract 11.1.6

R v Turner [1975] QB 834, 841–2 (CA)

LAWTON LJ: Jurors do not need psychiatrists to tell them how ordinary folk who are not suffering from any mental illness are likely to react to the stresses and strains of life. It follows that the proposed evidence was not admissible to establish that the defendant was likely to have been provoked. The same reasoning applies to its suggested admissibility on the issue of credibility. The jury had to decide what reliance they could put upon the defendant's evid-ence. He had to be judged as someone who was not mentally disordered. This is what juries are empanelled to do. The law assumes they can perform their duties properly. The jury in this case did not need, and should not have been offered the evidence of a psychiatrist to help them decide whether the defendant's evidence was truthful.

. . . In Lowery v The Queen the issues were unusual; and the accused to whose disadvantage the psychologist's evidence went had in effect said before it was called that he was not the sort of man to have committed the offence. . . . We adjudge Lowery v The Queen . . . to have been decided on its special facts. We do not consider that it is an authority for the proposition that in all cases psychologists and psychiatrists can be called to prove the probability of the accused's veracity. If any such rule was applied in our courts, trial by psychiatrists would be likely to take the place of trial by jury and magistrates. We do not find that prospect attractive and the law does not at present provide for it.

Similar views on the admissibility of expert opinion evidence on the issue of provocation were expressed by Lord Simon of Glaisdale in *R v Camplin*.[11] In a similar vein, the psychiatric evidence sought to be adduced in *R v Hurst*[12] to support the defence of duress by threats, in circumstances where the defendant did not suffer from psychiatric illness or disorder, was held to be inadmissible. It is important, however, that cases like *Turner* and *Hurst* should not be read as positing a rule requiring the automatic inadmissibility of all expert opinion evidence sought to be adduced in support of the defences of provocation and duress. Much must depend on the facts of the particular case, and the precise purpose for which it is proposed to adduce the evidence. It is notable that the Court of Appeal suggested in *R v Ahluwalia* that psychiatric evidence would be admissible where a condition such as post-traumatic stress disorder is relied upon as the basis for the defence of provocation.[13]

As the above extract from *Turner* also indicates, expert opinion evidence is, in general, inadmissible on the issue of a witness's credibility. And see generally *Re N (A Minor)*[14] and *Re M and R (Minors)*.[15] Where, however, the suggestion is that a witness is *incapable* of telling the truth because of mental illness, *medical*[16] evidence may be permitted:

Extract 11.1.7

Toohey v Metropolitan Police Commissioner [1965] AC 595, 608 (HL)

LORD PEARCE: Human evidence . . . is subject to many cross-currents such as partiality, prejudice, self-interest and, above all, imagination and inaccuracy. Those are matters with which the jury, helped by cross-examination and common sense, must do their best. But when a witness through physical (in which I include mental) disease or abnormality is not capable of giving a true or reliable account to the jury, it must surely be allowable for medical science to reveal this vital hidden fact to them. . . . it must . . . be allowable to call medical evidence of mental illness which makes a witness incapable of giving reliable evidence, whether through the existence of delusions or otherwise.

---

[11] [1978] AC 705, 727. Thus, 'problems can arise in directing the jury about the use of . . . psychiatric evidence, when, as sometimes happens, both [the defences of diminished responsibility and provocation] are run in tandem': G J Durston, 'Expert Opinion Evidence in Criminal Trials: A Review of the Current Position' (1996) 160 *Justice of the Peace* 837, 838.
[12] [1995] 1 Cr App R 82.
[13] [1992] 4 All ER 889, 898.
[14] [1996] 4 All ER 225.
[15] [1996] 4 All ER 239.
[16] See also *R v MacKenney* (1981) 76 Cr App R 271.

Is there really a clear-cut distinction between lack of credibility as a result of *incapacity* to tell the truth because of mental illness, and lack of credibility as a result of such factors as partiality, prejudice, self-interest, imagination or inaccuracy?

On the issue of expert opinion evidence pertaining to the credibility of a witness, the following decision of the Court of Appeal should also be noted:

Extract 11.1.8

R v Robinson [1994] 3 All ER 346, 352 (CA)

LORD TAYLOR OF GOSFORTH CJ: In our view the Crown cannot call a witness of fact and then, without more, call a psychologist or psychiatrist to give reasons why the jury should regard that witness as reliable.

. . . if the defence propose to call an expert witness to say that a witness of fact for the Crown should be regarded as unreliable due to some mental abnormality outwith the jury's experience, then, depending on the precise issue, it may be open to the Crown to call an expert in rebuttal, or even (anticipating the defence expert) as part of the prosecution case. It may even be open to the Crown to rebut by expert evidence a case put only in cross-examination that a prosecution witness is unreliable in a particular respect arising from mental abnormality. Much may depend upon the nature of the abnormality and of the cross-examination. If such evidence is admitted, great care would need to be taken to restrict the expert opinion to meeting the specific challenge and not to allow it to extend to 'oath-helping'.

The general approach of the courts to the admissibility of expert opinion evidence on the issues of the mens rea of the accused, defences raised by the accused, and the credibility of witnesses, may be easily criticised:

Extract 11.1.9

R D Mackay and A M Colman, 'Excluding Expert Evidence: A Tale of Ordinary Folk and Common Experience' [1991] *Criminal Law Review* 800, 809

In decisions regarding admissibility, the crucial question ought to be whether or not the expert evidence could make a significant contribution to the jury's understanding of the accused's state of mind. This must depend, of course, on the judge's assessment of the probative value of the evidence. If the expert evidence points to an abnormal state of mind or personality *of any degree* on the defendant's part at the time of the alleged offence, then we submit that the court ought to exercise its discretion in favour of admitting the evidence. There are many abnormal states of mind brought about by situational forces . . . which, although they do not involve mental disorders in any medical sense, none the less lie demonstrably beyond the understanding of ordinary people, and in relation to which expert evidence could therefore contribute significantly to a jury's understanding. . . . evidence on such matters ought in our view to be admitted, for to exclude it might deprive the jury of evidence that could help them to understand the defendant's state of mind at the material time.

That the orthodox approach of the English courts cannot withstand close scrutiny has been recognised in the High Court of Australia:

Extract 11.1.10

Murphy v R (1989) 167 CLR 94, 111 (HCA)

MASON CJ AND TOOHEY J: In *Reg v Turner* Lawton LJ expressed the basis upon which expert evidence is received in terms about which there can be no quarrel:

'An expert's opinion is admissible to furnish the court with scientific information which is likely to be outside the experience and knowledge of a judge or jury.'

Later, Lawton LJ added some remarks which may not be so unquestionable:

'Jurors do not need psychiatrists to tell them how ordinary folk who are not suffering from any mental illness are likely to react to the stresses and strains of life.'

There are difficulties with such a statement. To begin with, it assumes that 'ordinary' or 'normal' has some clearly understood meaning and, as a corollary, that the distinction between normal and abnormal is well recognized. Further, it assumes that the commonsense of jurors is an adequate guide to the conduct of people who are 'normal' even though they may suffer from some relevant disability. And it assumes that the expertise of psychiatrists (or, in the present case, psychologists) extends only to those who are 'abnormal'. None of these assumptions will stand close scrutiny.

See generally J Hunter and J Bargen, 'Diminished Responsibility: "Abnormal" Minds, Abnormal Murderers and What the Doctor Said' in S M H Yeo (ed), *Partial Excuses to Murder* (1990).

Even in England, however, there are signs that Lawton LJ's questionable remarks in *Turner* are being gradually diluted. In *R v Strudwick*, for example, the Court of Appeal observed:

It is not suggested here that the appellant is suffering from a mental illness, but that is not in itself conclusive against the admission of this evidence. The law is in a state of development in this area. There may well be other mental conditions about which a jury might require expert assistance in order to understand and evaluate their effect on the issues in a case.[17]

[17] (1993) 99 Cr App R 326, 332.

It is to be noted that the expert opinion evidence sought to be adduced on matters such as mens rea, defences and credibility is often exculpatory evidence sought to be introduced by defendants in their defence. Should this be a factor favouring the admissibility of the evidence?

Finally, it is interesting to note that the reluctance of English law to admit expert evidence on the issue of credibility is not mirrored in all jurisdictions:

Extract 11.1.11

J Hunter and K Cronin, *Evidence, Advocacy and Ethical Practice: A Criminal Trial Commentary* (1995) 363–4

In stark contrast to the common law approach, the German system has embraced psychological analysis because of its potential to provide accurate assessment of witness credibility. The process is known as *Glaubwürdigkeitsgutachten*, or the psychological expert report on credibility. This involves the court commissioning a psychological expert to assess a specific witness's credibility where there is doubt about the particular witness's veracity. According to Michaelis-Arntzen ['Die Glaubwürdigkeitsbegutachtung der Zeugenaussage durch einen Psychologischen Sachverständigen' in F Arntzen, *Vernehmungspsychologie* (2nd ed, Munich, 1989) 67–84] it is common to call for these reports where children (as young as five years) and adolescents are witnesses. Such reports are also considered appropriate where the criminal accusation amounts to one person's word against the accused, where there may be a motive to make a false accusation, where there are contradictions or vacillating views in the witness's pre-hearing statements or where the criminal *milieu* in which the allegations arise create doubt about credibility. It is not uncommon for it to be used to assess sexual assault victims. The defendant can request *Glaubwürdigkeitsgutachten* for a particular witness and the court will then choose the expert to conduct the testing.

In this process the expert tests the witness prior to the main hearing for consistency and detail in their story, ability to fabricate and ability to maintain a complex story. Imagination, memory, intelligence and personality are evaluated through the individual's demeanour, general behaviour and attitudes to form a credibility assessment. The assessment will typically take between 3–5 hours. Unlike a medical physical examination it loses its integrity if repeated. As a result it is important that the test be conducted professionally. The expert must prepare a credibility report which is presented in court through questioning of the witness or through an oral examination of the expert in the main hearing.

... *Glaubwürdigkeitsgutachten* is not without controversy. These is some controversy over the extent to which psychology invades the courtroom. Another disadvantage is that the broad-ranging and often sensitive nature of the inquiry into the witness's background by the psychologist means that the witness can be confronted with questions in the public environment of the courtroom about his/her life that are confidential and remote to the inquiry.

(c) Confessions

Similar principles are applied in determining whether the jury in a criminal case should be permitted to hear expert opinion evidence on the issue of the reliability of a confession. In *R v Weightman*, such evidence was held to be inadmissible on the basis that the defendant, although 'histrionic, theatrical and likely to say things to draw attention to herself', did not have a personality 'beyond the experience of normal non-medical people'. The jury, it was said, 'would not have been helped by having a psychiatrist talking about "emotional superficiality" and "impaired capacity to develop and sustain deep or enduring relationships"'.[18]

Extract 11.1.12

R v Ward [1993] 2 All ER 577, 641 (CA)

GLIDEWELL LJ: ... we conclude on the authorities as they now stand that the expert evidence of a psychiatrist or a psychologist may properly be admitted if it is to the effect that a defendant is suffering from a condition not properly described as mental illness, but from a personality disorder so severe as properly to be categorised as mental disorder. ... such evidence is admissible on the issue whether what a defendant has said in a confession or admission was reliable and therefore likely to have been true.

We emphasise that the occasions on which such evidence will properly be admissible will probably be rare. This decision is not to be construed as an open invitation to every defendant who repents of having confessed and seeks to challenge the truth of his confession to seek the aid of a psychiatrist.

Similar principles apply in relation to the admissibility of expert opinion evidence on a *voir dire* held to determine whether a confession should be excluded from evidence: see *R v Everett*;[19] *R v Silcott*;[20] *R v Heaton*[21] (expert opinion evidence inadmissible because there was no suggestion of mental handicap or retardation, and the defendant was within the normal range of intelligence albeit towards the lower end of it).

(d) Obscenity

In *R v Stamford*,[22] where the defendant was charged with posting packets containing indecent articles, the Court of Appeal held that 'evidence is not admissible on the issue whether a particular article is indecent or not, or

---

[18] (1990) 92 Cr App R 291, 297.
[19] [1988] Crim LR 826.
[20] (1991) *The Times*, 9 December.
[21] [1993] Crim LR 593.
[22] [1972] 2 QB 391.

whether it is obscene or not. That issue is a matter entirely for the jury, and it is one which they must decide without . . . the assistance of persons who may have views on the matter, or might be able to speak as to the effect on them of the article in question.'[23] This may be compared, however, with the earlier case of *DPP v A & BC Chewing Gum Ltd*,[24] where the defendant was charged with publishing for gain some obscene cards, which were sold with packets of bubble gum. Evidence of experts in child psychiatry about what effect the cards would be likely to have on children was held by the Divisional Court to be admissible. The court thought that, if adults had been at issue, expert opinion evidence might have been unnecessary, but in the case of children, such evidence was admissible, because the trier of fact would require all the assistance which it could get in considering the effect of the publication on children. The authority of this case is perhaps somewhat doubtful: the Court of Appeal in *Stamford* described it as 'a very special case',[25] and doubts about it were expressed by Viscount Dilhorne in *DPP v Jordan*.[26] It has recently, however, been referred to seemingly approvingly by the Court of Appeal:

> In cases involving children, expert medical and psychiatric evidence from paediatricians and allied disciplines is often quite indispensable to the court. As Lord Parker CJ said in *DPP v A & BC Chewing Gum Ltd* [1967] 2 All ER 504 at 506, [1968] 1 QB 159 at 165, when dealing with children, the court needs 'all the help [it] can get'. But that dependence in no way compromises the fact that the final decision in the case is the judge's and his alone.[27]

(e) DNA evidence

Extract 11.1.13

R v Doheny [1997] 1 Cr App R 369, 371–5 (CA)

PHILLIPS LJ:

DNA Testing

Deoxyribonucleic acid, or DNA, consists of long ribbon-like molecules, the chromosomes, 46 of which lie tightly coiled in nearly every cell of the body. These chromosomes – 23 provided from the mother and 23 from the father at conception, form the genetic blueprint of the body. Different sections of DNA have different identifiable and discrete characteristics. When a criminal

---

[23] At 398.
[24] [1968] 1 QB 159.
[25] [1972] 2 QB 391, 397.
[26] [1977] AC 699, 722.
[27] *Re M and R (Minors)* [1996] 4 All ER 239, 249.

leaves a stain of blood or semen at the scene of the crime it may prove possible to extract from that crime stain sufficient sections of DNA to enable a comparison to be made with the same sections extracted from a sample of blood provided by the suspect. This process is complex and we could not hope to describe it more clearly or succinctly than did Lord Taylor CJ in the case of *Deen* (transcript: December 21, 1993), so we shall gratefully adopt his description.

'The process of DNA profiling starts with DNA being extracted from the crime stain and also from a sample taken from the suspect. In each case the DNA is cut into smaller lengths by specific enzymes. The fragments produced are sorted according to size by a process of electrophoresis. This involves placing the fragments in a gel and drawing them electromagnetically along a track through the gel. The fragments with smaller molecular weight travel further than the heavier ones. The pattern thus created is transferred from the gel onto a membrane. Radioactive DNA probes, taken from elsewhere, which bind with the sequences of most interest in the sample DNA are then applied. After the excess of the DNA probe is washed off, an X-ray film is placed over the membrane to record the band pattern. This produces an auto-radiograph which can be photographed. When the crime stain DNA and the sample DNA from the suspect have been run in separate tracks through the gel, the resultant auto-radiographs can be compared. The two DNA profiles can then be said either to match or not.'

Even if a number of bands correspond exactly, any discrepancy between the profiles, unless satisfactorily explained, will show a mis-match and will exclude the suspect from complicity. Thus the first stage in seeking to prove identity by DNA profiling is to achieve a match.

The characteristics of an individual band of DNA will not be unique. The fact that the identical characteristic of a single band are to be found in the crime stain and the sample from the suspect does not prove that both have originated from the same source. Other persons will also have that identical band as part of their genetic make-up. Empirical research enables the analyst to predict the statistical likelihood of an individual DNA band being found in the genetic make-up of persons of particular racial groups 'the random occurrence ratio'.

As one builds up a combination of bands, the random occurrence ratio becomes increasingly more remote, by geometric progression. Thus, if two bands, each of which appear in 1 in 4 of the population are combined, the combination will appear in 1 in 16 of the population, and if to these are added a further band that is found in 1 in 4 of the population, the resultant combination will appear in 1 in 64 of the population. This process of multiplication is valid on the premise that each band is statistically independent from the others. The frequency ratio of the blood group is a factor which is statistically independent and thus this can also validly be used as a multiplier.

If the DNA obtained from the crime stain permits, it may be possible to demonstrate that there is a combination of bands common to the crime stain and the suspect which is very rare. For instance, it may be that the match achieved with the crime stain is one which has a statistical probability of existing in the case of only one in a million of the populace. We shall take a match probability, or random occurrence ratio, of one in a million as an example to demonstrate the conclusions that can properly be drawn from such data and those which cannot. We shall start with the latter.

'The Prosecutor's Fallacy'

It is easy, if one eschews rigorous analysis, to draw the following conclusion:
1. Only one person in a million will have a DNA profile which matches that of the crime stain.
2. The defendant has a DNA profile which matches the crime stain.
3. Ergo there is a million to one probability that the defendant left the crime stain and is guilty of the crime.

Such reasoning has been commended to juries in a number of cases by prosecuting counsel, by judges and sometimes by expert witnesses. It is fallacious and it has earned the title of 'The Prosecutor's Fallacy'. The propounding of the prosecutor's fallacy in the course of the summing-up was the reason, or at least one of the reasons, why the appeal against conviction was allowed in *Deen*. The nature of that fallacy was elegantly exposed by Balding and Donnelly in 'The Prosecutor's Fallacy and DNA Evidence' [1994] Crim LR 711. It should not, however, be thought that we endorse the calculations on pp 715 and 716 of that article.

Taking our example, the prosecutor's fallacy can be simply demonstrated. If one person in a million has a DNA profile which matches that obtained from the crime stain, then the suspect will be 1 of perhaps 26 men in the United Kingdom who share that characteristic. If no fact is known about the Defendant, other than that he was in the United Kingdom at the time of the crime the DNA evidence tells us no more than that there is a statistical probability that he was the criminal of 1 in 26.

The significance of the DNA evidence will depend critically upon what else is known about the suspect. If he has a convincing alibi at the other end of England at the time of the crime, it will appear highly improbable that he can have been responsible for the crime, despite his matching DNA profile. If, however, he was near the scene of the crime when it was committed, or has been identified as a suspect because of other evidence which suggests that he may have been responsible for the crime, the DNA evidence becomes very significant. The possibility that two of the only 26 men in the United Kingdom with the matching DNA should have been in the vicinity of the crime will seem almost incredible and a comparatively slight nexus between the defendant and the crime, independent of the DNA, is likely to suffice to present an overall picture to the jury that satisfies them of the defendant's guilt.

The reality is that, provided there is no reason to doubt either the matching data or the statistical conclusion based upon it, the random occurrence ratio deduced from the DNA evidence, when combined with sufficient additional evidence to give it significance, is highly probative. As the art of analysis progresses, it is likely to become more so, and the stage may be reached when a match will be so comprehensive that it will be possible to construct a DNA profile that is unique and which proves the guilt of the defendant without any other evidence. So far as we are aware that stage has not yet been reached.

The cogency of DNA evidence makes it particularly important that DNA testing is rigorously conducted so as to obviate the risk of error in the laboratory, that the method of DNA analysis and the basis of subsequent statistical calculation should – so far as possible – be transparent to the defence and that the true import of the resultant conclusion is accurately and fairly explained to the jury.

The role of the expert

Mr Alistair Webster QC, on behalf of Doheny, has made the following suggestions as to the procedure which should be followed in relation to DNA evidence:

1. The scientist should adduce the evidence of the DNA comparisons together with his calculations of the random occurrence ratio.
2. Whenever such evidence is to be adduced, the Crown should serve upon the defence details as to how the calculations have been carried out which are sufficient for the defence to scrutinise the basis of the calculations.
3. The Forensic Science Service ('FSS') should make available to a defence expert, if requested, the databases upon which the calculations have been based.

It seems to us that these suggestions are sound, and we would endorse them. We would add that it is important that any issue of expert evidence should be identified and, if possible, resolved before trial and this area should be explored by the court in the pre-trial review.

When the scientist gives evidence it is important that he should not overstep the line which separates his province from that of the jury.

He will properly explain to the jury the nature of the match ('the matching DNA characteristics') between the DNA in the crime stain and the DNA in the blood sample taken from the defendant. He will properly, on the basis of empirical statistical data, give the jury the random occurrence ratio – the frequency with which the matching DNA characteristics are likely to be found in the population at large. Provided that he has the necessary data, and the statistical expertise, it may be appropriate for him then to say how many people with the matching characteristics are likely to be found in the United Kingdom – or perhaps in a more limited relevant sub-group, such as, for instance, the caucasian, sexually active males in the Manchester area.

This will often be the limit of the evidence which he can properly and usefully give. It will then be for the jury to decide, having regard to all the relevant evidence, whether they are sure that it was the defendant who left the crime stain, or whether it is possible that it was left by someone else with the same matching DNA characteristics.

The scientist should not be asked his opinion on the likelihood that it was the defendant who left the crime stain, nor when giving evidence should he use terminology which may lead the jury to believe that he is expressing such an opinion.

It has been suggested that it may be appropriate for the statistician to expound to the jury a statistical approach to evaluating the likelihood that the defendant left the crime stain, using a formula which gives a numerical probability weighting to other pieces of evidence which bear on that question. This approach uses what is known as the Bayes Theorem. In the case of *Adams (Denis)* [1996] 2 Cr App R 467 this Court deprecated this exercise in these terms at p 482:

'To introduce Bayes Theorem, or any similar method, into a criminal trial plunges the jury into inappropriate and unnecessary realms of theory and complexity deflecting them from their proper task.'

We would strongly endorse that comment.

The summing-up

When the judge comes to sum-up, the jury are likely to need careful directions in respect of any issues of expert evidence and guidance to dispel any obfuscation that may have been engendered in relation to areas of expert evidence where no real issue exists. The judge should explain to the jury the relevance of the random occurrence ratio in arriving at their verdict and draw attention to the extraneous evidence which provides the context which gives that ratio its significance, and that which conflicts with the conclusion that the defendant was responsible for the crime stain. In so far as the random occurrence ratio is concerned, a direction along these lines may be appropriate, although any direction must always be tailored to the facts of the particular case:

'Members of the jury, if you accept the scientific evidence called by the Crown, this indicates that there are probably only four or five white males in the United Kingdom from whom that semen stain could have come. The defendant is one of them. If that is the position, the decision you have to reach, on all the evidence, is whether you are sure that it was the defendant who left that stain or whether it is possible that it was one of that other small group of men who share the same DNA characteristics.'

(f) Bayes Theorem

As stated in *Doheny*, the Court of Appeal in the following case was troubled by the fact that evidence of Bayes Theorem had been led before the jury:

Extract 11.1.14

R v Adams [1996] 2 Cr App R 467, 468, 470–7, 480–2 (CA)

ROSE LJ: On January 24, 1995, at the Central Criminal Court before His Honour Judge Gordon, this appellant was convicted of rape and was sentenced to seven years' imprisonment. He appeals against that conviction by leave of the single judge.

The victim of the offence was a Miss Marley who was walking home after an evening out on April 6, 1991. Her attacker was a stranger. He approached and asked her the time. She saw his face for a matter of seconds before looking at her watch. He raped her from behind. She reported the attack to the police and a DNA profile was obtained from semen on a high vaginal swab. In October 1993 she attended an identification parade but did not pick out the appellant or anyone else. At committal proceedings she said the appellant did not look like the man who had attacked her. The appellant was 37 and the complainant said at one stage in her evidence that he looked 40 to 42. The description which she had given was of a white, clean shaven, man with a local accent aged 20 to 25. The prosecution case rested entirely upon expert evidence in relation to the DNA sample which was challenged by the defence. In evidence, the defendant gave an alibi for the night of the attack which he said he had spent with his girlfriend who also gave evidence before the jury.

. . .

Doctor Harris for the Crown said that DNA profiles from the appellant and the crime's scene sample were compared and a visual match within one per cent declared. Computer calculation indicated that the chance of a randomly chosen unrelated man matching the DNA profile was one in 297 m rounded down in the interests of 'conservatism' to 200,000,000. That calculation was based on nine bands of DNA identified in the profile. Professor Donnelly for the defence gave evidence, by agreement, before the prosecution case was closed. He said it was logical and consistent for the jury to deal with the rest of the evidence in the case in statistical terms and for the jury to do this using the Bayes Theorem. He identified four types of evidence which could be evaluated in this way, namely the probability that the offence was committed by a local man (which the appellant was), the non identification evidence, the appellant's evidence and the alibi evidence. The Crown accepted that the Bayes Theorem was a valid method for looking at non-statistical matters in statistical terms and the judge directed the jury in relation to the Bayes Theorem in terms to which we shall shortly return. . . . The jury convicted unanimously after a retirement of some five hours.

. . .

The material part of Professor Donnelly's evidence-in-chief starts at Vol 2, pp 32D to 33C:

'Q. Now is it possible for the jury in this case to approach the evidence along statistical lines?

A. You mean the entirety of the evidence, or the DNA portions of it?

Q. The DNA evidence has been reduced to statistical estimates, so that we have got to deal with that, that is how it is expressed. Can they attempt if they want to do so, subject to the directions they will be given by the judge in due course, can they attempt to deal with the whole of this case in statistical terms?

A. That is possible, yes.

Q. Is it a logically sound approach?

A. It is and in fact more than that is true, it is the only logically sound and consistent approach to considering situations such as this.

Q. In your view is it, or may it be, a practical proposition for them to attempt that exercise?

A. I think it is practical, yes.

Q. So far as you are concerned if it is the only logical approach is that the approach, so far as you are qualified to do so, you would recommend them to take?

A.   I think my position would be that if one wanted to be logical and consistent there is no choice but to do it in the way that is recognised for these situations.

Q.   What does that involve by way of mathematical or statistical theory?

A.   There is a theory called Bayes Theorem, that is the name given to it, which explains how one should use different pieces of evidence – the DNA evidence is one example, there may be other pieces of evidence – to change one's assessment in the light of uncertainty.

Q.   If the jury wanted to work through to such a position, could they do it simply?

A.   I think relatively simply, yes.

Q.   How many questions would they have to ask themselves in relation to each piece of non-DNA evidence in the case?

A.   Broadly for each piece of similar type of evidence they have to ask two questions.

Q.   We have identified the following areas of evidence in the case. The probability that it was a local man who committed the offence: point number one. The non-identification evidence of the victim: point number two. The evidence of the defendant in due course himself: point number three. And the alibi evidence to be called on his behalf is point number four. Those are the four areas of evidence. Does it follow they would have eight questions?

A.   Effectively yes, maybe only seven because the first one is a starting point . . .'

At p 34 the evidence continued:

'Q.   So they would have seven questions, seven answers, and they could then be told how to deal with those answers?

A.   Yes.

Q.   And carry them forward to whatever their view was of the statistical estimate that was appropriate to apply in the context of the DNA evidence itself?

A.   Yes.

Q.   That would be logically consistent?

A.   Yes, in fact as I said that is the only logically consistent way.

Q.   The alternative is what, that they try in some way to balance non-statistical evidence against statistical evidence? Is there any formula, a simple formula that can be applied to that, or not?

A.   It is clear as I understand it that the problem in a case such as this is to compare the evidence which is not obviously statistical with the evidence that is statistical. There is one recognised and accepted way of doing that which avoids being inconsistent. I do not know of others, well, more than that is true, it has been shown that there is exactly one way of doing it that avoids inconsistency. Of course people reach decisions in the presence of uncertainty by other methods.

Q.   Without reference to any statistics at all?

A.   Yes.

Q.   But there is no formula that can combine the two if one remains in numerical quantities and the other remains in general expressions of evidence?

A.   That is right.

Q.   May we attempt to suggest the workings of this method hypothet-
ically for the jurors' later consideration, subject to the direction they
receive?

A.   I am happy to try and help.

Q.   Let us take our starting question, and if any member of the jury wish
to take it down this might be an appropriate moment for them to do it.
What is the starting question, question number one that you would pose
if you were approaching this on the Bayes Theorem basis?

A.   The first thing that I think one should ask is what is the chance,
having heard nothing about this particular case, what is the chance that
the real attacker, the rapist, comes from within the local area?

Q.   Have you got a figure, a working figure for us of the area we are
concerned with in this case of eligible men between the age of 15 and 60.

A.   Yes, my understanding from Hertfordshire County Council is that in
an area within 15 kilometres, that is their definition, that is about 10 miles,
of Hemel Hempstead there are just over 150,000, I think 153,000 men
between the age of 18 and 60.

Judge Gordon: That comes from some form of census, does it?

A.   I think so, my Lord, yes. That local area does not include either
Luton, which is to the north of the area where the offence occurred, or
London, which is to the south. In asking about the chance it is a local man
local would mean not including Luton or London or any of the other areas
outside that range of 15 kilometres or possibly just outside, from London,
or possibly a long way away.

Mr Thwaites: Would we as statisticians round that figure down to 150,000
for convenience of doing the sum, or does it not matter?

A.   I do not think the difference between 150,000 and 153,000 is going
to be significant.

Q.   So we have got that figure, do we now have to nominate the probability of it being a local man?

A.   One does, yes.

Q.   If I suggested it was a 75 per cent chance of being a local man.

Judge Gordon: That is the decision that the jury are going to have to
make, is it not?

A.   Absolutely.

Q.   This is an illustration.

Mr Thwaites: It is only for illustrative purposes, unless we have a probability we cannot make sense of it.

Judge Gordon: No, I follow that, but the jury are to put a question mark
if they are writing down.

Mr Thwaites: Oh, yes, they do not nominate my figures because they
are picked out of the air.

Judge Gordon: You are just showing us what happens on certain figures?

Mr Thwaites: Yes. Mr Lambert, I think, suggested 50 per cent. I pick the
figure 75 per cent.

Judge Gordon: 75 per cent chance that it is a local man?

Mr Thwaites: Yes. How do we translate that into our 153,000 to give us
a figure to carry forward to the next part of the sum?

A. Let me tell you the mechanics and then explain the rationale. The mechanics are that if one thought it was 75 per cent, 75 per cent is 75 over 100, you take the 150,000 and you multiply by what we call the inverse, you multiply 150,000 by 100 over 75. The effect of that would be to increase it by about a third. The reason for that is that the rationale is that if we were certain it was a local man and there are 153,000 relevant local men, the fact that it is a particular one, Mr Adams, we would assess as one over 150,000. If we are not certain it is a local man our assessment for a particular local man will be decreased a bit. The way that changes is that you take your 150,000 which are the odds, 150,000 to one are the odds on innocence, and you increase that by 100 divided by the percentage, 75 per cent. In this case, I think it was his Lordship yesterday took 50 per cent for the local man as a working example that would double the figure of 150,000 to 300,000, as Mr Lambert said.

Q. So when we have got this figure 150,000 times 100 over 75, do we do that little sum now or do we leave it until later?

A. Either is fine.

Q. Well, let us do it now and carry it forward?

A. May I use a calculator?

Judge Gordon: I do not mind you using a calculator.

A. That gives us 200,000.

Q. You take 150,000 as being the 75 per cent?

A. Exactly.

Q. So you then add another 25 per cent on to bring it up to 100?

A. You probably add a third on.

Q. Yes, 25 per cent is a third of 75.

A. Yes.

Mr Thwaites: So, what are we left with after this part of the calculation? How do we express what we have got?

A. We have now changed to a situation where our odds on a particular local man, Mr Adams is the one of interest, but a particular local man being the true rapist is 200,000 to one now.

Q. Is that the same as one in 200,000.

A. One way of putting it is to say that the odds are 200,000 to one, another way which is virtually identical is to say that the chance is one in 200,000.'

The witness then dealt with the non identification evidence at 37G to 38G:

'Q. You are saying if he was innocent what is the chance that he would not match her description?

Judge Gordon: Is this in percentage terms or in any way you like?

A. It is probably easiest to express probabilities as percentages, my Lord, with zero per cent representing completely impossible and 100 per cent representing absolutely certain, and 50 per cent is even odds, it is the chance of getting a head if we toss a fair coin, for example. That is the scale on which one should think about probability.

Mr Thwaites: What is the chance that if he is innocent he would not match the description I might put that at 90 per cent?

A. Very well.

Judge Gordon: Again I make clear this is a jury question. Can we just indicate each time which are the jury questions?

Mr Thwaites: Whenever I give a figure that is a matter for them to decide, that simple rule of thumb, my figures are only hypothetical. That is the first part of question. What is the second part?

A. The second question sounds similar, it is what is the chance of that evidence if in fact Mr Adams is guilty.

Q. You mean that he would not match the description?

A. Yes, if Mr Adams were the true rapist the question the jury must ask is what is the chance that the victim would say his description is different from Mr Adams, that the victim would identify someone and then soon afterwards not identify Mr Adams and make the statement at the Magistrates' Court.

Q. I would take the other percentage, my figure again, a matter for the jury, and I would say that there is only a 10 per cent chance of that.

A. Very well.

Q. So you have got those two figures?

A. I have, yes.

Q. How do we deal with them because this is the first time we have dealt with the double figure, in the first point we did not have that?

A. What matters is the ratio of those two figures. What matters is how much more likely one thinks the evidence is if Mr Adams is guilty than if he is innocent, or how much less likely? In this case if we put it that way round if we put the probability of the evidence given guilt on the top line, we have 10 per cent on the top line the hypothetical figure that has been suggested, and on the bottom line we have the probability of the evidence given innocence of 90 per cent, so 10 over 90 which is one over 9. We multiply that number, 1/9th, by our starting figure of one on 200,000.

Q. If we could do the sum what answer would we get?

A. I think we would get, being brave without a calculator, one in 1.8 m.

Q. Is that the same as we had in the first question, does that represent the chance that Adams is guilty?

A. Yes.'

The witness then dealt with the evidence of the defendant himself which Professor Donnelly assessed at 50 per cent, *ie* neutral. He was then asked to deal with the alibi evidence at just below 40D to 41C:

'Mr Thwaites: . . . What is the question. What is the chance that he would have an alibi if he was guilty?

A. More specifically what is the chance that whichever witness gives the alibi evidence would give that kind of evidence.

Q. If he were guilty?

A. Yes, if he were guilty. How likely is whatever evidence on the alibi the jury hear if he is guilty: that is the first question. The second question is how likely is that sort of evidence if he is innocent?

Q. So let us just nominate the figure of 1 in 4, 25 per cent in answer to the first question. And what is the chance that he would have an alibi if innocent let us say 50 per cent. I am giving him a greater, on my figures, I am giving him a greater probability of him having an alibi if he is an innocent man.

A. Yes, in fact your figures of 25 per cent and 50 per cent are saying that you think that particular alibi, or that sort of alibi evidence is twice as likely if he is innocent than if he is guilty. That piece of evidence you are saying points in favour of his innocence, you are saying is twice as likely if he is innocent than if he is guilty.

Q. Doing our little equation again we are going to put 25 over 50.

A. And get half.

Q. And we are going to multiply that by 1.8 m on the assumption . . .

Judge Gordon: Is that not twice as likely, I think we have done the mathematics, have we not?

Mr Thwaites: Some of us have, others may be slower. What is the figure that we come to?

A. We take the figure we had before this piece of evidence, which is one on 1,800,000, and we multiply it by one on 2, or 25 per cent on 50 per cent in your example, and the effect will be to change the one on 1,800,000, his Lordship will check my arithmetic, to one on 3,600,000.

Q. So on this entirely hypothetical basis we have got the figure of the probability of Adams being guilty from the non-DNA evidence as one in 3.6 m. I have done all the sums which the jury would do.

A. Yes, nothing hypothetical about the questions, they are the questions that need to be asked but the numbers to be put in to the formula are the jury's assessment and not mine.'

He then dealt at 42C with the DNA evidence:

'A. . . . Now the one in 200,000,000 is the chance of the DNA evidence, you will hear that I disagree with that figure, but if we accept that figure for the moment numerically, that is claimed to be the chance of the DNA evidence if Mr Adams is innocent. So we still ask the same two questions about the DNA. What is the chance of the DNA evidence if he is guilty? That is usually assumed that that is certain and I would not quarrel with that in this case. We ask the two questions and we have 100 per cent on the top line as the chance of the DNA evidence if he is guilty and accepting for the moment the figure we would have one on 200,000,000 on the bottom line. Now that ratio of effectively one divided by one divided by 200,000,000 gives you 200,000,000. So we do the same thing as before, we take our odds of one in 3,600,000 and we multiply them by the relevant figure for the DNA, which for the moment we will take to be 200,000,000. So we have one on 3,600,000 multiplied by 200,000,000 and we get about my calculation tells me about 55.

Q. What is that 55,000,000?

A. No, it is saying that the odds, it is much easier I think to think in terms of odds, the odds of him being guilty before the DNA evidence were one to 3,600,000. The DNA evidence has changed those and it is now 55 to one, on these figures, in favour of his guilt. So the final position we arrived at with this hypothetical scenario is to a view that he is 55 times more likely to be guilty than innocent.

Q. If the DNA figure in the jury view were to be reduced to 20,000,000 or 2,000,000 do we do a simple factoring exercise or do we have to do a different exercise to find out the percentage possibility?

A. Taking that figure of 55 we have got to just do a factoring exercise. So if the DNA number changed from 200,000,000 to 20,000,000 the 55 to one that he is guilty would change to 5 to one.

Q. And the 2,000,000?

A. To 2,000,000 it would change to being just under two times more likely that he is innocent than guilty. So when the DNA number is 200,000,000 we think, accepting the rest of the hypothesis, we would think that the chance that he is guilty is 55 to one. If the DNA evidence were 20,000,000 we would think the chance he was guilty was about five-and-a-half to one. If the DNA figure were about 2,000,000 we think that the chance of him being guilty is about one to two he is almost twice as likely to be innocent than guilty on that assessment.

Q. So the jury can see on a statistical analysis the crucial importance of trying to determine the correct starting figure for the DNA?

A. Yes, on that hypothetical assessment of the other evidence the changes of the sort you have suggested would actually make a big difference to the final outcome.'

. . .

It seems to us that the difficulties which arise in the present case stem from the fact that, at trial, the defence were permitted to lead before the jury evidence of the Bayes Theorem. No objection was taken by the prosecution. No argument on this point has been addressed to this Court. It would therefore be inappropriate for us to express a concluded view on the matter. But we have very grave doubt as to whether that evidence was properly admissible, because it trespasses on an area peculiarly and exclusively within the province of the jury, namely the way in which they evaluate the relationship between one piece of evidence and another. The Bayes Theorem may be an appropriate and useful tool for statisticians and other experts seeking to establish a mathematical assessment of probability. Even then, however, as the extracts from Professor Donnelly's evidence cited above demonstrate, the theorem can only operate by giving to each separate piece of evidence a numerical percentage representing the ratio between probability of circumstance A and the probability of circumstance B granted the existence of that evidence. The percentages chosen are matters of judgment: that is inevitable. But the apparently objective numerical figures used in the theorem may conceal the element of judgment on which it entirely depends. More importantly for present purposes, however, whatever the merits or demerits of the Bayes Theorem in mathematical or statistical assessments of probability, it seems to us that it is not appropriate for use in jury trials, or as a means to assist the jury in their task. In the first place, the theorem's methodology requires, as we have described, that items of evidence be assessed separately according to their bearing on the accused's guilt, before being combined in the overall formula. That in our view is far too rigid an approach to evidence of the type that a jury characteristically has to assess, where the cogency of (for instance) identification evidence may have to be assessed, at least in part, in the light of the strength of the chain of evidence in which it forms part. More fundamentally, however, the attempt to determine guilt or innocence on the basis of a mathematical formula, applied to each separate piece of evidence, is simply inappropriate to the jury's task. Jurors evaluate evidence and reach a conclusion

not by means of a formula, mathematical or otherwise, but by the joint application of their individual common sense and knowledge of the world to the
evidence before them. It is common for them to have to evaluate scientific
evidence, both as to its quality and as to its relationship with other evidence. Scientific evidence tendered as proof of a particular fact may establish
that fact to an extent which, in any particular case, may vary between slight
possibility and virtual certainty. For example, different blood spots on an accused's clothing may, on testing, reveal a range of conclusions from 'human
blood' via 'possibly the victim's blood' to 'highly likely to be the victim's blood'.
Such evidence is susceptible to challenge as to methodology and otherwise,
which may weaken or even, in some cases, strengthen the impact of the
evidence. But we have never heard it suggested that a jury should consider
the relationship between such scientific evidence and other evidence by
reference to probability formulas. That such a course would in any event be
impossible of sensible achievement by a jury, at least so far as the use of the
Bayes Theorem is concerned, is demonstrated by the practical application of
the stage of that theorem's methodology that involves numerical assessment
of the various items of evidence. Individual jurors might differ greatly not only
according to how cogent they found a particular piece of evidence (which
would be a matter for discussion and debate between the jury as a whole),
but also on the question of what percentage figure for probability should be
placed on that evidence. Since, as we have pointed out, the translation of
an assessment of cogency into a percentage probability of guilt is entirely a
matter of judgment and the conferring of a percentage probability of guilt upon
one item of evidence taken in isolation is an essentially artificial operation,
different jurors might well wish to select different numerical figures even when
they were broadly agreed on the weight of the evidence in question. They
could, presumably, only resolve any such difference by taking an average,
which would truly reflect neither party's view; and this point leaves aside the
even greater difficulty of how 12 jurors, applying Bayes as a single jury, are
to reconcile, under the mathematics of that formula, differing individual views
about the cogency of particular pieces of evidence. Quite apart from these
general objections, as the present case graphically demonstrates, to introduce
Bayes Theorem, or any similar method, into a criminal trial plunges the jury
into inappropriate and unnecessary realms of theory and complexity deflecting
them from their proper task.

It is these considerations which lead us to the provisional conclusion, un-
informed, as we have indicated, by argument, that evidence about the Bayes
Theorem ought not to have been admitted, without objection. The judge was
led into error in that, no doubt, he felt obliged to seek to sum up the evidence
to the jury.

That being so, it was, as it seems to us, incumbent upon him to direct the
jury both as to the substance of that evidence and as to the way in which it
was open to them to use that evidence. It seems to us that, in a summing-
up which was otherwise impeccable, he failed in these respects. Because of
his conscientious desire to try to ensure that the jury grasped what was, it
has to be remembered, the defence argument based on Bayes Theorem, he
concentrated his directions on that theorem, without indicating to the jury the
more commonsense and basic ways in which it would have been open to

them to weigh up the relative weight of the DNA evidence. The jury were not properly directed as to the meaning and implications for the prosecution case of an approach based on Bayes. If, as seems entirely possible, the jury abandoned the struggle to understand and apply Bayes, they were left by the summing-up with no other sufficient guidance as to how to evaluate the prosecution case (based as it was entirely on the DNA evidence), in the light of the other non-DNA evidence in the case. This means that their verdict cannot be regarded as safe.

Accordingly this appeal must be allowed and the conviction quashed.

The court ordered a retrial.

Adams may be compared with the classic Californian case of *People v Collins*.[28] As the opening paragraph of its judgment indicates, the Supreme Court of California was less dismissive than the English Court of Appeal of the concept of evidence of mathematical probability, but found on the facts of the case that such evidence had been improperly introduced. The opening paragraph reads as follows:

> We deal here with the novel question whether evidence of mathematical probability has been properly introduced and used by the prosecution in a criminal case. While we discern no inherent incompatibility between the disciplines of law and mathematics and intend no general disapproval or disparagement of the latter as an auxiliary in the fact-finding processes of the former, we cannot uphold the technique employed in the instant case. As we explain in detail *infra*, the testimony as to mathematical probability infected the case with fatal error and distorted the jury's traditional role of determining guilt or innocence according to long-settled rules. Mathematics, a veritable sorcerer in our computerized society, while assisting the trier of fact in the search for truth, must not cast a spell over him. We conclude that on the record before us defendant should not have had his guilt determined by the odds and that he is entitled to a new trial. We reverse the judgment.

The case concerned a robbery in an alley. The victim saw a young blond woman running from the scene. Another witness saw a blond woman with a ponytail run out of the alley and enter a yellow automobile driven by a black man wearing a moustache and beard. Janet and Malcolm Collins were arrested for the crime. They owned a yellow automobile with an off-white top. Janet had blond hair worn in a ponytail. Malcolm was a black man who at the time of his arrest had a moustache but no beard. The prosecutor called as a witness a mathematics instructor at a state college. This witness testified, in effect, to the 'product rule', which states that the probability that a number of mutually independent events will occur *together* is equal to the product of the individual probabilities that *each* of the events will occur. The prosecutor then asked the witness to assume that the following individual probabilities were applicable to the characteristics in question:

[28] 438 P 2d 33 (1968).

Characteristic	Individual Probability
A. Partially yellow automobile	1/10
B. Man with moustache	1/4
C. Woman with ponytail	1/10
D. Woman with blond hair	1/3
E. Black man with beard	1/10
F. Interracial couple in car	1/1000

The witness testified that, based on these figures, there was one chance in 12 million that any random couple would possess the distinctive characteristics of the defendants.

The difficulties with this evidence which were identified by the Californian Supreme Court included the following:

(1) '. . . the prosecution produced no evidence whatsoever showing, or from which it could be in any way inferred, that only one out of every ten cars which might have been at the scene of the robbery was partly yellow, that only one out of every four men who might have been there wore a mustache, that only one out of every ten girls who might have been there wore a ponytail, or that any of the other individual probability factors listed were even roughly accurate.'[29]

(2) No proof was presented that the characteristics in question were mutually independent, even though this was a prerequisite to the proper application of the 'product rule'. It is possible, for example, that most black men with beards (characteristic E) *also* have moustaches (characteristic B).[30]

(3) 'Confronted with an equation which purports to yield a numerical index of probable guilt, few juries could resist the temptation to accord disproportionate weight to that index; only an exceptional juror, and indeed only a defense attorney schooled in mathematics, could successfully keep in mind the fact that the probability computed by the prosecution can represent, *at best*, the likelihood that a random couple would share the characteristics testified to by the People's witnesses – *not necessarily the characteristics of the actually guilty couple.*'[31]

(4) Even if it could legitimately be accepted that there was one chance in 12 million of a *random* couple possessing the relevant characteristics of the guilty couple, this provided no assistance on the issue of whether the defendants were probably *the* guilty couple.[32]

In view of these considerations, therefore, the court thought

that under the circumstances the 'trial by mathematics' so distorted the role of the jury and so disadvantaged counsel for the defense, as to constitute in itself a

---

[29] At 38.
[30] At 39.
[31] At 40 (emphasis in original).
[32] Ibid.

miscarriage of justice. After an examination of the entire cause, including the evidence, we are of the opinion that it is reasonably probable that a result more favorable to defendant would have been reached in the absence of the above error. . . . The judgment against defendant must therefore be reversed.[33]

See also A Stein, 'Judicial Fact-Finding and the Bayesian Method: The Case for Deeper Scepticism about their Combination' (1996) 1 *International Journal of Evidence and Proof* 25.

(g) Further illustrations

Further illustrations of the general approach of the English courts are provided by a number of cases decided in recent years. In *R v Inch*[34] the defendant was accused of wounding the victim by striking him with a martial arts instrument. His defence was that the wound was caused when the victim head-butted him. At issue was the admissibility in evidence of the opinion of a medical orderly, who had attended the victim, that the wound, because of its depth and shape, had been caused by a blow from an instrument rather than by a collision of heads. The Courts-Martial Appeal Court held that this evidence was inadmissible: any evidence about the nature of the wound ought to have been given by someone qualified to express a professional opinion. In *R v Robb*, a case concerning voice identification, the Court of Appeal held that the evidence of an expert was admissible even though the auditory technique employed by him to identify the defendant's voice was not supplemented by acoustic analysis:

> We do not doubt that his judgment, based on close attention to voice quality, voice pitch and the pronunciation of vowels and consonants, would have a value significantly greater than that of the ordinary untutored layman, as the judgment of a hand-writing expert is superior to that of the man in the street. Dr Baldwin's reliance on the auditory technique must, on the evidence, be regarded as representing a minority view in his profession but he had reasons for his preference and on the facts of this case at least he was not shown to be wrong.[35]

At issue in *R v Theodosi*[36] was the following opinion of a police officer who had attended an accident scene and carried out an investigation involving the observation of markings in the road and various measurements. The officer in question was qualified at an advanced level in the investigation and reconstruction of road accidents, and the interpretation of evidence found at the scenes of such accidents.

> The onus for this accident lies wholly with Mr Theodosi, the driver of the Peugeot. We have a scenario of three young men, two of whom were driving very powerful

---

[33] At 41–2.
[34] (1989) 91 Cr App R 51.
[35] (1991) 93 Cr App R 161, 166.
[36] [1993] RTR 179.

cars. Mr Theodosi, who was the last vehicle of the three, may have allowed himself to be drawn into a manoeuvre beyond his limited driving experience in that he had to keep up with his friends, or he may have wanted to show off to the passengers that he had in his vehicle. Either way Mr Theodosi's actions in overtaking two other vehicles at a speed in the region of twice the legal speed limit for the road, amounts in my opinion to nothing less than a wanton act putting himself and others at risk.

The Court of Appeal held that, because 'the reference by the officer to peer groups was wholly outside his expertise', and because to admit the evidence would be to usurp the function of the jury, the opinion evidence in question was inadmissible.[37] This may be compared with the earlier decision of the Court of Appeal in *R v Oakley*,[38] where it was held that a police constable who had 15 years' experience in the traffic division, and had passed a qualifying examination as an accident investigator, had been rightly permitted to give expert opinion evidence on how a road accident had occurred.

What of evidence of 'facial mapping'?

Extract 11.1.15

R v Stockwell (1993) 97 Cr App R 260, 263–4 (CA)

THE LORD CHIEF JUSTICE: The prosecution sought before the learned judge to call a Mr Neave to assist the jury to determine whether the man shown on the security photographs at both scenes of crime was the appellant....

...

... Where, for example, there is a clear photograph and no suggestion that the subject has changed his appearance, a jury could usually reach a conclusion without help. Where, as here, however, it is admitted that the appellant had grown a beard shortly before his arrest, and it is suggested further that the robber may have been wearing clear spectacles and a wig for disguise, a comparison of photograph and defendant may not be straightforward. In such circumstances we can see no reason why expert evidence, if it can provide the jury with information and assistance they would otherwise lack, should not be given.

In the following case, the issue of evidence of 'video superimposition mapping' was considered:

Extract 11.1.16

R v Clarke [1995] 2 Cr App R 425, 428, 431 (CA)

STEYN LJ: ... there was evidence of video superimposition mapping ... Photographs from the scene in the bank were transferred to high quality video tape. The same was done with police identification photos of the appellant.

---

[37] At 184.
[38] (1979) 70 Cr App R 7.

Each was blown-up to about the same size. The machine was set to display both the head of the robber and the head of the suspect in exactly the same position on the television screen. Dr Vanezis then wiped a line up and down the screen: above the line was the appellant's face, below it was the face of the robber. As the line moved up and down so more of the one face and less of the other would be seen. Then the process was repeated but with a vertical line from side to side. Having compared the two photographs in this way, Dr Vanezis concluded that the appellant and the robber were the same man. . . .
. . .
. . . This is clearly a case like *Stockwell* where the comparison was not an entirely straightforward one. The process of enhancement that was used here enabled the jury to appreciate the similarity in configuration. As Mantell J observed, there was similarity of configuration between the ears, and the same point could be made in respect of the eyebrows. It is, therefore, not right to say that expert evidence could not have played a useful role here in assisting the jury in connection with the issue of identity.

In each of the above cases, do you consider the issue of necessity or that of reliability to have been the critical issue in the context of the particular case? Or are the two issues often so inextricably linked that there is little to be gained from attempting to separate them for analysis?

See also *R v Meads*[39] on expert evidence as to handwriting.

(h) Other jurisdictions

Extensive consideration was given to the issue of expert evidence in the landmark 1993 decision of the US Supreme Court in the following case, which contains valuable guidance as to the sorts of considerations which may be taken into account in determining admissibility.

Extract 11.1.17

Daubert v Merrell Dow Pharmaceuticals, Inc 113 S Ct 2786, 2792–9 (1993) (US Supreme Court)

BLACKMUN J: In the 70 years since its formulation in [*Frye v US* 54 App DC 46, 293 F 1013 (1923)], the 'general acceptance' test has been the dominant standard for determining the admissibility of novel scientific evidence at trial. . . .
The *Frye* test has its origin in a short and citation-free 1923 decision . . . In what has become a famous (perhaps infamous) passage, the then Court of Appeals for the District of Columbia . . . declared:

'Just when a scientific principle or discovery crosses the line between the experimental and demonstrable stages is difficult to define. Somewhere in

---

[39] [1996] Crim LR 519.

this twilight zone the evidential force of the principle must be recognized, and while courts will go a long way in admitting expert testimony deduced from a well-recognized scientific principle or discovery, *the thing from which the deduction is made must be sufficiently established to have gained general acceptance in the particular field in which it belongs.*' 54 App DC, at 47, 293 F, at 1014 (emphasis added).

. . .

. . . Petitioners' primary attack . . . is not on the content but on the continuing authority of the rule. They contend that the *Frye* test was superseded by the adoption of the Federal Rules of Evidence. We agree.

. . .

Here there is a specific Rule that speaks to the contested issue. Rule 702, governing expert testimony, provides:

> 'If scientific, technical, or other specialized knowledge will assist the trier of fact to understand the evidence or to determine a fact in issue, a witness qualified as an expert by knowledge, skill, experience, training, or education, may testify thereto in the form of an opinion or otherwise.'

Nothing in the text of this Rule establishes 'general acceptance' as an absolute prerequisite to admissibility. Nor does respondent present any clear indication that Rule 702 or the Rules as a whole were intended to incorporate a 'general acceptance' standard. . . . Given the Rules' permissive backdrop and their inclusion of a specific rule on expert testimony that does not mention 'general acceptance,' the assertion that the Rules somehow assimilated *Frye* is unconvincing. *Frye* made 'general acceptance' the exclusive test for admitting expert scientific testimony. That austere standard, absent from and incompatible with the Federal Rules of Evidence, should not be applied in federal trials.

That the *Frye* test was displaced by the Rules of Evidence does not mean, however, that the Rules themselves place no limits on the admissibility of purportedly scientific evidence. Nor is the trial judge disabled from screening such evidence. To the contrary, under the Rules the trial judge must ensure that any and all scientific testimony or evidence admitted is not only relevant, but reliable.

The primary focus of this obligation is Rule 702, which clearly contemplates some degree of regulation of the subjects and theories about which an expert may testify. '*If scientific*, technical, or other specialized *knowledge will assist the trier of fact* to understand the evidence or to determine a fact in issue' an expert 'may testify *thereto.*' The subject of an expert's testimony must be 'scientific . . . knowledge.' The adjective 'scientific' implies a grounding in the methods and procedures of science. Similarly, the word 'knowledge' connotes more than subjective belief or unsupported speculation. . . . Of course, it would be unreasonable to conclude that the subject of scientific testimony must be 'known' to a certainty; arguably, there are no certainties in science. . . . But, in order to qualify as 'scientific knowledge,' an inference or assertion must be derived by the scientific method. Proposed testimony must be supported by appropriate validation – *ie*, 'good grounds,' based on what is known. In short, the requirement that an expert's testimony pertain to 'scientific knowledge' establishes a standard of evidentiary reliability.

Rule 702 further requires that the evidence or testimony 'assist the trier of fact to understand the evidence or to determine a fact in issue.' This condition goes primarily to relevance. . . . The consideration has been aptly described . . . as one of 'fit.' . . . 'Fit' is not always obvious, and scientific validity for one purpose is not necessarily scientific validity for other, unrelated purposes. . . . The study of the phases of the moon, for example, may provide valid scientific 'knowledge' about whether a certain night was dark, and if darkness is a fact in issue, the knowledge will assist the trier of fact. However (absent creditable grounds supporting such a link), evidence that the moon was full on a certain night will not assist the trier of fact in determining whether an individual was unusually likely to have behaved irrationally on that night. Rule 702's 'helpfulness' standard requires a valid scientific connection to the pertinent inquiry as a precondition to admissibility.

That these requirements are embodied in Rule 702 is not surprising. Unlike an ordinary witness, see Rule 701, an expert is permitted wide latitude to offer opinions, including those that are not based on first-hand knowledge or observation. See Rules 702 and 703. Presumably, this relaxation of the usual requirement of first-hand knowledge . . . is premised on an assumption that the expert's opinion will have a reliable basis in the knowledge and experience of his discipline.

Faced with a proffer of expert scientific testimony, then, the trial judge must determine at the outset, pursuant to Rule 104(a), whether the expert is proposing to testify to (1) scientific knowledge that (2) will assist the trier of fact to understand or determine a fact in issue. This entails a preliminary assessment of whether the reasoning or methodology underlying the testimony is scientifically valid and of whether that reasoning or methodology properly can be applied to the facts in issue. We are confident that federal judges possess the capacity to undertake this review. Many factors will bear on the inquiry, and we do not presume to set out a definitive checklist or test. But some general observations are appropriate.

Ordinarily, a key question to be answered in determining whether a theory or technique is scientific knowledge that will assist the trier of fact will be whether it can be (and has been) tested. . . .

Another pertinent consideration is whether the theory or technique has been subjected to peer review and publication. Publication (which is but one element of peer review) is not a *sine qua non* of admissibility; it does not necessarily correlate with reliability, . . . and in some instances well-grounded but innovative theories will not have been published . . . Some propositions, moreover, are too particular, too new, or of too limited interest to be published. But submission to the scrutiny of the scientific community is a component of 'good science,' in part because it increases the likelihood that substantive flaws in methodology will be detected. . . . The fact of publication (or lack thereof) in a peer-reviewed journal thus will be a relevant, though not dispositive, consideration in assessing the scientific validity of a particular technique or methodology on which an opinion is premised.

Additionally, in the case of a particular scientific technique, the court ordinarily should consider the known or potential rate of error, . . . and the existence and maintenance of standards controlling the technique's operation. . . .

Finally, 'general acceptance' can yet have a bearing on the inquiry. . . . Widespread acceptance can be an important factor in ruling particular evidence admissible . . .

The inquiry envisioned by Rule 702 is, we emphasize, a flexible one. Its overarching subject is the scientific validity – and thus the evidentiary relevance and reliability – of the principles that underlie a proposed submission. The focus, of course, must be solely on principles and methodology, not on the conclusions that they generate.

Throughout, a judge assessing a proffer of expert scientific testimony under Rule 702 should also be mindful of other applicable rules. Rule 703 provides that expert opinions based on otherwise inadmissible hearsay are to be admitted only if the facts or data are 'of a type reasonably relied upon by experts in the particular field in forming opinions or inferences upon the subject.' Rule 706 allows the court at its discretion to procure the assistance of an expert of its own choosing. Finally, Rule 403 permits the exclusion of relevant evidence 'if its probative value is substantially outweighed by the danger of unfair prejudice, confusion of the issues, or misleading the jury. . . .' . . .

We conclude by briefly addressing what appear to be two underlying concerns of the parties and *amici* in this case. Respondent expresses apprehension that abandonment of 'general acceptance' as the exclusive requirement for admission will result in a 'free-for-all' in which befuddled juries are confounded by absurd and irrational pseudoscientific assertions. In this regard respondent seems to us to be overly pessimistic about the capabilities of the jury, and of the adversary system generally. Vigorous cross-examination, presentation of contrary evidence, and careful instruction on the burden of proof are the traditional and appropriate means of attacking shaky but admissible evidence. . . . Additionally, in the event the trial court concludes that the scintilla of evidence presented supporting a position is insufficient to allow a reasonable juror to conclude that the position more likely than not is true, the court remains free to direct a judgment, Fed Rule Civ Proc 50(a), and likewise to grant summary judgment . . . These conventional devices, rather than wholesale exclusion under an uncompromising 'general acceptance' test, are the appropriate safeguards where the basis of scientific testimony meets the standards of Rule 702.

Petitioners and, to a greater extent, their *amici* exhibit a different concern. They suggest that recognition of a screening role for the judge that allows for the exclusion of 'invalid' evidence will sanction a stifling and repressive scientific orthodoxy and will be inimical to the search for truth. . . . It is true that open debate is an essential part of both legal and scientific analyses. Yet there are important differences between the quest for truth in the courtroom and the quest for truth in the laboratory. Scientific conclusions are subject to perpetual revision. Law, on the other hand, must resolve disputes finally and quickly. The scientific project is advanced by broad and wide-ranging consideration of a multitude of hypotheses, for those that are incorrect will eventually be shown to be so, and that in itself is an advance. Conjectures that are probably wrong are of little use, however, in the project of reaching a quick, final, and binding legal judgment – often of great consequence – about a particular set of events in the past. We recognize that in practice, a gatekeeping role for the judge, no matter how flexible, inevitably on occasion will prevent the jury from learning of authentic insights and innovations. That, nevertheless, is the balance that is struck by Rules of Evidence designed not for the exhaustive search for cosmic understanding but for the particularized resolution of legal disputes.

To summarize: 'general acceptance' is not a necessary precondition to the admissibility of scientific evidence under the Federal Rules of Evidence, but the Rules of Evidence – especially Rule 702 – do assign to the trial judge the task of ensuring that an expert's testimony both rests on a reliable foundation and is relevant to the task at hand. Pertinent evidence based on scientifically valid principles will satisfy those demands.

Does the following synthesis of the approach taken recently in Australian cases provide a sound and useful rationalisation of this area of the law, incorporating both the necessity and reliability aspects?

Extract 11.1.18

S J Odgers and J T Richardson, 'Keeping Bad Science Out of the Courtroom – Changes in American and Australian Expert Evidence Law' (1995) 18 *University of New South Wales Law Journal* 108, 126–7

... it may be more appropriate to see the issue as an exercise in balancing. There are recent decisions in Australia which suggest such an approach, one in which the test renders inadmissible an expert opinion if the benefits to be derived from the opinion are outweighed by the disadvantages associated with it. According to this approach, relevant considerations would include:
- the reliability of the particular field of expertise;
- the reliability of the application of that field of expertise to the particular issue;
- the reliability of the expert's opinion (taking into account the expert's qualifications, experience, facilities and resources);
- the likely capacity of the tribunal of fact to understand and assimilate the evidence, without being misled or simply deferring to the expert opinion;
- the likely capacity of the tribunal of fact to properly determine the issue without the benefit of the expert opinion (thus, counter-intuitive expert testimony is more likely to be admitted than expert testimony which confirms common sense perceptions);
- the importance of the issue to which the evidence relates;
- the likely court time utilised if the opinion is admitted;
- the danger that the focus of the trial will shift from the evidence of the facts in dispute to the conflict between the competing theories of the various expert witnesses; and
- whether the evidence is being led against a defendant in a criminal trial.

In relation to the last consideration mentioned by Odgers and Richardson, one writer has gone so far as to argue that 'scientific evidence failing to satisfy the *Frye* ['general acceptance'] standard should *always* be excluded when offered against the defendant in a criminal case'.[40]

2. THE IMPLICATIONS OF THE RULE AGAINST HEARSAY

If an expert witness were to draw upon the work of others in reaching his or her conclusion, would he or she effectively be giving hearsay evidence? The issue was considered in the following three cases.

Extract 11.2.1

English Exporters v Eldonwall Ltd [1973] Ch 415, 420–1 (Ch D)

MEGARRY J: As an expert witness, the valuer is entitled to express his opinion about matters within his field of competence. In building up his opinions about values, he will no doubt have learned much from transactions in which he has himself been engaged, and of which he could give first-hand evidence. But he will also have learned much from many other sources, including much of which he could give no first-hand evidence. Textbooks, journals, reports of auctions and other dealings, and information obtained from his professional brethren and others, some related to particular transactions and some more general and indefinite, will all have contributed their share. Doubtless much, or most, of this will be accurate, though some will not; and even what is accurate so far as it goes may be incomplete, in that nothing may have been said of some special element which affects values. Nevertheless, the opinion that the expert expresses is none the worse because it is in part derived from the matters of which he could give no direct evidence. Even if some of the extraneous information which he acquires in this way is inaccurate or incomplete, the errors and omissions will often tend to cancel each other out; and the valuer, after all, is an expert in this field, so that the less reliable the knowledge that he has about the details of some reported transaction, the more his experience will tell him that he should be ready to make some discount from the weight that he gives it in contributing to his overall sense of values. Some aberrant transactions may stand so far out of line that he will give them little or no weight. No question of giving hearsay evidence arises in such cases; the witness states his opinion from his general experience.

Extract 11.2.2

R v Abadom [1983] 1 WLR 126, 129–30, 131–2 (CA)

KERR LJ: The point taken on this appeal was that the evidence of Mr Cooke, that the identical refractive index of the fragments of glass with that of the

---

[40] A Stein, 'The Refoundation of Evidence Law' (1996) 9 *Canadian Journal of Law and Jurisprudence* 279, 331 (emphasis added).

control sample occurred in only 4 per cent of all controlled glass samples analysed and statistically collated in the Home Office Central Research Establishment, was inadmissible because it constituted hearsay evidence. It was said to be hearsay because Mr Cooke had no personal knowledge of the analyses whose results were collated in these statistics, save possibly a few for which he may have been personally responsible. . . . In our view, the evidence was not inadmissible as hearsay. It is convenient to deal with this issue first on the basis of general principle and then to consider the authorities.

Mr Cooke was admittedly an expert, and was giving evidence as an expert, on the likelihood or otherwise of the fragments of glass having come from the control sample, the broken window. As an expert in this field he was entitled to express an opinion on this question, subject to laying the foundation for his opinion and subject, of course, to his evidence being tested by cross-examination for evaluation by the jury. In the context of evidence given by experts it is no more than a statement of the obvious that, in reaching their conclusion, they must be entitled to draw upon material produced by others in the field in which their expertise lies. Indeed, it is part of their duty to consider any material which may be available in their field, and not to draw conclusions merely on the basis of their own experience, which is inevitably likely to be more limited than the general body of information which may be available to them. Further, when an expert has to consider the likelihood or unlikelihood of some occurrence or factual association in reaching his conclusion, as must often be necessary, the statistical results of the work of others in the same field must inevitably form an important ingredient in the cogency or probative value of his own conclusion in the particular case. Relative probabilities or improbabilities must frequently be an important factor in the evaluation of any expert opinion and, when any reliable statistical material is available which bears upon this question, it must be part of the function and duty of the expert to take this into account.

However, it is also inherent in the nature of any statistical information that it will result from the work of others in the same field, whether or not the expert in question will himself have contributed to the bank of information available on the particular topic on which he is called upon to express his opinion. Indeed, to exclude reliance upon such information on the ground that it is inadmissible under the hearsay rule, might inevitably lead to the distortion or unreliability of the opinion which the expert presents for evaluation by a judge or jury. Thus, in the present case, the probative value or otherwise of the identity of the refractive index as between the fragments and the control sample could not be assessed without some further information about the frequency of its occurrence. If all glass of the type in question had the same refractive index, this evidence would have virtually no probative value whatever. The extent to which this refractive index is common or uncommon must therefore be something which an expert must be entitled to take into account, and indeed must take into account, before he can properly express an opinion about the likelihood or unlikelihood of the fragments of glass having come from the window in question. The cogency or otherwise of the expert's conclusion on this point, in the light of, inter alia, the available statistical material against which this conclusion falls to be tested, must then be a matter for the jury.

We therefore consider that Mr Cooke's reliance on the statistical information collated by the Home Office Central Research Establishment, before arriving at his conclusion about the likely relationship between the fragments of glass and the control sample, was not only permissible in principle, but that it was an essential part of his function as an expert witness to take account of this material.

. . .

. . . Once the primary facts on which [experts'] opinion is based have been proved by admissible evidence, they are entitled to draw on the work of others as part of the process of arriving at their conclusion. However, where they have done so, they should refer to this material in their evidence so that the cogency and probative value of their conclusion can be tested and evaluated by reference to it.

Thus, if in the present case the statistical tables of analyses made by the Home Office forensic laboratories had appeared in a textbook or other publication, it could not be doubted that Mr Cooke would have been entitled to rely upon them for the purposes of his evidence. Indeed, this was not challenged. But it does not seem to us, in relation to the reliability of opinion evidence given by experts, that they must necessarily limit themselves to drawing on material which has been published in some form. Part of their experience and expertise may well lie in their knowledge of unpublished material and in their evaluation of it. The only rule in this regard, as it seems to us, is that they should refer to such material in their evidence for the reasons stated above.

We accordingly conclude that Mr Cooke's reliance on the Home Office statistics did not infringe the rule against hearsay . . .

Extract 11.2.3

H v Schering Chemicals [1983] 1 WLR 143, 148, 149 (DC)

BINGHAM J: It is, as I have said, common ground that these articles can be referred to by experts as part of the general corpus of medical knowledge falling within the expertise of an expert in this field. That of course means that an expert who says (and I am looking at it from the plaintiffs' point of view for purposes of my example) 'I consider that there is a causal connection between the taking of the drug and the resulting deformity,' can fortify his opinion by referring to learned articles, publications, letters as reinforcing the view to which he has come. In doing so, he can make reference to papers in which a contrary opinion may be expressed but in which figures are set out which he regards as supporting his contention. In such a situation one asks: Are the figures and statistics set out in such an article strictly proved? and I think the answer is no. I think that they are nonetheless of probative value when referred to and relied on by an expert in the manner in which I have indicated. If an expert refers to the results of research published by a reputable authority in a reputable journal the court would, I think, ordinarily regard those results as supporting inferences fairly to be drawn from them, unless or until a different approach was shown to be proper.

. . .

Accordingly the plaintiffs are, in my judgment, entitled by means of expert evidence to incorporate the contents of the articles in their evidence in this case, and it will be given such weight as in the light of any other evidence and of any cross-examination appears to be proper.

See also *R v Jackson*.[41]

Are *English Exporters v Eldonwall Ltd*, *Abadom* and *H v Schering Chemicals* easily reconcilable with *Myers v DPP*[42] (see Chapter 7)? Or were the courts in these cases effectively creating a new exception to the hearsay rule, and, if so, were they justified in doing so? See generally A Ashworth and R Pattenden, 'Reliability, Hearsay Evidence and the English Criminal Trial' (1986) 102 *Law Quarterly Review* 292, 302–3.

Strict compliance with the hearsay rule would require that expert witnesses testify in court. However, this has been affected by the following statutory provision:

Extract 11.2.4

Criminal Justice Act 1988, s 30

30. Expert reports

(1) An expert report shall be admissible as evidence in criminal proceedings, whether or not the person making it attends to give oral evidence in those proceedings.

(2) If it is proposed that the person making the report shall not give oral evidence, the report shall only be admissible with the leave of the court.

(3) For the purpose of determining whether to give leave the court shall have regard –
   (a) to the contents of the report;
   (b) to the reasons why it is proposed that the person making the report shall not give oral evidence;
   (c) to any risk, having regard in particular to whether it is likely to be possible to controvert statements in the report if the person making it does not attend to give oral evidence in the proceedings, that its admission or exclusion will result in unfairness to the accused or, if more than one, to any of them; and
   (d) to any other circumstances that appear to the court to be relevant.

(4) An expert report, when admitted, shall be evidence of any fact or opinion of which the person making it could have given oral evidence.

(4A) Where the proceedings mentioned in subsection (1) above are proceedings before a magistrates' court inquiring into an offence as examining justices this section shall have effect with the omission of –
   (a) in subsection (1) the words 'whether or not the person making it attends to give oral evidence in those proceedings', and
   (b) subsections (2) to (4).

---

[41] [1996] 2 Cr App R 420.
[42] [1965] AC 1001.

(5) In this section 'expert report' means a written report by a person dealing wholly or mainly with matters on which he is (or would if living be) qualified to give expert evidence.

3. 'ULTIMATE ISSUES'

Is there a rule prohibiting experts from giving their opinions on 'ultimate issues'? What purpose, if any, would such a rule serve?

Extract 11.3.1

DPP v A & BC Chewing Gum Ltd [1968] 1 QB 159, 164 (DC)

LORD PARKER CJ: Those who practise in the criminal courts see every day cases of experts being called on the question of diminished responsibility, and although technically the final question 'Do you think he was suffering from diminished responsibility?' is strictly inadmissible, it is allowed time and time again without any objection.

Extract 11.3.2

R v Stockwell (1993) 97 Cr App R 260, 265 (CA)

THE LORD CHIEF JUSTICE: Mr Clegg's third and final argument is that even if Mr Neave was rightly allowed to state his findings, he should not have been permitted to give his opinion on the very issue before the jury. He said: 'My conclusion on count 1 is that the photos strongly support the view that the suspect and the robber are the same man.' He went on: 'There is limited information, but I think the exhibits reveal that there is support for the view that the robber and the suspect are the same man on count 2, but it is not anything like as strong as the support on count 1.'

Whether an expert can give his opinion on what has been called the ultimate issue, has long been a vexed question. There is a school of opinion supported by some authority doubting whether he can (see *Wright* (1821) Russ & Ry 456, 458). On the other hand, if there is such a prohibition, it has long been more honoured in the breach than the observance . . .
. . .

The rationale behind the supposed prohibition is that the expert should not usurp the functions of the jury. But since counsel can bring the witness so close to opining on the ultimate issue that the inference as to his view is obvious, the rule can only be . . . a matter of form rather than substance.[43]

---

[43] And see generally *Re M and R (Minors)* [1996] 4 All ER 239, 251. The Supreme Court of Canada has recently stated that 'expert testimony is admissible even if it relates directly to the ultimate question which the trier of fact must answer': *R v R(D)* (1996) 107 CCC (3d) 289, 304.

The point made in the last sentence in the extract – that an ultimate issue rule can easily be circumvented – is well illustrated by reference to the United States experience. Rule 704 of the Federal Rules of Evidence provides:

Extract 11.3.3

US Federal Rules of Evidence, Rule 704

Rule 704. Opinion on Ultimate Issue

(a) Except as provided in subdivision (b), testimony in the form of an opinion or inference otherwise admissible is not objectionable because it embraces an ultimate issue to be decided by the trier of fact.

(b) No expert witness testifying with respect to the mental state or condition of a defendant in a criminal case may state an opinion or inference as to whether the defendant did or did not have the mental state or condition constituting an element of the crime charged or of a defense thereto. Such ultimate issues are matters for the trier of fact alone.

Thus, the ultimate issue rule does not apply, *except* in relation to those issues specified in Rule 704(b). Rule 704(b) was considered in the following case:

Extract 11.3.4

US v Thigpen 4 F 3d 1573, 1580 (11th Cir 1993), cert denied 114 S Ct 2746 (1994)

BIRCH J: The psychiatric experts offered by the government and the defense both testified that Thigpen suffered from schizophrenia. When cross-examining the defense's expert, the prosecutor asked a series of questions to elicit an opinion as to whether such a condition by necessity implies that a person would be unable to appreciate the nature and quality of his acts. The prosecutor asked a similar question of its psychiatric expert on direct examination. No question by the prosecutor asked the witness to opine whether Thigpen was able to appreciate his actions.

Expert testimony concerning the nature of a defendant's mental disease or defect, including its typical effect on a person's mental state is admissible. *United States v Davis*, 835 F 2d 274, 276 (11th Cir), *cert denied*, 487 US 1219, 108 S Ct 2874, 101 L Ed 2d 909 (1988)....

In *United States v Manley*, 893 F 2d 1221, 1224 (11th Cir) (per curiam), *cert denied*, 498 US 901, 111 S Ct 259, 112 L Ed 2d 216 (1990), we upheld the exclusion of opinion testimony by a defense expert where counsel inquired as to the mental capacity of a hypothetical person with each of the pertinent characteristics of the defendant. While 'a thinly veiled hypothetical' may not be used to circumvent Rule 704(b), the rule does not bar 'an explanation of the disease and its typical effect on a person's mental state.' *Manley*, 893 F 2d at 1224 (citing *Davis*, 835 F 2d at 276). The government's questions in Thigpen's case sought the latter and were therefore allowed without error.

It was possible, therefore, for Rule 704(b) to be circumvented simply by eliciting an opinion that the defendant suffered from schizophrenia, and then eliciting an opinion as to whether such a condition *necessarily* implies that a person would be unable to appreciate the nature and quality of his acts. What would have been forbidden was to elicit a direct opinion as to whether the defendant was able to appreciate the nature and quality of his acts. Surely, however, there is effectively no difference between the two approaches. See generally R Slovenko, 'Surveying the Attacks on Psychiatry in the Legal Process' (1996) 1 *International Journal of Evidence and Proof* 48, 59–60.

In civil proceedings in England, the ultimate issue rule has been expressly abolished by statute:

Extract 11.3.5

Civil Evidence Act 1972, s 3

3. Admissibility of expert opinion and certain expressions of non-expert opinion

(1) Subject to any rules of court made in pursuance of this Act, where a person is called as a witness in any civil proceedings, his opinion on any relevant matter on which he is qualified to give expert evidence shall be admissible in evidence.

(2) ...

(3) In this section 'relevant matter' includes an issue in the proceedings in question.

A similar express abolishment of the ultimate issue rule in criminal proceedings is long overdue.

4. DUTIES AND RESPONSIBILITIES OF EXPERT WITNESSES

While the following observations were made with civil cases in mind, they are clearly applicable, mutatis mutandis, in criminal cases as well:

Extract 11.4.1

The 'Ikarian Reefer' [1993] FSR 563, 565–6 (Commercial Court)

CRESSWELL J: The duties and responsibilities of expert witnesses in civil cases include the following:
   1. Expert evidence presented to the court should be, and should be seen to be, the independent product of the expert uninfluenced as to form or content by the exigencies of litigation: *Whitehouse v Jordan* [1981] 1 WLR 246 at 256, *per* Lord Wilberforce.

2. An expert witness should provide independent assistance to the court by way of objective, unbiased opinion in relation to matters within his expertise: *Polivitte Ltd v Commercial Union Assurance Co plc* [1987] 1 Lloyd's Rep 379 at 386, Garland J and *Re J* [1990] FCR 193, Cazalet J. An expert witness in the High Court should never assume the role of an advocate.

3. An expert witness should state the facts or assumptions upon which his opinion is based. He should not omit to consider material facts which could detract from his concluded opinion (*Re J, supra*).

4. An expert witness should make it clear when a particular question or issue falls outside his expertise.

5. If an expert's opinion is not properly researched because he considers that insufficient data is available, then this must be stated with an indication that the opinion is no more than a provisional one (*Re J, supra*). In cases where an expert witness, who has prepared a report, could not assert that the report contained the truth, the whole truth and nothing but the truth without some qualification, that qualification should be stated in the report: *Derby & Co Ltd and others v Weldon and others, The Times*, 9 November 1990, *per* Staughton LJ.

6. If, after exchange of reports, an expert witness changes his view on a material matter having read the other side's expert's report or for any other reason, such change of view should be communicated (through legal representatives) to the other side without delay and when appropriate to the court.

7. Where expert evidence refers to photographs, plans, calculations, analyses, measurements, survey reports or other similar documents, these must be provided to the opposite party at the same time as the exchange of reports (see 15.5 of the Guide to Commercial Court Practice).

5. REFORM

The Runciman Royal Commission devoted considerable attention to the issue of expert evidence, making a large number of suggestions for reform. The following are some of the recommendations of the Commission pertaining to the trial stage of the criminal justice process:

Extract 11.5.1

Royal Commission on Criminal Justice, *Report* (1993) 159–61

71. ...we recommend that far more use is made of written summaries of such expert evidence as is not contested. All too often, expert evidence is given orally by witnesses in order, it would seem, to enhance the value of the evidence in the eyes of the jury. But where the defence have agreed the evidence, there should be no question of cross-examination and the attendance of the witness and his or her appearance in the box is unnecessary. We

have been told that nevertheless some judges insist on the appearance of expert witnesses in such circumstances because they believe that this makes the trial more comprehensible to the jury. We do not, however, agree that such a course is necessary or justified. We therefore recommend that, where the expert evidence is agreed, it should be presented to the jury as clearly as possible, normally by written statement. It would be for counsel to speak to such a statement in their opening and closing speeches.

72.   Where the evidence is in dispute and the expert witness goes into the witness box, his or her evidence can often be greatly assisted by the use of visual and other technical aids and we recommend that these are used wherever possible. . . .

73.   . . . many experts feel that they are not always given a proper opportunity to explain what the scientific evidence really means. This may be because counsel stop short of asking vital questions from lack of scientific knowledge or inadequate briefing or because they make inadequate use of the opportunity to re-examine after cross-examination or because they do not want the answer to be heard. We recommend that trial judges, where the evidence is disputed, ask expert witnesses before they leave the witness box whether there is anything else that they wish to say. To avoid inadmissible evidence being heard, the judge should put this question in the absence of the jury and, if the expert witness does indicate a wish to clarify the evidence, it should be heard before the jury returns. If the judge is satisfied that there can be no objection to the evidence, it should be put before the jury. Expert witnesses should on the same basis be readier to ask the judge to be allowed to add to what they have said in examination or cross-examination in order to make themselves clear. They might best do this by telling their solicitor on leaving the witness box that they wish to clarify the evidence just given. The solicitor would be under an obligation to inform counsel and counsel to tell the judge. The judge would then explore the admissibility of the evidence in the absence of the jury as we propose above and, if appropriate, the witness would be recalled to clarify the earlier evidence.

74.   Some of our witnesses would go further than the recommendations we have made above. In their view expert evidence should be given by a court expert, either instead of or in addition to the experts who appear for the prosecution and the defence. Alternatively, some would recommend that judges should sit in the relevant cases with an expert assessor or assessors. We have considered these suggestions but are not in favour of them. A court expert, even if subject to examination and cross-examination, would by implication carry more weight than an expert for the prosecution or the defence. There would, however, be no guarantee that he or she was any nearer to the truth of the matter than the expert witnesses for the parties. A court expert should not in our view be the only expert, since that would deprive the parties of the opportunity of leading their own expert evidence. But to have a court expert in addition to the experts for the parties would greatly extend the amount of time spent in examination and cross-examination of all three experts without making discovery of the truth any more certain. The worst solution of all, in our view, would be to have the expert sitting with the judge as an assessor, since his or her evidence would not be susceptible to examination or cross-examination by either side.

75. Expert witnesses need to be identified as such by reference to their experience and qualifications. At present, this is a matter for the courts to assess and we think that it should continue to be so. The courts should be guided, where there is any doubt, by whether the witness possesses a professional qualification guaranteed by membership of the appropriate professional body or the possession of a relevant professional or vocational degree, diploma or certificate. We see no need for a system of statutory certification or accreditation of expert witnesses nor for the maintenance of a register of experts by a Government Department. We do, however, recommend that the professional bodies assist the courts in their task of assessment by maintaining a special register of their members who are suitably qualified to act as expert witness in particular areas of expertise. We do not see professional bodies as guaranteeing the competence of individuals. But they might be asked to give advice to legal representatives on the qualifications that witnesses should hold if they are to be considered expert in a particular field.

The recommendations in paragraph 73 are obviously intended to invest expert witnesses with greater latitude in providing their testimony. It has been suggested that, at present, there are powerful reasons why an expert witness might choose to remain 'deferential' in court:

Extract 11.5.2

C A G Jones, *Expert Witnesses: Science, Medicine, and the Practice of Law* (1994) 126–7

The law . . . retains a number of powers to which even the most eminent of experts may be subjected. It can insist that they prove their expertise in open court and it can, if it so desires, deny their province. In doing so, it can subject them to an unfamiliar and humiliating examination of their credit and status. It may require them to undergo challenges to their professional integrity and the validity of their views. It requires their professional deference and it can publicly chastise them when this is not forthcoming.

Having these rules on the books provides something more than the mere semblance of power. In appearance as well as in reality judicial control is exercised over (1) the verdict; (2) the style, form and content of expert evidence; and (3) the recognition of a man of science as a professional expert. The law still holds some sway over the making and breaking of professional reputations . . . On occasion, its pronouncements have had a devastating effect upon the professional careers of experts who have appeared as witnesses. The fact is that the judiciary retains the power to confer or deny professional status, to humiliate and control expert witnesses, to reveal the interpretative uncertainties of their work, to shape the form and content of their evidence, and to insist upon their deference throughout the legal process. This acts as a significant brake on the conduct of experts in court. If they want recognition, they must abide by the rules of the club. One of these rules is that they must not speak out of turn.

The issue of whether a system of court experts should be introduced in England has precipitated considerable debate in recent times. As the extract from its *Report* indicates, the idea did not find favour with the Runciman Royal Commission. Yet the Commission's fear that the use of court experts may result in great weight being placed by the jury on evidence which may be no more reliable than evidence given by experts called by the parties is unjustified. The point, as Alldridge succinctly puts it, is surely that 'court-appointed witnesses *should* carry more weight, because there is every reason to believe that their evidence will be better evidence'.[44] Court experts are common in Continental jurisdictions. The French system of court experts, for example, seeks to eliminate the 'battle of the experts' in the courtroom by emphasising consensualism rather than confrontation. In order to be eligible to serve the court in a particular case, court experts have to be licensed. The *juge d'instruction* typically makes the decision about whether an expert is to be appointed, and if so which expert. In most cases, a single expert will be appointed, although there will often be a panel in difficult cases. On completion, the expert's report is delivered to the *juge d'instruction* for communication to the parties, who may ask the *juge d'instruction* to direct the expert to perform further tests or provide more information, or to appoint another expert for a second opinion.[45]

It has been suggested that procedures based on a 'didactic' approach to the presentation of expert evidence be introduced:

Extract 11.5.3

E J Imwinkelried, 'The Next Step in Conceptualizing the Presentation of Expert Evidence as Education: The Case for Didactic Trial Procedures' (1997) 1(2) *International Journal of Evidence and Proof* 128, 132

[It is] propose[d] [that] trial procedures [be revised] to improve the educational component of the presentation of expert evidence to the trier of fact. . . . In [a classroom] setting, the cast of characters often includes a principal teacher, a teaching assistant, and students. The principal teacher lectures to the group of students; and to enhance the students' understanding of the material covered in the lecture, the students have subsequent 'interactive exchanges' with the teaching assistant. [It is] propose[d] [that] the courtroom procedures for judges, court-appointed experts and jurors [be revised] to enable them to adopt the educational roles of teacher, teaching assistant and student. . . .

---

[44] P Alldridge, 'Forensic Science and Expert Evidence' (1994) 21 *Journal of Law and Society* 136, 142 (emphasis added). Cf P Roberts, 'Forensic Science Evidence after Runciman' [1994] *Criminal Law Review* 780, 788–91.

[45] The source of this information is J R Spencer, 'Court Experts and Expert Witnesses: Have We a Lesson to Learn from the French?' (1992) 45 *Current Legal Problems* 213, which may be consulted for a very readable account of the French system.

as teachers, trial judges should make more extensive use of their power to judicially notice facts to lecture the jury on relatively indisputable scientific propositions. . . . court-appointed experts should in effect serve as teaching assistants working with jurors to ensure jurors understand the propositions covered in the judge's lecture. Lastly, . . . like students, jurors [should] be both permitted and encouraged to question court-appointed experts to increase jury comprehension of the scientific proposition.

. . . these proposed procedures would supplement rather than supplant attorney examination of experts called by the opposing sides. Given the benefit of enhanced educational roles of the judge and court-appointed expert, the jurors would not only be more likely to understand the testimony by the partisan experts; more importantly, they would also be in a better position to arbitrate the points of disagreement between those experts.

Whatever the intrinsic merits of such proposals, the prospect of their being accorded serious consideration in England must be regarded as remote.

Further reading

P Alldridge, 'Forensic Science and Expert Evidence' (1994) 21 *Journal of Law and Society* 136

M Beaumont, 'Psychiatric Evidence: Over-Rationalising the Abnormal' [1988] *Criminal Law Review* 290

J Creaton, 'DNA Profiling and the Law: A Critique of the Royal Commission's Recommendations' in M McConville and L Bridges (eds), *Criminal Justice in Crisis* (1994)

G J Durston, 'Expert Opinion Evidence in Criminal Trials: A Review of the Current Position' (1996) 160 *Justice of the Peace* 837

J D Jackson, 'The Ultimate Issue Rule: One Rule Too Many' [1984] *Criminal Law Review* 75

C A G Jones, *Expert Witnesses: Science, Medicine, and the Practice of Law* (1994)

A Kenny, 'The Expert in Court' (1983) 99 *Law Quarterly Review* 197

R D Mackay and A M Colman, 'Equivocal Rulings on Expert Psychological and Psychiatric Evidence: Turning a Muddle into a Nonsense' [1996] *Criminal Law Review* 88

— 'Excluding Expert Evidence: A Tale of Ordinary Folk and Common Experience' [1991] *Criminal Law Review* 800

S J Odgers and J T Richardson, 'Keeping Bad Science out of the Courtroom – Changes in American and Australian Expert Evidence Law' (1995) 18 *University of New South Wales Law Journal* 108

R Pattenden, 'Conflicting Approaches to Psychiatric Evidence in Criminal Trials: England, Canada and Australia' [1986] *Criminal Law Review* 92

— 'Expert Opinion Evidence Based on Hearsay' [1982] *Criminal Law Review* 85

E Phillips, 'Testing the Truth: The Alliance of Science and Law' in M McConville and L Bridges (eds), *Criminal Justice in Crisis* (1994)

M Redmayne, 'The Royal Commission and the Forensic Science Market' in M McConville and L Bridges (eds), *Criminal Justice in Crisis* (1994)

P Roberts, 'Forensic Science Evidence after Runciman' [1994] *Criminal Law Review* 780

— 'Science in the Criminal Process' (1994) 14 *Oxford Journal of Legal Studies* 469

— and C Willmore, *The Role of Forensic Science Evidence in Criminal Proceedings* (Royal Commission on Criminal Justice Research Study No 11) (1993)

B Robertson and G A Vignaux, 'Expert Evidence: Law, Practice and Probability' (1992) 12 *Oxford Journal of Legal Studies* 392

Royal Commission on Criminal Justice, *Report* (Cm 2263) (1993) Ch 9

A Samuels, 'Psychiatric Evidence' [1981] *Criminal Law Review* 762

J R Spencer, 'Court Experts and Expert Witnesses: Have We a Lesson to Learn from the French?' (1992) 45 *Current Legal Problems* 213

B Steventon, *The Ability to Challenge DNA Evidence* (Royal Commission on Criminal Justice Research Study No 9) (1993)

12

PUBLIC INTEREST IMMUNITY

It will have been seen from the examination of improperly obtained evidence in Chapter 9 that involved in that topic is a clash of two competing public interests: on the one hand, the public interest in allowing the admission of all relevant and reliable evidence, in order that those guilty of crimes may be brought to conviction, and, on the other hand, the public interest in maintaining the moral integrity of the criminal justice process. A similar clash of competing public interests underlies the doctrine of public interest immunity. The law takes the view that, in appropriate circumstances, material which would otherwise be disclosed in the course of litigation may be withheld on the basis that disclosure would undermine the public interest[1] – by, for example, compromising national security or the proper functioning of the public service. A claim to public interest immunity may be made by the party in possession of the material (either on its own initiative or at the request of the relevant government department), or directly by the head of the department or the Attorney-General. It appears, too, that the court has a duty to raise the issue of public interest immunity itself if no other person has done so.[2] The issue of public interest immunity, in the light of such events as the Matrix Churchill case and the publication of the Scott Report, has been subjected to intense scrutiny in recent years. In the Matrix Churchill case, three directors of Matrix Churchill, a company manufacturing and exporting machine tools, were charged with supplying arms-making equipment to Iraq, in breach of the government's published export guidelines. The directors' defence was that government ministers were aware of, and authorised, the exporting, and that MI6 also knew. Four ministers signed public interest immunity certificates in relation to documents of which the defence sought disclosure. The trial judge ordered disclosure of some of these. The prosecution then discontinued the trial, because Alan Clark, the then Minister of State at the Department of Trade and Industry, admitted under cross-examination that the government had been fully aware of the intended use

---

[1] See, eg, Criminal Procedure and Investigations Act 1996, ss 3(6), 7(5), 8(5), 9(8) (all reproduced in Ch 4).
[2] *Duncan v Cammell, Laird & Co* [1942] AC 624, 642.

537

of the equipment.[3] In the light of the Matrix Churchill case, the Scott inquiry was instituted, culminating in the publication of the Scott Report[4] in February 1996.

1. A SHIFT IN JUDICIAL ATTITUDES

The following extract from the most recent decision of the House of Lords on public interest immunity provides a clear analysis of the development of the law in this area:

Extract 12.1.1

R v Chief Constable, W Midlands, ex p Wiley [1995] 1 AC 274, 288–91 (HL)

LORD WOOLF: The decision of *Duncan v Cammell, Laird & Co Ltd* [1942] AC 624 is usually regarded as being a convenient starting point for consideration of the development of the law as to public interest immunity or, as it was then known, 'Crown privilege' because the decision reflected the high water mark of judicial acceptance of the immunity of documents from disclosure in order to protect the public interest. On the facts which were involved in that case the decision of the House was perfectly understandable since the documents related to the sinking of a submarine, on which secret equipment was installed during her trials in 1939, with the loss of her crew. However, this House in sweeping terms unanimously laid down that a court could never question a claim to Crown privilege by the Crown if the claim was made in proper form. This applied both to the contents of individual documents and classes of documents. The dangerous consequences which could follow from this approach were clearly identified by Lord Pearce in *Conway v Rimmer* [1968] AC 910, 985:

> 'Any department quite naturally and reasonably wishes, as any private business or any semi-state board must also wish, that its documents or correspondence should never be seen by any outside eye. If it can obtain this result by putting forward a general vague claim for protection on the ground of candour it can hardly be blamed for doing so. "It is not surprising" it has been said (*Wade, Administrative Law*, 2nd ed (1967), p 285) "that the Crown, having been given a blank cheque, yielded to the temptation to overdraw." And the defect of such an argument is that discrimination and relaxation of the claim could not be acknowledged by the Crown lest it jeopardise the claim of the whole class of documents and of other classes

---

[3] See generally I Leigh, 'Matrix Churchill, Supergun and the Scott Inquiry' [1993] *Public Law* 630; I Leigh, 'Reforming Public Interest Immunity' in M J Allen (ed), *Web Journal of Current Legal Issues Yearbook 1995* (1996); A Tomkins, 'Public Interest Immunity after Matrix Churchill' [1993] *Public Law* 650.

[4] R Scott, *Report of the Inquiry into the Export of Defence Equipment and Dual-Use Goods to Iraq and Related Prosecutions* (1996).

of document. No weighing of the injury done to particular litigants (and thereby to the public at large) by a resulting denial of justice can be made. The ministry puts forward the rigid general claim. The court accepts it. The litigant ruefully leaves the lists, a victim of an injustice, great or small. In some cases this injustice is a necessary evil for the public good, in others it is unnecessary. Yet the court has not weighed the balance or considered whether the public interest in the well-being or routine of the ministry or the public interest in the fair administration of justice should have prevailed in that particular case.'

In *Conway v Rimmer* the House alleviated this undesirable legal situation established by *Duncan v Cammell, Laird & Co Ltd*. Having regard to the facts with which these appeals are concerned, it is of interest to note that in *Conway v Rimmer* [1968] AC 910, the House was concerned with a case in which a former police constable began an action for malicious prosecution against his former superintendent and the documents which gave rise to the appeal included four reports made by the superintendent about the plaintiff during his period of probation and a report by him to his chief constable for transmission to the Director of Public Prosecutions in connection with the prosecution of the plaintiff on a criminal charge on which he was acquitted. The House, in that case, made it clear that, even though there was objection by the Secretary of State in proper form to the production of the documents, the courts, in the appropriate circumstances, could, if necessary, inspect the documents. It was also entitled to balance the public interest in avoiding harm being done to the nation or the public service as against the public interest that the administration of justice should not be frustrated by the withholding of the production of the documents. If the court came to the conclusion that the public interest in the disclosure of the documents was greater than the public interest in their immunity, then the court could order that the documents be disclosed. The House having inspected the documents came to the conclusion that they contained nothing which would be in any way prejudicial to the public interest and they should be disclosed.

In the course of his speech, Lord Reid, at pp 941–942, referred to a statement made by the then Lord Chancellor, Lord Kilmuir, in this House on 6 June 1956 which explained the difference between a claim for public interest immunity based on the contention that the contents of a particular document would injure the public interest if disclosed and a class claim. With regard to a class claim which is the type of claim with which we are concerned with here, Lord Reid said that he regarded a proper test to be applied as being that used by Lord Simon LC in *Duncan v Cammell, Laird & Co Ltd*, and involved asking whether the withholding of a document because it belongs to a particular class is really 'necessary for the proper functioning of the public service.' Lord Reid added, at pp 953–954:

'The police are carrying on an unending war with criminals many of whom are today highly intelligent. So it is essential that there should be no disclosure of anything which might give any useful information to those who organise criminal activities. And it would generally be wrong to require disclosure in a civil case of anything which might be material in a pending prosecution: but after a verdict has been given or it has been decided to take no proceedings there is not the same need for secrecy. With regard to other documents there seems to be no greater need for protection than in the case of departments of government. It appears to me to be most improbable that any harm would be done by disclosure of the probationary reports on the appellant or of the report from the police training centre. With regard to the report which the respondent made to his chief constable with a view to the prosecution of the appellant there could be more doubt, although no suggestion was made in argument that disclosure of its contents would be harmful now that the appellant has been acquitted. And, as I have said, these documents may prove to be of vital importance in this litigation.'

The next case to which it is desirable to refer is *Reg v Lewes Justices, Ex parte Secretary of State for the Home Department* [1973] AC 388. The case is primarily significant in the development of the law in relation to public interest immunity because of another passage in a speech of Lord Reid, at p 400, which as it is relevant to the issues with which we are concerned, I will set out:

'The ground put forward has been said to be Crown privilege. I think that that expression is wrong and may be misleading. There is no question of any privilege in the ordinary sense of the word. The real question is whether the public interest requires that the letter shall not be produced and whether that public interest is so strong as to override the ordinary right and interest of a litigant that he shall be able to lay before a court of justice all relevant evidence. A Minister of the Crown is always an appropriate and often the most appropriate person to assert this public interest, and the evidence or advice which he gives to the court is always valuable and may sometimes be indispensable. But, in my view, it must always be open to any person interested to raise the question and there may be cases where the trial judge should himself raise the question if no one else has done so. In the present case the question of public interest was raised by both the Attorney-General and the Gaming Board. In my judgment both were entitled to raise the matter. Indeed I think that in the circumstances it was the duty of the board to do as they have done. The claim in the present case is not based on the nature of the contents of this particular letter. It is based on the fact that the board cannot adequately perform their statutory duty unless they can preserve the confidentiality of all communications to them regarding the character, reputation or antecedents of applicants for their consent. Claims for "class privilege" were fully considered by this House in *Conway v Rimmer* [1968] AC 910. It was made clear that there is a heavy burden of proof on any authority which makes such a claim. But the possibility of establishing such a claim was not ruled out.'

In addition to the fact that this passage explains why it is now the practice to refer to public interest immunity rather than Crown privilege, I draw attention to what Lord Reid said about the role of the Crown and also what he said about the burden of proof on any authority which makes a claim on a class basis.

In *Ex p Wiley*, all the parties in the House of Lords accepted, and the House agreed, that a class claim could not be made in respect of documents created in the course of investigating a complaint about police misconduct. The House left open the question, however, whether a class claim could be made in relation to the actual *reports* of the investigating officers. In *Taylor v Anderton*,[5] the Court of Appeal held that such a claim could indeed be made.

The following extract addresses two issues: first, the distinction between 'class' and 'contents' claims to public interest immunity, and, secondly, the necessity in certain circumstances for courts to inspect documents before making a decision on whether disclosure should be ordered.

Extract 12.1.2

***Burmah Oil Co v Bank of England* [1980] AC 1090, 1144–5 (HL)**

LORD SCARMAN: I do not therefore accept that there are any classes of documents which, however harmless their contents and however strong the requirement of justice, may never be disclosed until they are only of historical interest. In this respect I think there may well be a difference between a 'class' objection and a 'contents' objection – though the residual power to inspect and to order disclosure must remain in both instances. A Cabinet minute, it is said, must be withheld from production. Documents relating to the formulation of policy at a high level are also to be withheld. But is the secrecy of the 'inner workings of the government machine' so vital a public interest that it must prevail over even the most imperative demands of justice? If the contents of a document concern the national safety, affect diplomatic relations or relate to some state secret of high importance, I can understand an affirmative answer. But if they do not . . . , what is so important about secret government that it must be protected even at the price of injustice in our courts?

. . .

Inspection by the court is, I accept, a power to be exercised only if the court is in doubt, after considering the certificate, [about] the issues in the case and the relevance of the documents whose disclosure is sought. Where documents are relevant . . . , I would think a pure 'class' objection would by itself seldom quieten judicial doubts – particularly if . . . a substantial case can be made out for saying that disclosure is needed in the interest of justice.

The issue of inspection by the court was considered again by the House of Lords in the following case:

Extract 12.1.3

***Air Canada v Secretary of State for Trade* [1983] 2 AC 394, 435–6, 438–9, 444–6, 449 (HL)**

LORD FRASER OF TULLYBELTON: The most that can usefully be said is that, in order to persuade the court even to inspect documents for which

---

[5] [1995] 1 WLR 447.

public interest immunity is claimed, the party seeking disclosure ought at least to satisfy the court that the documents are very likely to contain material which would give substantial support to his contention on an issue which arises in the case, and that without them he might be 'deprived of the means of . . . proper presentation' of his case: see *Glasgow Corporation v Central Land Board*, 1956 SC (HL) 1, 18, *per* Lord Radcliffe. . . .

. . . When the claim is a 'class' claim judges will often not be well qualified to estimate its strength, because they may not be fully aware of the importance of the class of documents to the public administration as a whole. Moreover, whether the claim is a 'class' claim or a 'contents' claim, the court will have to make its decision on whether to order production, after having inspected the documents privately, without having the assistance of argument from counsel. It should therefore, in my opinion, not be encouraged to 'take a peep' just on the offchance of finding something useful. It should inspect documents only where it has definite grounds for expecting to find material of real importance to the party seeking disclosure.

[Lord Edmund-Davies agreed with the views of Lord Fraser of Tullybelton.]

LORD WILBERFORCE: What then are the criteria upon which a decision should be made to inspect, or not to do so? . . . there are three questions which have now to be answered. (1) What is it that the documents must be likely (in whatever degree) to support? (2) What is the degree of likelihood that must be shown? (3) Is that degree of likelihood attained?

(1)   On this point there was a difference in opinion between Bingham J and the Court of Appeal. The learned judge held that documents would be necessary for fairly disposing of a case or (his gloss) for the due administration of justice, if they give substantial assistance to the court in determining the facts upon which the decision in the case would depend. He considered that they were very likely to affect the outcome 'one way or the other.' The Court of Appeal, on the other hand, held that there must be a likelihood that the documents would support the case of the party seeking discovery.

On this point I agree with the Court of Appeal. In a contest purely between one litigant and another, . . . the task of the court is to do, and be seen to be doing, justice between the parties . . . There is no higher or additional duty to ascertain some independent truth. It often happens, from the imperfection of evidence, or the withholding of it, sometimes by the party in whose favour it would tell if presented, that an adjudication has to be made which is not, and is known not to be, the whole truth of the matter: yet if the decision has been in accordance with the available evidence and with the law, justice will have been fairly done. It is in aid of justice in this sense that discovery may be ordered, and it is so ordered upon the application of one of the parties who must make out his case for it. If he is not able to do so, that is an end of the matter. There is no independent power in the court to say that, nevertheless, it would like to inspect the documents, with a view to possible production, for its own assistance.

. . .

(2)   The degree of likelihood (of providing support for the plaintiff's case) may be variously expressed: 'likely' was the word used by Lord Edmund-Davies in

Burmah Oil: a 'reasonable probability' by Lord Keith of Kinkel. Both expressions must mean something beyond speculation, some concrete ground for belief which takes the case beyond a mere 'fishing' expedition. One cannot attain greater precision in stating what must be a matter of estimation. I would accept either formula.

(3) . . .

LORD SCARMAN: The issue is specific and within a small compass. The Crown having made its objection to production in proper form, in what circumstances should the court inspect privately the documents before determining whether they, or any of them, should be produced?

The court, of course, has a discretion: but the discretion must be exercised in accordance with principle. The principle governing the production of disclosed documents is embodied in RSC, Ord 24, r 13. No order for the production of any documents for inspection or to the court shall be made unless the court is of the opinion that the order is necessary either for disposing fairly of the cause or matter or for saving costs: r 13(1). And the court may inspect the document for the purpose of deciding whether the objection to production is valid: r 13(2). The rule provides a measure of protection for a party's documents irrespective of their class or contents and independently of any privilege or immunity. While the existence of all documents in a party's possession or control relating to matters in question in the action must be 'discovered,' that is to say disclosed, to the other party (or parties), he is not obliged to produce them unless the court is of the opinion that production is necessary.

. . .

Faced with a properly formulated certificate claiming public interest immunity, the court must first examine the grounds put forward. If it is a 'class' objection and the documents (as in *Conway v Rimmer* [1968] AC 910) are routine in character, the court may inspect so as to ascertain the strength of the public interest in immunity and the needs of justice before deciding whether to order production. If it is a 'contents' claim, eg, a specific national security matter, the court will ordinarily accept the judgment of the minister. But if it is a class claim in which the objection on the face of the certificate is a strong one . . . the court will pay great regard to the minister's view (or that of the senior official who has signed the certificate). It will not inspect unless there is a likelihood that the documents will be necessary for disposing fairly of the case or saving costs. Certainly, if . . . the court should think that the documents might be 'determinative' of the issues in the action to which they relate, the court should inspect: for in such a case there may be grave doubt as to which way the balance of public interest falls: *Burmah Oil Co Ltd v Governor and Company of the Bank of England* [1980] AC 1090, 1134–5, 1145. But, unless the court is satisfied on the material presented to it that the documents are likely to be necessary for fairly disposing of the case, it will not inspect for the simple reason that unless the likelihood exists there is nothing to set against the public interest in immunity from production.

. . .

The learned judge rejected, in my view rightly, the view which has commended itself to the Court of Appeal and to some of your Lordships that the criterion for determining whether to inspect or not is whether the party seeking production can establish the likelihood that the documents will assist his case or damage that of his opponent. No doubt that is what he is seeking; no doubt also, it is a very relevant consideration for the court. But it would be dangerous to elevate it into a principle of the law of discovery. Discovery is one of the few exceptions to the adversarial character of our legal process. It assists parties and the court to discover the truth. By so doing, it not only helps towards a just determination: it also saves costs. A party who discovers timeously a document fatal to his case is assisted as effectively, although less to his liking, as one who discovers the winning card; for he can save himself and others the heavy costs of litigation. There is another important aspect of the matter. The Crown, when it puts forward a public interest immunity objection, is not claiming a privilege but discharging a duty. The duty arises whether the document assists or damages the Crown's case or if, as in a case to which the Crown is not a party, it neither helps nor injures the Crown. It is not for the Crown but for the court to determine whether the document should be produced. Usually, but not always, the critical factor will be whether the party seeking production has shown the document will help him. But it may be necessary for a fair determination or for saving costs, even if it does not. . . . Basically, the reason for selecting the criterion of justice, irrespective of whether it assists the party seeking production, is that the Crown may not have regard to party advantage in deciding whether or not to object to production on the ground of public interest immunity. It is its duty to bring the objection, if it believes it to be sound, to the attention of the court. It is for the court, not the Crown, to balance the two public interests, that of the functioning and security of the public service, which is the sphere within which the executive has the duty to make an assessment, and that of justice, upon which the executive is not competent to pass judgment.

LORD TEMPLEMAN: I agree with my noble and learned friend, Lord Scarman, for the reasons he has deployed that the court should inspect the documents if the court considers the disclosure of the documents may materially assist any of the parties to the proceedings. If the plaintiff seeks discovery against the assertion which the defendant feels under a duty to put forward of public interest immunity, the judge may find the documents are wholly or partly favourable to the plaintiff's case or wholly or partly fatal to the plaintiff's case. In either event the judge must decide whether the public interest in maintaining the confidential nature of the document prevails over the public interest in ensuring that justice is achieved. If the public interest in confidentiality prevails the judge will decline to allow the plaintiff to see the documents. If the judge decides in all the circumstances that the claim for public interest immunity is not strong enough to prevail over the public interest in justice, the judge will allow the plaintiff to inspect the documents. In that case either party is free to use the documents for the purposes of the proceedings but is not bound to do so. If both parties in their discretion for the same or different reasons decide not to rely on the documents, the documents will not be revealed to the public. The plaintiff who will only have inspected the documents in order to determine whether or not to make use of them in the proceedings will not be allowed to make use of the documents for any other purpose.

Which do you prefer – the narrower views of Lord Fraser of Tullybelton, Lord Edmund-Davies and Lord Wilberforce, or the broader views of Lords Scarman and Templeman?

See also *R v K*[6] and *Wallace Smith Trust Co v Deloitte*[7] on the importance of inspection by the court. But compare *Balfour v Foreign Office*,[8] discussed later in the chapter.

The following statutory provision is meant to reflect the common law on public interest immunity. Does it provide a useful rationalisation of the law, and, in particular, of the factors to be taken into account by the court?

Extract 12.1.4

Evidence Act 1995 (Australia), s 130

130. Exclusion of evidence of matters of state

(1) If the public interest in admitting into evidence information or a document that relates to matters of state is outweighed by the public interest in preserving secrecy or confidentiality in relation to the information or document, the court may direct that the information or document not be adduced as evidence.

(2) The court may give such a direction either on its own initiative or on the application of any person (whether or not the person is a party).

(3) In deciding whether to give such a direction, the court may inform itself in any way it thinks fit.

(4) . . .

(5) Without limiting the matters that the court may take into account for the purposes of subsection (1), it is to take into account the following matters:

    (a) the importance of the information or the document in the proceeding;

    (b) if the proceeding is a criminal proceeding – whether the party seeking to adduce evidence of the information or document is a defendant or the prosecutor;

    (c) the nature of the offence, cause of action or defence to which the information or document relates, and the nature of the subject matter of the proceeding;

    (d) the likely effect of adducing evidence of the information or document, and the means available to limit its publication;

    (e) whether the substance of the information or document has already been published;

    (f) if the proceeding is a criminal proceeding and the party seeking to adduce evidence of the information or document is a defendant – whether the direction is to be made subject to the condition that the prosecution be stayed.

(6) . . .

[6] (1992) 97 Cr App R 342.
[7] [1996] 4 All ER 403, 413.
[8] [1994] 1 WLR 681.

So far in this chapter, we have essentially been concerned with the following issues:

- the courts' move away from the old approach of deferring to the views of the executive;
- the 'balancing approach' now adopted by the courts;
- the distinction drawn in the law between 'contents claims' and 'class claims';
- the power of the courts to inspect documents to determine whether disclosure should be ordered.

We shall now examine a number of different contexts in which litigation concerning public interest immunity has arisen.

2. NATIONAL SECURITY AND ANALOGOUS CONCERNS

Public interest immunity may be claimed on the basis of national security, or the maintenance of good diplomatic relations and international comity. The decision of the House of Lords in *Duncan v Cammell, Laird & Co*[9] provides a classic illustration of a claim based on national security concerns.[10] Although, as we have seen, the reasoning of the House of Lords in *Duncan* was subsequently disapproved by the House of Lords in *Conway v Rimmer*, the view was expressed in *Conway* that the actual result reached in *Duncan* was justifiable.[11]

It has been seen earlier that courts have a general discretion to inspect documents to determine whether they should be disclosed or whether, instead, the claim to public interest immunity should be upheld. There may, however, be an exception to this in the case of claims to public interest immunity on the basis of risk to national security. The Court of Appeal held in *Balfour v Foreign Office* that 'once there is an actual or potential risk to national security demonstrated by an appropriate certificate the court should not exercise its right to inspect'.[12] Is this justifiable?

Public interest immunity may also be claimed in the interests of protection of good diplomatic relations and international comity. In *Buttes Oil Co v Hammer (No 3)*,[13] Brightman LJ said:

> In my view it is in the public interest of the United Kingdom that the contents of confidential documents addressed to, or emanating from sovereign states, or concerning the interests of sovereign states, arising in connection with an international territorial dispute between sovereign states, shall not be ordered by the courts of this country to be disclosed by a private litigant without the consent of

---

[9] [1942] AC 624.
[10] See also *Hennessy v Wright* (1888) 21 QBD 509; *Asiatic Petroleum Co Ltd v Anglo-Persian Oil Co Ltd* [1916] 1 KB 822.
[11] [1968] AC 910, 938.
[12] [1994] 1 WLR 681, 688.
[13] [1981] QB 223.

the sovereign states concerned. I think that such an immunity is a public interest of the United Kingdom and I think that it outweighs the public interest that justice shall be administered on the basis of full disclosure of all relevant unprivileged documents. It is analogous to, but is clearly distinguishable from the public interest immunity which may attach to confidential documents of Her Majesty's Government. The resolution of a territorial dispute between sovereign states is a political question and it is undesirable that an English court should be seen to be forcing the disclosure of documents, prima facie of a confidential nature, for the ostensible purpose of pronouncing, albeit indirectly, on the merits of such a dispute.[14]

In a similar vein, inter-departmental memoranda between officials in a foreign embassy may also be subject to public interest immunity.[15]

3. PROPER FUNCTIONING OF THE PUBLIC SERVICE

The decision of the House of Lords in *Ex p Wiley*, as well as the earlier decisions of the House in *Conway v Rimmer*,[16] *Burmah Oil Co v Bank of England*[17] and *Air Canada v Secretary of State for Trade*,[18] provide authoritative judicial acknowledgement that considerations pertaining to the proper functioning of departments of central government, or the police, may found a claim of public interest immunity. But it is not just departments of central government or police departments which may be entitled to claim public interest immunity. In *D v NSPCC*,[19] the plaintiff claimed damages from the NSPCC for the injury to her health caused by the negligence of the NSPCC in pursuing the allegations of an informant that she had maltreated her child. These allegations had proved groundless. The NSPCC argued that documents which revealed the informant's identity were subject to public interest immunity. The House of Lords agreed, holding that the public interest in protecting the flow of information justified the refusal to order disclosure of the documents, since a consequence of disclosure might well be that the NSPCC's sources of information would dry up. The significance of this case, as Lord Woolf put it in *Ex p Wiley*, 'is that it made clear that the immunity does not only exist to protect the effective functioning of departments or organs of central government or the police, but also could protect the effective functioning of an organisation such as the NSPCC which was authorised under an Act of Parliament to bring legal proceedings for the welfare of children'.[20]

---

[14] At 265. The case was reversed on other grounds in [1982] AC 888.
[15] Cf *Fayed v Al-Tajir* [1987] 2 All ER 396.
[16] [1968] AC 910.
[17] [1980] AC 1090.
[18] [1983] 2 AC 394.
[19] [1978] AC 171.
[20] [1995] 1 AC 274, 291.

Other bodies which have been acknowledged by the courts as being potentially able to claim public interest immunity include local authorities,[21] the Gaming Board,[22] the Customs and Excise Commissioners[23] and the Law Society.[24] Whether such bodies can in fact claim public interest immunity in a particular case is dependent, of course, on the outcome of the 'balancing exercise' in the context of the case.

4. CRIMINAL CASES

Traditionally, the issue of public interest immunity has tended to arise in non-criminal litigation. Recently, however, it has had to be considered in a number of criminal cases, of which the Matrix Churchill case is perhaps the best known. In the criminal sphere, the issue of public interest immunity acquires a special dimension. Where, as is typically the case, it is the defence that is seeking disclosure of information held by the prosecution, a decision not to order disclosure may well result in the withholding of information which shows the defendant's innocence. The right of the defendant not to be convicted of an offence of which he or she is innocent may accordingly be compromised. As we shall see, the same approach of performing a 'balancing exercise' is adopted by criminal courts as is adopted by the civil courts. Is this a meaningful approach in the criminal context?

We shall examine now the two main contexts in which public interest immunity disputes in criminal cases have arisen: the disclosure of the identity of police informers, and the disclosure of the location of police observation points.

(a) Disclosure of the identity of police informers

Extract 12.4.1

R v Turner [1995] 1 WLR 264, 265–8 (CA)

LORD TAYLOR OF GOSFORTH CJ: The facts are as follows. At about 5.50 pm on 7 December 1992, a man armed with what appeared to be a gun committed a robbery at the Scampton Way Stores, a corner shop in Gainsborough. He stole about £200 in cash. Several witnesses described the

---

[21] *Re D (Infants)* [1970] 1 WLR 599; *Gaskin v Liverpool Council* [1980] 1 WLR 1549; *R v City of Birmingham DC, ex p O* [1982] 2 All ER 356; *Re M (A Minor) (Disclosure of Material)* [1990] 2 FLR 36.
[22] *R v Lewes JJ, ex p Home Secretary* [1973] AC 388.
[23] *A Crompton Ltd v Customs & Excise* [1974] AC 405; *Norwich Pharmacal v Customs & Excise* [1974] AC 133.
[24] *Buckley v Law Society (No 2)* [1984] 3 All ER 313.

robber. There were slight differences in those descriptions, particularly of his clothing, but it was generally agreed that he was wearing a black or navy donkey jacket, jeans, a flying hat with flaps, and a scarf or large handkerchief covering his lower face. It follows from that that no one at the scene was able to see his full face. Clothing and a gun were found by the police following a tip-off by an informer, who was not named in the proceedings. Those items were found a day or two after the robbery in fields about 1 1/2 miles from the scene. They were found on two separate occasions, the clothes on one and the gun on another. It was common ground that the clothing found had belonged to the appellant. Indeed, his fingerprint was on an article in the pocket of one of the items of clothing.

. . .

The appellant gave evidence on his own behalf. He accepted that the clothes found by the police were his; they were old clothes he had used when drain-laying. He had discarded them several months before his arrest; he had put them in bags, which he kept in a shed.

On the day of the robbery, he said he had been in a public house and met an acquaintance called Mitch who said he was going to sort out someone who had been 'knocking off' his girlfriend. The appellant offered to get him a cheap gun. They went to another friend of the appellant, Mr Dargen. There the appellant bought the gun from Dargen whilst Mitch waited outside. The appellant sold the gun on to Mitch, making £5 on the deal. He also provided the old clothes for £5 to Mitch, because Mitch was wearing bright-coloured and readily recognisable clothes at the time. After the transaction, the appellant went home. He still contended that he had an alibi for the relevant period.

. . .

The prosecution did not wish to disclose the details of the informant who had alerted the police. . . .

. . .

Coming to the balancing exercise which the judge has to conduct on such an application, we refer again to *Reg v Keane* [1994] 1 WLR 746, where the principles are set out. The judgment states, at pp 751–752:

> 'If the disputed material may prove the defendant's innocence or avoid a miscarriage of justice, then the balance comes down resoundingly in favour of disclosing it.'

The judgment continues, at p 752:

> 'when the court is seized of the material, the judge has to perform the balancing exercise by having regard on the one hand to the weight of the public interest in non-disclosure. On the other hand, he must consider the importance of the documents to the issues of interest to the defence, present and potential, so far as they have been disclosed to him or he can foresee them.'

Since *Reg v Ward* [1993] 1 WLR 619 there has been an increasing tendency for defendants to seek disclosure of informants' names and roles, alleging that those details are essential to the defence. Defences that the accused has been set up, and allegations of duress, which used at one time to be rare, have multiplied. We wish to alert judges to the need to scrutinise applications for disclosure of details about informants with very great care. They will need to be astute to see that assertions of a need to know such details, because they are essential to the running of the defence, are justified. If they are not so justified, then the judge will need to adopt a robust approach in declining to order disclosure. Clearly, there is a distinction between cases in which the circumstances raise no reasonable possibility that information about the informant will bear upon the issues and cases where it will. Again, there will be cases where the informant is an informant and no more; other cases where he may have participated in the events constituting, surrounding, or following the crime. Even when the informant has participated, the judge will need to consider whether his role so impinges on an issue of interest to the defence, present or potential, as to make disclosure necessary.

. . .

It is sufficient for us to say that in this case we are satisfied that the information concerning the informant showed a participation in the events concerning this crime which, coupled with the way in which the defence was raised from the very first moment by the defendant when he said that he was being set up, gave rise to the need for the defence to be aware of the identity of the informant and his role in this matter. We, therefore, conclude that if one applies the principle which has been quoted from *Reg v Keane* [1994] 1 WLR 746, 751–752 to the facts of the present case, there could only be one answer to the question as to whether the details concerning this informer were so important to the issues of interest to the defence, present and potential, that the balance which the judge had to strike came down firmly in favour of disclosure.

The following decision of the Supreme Court of Canada provides an articulate discussion of the issues pertaining to disclosure of the identity of police informers. Specifically, the court had to address the interesting question of whether non-disclosure would infringe an accused's right to make full answer and defence under the Canadian Charter of Rights and Freedoms.

<hr>

Extract 12.4.2

<hr>

R v Leipert (1997) 143 DLR (4th) 38, 43–52 (SCC)

McLACHLIN J:

(a) *The Importance of Informer Privilege*
A court considering this issue must begin from the proposition that informer privilege is an ancient and hallowed protection which plays a vital role in law enforcement. It is premised on the duty of all citizens to aid in enforcing the law. The discharge of this duty carries with it the risk of retribution from those involved in crime. The rule of informer privilege was developed to protect citizens who assist in law enforcement and to encourage others to do the same. As Cory JA (as he then was) stated in *R v Hunter* (1987), 57 CR (3d) 1 at pp 5–6, 34 CCC (3d) 14 (Ont CA):

The rule against the non-disclosure of information which might identify an informer is one of long standing. It developed from an acceptance of the importance of the role of informers in the solution of crimes and the apprehension of criminals. It was recognized that citizens have a duty to divulge to the police any information that they may have pertaining to the commission of a crime. It was also obvious to the courts from very early times that the identity of an informer would have to be concealed, both for his or her own protection and to encourage others to divulge to the authorities any information pertaining to crimes. It was in order to achieve these goals that the rule was developed.

The rule is of fundamental importance to the workings of a criminal justice system. As described in *Bisaillon v Keable*, [1983] 2 SCR 60 at p 105, 7 CCC (3d) 385, 2 DLR (4th) 193:

> The rule gives a peace officer the power to promise his informers secrecy expressly or by implication, with a guarantee sanctioned by the law that this promise will be kept even in court, and to receive in exchange for this promise information without which it would be extremely difficult for him to carry out his duties and ensure that the criminal law is obeyed.

In *R v Scott*, [1990] 3 SCR 979 at p 994, 61 CCC (3d) 300, Cory J stressed the heightened importance of the rule in the context of drug investigations:

> The value of informers to police investigations has long been recognized. As long as crimes have been committed, certainly as long as they have been prosecuted, informers have played an important role in their investigation. It may well be true that some informers act for compensation or for self-serving purposes. Whatever their motives, the position of informers is always precarious and their role is fraught with danger.
>
> The role of informers in drug-related cases is particularly important and dangerous. Informers often provide the only means for the police to gain some knowledge of the workings of the drug trafficking operations and networks.... The investigation often will be based upon a relationship of trust between the police officer and the informer, something that may take a long time to establish. The safety, indeed the lives, not only of informers but also of the undercover police officers will depend on that relationship of trust.

In most cases, the identity of the informer is known to the police. However, in cases like the instant one, the identity of the informer is unknown to everyone including the Crime Stoppers' agent who received the call. The importance of the informer privilege rule in cases where the identity of the informer is anonymous was stressed by the California Court of Appeal in *People v Callen*, 194 Cal App 3d 558 (1987). The court, in holding that the police have no duty to determine or disclose the identity of anonymous informers, stated at p 587:

> Such an investigatory burden would not only be onerous and frequently futile, it would destroy programs such as Crimestoppers by removing the guarantee of anonymity. Anonymity is the key to such a program. It is the promise of anonymity which allays the fear of criminal retaliation which

otherwise discourages citizen involvement in reporting crime. In turn, by guaranteeing anonymity, Crimestoppers provides law enforcement with information it might never otherwise obtain. We are satisfied the benefits of a Crimestoppers-type program – citizen involvement in reporting crime and criminals – far outweigh any speculative benefits to the defense arising from imposing a duty on law enforcement to gather and preserve evidence of the identity of informants who wish to remain anonymous.

Informer privilege is of such importance that once found, courts are not entitled to balance the benefit enuring from the privilege against countervailing considerations, as is the case, for example, with Crown privilege or privileges based on Wigmore's four-part test: J Sopinka, S N Lederman and A W Bryant, *The Law of Evidence in Canada* (Toronto: Butterworths, 1992), at pp 805–6. In *Bisaillon v Keable, supra*, this Court contrasted informer privilege with Crown privilege in this regard. In Crown privilege, the judge may review the information and in the last resort revise the minister's decisions by weighing the two conflicting interests, that of maintaining secrecy and that of doing justice. The Court stated at pp 97–98:

> This procedure, designed to implement Crown privilege, is pointless in the case of secrecy regarding a police informer. In this case, the law gives the Minister, and the Court after him, no power of weighing or evaluating various aspects of the public interest which are in conflict, since it has already resolved the conflict itself. It has decided once and for all, subject to the law being changed, that information regarding police informers' identity will be, because of its content, a class of information which it is in the public interest to keep secret, and that this interest will prevail over the need to ensure the highest possible standard of justice.
>
> Accordingly, the common law has made secrecy regarding police informers subject to a special system with its own rules, which differ from those applicable to Crown privilege.

The Court in *Bisaillon v Keable* summed the matter up by asserting that the application of informer privilege 'does not depend on the judge's discretion, as it is a legal rule of public order by which the judge is bound' (p 93).

In summary, informer privilege is of such importance that it cannot be balanced against other interests. Once established, neither the police nor the court possesses discretion to abridge it.

(b) *Who may Claim Informer Privilege?*
The privilege belongs to the Crown: *Solicitor General of Canada v Royal Commission of Inquiry into Confidentiality of Health Records in Ontario*, [1981] 2 SCR 494, 62 CCC (2d) 193, 128 DLR (3d) 193. However, the Crown cannot, without the informer's consent, waive the privilege either expressly or by implication by not raising it: *Bisaillon v Keable, supra*, at p 94. In that sense, it also belongs to the informer. This follows from the purpose of the privilege, being the protection of those who provide information to the police and the encouragement of others to do the same. This is the second reason why the police and courts do not have a discretion to relieve against the privilege.

The fact that the privilege also belongs to the informer raises special concerns in the case of anonymous informants, like those who provide telephone tips to Crime Stoppers. Since the informer whom the privilege is designed to protect and his or her circumstances are unknown, it is often difficult to predict with certainty what information might allow the accused to identify the informer. A detail as innocuous as the time of the telephone call may be sufficient to permit identification. In such circumstances, courts must exercise great care not to unwittingly deprive informers of the privilege which the law accords to them.

(c) *The Scope of Informer Privilege*
Connected as it is to the essential effectiveness of the criminal law, informer privilege is broad in scope. While developed in criminal proceedings, it applies in civil proceedings as well: *Bisaillon v Keable, supra.* It applies to a witness on the stand. Such a person cannot be compelled to state whether he or she is a police informer: *Bisaillon v Keable, supra.* And it applies to the undisclosed informant, the person who although never called as a witness, supplies information to the police. Subject only to the 'innocence at stake' exception, the Crown and the court are bound not to reveal the undisclosed informant's identity.

Informer privilege prevents not only disclosure of the name of the informant, but of any information which might implicitly reveal his or her identity. Courts have acknowledged that the smallest details may be sufficient to reveal identity. In *R v Garofoli*, [1990] 2 SCR 1421 at p 1460, 60 CCC (3d) 161, Sopinka J suggested that trial judges, when editing a wire-tap packet, consider:

> '. . . whether the identities of confidential police informants, and consequently their lives and safety, may be compromised, bearing in mind that such disclosure may occur as much by reference to the nature of the information supplied by the confidential source as by the publication of his or her name;' [*R v Parmar* (1987), 34 CCC (3d) 260 (Ont HCJ) at p 281.]

This principle was also confirmed by the British Columbia Court of Appeal in *R v Hardy* (1994), 45 BCAC 146 at p 149:

> It is well recognized that information which might identify a confidential informant need not be disclosed to the Justice of the Peace or at trial.

Similarly, McEachern CJBC in the case at bar suggested (at para 35) that an 'accused may know that only some very small circle of persons, perhaps only one, may know an apparently innocuous fact that is mentioned in the document'. He noted: 'The privilege is a hallowed one, and it should be respected scrupulously'.

The jurisprudence therefore suggests that the Crown must claim privilege over information that reveals the identity of the informant or that may implicitly reveal identity. In many cases, the Crown will be able to contact the informer to determine the extent of information that can be released without jeopardizing the anonymity of the tipster. The informer is the only person who knows the potential danger of releasing those facts to the accused. The difficulty in this case is that the identity of the informer is unknown. Therefore, the Crown is not in a position to determine whether any part of the information could reveal his or her identity. This led the Crown in the case at bar to claim privilege for all of the information provided by the informer. The extension of privilege to all information that could identify an informant justifies this claim in the case of an anonymous informant.

(d) *The 'Innocence at Stake' Exception*

Informer privilege is subject only to one exception, known as the 'innocence at stake' exception. Lord Esher, MR, described this exception in *Marks v Beyfus* (1890), 25 QBD 494 (CA) at p 498:

> ... if upon the trial of a prisoner the judge should be of opinion that the disclosure of the name of the informant is necessary or right in order to shew the prisoner's innocence, then one public policy is in conflict with another public policy, and that which says that an innocent man is not to be condemned when his innocence can be proved is the policy that must prevail.

In *Bisaillon v Keable, supra*, this Court held (at p 93):

> The rule is subject to only one exception, imposed by the need to demonstrate the innocence of an accused person.

As Cory J stated in *Scott, supra*, at pp 995–96:

> In our system the right of an individual accused to establish his or her innocence by raising a reasonable doubt as to guilt has always remained paramount.

In order to raise the 'innocence at stake' exception to informer privilege, there must be a basis on the evidence for concluding that disclosure of the informer's identity is necessary to demonstrate the innocence of the accused: *R v Chiarantano*, [1990] OJ No 2603 (QL) (Ont CA), *per* Brooke JA, affirmed [1991] 1 SCR 906. In *Chiarantano, supra*, the possibility that the information provided by the informer regarding the arrival at a residence of drugs later found in the possession of the accused might conflict with the evidence of the accused was held not to raise a basis for disclosure pursuant to the 'innocence at stake' exception. The court held that the usefulness of the information was speculative and that mere speculation that the information might assist the defence is insufficient. If speculation sufficed to remove the privilege, little if anything would be left of the protection which the privilege purports to accord.

On the other hand, circumstances may arise where the evidence establishes a basis for the exception, as where the informer is a material witness to the crime or acted as an *agent provocateur*: see *Scott, supra*. Where such a basis is established, the privilege must yield to the principle that a person is not to be condemned when his or her innocence can be proved.

(e) *Informer Privilege and the Charter*

It has been suggested (although not by the appellant) that the *Canadian Charter of Rights and Freedoms*, as interpreted in [*R v Stinchcombe* [1991] 3 SCR 326] has introduced another exception to the informer privilege rule based on the right to full disclosure of documents in the Crown's possession in aid of the *Charter* guarantee of the right to make full answer and defence:

D M Tanovich 'When Does *Stinchcombe* Demand that the Crown Reveal the Identity of a Police Informer?' (1995), 38 CR (4th) 202. According to this argument, 'innocence at stake' would no longer be the only exception to the informer privilege rule.

This argument rests on a right to disclosure broader than any which this Court has enunciated. In *Stinchcombe, supra*, the right to disclosure of Crown documents was expressly made subject to two conditions: relevance (to be interpreted generously as including all that is not clearly irrelevant) and privilege. The right to disclosure was not to trump privilege. Any doubt about its application to informer privilege was expressly negated [at p 335 SCR]:

> . . . it is suggested that disclosure may put at risk the security and safety of persons who have provided the prosecution with information. No doubt measures must occasionally be taken to protect the identity of witnesses and informers. *Protection of the identity of informers is covered by the rules relating to informer privilege and exceptions thereto* . . . [Emphasis added.]

In *R v O'Connor*, [1995] 4 SCR 411, 103 CCC (3d) 1, 130 DLR (4th) 235, and *A (LL) v B (A)*, [1995] 4 SCR 536, 103 CCC (3d) 92, 130 DLR (4th) 422, *sub nom R v Beharriell*, this Court in dealing with disclosure of third party medical and therapeutic records, did not suggest that the informer privilege rule had been altered by the requirement of Crown disclosure, under the *Charter*. Rather, it appears to have endorsed the common law rule: 'so important is the societal interest in preventing a miscarriage of justice that our law requires the state to disclose the identity of an informer in certain circumstances, despite the fact that the revelation may jeopardize the informer's safety': *O'Connor, supra*, at para 18, *per* Lamer CJC and Sopinka J. The comments of L'Heureux-Dubé J in *A (LL) v B (A)*, *supra*, at paras 37 and 69, are to the same effect. This Court has consistently affirmed that it is a fundamental principle of justice, protected by the *Charter*, that the innocent must not be convicted: *R v Seaboyer*, [1991] 2 SCR 577 at p 611, 66 CCC (3d) 321, 83 DLR (4th) 193; *Stinchcombe, supra*; *O'Connor, supra*. To the extent that rules and privileges stand in the way of an innocent person establishing his or her innocence, they must yield to the *Charter* guarantee of a fair trial. The common law rule of informer privilege, however, does not offend this principle. From its earliest days, the rule has affirmed the priority of the policy of the law 'that an innocent man is not to be condemned when his innocence can be proved' by permitting an exception to the privilege where innocence is at stake: *Marks v Beyfus, supra*. It is therefore not surprising that this Court has repeatedly referred to informer privilege as an example of the policy of the law that the innocent should not be convicted, rather than as a deviation from it.

I find no inconsistency between the *Charter* right to disclosure of Crown documents affirmed in *Stinchcombe, supra*, and the common law rule of informer privilege.

(f) . . .

. . .

(g) . . .

. . .

(h) *Procedure*

When an accused seeks disclosure of privileged informer information on the basis of the 'innocence at stake' exception, the following procedure will apply. First, the accused must show some basis to conclude that without the disclosure sought his or her innocence is at stake. If such a basis is shown, the court may then review the information to determine whether, in fact, the information is necessary to prove the accused's innocence. If the court concludes that disclosure is necessary, the court should only reveal as much information as is essential to allow proof of innocence. Before disclosing the information to the accused, the Crown should be given the option of staying the proceedings. If the Crown chooses to proceed, disclosure of the information essential to establish innocence may be provided to the accused.

What is notable about this decision, therefore, is the particular weight which it attaches, even in the face of a constitutional bill of rights, to the public interest in the non-disclosure of the identity of police informers. Determination that the 'innocence at stake' exception is inapplicable leads automatically to the conclusion that the accused's right to make full answer and defence under the Charter is not infringed.

The English Court of Appeal has held that a police informer wishing to sacrifice his or her anonymity is not prevented by the doctrine of public interest immunity from doing so:

Extract 12.4.3

Savage v Chief Constable of Hampshire **[1997] 2 All ER 631, 632–6 (CA)**

JUDGE LJ: On 17 August 1994 the plaintiff, David James Savage, began the present proceedings in Portsmouth County Court. He was acting in person. His pleading was inadequate and defective. A draft amended particulars of claim was prepared by counsel. Leave to amend was sought. The defendant, the Chief Constable of the Hampshire Constabulary, opposed the application on the ground that, even in its proposed amended form, the action was frivolous, vexatious and an abuse of the process of the court.

On 27 July 1995 Judge Martin Tucker QC sitting as a deputy judge of the High Court, concluded that the amended claim was properly stigmatised as frivolous and vexatious. He, therefore, refused the application for leave to amend and struck out the claim. Leave to appeal from his decision has been granted by this court.

The plaintiff's claim in its amended form asserted that the defendant, as Chief Constable of the Hampshire Constabulary, was liable to pay him on a contractually agreed basis for his work as a police informer. For the purposes of this appeal, it must be assumed that the plaintiff did indeed work as a police informer who, following his arrest in 1990 for unlawful possession of drugs, was invited to assist the police and agreed to do so after discussions which culminated in an oral agreement with a chief inspector of the Hampshire constabulary that he would be paid for information leading to the arrest and conviction of persons

556

involved in serious crime, or the prevention of serious crime, or the recovery of property. Payment would be calculated on the basis of 10% of the value of any property concerned, less any insurance reward. Alternatively, if payment could not be calculated in this way, then a reasonable sum would be payable. The plaintiff claims that the chief inspector was acting within the scope of his actual or apparent authority as agent for the chief constable.

Subsequently, in performance of this agreement, the plaintiff provided appropriate assistance and information, and has not received the agreed or any reasonable payment. If the case proceeds to a hearing, an alternative view of these crucial facts is likely to be pursued, but as the appeal is not concerned with the factual merits or otherwise of the plaintiff's claim but with the single question whether or not it is legally tenable, nothing more need be said about the facts.

In essence, the question for decision is whether a police informer is precluded from taking proceedings to recover moneys promised to him by a police officer in exchange for information. . . .

Ignoring for the moment the unsuccessful arguments deployed on behalf of the defendant, the successful submission was concisely summarised by the judge. The claim was not admissible as it involved an assertion by the plaintiff in open court that he was a police informer. He was not permitted to allege or give evidence to establish any such case. The plaintiff argues that this conclusion was wrong in law.

It is well understood that on occasion the public interest requires that evidence which would otherwise be relevant and admissible in litigation should nevertheless not be disclosed or adduced in court. The need to conceal the identity of informers is justified, 'not only for their own safety but to ensure that the supply of information about criminal activities does not dry up' (see *R v Hennessy* (1978) 68 Cr App R 419 at 426 per Lawton LJ; see also *D v National Society for the Prevention of Cruelty to Children* [1977] 1 All ER 589, [1978] AC 171).

These are not the only considerations. In a limited number of cases, the claim for concealment is justified on the basis that the police service could not otherwise function properly and perform their public duty. . . . The principle is long-standing:

'. . . the rule clearly established and acted on is this, that, in a public prosecution a witness cannot be asked such questions as will disclose the informer, if he be a third person. This has been a settled rule for fifty years . . . we think the principle of the rule applies to the case where a witness is asked if he himself is the informer . . .' (See *A-G v Briant* (1846) 15 M & W 169 at 183, 153 ER 808 at 815.)

As the language demonstrates, this case was not concerned with civil proceedings but with a criminal prosecution. In *Marks v Beyfus* (1890) 25 QBD 494 the plaintiff issued civil proceedings for damages for malicious prosecution. He called the Director of Public Prosecutions as a witness. He refused to identify the name of the person who had given him the information on which he had acted against the plaintiff. The Court of Appeal upheld the judge's decision that he should not do so. Lord Esher MR explained (at 498):

'. . . this rule as to public prosecutions was founded on grounds of public policy, and if this prosecution was a public prosecution the rule attaches . . . I do not say it is a rule which can never be departed from; if upon the trial of a prisoner the judge should be of opinion that the disclosure of the name of the informant is necessary or right in order to shew the prisoner's innocence, then one public policy is in conflict with another public policy, and that which says that an innocent man is not to be condemned when his innocence can be proved is the policy that must prevail. But except in that case, this rule of public policy is not a matter of discretion; it is a rule of law, and as such should be applied by the judge at the trial, who should not treat it as a matter of discretion . . .'

At the end of his judgment he added that the rule applied –

'not only to the trial of the prisoner, but also to a subsequent civil action between the parties on the ground that the criminal prosecution was maliciously instituted or brought about.' (See (1890) 25 QBD 494 at 499.)

The principle firmly established and constantly repeated thereafter was that immunity from disclosure was not a privilege to be waived by one or other party to the proceedings (see also *Rogers v Secretary of State for the Home Dept, Gaming Board for GB v Rogers* [1972] 2 All ER 1057, [1973] AC 388 and *D v National Society for the Prevention of Cruelty to Children* [1977] 1 All ER 589, [1978] AC 171). Secondly, non-disclosure was not limited to criminal prosecutions but extended in some circumstances to civil proceedings as well. However, Lord Esher MR did not use language to suggest that the principle applied to every civil action in whatever form the proceedings might take. . . .

Although there are numerous authorities which deal with the application and, indeed, the continuing development of the essential principles, one question not yet decided is whether the public interest requires that the principle should be applied when the informer himself positively wishes his activities to be identified. In such circumstances, and assuming that the informer is adult and of reasonable intelligence, it is difficult to see why the court should prevent disclosure of his activities on the basis that his personal safety would be in danger. Disclosure at his insistence could not serve to undermine one of the essential features of arrangements between the police and their informers that the informers and their identity will normally be protected from disclosure.

This approach is consistent with the authorities. In *R v Rankine* [1986] 2 All ER 566, [1986] QB 861, the court had to consider the problem of police surveillance from observation posts. It was decided that the reasons which protected the informer from being identified applied –

'with equal force to the identification of the owner or occupier of premises used for surveillance and to the identification of the premises themselves. The cases are indistinguishable, and the same rule must apply to each.' (See [1986] 2 All ER 566 at 570, [1986] QB 861 at 867.)

In *R v Johnson* [1989] 1 All ER 121, [1988] 1 WLR 1377 general guidance was given about the information to be placed before the trial judge when the prosecution sought to exclude evidence which would identify places of observation and occupiers of such premises. . . .

If the views of the individuals whose safety was most in need of protection could be considered in relation to an observation post case, in my judgment, the wish of an informer that his identity should be disclosed could not without more be ignored on the basis of the immunity principle, certainly in relation to civil proceedings taken by him after the conclusion of any relevant criminal prosecutions.

The developing law in relation to observation posts coincided with a separate line of authorities relating to complaints against police officers. A series of decisions in the Court of Appeal beginning with *Neilson v Laugharne* [1981] 1 All ER 829, [1981] QB 736, followed and adopted in *Hehir v Comr of Police of the Metropolis* [1982] 2 All ER 335, [1982] 1 WLR 715, *Makanjuola v Comr of Police of the Metropolis* [1992] 3 All ER 617 and *Halford v Sharples* [1992] 3 All ER 624, [1992] 1 WLR 736 were overruled in *R v Chief Constable of the West Midlands Police, ex p Wiley, R v Chief Constable of Nottinghamshire Constabulary, ex p Sunderland* [1994] 3 All ER 420, [1995] 1 AC 274. . . .

. . .

In my judgment, it follows from both these lines of authority that, if a police informer wishes personally to sacrifice his own anonymity, he is not precluded from doing so by the automatic application of the principle of public interest immunity at the behest of the relevant police authority. This follows, not from waiver of privilege attaching personally to the informer, but from the disappearance of the primary justification for the claim for public interest immunity.

That, of course, is not an end of the matter. It is possible that, notwithstanding the wishes of the informer, there remains a significant public interest, extraneous to him and his safety and not already in the public domain, which would be damaged if he were allowed to disclose his role. However, I am unable to understand why the court should infer, for example, that disclosure might assist others involved in criminal activities, or reveal police methods of investigation, or hamper their operations, or indicate the state of their inquiries into any particular crime, or even that the police are in possession of information which suggests extreme and urgent danger to the informer if he were to proceed. Considerations such as these might, in an appropriate case, ultimately tip the balance in favour of preserving the informer's anonymity against his wishes in the public interest. There is no evidence that any such consideration applies to the present case.

(b) Disclosure of the location of police observation points

To what extent are the police required to disclose the location of premises used by them for surveillance purposes?

Extract 12.4.4

R v Johnson [1988] 1 WLR 1377, 1385–6 (CA)

WATKINS LJ: Clearly a trial judge must be placed by the Crown which seeks to exclude evidence of the identification of places of observation and occupiers of premises, in the best possible position to enable him properly in the interests of justice, which includes providing a defendant with a fair trial, to determine whether he will afford to the police the protection sought. At the heart of this problem is the desirability, as far as that can properly be given, of re-assuring people who are asked to help the police that their identities will never be disclosed lest they become the victims of reprisals by wrongdoers for performing a public service.

The minimum evidential requirements seem to us to be the following.

(a) The police officer in charge of the observations to be conducted, no one of lower rank than a sergeant should usually be acceptable for this purpose, must be able to testify that beforehand he visited all observation places to be used and ascertained the attitude of occupiers of premises, not only to the use to be made of them, but to the possible disclosure thereafter of the use made and facts which could lead to the identification of the premises thereafter and of the occupiers. He may of course in addition inform the court of difficulties, if any, usually encountered in the particular locality of obtaining assistance from the public.

(b) A police officer of no lower rank than a chief inspector must be able to testify that immediately prior to the trial he visited the places used for observations, the results of which it is proposed to give in evidence, and ascertained whether the occupiers are the same as when the observations took place and whether they are or are not, what the attitude of those occupiers is to the possible disclosure of the use previously made of the premises and of facts which could lead at the trial to identification of premises and occupiers.

Such evidence will of course be given in the absence of the jury when the application to exclude the material evidence is made. The judge should explain to the jury, as this judge did, when summing up or at some appropriate time before that, the effect of his ruling to exclude, if he so rules.

See also *R v Hewitt*.[25] In *Blake v DPP*,[26] it was held that fear of harassment, as opposed to violence, by the occupiers of the premises is a sufficient basis for a public interest immunity claim.

(c) General comments

The following are some of the observations and recommendations made in the Scott Report in relation to public interest immunity in criminal cases:

Extract 12.4.5

R Scott, *Report of the Inquiry into the Export of Defence Equipment and Dual-Use Goods to Iraq and Related Prosecutions* (1996) 1789–91

. . .

(ii) PII claims on a class basis should not in future be made. PII contents claims should not be made in respect of documents which it is apparent are documents which might be of assistance to the defence.

. . .

[25] (1991) 95 Cr App R 81.
[26] (1992) 97 Cr App R 169.

(viii) . . . the judge should be asked to decide whether the documents might be of assistance to the defence. If a document satisfies this test, the document ought not to be withheld from a defendant on PII grounds. There is no true balance to be struck. The weight of public interest factors underlying the PII claim is immaterial. However, existing authority, with its apparent endorsement of the 'balancing exercise' while at the same time requiring the disclosure of any document which 'may prove the defendant's innocence to avoid a miscarriage of justice', suffers, in my opinion, from some degree of ambiguity. It would be important, in my opinion, if disclosure of a material document is to be withheld, that the defendant should know whether the decision was based on the judge's conclusion that the document would not be of any assistance to the defence or on the judge's conclusion that, despite meeting that test, the weight of public interest factors precludes disclosure. The latter conclusion would, in my opinion, be wrong in principle and contrary to authority.

(ix) For the purposes of any argument on the assistance that a document might give the defence, the defendant should specify the line or lines of defence which, in the defendant's contention, give the document its requisite materiality.

(x) If the documents, although relevant and *prima facie* disclosable, do not appear to be documents that might assist the defence, the judge may conclude that in view of the public interest factors underlying the PII claim, the documents need not be disclosed.

See also R Scott, 'The Acceptable and Unacceptable Use of Public Interest Immunity' [1996] *Public Law* 427. Do you agree with Scott that it is meaningless, in the context of criminal litigation, to speak in terms of a 'balancing exercise'? Scott's contention that class claims are inappropriate in criminal cases is echoed by Leigh,[27] who also argues that 'a mandatory statutory requirement of judicial inspection should apply to PII claims in criminal proceedings'.[28]

In the following case, the Court of Appeal made a number of observations on public interest immunity claims in criminal cases:

Extract 12.4.6

R v Davis [1993] 1 WLR 613, 617–18 (CA)

LORD TAYLOR OF GOSFORTH CJ: . . . Mr Mansfield submits that in all cases where the prosecution contend public interest immunity or sensitivity justifies non-disclosure: (a) they must give notice to the defence that they are applying for a ruling by the court; (b) they must indicate to the defence at least the category of the material they hold; and (c) the defence must have the

[27] I Leigh, 'Reforming Public Interest Immunity' in M J Allen (ed), *Web Journal of Current Legal Issues Yearbook 1995* (1996).
[28] At 104.

opportunity to make representations to the court. In other words, he contends for an inter partes hearing in all cases with disclosure of at least the category of the material. . . .

Mr Bevan accepts that in the majority of cases these requirements should be met. The problem arises where, exceptionally, the sensitivity of the material is such that to reveal the category, or, still more exceptionally, the very fact that an application is being made to the court, will defeat the public interest in non-disclosure.

In our judgment, the proper approach is as follows. (1) . . . (2) If the prosecution wish to rely on public interest immunity or sensitivity to justify non-disclosure, then, whenever possible, which will be in most cases, (a), (b) and (c) of Mr Mansfield's formulation above will apply. (3) Where, however, to disclose even the category of the material in question would in effect be to reveal that which the Crown contends should not in the public interest be revealed, a different procedure will apply. The Crown should still notify the defence that an application to the court is to be made, but the category of the material need not be specified and the application will be ex parte. If the court, on hearing the application, considers that the normal procedure under (2) above ought to have been followed, it will so order. If not, it will rule on the ex parte application. (4) It may be that, in a highly exceptional case, to reveal even the fact that an ex parte application is to be made, could 'let the cat out of the bag' so as to stultify the application. Such a case would be rare indeed, but we accept Mr Bevan's contention that it could occur. In that event, the prosecution should apply to the court, ex parte, without notice to the defence. Again, if the court, on hearing the application, considered that at least notice of the application should have been given to the defence or even that the normal inter partes procedure should have been adopted, it will so order.
. . .

We should add that where the court, on application by the Crown, rules in favour of non-disclosure before the hearing of a case begins, that ruling is not necessarily final. In the course of the hearing, the situation may change. Issues may emerge so that the public interest in non-disclosure may be eclipsed by the need to disclose in the interests of securing fairness to the defendant. If that were to occur, the court would have to indicate to the Crown its change of view. The Crown would then have to decide whether to disclose or offer no further evidence.

It will therefore be necessary for the court to continue to monitor the issue. For that reason, it is desirable that the same judge or constitution of the court which decides the application should conduct the hearing. If that is not possible, the judge or constitution which does conduct the hearing should be apprised at the outset of the material upon which non-disclosure was upheld on the Crown's earlier application.

In the later case of *R v Keane*, the Court of Appeal made the point that 'the more full and specific the indication the defendant's lawyers give of the defence or issues they are likely to raise, the more accurately both prosecution and judge will be able to discuss the value to the defence of the material'.[29]

---

[29] [1994] 1 WLR 746, 752.

The approach advocated in *Davis* is now encapsulated in the Crown Court (Criminal Procedure and Investigations Act 1996) (Disclosure) Rules 1997 and in the Magistrates' Courts (Criminal Procedure and Investigations Act 1996) (Disclosure) Rules 1997.

It should be noted that, in a criminal case, the Crown Prosecution Service may be able to disclose voluntarily to the defence, without obtaining a court order, documents in respect of which a class claim to public interest immunity can be made. However, the prior express written approval of the Treasury Solicitor to the voluntary disclosure must be obtained. To seek such approval the CPS should submit to the Treasury Solicitor copies of the relevant documents, identify the public interest immunity class into which they fall, and indicate the materiality of the documents to the proceedings. 'Before giving his approval, the Treasury Solicitor should consult any other relevant government department and satisfy himself that the balance in his view falls clearly in favour of disclosing the documents. In making that assessment he will inevitably have regard, inter alia, to (a) the particular class of documents involved, (b) their materiality to the proceedings and (c) the extent to which disclosure will damage the public interest in the integrity of the class claim. The Treasury Solicitor should be the readier to approve disclosure of documents likely to assist the defence case than those which the CPS wish to disclose with a view to furthering the interests of the prosecution.'[30]

5. CONFIDENTIALITY

Certain relationships – such as the relationship between doctor and patient, priest and penitent, banker and customer, or journalist and source – are carried on with the expectation that they are confidential relationships. To what extent are such relationships protected by the doctrine of public interest immunity?

Extract 12.5.1

Science Research Council v Nassé [1980] AC 1028, 1065–6 (HL)

LORD WILBERFORCE:

1. There is no principle of public interest immunity, as that expression was developed from *Conway v Rimmer* [1968] AC 910, protecting . . . confidential documents . . .
2. There is no principle in English law by which documents are protected from discovery by reason of confidentiality alone. But there is no reason why, in the exercise of its discretion to order discovery, the tribunal should not have

---

[30] *R v Horseferry Road Magistrates' Court, ex p Bennett (No 2)* [1994] 1 All ER 289, 297.

regard to the fact that documents are confidential, and that to order disclosure would involve a breach of confidence. . . .

3. As a corollary to the above, it should be added that relevance alone, though a necessary ingredient, does not provide an automatic sufficient test for ordering discovery. The tribunal always has a discretion. . . .

4. The ultimate test . . . is whether discovery is necessary for disposing fairly of the proceedings. If it is, then discovery must be ordered notwithstanding confidentiality. But where the court is impressed with the need to preserve confidentiality in a particular case, it will consider carefully whether the necessary information has been or can be obtained by other means, not involving a breach of confidence.

5. In order to reach a conclusion whether discovery is necessary notwithstanding confidentiality the tribunal should inspect the documents. It will naturally consider whether justice can be done by special measures such as 'covering up', substituting anonymous references for specific names, or, in rare cases, hearing in camera.

6. The procedure by which this process is to be carried out is one for tribunals to work out in a manner which will avoid delay and unnecessary applications.

See also *Lonrho PLC v Fayed (No 4)*[31] and *Wallace Smith Trust Co v Deloitte*.[32]

The following statutory provision relates to the disclosure of sources of information contained in *publications*.

Extract 12.5.2

Contempt of Court Act 1981, s 10

10. Sources of information

No court may require a person to disclose, nor is any person guilty of contempt of court for refusing to disclose, the source of information contained in a publication for which he is responsible, unless it be established to the satisfaction of the court that disclosure is necessary in the interests of justice or national security or for the prevention of disorder or crime.

This provision was the subject of detailed consideration by the House of Lords in *X Ltd v Morgan-Grampian Ltd*,[33] in which a number of earlier authorities were discussed. *X Ltd v Morgan-Grampian Ltd* concerned Goodwin, a trainee journalist on the staff of *The Engineer*, which was published by Morgan-Grampian Ltd. Goodwin was telephoned by a person who informed him that a company, Tetra Ltd, was in the process of raising a £5 million loan and had financial problems as a result of an expected loss of £2,100,000 for 1989 on a turnover of £20,300,000. This information came from a draft of Tetra

---

[31] [1994] 2 WLR 209.
[32] [1996] 4 All ER 403, 412–3.
[33] [1991] 1 AC 1.

Ltd's confidential corporate plan, a copy of which had been stolen. On application by Tetra Ltd, the High Court ordered that Goodwin disclose the identity of his source on the ground that such disclosure was 'necessary in the interests of justice'. After an unsuccessful appeal to the Court of Appeal, Goodwin appealed to the House of Lords.

Extract 12.5.3

X Ltd v Morgan-Grampian Ltd [1991] 1 AC 1, 40–4 (HL)

LORD BRIDGE OF HARWICH: The courts have always recognised an important public interest in the free flow of information. How far and in what circumstances the maintenance of this public interest operated to confer on journalists any privilege from disclosure of their sources which the common law would recognise admitted of no short and simple answer on the authorities. But the matter is no longer governed by the common law and I do not think any assistance is to be gained from the authorities preceding the coming into force of section 10 of the Contempt of Court Act 1981 . . .

It has been accepted in this case at all levels that the section applies to the circumstances of the instant case notwithstanding that the information obtained by Mr Goodwin from the source has not been 'contained in a publication.' The information having been communicated and received for the purposes of publication, it is clearly right to treat it as subject to the rule which the section lays down, since the purpose underlying the statutory protection of sources of information is as much applicable before as after publication. It is also now clearly established that the section is to be given a wide, rather than a narrow, construction in the sense that the restriction on disclosure applies not only to direct orders to disclose the identity of a source but also to any order for disclosure of material which will indirectly identify the source and applies notwithstanding that the enforcement of the restriction may operate to defeat rights of property vested in the party who seeks to obtain that material: *Secretary of State for Defence v Guardian Newspapers Ltd* [1984] Ch 156, 166–167, *per* Griffiths LJ; [1985] AC 339, 349–350, *per* Lord Diplock. As a statement of the rationale underlying this wide construction I cannot do better than quote from the passage in the judgment of Griffiths LJ to which I have referred, where he said:

> 'The press have always attached the greatest importance to their ability to protect their sources of information. If they are not able to do so, they believe that many of their sources would dry up and this would seriously interfere with their effectiveness. It is in the interests of us all that we should have a truly effective press, and it seems to me that Parliament by enacting section 10 has clearly recognised the importance that attaches to the ability of the press to protect their sources. . . . I can see no harm in giving a wide construction to the opening words of the section because by the latter part of the section the court is given ample powers to order the source to be revealed where in the circumstances of a particular case the wider public interest makes it necessary to do so.'

565

It follows then that, whenever disclosure is sought, as here, of a document which will disclose the identity of a source within the ambit of section 10, the statutory restriction operates unless the party seeking disclosure can satisfy the court that 'disclosure is necessary' in the interests of one of the four matters of public concern that are listed in the section. I think it is indisputable that where a judge asks himself the question: 'Can I be satisfied that disclosure of the source of *this* information is necessary to serve *this* interest?' he has to engage in a balancing exercise. He starts with the assumptions, first, that the protection of sources is itself a matter of high public importance, secondly, that nothing less than necessity will suffice to override it, thirdly, that the necessity can only arise out of concern for another matter of high public importance, being one of the four interests listed in the section.

What assistance is to be derived from the authorities as to the proper tests to be applied in carrying out this balancing exercise? In *Secretary of State for Defence v Guardian Newspapers Ltd* [1985] AC 339, 345, Lord Diplock said:

'The section is so drafted as to make it a question of fact not of discretion as to whether in the particular case a requirement for disclosure of sources of information falls within one of the express exceptions introduced by the word "unless."'

In the same case I said, at p 372:

'There is no ambiguity in the phrase "necessary in the interests of national security." Whether such a necessity is established by the evidence, and, in the case of an interlocutory application, whether the necessity is established at the interlocutory stage, are both questions of fact which must always depend on the evidence adduced in any particular case.'

In *In re An Inquiry under the Company Securities (Insider Dealing) Act 1985* [1988] AC 660, 704, Lord Griffiths said:

'What then is meant by the words "necessary . . . for the prevention of . . . crime" in section 10? I do not think that much light is thrown upon this question by an elaborate discussion of the meaning of the word "necessary." "Necessary" is a word in common usage in everyday speech with which everyone is familiar. Like all words, it will take colour from its context; for example, most people would regard it as "necessary" to do everything possible to prevent a catastrophe but would not regard it as "necessary" to do everything possible to prevent some minor inconvenience. Furthermore, whether a particular measure is necessary, although described as a question of fact for the purpose of section 10, involves the exercise of a judgment upon the established facts. In the exercise of that judgment different people may come to different conclusions on the same facts; for an example of this one has to look no further than *Secretary of State for Defence v Guardian Newspapers Ltd.* But this cannot be avoided and the task of the judge will not be lightened by substituting for the familiar word "necessary" some other set of words with a similar meaning. I do not myself think that it helps to consider the meaning of "necessary" when used in the narrow context of discovery of documents and then apply it to the very broad considerations that will arise when considering the four heads of public interest identified in section 10. I therefore derive no assistance from the discussion of the word "necessary" in *Air Canada v Secretary of State for Trade* [1983] 2 AC 394. I doubt if it is possible to go further than to say that "necessary" has a meaning that lies somewhere between "indispensable" on the one hand, and "useful" or "expedient" on the other, and to leave it to the judge to decide towards which end of the scale of meaning he will place it on the facts of any particular case. The nearest paraphrase I can suggest is "really needed."'

Lord Oliver of Aylmerton said, at pp 708–709:

'Thus the essential question raised by this appeal is whether . . . it is information which is "necessary . . . for the prevention of . . . crime." That is a question which the judge before whom it arises can determine only in the context of the particular facts proved before him and I share the doubt expressed by my noble and learned friend whether it is either possible or desirable to seek to provide for him, by reference to other more or less synonymous adjectives, some absolute yardstick by which the question is to be answered. Necessity is a relative concept and the degree of need before an act or measure can be said to be "necessary," although not, clearly, a question which is to be answered without reference to some objective standards, must, in the end, be and remain a matter of judgment.'

I cannot help wondering whether these dicta do not concentrate attention too much on only one side of the picture. They suggest that in determining whether the criterion of necessity is established one need only look at, in the one case, the interests of national security and, in the other case, the prevention of crime. In the context of cases dealing with those two grounds of exception to the protection of sources, it is perfectly understandable that they should do so. For if non-disclosure of a source of information will imperil national security or enable a crime to be committed which might otherwise be prevented, it is difficult to imagine that any judge would hesitate to order disclosure. These two public interests are of such overriding importance that once it is shown that disclosure will serve one of those interests, the necessity of disclosure follows almost automatically; though even here if a judge were asked to order disclosure of a source of information in the interests of the prevention of crime, he 'might properly refuse to do so if, for instance, the crime was of a trivial nature:' see [1988] AC 660, 703, *per* Lord Griffiths.

But the question whether disclosure is necessary in the interests of justice gives rise to a more difficult problem of weighing one public interest against another. A question arising under this part of section 10 has not previously come before your Lordships' House for decision. In discussing the section generally Lord Diplock said in *Secretary of State for Defence v Guardian Newspapers Ltd* [1985] AC 339, 350:

'The exceptions include no reference to "the public interest" generally and I would add that in my view the expression "justice," the interests of which are entitled to protection, is not used in a general sense as the antonym of "injustice" but in the technical sense of the administration of justice in the course of legal proceedings in a court of law, or, by reason of the extended definition of "court" in section 19 of the Act of 1981 before a tribunal or body exercising the judicial power of the state.'

I agree entirely with the first half of this dictum. To construe 'justice' as the antonym of 'injustice' in section 10 would be far too wide. But to confine it to 'the technical sense of the administration of justice in the course of legal proceedings in a court of law' seems to me, with all respect due to any dictum of the late Lord Diplock, to be too narrow. It is, in my opinion, 'in the interests of justice,' in the sense in which this phrase is used in section 10, that persons should be enabled to exercise important legal rights and to protect themselves from serious legal wrongs whether or not resort to legal proceedings in a court of law will be necessary to attain these objectives. Thus, to take a very obvious example, if an employer of a large staff is suffering grave damage from the activities of an unidentified disloyal servant, it is undoubtedly in the interests of justice that he should be able to identify him in order to terminate his contract of employment, notwithstanding that no legal proceedings may be necessary to achieve that end.

Construing the phrase 'in the interests of justice' in this sense immediately emphasises the importance of the balancing exercise. It will not be sufficient, per se, for a party seeking disclosure of a source protected by section 10 to show merely that he will be unable without disclosure to exercise the legal right or avert the threatened legal wrong on which he bases his claim in order to establish the necessity of disclosure. The judge's task will always be to weigh in the scales the importance of enabling the ends of justice to be attained in the circumstances of the particular case on the one hand against the importance of protecting the source on the other hand. In this balancing exercise it is only if the judge is satisfied that disclosure in the interests of justice is of such preponderating importance as to override the statutory privilege against disclosure that the threshold of necessity will be reached.

Whether the necessity of disclosure in this sense is established is certainly a question of fact rather than an issue calling for the exercise of the judge's discretion, but, like many other questions of fact, such as the question whether somebody has acted reasonably in given circumstances, it will call for the exercise of a discriminating and sometimes difficult value judgment. In estimating the weight to be attached to the importance of disclosure in the interests of justice on the one hand and that of protection from disclosure in pursuance of the policy which underlies section 10 on the other hand, many factors will be relevant on both sides of the scale.

It would be foolish to attempt to give comprehensive guidance as to how the balancing exercise should be carried out. But it may not be out of place to indicate the kind of factors which will require consideration. In estimating the importance to be given to the case in favour of disclosure there will be a wide spectrum within which the particular case must be located. If the party seeking disclosure shows, for example, that his very livelihood depends upon it, this will put the case near one end of the spectrum. If he shows no more than that what he seeks to protect is a minor interest in property, this will put the case at or near the other end. On the other side the importance of protecting a source from disclosure in pursuance of the policy underlying the statute will also vary within a wide spectrum. One important factor will be the nature of the information obtained from the source. The greater the legitimate public interest in the information which the source has given to the publisher or intended publisher, the greater will be the importance of protecting the source.

But another and perhaps more significant factor which will very much affect the importance of protecting the source will be the manner in which the information was itself obtained by the source. If it appears to the court that the information was obtained legitimately this will enhance the importance of protecting the source. Conversely, if it appears that the information was obtained illegally, this will diminish the importance of protecting the source unless, of course, this factor is counterbalanced by a clear public interest in publication of the information, as in the classic case where the source has acted for the purpose of exposing iniquity. I draw attention to these considerations by way of illustration only and I emphasise once again that they are in no way intended to be read as a code.

In the result, the House of Lords agreed with the lower courts that disclosure in this case was 'necessary in the interests of justice'. Following the decision of the House of Lords, the High Court fined Goodwin £5,000 for contempt of court. When the case reached the European Court of Human Rights, however, it was held that there had been an unjustified violation of Goodwin's right to freedom of expression under art 10 of the European Convention on Human Rights.

Extract 12.5.4

Goodwin v UK (1996) 22 EHRR 123, 139, 143–6 (ECHR)

27. The applicant alleged that the disclosure order requiring him to reveal the identity of his source and the fine imposed upon him for having refused to do so constituted a violation of Article 10 of the Convention, which reads:
   1. Everyone has the right to freedom of expression. This right shall include freedom to hold opinions and to receive and impart information and ideas without interference by public authority and regardless of frontiers. This Article shall not prevent States from requiring the licensing of broadcasting, television or cinema enterprises.
   2. The exercise of these freedoms, since it carries with it duties and responsibilities, may be subject to such formalities, conditions, restrictions or penalties as are prescribed by law and are necessary in a democratic society, in the interests of national security, territorial integrity or public safety, for the prevention of disorder or crime, for the protection of health or morals, for the protection of the reputation or rights of others, for preventing the disclosure of information received in confidence, or for maintaining the authority and impartiality of the judiciary.
28. It was undisputed that the measures constituted an interference with the applicant's right to freedom of expression as guaranteed by Article 10(1) and the Court sees no reason to hold otherwise. It must therefore examine whether the interference was justified under Article 10(2).
. . .

39. The Court recalls that freedom of expression constitutes one of the essential foundations of a democratic society and that the safeguards to be afforded to the press are of particular importance.

Protection of journalistic sources is one of the basic conditions for press freedom, as is reflected in the laws and the professional codes of conduct in a number of Contracting States and is affirmed in several international instruments on journalistic freedoms. Without such protection, sources may be deterred from assisting the press in informing the public on matters of public interest. As a result the vital public watchdog role of the press may be undermined and the ability of the press to provide accurate and reliable information may be adversely affected. Having regard to the importance of the protection of journalistic sources for press freedom in a democratic society and the potentially chilling effect an order of source disclosure has on the exercise of that freedom, such a measure cannot be compatible with Article 10 of the Convention unless it is justified by an overriding requirement in the public interest.

These considerations are to be taken into account in applying to the facts of the present case the test of necessity in a democratic society under Article 10(2).

40. As a matter of general principle, the 'necessity' for any restriction on freedom of expression must be convincingly established. Admittedly, it is in the first place for the national authorities to assess whether there is a 'pressing social need' for the restriction and, in making their assessment, they enjoy a certain margin of appreciation. In the present context, however, the national margin of appreciation is circumscribed by the interest of democratic society in ensuring and maintaining a free press. Similarly, that interest will weigh heavily in the balance in determining, as must be done under Article 10(2), whether the restriction was proportionate to the legitimate aim pursued. In sum, limitations on the confidentiality of journalistic sources call for the most careful scrutiny by the Court.

The Court's task, in exercising its supervisory function, is not to take the place of the national authorities but rather to review under Article 10 the decisions they have taken pursuant to their power of appreciation. In so doing, the Court must look at the 'interference' complained of in the light of the case as a whole and determine whether the reasons adduced by the national authorities to justify it are 'relevant and sufficient'.

41. In the instant case, as appears from Lord Bridge's speech in the House of Lords, Tetra was granted an order for source disclosure primarily on the grounds of the threat of severe damage to their business, and consequently to the livelihood of their employees, which would arise from disclosure of the information in their corporate plan while their refinancing negotiations were still continuing. This threat, 'ticking away beneath them like a time bomb', as Lord Donaldson put it in the Court of Appeal, could only be defused, Lord Bridge considered, if they could identify the source either as himself the thief of the stolen copy of the plan or as a means to lead to identification of the thief and thus put the company in a position to institute proceedings for the recovery of the missing document. The importance of protecting the source, Lord Bridge concluded, was much diminished by the source's complicity, at the very least, in a gross breach of confidentiality which was not counterbalanced by any legitimate interest in publication of the information.

42. In the Court's view, the justifications for the impugned disclosure order in the present case have to be seen in the broader context of the *ex parte*

interim injunction which had earlier been granted to the company, restraining not only the applicant himself but also the publishers of *The Engineer* from publishing any information derived from the plan. That injunction had been notified to all the national newspapers and relevant journals. The purpose of the disclosure order was to a very large extent the same as that already being achieved by the injunction, namely to prevent dissemination of the confidential information contained in the plan. There was no doubt, according to Lord Donaldson in the Court of Appeal, that the injunction was effective in stopping dissemination of the confidential information by the press. Tetra's creditors, customers, suppliers and competitors would not therefore come to learn of the information through the press. A vital component of the threat of damage to the company had thus already largely been neutralised by the injunction. This being so, in the Court's opinion, in so far as the disclosure order merely served to reinforce the injunction, the additional restriction on freedom of expression which it entailed was not supported by sufficient reasons for the purposes of Article 10(2) of the Convention.

43. What remains to be ascertained by the Court is whether the further purposes served by the disclosure order provided sufficient justification.

44. In this respect it is true, as Lord Donaldson put it, that the injunction 'would not effectively prevent publication to [Tetra's] customers or competitors' directly by the applicant journalist's source (or that source's source). Unless aware of the identity of the source, Tetra would not be in a position to stop such further dissemination of the contents of the plan, notably by bringing proceedings against him or her for recovery of the missing document, for an injunction against further disclosure by him or her and for compensation for damage.

It also had a legitimate reason as a commercial enterprise in unmasking a disloyal employee or collaborator who might have continuing access to its premises in order to terminate his or her association with the company.

45. These are undoubtedly relevant reasons. However, as also recognised by the national courts, it will not be sufficient, *per se*, for a party seeking disclosure of a source to show merely that he or she will be unable without disclosure to exercise the legal right or avert the threatened legal wrong on which he or she bases his or her claim in order to establish the necessity of disclosure. In that connection, the Court would recall that the considerations to be taken into account by the Convention institutions for their review under Article 10(2) tip the balance of competing interests in favour of the interest of democratic society in securing a free press. On the facts of the present case, the Court cannot find that Tetra's interests in eliminating, by proceedings against the source, the residual threat of damage through dissemination of the confidential information otherwise than by the press, in obtaining compensation and in unmasking a disloyal employee or collaborator were, even if considered cumulatively, sufficient to outweigh the vital public interest in the protection of the applicant journalist's source. The Court does not therefore consider that the further purposes served by the disclosure order, when measured against the standards imposed by the Convention, amount to an overriding requirement in the public interest.

46. In sum, there was not, in the Court's view, a reasonable relationship of proportionality between the legitimate aim pursued by the disclosure order

and the means deployed to achieve that aim. The restriction which the disclosure order entailed on the applicant journalist's exercise of his freedom of expression cannot therefore be regarded as having been necessary in a democratic society, within the meaning of Article 10(2), for the protection of Tetra's rights under English law, notwithstanding the margin of appreciation available to the national authorities.

Accordingly, the Court concludes that both the order requiring the applicant to reveal his source and the fine imposed upon him for having refused to do so gave rise to a violation of his right to freedom of expression under Article 10.

Do you agree with the decision of the European Court of Human Rights? Or do you agree with the view of the dissenting judges that 'the domestic courts were . . . better placed to evaluate, on the basis of the evidence before them, the strength of [Tetra's] interests [in securing the additional measures of protection sought through the disclosure order], and . . . the conclusion which they reached as to where, in the light of their evaluation, the corresponding balance should be struck was within the margin of appreciation allowed to the national authorities'?[34]

Further reading

T R S Allan, 'Public Interest Immunity and Ministers' Responsibilities' [1993] *Criminal Law Review* 660

J A Andrews, 'Public Interest and Criminal Proceedings' (1988) 104 *Law Quarterly Review* 410

D H Clark, 'The Last Word on the Last Word' (1969) 32 *Modern Law Review* 142

C Forsyth, 'Public Interest Immunity: Recent and Future Developments' [1997] *Cambridge Law Journal* 51

G Ganz, '*Matrix Churchill* and Public Interest Immunity: A Postscript' (1995) 58 *Modern Law Review* 417

I Leigh, 'Matrix Churchill, Supergun and the Scott Inquiry' [1993] *Public Law* 630

A R Ostrin, 'Police Observation Points' (1992) 156 *Justice of the Peace* 423

R Scott, 'The Acceptable and Unacceptable Use of Public Interest Immunity' [1996] *Public Law* 427

— *Report of the Inquiry into the Export of Defence Equipment and Dual-Use Goods to Iraq and Related Prosecutions* (1996)

A T H Smith, 'Public Interest Immunity and Sensitive Material' [1993] *Cambridge Law Journal* 357

— 'Public Interest Immunity in Criminal Cases' [1993] *Cambridge Law Journal* 1

---

[34] *Goodwin v UK* (1996) 22 EHRR 123, 151.

C Tapper, 'The Open Society and its Enemy' (1978) 41 *Modern Law Review* 192

— 'Privilege and Policy' (1974) 37 *Modern Law Review* 92

A Tomkins, 'Public Interest Immunity after Matrix Churchill' [1993] *Public Law* 650

A A S Zuckerman, 'Privilege and Public Interest' in C F H Tapper (ed), *Crime, Proof and Punishment: Essays in Memory of Sir Rupert Cross* (1981)

— 'Public Interest Immunity – A Matter of Prime Judicial Responsibility' (1994) 57 *Modern Law Review* 703

13

LEGAL PROFESSIONAL PRIVILEGE

1. THE CONCEPT OF PRIVILEGE

Generally, a person entitled to claim 'privilege' is not required to disclose the privileged material or to give evidence of that material. Such material is allowed to be withheld not because of its actual or potential unreliability, but rather, as in the case of material subject to public interest immunity, because of considerations of extrinsic policy. There are three main categories of privilege, sometimes termed the 'heads of privilege': (1) the privilege against self-incrimination; (2) 'without prejudice' negotiations; and (3) most importantly, legal professional privilege. The privilege against self-incrimination permits a witness in a trial to refuse to answer questions in certain circumstances. In *Blunt v Park Lane Hotel Ltd* Goddard LJ stated that 'the rule is that no one is bound to answer any question if the answer thereto would, in the opinion of the judge, have a tendency to expose the deponent to any criminal charge, penalty, or forfeiture which the judge regards as reasonably likely to be preferred or sued for'.[1] This rule has been affected, however, by numerous statutory provisions, such as, in criminal proceedings, s 1(e) and (f) of the Criminal Evidence Act 1898, discussed in Chapter 6. The position with respect to 'without prejudice' negotiations has been explained by the House of Lords as follows:

Extract 13.1.1

Rush & Tomkins v GLC [1989] AC 1280, 1299–300 (HL)

LORD GRIFFITHS: The 'without prejudice' rule is a rule governing the admissibility of evidence and is founded upon the public policy of encouraging litigants to settle their differences rather than litigate them to a finish. . . .

The rule applies to exclude all negotiations genuinely aimed at settlement whether oral or in writing from being given in evidence. A competent solicitor will always head any negotiating correspondence 'without prejudice' to make

[1] [1942] 2 KB 253, 257.

clear beyond doubt that in the event of the negotiations being unsuccessful they are not to be referred to at the subsequent trial. However, the application of the rule is not dependent upon the use of the phrase 'without prejudice' and if it is clear from the surrounding circumstances that the parties were seeking to compromise the action, evidence of the content of those negotiations will, as a general rule, not be admissible at the trial and cannot be used to establish an admission or partial admission.

Detailed treatments of the privilege against self-incrimination and 'without prejudice' negotiations may be found in the standard textbooks. The focus of this chapter is on an examination of legal professional privilege. When proceeding through this chapter, the following questions should be borne in mind. What exactly are the extrinsic policy considerations underlying the doctrine of legal professional privilege? Does the current state of the law reflect these considerations in a coherent manner?

2. WHAT IS LEGAL PROFESSIONAL PRIVILEGE?

Two types of communications will be subject to legal professional privilege:

(1) Communications between *client and legal adviser* which have, as their purpose, the obtaining and giving of legal advice. (The privilege extends also to documents, or other items, which are brought into existence for the purpose of obtaining or giving legal advice.)
(2) Communications between *client or legal adviser and third parties* which have preparation for litigation as their sole or dominant purpose. (The privilege extends also to documents, or other items, which are brought into existence for the sole or dominant purpose of preparing for litigation.)

These principles are also articulated in section 10 of the Police and Criminal Evidence Act 1984, which has been held[2] to encapsulate the common law.

Extract 13.2.1

Police and Criminal Evidence Act 1984, s 10

10. Meaning of 'items subject to legal privilege'
   (1) Subject to subsection (2) below, in this Act 'items subject to legal privilege' means –
      (a) communications between a professional legal adviser and his client or any person representing his client made in connection with the giving of legal advice to the client;

---

[2] *R v CCC, ex p Francis & Francis* [1989] AC 346, 382, 384–5 per Lord Griffiths; 395 per Lord Goff of Chieveley.

(b) communications between a professional legal adviser and his client or any person representing his client or between such an adviser or his client or any such representative and any other person made in connection with or in contemplation of legal proceedings and for the purposes of such proceedings; and

(c) items enclosed with or referred to in such communications and made –

(i) in connection with the giving of legal advice; or

(ii) in connection with or in contemplation of legal proceedings and for the purposes of such proceedings,

when they are in the possession of a person who is entitled to possession of them.

(2) Items held with the intention of furthering a criminal purpose are not items subject to legal privilege.

The privilege is that of the client, and of the client's successors in title. In addition, there is a principle that 'once privileged, always privileged'.[3] It may be possible, therefore, for privilege to be claimed in subsequent proceedings. The extent to which privilege may be claimed in subsequent proceedings by the client, or by the client's successor in title, was discussed in the following case:

Extract 13.2.2

The 'Aegis Blaze' [1986] 1 Lloyd's Rep 203, 209–10 (CA)

CROOM-JOHNSON LJ: The matter in the end appears to me to stand thus. Unless the party claiming the privilege or his successor is a party to the subsequent action, no question of a claim to privilege will arise. . . . If, however, the party claiming privilege in the second action is the person entitled to privilege in the first action, but there is no connection of subject matter whatever, it is most improbable that the question will arise, for in such circumstances the document will not be relevant and will not therefore be disclosable, and there will therefore be no question of production. If, however, there is a sufficient connection for the document to be relevant, then it is, in my view, right that the party entitled to the privilege should be able to assert it in the second action. I accept, of course, that that may mean that the Court trying the second action is deprived of full information, but so would the Court have been in the first action, and so also may it be in any case where privilege is asserted.

Privilege may therefore be invoked in subsequent litigation, by the client or his or her successor in title, even if the subject matter of the subsequent litigation, or the parties to it, are not the same as in the original litigation.

---

[3] *R v Derby Magistrates' Court, ex p B* [1995] 3 WLR 681, 692.

(a) Collateral facts and pre-existing documents

Privilege does not extend to what may be termed 'collateral facts', and, thus, evidence of such facts is admissible.[4] A legal adviser is permitted, for example, to give evidence that he or she had a meeting with the client; to give evidence about the physical or mental state of the client;[5] and to give evidence about the client's handwriting.[6] Equally, it is clear that pre-existing documents – that is, documents not actually brought into existence for the purpose either of obtaining/giving legal advice or of preparing for litigation – are not privileged.[7] The following extract is taken from a decision of the Court of Appeal on s 10(1)(c) of the Police and Criminal Evidence Act 1984 (reproduced above).

Extract 13.2.3

R v R [1994] 1 WLR 758, 763 (CA)

EVANS LJ: The object in question in the present case was a sample of the appellant's blood provided by him to his general practitioner at the request of his solicitors and for the purposes of his defence in these criminal proceedings. It was given in circumstances of confidence. That factor is a precondition of privilege, although it is not enough to create privilege on its own. We hold that the sample so obtained was an 'item' which was subject to legal privilege in these proceedings, provided that it falls within the express wording of section 10.

Mr Hotten submitted that section 10 is limited to items which are 'made' and that a blood sample cannot be said to have been 'made.' It is even more difficult, he submits, to say that other kinds of samples, such as nail clippings or individual hairs taken as samples, in common parlance are 'made.' In our judgment, however, the word was used in a general sense, certainly wide enough to include 'brought into existence,' and a sample of blood obtained and held in a particular container does constitute an 'item . . . made' for the purposes of legal proceedings etc. If his submission were correct, it is difficult to identify any kind of object which would be subject to legal privilege under section 10(1)(*c*), except perhaps a model, made for the purpose of obtaining expert advice. (Documents are communications within section 10(1)(*a*) and (*b*).) The significance of 'made,' meaning 'brought into existence,' in our judgment, is that the privilege does not extend to objects which did not come into existence for the purpose of obtaining legal advice, etc: cf *Ventouris v Mountain* [1991] 1 WLR 607.

A pre-existing document *will*, however, be privileged if to disclose it would have the effect of revealing the nature of the legal advice given to the client.[8]

---

[4] See generally A Keane, *The Modern Law of Evidence* (4th ed 1996) 526, for a fuller discussion.
[5] *Jones v Godrich* (1845) 5 Moo PC 16; 13 ER 394.
[6] *Dwyer v Collins* (1852) 21 LJ Ex 225, 227.
[7] *Brown v Foster* (1857) 1 H & N 736; 156 ER 1397; *R v Peterborough Justice, ex p Hicks* [1977] 1 WLR 1371; *R v King* [1983] 1 WLR 411; *Ventouris v Mountain* [1991] 1 WLR 607.
[8] *Dubai Bank Ltd v Galadari (No 7)* [1992] 1 WLR 106, 110. See also *Lyell v Kennedy* (1884) 27 Ch D 1, 26.

(b) 'Legal adviser'

At issue in *New Victoria Hospital v Ryan*[9] was correspondence between the hospital and a firm of personnel consultants which at the time did not employ any legally qualified staff. The Employment Appeal Tribunal held that privilege did not attach to the documents 'because in our opinion the privilege should be strictly confined to legal advisers such as solicitors and counsel, who are professionally qualified, who are members of professional bodies, who are subject to the rules and etiquette of their professions, and who owe a duty to the court. This is a clearly defined and easily identifiable qualification for the attachment of privilege. To extend the privilege to unqualified advisers such as personnel consultants is in our opinion unnecessary and undesirable.'[10]

The general position is, however, affected by a number of specific statutory provisions. For example, the effect of s 33 of the Administration of Justice Act 1985 is that licensed conveyancers are to be treated as solicitors for the purposes of legal professional privilege. Note also the following provision:

Extract 13.2.4

Copyright, Designs and Patents Act 1988, s 280

280. Privilege for communications with patent agents

(1) This section applies to communications as to any matter relating to the protection of any invention, design, technical information, or trade mark, or as to any matter involving passing off.

(2) Any such communication –

    (a) between a person and his patent agent, or

    (b) for the purpose of obtaining, or in response to a request for, information which a person is seeking for the purpose of instructing his patent agent,

is privileged from disclosure in legal proceedings in England, Wales or Northern Ireland in the same way as a communication between a person and his solicitor or, as the case may be, a communication for the purpose of obtaining, or in response to a request for, information which a person seeks for the purpose of instructing his solicitor.

. . .

(c) Communications between client and legal adviser

Precisely what communications between client and legal adviser will be subject to legal professional privilege?

---

[9] [1993] ICR 201.
[10] At 203–4.

Extract 13.2.5

Minter v Priest **[1930] AC 558, 568, 581, 584 (HL)**

LORD BUCKMASTER: The relationship of solicitor and client being once established, it is not a necessary conclusion that whatever conversation ensued was protected from disclosure. The conversation to secure this privilege must be such as, within a very wide and generous ambit of interpretation, must be fairly referable to the relationship, but outside that boundary the mere fact that a person speaking is a solicitor, and the person to whom he speaks is his client affords no protection.

LORD ATKIN: . . . communications between solicitor and client which do not pass for the purpose of giving or receiving professional advice are not protected. It follows that client and solicitor may meet for the purpose of legal advice and exchange protected communications, and may yet in the course of the same interview make statements to each other not for the purpose of giving or receiving professional advice but for some other purpose. Such statements are not within the rule: see per Lord Wrenbury in *O'Rourke v Darbishire* [1920] AC 581, 629.

. . .

. . . It is not necessary that the relations should have reached the definite status of solicitor and client. The solicitor may not be willing to be employed as a solicitor by the person with whom he may be communicating. If a person goes to a professional legal adviser for the purpose of seeing whether the professional person will give him professional advice, communications made for the purpose of indicating the advice required will be protected.

O'Rourke v Darbishire, referred to by Lord Atkin, also makes it clear that legal professional privilege does attach in a situation where the legal adviser gives legal advice to a body of which he or she happens to be a member, such as a board of trustees:

> Trustees are entitled to consult a solicitor with reference to the affairs of the trust, and the communications between them and their legal adviser are privileged if for the purpose of obtaining legal advice. Why should such communications be less privileged because the solicitor is himself one of the trustees? There is no valid distinction between such communications with the solicitor who is himself a trustee, and such communications with a solicitor who is outside the trust altogether. Of course the privilege is confined to communications genuinely for the purpose of getting legal advice. It would not extend to mere business communications with reference to the trust, not for the purpose of getting legal advice.[11]

[11] [1920] AC 581, 602.

579

Extract 13.2.6

Balabel v Air India [1988] Ch 317, 330–1 (CA)

TAYLOR LJ: In my judgment, . . . the test is whether the communication or other document was made confidentially for the purposes of legal advice. Those purposes have to be construed broadly. Privilege obviously attaches to a document conveying legal advice from solicitor to client and to a specific request from the client for such advice. But it does not follow that all other communications between them lack privilege. In most solicitor and client relationships, especially where a transaction involves protracted dealings, advice may be required or appropriate on matters great or small at various stages. There will be a continuum of communication and meetings between the solicitor and client. . . . Where information is passed by the solicitor or client to the other as part of the continuum aimed at keeping both informed so that advice may be sought and given as required, privilege will attach. A letter from the client containing information may end with such words as 'please advise me what I should do.' But, even if it does not, there will usually be implied in the relationship an overall expectation that the solicitor will at each stage, whether asked specifically or not, tender appropriate advice. Moreover, legal advice is not confined to telling the client the law; it must include advice as to what should prudently and sensibly be done in the relevant legal context.

It may be that applying this test to any series of communications might isolate occasional letters or notes which could not be said to enjoy privilege. But to be disclosable such documents must be not only privilege-free but also material and relevant. Usually a letter which does no more than acknowledge receipt of a document or suggest a date for a meeting will be irrelevant and so non-disclosable. In effect, therefore, the 'purpose of legal advice' test will result in most communications between solicitor and client in, for example, a conveyancing transaction being exempt from disclosure, either because they are privileged or because they are immaterial or irrelevant.

Extract 13.2.7

Nederlandse Reassurantie Groep Holding NV v Bacon & Woodrow [1995] 1 All ER 976, 982–3 (Commercial Court)

COLMAN J: . . . legal professional privilege only attaches to such communications as pass between the solicitor and client which are brought into existence or occur in the course of the performance of the solicitor's professional duty or function as solicitor retained to give professional advice, as distinct from some other capacity unrelated to the giving of legal professional advice . . . if a solicitor is instructed for the purpose of getting legal advice in relation to a particular transaction or series of transactions, then all the communications between the solicitor and the client relating to that transaction will be privileged notwithstanding they do not contain advice on matters of law or construction, provided that they are directly related to the performance by the solicitor of his professional duty as legal adviser of the client. . . .

... a solicitor's professional duty or function is frequently not exclusively related to the giving of advice on matters of law or ... on drafting or construction of documents. It not infrequently relates to the commercial wisdom of entering into a given transaction in relation to which legal advice is also sought.

It has been held that 'if legal advice obtained by one person is passed on to another person for the sake of informing that other person in confidence of legal advice which that person needs to know by reason of a *sufficient common interest* between them', the legal advice remains privileged.[12]

(d) Communications with third parties

Communications with third parties are privileged only if they have preparation for litigation as their sole or dominant purpose. In *Wheeler v Le Marchant*,[13] the question arose whether certain reports made to the defendant's solicitor by a surveyor were privileged. It was held that they were not, because although the reports did relate to the subject matter of the litigation, they had been made at a time when no litigation was actually contemplated. But even if litigation was contemplated, preparation for the litigation must have been at least the dominant purpose of the communications. In *Woolley v North London Railway Co*,[14] it was held that even though litigation was contemplated, certain reports to the general manager of the railway company were not privileged, because they were made simply for the purpose of conveying information.

Extract 13.2.8

Waugh v British Railways Board [1980] AC 521, 531–3, 534–7 (HL)

The plaintiff's husband, an employee of the British Railways Board, was killed in a railway accident. The plaintiff brought an action for damages, and sought discovery of an internal inquiry report made by two officers of the Board two days after the accident. The Board refused discovery on the ground of legal professional privilege.

LORD WILBERFORCE: ... while privilege may be required in order to induce candour in statements made for the purposes of litigation it is not required in relation to statements whose purpose is different – for example to enable a railway to operate safely.

---

[12] *Svenska v Sun Alliance* [1995] 2 Lloyd's Rep 84, 88 (emphasis added).
[13] (1881) 17 Ch D 675.
[14] (1869) LR 4 CP 602.

It is clear that the due administration of justice strongly requires disclosure and production of this report: it was contemporary; it contained statements by witnesses on the spot; it would be not merely relevant evidence, but almost certainly the best evidence as to the cause of the accident. If one accepts that this important public interest can be overridden in order that the defendant may properly prepare his case, how close must the connection be between the preparation of the document and the anticipation of litigation? On principle I would think that the purpose of preparing for litigation ought to be either the sole purpose or at least the dominant purpose of it: to carry the protection further into cases where that purpose was secondary or equal with another purpose would seem to be excessive, and unnecessary in the interest of encouraging truthful revelation. At the lowest such desirability of protection as might exist in such cases is not strong enough to outweigh the need for all relevant documents to be made available.

. . .

It appears to me that unless the purpose of submission to the legal adviser in view of litigation is at least the dominant purpose for which the relevant document was prepared, the reasons which require privilege to be extended to it cannot apply. . . . I would allow the appeal and order disclosure of the joint report.

LORD SIMON OF GLAISDALE: The appellant argues that the correct test is . . . the sole purpose [test]; or, alternatively, . . . the dominant purpose [test]. The respondents argue that *Ankin v London and North Eastern Railway Co* [1930] 1 KB 527 and *Ogden v London Electric Railway Co*, 49 TLR 542, were correctly decided, and that it is sufficient to attract privilege from disclosure if one of the purposes (however subsidiary) is with a view to apprehended litigation.

The issue exemplifies a situation which frequently causes difficulties – where the forensic situation is covered by two valid legal principles which point each to a different forensic conclusion. Here, indeed, both principles subserve the same legal end – the administration of justice. The first principle is that the relevant rules of law should be applied to the whole body of relevant evidence – in other words, in principle all relevant evidence should be adduced to the court. The report in question in this appeal undoubtedly contains information relevant to the matters in issue in the litigation here. The first principle thus indicates that it should be disclosed, so that the appellant may make use of it if she wishes.

The second general principle arises out of the adversary (in contradiction to the inquisitorial) system of administration of justice. Society provides an objective code of law and courts where civil contentions can be decided. But it contents itself with so providing a forum and a code (and nowadays some finance for those who could not otherwise get justice). Having done so much, society considers that it can safely leave each party to bring forward the evidence and argument to establish his/her case, detaching the judge from the hurly-burly of contestation and so enabling him to view the rival contentions dispassionately. It is true that this does not in itself give rise to legal professional privilege. Sir Thomas More, before his time for judicial and administrative responsibility, had a different system for the Utopians:

'For they thinke it most mete, that euery man shuld pleade his owne matter, and tell the same tale before the iudge, that he would tel to his man of lawe. So shall there be lesse circumstance of wordes, and the trwth shal soner cum to light; whiles the iudge with a discrete judgement doth waye the wordes of hym whom no lawier hath instruct with deceit; and whiles he helpeth and beareth out simple wittes agaynst the false and malicious circumuertions of craftie chyldren.' (*Utopia*, 1516, tr Ralph Robinson, 1551, Bk 2, [ch 7].)

This is all very fine; but that great moralist and master of common sense, Dr Johnson, saw the snag. Quite apart from the descent of the judge into the arena:

'As it rarely happens that a man is fit to plead his own cause, lawyers are a class of the community, who, by study and experience, have acquired the art and power of arranging evidence, and of applying to the points at issue what the law has settled. A lawyer is to do for his client all that his client might fairly do for himself, if he could.' (Boswell, *Life of Johnson*, ed Birkbeck Hill (1950), vol v, 26).

So the adversary system calls for legal representation if it is to operate with such justice as is vouchsafed to humankind.

This system of adversary forensic procedure with legal professional advice and representation demands that communications between lawyer and client should be confidential, since the lawyer is for the purpose of litigation merely the client's alter ego. So too material which is to go into the lawyer's (ie the client's) brief or file for litigation. This is the basis for the privilege against disclosure of material collected by or on behalf of a client for the use of his lawyer in pending or anticipated litigation: see Cotton LJ in *Southwark and Vauxhall Water Co v Quick* (1878) 3 QBD 315, 321–322; *D v National Society for the Prevention of Cruelty to Children* [1978] AC 171, 231; Sixteenth Report of the Law Reform Committee, paras 17–21. Apart from the limited exception of some expert evidence, for which the Rules of the Supreme Court make express provision (Ord 38, r 37), a party in civil litigation is not entitled to see the adversary's proofs of what his witnesses will say at the trial; there has been no suggestion that he should be so entitled; and any such development would require the most careful consideration based on widespread consultation. The report in question in this appeal undoubtedly contains material collected by or on behalf of the respondents for the use of their solicitors in anticipated litigation. The second principle thus indicates that the respondents are entitled to claim that it is confidential as between themselves and their solicitors and that they are not bound to disclose it.

Historically, the second principle – that a litigant must bring forward his own evidence to support his case, and cannot call on his adversary to make or aid it – was fundamental to the outlook of the courts of common law. The first principle – that the opponent might be compelled to disclose relevant evidence in his possession – was the doctrine of the Chancery, a court whose conscience would be affronted by forensic success contrary to justice obtained merely through the silent non-cooperation of the defendant (see YB 9 Ed IV, Trin 9), and which therefore had some inclination to limited inquisitorial procedures.

The conflict between the Chancery and the courts of common law was, here as elsewhere, ultimately resolved by compromise and accommodation.

I can see no intrinsic reason why the one principle rather than the other should prevail in a situation where they are counter-indicative. Neither is absolute: both are subject to numerous exceptions. For example, if a document protected by legal professional privilege (or secondary evidence of it) has been obtained by the opposite party independently – even through the default of the legal adviser – even by dishonesty – either will probably be admissible: *Phipson on Evidence*, 12th ed (1976), p 241, para 584; Sixteenth Report of the Law Reform Committee, para 31. The numerous exceptions to the principle that all relevant evidence should be disclosed arise partly from historical reasons (the tensions between the courts of common law, where questions of fact were tried, and the Court of Chancery, where the remedy of discovery was developed), partly from considerations of justice, partly from wider social considerations: see *D v National Society for the Prevention of Cruelty to Children* [1978] AC 171, at pp 231 et seq. Thus the historical exclusion of hearsay evidence, 'the best evidence' rule and 'without prejudice' communications are examples of exceptions to the principle of adduction of all relevant evidence. So too is the rule excluding, in general, evidence going merely to the discredit of a witness, even though the credibility of the witness may be decisive of the case. But the exception which most nearly touches the issue facing your Lordships was cogently invoked in this very connection by James LJ in *Anderson v Bank of British Columbia*, 2 ChD 644, 656:

> '. . . as you have no right to see your adversary's brief, you have no right to see that which comes into existence merely as the materials for the brief.'

The adversary's brief will contain much relevant material; nevertheless, you cannot see it because that would be inconsistent with the adversary forensic process based on legal representation. I would, though, draw attention to the word 'merely' in James LJ's dictum.

There is, then, no a priori reason why the one general principle should yield to the other. But in my judgment each party's main contention would virtually result in the total exclusion of the principle relied on by the other. The rule in *Ogden* in effect means that reports such as that in the instant case will always be excluded, because it is unlikely that there is not in such circumstances even the subsidiary purpose of informing the legal advisers. On the other hand, to enjoin that privilege can only be claimed if the information of legal advisers is the sole purpose of the report will in effect mean that such reports must always be disclosed, because it is unlikely that in such circumstances there will not be even the subsidiary purpose of ascertaining whether the system of work can be improved. Indeed, in this type of report causation and fault can hardly be kept apart.

Your Lordships will therefore, I apprehend, be seeking some intermediate line which will allow each of the two general principles scope in its proper sphere. Various intermediate formulae as a basis for the privilege have been canvassed in argument before your Lordships, most based on some authority – the obtaining of legal advice was 'an appreciable purpose'; 'a substantial purpose'; '*the* substantial purpose'; it was 'wholly or mainly' for that purpose; that was its 'dominant' purpose; that was its 'primary' purpose.

Some of these are in my view too vague. Some give little or no scope to the principle of open litigation with the minimum exclusion of relevant evidence. The one that appeals most to me is 'dominant' purpose ... It allows scope to each of the governing principles. It seems to me less quantitative than 'mainly'; and I think it would be easier to apply – the law is already cognisant of the concept of a dominant purpose – in the law of conspiracy, for example (see *Crofter Hand Woven Harris Tweed Co Ltd v Veitch* [1942] AC 435, especially at pp 445 (Viscount Simon LC), 452 (Viscount Maugham)), and in the law as to fraudulent preference in bankruptcy (see *Halsbury's Laws of England*, 4th ed, vol 3 (1973), pp 496, 499, paras 908, 913).

See also *Melik & Co v Norwich Union*.[15]

In 1976, the High Court of Australia adopted, by a majority, a 'sole purpose' test in preference to a 'dominant purpose' one.[16] The House of Lords in *Waugh* was, however, unpersuaded by this approach, Lord Wilberforce commenting that 'to hold that the purpose ... must be the sole purpose would, apart from difficulties of proof, in my opinion, be too strict a requirement, and would confine the privilege too narrowly'.[17] It is notable that the 'sole purpose' test has been abandoned in favour of a 'dominant purpose' one in the Australian Evidence Act 1995.[18]

The following case contains an important discussion of how it is to be determined what the dominant purpose of a document was.

Extract 13.2.9

Guinness Peat Ltd v Fitzroy Robinson [1987] 1 WLR 1027, 1036–7 (CA)

The plaintiffs, Guinness Peat Properties Ltd, were building developers who engaged the defendants, Fitzroy Robinson Partnership, as architects. The plaintiffs informed the defendants of an alleged design fault. Because the defendants' insurance policy required them to notify claims immediately, the defendants wrote a letter to their insurers expressing their own views on the merits of the claim. The question was whether this letter was privileged.

SLADE LJ: ... the dominant purpose of a document does not necessarily fall to be ascertained by reference to the intention of its actual composer ... Barwick CJ's formulation of the test itself in *Grant v Downs* (1976) 135 CLR 674, 677, refers to the dominant purpose of its author 'or of the person or authority under whose direction, whether particular or general, it was produced or brought into existence.' These words are not to be read as if they had statutory force. Nevertheless, I think that in the present case the insurers

---

[15] [1980] 1 Lloyd's Rep 523.
[16] *Grant v Downs* (1976) 135 CLR 674.
[17] [1980] AC 521, 533.
[18] Section 119.

are to be regarded as the persons under whose direction the McLeish letter was brought into existence, within the sense and spirit of this formulation.
. . .

In the light of [the] authorities, I accept that the dominant purpose of the McLeish letter must be viewed objectively on the evidence, particularly by reference to the intentions of the insurers who procured its genesis. Subject to what is said below, I accept that, so viewed, the dominant purpose was to produce a letter of notification which would be used in order to obtain legal advice or to conduct or aid in the conduct of litigation which was at the time of its production in reasonable prospect.

3. WAIVER

As the privilege is that of the client, he or she may waive it, either expressly or impliedly. Reference to a privileged document in the pleadings may, depending on the circumstances, constitute waiver: 'It must be right that a bare reference to a document in a pleading does not waive any privilege attaching to it . . . If, on the other hand, a document is reproduced in full in the pleading, its confidentiality is gone and no question of privilege could arise. Where the line is drawn between these two extremes may be a matter of some nicety . . .'.[19] In a similar vein, what precisely is waived by the adduction in court of evidence of privileged material would be dependent on the circumstances: 'If the evidence is adduced then the extent of the waiver relates to the transaction to which that evidence goes. The extent of the transaction has to be examined and where it is what somebody said on a particular occasion, then that is the transaction. It is not the subject matter of those conversations. It does not extend to all matters relating to the subject matter of those conversations.'[20]

It is not generally possible to waive privilege in relation only to part of a document. 'Waiver of part of a document is bound to lead to grave difficulties for all parties and to many unjustified suspicions.'[21] An exception to this is recognised, however, where the remainder of the document relates to such a distinct subject matter that severance is possible:

> The second question is whether, the whole of the memorandum being a privileged communication between legal adviser and client, the plaintiffs may waive the privilege with regard to the first two paragraphs of the memorandum but assert privilege over the additional matter. In my judgment, severance would be possible if the memorandum dealt with entirely different subject matters or different incidents and could in effect be divided into two separate memoranda each dealing with a separate subject matter.[22]

[19] *Buttes Gas and Oil Co v Hammer (No 3)* [1981] QB 223, 252, revd in [1982] AC 888 on different grounds.
[20] *General Accident Corpn v Tanter* [1984] 1 WLR 100, 114–15. See also *Balkanbank v Taher* (1994) *The Times*, 19 February.
[21] *Great Atlantic Insurance v Home Insurance* [1981] 1 WLR 529, 537 per Templeman LJ.
[22] At 536.

In *Lillicrap v Nalder & Son*,[23] the plaintiffs were property developers who engaged the defendants, a firm of solicitors, to act for them in a series of transactions. The plaintiffs brought an action against the defendants in respect of one of those transactions, alleging negligence on the part of the defendants in failing to provide proper advice. The Court of Appeal held that the institution by a client of civil proceedings against his or her solicitor constitutes an implied waiver of legal professional privilege to the extent necessary to enable the court to adjudicate the dispute fully and fairly. Such waiver would extend only to documents relevant to an issue in the action. The waiver must extend sufficiently far, however, not only to enable the plaintiff to establish his or her cause of action, but also to enable the defendant to establish a defence to the cause of action if one exists. Here, the issue between the parties concerned causation of loss; the defendants admitted negligence but denied that this had caused the loss, and thus the plaintiffs had to establish such causation before they could be awarded substantial damages. It would be a defence for the defendants to establish, with reference to earlier transactions, that the plaintiffs would have proceeded with the transaction in question whatever advice they received. The documents in the other transactions were therefore relevant. Accordingly, the plaintiffs' implied waiver of privilege extended to the documents in the other transactions.

What is the rationale for the principle that a client may impliedly waive privilege by bringing an action against his or her solicitor?

Extract 13.3.1

Nederlandse Reassurantie Groep Holding NV v Bacon & Woodrow [1995] 1 All ER 976, 986 (Commercial Court)

COLMAN J: The true analysis of what the courts are doing in such cases of so-called implied waiver of privilege is, in my judgment, to prevent the unfairness which would arise if the plaintiff were entitled to exclude from the court's consideration evidence relevant to a defence by relying upon the privilege arising from the solicitor's duty of confidence. The client is thus precluded from *both* asserting that the solicitor has acted in breach of duty and thereby caused the client loss and, to make good that claim, opening up the confidential relationship between them and at the same time seeking to enforce against that same solicitor a duty of confidence arising from their professional relationship in circumstances where such enforcement would deprive the solicitor of the means of defending the claim. It is fundamental to this principle that the confidence which privilege would otherwise protect arises by reason of the same professional relationship between the parties to the litigation. The underlying unfairness which the principle aims to avoid arises because the claim is asserted and the professional relationship opened for investigation against the very party whose duty of confidence is the basis of the privilege.

---

[23] [1993] 1 WLR 94.

It is against the unfairness of both opening the relationship by asserting the claim and seeking to enforce the duty of confidence owed by the defendant that the principle is directed.

See also *Kershaw v Whelan*.[24]

It has been held that, if X makes a privileged document available to the police for the limited purpose of assisting in the conduct of criminal proceedings against Y, this cannot properly be construed as waiver of privilege for the purposes of X's subsequent civil action against Y. 'Indeed, it would . . . be contrary to public policy if the plaintiff's action in making the documents available in the criminal proceedings had the effect of automatically removing the cloak of privilege which would otherwise be available to it in the civil litigation for which the cloak was designed.'[25]

See also, on the issue of waiver of legal professional privilege in the context of s 34 of the Criminal Justice and Public Order Act 1994, *R v Condron*[26] (extracted in Chapter 8).

4. FACILITATION OF CRIME OR FRAUD

Extract 13.4.1

R v Cox (1884) 14 QBD 153, 165–6 (CCR)

STEPHEN J: The question, therefore is, whether, if a client applies to a legal adviser for advice intended to facilitate or to guide the client in the commission of a crime or fraud, the legal adviser being ignorant of the purpose for which his advice is wanted, the communication between the two is privileged? We expressed our opinion at the end of the argument that no such privilege existed. If it did, the result would be that a man intending to commit treason or murder might safely take legal advice for the purpose of enabling himself to do so with impunity, and that the solicitor to whom the application was made would not be at liberty to give information against his client for the purpose of frustrating his criminal purpose. Consequences so monstrous reduce to an absurdity any principle or rule in which they are involved.

In *Butler v Board of Trade*, it was held that 'what has to be shown prima facie is not merely that there is a bona fide and reasonably tenable charge of crime or fraud but a prima facie case that the communications in question were made in preparation for or in furtherance or as part of it'.[27]

---

[24] [1996] 1 WLR 358.
[25] *British Coal Corpn v Dennis Rye Ltd* [1988] 1 WLR 1113, 1122.
[26] (1996) 161 JPR 1.
[27] [1971] Ch 680, 689.

Extract 13.4.2

Barclays Bank v Eustice [1995] 4 All ER 511, 521, 524, 525 (CA)

SCHIEMANN LJ: ... advice sought or given for the purpose of effecting iniquity is not privileged. The present appeal is concerned essentially with the question whether the effecting of transactions at an undervalue for the purpose of prejudicing the interests of a creditor can be regarded as 'iniquity' in this context. . . .

. . .

. . . For reasons given earlier in this judgment we start here from a position in which, on a prima facie view, the client was seeking to enter into transactions at an undervalue the purpose of which was to prejudice the bank. I regard this purpose as being sufficiently iniquitous for public policy to require that communications between him and his solicitor in relation to the setting up of these transactions be discoverable.

. . .

I do not consider that the result of upholding the judge's order in the present case will be to discourage straightforward citizens from consulting their lawyers. Those lawyers should tell them that what is proposed is liable to be set aside and the straightforward citizen will then not do it and so the advice will never see the light of day. In so far as those wishing to engage in sharp practice are concerned, the effect of the present decision may well be to discourage them from going to their lawyers. This has the arguable public disadvantage that the lawyers might have dissuaded them from the sharp practice. However, it has the undoubted public advantage that the absence of lawyers will make it more difficult for them to carry out their sharp practice. In my judgment the balance of advantage is in permitting inspection of the material as ordered by the judge. I would dismiss the appeal.

Section 10(2) of the Police and Criminal Evidence Act 1984, which, as seen above, provides that 'items held with the intention of furthering a criminal purpose' are not subject to legal professional privilege, was considered by the House of Lords in the following case.

Extract 13.4.3

R v CCC, ex p Francis & Francis [1989] AC 346, 379–81, 378–9 (HL)

LORD BRANDON OF OAKBROOK: My Lords, Part II of the Police and Criminal Evidence Act 1984, which comprises sections 8 to 22, is headed 'Powers of entry, search and seizure.' Under section 8 a justice of the peace, if satisfied of certain specified matters, may issue a warrant authorising a constable to enter and search premises for material likely to be of evidential value in relation to a serious arrestable offence, and a constable, acting on such a warrant, may seize and retain any such material. Items subject to legal privilege, however, are expressly excluded from the ambit of material which may be the subject matter of such a warrant.

The expression 'items subject to legal privilege' as used in section 8 is defined in section 10. . . . It is clear that the person by whom items are held in terms of subsection (2) is the person in whose possession they are and who is entitled to possession of them in terms of subsection (1). That person is the holder of the items and will in most cases be a solicitor.

The question for decision in this appeal is to whose intention the expression 'with the intention of furthering a criminal purpose' contained in subsection (2) refers. Does it refer to the intention of the holder only ('the first meaning')? Or does it refer to the intention of any person including the holder ('the second meaning')?

It has been suggested that the first meaning is the literal meaning of the expression, and even that it is the only meaning which the expression is, as a matter of grammar, capable of having. With great respect to those of your Lordships who are of that opinion, I do not agree with it. It would have been possible for the draftsman to have inserted the qualifying words 'of the holder' between the word 'intention' and the words 'of furthering.' Subsection (2) would then have read 'Items held with the intention of the holder of furthering a criminal purpose are not items subject to legal privilege,' and the first meaning would then with certainty have been the meaning intended. The draftsman could on the other hand have inserted the qualifying words 'of the holder or any other person' in the same place. Subsection (2) would then have read 'Items held with the intention of the holder or any other person of furthering a criminal purpose are not items subject to legal privilege.' There would have been nothing ungrammatical in making the latter insertion, and the result of it would have been that the second meaning would with certainty have been intended.

What then is the consequence of the draftsman having inserted no qualifying words between the word 'intention' and the words 'of furthering?' It is not, in my view, that the expression is only capable of having the first meaning. It is rather that the expression is capable of having either the first meaning or the second meaning, and that a choice between the two meanings has to be made by reference to the purpose of Part II of the Act.

That purpose is to give the police the power, when so authorised on proper grounds by the appropriate judicial authority to enter premises, search for material likely to be of evidential value in relation to a serious offence, and to seize and retain such material. That power is conferred on the police in the public interest, so that serious crimes may be more easily and effectively investigated and the perpetrators of them more easily and effectively prosecuted. If the first meaning of the expression 'with the intention of furthering a criminal purpose' is adopted, the result will be that items held by a solicitor will only be subject to search, seizure and retention if the solicitor himself has the intention concerned. If the second meaning of the expression is adopted, the result will be that items held by a solicitor will be subject to search, seizure and retention not only in cases where a solicitor himself has the intention concerned, but also in cases where a client, or another person making use of a client as an intermediary, has the intention concerned.

Because cases of solicitors having the intention of furthering a criminal purpose are happily rare, the first result referred to above would do little to assist in achieving the purpose of Part II of the Act, and would allow the principle of legal privilege to be used to protect the perpetrators of serious crimes. By contrast, the second result referred to above would materially assist in achieving the purpose of Part II of the Act, and would prevent the principle of legal privilege being used to protect the perpetrators of serious crimes.

The conclusion to which I am led by these considerations is that the legislature must have intended to bring about the second result rather than the first, and that the expression 'with the intention of furthering a criminal purpose' should therefore be given the second meaning rather than the first.

I would therefore answer the certified question as follows:

'On the true construction of section 10(2) of the Police and Criminal Evidence Act 1984 items which would otherwise come within the definition of 'items subject to legal privilege' contained in section 10(1) are excluded from that definition if they are held with the intention of either the holder or any other person of furthering a criminal purpose.'

[Lord Griffiths and Lord Goff of Chieveley were also in the majority.]

LORD BRIDGE OF HARWICH [dissenting]: But your Lordships take the very large further step of deciding that otherwise privileged communications between an innocent solicitor and his innocent client may lose their privilege, both under the statute and at common law, by reference to the intention of some third party to further a criminal purpose. As the case has been presented throughout, this is a necessary step if the decision of the Divisional Court is to be upheld and I well understand your Lordships' concern to give every assistance to the police in pursuit of drug traffickers, who are rightly regarded as enemies of society scarcely less deadly than terrorists. But this development of the law goes well beyond any previous authority and, if it is a legitimate extension of a previously accepted principle, it should be capable of being expressed in language sufficiently precise to make clear the boundary within which the new principle is to apply that the criminal intention of one party may operate to deprive another innocent party seeking legal advice of the protection of legal professional privilege. The answer proposed by your Lordships to the certified question in terms suggests that the relevant intention for the purposes of section 10(2) may be that of 'any other person' without limitation. The only other language which I find in any of your Lordships' speeches to indicate the required nexus between the criminal party and the innocent party, who is to be deprived of legal professional privilege for communications with his legal adviser, is that the latter is the 'innocent tool' of the former. If this is intended to serve as a sufficient definition of a new legal principle, I must say, with all respect, that I find it totally inadequate.

... the result in the instant case is of minor importance compared to the use which will be made of your Lordships' decision in future unforeseen and unforeseeable circumstances. Mr Worsley, in his forceful submissions for the respondent, made no secret of the fact that the police regard this as a test case of crucial importance and seek to open a very wide door in favour of criminal investigation at the expense of privilege. If section 10(2) were to be construed as embodying his suggested implied terms at their widest, it would seem to give the police unlimited access to privileged material which they could plausibly suggest to be intended to serve a criminal purpose irrespective of any connection between the party claiming privilege and the party whose criminal purpose was alleged to be served.

It is for these reasons that I am apprehensive that your Lordships' decision will open the door to a spate of applications to obtain access to privileged material on the ground that the privilege is vitiated by a criminal intention on the part of some third party. It will then fall to circuit judges, on a case by case basis, to seek to define the limits of application of the new principle in the absence of guidance from your Lordships. It is for their benefit that I feel obliged to sound this note of warning. Whilst loyally accepting the authority of your Lordships' decision on the facts, I cannot for a moment accept the wide terms of your Lordships' answer to the certified question as a satisfactory statement of the law without further limitation and definition.

. . . I would answer the certified question as follows:

'Upon the true construction of section 10(2) of the Police and Criminal Evidence Act 1984 items which would otherwise fall within the definition of "items subject to legal privilege" are excluded from that definition if, but only if, the solicitor or other person holding the item in question has the intention of furthering a criminal purpose.'

[Lord Oliver of Aylmerton also dissented.]

Do you find the majority or minority view more persuasive? Consider, for example, the arguments advanced in the following extract:

Extract 13.4.4

A L E Newbold, 'The Crime/Fraud Exception to Legal Professional Privilege' (1990) 53 *Modern Law Review* 472, 481–3

It would seem that [the House of Lords] overlooked the fact that there is an indestructible link between the making of the communication and the intention to further a criminal purpose. Furthermore, they ignored the fact that the relevant communication must be between lawyer and client and the communication itself must relate to that purpose. . . . if both the client and the lawyer are innocent, there are no grounds for attacking legal privilege.

. . . To whom does one look to discover with what intention a communication was made? Surely it can be only to the communicators themselves, ie lawyer and client. Who else can be relevant? Lord Goff, with whom the majority agreed, says that a third party's intention is relevant. It is very difficult to understand how it can be relevant. It is impossible to make a communication with someone else's intention. Lord Goff 'overlooks' the communication aspect and concentrates entirely on the intention to further any criminal purpose. . . . Intention without communication must be irrelevant. . . .

. . .

... At one time the law said, and quite rightly said, a person is answerable for his or her own state of mind. If he or she seeks legal advice for a criminal purpose either by duping or conniving with the lawyer, then he or she is not entitled to the protection of privilege since by dishonesty he or she can have had no exception of it in the first place. So the lawyer could say to the client when he or she was approached for legal advice that all communications between them were protected from disclosure except those which were intended by the client to further some criminal purpose. The client knew the position. Now this is no longer the case. The law now expects a client to be aware of the state of someone else's mind. A lawyer must now say to a client that nothing the client says will be protected from disclosure if anyone else in the world has a dishonest intention in relation to the subject matter and is using the client as an innocent tool. And the client might well point out that he or she has no dishonest intention and that he or she cannot know what anyone else intends. The lawyer will be forced to agree. The net result is that no client communication is ever guaranteed to be protected from disclosure even if both lawyer and client are acting in good faith. Furthermore, there is a very serious question of limitation. Under the common law, the communication which was intended to further a criminal purpose was not protected. Now that the House of Lords has removed the nexus between the making of the communication and the intention to further a criminal purpose, there is no obvious limitation on which communications must be disclosed.

5. AN 'ABSOLUTE' DOCTRINE?

The question whether legal professional privilege constitutes an 'absolute' doctrine, or whether, instead, it is subject to a 'balancing' exercise, was considered recently by the House of Lords in two cases.

Extract 13.5.1

***R v Derby Magistrates' Court, ex p B* [1995] 3 WLR 681, 690–7 (HL)**

LORD TAYLOR OF GOSFORTH CJ: The stipendiary magistrate considered that it was his duty to weigh the public interest which protects confidential communications between a solicitor and his client against the public interest in securing that all relevant and admissible evidence is made available to the defence. In his view the balance came down firmly in favour of production. The applicant could no longer be regarded as having any recognisable interest in asserting privilege. The overriding consideration was the need to secure a fair trial for the stepfather. In holding that he was obliged to weigh competing public interests against each other, the stipendiary magistrate was following the decision of the Court of Appeal (Criminal Division) in *Reg v Ataou* [1988] QB 798. ...

The important question remains, however, whether *Reg v Ataou* was correctly decided, and in particular whether when there is a claim for privilege in respect of confidential communications between solicitor and client there is a balancing exercise to be performed at all. . . .

. . .

. . . under the principle stated in *Reg v Ataou*, if it be correct, the judge is required to approach an application for production of documents protected by legal privilege in two stages. First he must ask whether the client continues to have any recognisable interest in asserting the privilege and, secondly whether, if so, his interest outweighs the public interest that relevant and admissible documents should be made available to the defence in criminal proceedings.

So stated, the principle seems to conflict with the long established rule that a document protected by privilege continues to be protected so long as the privilege is not waived by the client: once privileged, always privileged. It also goes against the view that the privilege is the same whether the documents are sought for the purpose of civil or criminal proceedings, and whether by the prosecution or the defence, and that the refusal of the client to waive his privilege, for whatever reason, or for no reason, cannot be questioned or investigated by the court. . . .

. . .

The principle which runs through [the] cases . . . is that a man must be able to consult his lawyer in confidence, since otherwise he might hold back half the truth. The client must be sure that what he tells his lawyer in confidence will never be revealed without his consent. Legal professional privilege is thus much more than an ordinary rule of evidence, limited in its application to the facts of a particular case. It is a fundamental condition on which the administration of justice as a whole rests.

. . .

. . . once any exception to the general rule is allowed, the client's confidence is necessarily lost. The solicitor, instead of being able to tell his client that anything which the client might say would never in any circumstances be revealed without his consent, would have to qualify his assurance. He would have to tell the client that his confidence might be broken if in some future case the court were to hold that he no longer had 'any recognisable interest' in asserting his privilege. One can see at once that the purpose of the privilege would thereby be undermined.

As for the analogy with public interest immunity, . . . it by no means follows that because a balancing exercise is called for in one class of case, it may also be allowed in another. Legal professional privilege and public interest immunity are as different in their origin as they are in their scope. Putting it another way, if a balancing exercise was ever required in the case of legal professional privilege, it was performed once and for all in the 16th century, and since then has applied across the board in every case, irrespective of the client's individual merits.

. . . it is not for the sake of the applicant alone that the privilege must be upheld. It is in the wider interests of all those hereafter who might otherwise be deterred from telling the whole truth to their solicitors. For this reason I am of the opinion that no exception should be allowed to the absolute nature of legal professional privilege, once established. It follows that *Reg v Barton* [1973] 1 WLR 115 and *Reg v Ataou* [1988] QB 798 were wrongly decided, and ought to be overruled.

This decision is open to criticism on the ground that it overlooks the importance of the need to protect the innocent from wrongful conviction. To distinguish legal professional privilege from public interest immunity is not convincing, since in both cases the issue is whether the need to ensure that a defendant is able to establish his or her innocence may be overridden by extrinsic policy considerations. The fact that in the 16th century the balance may have come down in favour of upholding the privilege whatever the circumstances does not dictate that this should still be the case at the end of the 20th century. Lord Taylor's fear that 'once any exception to the general rule is allowed, the client's confidence is necessarily lost', and that clients 'might . . . be deterred from telling the whole truth to their solicitors', is based merely on an assumption which lacks empirical support. Do you agree with these criticisms of *Ex p B*? See generally M Bowes, 'The Supremacy of Legal Professional Privilege: The *Derby Magistrates* Case', *Archbold News*, 3 May 1996, 5; C Tapper, 'Prosecution and Privilege' (1996) 1 *International Journal of Evidence and Proof* 5; A A S Zuckerman, 'Legal Professional Privilege – The Cost of Absolutism' (1996) 112 *Law Quarterly Review* 535.

Extract 13.5.2

Re L (A Minor) [1996] 2 WLR 395, 397, 399–403 (HL)

LORD JAUNCEY OF TULLICHETTLE: My Lords, this appeal by a mother involves consideration of the extent to which [legal professional privilege] is applicable in care proceedings under Part IV of the Children Act 1989.
. . .

The order of the district judge was in the form of one approved by the Court of Appeal in *Oxfordshire County Council v M* [1994] Fam 151 after an unsuccessful challenge thereto by parents. Sir Stephen Brown P, after pointing out that proceedings under the Act were not adversarial, stated, at p 161, that children's cases 'fall into a special category where the court is bound to undertake all necessary steps to arrive at an appropriate result in the paramount interests of the welfare of the child.' The reference to 'paramount interest' was a reference to section 1(1) of the Act which is in, inter alia, the following terms:

'When a court determines any question with respect to – (*a*) the upbringing of a child; or (*b*) . . . the child's welfare shall be the court's paramount consideration.'

The President concluded his judgment in the following passage, at p 162:

'Children's cases are to be regarded as being in a special category. In these circumstances, the court has power to override legal professional privilege in relation to experts' reports when it gives leave to parties to obtain them.'

Their Lordships were informed that since the *Oxfordshire* case orders in that form have regularly been made by judges in the Family Division.

Miss Kushner submitted that Dr France's report was the subject of legal professional privilege, that such privilege was absolute (*Reg v Derby Magistrates' Court, Ex parte B* [1995] 3 WLR 681) and that it could be overridden neither in the public interest nor in furtherance of the paramountcy of the child's interests. The *Oxfordshire* case was wrongly decided.

. . .

It is clear from the reasoning of the Lord Chief Justice and of the other members of the committee [in *Ex p B*] that the reference to legal professional privilege was in the context of the relationship between solicitor and client. Indeed, there was no occasion to consider whether and in what other circumstances absolute legal professional privilege might apply. Notwithstanding this, Miss Kushner maintained that the absolute nature of the privilege attaching to the solicitor-client relationship extended equally to all other forms of legal professional privilege.

My Lords, I reject this contention. There is . . . a clear distinction between the privilege attaching to communications between solicitor and client and that attaching to reports by third parties prepared on the instructions of a client for the purposes of litigation. In the former case the privilege attaches to all communications whether related to litigation or not, but in the latter case it attaches only to documents or other written communications prepared with a view to litigation: *Waugh v British Railways Board* [1980] AC 521, 533B, 537G and 544B. There is this further distinction that whereas a solicitor could not without his client's consent be compelled to express an opinion on the factual or legal merits of the case, a third party who has provided a report to a client can be subpoenaed to give evidence by the other side and cannot decline to answer questions as to his factual findings and opinion thereon. There is no property in the opinion of an expert witness: *Harmony Shipping Co SA v Saudi Europe Line Ltd* [1979] 1 WLR 1380, 1386G, *per* Lord Denning MR.

Litigation privilege, as it has been called, is an essential component of adversarial procedure. In *Worrall v Reich* [1955] 1 QB 296 it was held that one party to a litigation could not be compelled to produce to the other party a medical report obtained for the purposes of the action. This case was followed in *In re Saxton, decd* [1962] 1 WLR 968 in relation to the report of a handwriting expert where Lord Denning MR said, at p 972: 'In short, it is one of our notions of a fair trial that, except by agreement, you are not entitled to see the proofs of the other side's witnesses.' In *Causton v Mann Egerton (Johnsons) Ltd* [1974] 1 WLR 162, 170, which concerned the disclosure of medical reports in a personal injury action, Roskill LJ said:

'I am clearly of the view that this court has no power to order production of privileged documents. . . . so long as we have an adversary system, a party is entitled not to produce documents which are properly protected by privilege if it is not to his advantage to produce them, and even though their production might assist his adversary . . .'

Finally, in *Waugh v British Railways Board* [1980] AC 521, 536 Lord Simon of Glaisdale said:

'This system of adversary forensic procedure with legal professional advice and representation demands that communications between lawyer and client should be confidential, since the lawyer is for the purpose of litigation merely the client's alter ego. So too material which is to go into the lawyer's (ie the client's) brief or file for litigation. This is the basis for the privilege against disclosure of material collected by or on behalf of a client for the use of his lawyer in pending or anticipated litigation . . .'

Lord Denning MR, Roskill LJ and Lord Simon of Glaisdale all emphasised the important part which litigation privilege plays in a fair trial under the adversarial system. This raises the question of whether proceedings under Part IV of the Act are essentially adversarial in their nature. If they are, litigation privilege must continue to play its normal part. If they are not, different considerations may apply.

In *In re K (Infants)* [1965] AC 201, which concerned disclosure of a guardian ad litem's report in wardship proceedings, Lord Evershed, at p 218E, pointed out that the purpose of the judicial inquiry was to make a decision about the future upbringing of the infant, whereby the infant was in a special position distinct from that of other parties. Lord Devlin, at p 240, quoted with approval the following dictum of the trial judge, Ungoed-Thomas J:

'The jurisdiction regarding wards of court which is now exercised by the Chancery Division is an ancient jurisdiction deriving from the prerogative of the Crown as parens patriae. It is not based on the rights of parents, and its primary concern is not to ensure their rights but to ensure the welfare of the children.'

He later stated, at p 241:

'Where the judge is not sitting purely, or even primarily, as an arbiter but is charged with the paramount duty of protecting the interests of one outside the conflict, a rule that is designed for just arbitrament cannot in all circumstances prevail.'

Lord Scarman, in *In re E (SA) (A Minor) (Wardship: Court's Duty)* [1984] 1 WLR 156, 158–159, pointed out that a court in wardship proceedings was not exercising an adversarial jurisdiction and that:

'Its duty is not limited to the dispute between the parties: on the contrary, its duty is to act in the way best suited in its judgment to serve the true interest and welfare of the ward. In exercising a wardship jurisdiction, the court is a true family court. Its paramount concern is the welfare of the ward. It will, therefore, sometimes be the duty of the court to look beyond the submissions of the parties in its endeavour to do what it judges to be necessary.'

Since the judgment in *In re K (Infants)* [1965] AC 201 there have been numerous pronouncements by judges of the Family Division stressing that proceedings in wardship are non-adversarial. It is not necessary to refer to these and I simply refer back to the passages which I have already quoted from the judgment of Sir Stephen Brown P in the *Oxfordshire* case [1994] Fam 151. In these passages the President was, as I understand him, equating the position in Children Act proceedings to wardship proceedings. The above dictum would appear to provide firm support for the proposition that proceedings under Part IV of the Act are, like wardship proceedings, essentially non-adversarial in their nature.

However, Miss Kushner argued that such statutory proceedings were not to be equiparated to wardship proceedings. This submission goes too far. It is, of course, true that once a care order under Part IV of the Act has been made it is the local authority and not the court which has the direct responsibility for the child, but until such an order has been made the role of the court under the Act does not differ significantly from its role in wardship proceedings. In reaching a decision in either case the primary consideration was and is the welfare of the child.

I agree with Sir Stephen Brown P that care proceedings are essentially non-adversarial. Having reached that conclusion, and also that litigation privilege is essentially a creature of adversarial proceedings, it follows that the matter is at large for this House to determine what if any role it has to play in care proceedings.

... in these proceedings, which are primarily non-adversarial and investigative as opposed to adversarial, the notion of a fair trial between opposing parties assumes far less importance. In the latter case the judge must decide the case in favour of one or other party upon such evidence as they choose to adduce, however much he might wish for further evidence on any point. In the former case the judge is concerned to make a decision which is in the best interest of the child in question and may make orders which are sought by no party to the proceedings: sections 10(1)(b), 31(5), 34(5) of the Act. Furthermore, the court has wide powers under rule 4.11(9)(10) of the Rules to require the guardian ad litem to obtain expert reports and other assistance. Thus the court is seeking to reach a decision which will be in the best interests of someone who is not a direct party and is granted investigative powers to achieve that end. In these circumstances I consider that care proceedings under Part IV of the Act are so far removed from normal actions that litigation privilege has no place in relation to reports obtained by a party thereto which could not have been prepared without the leave of the court to disclose documents already filed or to examine the child. In reaching this conclusion I attach considerable importance to the following dictum of Sir Stephen Brown P in the *Oxfordshire* case [1994] Fam 151, 161:

> 'If a party, having obtained the leave of the court, were to be able to conceal, or withhold from the court, matters which were of importance and were relevant to the future of the child, there would be a risk that the welfare of the child would not be promoted as the Children Act 1989 requires.'

...

I differ from Sir Stephen Brown P, with his great experience of proceedings under the Act, only in as much as he concluded that in the foregoing circumstances the court had power to *override* the privilege. The *Oxfordshire* case was, however, argued on the assumption that the privilege existed but could be overridden. This case was also argued on the same assumption in the Court of Appeal, but Sir Thomas Bingham MR expressed doubt as to whether the assumption was rightly made. His doubts were in my view well founded. The better view is that litigation privilege never arose in the first place rather than that the court has power to override it. It is excluded by necessary implication from the terms and overall purpose of the Act. This does not of course affect privilege arising between solicitor and client.

Do you find the distinction drawn between legal advice privilege and litigation privilege convincing? Or are they in reality, as Lord Nicholls of Birkenhead thought in his dissenting speech,[28] 'integral parts of a single privilege'? Should the House of Lords in *Re L (A Minor)* have taken the bold step of declaring *Ex p B* to have been wrongly decided, and not simply have confined the decision to cases of legal advice privilege? After all, 'if the House of Lords places child welfare above the litigant's interest why should the removal of legal professional privilege be confined to its litigation limb? In other words, should not communications between client and lawyer also be disclosable for the sake of protecting children from harm?'[29] See generally D Burrows, 'Privilege and Disclosure after *Re L*' (1996) 140 *Solicitors Journal* 560; J McEwan, 'The Uncertain Status of Privilege in Children Act Cases: *Re L*' (1996) 1 *International Journal of Evidence and Proof* 80; C Passmore, 'Privilege in the Lords' (1996) 146 *New Law Journal* 921.

6. SECONDARY EVIDENCE

The general principle, affirmed in *Calcraft v Guest*,[30] is that where privileged information has become known to a person not entitled to it (that is, a person other than the client, the legal adviser, any relevant third parties, or any agents for communication such as clerks and secretaries), then it may be used by that person in evidence. It is irrelevant how that person came by this information. Equity has, however, stepped in to ameliorate the harshness of the rule in *Calcraft*. If the information has not already been used in evidence, an injunction may be able to be obtained to prevent its use. In *Lord Ashburton v Pape*,[31] Pape, a party to bankruptcy proceedings, obtained by a trick copies of privileged correspondence between Lord Ashburton and his solicitor. The Court of Appeal granted an injunction to prevent Pape from using the copies in the bankruptcy proceedings. The cases of *Goddard v Nationwide*,[32] *English & American Insurance Co Ltd v Herbert Smith*[33] and *Guinness Peat Ltd v Fitzroy Robinson*[34] make it clear that the privileged information does not have

---

[28] [1996] 2 WLR 395, 408.
[29] A A S Zuckerman, 'Legal Professional Privilege – The Cost of Absolutism' (1996) 112 *Law Quarterly Review* 535, 538.
[30] [1898] 1 QB 759.
[31] [1913] 2 Ch 469.
[32] [1986] 3 WLR 734.
[33] [1988] FSR 232.
[34] [1987] 1 WLR 1027.

to have been obtained by trickery or fraud before an injunction can be granted – it is sufficient if it was obtained by taking advantage of an obvious mistake. In *Goddard*, the plaintiff's solicitor accidentally sent the defendant a copy of a document which recorded conversations between the plaintiff's solicitor and the plaintiff. The plaintiff applied for, and was granted, an injunction. Similarly, in *English & American Insurance*, the clerk of a certain barrister whom the plaintiffs' solicitors were instructing handed over to the defendants' solicitors, by mistake, some documents which included instructions to counsel, an opinion of counsel, counsel's notes, letters from the plaintiffs' solicitors to the plaintiffs, and witness statements. The plaintiffs applied for and obtained an injunction.

The issue of to whom the mistake must have been 'obvious' was considered in the following case:

Extract 13.6.1

IBM Corp v Phoenix International [1995] 1 All ER 413, 421, 422, 424, 426 (Ch D)

ALDOUS J: I believe that the following propositions of law cannot be doubted.

(1) The privilege is that of the client, namely Phoenix, and not its solicitors.

(2) Privilege can only be waived by Phoenix and not by its solicitors unless authorised to do so.

(3) A party giving discovery is under a duty to ensure that only documents in respect of which no claim for privilege is made are disclosed.

(4) After inspection has taken place, the court can intervene by way of injunction to prevent use of privileged documents.

(5) When deciding whether to intervene to prevent use of privileged documents, the court is exercising an equitable jurisdiction and is therefore not confined to rigid rules. But when fraud is not established, the general rule is that no injunction will be granted after inspection, unless (a) the document is privileged, and (b) disclosure has occurred as a result of an obvious mistake.

(6) At all times the onus is upon the person claiming the relief to establish that the relief sought should be granted.

The parties do not agree as to the nature of the person to whom the mistake must be obvious. IBM submitted that the relevant person was the recipient of the disclosed document; whereas Phoenix submitted that the relevant person was a notional solicitor with reasonable skill, knowledge and judgment, to which I will refer as the reasonable solicitor. The difference is of importance as inspection does not have to be conducted by a legally trained person and in some cases will be carried out by litigants in person who may not know anything about the law.

. . .

. . . I believe that Phoenix's submission is correct. The court must adopt the mantle of the reasonable solicitor. The evidence of what a solicitor thought at the time can be relevant. However the decision is for the court. The court must decide whether it is satisfied, on the balance of probabilities, that the reasonable solicitor would have realised that privilege had not been waived.

. . .

As I have said, I cannot think of any good reason why the reasonable solicitor should conclude that Phoenix had decided to waive privilege in the legal bills. They are clearly privileged; they seem to be irrelevant to proceedings in this country; they fall within the category of documents for which privilege is claimed; the method of giving discovery was not meticulously carried out; the amount of discovery was very substantial and it was done in a hurry. From that and the absence of any reasonable reason why Phoenix should waive privilege, I conclude that the reasonable solicitor would believe that the legal bills had been disclosed by mistake and that would be evident to him.

An injunction being an equitable remedy, the usual principles relating to the granting of discretionary remedies apply here. Thus an injunction may be refused on the ground, for example, that there has been inordinate delay on the part of the party seeking the remedy. It would appear, too, that an injunction cannot be granted to an accused in a public prosecution to prevent the Crown from adducing admissible evidence relevant to the offence charged.[35]

Apart from an injunction, one other possible remedy may be available. The availability of this remedy would appear to be limited to situations in which the privileged document was improperly obtained within the four walls of the courtroom:

Extract 13.6.2

ITC Ltd v Video Exchange Ltd [1982] Ch 431, 440–1 (Ch D)

WARNER J: That submission is in a nutshell that, in the circumstances of this case, I must balance the public interest that the truth should be ascertained, which is the reason for the rule in *Calcraft v Guest* [1898] 1 QB 759, against the public interest that litigants should be able to bring their documents into court without fear that they may be filched by their opponents, whether by stealth or by a trick, and then used by them in evidence. . . . I do not overlook that for a party to litigation to take possession by stealth or by a trick of documents belonging to the other side within the precincts of the court is probably contempt of court, so that there may be another sanction. But it seems to me that, if it is contempt of court, then the court should not countenance it by admitting such documents in evidence.

A list of propositions relating to this area of the law was provided by Nourse LJ in *Goddard v Nationwide*:

---

[35] *Butler v Board of Trade* [1971] Ch 680, 690.

Extract 13.6.3

Goddard v Nationwide [1986] 3 WLR 734, 744–6 (CA)

NOURSE LJ: The following observations are not made in any order of logic or importance. They are in general confined to a case, such as the present, where the communication is both confidential and privileged and the privilege has not been waived.

First, it is desirable to emphasise that the proceedings in which the rule of evidence denies protection to the confidential communication are not proceedings whose purpose is to seek that protection. The question is an incidental one which arises when the party who desires the protection asserts a right to it as if he were the plaintiff in an action seeking to invoke the equitable jurisdiction. When *Lord Ashburton v Pape* was decided, the practice and procedures of our courts were no doubt such that it was first necessary to issue fresh proceedings. Nowadays I think that we would at the most require an undertaking to issue a pro forma writ, perhaps not even that, a consideration which no doubt explains the agreement not to require fresh proceedings in the present case. The crucial point is that the party who desires the protection must seek it before the other party has adduced the confidential communication in evidence or otherwise relied on it at trial.

Secondly, although the equitable jurisdiction is of much wider application, I have little doubt that it can prevail over the rule of evidence only in cases where privilege can be claimed. The equitable jurisdiction is well able to extend, for example, to the grant of an injunction to restrain an unauthorised disclosure of confidential communications between priest and penitent or doctor and patient. But those communications are not privileged in legal proceedings and I do not believe that equity would restrain a litigant who already had a record of such a communication in his possession from using it for the purposes of his litigation. It cannot be the function of equity to accord a de facto privilege to communications in respect of which no privilege can be claimed. Equity follows the law.

Thirdly, the right of the party who desires the protection to invoke the equitable jurisdiction does not in any way depend on the conduct of the third party into whose possession the record of the confidential communication has come. Thus, several eminent judges have been of the opinion that an injunction can be granted against a stranger who has come innocently into the possession of confidential information to which he is not entitled: see *Rex Co v Muirhead* (1926) 136 LT 568, 573, *per* Clauson J; *Printers & Finishers Ltd v Holloway* [1965] 1 WLR 1, 7, *per* Cross J; and *Butler v Board of Trade* [1971] Ch 680, 690, *per* Goff J. This view seems to give effect to the general rule that equity gives relief against all the world, including the innocent, save only a bona fide purchaser for value without notice. It is directly in point in the present case and our decision necessarily affirms it.

Fourthly, once it is established that a case is governed by *Lord Ashburton v Pape* [1913] 2 Ch 469 there is no discretion in the court to refuse to exercise the equitable jurisdiction according to its view of the materiality of the communication, the justice of admitting or excluding it or the like. ... In saying this, I do not intend to suggest that there may not be cases where an injunction can properly be refused on general principles affecting the grant of a discretionary remedy, for example on the ground of inordinate delay.

Fifthly, in a case to which *Lord Ashburton v Pape* can no longer apply, public policy may nevertheless preclude a party who has acted improperly in the proceedings from invoking the rule of evidence: see *ITC Film Distributors Ltd v Video Exchange Ltd* [1982] Ch 431, where the defendant had at an earlier hearing obtained some of the plaintiff's privileged documents by a trick. Warner J, having expressed the view that there were by that stage in the case difficulties in the way of his granting the plaintiff relief on the basis of *Lord Ashburton v Pape*, held, at p 441, that the greater public interest that litigants should be able to bring their documents into court without fear that they may be filched by their opponents, whether by stealth or by a trick, and then used in evidence required an exception to the rule in *Calcraft v Guest* [1898] 1 QB 759, save in regard to documents at which he (the judge) had already looked. I emphasise that that decision proceeded not on an exercise of the court's discretion but on grounds of public policy.

Sixthly, the distinction between civil proceedings and public prosecutions made in *Butler v Board of Trade* [1971] Ch 680 was again one which was made on grounds of public policy. The distinction has since been adopted and applied by the Criminal Division of this court in *Reg v Tompkins*, 67 Cr App R 181. It can now be disregarded only by the House of Lords.

Finally, it is to be noted that the Court of Appeal in New Zealand, after an extensive consideration of the authorities, including *Calcraft v Guest, Butler v Board of Trade* and *Reg v Tompkins*, recently declined to apply the rule of evidence in a criminal case and held that the evidence of a police constable who had happened to overhear a privileged conversation between the accused and his solicitor (ie one which was not itself part of a criminal or unlawful proceeding: see *Reg v Cox and Railton* (1884) 14 QBD 153) was not admissible: see *Reg v Uljee* [1982] 1 NZLR 561. The practical result of the decision would seem to be to leave the spirit of *Lord Ashburton v Pape* [1913] 2 Ch 469 supreme in both civil and criminal proceedings in that jurisdiction, a supremacy for which in my respectful opinion there is much to be said in this.

In *Webster v James Chapman & Co*, Scott J expressed doubts about Nourse LJ's third and fourth propositions. Scott J thought that in deciding whether to grant an injunction, the court should perform a balancing exercise, taking into account considerations such as the circumstances in which the privileged information came into the hands of the third party, and the materiality of the privileged information.[36] Presumably, therefore, a court should be slower to grant an injunction where the information was obtained simply by taking advantage of an obvious mistake than where it was obtained by fraud. Equally, the more important the privileged information, the slower a court should be to grant an injunction. In the subsequent case of *Derby & Co Ltd v Weldon (No 8)*, however, it was considered inappropriate for a court to perform such a balancing exercise in deciding whether to grant an injunction:

[36] [1989] 3 All ER 939, 945.

The court does not, so far as privileged documents are concerned, weigh the privilege and consider whether the privilege should outweigh the importance that the document should be before the court at the trial, or the importance that possession of the document and the ability to use it might have for the advocate; and, again, where the privilege is being restored because the inspection was obtained by fraud or by taking advantage of a known mistake, there is to my mind no logic at all in qualifying the restoration of the status quo by reference to the importance of the document. 'You have taken advantage of an obvious mistake to obtain copies of documents; we will order you to return all the ones that are unimportant but you can keep the ones that are important' would be a nonsensical attitude for the court to adopt.[37]

It would seem, therefore, that the propositions laid down by Nourse LJ in *Goddard v Nationwide* do represent the law today.

The following comment has been made on this area of the law:

Extract 13.6.4

C Tapper, *Cross and Tapper on Evidence* (8th ed 1995) 483

The resultant law can be criticised on two grounds: (1) the contrast between *Calcraft v Guest* and *Lord Ashburton v Pape* makes the client's success in getting evidence excluded depend on the date at which he found out that he was the victim of a wrongdoer; (2) the distinction between public prosecutions and other legal proceedings is unjustified. If they can be answered, the answer to the first criticism seems to be that trials at which it was claimed that the contents of a confidential document ought not to be put in evidence, although no previous injunction had been obtained, would be unduly protracted by the collateral inquiry into the circumstances in which the document was obtained; while the answer to the second criticism may be that, in criminal proceedings, the accused receives as much protection as he should receive from the law of privilege in the strict sense and it would be going too far to afford him the protection afforded by the law of confidentiality.

What do you make of this comment?

Further reading

T R S Allan, 'Filching Your Opponent's Papers in Court: When Privilege Cannot be Defeated by a Trick' (1983) 133 *New Law Journal* 665

— 'Legal Privilege and the Principle of Fairness in the Criminal Trial' [1987] *Criminal Law Review* 449

N H Andrews, 'The Influence of Equity upon the Doctrine of Legal Professional Privilege' (1989) 105 *Law Quarterly Review* 608

---

[37] [1990] 3 All ER 762, 783.

D J Boniface, 'Legal Professional Privilege and Disclosure Powers of Investigative Agencies: Some Interesting and Troubling Issues Regarding Competing Public Policies' (1992) 16 *Criminal Law Journal* 320

J D Heydon, 'Legal Professional Privilege and Third Parties' (1974) 37 *Modern Law Review* 601

A L E Newbold, 'The Crime/Fraud Exception to Legal Professional Privilege' (1990) 53 *Modern Law Review* 472

C Tapper, 'Privilege and Confidence' (1972) 35 *Modern Law Review* 83

BIBLIOGRAPHY

Acorn, A E, 'Similar Fact Evidence and the Principle of Inductive Reasoning: Makin Sense' (1991) 11 *Oxford Journal of Legal Studies* 63

Adler, Z, *Rape on Trial* (London: Routledge & Kegan Paul, 1987)

Allan, J, 'The Working and Rationale of the Hearsay Rule and the Implications of Modern Psychological Knowledge' (1991) 44 *Current Legal Problems* 217

Allan, T R S, 'Filching Your Opponent's Papers in Court: When Privilege Cannot be Defeated by a Trick' (1983) 133 *New Law Journal* 665

— 'Legal Privilege and the Principle of Fairness in the Criminal Trial' [1987] *Criminal Law Review* 449

— 'Public Interest Immunity and Ministers' Responsibilities' [1993] *Criminal Law Review* 660

— 'Similar Fact Evidence and Disposition: Law, Discretion and Admissibility' (1985) 48 *Modern Law Review* 253

— 'Some Favourite Fallacies about Similar Facts' (1988) 8 *Legal Studies* 35

Alldridge, P, 'Forensic Science and Expert Evidence' (1994) 21 *Journal of Law and Society* 136

Allen, C J W, 'Discretion and Security: Excluding Evidence under Section 78(1) of the Police and Criminal Evidence Act 1984' [1990] *Cambridge Law Journal* 80

Allport, G W, and Postman, L, *The Psychology of Rumor* (Henry Holt and Co, 1947) (reprinted New York: Russell & Russell, 1965)

Andrews, J A, 'Public Interest and Criminal Proceedings' (1988) 104 *Law Quarterly Review* 410

— and Hirst, M, *Criminal Evidence* (2nd ed, London: Sweet & Maxwell, 1992)

Andrews, N H, 'The Influence of Equity upon the Doctrine of Legal Professional Privilege' (1989) 105 *Law Quarterly Review* 608

Ashworth, A J, 'Evidence of Previous Misconduct' [1996] *Criminal Law Review* 681

— 'Excluding Evidence as Protecting Rights' [1977] *Criminal Law Review* 723

— and Blake, M, 'The Presumption of Innocence in English Criminal Law' [1996] *Criminal Law Review* 306

— and Pattenden, R, 'Reliability, Hearsay Evidence and the English Criminal Trial' (1986) 102 *Law Quarterly Review* 292

Australian Law Reform Commission, *Evidence (Vol 1)* (Report No 26: Interim) (Canberra: Australian Government Publishing Service, 1985)

Bagshaw, R, *Cross and Wilkins: Outline of the Law of Evidence* (London: Butterworths, 1996)

Bainham, A, 'Sexual Abuse in the Lords' [1996] *Cambridge Law Journal* 209

Baker, K K, 'Once a Rapist? Motivational Evidence and Relevancy in Rape Law' (1997) 110 *Harvard Law Review* 563

Beale, S S, 'Prior Similar Acts in Prosecutions for Rape and Child Sex Abuse' (1993) 4 *Criminal Law Forum* 307

Beaumont, M, 'Psychiatric Evidence: Over-Rationalising the Abnormal' [1988] *Criminal Law Review* 290

Bennion, F, 'Statutory Exceptions: A Third Knot in the Golden Thread?' [1988] *Criminal Law Review* 31

Bentham, J, *Rationale of Judicial Evidence, Specially Applied to English Practice (Vol 1)* (London: Hunt and Clarke, 1827) (reprinted New York: Garland Publishing, Inc, 1978)

Birch, D J, 'Corroboration: Goodbye to all that?' [1995] *Criminal Law Review* 524

— 'The Criminal Justice Act 1988: (2) Documentary Evidence' [1989] *Criminal Law Review* 15

— 'The Criminal Justice Act 1991: (4) Children's Evidence' [1992] *Criminal Law Review* 262

— 'Excluding Evidence from Entrapment: What is a "Fair Cop"?' (1994) 47 *Current Legal Problems* 73

— 'Hearsay-Logic and Hearsay-Fiddles: *Blastland* Revisited' in P Smith (ed), *Criminal Law: Essays in Honour of J C Smith* (London: Butterworths, 1987)

— 'Hunting the Snark: The Elusive Statutory Exception' [1988] *Criminal Law Review* 221

— 'The Pace Hots up: Confessions and Confusions under the 1984 Act' [1989] *Criminal Law Review* 95

— 'Play it Again! Replaying Children's Video Evidence', *Archbold News*, 4 April 1996, 6

Black, J S W, 'Breath Testing Devices and Computer Evidence' (1997) 141 *Solicitors Journal* 236

Boniface, D J, 'Legal Professional Privilege and Disclosure Powers of Investigative Agencies: Some Interesting and Troubling Issues Regarding Competing Public Policies' (1992) 16 *Criminal Law Journal* 320

Bowes, M, 'The Supremacy of Legal Professional Privilege: The *Derby Magistrates* Case', *Archbold News*, 3 May 1996, 5

Browne, K, 'An Inference of Guilt?' (1997) 141 *Solicitors Journal* 202

— 'Primed, Stated and Seconded' (1997) 141 *Solicitors Journal* 336

Bryden, D P, and Park, R C, '"Other Crimes" Evidence in Sex Offense Cases' (1994) 78 *Minnesota Law Review* 529

Bull, R, 'Obtaining Evidence Expertly: The Reliability of Interviews with Child Witnesses' (1992) 1 *Expert Evidence* 5

Burrows, D, 'Care Proceedings after *Re H*' (1996) 140 *Solicitors Journal* 94

— 'Privilege and Disclosure after *Re L*' (1996) 140 *Solicitors Journal* 560

Campbell, B, 'If Children Accuse, Can there be Justice?', *The Independent*, 17 January 1995, 15

Carmody, T, 'Recent and Proposed Statutory Reforms to the Common Law Exclusionary Discretions' (1997) 71 *Australian Law Journal* 119

Carter, P B, 'Forbidden Reasoning Permissible: Similar Fact Evidence a Decade after *Boardman*' (1985) 48 *Modern Law Review* 29

— 'Hearsay, Relevance and Admissibility: Declarations as to State of Mind and Declarations against Penal Interest' (1987) 103 *Law Quarterly Review* 106
— 'Hearsay: Whether and Whither?' (1993) 109 *Law Quarterly Review* 573
— *Cases and Statutes on Evidence* (2nd ed, London: Sweet & Maxwell, 1990)
Choo, A L-T, 'Confessions and Corroboration: A Comparative Perspective' [1991] *Criminal Law Review* 867
— 'Corroboration of Disputed Confessions' (1991) 107 *Law Quarterly Review* 544
— 'Halting Criminal Prosecutions: The Abuse of Process Doctrine Revisited' [1995] *Criminal Law Review* 864
— 'The Hearsay Rule and Confessions Relied upon by the Defence: *R v Myers*' (1997) 1(3) *International Journal of Evidence and Proof* 158
— 'Reform of the Hearsay Rule: Developments in Commonwealth Jurisdictions' in J F Nijboer and J M Reijntjes (eds), *Proceedings of the First World Conference on New Trends in Criminal Investigation and Evidence* (Lelystad: Open University of the Netherlands, 1997)
— *Abuse of Process and Judicial Stays of Criminal Proceedings* (Oxford: Clarendon Press, 1993)
— *Hearsay and Confrontation in Criminal Trials* (Oxford: Clarendon Press, 1996)
— and Mellors, M, 'Undercover Police Operations and What the Suspect Said (or Didn't Say)' in M Allen (ed), *Web Journal of Current Legal Issues Yearbook 1995* (London: Blackstone Press Ltd, 1996)
'The Civil Evidence Act 1995' (1996) 160 *Justice of the Peace* 82
Clark, D H, 'The Last Word on the Last Word' (1969) 32 *Modern Law Review* 142
Cleary, E W, *McCormick on Evidence* (3rd ed, St Paul, Minn: West Publishing Co, 1984)
Creaton, J, 'DNA Profiling and the Law: A Critique of the Royal Commission's Recommendations' in M McConville and L Bridges (eds), *Criminal Justice in Crisis* (Aldershot: Edward Elgar, 1994)
Creighton, P, 'Spouse Competence and Compellability' [1990] *Criminal Law Review* 34
'Criminal Procedure and Investigations Act 1996', *Archbold News*, 15 August 1996, 5
Cross, R, 'The Periphery of Hearsay' (1969) 7 *Melbourne University Law Review* 1
Cutler, B L, and Penrod, S D, *Mistaken Identification: The Eyewitness, Psychology, and the Law* (Cambridge: CUP, 1995)

Damaška, M R, 'Propensity Evidence in Continental Legal Systems' (1994) 70 *Chicago-Kent Law Review* 55
— *The Faces of Justice and State Authority: A Comparative Approach to the Legal Process* (New Haven: Yale University Press, 1986)
Davies, G, Wilson, C, Mitchell, R, and Milsom, J, *Videotaping Children's Evidence: An Evaluation* (London: Home Office, 1995)
Dennis, I H, 'Codification and Reform of Evidence Law in Australia' [1996] *Criminal Law Review* 477
— 'The Criminal Justice and Public Order Act 1994: The Evidence Provisions' [1995] *Criminal Law Review* 4
— 'Evidence against a Co-Accused' (1983) 36 *Current Legal Problems* 177
— 'Miscarriages of Justice and the Law of Confessions: Evidentiary Issues and Solutions' [1993] *Public Law* 291
— 'Reconstructing the Law of Criminal Evidence' (1989) 42 *Current Legal Problems* 21

Dent, H, and Flin, R (eds), *Children as Witnesses* (Chichester: John Wiley & Sons, 1992)

Doob, A N, and Kirshenbaum, H M, 'Some Empirical Evidence on the Effect of S 12 of the Canada Evidence Act upon an Accused' (1972) 15 *Criminal Law Quarterly* 88

Doran, S, 'Character Evidence and the Threat of Collusion: Free Evaluation or Judicial Responsibility?' in J F Nijboer and J M Reijntjes (eds), *Proceedings of the First World Conference on New Trends in Criminal Investigation and Evidence* (Lelystad: Open University of the Netherlands, 1997)

— 'Similar Facts and the Shadow of Collusion: A Matter of Judicial Responsibility', *Archbold News*, 12 December 1995, 5

Durston, G J, 'A Brief Recap on the Implications of the Abolition of the Right to Silence in the Criminal Justice and Public Order Act 1994' (1996) 160 *Justice of the Peace* 62

— 'Character Evidence Going to Credit: Recent Developments with Reference to Section 1(f)(ii) (the Second Limb) of the Criminal Evidence Act 1898' (1996) 160 *Justice of the Peace* 439

— 'Expert Opinion Evidence in Criminal Trials: A Review of the Current Position' (1996) 160 *Justice of the Peace* 837

— 'Is it Hearsay?' (1996) 160 *Justice of the Peace* 535

Dworkin, R, *A Matter of Principle* (Oxford: Clarendon Press, 1986)

Easton, S, 'The Right to Silence and the Pursuit of Truth' in E Attwooll and D Goldberg (eds), *Criminal Justice: United Kingdom Association for Legal and Social Philosophy – Twentieth Annual Conference at Glasgow. 24–26 March, 1994* (Stuttgart: Steiner, 1995)

Edwards, A, 'The Criminal Procedure and Investigations Act 1996: (2) The Procedural Aspects' [1997] *Criminal Law Review* 321

Edwards, S, 'Compelling a Reluctant Spouse' (1989) 139 *New Law Journal* 691

Ekman, P, *Telling Lies: Clues to Deceit in the Marketplace, Politics, and Marriage* (New York: W W Norton & Co, 1992)

Elliott, D W, 'Cut Throat Tactics: The Freedom of an Accused to Prejudice a Co-Accused' [1991] *Criminal Law Review* 5

Finman, T, 'Implied Assertions as Hearsay: Some Criticisms of the Uniform Rules of Evidence' (1962) 14 *Stanford Law Review* 682

Forsyth, C, 'Public Interest Immunity: Recent and Future Developments' [1997] *Cambridge Law Journal* 51

Frank, J, *Courts on Trial: Myth and Reality in American Justice* (Princeton, NJ: Princeton University Press, 1950)

Galligan, D J, 'More Scepticism about Scepticism' (1988) 8 *Oxford Journal of Legal Studies* 249

Ganz, G, '*Matrix Churchill* and Public Interest Immunity: A Postscript' (1995) 58 *Modern Law Review* 417

Gelowitz, M A, 'Section 78 of the Police and Criminal Evidence Act 1984: Middle Ground or No Man's Land?' (1990) 106 *Law Quarterly Review* 327

Gleeson, A M, 'Individualised Justice – The Holy Grail' (1995) 69 *Australian Law Journal* 421

Goldman, S A, 'Not So "Firmly Rooted": Exceptions to the Confrontation Clause' (1987) 66 *North Carolina Law Review* 1

Gooderson, R N, 'Previous Consistent Statements' [1968] *Cambridge Law Journal* 64

Graham, K W, Jr, 'The Right of Confrontation and the Hearsay Rule: Sir Walter Raleigh Loses Another One' (1972) 8 *Criminal Law Bulletin* 99

Graham, M H, ' "Stickperson Hearsay": A Simplified Approach to Understanding the Rule against Hearsay' [1982] *University of Illinois Law Review* 887

Grainger, I, 'Hearsay Evidence Admissible' (1996) 140 *Solicitors Journal* 536

— 'New Rules on Hearsay Notices' (1997) 141 *Solicitors Journal* 112

Greer, S, 'The Right to Silence, Defence Disclosure, and Confession Evidence' (1994) 21 *Journal of Law and Society* 102

Grevling, K, 'Undercover Operations: Balancing the Public Interest?' (1996) 112 *Law Quarterly Review* 401

Gross, H, *A Theory of Criminal Justice* (New York: OUP, 1979)

Guest, S, 'Hearsay Revisited' (1988) 41 *Current Legal Problems* 33

— 'The Scope of the Hearsay Rule' (1985) 101 *Law Quarterly Review* 385

Hamer, D, 'The Civil Standard of Proof Uncertainty: Probability, Belief and Justice' (1994) 16 *Sydney Law Review* 506

Hans, V P, and Doob, A N, 'Section 12 of the Canada Evidence Act and the Deliberations of Simulated Juries' (1976) 18 *Criminal Law Quarterly* 235

Healy, P, 'Proof and Policy: No Golden Threads' [1987] *Criminal Law Review* 355

Heydon, J D, 'Legal Professional Privilege and Third Parties' (1974) 37 *Modern Law Review* 601

— and Ockelton, M, *Evidence: Cases and Materials* (4th ed, London: Butterworths, 1996)

Hoffmann, L H, 'Similar Facts after *Boardman*' (1975) 91 *Law Quarterly Review* 193

Hogan, A, 'The Civil Evidence Act 1995' (1997) 147 *New Law Journal* 226

Howard, M N, 'Refreshment of Memory out of Court' [1972] *Criminal Law Review* 351

Hunter, J, ' "Tainted" Proceedings: Censuring Police Illegalities' (1985) 59 *Australian Law Journal* 709

— 'Unreliable Memoirs and the Accused: Bending and Stretching Hearsay – Part One' (1994) 18 *Criminal Law Journal* 8

— and Bargen, J, 'Diminished Responsibility: "Abnormal" Minds, Abnormal Murderers and What the Doctor Said' in S M H Yeo (ed), *Partial Excuses to Murder* (Sydney: Federation Press, 1990)

— and Cronin, K, *Evidence, Advocacy and Ethical Practice: A Criminal Trial Commentary* (Sydney: Butterworths, 1995)

Hunter, M, 'Judicial Discretion: Section 78 in Practice' [1994] *Criminal Law Review* 558

Imwinkelried, E J, 'The Next Step in Conceptualizing the Presentation of Expert Evidence as Education: The Case for Didactic Trial Procedures' (1997) 1(2) *International Journal of Evidence and Proof* 128

Jackson, J D, 'Interpreting the Silence Provisions: The Northern Ireland Cases' [1995] *Criminal Law Review* 587

— 'Judicial Responsibility in Criminal Proceedings' (1996) 49 *Current Legal Problems* 59

— 'The Ultimate Issue Rule: One Rule Too Many' [1984] *Criminal Law Review* 75

Jennings, A F, 'Resounding Silence' (1996) 146 *New Law Journal* 725

— 'Resounding Silence – 2' (1996) 146 *New Law Journal* 764

— 'Resounding Silence – 3' (1996) 146 *New Law Journal* 821

Jerrard, R R, 'The Police Officer's Notebook' (1993) 157 *Justice of the Peace* 5

Jones, C A G, *Expert Witnesses: Science, Medicine, and the Practice of Law* (Oxford: Clarendon Press, 1994)

Jones, T H, 'Insanity and the Burden of Proof on the Accused: A Human Rights Approach' in J F Nijboer and J M Reijntjes (eds), *Proceedings of the First World Conference on New Trends in Criminal Investigation and Evidence* (Lelystad: Open University of the Netherlands, 1997)

— 'Insanity, Automatism, and the Burden of Proof on the Accused' (1995) 111 *Law Quarterly Review* 475

Jörg, N, Field, S, and Brants, C, 'Are Inquisitorial and Adversarial Systems Converging?' in P Fennell, C Harding, N Jörg and B Swart (eds), *Criminal Justice in Europe: A Comparative Study* (Oxford: Clarendon Press, 1995)

Kalven, H, Jr, and Zeisel, H, *The American Jury* (Boston: Little, Brown and Company, 1966)

Keane, A, *The Modern Law of Evidence* (4th ed, London: Butterworths, 1996)

Kenny, A, 'The Expert in Court' (1983) 99 *Law Quarterly Review* 197

King, I, 'SFO Chief Seeks Review of Jury Role in Fraud Cases', *The Guardian*, 25 June 1996, 18

Kovera, M B, Park, R C, and Penrod, S D, 'Jurors' Perceptions of Eyewitness and Hearsay Evidence' (1992) 76 *Minnesota Law Review* 703

Landsman, S, and Rakos, R F, 'Research Essay: A Preliminary Empirical Enquiry Concerning the Prohibition of Hearsay Evidence in American Courts' (1991) 15 *Law and Psychology Review* 65

Langbein, J H, 'Historical Foundations of the Law of Evidence: A View from the Ryder Sources' (1996) 96 *Columbia Law Review* 1168

Langdon-Down, G, 'Hung on the Issue of Juries', *The Independent*, Section Two, 24 January 1996, 14

Law Commission (Consultation Paper No 138), *Criminal Law – Evidence in Criminal Proceedings: Hearsay and Related Topics – A Consultation Paper* (London: HMSO, 1995)

— (Consultation Paper No 141), *Criminal Law – Evidence in Criminal Proceedings: Previous Misconduct of a Defendant – A Consultation Paper* (London: HMSO, 1996)

— (Law Com No 245), *Evidence in Criminal Proceedings: Hearsay and Related Topics* (London: HMSO, 1997)

Lees, S, *Ruling Passions: Sexual Violence, Reputation and the Law* (Buckingham: Open University Press, 1997)

Leigh, I, 'Matrix Churchill, Supergun and the Scott Inquiry' [1993] *Public Law* 630

— 'Reforming Public Interest Immunity' in M J Allen (ed), *Web Journal of Current Legal Issues Yearbook 1995* (London: Blackstone Press Ltd, 1996)

Lempert, R O, and Saltzburg, S A, *A Modern Approach to Evidence: Text, Problems, Transcripts and Cases* (2nd ed, St Paul, Minn: West Publishing Co, 1982)

Leng, R, and Taylor, R D, *Blackstone's Guide to the Criminal Procedure and Investigations Act 1996* (London: Blackstone Press Ltd, 1996)

Levi, M, 'When the Quality of Mercy is Strained', *The Times Higher Education Supplement*, 4 October 1996, 20

Lewis, P, 'Corroboration Reborn' (1996–7) 7 *King's College Law Journal* 140

Libling, D F, 'Evidence of Past Identification' [1977] *Criminal Law Review* 268

Loftus, E F, *Eyewitness Testimony* (Cambridge, Mass: Harvard University Press, 1979)

LSE Jury Project, 'Juries and the Rules of Evidence' [1973] *Criminal Law Review* 208

McColgan, A, 'Common Law and the Relevance of Sexual History Evidence' (1996) 16 *Oxford Journal of Legal Studies* 275

McConville, M, *Corroboration and Confessions: The Impact of a Rule Requiring that no Conviction Can be Sustained on the Basis of Confession Evidence Alone* (Royal Commission on Criminal Justice Research Study No 13) (London: HMSO, 1993)

—, Hodgson, J, Bridges, L, and Pavlovic, A, *Standing Accused: The Organisation and Practices of Criminal Defence Lawyers in Britain* (Oxford: Clarendon Press, 1994)

McCormick, C T, 'The Borderland of Hearsay' (1930) 39 *Yale Law Journal* 489

McEwan, J, 'The Law Commission Consultation Paper on Previous Misconduct: (2) Law Commission Dodges the Nettles in Consultation Paper No 141' [1997] *Criminal Law Review* 93

— 'The Uncertain Status of Privilege in Children Act Cases: *Re L*' (1996) 1 *International Journal of Evidence and Proof* 80

— *Evidence and the Adversarial Process: The Modern Law* (Oxford: Blackwell, 1992)

Mack, K, 'Continuing Barriers to Women's Credibility: A Feminist Perspective on the Proof Process' (1993) 4 *Criminal Law Forum* 327

Mackay, R D, and Colman, A M, 'Equivocal Rulings on Expert Psychological and Psychiatric Evidence: Turning a Muddle into a Nonsense' [1996] *Criminal Law Review* 88

— and Colman, A M, 'Excluding Expert Evidence: A Tale of Ordinary Folk and Common Experience' [1991] *Criminal Law Review* 800

Manchester, C, 'Admissibility of Spent Convictions in Civil Cases: *Thomas v Commissioner of Police for the Metropolis*' (1997) 1(3) *International Journal of Evidence and Proof* 152

Michael, J, and Emmerson, B, 'Current Topic: The Right to Silence' [1995] *European Human Rights Law Review* 4

Miene, P, Park, R C, and Borgida, E, 'Juror Decision Making and the Evaluation of Hearsay Evidence' (1992) 76 *Minnesota Law Review* 683

Milich, P S, 'Hearsay Antinomies: The Case for Abolishing the Rule and Starting Over' (1992) 71 *Oregon Law Review* 723

— 'Re-Examining Hearsay under the Federal Rules: Some Method for the Madness' (1991) 39 *University of Kansas Law Review* 893

Miller, C J, 'Proof of Civil Contempt' (1996) 112 *Law Quarterly Review* 539

Mirfield, P, 'The Argument from Consistency for Overruling *Selvey*' [1991] *Cambridge Law Journal* 490

— ' "Corroboration" after the 1994 Act' [1995] *Criminal Law Review* 448

— 'The Legacy of *Hunt*' [1988] *Criminal Law Review* 19

— 'Proof and Prejudice in the House of Lords' (1996) 112 *Law Quarterly Review* 1

— 'Similar Facts – *Makin* Out?' [1987] *Cambridge Law Journal* 83

— 'Successive Confessions and the Poisonous Tree' [1996] *Criminal Law Review* 554

— 'Two Side-Effects of Sections 34 to 37 of the Criminal Justice and Public Order Act 1994' [1995] *Criminal Law Review* 612

— 'An Ungrateful Reply' [1988] *Criminal Law Review* 233

— *Confessions* (London: Sweet & Maxwell, 1985)

Mortimore, C, 'Severance Revisited' (1996) 140 *Solicitors Journal* 611

Munday, R, 'Comparative Law and English Law's Character Evidence Rules' (1993) 13 *Oxford Journal of Legal Studies* 589

— '*Cum Tacent Clamant:* Drawing Proper Inferences from a Defendant's Failure to Testify' [1996] *Cambridge Law Journal* 32

— 'Handling Convictions Admissible under S 27(3) of the Theft Act 1968: Part 1' (1995) 159 *Justice of the Peace* 223

— 'Handling Convictions Admissible under S 27(3) of the Theft Act 1968: Part 2' (1995) 159 *Justice of the Peace* 261

— 'Inferences from Silence and European Human Rights Law' [1996] *Criminal Law Review* 370

— 'Musings on the Dying Declaration' (1993) 22 *Anglo-American Law Review* 42

— 'The Paradox of Cross-Examination to Credit – Simply too Close for Comfort' [1994] *Cambridge Law Journal* 303

— 'The Proof of Fear: Part 1' (1993) 143 *New Law Journal* 542

— 'The Proof of Fear: Part 2' (1993) 143 *New Law Journal* 587

— 'Section 1(f)(ii) of the Criminal Evidence Act 1898: When should a Judge Stiffen a Prosecutor's Fibre?' (1997) 161 *Justice of the Peace* 155

— 'Similar Fact Evidence and the Risk of Contaminated Testimony' [1995] *Cambridge Law Journal* 522

— 'Vaguely Similar Facts and Severance of Counts' (1996) 160 *Justice of the Peace* 663

— 'What Constitutes a Good Character?' [1997] *Criminal Law Review* 247

— 'Who Qualifies as a "Witness" for the Purpose of Imputations Made under Section 1(f)(ii) of the Criminal Evidence Act 1898' (1997) 161 *Justice of the Peace* 379

Murphy, P, 'Hearsay: The Road to Reform' (1997) 1(2) *International Journal of Evidence and Proof* 107

— 'Practising Safe Hearsay: Surrender may be Inevitable, but Shouldn't We Take Precautions?' (1997) 1(3) *International Journal of Evidence and Proof* 105

Murray, C, 'Fair is Foul and Foul is Fair' (1996) 146 *New Law Journal* 1288

Myers, M A, 'Rule Departures and Making Law: Juries and their Verdicts' (1979) 13 *Law and Society Review* 781

Nair, R, 'Weighing Similar Fact and Avoiding Prejudice' (1996) 112 *Law Quarterly Review* 262

Nance, D A (ed), 'Symposium on the Admission of Prior Offense Evidence in Sexual Assault Cases' (1994) 70 *Chicago-Kent Law Review* 1

Nash, S, and Furse, M, '*Murray* and the Right to Silence' (1996) 146 *New Law Journal* 261

— and Solley, S, 'Limitations on the Right to Silence and Abuse of Process' (1997) 61 *Journal of Criminal Law* 95

Newark, M, 'The Hostile Witness and the Adversary System' [1986] *Criminal Law Review* 441

— 'Opening up the Collateral Issue Rule' (1992) 43 *Northern Ireland Legal Quarterly* 166

— and Samuels, A, 'Refreshing Memory' [1978] *Criminal Law Review* 408

Newbold, A L E, 'The Crime/Fraud Exception to Legal Professional Privilege' (1990) 53 *Modern Law Review* 472

Nijboer, J F, 'Common Law Tradition in Evidence Scholarship Observed from a Continental Perspective' (1993) 41 *American Journal of Comparative Law* 299

O'Brien, D, 'The Rule against Hearsay RIP' (1996) 146 *New Law Journal* 153

Odgers, S J, and Richardson, J T, 'Keeping Bad Science out of the Courtroom – Changes in American and Australian Expert Evidence Law' (1995) 18 *University of New South Wales Law Journal* 108

Ormerod, D C, 'Law Commission Consultation Paper No 138 on Hearsay: (2) The Hearsay Exceptions' [1996] *Criminal Law Review* 16

— 'Reform of Implied Assertions' (1996) 60 *Journal of Criminal Law* 201

Osborne, C, 'Hearsay and the European Court of Human Rights' [1993] *Criminal Law Review* 255

Ostrin, A R, 'Police Observation Points' (1992) 156 *Justice of the Peace* 423

Paciocco, D M, 'The Judicial Repeal of S 24(2) and the Development of the Canadian Exclusionary Rule' (1990) 32 *Criminal Law Quarterly* 326

Packer, H L, *The Limits of the Criminal Sanction* (Stanford: Stanford University Press, 1969)

Palmer, A, 'The Scope of the Similar Fact Rule' (1994) 16 *Adelaide Law Review* 161

Park, R C, 'Sexual Assault and the Rule against Character Reasoning' in J F Nijboer and J M Reijntjes (eds), *Proceedings of the First World Conference on New Trends in Criminal Investigation and Evidence* (Lelystad: Open University of the Netherlands, 1997)

— 'A Subject Matter Approach to Hearsay Reform' (1987) 86 *Michigan Law Review* 51

Passmore, C, 'Privilege in the Lords' (1996) 146 *New Law Journal* 921

Pattenden, R, 'Conceptual versus Pragmatic Approaches to Hearsay' (1993) 56 *Modern Law Review* 138

— 'Conflicting Approaches to Psychiatric Evidence in Criminal Trials: England, Canada and Australia' [1986] *Criminal Law Review* 92

— 'Evidence of Previous Malpractice by Police Witnesses and R v Edwards' [1992] *Criminal Law Review* 549

— 'Expert Opinion Evidence Based on Hearsay' [1982] *Criminal Law Review* 85

— 'The Hostile Witness' (1992) 56 *Journal of Criminal Law* 414

— 'Inferences from Silence' [1995] *Criminal Law Review* 602

— 'The Purpose of Cross-Examination under Section 1(f) of the Criminal Evidence Act 1898' [1982] *Criminal Law Review* 707

— 'Should Confessions be Corroborated?' (1991) 107 *Law Quarterly Review* 317

— 'Similar Fact Evidence and Proof of Identity' (1996) 112 *Law Quarterly Review* 446

— 'The Submission of No Case – Some Recent Developments' [1982] *Criminal Law Review* 558

— *Judicial Discretion and Criminal Litigation* (Oxford: Clarendon Press, 1990)

Phillips, E, 'Testing the Truth: The Alliance of Science and Law' in M McConville and L Bridges (eds), *Criminal Justice in Crisis* (Aldershot: Edward Elgar, 1994)

Phillips, J H, 'The Voir Dire' (1989) 63 *Australian Law Journal* 46

Plotnikoff, J, and Woolfson, R, *Prosecuting Child Abuse: An Evaluation of the Government's Speedy Progress Policy* (London: Blackstone Press Ltd, 1995)

'Previous Misconduct of a Defendant', *Archbold News*, 15 August 1996, 6

Prithipaul, R, 'Observations on the Current Status of the Hearsay Rule' (1996) 39 *Criminal Law Quarterly* 84

Purnell, N, 'A Brief Guide to Part 1 of the Criminal Procedure and Investigations Act 1996', *Archbold News*, 10 February 1997, 4

Rakos, R F, and Landsman, S, 'Researching the Hearsay Rule: Emerging Findings, General Issues, and Future Directions' (1992) 76 *Minnesota Law Review* 655

Re, L, 'Oral v Written Evidence: The Myth of the "Impressive Witness"' (1983) 57 *Australian Law Journal* 679

Redmayne, M, 'Process Gains and Process Values: The Criminal Procedure and Investigations Act 1996' (1997) 60 *Modern Law Review* 79

— 'The Royal Commission and the Forensic Science Market' in M McConville and L Bridges (eds), *Criminal Justice in Crisis* (Aldershot: Edward Elgar, 1994)

Reed, T J, 'Evidentiary Failures: A Structural Theory of Evidence Applied to Hearsay Issues' (1994) 18 *American Journal of Trial Advocacy* 353

Reeves, P, 'Video Recorded Evidence of Children' (1993) 157 *Justice of the Peace* 229

Rein, A, 'The Scope of Hearsay' (1994) 110 *Law Quarterly Review* 431

Reiter, H, 'Hearsay Evidence and Criminal Process in Germany and Australia' (1984) 10 *Monash University Law Review* 51

Report of the Advisory Group on Video Evidence (London: Home Office, 1989)

Roberts, P, 'Forensic Science Evidence after Runciman' [1994] *Criminal Law Review* 780

— 'The Law Commission Consultation Paper on Previous Misconduct: (1) All the Usual Suspects: A Critical Appraisal of Law Commission Consultation Paper No 141' [1997] *Criminal Law Review* 75

— 'Science in the Criminal Process' (1994) 14 *Oxford Journal of Legal Studies* 469

— 'Taking the Burden of Proof Seriously' [1995] *Criminal Law Review* 783

— and Willmore, C, *The Role of Forensic Science Evidence in Criminal Proceedings* (Royal Commission on Criminal Justice Research Study No 11) (London: HMSO, 1993)

Robertson, B, and Vignaux, G A, 'Expert Evidence: Law, Practice and Probability' (1992) 12 *Oxford Journal of Legal Studies* 392

Robertson, G, 'Entrapment Evidence: Manna from Heaven, or Fruit of the Poisoned Tree?' [1994] *Criminal Law Review* 805

Roskill, *Fraud Trials Committee Report* (London: HMSO, 1986)

Royal Commission on Criminal Justice, *Report* (Cm 2263) (London: HMSO, 1993)

Saltzburg, S A, 'A Special Aspect of Relevance: Countering Negative Inferences Associated with the Absence of Evidence' (1978) 66 *California Law Review* 1011

Samuels, A, 'No Case to Answer: The Judge Must Stop the Case: *Galbraith*', *Archbold News*, 14 November 1996, 6

— 'Psychiatric Evidence' [1981] *Criminal Law Review* 762

Sanders, A, and Young, R, *Criminal Justice* (London: Butterworths, 1994)

Sattar, G, and Bull, R, 'Child Witnesses in Court: Psycho-Legal Issues' (1996) 140 *Solicitors Journal* 401

Scallen, E A, 'Constitutional Dimensions of Hearsay Reform: Toward a Three-Dimensional Confrontation Clause' (1992) 76 *Minnesota Law Review* 623

Schaitkin, K A, '"Negative Hearsay" – The Sounds of Silence' (1980) 84 *Dickinson Law Review* 605

Schneider, C E, 'Discretion and Rules: A Lawyer's View' in K Hawkins (ed), *The Uses of Discretion* (Oxford: Clarendon Press, 1992)

Scott, R, 'The Acceptable and Unacceptable Use of Public Interest Immunity' [1996] *Public Law* 427

— *Report of the Inquiry into the Export of Defence Equipment and Dual-Use Goods to Iraq and Related Prosecutions* (London: HMSO, 1996)

Scottish Law Commission, *Evidence: Report on Hearsay Evidence in Criminal Proceedings* (Scot Law Com No 149) (Edinburgh: HMSO, 1995)

Seidelson, D E, 'Implied Assertions and Federal Rule of Evidence 801: A Quandary for Federal Courts' (1986) 24 *Duquesne Law Review* 741

Sharpe, S, 'Covert Police Operations and the Discretionary Exclusion of Evidence' [1994] *Criminal Law Review* 793

— 'Covert Policing: A Comparative View' (1996) 25 *Anglo-American Law Review* 163

— 'Electronic Eavesdropping: A Chance for Accountability?' (1996) 146 *New Law Journal* 1088

— 'Judicial Discretion and Investigative Impropriety' (1997) 1(2) *International Journal of Evidence and Proof* 149

Slovenko, R, 'Surveying the Attacks on Psychiatry in the Legal Process' (1996) 1 *International Journal of Evidence and Proof* 48

Smith, A T H, 'Public Interest Immunity and Sensitive Material' [1993] *Cambridge Law Journal* 357

— 'Public Interest Immunity in Criminal Cases' [1993] *Cambridge Law Journal* 1

Smith, J C, 'The Presumption of Innocence' (1987) 38 *Northern Ireland Legal Quarterly* 223

— 'Satisfying the Jury' [1988] *Criminal Law Review* 335

— 'Sections 23 and 24 of the Criminal Justice Act 1988: (1) Some Problems' [1994] *Criminal Law Review* 426

Solnit, A J, 'Truth Telling: The Child as Witness' (1994) 2 *International Journal of Children's Rights* 61

Spencer, J N, 'The Current Hearsay Rule and Proposals for Reform' (1996) 60 *Journal of Criminal Law* 77

— 'The Right of Silence, Legal Privilege and the Decision in *Condron*' (1996) 160 *Justice of the Peace* 1167

Spencer, J R, 'Bugging and Burglary by the Police' [1997] *Cambridge Law Journal* 6

— 'Court Experts and Expert Witnesses: Have We a Lesson to Learn from the French?' (1992) 45 *Current Legal Problems* 213

— 'Hearsay, Relevance and Implied Assertions' [1993] *Cambridge Law Journal* 40

— 'Law Commission Consultation Paper No 138 on Hearsay: (3) Hearsay Reform: A Bridge Not Far Enough?' [1996] *Criminal Law Review* 29

— 'Orality and the Evidence of Absent Witnesses' [1994] *Criminal Law Review* 628

— and Flin, R H, *The Evidence of Children: The Law and the Psychology* (2nd ed, London: Blackstone Press Ltd, 1993)

Sprack, J, 'The Criminal Procedure and Investigations Act 1996: (1) The Duty of Disclosure' [1997] *Criminal Law Review* 308

Stein, A, 'After *Hunt*: The Burden of Proof, Risk of Non-Persuasion and Judicial Pragmatism' (1991) 54 *Modern Law Review* 570

— 'Judicial Fact-Finding and the Bayesian Method: The Case for Deeper Scepticism about their Combination' (1996) 1 *International Journal of Evidence and Proof* 25

— 'The Refoundation of Evidence Law' (1996) 9 *Canadian Journal of Law and Jurisprudence* 279

Stein, P, and Shand, J, *Legal Values in Western Society* (Edinburgh: Edinburgh University Press, 1974)

Stephen, Sir J F, *A Digest of the Law of Evidence* (12th ed by Sir H L Stephen and L F Sturge, London: Macmillan and Co, Ltd, 1946)

Stevens, R, 'Getting over the Threshold – An Exegesis of Section 31(2) of the Children Act 1989' (1996) 160 *Justice of the Peace* 111

Steventon, B, *The Ability to Challenge DNA Evidence* (Royal Commission on Criminal Justice Research Study No 9) (London: HMSO, 1993)

Stone, J, 'Burden of Proof and the Judicial Process: A Commentary on *Joseph Constantine Steamship, Ltd v Imperial Smelting Corporation, Ltd*' (1944) 60 *Law Quarterly Review* 262

— 'The Rule of Exclusion of Similar Fact Evidence: England' (1933) 46 *Harvard Law Review* 954

— (rev Wells, W A N), *Evidence: Its History and Policies* (Sydney: Butterworths, 1991)

Stone, M, 'Instant Lie Detection? Demeanour and Credibility in Criminal Trials' [1991] *Criminal Law Review* 821

Stone, R, 'Exclusion of Evidence under Section 78 of the Police and Criminal Evidence Act: Practice and Principles' in M J Allen (ed), *Web Journal of Current Legal Issues Yearbook 1995* (London: Blackstone Press Ltd, 1996)

Strong, J W (ed), *McCormick on Evidence* (4th ed, St Paul, Minn: West Publishing Co, 1992)

Sunstein, C R, 'Problems with Rules' (1995) 83 *California Law Review* 953

Swift, E, 'A Foundation Fact Approach to Hearsay' (1987) 75 *California Law Review* 1339

— 'Smoke and Mirrors: The Failure of the Supreme Court's Accuracy Rationale in *White v Illinois* Requires a New Look at Confrontation' (1993) 22 *Capital University Law Review* 145

Symposium on Hearsay and Implied Assertions: How would (or should) the Supreme Court Decide the *Kearley* Case?, (1995) 16 *Mississippi College Law Review* 1

Tain, P, 'Covert Surveillance, *R v Khan* and the European Convention' (1996) 140 *Solicitors Journal* 785

Tapper, C F H, '*Hillmon* Rediscovered and Lord St Leonards Resurrected' (1990) 106 *Law Quarterly Review* 441

— 'The Meaning of Section 1(f)(i) of the Criminal Evidence Act 1898' in C F H Tapper (ed), *Crime, Proof and Punishment: Essays in Memory of Sir Rupert Cross* (London: Butterworths, 1981)

— 'The Open Society and its Enemy' (1978) 41 *Modern Law Review* 192

— 'Overhearing and Oversight' (1997) 1(2) *International Journal of Evidence and Proof* 162

— 'Privilege and Confidence' (1972) 35 *Modern Law Review* 83

— 'Privilege and Policy' (1974) 37 *Modern Law Review* 92

— 'Prosecution and Privilege' (1996) 1 *International Journal of Evidence and Proof* 5

— *Cross and Tapper on Evidence* (8th ed, London: Butterworths, 1995)

Temkin, J, 'Sexual History Evidence – The Ravishment of Section 2' [1993] *Criminal Law Review* 3

— (ed), *Rape and the Criminal Justice System* (Aldershot: Dartmouth, 1995)

— *Rape and the Legal Process* (London: Sweet & Maxwell, 1987)

Thayer, J B, *A Preliminary Treatise on Evidence at the Common Law* (Boston: Little, Brown and Co, 1898)

Tiersma, P M, 'Reforming the Language of Jury Instructions' (1993) 22 *Hofstra Law Review* 37

Tomkins, A, 'Public Interest Immunity after Matrix Churchill' [1993] *Public Law* 650

Tribe, L H, 'Triangulating Hearsay' (1974) 87 *Harvard Law Review* 957

Twining, W, *Rethinking Evidence: Exploratory Essays* (Evanston, Illinois: Northwestern University Press, 1994)

— *Theories of Evidence: Bentham and Wigmore* (London: Weidenfeld & Nicolson, 1985)

Victim Support, *Women, Rape and the Criminal Justice System* (London: Victim Support, 1996)

Walker, S, *Taming the System: The Control of Discretion in Criminal Justice 1950–1990* (New York: OUP, 1993)

Wellborn, O G III, 'The Definition of Hearsay in the Federal Rules of Evidence' (1982) 61 *Texas Law Review* 49

— 'Demeanor' (1991) 76 *Cornell Law Review* 1075

Wigmore, J H, 'The American Law Institute Code of Evidence Rules: A Dissent' (1942) 28 *American Bar Association Journal* 23

— (rev Tillers, P), *Evidence in Trials at Common Law (Vol 1A)* (Boston: Little, Brown and Co, 1983)

— (rev Chadbourn, J H), *Evidence in Trials at Common Law (Vol 5)* (Boston: Little, Brown and Co, 1974)

— (rev Chadbourn, J H), *Evidence in Trials at Common Law (Vol 7)* (Boston: Little, Brown and Co, 1978)

Williams, K D, Loftus, E F, and Deffenbacher, K A, 'Eyewitness Evidence and Testimony' in D K Kagehiro and W S Laufer (eds), *Handbook of Psychology and Law* (New York: Springer-Verlag, 1992)

Wissler, R L, and Saks, M J, 'On the Inefficacy of Limiting Instructions: When Jurors Use Prior Conviction Evidence to Decide on Guilt' (1985) 9 *Law and Human Behavior* 37

Wolchover, D, and Heaton-Armstrong, A, *Wolchover and Heaton-Armstrong on Confession Evidence* (London: Sweet & Maxwell, 1996)

Yarmey, A D, *The Psychology of Eyewitness Testimony* (New York: The Free Press, 1979)

Zander, M, *Cases and Materials on the English Legal System* (7th ed, London: Butterworths, 1996)

— and Henderson, P, *The Royal Commission on Criminal Justice: Crown Court Study* (London: HMSO, 1993)

Zuckerman, A A S, 'Evidence' [1985] *All ER Review* 155

— 'Law Commission Consultation Paper No 138 on Hearsay: (1) The Futility of Hearsay' [1996] *Criminal Law Review* 4

— 'Legal Professional Privilege – The Cost of Absolutism' (1996) 112 *Law Quarterly Review* 535

— 'Miscarriage of Justice and Judicial Responsibility' [1991] *Criminal Law Review* 492
— 'No Third Exception to the Woolmington Rule' (1987) 103 *Law Quarterly Review* 170
— 'Privilege and Public Interest' in C F H Tapper (ed), *Crime, Proof and Punishment: Essays in Memory of Sir Rupert Cross* (London: Butterworths, 1981)
— 'Public Interest Immunity – A Matter of Prime Judicial Responsibility' (1994) 57 *Modern Law Review* 703
— 'The Third Exception to the Woolmington Rule' (1976) 92 *Law Quarterly Review* 402
— *The Principles of Criminal Evidence* (Oxford: Clarendon Press, 1989)

INDEX

Accomplices
corroboration and, 92
Accused
character of, 207 *et seq*, 252, 254–79
competence and compellability of,
75–81
confessions by, *see* Confessions
convictions of, 195–203, 245,
252–3
cross-examination
character, as to, 245 *et seq*
co-accused, by, 77, 284–8
failure to testify *see* Right to silence
former spouse of
competence and compellability,
82
spouse of
competence and compellability,
81–4
testify, point at which to, 154
Admissibility, general concept of,
3–8
see also Relevance
see also Weight of evidence
Adversarial tradition
definition, 131–2
see also Inquisitorial model
Adverse inferences *see* Right to silence
Alibi
defence of, 104
notice of, 142–3, 146

Balance of probability
definition of, 57–60
Bankers
compellability of, 88

Bayes Theorem, 506–17
Burden of proof, 40–57
definition, 40–1
evidential, 40
legal burden, 40
incidence of in civil trial, 54–7
incidence of in criminal trials,
41–54
duress, 41, 43
express statutory exceptions,
44–5
general rule *see* Woolmington
rule
implied statutory exceptions,
45–54
insane automatism, 42–3
insanity, 42–4
see also M'Naghten rules
M'Naghten rules, 42–3
non-insane automatism, 41, 43
provocation, 41, 43
self-defence, 41, 43
unfitness to plead, 42, 43
Woolmington rule, 41–3
misdirection, 54
presumption of innocence, 42
probative burden *see* legal burden
provisional burden *see* evidential
burden

Children
competence of, 86–8, 120
protection of,
within criminal proceedings, 119–28
cross-examination of, 128
live television link, 121–3

notice of transfer, 128–9
screens and social workers,
120–1
video recordings, 123–8
sworn evidence and, 86
unsworn evidence and, 86–8
Circumstantial evidence, 12–16
definition, 12
examples of –
adverse inferences, 14–16
intimate samples,
refusal of consent, 15
see also Right to silence
continuance, 13
fingerprints, 13
motive, 14
opportunity, 13
reactions of tracker dogs, 13–14
Close of case
adducing evidence following, 154–5
Co-accused
competence and compellability, 75,
77
confessions by, 306–15
evidence against by accused, 284–8
Co-defendant *see* Co-accused
Collateral finality rule *see* Cross-
examination
Compellability *see* Competence and
compellability
Competence and compellability, 73–88
accused, 75–81
bankers, 88
children
civil trials, 86
criminal trials, 86–8, 120
expert evidence as to, 74
see also Expert opinion evidence
former spouse of accused, 82
judges, 88
mental disability, 84–6
perjury, 74
spouse of accused, 81–4
sworn evidence, 73–4
Confessions, 16, 396–432
co-defendant, by, 307–15
corroboration and supporting
evidence, 371–2
definition of, 369–70

discretionary exclusion, 385–6
common law, 387
denial of access to legal advice,
389–96
improperly obtained confessions,
385–6
limitation to, 402–3
police lies, 387–8
recording requirements, 396–402
statute, 386–7
inadmissible confession –
facts discovered in consequence of,
408–10
legal professional privilege, 417
see also Legal professional privilege
mandatory exclusion, 373
involuntary confessions, 373
oppression, 272–7
unreliability, 373, 378–85
mental disability, 405–7
mixed statements, 407–8
partly adverse statements *see* mixed
statements
right to silence, erosion of, 410–30
see also Right to silence
role of judge and jury, 403–4, 407
third parties, by, 307
voir dire and, 404
Contempt of court, 33, 62, 564
Convictions *see* Previous convictions
Corroboration
general rule, 89
exceptions –
attempts, 92
perjury, 89, 91–2
speeding offences, 89–90
treason, 89
warning, 92
abolition of, 93
accomplices, 92
alibi, 104
confessions, 104 *see also*
Confessions
criminal connections, 101
improper motive, 101
judge's discretion, 93–104
Lucas direction, 103–4
mental condition, 101–3
sexual cases, 92, 94–100, 105

Cross-examination, 134, 184–9,
  245–88
accused, of, 245–90
  credit, as to, 279, 288–9
  Criminal Evidence Act 1898, 245
  et seq
  s.1 – competency, 245
  s.1(e) – liability to cross-
    examination, 245
  s.1(f) – shield, 245
    bad character, 145, 252
      meaning as to, 254
    previous offences
      charged, 245, 252–3
      commission, 245, 252
      convicted of, 245, 252
  s.1(f)(i)–(iii) – loss of shield
    admissible evidence of guilt,
      246, 254–5
    see also Similar-fact evidence
    character in issue, 246, 255–7
    good character –
      meaning of, 263–4
      rebuttal of, 264
      relevance of –
        see Vye direction
      Vye direction, 257–63
    co-accused, evidence against,
      246, 284–8
    imputations cast, 246, 265–84
      practical implications of
        rule, 279–82
      reform, 283–4
      witness for prosecution –
        definition, 265–7
    general evaluation, 288–90
    leave requirements, 254–5
    relationship between provisos (e)
      and (f), 246–52
  child victims, of, 128
collateral finality rule, 189–206
  exceptions to –
    bias, 201–3
    incapacity, 203
    prior convictions, 191–5
    prior inconsistent statements,
      191–5
    reputation for lack of veracity,
      203–4

finality of answers to collateral
    questions, 190
  meaning of, 189–91
  credit, as to, 188–9 *see also* Collateral
    finality rule
  facts in issue, 184, 190–1
  leading questions, 184
  limitations to, 187–9
  probative value of, 188
  purpose of, 184–7
  rule in *Browne v Dunn*, 189

DNA evidence, 502–6
Deceased
  statements of persons since, 321–5
    declarations against pecuniary or
      proprietary interest, 321–2
    declarations in the course of duty,
      322–3
    dying declarations, 323–5
Defendant *see* Accused
Discovery *see* Pre-trial disclosure
Documents
  bankers' books, production of, 88
  business documents, 338–42
  computer produced documents,
    347–55
  depositions admitted in evidence in
    committal proceedings, 355
  documents, pre-existing, within legal
    professional privilege, 577
  documents prepared for purpose of
    criminal proceedings, 343
  documents protected by public
    interest immunity *see* Public
    interest immunity
  documents to be disclosed, pre-trial,
    139–46
  documents used by expert witnesses,
    hearsay and, 524–8
  documents used to refresh memory,
    requirements of, 175–83
  first hand documentary hearsay,
    332–8
  reports by experts, 527–8
    advance disclosure of findings,
      140
Duress
  defence of, burden of proof, 41–3

Entrapment, 442–58
Evidence
  civil, 27
  criminal, 27
    underlying principles of, 28–33
  definition, 1
  development of law of, 3
  reform of laws of, 38
Evidential burden *see* Burden of proof
Examination-in-chief, 134, 155–75
  general rule, 155
  hostile witness, 158–61
    prior inconsistent statements in
      relation to, 159, 160
  leading questions, 155–8
  prior consistent statements
    civil trial, 174–5
    criminal trial
      complaint in sexual cases, 161–2
      reform, 173–4
      statement admissible as part of
        res gestae, 173
        see also Hearsay
      statement made on accusation,
        170–1
      statement made on discovery of
        incriminating articles, 172
      statement of prior identification
        of accused, 173
      statement rebutting allegation of
        recent fabrication, 162–9
  refreshing memory
    in court, 175, 180
    out of court, 181–4
    see also Refreshing memory
  unfavourable witness, 158
Exclusionary discretion *see* Judicial
  discretion
Exclusionary rules *see* Hearsay and
  Confessions
Expert opinion evidence, 490 *et seq*
  admissibility, 493–524
    necessity, 493
    reliability, 493
    statutory provisions, 494
  advance notice rules, 149–50
  assault and, 517
  Bayes Theorem, 506–17
  confessions, admissibility of, and, 501

credibility, issue of, and, 494–500
DNA, 502–6
defence raised and, 494–500
duties of expert, 530–1
foreign law, 519–35
handwriting, 518
hearsay and, 355, 524–8
impartiality, need for, 490–1
mens rea, issue of, and, 494–500
mental disorders and, 495–500
obscenity, 501–2
photographs, 518
reform, 531–5
ultimate issues, 528–30
voice identification, 517

Finality of answers to collateral
  questions *see* Cross-examination
Former spouses *see* Competence and
  compellability

Galbraith principle *see* No case to answer

Hearsay evidence, 5, 12, 16, 292–368
  admissibility by statute, 292–5
  civil proceedings – rule governing,
    295–300
    adducing, notice of proposal,
      295–6, 298–9
    admissibility, 295
    competence and credibility of
      witness, 296–7, 299
    formerly admissible at common
      law, 297
    Ogden tables, admissibility and
      proof, 298
    preservation of existing statutory
      rules, 298
    weight of evidence, 296
    witnesses for cross-examination on,
      power to call, 296, 299
  common law exceptions to rule,
    292–5, 321
    statements forming part of *res
      gestae*, 325–31
    spontaneous statements, 325–7
    statements accompanying and
      explaining a relevant act,
      327–8

statements concerning
contemporaneous physical
state, 330–1
statements concerning
contemporaneous state of
mind, 328–30
statements in public documents,
331–2
statements in works of reference, 332
statements made in former
proceedings, 332
statements of deceased persons,
321–5
declarations against pecuniary or
proprietary interest, 321–2
declarations in course of duty,
322–3
dying declarations, 323–5
criminal proceedings – rule
governing, 140
application of rule, 300–3
European Convention on Human
Rights, implication of, 358–60
evasion of, 304–16
confessions by third parties and
co-defendants, 306–15
factual assertion, air ticket
containing, 304
identification parade, evidence of,
305
photofit evidence, 305–6
see also Confessions – mixed
statements
see also Expert opinion evidence –
hearsay and
implied assertions, 316–21
reform, 360–7
statutory exceptions to rule, 332–58
computer produced documents,
347–55
Criminal Justice Act 1988 – Pt II
business documents (s.24),
338–42
documents prepared for criminal
proceedings or investigation,
343–4
first hand documentary hearsay
(s.23), 332–8
judicial discretion (s.25), 342–6

Criminal Justice Act 1988 – Sched. 2
credibility and weight, 347
expert reports, 358 see also Expert
opinion evidence, hearsay and
further exceptions, 358
proof of written documents,
357–8
statements made within committal
proceedings, 355–6
video recordings of child witness,
358 see also Children, protection
of
Hostile witnesses, 158–61

Identification evidence see also Similar
fact evidence, identification
and
Code D requirements, 471, 479–82
confrontation, 479, 481
group identification, 479, 480
identification parade, 479, 480
see also Hearsay and
photographs and photofit, 482
see also Hearsay and
video film, 479, 480
exclusionary discretion, 471, 479,
482–7
need of caution, 467–8
event factors, 469–70
crime seriousness, 469
cross-gender identification, 470
cross-race identification, 470
exposure duration, 469
presence of weapon, 469
stress, arousal and violence,
470
post-event factors, 470–1
time lapse between crime and
identification, 470–1
witness factors, 468–9
biases and prejudices, 468
expectations from past
experience, 468
momentary or temporary
expectations, 468
perceptual activity, 469
vision, 468
relationship between Code D
breaches and warning, 487–9

Turnbull guidelines, 471–9
warning requirements *see* Turnbull
    guidelines
Inquisitorial model
    definition, 131–2 *see also* Adversarial
        tradition
Insane automatism
    defence of, burden of proof, 42–3

Joinder and severance *see* Similar-fact
    evidence
Judicial discretion, 23–6
    child victims, as to, 120–8
    confessions and, 385–402
    corroboration and, 93–104
    cross-examination and, 254, 257–63,
        279, 288–9
    hearsay and, 342–6
    hostile witnesses, leave to cross-
        examine, 159
    illegally or unfairly obtained
        evidence, 433–65
    no case to answer and, 134–9
    similar-fact evidence, 217

Legal advice
    denial of access to, 389–93
Legal burden *see* Burden of proof
Legal professional privilege, 574–604
    see also Privilege and Public
        interest immunity
    absolute doctrine, 593–9
    collateral facts, 577
    communications protected by –
        client and legal adviser, between,
            575–81
        third parties, with, 575–7, 581–6
    exceptions to –
        crime facilitation, 588–93
        fraud facilitation, 588–93
    pre-existing documents, 577
    secondary evidence and, 599–604
    unqualified advisers
        general position, 578
        statutory position, 578
    waiver, 586–8
Lies *see* Corroboration – Lucas direction
Lucas direction *see* Corroboration

Memory refreshing documents *see*
    Refreshing memory
M'Naghten rules *see* Burden of proof

National security *see* Public interest
    immunity
No case to answer
    submission of, 134–9
Non-confessional evidence improperly
    obtained, 433–65 *see also*
    Identification evidence
    discretionary exclusion, 433–4
    electronic listening devices, 442–58
    entrapment, 442–58
    general rule, 433
    obtained outside of jurisdiction, 458
    rationale for exclusion, 458–65
    road traffic cases, 434–8
    undercover police activity, 442–58
    violation of PACE, 438–42 *see also*
        Confessions
Non-insane automatism
    defence of, burden of proof, 41, 43

Ogden tables *see* Hearsay evidence
Opinion evidence
    general rule, 490
    see Expert opinion evidence
Oppression *see* Confessions
Oral evidence *see* Testimony

Police informers
    identification of, 548–59
Pre-trial disclosure
    civil, 139–40
    criminal, 140–50
Pre-trial hearing, 17–23
    rules governing, 17–18
Previous consistent statements, 161–75
    accusation, statements made on,
        170–2
    civil trial, within, 174–5
    complaints in sex cases, 162–9
    incriminating articles, discovery of,
        statements made on, 172
    prior identification of accused, 173
    recent fabrication, rebuttal of
        allegations, 169–70

reform of, 173–4
res gestae statements, 173
Previous convictions, 195–203, 245,
    252–3
Previous inconsistent statements,
    191–5
examination of written statements,
    192
hostile witness and, 159–60
Prior consistent statements *see* Previous
    consistent statements
Prior inconsistent statements *see*
    Previous inconsistent statements
Privilege
legal professional privilege *see* Legal
    professional privilege
self-incrimination, against, 574 *see*
    also Cross-examination, accused,
    of
without prejudice negotiations,
    574–5
Provocation
defence of, burden of proof, 41, 43
Public interest immunity, 537–72
confidential relationships and, 563 *see*
    also Legal professional privilege
criminal cases, 548
informers, identification of, 548–59
observation points – disclosure,
    559–60
Scott report and recommendations,
    560–3
definition, 537–8
judicial attitude to, 538–46
national security and, 546–7
public service, proper functioning of,
    547–8
Public policy *see* Public interest
    immunity

Questions of fact
definition of, 16
examples of, 16
Questions of Law
definition of, 16
examples of, 16

Rationalist approach *see* Evidence –
    development of law of

Real evidence, 8–12
definition of, 8
out-of-court inspections, 9–11
Reasonable doubt
definition of, 60–2
Re-examination, 134, 206
limits on, 206
see also Examination in chief
Refreshing memory
hearsay rule and, 331–2, 355
in court, 172
contemporaneity, requirement of,
    176–8
making or verification of entry,
    175–6
status of documents used for,
    178–81
out of court, 181–3
Relevance, general concept of, 3–8
admissibility and, *see* Admissibility
probative value, 3–8
Wigmore approach, 5–6
Res gestae
Hearsay rule and, 325
contemporaneous physical state,
    statements concerning, 330–1
contemporaneous state of mind,
    statements concerning, 328–30
relevant act, statements
    accompanying and explaining,
    327–8
spontaneous statements, 325–7
previous consistent statements and, 173
Right to silence
adverse inferences, 14–16, 75–81, 268
erosion of, 410–30
Role of Judge
confessions and, 403–4, 407
expert opinion evidence and, 493 *et seq*
judicial warning as to relevance, 7, 8
submission of no case to answer, on
    a, 134–9
trier of law, as, 16
Role of jury
confessions and, 403–4, 407
expert evidence and, 493 *et seq*
trial, within, 33–7
triers of fact, as, 16
weight of evidence, as to, 7

Rule against self-corroboration or narrative *see* Previous consistent statements

Sanity
expert evidence and, 494–501
presumption of, 43
Secondary evidence, 599–604
Self-defence
defence of, burden of proof, 41–3
Similar-fact evidence, 5, 207–44
admissibility of, 207–23
civil trials, 242
contamination, 223–30
dissimilarities, 219, 220
identification and, 219, 230–5
see also Identification evidence
joinder and severance and, 235–7
possession of incriminating articles, 237–41
relevance and, 222
statutory exceptions to general prohibition, 241–2
spying, 241
theft, 242
striking similarity, 208–19
Standard of proof, 40, 57–72
balance of probabilities – definition, 57–60
beyond reasonable doubt – definition, 60–2
discharge within civil trials –
allegations of criminal conduct, 63
care proceedings, allegation of sexual abuse, 66–8
contempt of court, 62–3
general rule, 61–2
quasi-criminal proceedings, 63–6
discharge within criminal trials, 57–61
misdirection, 61
third standard, 68–72

Testimony
benefits of, 132–4
definition of, 8
direct evidence, 12
Trial – criminal
general principles of, 132–4
Trial within a trial *see* Voir dire
Turnbull guidelines *see* Identification evidence

Unfitness to plead, 42, 43
statutory provision, 494

Voir dire, 16–23, 74, 404

Weight of evidence, general concept of, 3–8
see also Admissibility
see also Relevance
Wigmore approach *see* Relevance
Witnesses
civil trial
judge's power to call, 140
competence and compellability *see* Competence and compellability
corroboration *see* Corroboration
criminal trial
court's power to call, 152–3
court's power to question, 153
hostile, 158–61
prosecution obligation to call, 150
unfavourable, 158
vulnerable
children, 119
competence *see* Competence and compellability
protection within criminal proceedings, 120–8
complainant in sexual cases, 105–19
admissibility of previous sexual conduct, 105–8
Victim Support findings, 108–11
Woolmington rule *see* Burden of proof